AF880230

LONGMAN

CORNERSTONE C

Teacher's Edition

Anna Uhl Chamot

Jim Cummins

Sharroky Hollie

PEARSON
Longman

Longman Cornerstone C

TEACHER'S EDITION

Pearson Education, 10 Bank Street, White Plains, NY 10606

Staff credits: The people who made up the *Longman Cornerstone* team, representing editorial, production, design, manufacturing, and marketing, are John Ade, Rhea Banker, Liz Barker, Kenna Bourke, Jeffrey Buckner, Brandon Carda, Daniel Comstock, Martina Deignan, Gina DiLillo, Nancy Flaggman, Cate Foley, Patrice Fraccio, Tracy Grenier, Zach Halper, Henry Hild, Sarah Hughes, Karen Kawaguchi, Lucille Kennedy, Ed Lamprich, Jamie Lawrence, Niki Lee, Christopher Leonowicz, Tara Maceyak, Katrinka Moore, Linda Moser, Liza Pleva, Edie Pullman, Monica Rodriguez, Tara Rose, Tania Saiz-Sousa, Chris Siley, Heather St. Clair, Loretta Steeves, and Andrew Vaccaro.

Text design and composition: The Quarasan Group, Inc.

ISBN-13: 978-0-13-713155-6
ISBN-10: 0-13-713155-0

Printed in the United States of America

4 5 6 7 8 9 10–DME–12 11 10 09

About the Authors

Anna Uhl Chamot is a professor of secondary education and a faculty advisor for ESL in George Washington University's Department of Teacher Preparation. She has been a researcher and teacher trainer in content-based second-language learning and language-learning strategies. She co-designed and has written extensively about the Cognitive Academic Language Learning Approach (CALLA) and spent seven years implementing the CALLA model in the Arlington Public Schools in Virginia.

Jim Cummins is the Canada Research Chair in the Department of Curriculum, Teaching, and Learning of the Ontario Institute for Studies in Education at the University of Toronto. His research focuses on literacy development in multilingual school contexts, as well as on the potential roles of technology in promoting language and literacy development. His recent publications include: *The International Handbook of English Language Teaching* (co-edited with Chris Davison), and *Literacy, Technology, and Diversity: Teaching for Success in Changing Times* (with Kristin Brown and Dennis Sayers).

Sharroky Hollie is an assistant professor in teacher education at California State University, Dominguez Hills. His expertise is in the field of professional development, African-American education, and second-language methodology. He is an urban literacy visiting professor at Webster University, St. Louis. Sharroky is the Executive Director of the Center for Culturally Responsive Teaching and Learning (CCRTL) and the co-founding director of the nationally acclaimed Culture and Language Academy of Success (CLAS).

Thematic Organization

Six thematic units per level organized around a **Big Question** provide a starting point for building understanding of key concepts and academic vocabulary. Each reading in the unit asks students to consider different aspects of the **Big Question**, leading to deeper levels of understanding.

Systematic Skills Development

Three readings per unit develop academic skills logically and systematically in a clear and consistent sequence.

UNIT 1 Contents

Helping Others

The Big Question

viii

Bonus Reading

High interest **Bonus Readings** at the end of each unit serve as a built-in library for independent reading and help build students' reading confidence.

UNIT 2 Contents

Heroes and Their Journeys

Front-Loading Instruction

Unit level **Words to Know** and high-interest **Mini-Autobiographies** introduce students to the key terms they'll explore and provide a context for learning.

Academic Vocabulary

Critical academic vocabulary and key terms are explicitly taught with each reading, with multiple opportunities to practice.

The Big Question

x

xi

Reading Strategies

Reading strategies are explicitly taught in a step-by-step format, ensuring students know when and how to apply the strategies to their reading.

Reading Review and Practice

Clear, consistent, explicit instruction and practice in phonics, fluency, word analysis, and comprehension follow each reading, ensuring learners have plenty of opportunities to master critical reading skills.

UNIT 3 Contents

Building a New Country

The Big Question

xii

xiii

Grammar and Writing

Grammar concepts are explicitly taught with each reading, with extensive use of modeling and providing plenty of practice. Modeled writing activities with each reading give students guided practice in key writing skills in each of the writing domains.

Picture Walk

A photo essay for one of the readings in the unit helps develop visual literacy and builds additional background knowledge about the topic of the reading. Extension activities typically involve conducting further research and reporting on the topic.

UNIT 4

Contents

Your Environment

The Big Question

xiv

UNIT 5

Contents

Sounds and Music

The Big Question

Built-in Differentiated Instruction

As they discuss the **Big Question**, students demonstrate their understanding of key concepts, and their ability to transfer and apply newly-acquired skills to a series of unit projects that range in level of difficulty for built-in differentiated instruction.

UNIT 6

Contents

Visiting National Parks

The Big Question

Skills Handbooks

Features 30 pages of additional support in reading, writing, grammar, technology, and study skills and more. These handbooks provide easy-to-use and easy-to-understand support in the critical academic skills that students need for success.

LEVEL C

Cornerstone Scope & Sequence

	Selection	Reading Strategy	Key Words	Academic Words
Unit 1 **Helping Others** The Big Question In what ways can people or groups help others?	1 **Everybody Wins** **Genre:** Literature/Realistic fiction 2 **Doctors Without Borders** **Genre:** Informational text/Newspaper article 3 **Stone Soup** **Genre:** Literature/Folktale **Bonus Reading** **A Team Crosses the Finish Line** **Genre:** Informational text/Magazine article	• Preview and predict • Activate prior knowledge • Identify events in a plot	important, complete, exclaimed, clumsy, improve, suspicious emergency, courageous, teamwork, training, intervene, refugees carry, scarce, share, peeked, cottage, charge	conduct project evaluate task attitude item
Unit 2 **Heroes and Their Journeys** The Big Question What does it take to be a hero?	1 **The Three Gifts** **Genre:** Literature/Folktale 2 **Brave Androcles** **Genre:** Literature/Poetry 3 **The Wizard of Oz** **Genre:** Literature/Fantasy **Bonus Reading** **The Elephant Shepherd** **Genre:** Literature/Short story	• Identify characters and plot • Make connections • Identify problems and solutions	bore, cooperate, marvelous, millet, virtue, grateful chased, arena, swollen, wander, criminal blister, contained, broad, midst, merry, startle	assess error motive principle distinct interact
Unit 3 **Building a New Country** The Big Question How do people create new countries?	1 **Writing a Great Speech** **Genre:** Informational text/Speeches 2 **One Hot Summer in Philadelphia** **Genre:** Informational text/Social studies 3 **One Out of Many** **Genre:** Literature/Play **Bonus Reading** **The Real Soldier** **Genre:** Literature/Historical fiction	• Compare and contrast • Identify Main idea and details • Make inferences	colonies, crown, adversary, taxes, liberty, representation delegates, confidential, privy, secrecy, merchants, tailors, cobblestone, curious surrender, veteran, republic, federal, separate, legislature	contract compensate individual legal convention debate

Word Analysis	Phonics	Spelling Tip	Graphic Organizers	Grammar	Writing Modes/ Assignments	Writing Models	Reading Fluency
• Multiple meaning words	• Short vowels • Long vowels with silent *e*	• Use a dictionary to check spelling • Add *s* to make nouns plural • Compound words	• Problem and Solution Chart • KWL Chart • Sequence Chart	• Singular and plural nouns • Past tense verbs • Future tense verbs	• Write a narrative • Write a paragraph with a topic sentence • Write a paragraph	• Narrative about a NASCAR race • Paragraph that tells how you solved a problem • Paragraph that describes a future weekend event	• Look ahead • Speed and accuracy • Read with expression
• Word origins	• Long vowel pairs • Vowel pair: *ea*	• The letters *c* and *h* or *s* and *h* stand for one sound. • Spelling for the sound /k/ • The apostrophe (') takes the place of letters that are left out	• Cause and Effect Chart • Story Map • Idea Web	• Adjectives and adverbs • Pronouns • Possessive nouns	• Write about causes and effects • Write a poem • Write a descriptive paragraph	• Description of a cause and effect from the reading • Poem about a favorite hero • Description of favorite room	• Look ahead • Read with expression • Speed and accuracy
• Synonyms and antonyms	• *r*-controlled: *ar*, *or*, *ore* • Consonant digraphs *ch*, *sh*, *th*	• *i* before *e* • *-le* endings • Words with silent letters *gh*	• Venn Diagram • Main Idea and Details Chart • 5 W Chart	• Subject-verb agreement • Letters • Commas in a series	• Write a persuasive speech • Write a persuasive letter • Write an historical speech	• Paragraphs about freedom of speech • Letter about Philadelphia • Persuasive speech on accepting the Constitution	• Speed and accuracy • Look ahead • Read with expression

	Selection	Reading Strategy	Key Words	Academic Words
Unit 4 Your Environment The Big Question How do people and environments affect each other?	1 **Biomes All Over the World** **Genre:** Informational text/ Science 2 **Springer Goes Home** **Genre:** Informational text/ Magazine article 3 **After the Hurricane** **Genre:** Informational text/ Social studies Bonus Reading **Marine Food Web** **Genre:** Informational text/ Science	• Visualize • Problem and solution • Sequence	biome, desert, equator, grasslands, ocean, tropical, tundra migrated, orphan, pods, predator, reunite, starvation assistance, damage, handle, relief, stranded, assess	adapt classify consume goal authorities establish
Unit 5 Sounds and Music The Big Question How do people make and use music?	1 **Touching Sound with Evelyn Glennie** **Genre:** Informational text/ Internet article 2 **A Song Map** **Genre:** Literature/Song 3 **Homemade Music** **Genre:** Informational text/ Music Bonus Reading **The Radio Storm** **Genre:** Literature/Realistic fiction	• Identify Main idea and details • Summarize • Identify Author's purpose	musicians, percussion, sounds, hearing, vibrations, instruments code, escape, landmarks, secret, riverbank, tracks rhythms, kazoo, harmonies, flea market, improvisation	context demonstrate assist accompany complexity variety
Unit 6 Visiting National Parks The Big Question Why are national parks important?	1 **Yosemite National Park** **Genre:** Functional writing/ Newspaper article 2 **How to Prepare for a Trip to Yosemite** **Genre:** Functional writing/E-mail 3 **My Trip to Yosemite** **Genre:** Functional writing/ Scrapbook Bonus Reading **Jay Writes a Research Paper** **Genre:** Functional writing/E-mail	• Make connections • Draw conclusions • Review and retell	tributaries, national parks, cliffs, sequoias, grove environment, ecosystem, alpine, landslide, conservation, secluded, scenic cascade, meadow, peak, ascend, forest, valley	area region specific features comment correspond

Word Analysis	Phonics	Spelling Tip	Graphic Organizers	Grammar	Writing Modes/ Assignments	Writing Models	Reading Fluency
• Homophones	• Final /s/ and /z/ sounds • Consonant clusters	• *tch* endings • Adding *-ed* and *-ing* • Spelling homophones	• Compare and Contrast Chart • Problem and Solution Chart • Sequence Chart	• Conjunctions and transitions • Complete and incomplete sentences • Prepositions	• Write a paragraph • Write an explanation • Make a poster	• Expository paragraph on a biome • Expository paragraph to explain a decision • How-to poster on helping after an emergency	• Look ahead • Read with expression • Speed and accuracy
• Figurative language	• Final *-ed* • Words with *ow* and *ou*	• Using a related word to spell an unknown word • When the /j/ sound is spelled with a *g*, the *g* is followed by e, i, or y • Spell with silent letters by saying them aloud	• Main Idea and Details Chart • Inference Chart • Compare and Contrast Chart	• Appositives and prepositional phrases • Dependent and independent clauses • Commonly misused verbs	• Write an introductory paragraph • Write a compare and contrast essay • Write a descriptive paragraph	• Introductory paragraph that compares and contrasts • Comparison of two types of music • Description of a musical instrument	• Look ahead • Read with expression • Speed and accuracy
• Latin word roots	• Words with *v* and *w* • Variant vowel: *oo*	• Prefixes and suffixes • Using a computer's spell check • Keep a personal word list of difficult words	• 5 W Chart • KWL Chart • Main Idea and Details Chart	• Four types of sentences • Active and passive voice • Articles	• Write a business letter • Write in active voice • Write a concluding paragraph	• Letter of inquiry about a visit • Paragraph about a visit to the Andes Mountains • Concluding paragraph in the form of an e-mail	• Look ahead • Read with expression • Speed and accuracy

Research Bibliography

Reading

Anderson, Neil J. *Exploring Second Language Reading: Issues and Strategies*. Boston, Mass.: Heinle & Heinle, 1999.

Anderson, Thomas, and B. Armbruster. "Readable Textbooks (or, Selecting a Textbook is Not Like Buying a Pair of Shoes)." In *Reading Comprehension: From Research to Practice*. Edited by Judith Orasanu. Mahwah, N.J.: Lawrence Erlbaum Associates, 1986, 151-162.

Cummins, Jim. "Language Proficiency, Bilingualism, and Academic Achievement." In *The Multicultural Classroom: Readings for Content-Area Teachers*, edited by P.A. Richard-Amato and M.A. Snow. White Plains, N.Y.: Longman, 1992.

Grabe, W. "Current Developments in Second Language Reading Research." In *TESOL Quarterly* 25 (1991): 375–406.

———. "Dilemmas for the Development of Second Language Reading Abilities." In *Prospect* 10 (1995): 38–51.

———. "Reading research and its implications for reading assessment." In *Fairness and Validation in Language Assessment*, edited by A. Kunnan (Cambridge: Cambridge University Press, 2000), 226-262.

National Reading Panel of the National Institute of Child Health & Human Development. *Teaching Children to Read: An Evidence-Based Assessment of the Scientific Research Literature on Reading and its Implications for Reading Instruction. Reports of the Subgroups.* NIH Publication No. 00-4754. Washington, DC: U.S. Government Printing Office, 2000.

Rumelhart, D.E. "Schemata: The Building Blocks of Cognition." In *Theoretical Issues in Reading Comprehension: Perspectives from Cognitive Psychology, Linguistics, Artificial Intelligence, and Education*, edited by R.J. Spiro, B.C. Bruce, and W.F. Brewer. Mahwah, N.J.: Lawrence Erlbaum Associates, 1980.

Spangenberg-Urbschat, Karen, and R. Pritchard, eds. *Kids Come in All Languages: Reading Instruction for ESL Students*. Newark, Del.: International Reading Association, 1994.

Stanovich, K. *Progress in Understanding Reading: Scientific Foundations and New Frontiers*. New York: Guilford Press, 2000.

Stanovich, P.J., and K. Stanovich. *Using Research and Reason in Education: How Teachers Can Use Scientifically Based Research to Make Curricular and Instructional Decisions.* Washington, DC: National Institute for Literacy, 2003.

Vocabulary

Chamot, A.U. and J.M. O'Malley. "The Cognitive Academic Language Learning Approach: A Bridge to the Mainstream." In *The Multicultural Classroom: Readings for Content-Area Teachers*, edited by P.A. Richard-Amato and M.A. Snow. New York: Longman, 1992, 39-57.

Fathman, A.K., M.E. Quinn, and C. Kessier. *Teaching Science to English Learners, Grades 4–8.* Program Information Guide Series, No. 11 from the National Clearinghouse for Bilingual Education, 1992.

Miller, G. "How School Children Learn Words." In *Proceedings of the Third Eastern States Conference on Linguistics*, edited by F. Marshall. Columbus, Ohio: The Ohio State University, 1986.

Nation, I.S.P. *Learning Vocabulary in Another Language*. New York: Cambridge University Press, 2001.

Schmitt, Norbert. *Vocabulary in Language Teaching.* New York: Cambridge University Press, 2000.

Schmitt, Norbert and M. McCarthy, eds. *Vocabulary: Description, Acquisition, and Pedagogy*. New York: Cambridge University Press, 1997.

Short, D.J. "Assessing Integrated Language and Content Instruction." In *TESOL Quarterly* 27 (4), 1993.

Snow, M.A., and D. Brinton. *The Content-Based Classroom: Perspectives on Integrating Language and Content.* White Plains, N.Y.: Longman, 1997.

English Learners

Bartlett, F.C., Sir. *Remembering: A Study in Experimental and Social Psychology.* 1932; Reprint New York: Cambridge University Press, 1995.

Berg, E.C. "Preparing ESL Students for Peer Response." In *TESOL Journal* 8 (2), 1999.

Breen, Michael P., ed. *Learner Contributions to Language Learning: New Directions in Research.* New York: Longman, 2001.

Brinton, Donna M., and Peter Master, eds. *New Ways in Content-Based Instruction.* Alexandria, VA.: Teachers of English to Speakers of Other Languages, 1997.

Chamot, A.U., and J.M. O'Malley. *The CALLA Handbook: Implementing the Cognitive Academic Language Learning Approach.* 2nd edition. White Plains, NY: Pearson-Longman, 2008.

Chamot, A. U., et al. *The Learning Strategies Handbook.* White Plains, N.Y.: Longman, 1999.

Chamot, A. U., and C. Keatley. *Sailing the 5 Cs with Learning Strategies: A Resource Guide for Secondary Foreign Language Educators.* Washington, DC: National Capital Language Resource Center, 2004. http://nclrc.org/sailing/

Cohen, Andrew D. *Strategies in Learning and Using a Second Language.* New York: Longman, 1998.

Cummins, Jim. *Empowering Minority Students.* Sacramento, Calif.: California Association for Bilingual Education, 1989.

———. "Linguistic Interdependence and the Educational Development of Bilingual Children." In *Review of Educational Research* 49 (2), 1979, 222–251.

———. *Negotiating Identities: Education for Empowerment in a Diverse Society.* California Association for Bilingual Education, 1996.

Doughty, C., and J. Williams. *Focus on Form in Classroom Second Language Acquisition.* New York: Cambridge University Press, 1998.

Freeman, David E., and Y.S. Freeman. *Between Worlds: Access to Second Language Acquisition.* Portsmouth, N.H.: Heinemann, 1994.

Kessler, Carolyn, ed. *Cooperative Language Learning: A Teacher's Resource Book.* Englewood Cliffs, N.J.: Prentice Hall Regents, 1992.

Labov, William S. Ash, and C. Boberg. *Atlas of North American English: Phonetics, Phonology, and Sound Change.* Berlin: Mouton de Gruyter, 2006.

Larsen-Freeman, Diane, and M.H. Long. *An Introduction to Second Language Acquisition Research.* New York: Longman, 1991.

Lightbown, Patsy, and N. Spada. *How Languages Are Learned*, 2nd. ed. New York: Oxford University Press, 1993.

Mccaleb, Sudia P. *Building Communities of Learners: A Collaboration Among Teachers, Students, Families, and Community.* New York: St. Martin's Press, 1994.

O'Malley, J.M., and A.U. Chamot. *Learning Strategies in Second Language Acquisition.* New York: Cambridge University Press, 1990. O'Malley, J.M., and L. Valdez Pierce. *Authentic Assessment for English Language Learners: Practical Approaches for Teachers.* Reading, Mass.: Addison-Wesley, 1996.

Reid, J. M., ed. *Learning Styles in the ESL/EFL Classroom*. Boston, Mass.: Heinle and Heinle, 1995.

Rubin, J. "A Review of Second Language Listening Comprehension Research." In *Modern Language Journal* 78 (1994): 199-221.

Short, D. J. *New Ways of Teaching English at the Secondary Level.* Alexandria, VA.: Teachers of English to Speakers of Other Languages, 1999.

Differentiated Instruction

Anderson, Thomas, and B. Armbruster. "On Selecting 'Considerate' Content Area Textbooks." In *Remedial and Special Education* (January/February 1988): 9, 47.

Cummins, Jim, and D. Sayers. *Brave New Schools: Challenging Cultural Illiteracy Through Global Learning Networks.* New York: St. Martin's Press, 1995.

Dole, J. A., K. J. Brown, and W. Trathen. "The Effects of Strategy Instruction On the Comprehension Performance of At-Risk Students." In *Reading Research Quarterly* 31 (1996): 62–88.

Gardner, Howard. *Frames of Mind: The Theory of Multiple Intelligences.* New York: Basic Books, 1993.

Gay, Geneva. *Culturally Responsive Teaching: Theory, Research, and Practice.* New York: Teachers College Press, 2000.

Gonzalez, Virginia, et al. *Assessment and Instruction of Culturally and Linguistically Diverse Students with or At-Risk of Learning Problems: From Research to Practice.* Boston, Mass.: Allyn & Bacon, 1997.

Ladson-Billings, Gloria. *The Dreamkeepers: Successful Teachers of African American Children.* San Francisco, Calif.: Jossey-Bass Inc., 1994.

Oxford, Rebecca, ed. *Language Learning Strategies Around the World: Cross-Cultural Perspectives.* Honolulu, Hawaii: University of Hawaii Press, 1996.

Pressley, Michael J., and V. Woloshyn, eds. *Cognitive Strategy Instruction That Really Improves Children's Academic Performance*, 2d ed. Cambridge, Mass.: Brookline Books, 1995.

Richard-Amato, Patricia A., and Marguerite Ann Snow, eds. *The Multicultural Classroom: Readings for Content-Area Teachers.* White Plains, N.Y.: Longman, 1992.

Rigg, Pat, and V.G. Allen, eds. *When They Don't All Speak English: Integrating the ESL Student into the Regular Classroom.* Urbana, Ill.: National Council of Teachers of English, 1989.

Rong, Xue Lan, and J. Preissle. *Educating Immigrant Students: What We Need to Know to Meet the Challenges.* Thousand Oaks, Calif.: Corwin Press, 1998.

Scarcella, Robin. *Teaching Language Minority Students in the Multicultural Classroom.* Englewood Cliffs, N.J.: Prentice Hall Regents, 1990.

Sternberg, Robert J. *The Triarchic Mind: A New Theory of Human Intelligence.* New York: Viking Press, 1988.

Wendt, Dirk, "An Experimental Approach to the Improvement of the Typographic Design of Textbooks." In *Visible Language* 13 (2), 1979.

Writing

Clemmons, J., et al. *Portfolios in the Classroom: A Teacher's Sourcebook.* New York: Scholastic Professional Books, 1993.

Glazer, S.M., and C.S. Brown. *Portfolios and Beyond: Collaborative Assessment in Reading and Writing.* Norwood, Mass.: Christopher-Gordon, 1993.

Hudelson, Sarah. *Write On: Children Writing in ESL.* Englewood Cliffs, N.J.: Prentice Hall Regents, 1989.

Spandel, Vicki. *Creating Writers: Through 6-Trait Writing Assessment and Instruction*, 3d ed. New York: Longman, 2001.

Reviewers

Rebecca Anselmo
Sunrise Acres Elementary School
Las Vegas, NV

Ana Applegate
Redlands School District
Redlands, CA

Terri Armstrong
Houston ISD
Houston, TX

Jacqueline Avritt
Riverside County Office of Ed.
Riverside, CA

Mitchell Bobrick
Palm Beach County School
West Palm Beach, FL

Victoria Brioso-Saldala
Broward County Schools
Fort Lauderdale, FL

Brenda Cabarga Schubert
Creekside Elementary School
Salinas, CA

Joshua Ezekiel
Bardin Elementary School
Salinas, CA

Veneshia Gonzalez
Seminole Elementary School
Okeechobee, FL

Carolyn Grigsby
San Francisco Unified School District
San Francisco, CA

Julie Grubbe
Plainfield Consolidated Schools
Chicago, IL

Yasmin Hernandez-Manno
Newark Public Schools
Newark, NJ

Janina Kusielewicz
Clifton Public Schools/
Bilingual Ed. &
Basic Skills Instruction Dept.
Clifton, NJ

Mary Helen Lechuga
El Paso ISD
El Paso, TX

Gayle P. Malloy
Randolph School District
Randolph, MA

Randy Payne
Patterson/Taft Elementaries
Mesa, AZ

Marcie L. Schnegelberger
Alisal Union SD
Salinas, CA

Lorraine Smith
Collier County Schools
Naples, FL

Shawna Stoltenborg
Glendale Elementary School
Glen Burnie, MD

Denise Tiffany
West High School
Iowa City, IA

Teaching and Learning Strategies

Anna Uhl Chamot

Many students face challenges to academic achievement. These include English Language Learners (ELLs), Struggling Readers (SRs), and Standard English Learners (SELs). Not only must these students learn standard academic English, but they must do so while also learning content subject matter and skills. In addition, all students are now expected to meet the same national and state standards and assessments as proficient speakers, readers, and writers of standard academic English. ***Cornerstone*** provides challenging content-based language development and learning strategies that help students achieve academic goals.

Why teach learning strategies?

Learning strategies accelerate standard academic language learning for all students more effectively and efficiently. Learning strategies are techniques for understanding, remembering, and using information and skills. They are particularly important for students seeking to master academic language and content simultaneously, as they do in ***Cornerstone***.

Learning strategy instruction can help students by:

- showing them techniques for "how to learn,"
- developing their independence as learners,
- increasing their academic motivation, and
- developing their awareness of their own thinking and learning processes.

Research has shown that when students develop metacognition, the awareness of the learning processes and strategies that lead to success, they are more likely to plan how to proceed with a learning task, monitor their own performance, find solutions to problems encountered, and evaluate themselves upon task completion.

All kinds of fiction, poetry, and informational texts provide students with models of academic and literary language. However, to make full use of these models, students need to comprehend what they read. Reading strategies presented in ***Cornerstone*** provide detailed instructions on how to apply the strategy to the text they are about to read.

Many of the reading strategies in ***Cornerstone*** have broader applications and can be used as learning strategies for listening, speaking, writing, and remembering both vocabulary and content information. Some examples are:

- *Predict*—Anticipate what is coming next during a listening activity.
- *Visualize / Use Visuals*—Make a mental image of the events and characters in a story you are writing; use or draw a visual aid to learn vocabulary.
- *Make Inferences*—Use the context of a listening activity and what you know about the topic to figure out the meaning of new words or ideas.
- *Ask Questions*—Ask the teacher or others to explain what you do not understand; after speaking or writing, ask yourself or others how well you communicated your meaning.
- *Scan / Selective Attention*—Focus on specific content information, academic words, or literary words as you read, listen, speak, and write.
- *Take Notes*—Write down important ideas as you listen and as you prepare to write.
- *Summarize*—Create a mental, oral, or written summary of information you learn.
- *Classify / Sequence*—Classify new words and ideas according to their similarities; sequence events, directions, and steps to solve a problem.

Additional learning strategies that are especially helpful to ELLs, SRs, and SELs in acquiring standard academic English and content are the following three metacognitive strategies and a strategy for using prior knowledge:

- *Plan*—Set goals and identify steps needed to accomplish a learning task.
- *Monitor / Identify Problems*—While working on a learning task, check your comprehension or production and identify any problems you are having.
- *Evaluate*—After completing a learning task, assess how well you have done.
- *Use What You Know*—Use your own knowledge and experiences to understand and learn something new; brainstorm words and ideas; make associations and analogies; explain your prior knowledge about a topic.

Guidelines for teaching learning strategies

Since learning strategies are mental processes with few observable manifestations, it is difficult to tell whether a student is learning how to use them. ***Cornerstone*** offers these suggestions to help teachers make strategy instruction more explicit:

- Model the strategy by "thinking aloud" as you perform a task similar to the one students will perform.
- Use the strategy names and refer to them consistently by name.
- Tell students why the strategy is important and how it can help them.
- Remind students to use strategies as they read, listen, brainstorm, write, focus on grammar, learn vocabulary, and work on projects.

- Provide opportunities for students to discuss strategies—how they use them, additional strategies they use, and which strategies they prefer.

The five-phase instructional sequence developed for the Cognitive Academic Language Learning Approach (CALLA) has provided a useful framework for teaching learning strategies. In this approach, highly explicit instruction in applying strategies to learning tasks is gradually faded so that the students can begin to assume greater responsibility in selecting and applying their own preferred learning strategies. An important feature of the CALLA instructional sequence is that the needs and thoughts of students are central to all instruction. The sequence guides students towards increasing levels of independence, thus fostering attitudes of academic self-efficacy. The five phases of the CALLA instructional sequence are:

Preparation Students identify strategies they are already using and develop their metacognitive awareness of the relationship between their own mental processes and effective learning. Activities in the Preparation stage can include class discussions about strategies used for recent learning tasks, group or individual interviews about strategies used for particular tasks, think-aloud sessions in which students describe their thought processes while they work on a task, questionnaires or checklists about strategies used, and diary entries about individual approaches to language and content learning.

Presentation This phase focuses on explaining and modeling the new learning strategy. The teacher describes the characteristics, usefulness, and applications of the strategy. The most effective way to present the new strategy is for teachers to model their own use of the strategy by "thinking aloud" (see above). Teachers can then ask students to name the strategy and explain when and how to use it. Modeling helps students visualize themselves working successfully on a similar learning task.

Practice Students now practice the new learning strategy with an authentic learning task, such as those presented in ***Cornerstone***. For example, a group of students might read a story, then describe the images the story evoked, discuss unfamiliar words encountered and infer meanings through context clues, and take turns summarizing the main points of the story. In a content-based academic language program such as ***Cornerstone***, strategies can be used to understand and remember concepts and skills from curriculum areas such as science, social studies, and language arts.

Self-Evaluation Students evaluate their success in using learning strategies, thus developing metacognitive awareness of their own learning processes. Activities that develop students' ability to evaluate themselves include debriefing discussions after strategy practice, learning logs in which students record the results of their learning strategies applications, checklists of strategies used, and open-ended questionnaires in which students express their opinions about the usefulness of particular strategies.

Expansion Finally, students make personal decisions about the strategies that they find most effective, apply these strategies to new contexts in other classes, and devise their own individual combinations and interpretations of learning strategies. By this stage, the goal of learning strategies instruction has been achieved.

Ongoing monitoring of students' use of both instructed and individually developed strategies is essential if teachers are to scaffold their instruction successfully. In scaffolded instruction, teachers begin with explicit instruction and gradually reduce prompts and cues to students. In this way, students begin to assume responsibility for the regulation of their own learning. Individual students may need greater or lesser amounts of explicit strategies instruction, depending on the degree to which they have already developed strategies independently. When students are able to use instructed strategies without prompting, they are ready to explore new strategies, new applications, and new opportunities for self-regulated learning.

Suggested Reading

Chamot, A.U. *The CALLA Handbook: Implementing the Cognitive Academic Learning Language Approach,* 2d ed. White Plains, N.Y.: Longman, 2008.

Chamot, A.U. "Accelerating Academic Achievement of English Language Learners: A Synthesis of Five Evaluations of the CALLA Model." In *The International Handbook of English Language Learning, Part I,* edited by J. Cummins and C. Davison (Norwell, Mass.: Springer Publications, 2007), 317–331.

Chamot, A.U. "Language Learning Strategy Instruction: Current Issues and Research." In *Annual Review of Applied Linguistics.* New York: Cambridge University Press, 2005.

The Challenge of Learning Academic English

Jim Cummins

What is academic English?

Children with normal language development come to school at age four or five fluent in their home language. We spend another 12 years attempting to expand this linguistic competence into the sphere of literacy. In the early grades, instruction focuses on teaching students how to decode. Early reading instruction focuses on how the sounds of the language map to written symbols and also encourages them to apply these skills in reading and writing extensively. These early years are crucial in helping students forge an affective connection to reading and writing.

However, the acquisition of fluent decoding skills in the primary grades is only the first step to becoming a strong reader. As students progress through the grades, they are required to read increasingly complex texts and academic language becomes increasingly complex. The complexity of academic language reflects:

- The difficulty of the concepts;
- The vocabulary in content texts that include many low frequency and technical words rarely used in conversation; many of these words come from Latin and Greek.;
- Increasingly sophisticated grammatical constructions.

Students are not only required to read this language, but also to use it in an accurate and coherent way in their own writing.

We find academic language predominantly in books. Therefore, students who read extensively both inside and outside the school have far greater opportunities to acquire academic language.

Why is conversational English faster to acquire than academic English?

Linguists estimate that knowledge of about 2,000 words is enough to get by in most conversational situations. There are many clues to meaning in face-to-face conversation—eye contact, gestures, facial expressions, intonation, etc. So we don't need to know as much of the language to understand the meaning or make ourselves understood. By contrast, the language used in schools and formal situations lacks these supports and entails many more low frequency words and difficult grammatical constructions.

What challenges do Struggling Readers face?

The learning difficulties faced by Struggling Readers can derive from a variety of sources regardless of whether their home language is English or a language other than English. Some students experience difficulties in acquiring decoding skills and fall behind from an early stage; other students acquire reasonably fluent decoding skills but experience difficulties around Grades 3 or 4 when the conceptual and linguistic load of the curriculum becomes significantly more intense. If the problems lie in decoding, then provide support to help students acquire the sound symbol relationships that characterize English written text. If the problems lie in reading comprehension, focus on building vocabulary and encouraging students to read extensively. In both cases, we should strive for a balanced approach—build awareness of how written language works while simultaneously encouraging reading and writing.

What strategies help develop academic language?

Growth in reading and writing skills is strongly related to students' level of literacy engagement. Reading researcher John Guthrie (2004) summarized this research by noting that students whose family background was characterized by low income and low education, but who were highly engaged readers, substantially outscored students who came from backgrounds with higher education and higher income, but who themselves were less engaged readers. This finding suggests the stunning conclusion that engaged reading can overcome traditional barriers to reading achievement. (p. 5)

We can promote literacy engagement by using scaffolds to make the input more comprehensible. It is also important to scaffold students' use of language, particularly their written language. For example, newcomer students can be encouraged to write initially in their first language (L1) and then work from L1 to English.

Effective instruction will also activate prior knowledge and build background. Learning can be defined as the integration of new knowledge or skills with the knowledge or skills we already possess. Therefore it is crucial to activate preexisting knowledge so that students can relate new information to what they already know.

Identity affirmation is also crucial for literacy engagement. Students who feel their culture and identity validated in the classroom are much more likely to engage with literacy than those who perceive their culture and identity ignored or devalued. Writing for authentic purposes and for real audiences, together with creative project work that will be published (e.g., on a school web site), are excellent ways of reinforcing students' academic and cultural identities.

Finally, literacy engagement requires that teachers across the curriculum explain how language works and stimulate students' curiosity about language. Students who gain a sense of control over language will want to use it for powerful purposes.

Reference

Guthrie, J. T. (2004). Teaching for literacy engagement. Journal of Literacy Research, 36, 1-30.

Using Culturally and Linguistically Responsive Teaching to Enhance Learning for All Students

Sharroky Hollie

What is culturally and linguistically responsive teaching?

Geneva Gay, in *Culturally Responsive Teaching—Theory, Practice, and Pedagogy* (2004), defines it as the use of cultural knowledge, prior experiences, frames of reference, and performance styles of ethnically diverse students to make learning encounters more relevant to and effective for them. It teaches to and through the strengths of these students. It is culturally validating and affirming. CLR validates and affirms the home language and culture of students through the use of responsive instructional strategies, which act as bridges to acceptance, achievement, and empowerment in academic settings and mainstream culture at large.

Who benefits from CLR?

All students is the simple answer. The more precise question is which students benefit *most* from culturally and linguistically responsive teaching? A precise answer delves into who these students are most likely to be. A survey of any recent or past standardized data gives the answer of who is achieving and who is not. In this context, culturally and linguistically responsive teaching would most benefit those students who are termed underserved as opposed to underachieving.

What is a Standard English Learner (SEL)?

A Standard English Learner is a student whose home language differs enough from Standard English and Academic English in these ways: phonologically, morpho-syntactically, syntactically, semantically, pragmatically, and rhetorically. Commonly known as non-standard languages, African American Vernacular, Chicano English, Hawaiian Pidgin English, and Native American dialects represent the languages of many underserved students. Superficially, these students have an apparent proficiency in Standard English and Academic English, but a deep examination of their reading and written skills coupled with the demands of school language posit a different picture. Unfortunately, the students are many times seen as language deficient, not language different, and are skipped over in terms of their linguistic needs.

What are the key strands for culturally and linguistically responsive teaching and learning?

Teaching Using Culturally Relevant Literature

- Purposefully using texts that affirm and validate students' backgrounds, cultures, languages, and experiences
- Using effective literacy and language strategies made culturally responsive

Systematic Teaching of Situational Appropriateness

- Addressing language variation among SELs (Standard English Learners) and ELs (English Learners)
- Using strategies to support Standard English mastery

Cultural Behaviors for a Positive Classroom Community

- Engaging the students in rigorous activities which tap into the personal learning styles
- Providing protocols for discussion and participation that validate and affirm cultural behaviors and teach situational appropriateness

Academic Vocabulary Through Conceptually Coded Words

- Validating students' knowledge and home vocabulary
- Linking cultural concepts to academic words
- Applying understanding of synonyms/antonyms

A Validating and Affirming Learning Environment

- Accepting, affirmative, risk-free classroom environment
- Including in the room environment images that are reflective of students' cultures, from the instructional texts and materials to the instructional activities, from the classroom walls to the classroom library

How do I become culturally responsive?

Some steps to becoming culturally and linguistically responsive:

- Recognize your student population in terms of who is being underserved, who is not being responded to culturally and/or linguistically.
- Assess if these students' underachievement is related to their language proficiency and/or lack of responsiveness on the part of the instruction in relation to engagement, motivation, and/or skills development.
- Using the instructional strands as an umbrella, identify key strategies (labeled like this CRI) that would be culturally and linguistically responsive and act as bridges to achievement.
- Infuse the strategies into your teaching, creating consistent moments for students to connect to what is being taught culturally and linguistically.

Introduction to Linguistics

How People Speak

All languages have both consonants and vowels. Consonants are made with some obstruction of the vocal tract, either a complete stoppage of air or enough constriction to create friction. Vowels are produced with the vocal tract more open; they have no constriction that might cause friction.

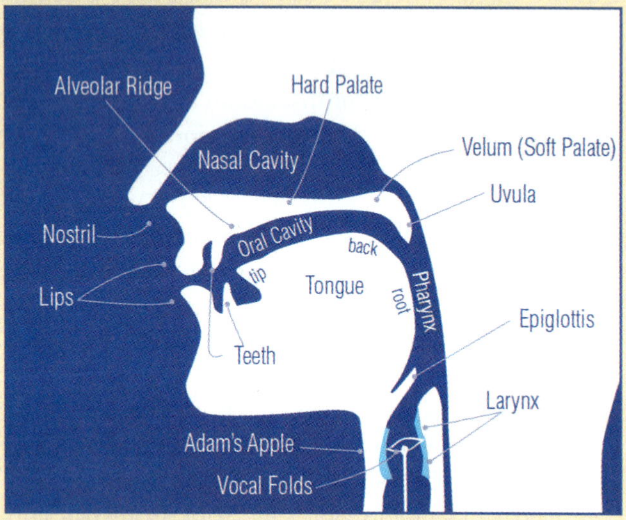

Figure 1: The human vocal tract makes the sounds of speech.

Consonants

Every consonant can be described by noting three characteristics: voicing, place of articulation, and manner of articulation.

Voicing

Many sounds of language, including all vowels, employ vibration of the vocal folds in the larynx. This creates more resonance and energy for the sound. All speech sounds are characterized as either voiced (with vocal fold vibration) or voiceless (with no vocal fold vibration). Feeling the vibration around the Adam's apple can help you understand this difference. If you say "sssss" and then "zzzzz," you can feel the distinction: /s/ is voiceless and /z/ is voiced.

Place of Articulation

This is the location in the vocal tract where the air stream may be constricted. The /s/ sound, for example, is made with the tongue tip close to the alveolar ridge (see Figure 1).

Place of Articulation Terms

Bilabial: using both lips

Glottal: produced at the larynx

Interdental: tongue tip between upper and lower teeth

Labio-dental: upper teeth and lower lip

Labio-velar: rounding of lips; tongue body raised toward velum

Palatal: body of tongue and high part of palate

Palato-alveolar: tongue tip and palate behind alveolar ridge

Velar: body of tongue and velum (soft palate)

Manner of Articulation

This is the type or degree of constriction that occurs in an articulation. For example, the /t/ sound completely stops the airflow with the tongue tip at the alveolar ridge, but /s/ allows air to pass noisily through a small opening.

Manner of Articulation Terms

Alveolar: tongue tip and ridge behind teeth

Affricate: complete constriction followed by slow separation of the articulators resulting in friction

Approximant: close constriction, but not enough for friction

Fricative: narrow constriction; turbulent airflow causing friction

Glottal: produced at the larynx

Lateral: air passes over sides of tongue

Nasal: lowered velum to let air escape through the nose

Stop: complete constriction, closure so that air cannot escape through the oral cavity

Tap: brief contact between tongue tip and alveolar ridge

Vowels

Vowels are open, sonorous sounds. Each vowel can be uniquely described by noting the position of the tongue, the tension of the vocal tract, and the position of the lips. Vowels are described by ***height,*** where the tongue is relative to the roof of the mouth. They can be high, mid, or low. Tongue backness tells if the tongue articulation is in the front or back of the mouth.

Tense vowels are more common around the world. In English, they are longer and include an expansion of the throat at the pharynx. Lax vowels are shorter with a more neutral pharynx. An example is the tense long *e* as in *meet* versus the lax short *i* as in *mitt.* The lips can be either in a spread or a neutral position, or they can be rounded and protrude slightly.

Speaking English

English is the third most widely spoken native language in the world, after Mandarin and Spanish. There are about 330 million native speakers of English and 600 million who speak it as a foreign language.

English Consonant Sounds

The following chart gives the International Phonetic Alphabet (IPA) symbol for each English consonant along with its voicing, place, and manner of articulation. This information can be used to understand and help identify problems that non-native speakers may encounter when learning to speak English.

CONSONANTS OF ENGLISH

IPA	Articulation	Example
p	voiceless bilabial stop	**p**it
b	voiced bilabial stop	**b**it
m	voiced bilabial nasal stop	**m**an
w	voiced labio-velar approximant	**w**in
f	voiceless labio-dental fricative	**f**un
v	voiced labio-dental fricative	**v**ery
θ	voiceless interdental fricative	**th**ing
ð	voiced interdental fricative	**th**ere
t	voiceless alveolar stop	**t**ime
d	voiced alveolar stop	**d**ime
n	voiced alveolar nasal stop	**n**ame
s	voiceless alveolar fricative	**s**oy
z	voiced alveolar fricative	**z**eal
ɾ	voiced alveolar tap	bu**tt**er
l	voiced alveolar central approximant	**l**oop
ɹ	voiced palato-alveolar affricate	**r**ed
ʃ	voiceless palato-alveolar fricative	**sh**allow
ʒ	voiced palato-alveolar affricate	vi**s**ion
ʧ	voiceless palato-alveolar affricate	**ch**irp
ʤ	voiced palato-alveolar affricate	**j**oy
j	voiced palatal approximant	**y**ou
k	voiceless velar stop	**k**ite
g	voiced velar stop	**g**oat
ŋ	voiced velar nasal stop	ki**ng**
h	voiceless glottal fricative	**h**ope

English Vowel Sounds

Most languages in the world have around five vowel sounds. English has 13 common vowel sounds, which means that many students of English must learn more vowel distinctions than there are in their native language. The lax vowels are most difficult. Some vowels are diphthongs, meaning the tongue is in one position at the beginning of the sound, and it moves to another position by the end of it.

VOWELS OF ENGLISH

IPA	Sound	Example
i	ē	b**ea**t
ɪ	ĭ	b**i**t
e	ā	b**ai**t
ɛ	ĕ	b**e**t
æ	ă	b**a**t
u	o͞o	b**oo**t
ʊ	o͝o	c**ou**ld
o	ō	b**oa**t
ɔ	aw	**law**
ɑ	ŏ	h**o**t
ə	ə	**a**bout
ʌ	ŭ	c**u**t
ɝ	er	b**ir**d
ɑ ʊ	ow	h**ou**se
ɔ ɪ	oy	b**oy**
ɑ ɪ	ī	b**i**te

Figure 2 is a schematic of the mouth. The left is the front of the mouth; the right is the back. The top is the roof of the mouth and the bottom is the floor. Placement of the vowel shows where the tongue reaches its maximum in the English articulation.

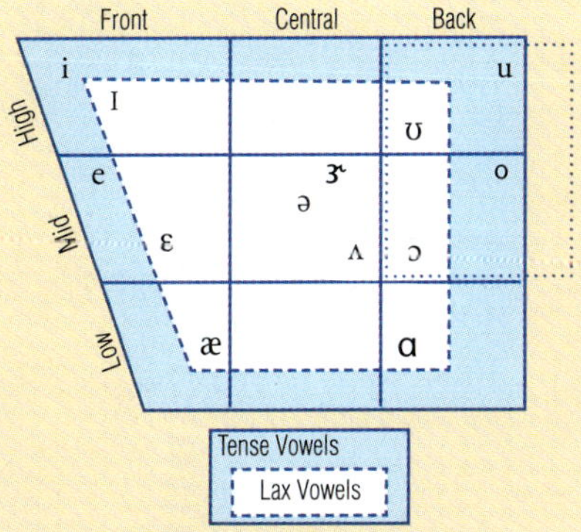

Figure 2: English vowel sounds

Introduction to Linguistics

Transference

Pronunciation

All languages build on the same fundamentals. All languages contrast voiced and voiceless sound, and have stops and fricatives. Many languages use the same places of articulation for consonants as well. The majority of sounds will easily transfer from another language to English.

However, there will always be some sounds that are not found in a person's native language that can pose a challenge to the English language learner. English has a few relatively rare sounds, such as the interdental sounds spelled with *th*, /θ/ and /ð/. The /r/ sound in English is also a very rare type of sound. Most other languages use a tap or trill articulation for an /r/ sound.

In some languages, the /l/ and /r/ sounds belong to one psychological category. This means that they count as the same sound in that language. In this case, it is not the articulation that is difficult, but the perception of the difference and consistent use of one versus the other in any word context. This type of psychological category is called a *phoneme,* and multiple speech sounds all can be categorized as the same phoneme in that language.

This is true for English as well, where, for example, the alveolar lateral /l/ as in *lob* and the velarized lateral /ɫ/ as in *ball* are both counted as the same sound—an *l*—to native speakers of English. It is important to keep in mind that both the phonetic articulation of a sound and its psychological, phonemic category factor into the learning of a new language.

Grammar

Pronouncing English is not the only stumbling block for English learners. The grammar and usage, or syntax, of English may present distinctions that are unique to the language. For example, English syntax requires adjectives to precede the nouns they modify, as in *the tall girl.* In other languages, such as Spanish, Hmong, and Vietnamese, adjectives follow nouns, as in *la chica alta* (literally *the girl tall* in Spanish). This may cause word-order problems, particularly for less advanced English learners.

Other syntactic differences are less obvious and may cause problems even for advanced learners. For example, many East Asian languages (such as Mandarin, Cantonese, and Korean) do not mark agreement between subject and verb. Speakers of these languages may therefore leave out agreement markers such as the *-s* in *The girl like cats.*

The use of articles varies across languages. For instance, Spanish uses the definite article more often than English, while Mandarin and Cantonese do not have articles. A Spanish-speaking English learner might say *The girl likes the cats* instead of *The girl likes cats,* and a Mandarin or Cantonese speaker might say *Girl like cat.*

Plural marking is another potential trouble spot: Vietnamese, Filipino, Cantonese, and Mandarin do not add plural markers to nouns. Learners speaking these languages may have difficulty with English plurals, saying *cat* instead of *cats.*

Grammar Hot Spots

Look for Grammar Hot Spots on the following pages for tips on the most common syntax errors made by speakers of languages other than English.

Common First Languages

In the Common First Languages section, you will find details of some common non-English languages spoken in the United States. They are:

- Spanish
- Vietnamese
- Cantonese
- Hmong
- Filipino
- Korean
- Mandarin

You can use the fundamentals of speech articulation already covered to help you understand where the languages differ from English. Differences in the spoken language and in the writing systems are explored as well. These sections pinpoint common trouble spots specific to learners of English.

Culture Clues

Look to Culture Clues for insights into the cultural differences of each language learner as well as ideas for ways to embrace students' diversity.

African American Vernacular English

While not a non-English language, African American Vernacular English (AAVE) is spoken commonly in many student populations and can present barriers to success in reading and writing similar to those facing English language learners. This section provides details on this unique English dialect and suggestions for addressing potential learning problems you may encounter with speakers of AAVE.

Linguistic Contrastive Analysis

The Linguistic Contrastive Analysis Charts provide a quick reference for comparing English sounds with those of other languages. The charts allow you to check at a glance which sounds have equivalents in other languages. For those sounds that don't have equivalents, you can find the closest sound used as a substitute and suggestions for helping someone gain a native English articulation.

In these charts, the sounds are notated using the International Phonetic Alphabet (IPA). This is the most widely recognized and used standard for representing speech sounds in any language. A guiding principle of the IPA across all languages is that each sound is uniquely represented by one symbol, and each symbol represents only one sound.

The chart has columns for each native language with rows corresponding to each English phoneme. Each cell in the chart gives an example word using that sound in the native language, a definition in parenthesis, and transference tips below. If there is no sound equivalent to English, a common substitution used by speakers of that language may be provided.

Transference Tips

Transference tips give you ideas of how the sound will be produced by the learner. Cells highlighted in yellow note where the English learner will have particular difficulty with the English sound.

Common First Languages

Spanish

Background

Spanish is the second most widely spoken language in the world. There are more than 400 million native Spanish speakers in 20-plus countries on three continents. Spanish vocabulary and pronunciation differ from country to country. While most dialect differences in English are in vowel sounds, Spanish dialects differ in their consonants.

Spoken

Spanish sounds are similar to those found in English, so there is a strong foundation for the native Spanish speaker learning English. However, there are three key differences between English and Spanish consonants:

1. Most of the alveolar sounds in English, such as /t/, /d/, and /n/ are produced farther forward in the mouth in Spanish. Instead of the tongue touching the alveolar ridge as in English, in Spanish it touches the back of the teeth.
2. Another difference is that the /r/ sound in English is not found in Spanish. There are two /r/ sounds in Spanish. One is the tap /r/, which occurs in English as the quick sound in the middle of the name *Betty*. Psychologically, this tap sound is a kind of /t/ or /d/ sound in English, while in Spanish it is perceived as an /r/. The other /r/ sound in Spanish is a trill, or series of tongue taps on the alveolar ridge. This does not occur in English.
3. The third key difference between English and Spanish can be found in the English production of the voiceless stops /p/, /t/, and /k/. In English these sounds are aspirated, with an extra puff of air at the end, when the sound occurs at the beginning of a word or stressed syllable. So, /p/ is aspirated in *pit*. Learners can add a puff of air to such sounds to sound more like native English speakers.

Culture Clues

The Spanish language covers many countries, dialects, and cultures. Always encourage students to share special things about their culture, such as foods, festivals, or social customs.

There are five vowels in Spanish, which are a subset of the English vowels. Spanish vowels include tense vowel sounds /a/ /e/ /i/ /o/ /u/. Lax vowel sounds in English are the problematic ones for native Spanish speakers.

Written

Like English, written Spanish uses the Roman alphabet, so both writing systems are similar. There are a few orthographic differences to note, however:

- The letter *h* in Spanish is silent, but the sound /h/ is written as *j* or *g*.
- A single letter *r* in Spanish represents a tap, while the double *rr* represents a trill.
- Accents are used to show the stress on a syllable when the stress is different from the usual rules. In some cases, words change meaning according to the accents. For example, *el* means *the* while *él* means *he*.

Written Spanish vowels are pronounced like the symbols in the IPA. So, the Spanish "i" is pronounced with the long ē as in the word *beat*. The IPA and Spanish symbol for this letter is the same: /i/.

Grammar Hot Spots

- Double negatives are part of standard grammar in Spanish. Stress the single negative construction in English.
- English prepositions are a common stumbling point for Spanish speakers.

Vietnamese

Background

Approximately 80 million people in Vietnam speak Vietnamese. The northern dialect is the standard, though central and southern dialects also exist. Most Vietnamese speakers in the United States are from southern Vietnam and speak the southern dialect.

Spoken

Vietnamese is a tonal language, so each syllable is pronounced with a distinctive tone that affects meaning. Vietnamese has a complex vowel system of 12 vowels and 26 diphthongs. Its consonants are simpler, but Vietnamese syllable structure allows few possibilities for final consonants.

Students may need help noticing and learning to reproduce final consonant sounds in English words and syllables. Vietnamese syllable structure allows for limited combinations of initial consonants. Students also may need help with the more complex initial consonant clusters of English words and syllables.

Culture Clues

In traditional Vietnamese education, there is a strict division between the roles of student and teacher. Students may be confused if asked to direct a part of their own study, so encourage group work.

Written

Since the 1600s, Vietnamese has used a Romanized alphabet. Many characters written in Vietnamese have sounds different from their English counterparts, such as *d, x, ch, nh, kh, g, tr, r,* and *e.*

Grammar Hot Spots

- Like English, Vietnamese uses Subject-Verb-Object (SVO) syntax, or word order.
- Vietnamese does not use affixes; instead, syntax expresses number, case, and tense.

Cantonese

Background

Cantonese is one of the seven major Chinese languages, not all of which are mutually intelligible. Cantonese is mostly spoken in China's southern provinces, Hong Kong, and Macau by about 66 million people. It is a tonal language, and the same sequence of letters can have different meanings depending on their pitch.

Spoken

Cantonese has six stops, aspirated and non-aspirated /p/, /t/, /k/; three fricatives /f/, /s/, /h/, and two affricates /ts/, /ts^h/. Some sounds which do not exist in Cantonese can be difficult for the English language learner. The /v/ often gets pronounced as /f/ or /w/; the /z/ is often said as /s/, the sounds spelled with *th* are often said as /t/, /d/, or /f/. Cantonese speakers have difficulty distinguishing between /l/ and /r/, since /r/ is not present in their language. They tend to produce an /l/-like sound for both English sounds in words such as *ride* and *lied.*

Cantonese has 11 vowels and 10 diphthongs. One of the major problems for Cantonese speakers is distinguishing between English tense and lax vowels, because the distribution of Cantonese short and long vowels is determined by the sound context.

Syllables in Cantonese don't have consonant clusters. English consonant clusters are often deleted or broken up by vowel insertion (e.g., *list* becomes *lis*). This may be especially problematic when producing English past tense (e.g., *baked*).

Culture Clues

"Chinese" isn't a language of its own. There are many regional languages spoken in this large country, including Cantonese. For each language spoken, there may be different cultural traditions and beliefs. Talk about where in China students are from and the celebrations and norms that make them unique.

Written

Cantonese is written with standard Chinese characters known as *Hànzi* where each character represents a syllable and has a meaning. Additional Cantonese-specific characters were also added. Cantonese speakers may have difficulty with sound-letter correspondences in English.

Grammar Hot Spots

- English articles and prepositions are difficult for Cantonese speakers. *In, on,* and *at,* for instance, can be translated as the same preposition in Cantonese.
- Plurals, tenses, and gerund endings are difficult for Cantonese speakers to transfer to English.

Common First Languages

Hmong

Background

Hmong is a group of approximately 18 languages within the Hmong-Mien family. There are roughly four million speakers of Hmong, including 200,000 in the United States. They are mainly from two groups with mutually intelligible dialects—Hmong Daw and Mong Leng.

Spoken

Hmong vowels are few and simple, but its consonants are complex and differ from those of English. Notable features of Hmong phonology absent from English include consonantal pre-nasalization (the /m/n/ŋ/ sound before a consonant) and the contrast between nasalized and non-nasalized vowels. Hmong is tonal. Each syllable is pronounced with a distinctive pitch.

Culture Clues

In traditional Hmong culture, learning takes place through hands-on experience. Students may find it difficult to adjust to the use of graphics or print media. Competition, personal achievement, and self-directed instruction may be unfamiliar concepts, so students may prefer group work.

Written

The Romanized Popular Alphabet (RPA), developed in the 1950s, is the usual way of transcribing Hmong. Syllable-final consonants are absent in pronunciation but are used to represent orthographically the tonal value of a given syllable. Students may need particular help in identifying and learning to reproduce the final consonant sounds of English words and syllables.

Grammar Hot Spots

- Like English, Hmong is an SVO language. Personal pronouns are marked for number, including inflection for singular, dual, and plural, though they are not marked for case.
- Because Hmong and English prepositions often have different semantic qualities, students may need help mastering uses of English prepositions. For example, it is correct to say "think <u>about</u> [something]" rather than "think <u>on</u> [something]."

Filipino

Background

Filipino and English are the official languages of the Philippines, where 175 languages are spoken. There are about 24 million native speakers of Filipino, and more than 50 million people speak Filipino as a second language. You may hear the terms Filipino and Tagalog being used interchangeably.

Spoken

Filipino has many similar speech sounds to English. The notable exceptions are the lack of the consonant sounds /f/, /v/, and those spelled with *th.* Of these, the English /f/ and /v/ cause the most difficulty for learners. The distinction between long *e* (as in *beat*) and short *i* (as in *bit*) is also a trouble spot. Filipino does not allow consonant clusters at the end of syllables, so *detect* may be simplified to just one consonant (*detec*).

Culture Clues

Most people from the Philippines can speak Filipino, but for many it is not their first language. Ask Filipino students about other languages they speak. Because English is used alongside Filipino as the language of instruction in the Philippines, most Filipinos are familiar with English.

Written

The Filipino alphabet has 28 letters and is based on the Spanish alphabet, so the English writing system poses little problem.

Grammar Hot Spots

- Filipino word order is Verb-Subject-Object (VSO), which does not transfer well to English.
- Inflectional verb endings, such *as -s, -en, -ed,* and *-ing* do not exist in Filipino, so it is common to leave out the third person singular verb marker (*"He walk,"* not *"He walks"*).

Korean

Background
Korean is spoken by 71 million people in North and South Korea. Standard Korean is based on the speech in and around Seoul.

Spoken
Korean does not have corresponding sounds for English /f/, /v/, /θ/, /ð/, and /ʤ/. In word-initial position, all Korean stops are voiceless. Voiced stops /b/, /d/, and /g/ are only produced between two vowels. Korean speakers may have difficulty producing /s/, /ʃ/, and /z/ in some contexts, in addition to English /r/ and /l/ sounds (e.g., *rock* and *lock*). They may have problems in producing English consonant clusters (e.g., *str-, sk-*). These problems can often be eliminated by vowel insertion or consonant deletion. In addition, the distinction between English tense and lax vowels (e.g., /i/ as in *beat* vs. /ɪ/ as in *bit*) may be problematic for Korean speakers.

Culture Clues

Korean uses a complex system of honorifics, so it is unusual for Korean students to use the pronoun *you* or call their teachers by their first name.

Written
Modern Korean uses the Korean alphabet (*Hangul*) or a mixed script of *Hangul* and Chinese. *Hangul* is an alphabetic script organized into syllabic blocks.

Grammar Hot Spots

- In contrast to English, Korean word order is Subject-Object-Verb (SOV). The verb always comes at the end of a sentence.
- Korean syllable stress is different, so learners may have difficulties with the rhythm of English.

Mandarin

Background
Chinese encompasses a wide range of dialects and is the native language of two-thirds of China. There are approximately 870 million Mandarin speakers worldwide. North Mandarin, as found in Beijing, is the basis of the modern standard language.

Spoken
Mandarin Chinese and English differ substantially in their sound structure. Mandarin lacks voiced obstruent consonants (/b/, /d/, /g/, /ʤ/), causing difficulty for speakers in perceiving and producing English voiced consonants (e.g., *buy* may be pronounced and perceived as *pie*). The sounds spelled with *th* are not present in Mandarin, so they are often substituted with /s/ or /t/ causing, for example, *fourth* to be pronounced as *fours.* Mandarin Chinese has five vowels. Due to the relatively small vowel inventory and contextual effects on vowels in Mandarin, many English vowels and tense/lax distinctions present problems for speakers of Mandarin Chinese. Mandarin allows only a very simple syllable structure, causing problems in producing consonant clusters in English. Speakers may drop consonants or insert vowels between them (e.g., *film* may become /filəm/). The use of tones in Mandarin may result in the rising and falling of pitch when speaking English.

Culture Clues

The use of formal and informal forms of English is hard to master for Mandarin speakers. Chinese speakers will often play down compliments they receive.

Written
Chinese is written with characters known as *Hànzi.* Each character represents a syllable and also has a meaning. A Romanized alphabet called *Pinyin* marks pronunciation of characters. Chinese speakers may have problems mastering letter-sound correspondences in written English, especially for sounds that are not present in Mandarin.

Grammar Hot Spots

- The non-inflected nature of Chinese causes Mandarin speakers to have problems with plurals, past tense markers, and gerund forms (*-s, -ed, -ing*).
- Mastering English tenses and passive is difficult. Students should be familiarized with correct lexical and syntactic features as well as appropriate situations for the use of various tenses and passives.

AAVE

African American Vernacular English in the Classroom

To effectively address AAVE in the classroom, the first and most important step for the teacher is to acknowledge the student's use of home language or AAVE as "language different, not language deficit." To accomplish this, a teacher replaces deficit terminology and phrases such as *correct, fix, make better, proper,* or *say it right* with affirming language such as *translate, code-switch, put it in another way,* or *say it for an academic audience.* The second step involves modifying the instruction, focusing on an established technique for second-language instruction called contrastive analysis. With this methodology, teachers have students focus on the rules of the target language through the lens of their home language. The process for doing so is outlined below:

1. **Pre-assessment:** Determine the students' needs for instruction regarding a particular linguistic feature. Use both formal and informal assessments. Listen to students talk; read their writing. In addition, assess the degree to which a student uses a particular linguistic feature. Not all Standard English Learners (SELs) use all Home Language features.
2. **Introduce the AAVE linguistic rule:** For example, explain that multiple negation is the use of multiple negative words in a sentence. The more negative intensifiers in a sentence, the greater the negative sentiment being expressed.
3. **Identify the use of the rule with authentic samples:** For example, explain that the statement *"We don't never have no homework on Friday"* is an example of multiple negation because it contains more than one negative word.
4. **Distinguish between AAVE and the target language:** Give as the SE equivalent *We don't normally have any homework on Friday.* Point out that in Standard English, usage requires one negative word and use of intensifiers (adjectives and adverbs).
5. **Explicitly teach the code switch:** Explain that *We don't never have no homework on Friday. = We don't normally have any homework on Friday.* Point out that Standard English intensifiers *normally* and *any* accurately translate the use of the three negatives in the Home Language sentence.
6. **Address the issue of situational appropriateness:** Emphasize that Standard English is required in many contexts, such as schoolwork, job interviews, and so on.
7. **Assessment:** Assess students to determine their ability to 1) accurately identify the use of AAVE rules, 2) differentiate between home and school language, and 3) code-switch between the two.

AAVE Linguistic Contrastive Analysis Chart

PHONICS	MARKERS	GRAMMAR	VOCABULARY
Digraph /th/ There is no /th/, similar to French as well as other languages. Examples AAVE: *dat* SE: *that* AAVE: *mouf* SE: *mouth*	**Past Tense Marker** /ed/ Markers, such as verb tense, are sometimes indicated by tonality versus a use of a morpheme in Standard English. Examples AAVE: *cook yesterday* SE: *cooked* AAVE: *move last night* SE: *moved*	**Regularization** "Hypercorrection" or over-generalizing of the rule linked to the irregular patterns of Standard English with number agreement and subject/objective pronouns Subject verb agreement Examples AAVE: *She walk home sometimes* SE: *She walks home sometimes* Reflexive pronoun AAVE: *hisself (subject pronoun is regularized object pronoun as well)* SE: *himself*	**Culturally Specific Static Vocabulary** Vocabulary specific to the community that is passed down generation to generation Terms like: *kitchen* (back of the hair) or *tripping* (being bothersome)
Same Voicing Consonant Clusters Voiced Clusters *ld, nd, ng* Unvoiced Clusters *sk, st, ft, kt* Examples AAVE: *col* SE: *cold* AAVE: *des* SE: *desk*	**Possessive Marker** Possession marked by location of possessor and intonation of word when verbalized Examples AAVE: *Bobby toy* SE: *Bobby's toy*	**Use of *Be*** Habitual *Be* The *be* form is durative, referring to an ongoing state. Examples AAVE: *I be talking with them.* SE: *I often talk with them.*	**Dynamic Uses of Slang** Vocabulary of the youth that changes frequently and can be tied to one specific generation Note: terms for money based on the decade 70s—bread 80s—mula 90s—benjimans 2000—cheddar
Vowel Pairs /I/ /i/ Mixing of short and long vowels Examples AAVE: *Ah* SE: *I* AAVE: Thank SE: Th*i*nk	**Plural Marker** Unnecessary when numerically defined Examples AAVE: *fifty cent* SE: *fifty cents*	**Topicalization** Subject announced or "topicalized." Examples AAVE: *That teacher she mean.* SE: *That teacher is mean.*	
Reflexive *R* and *L* *R* and *L* before controlled vowels that do not appear; same occurrence in Asian languages Examples: AAVE: *Sista', Motha'* SE: *Sister, mother* AAVE: *mi'ion, ye'ow* SE: *million, yellow*	**Negation** Uses of multiple negatives to intensify negative in sentences; not equivalent to double negative in Standard English Examples AAVE: *Don't never do that more.* SE: *Don't do that anymore.*	***Is/Are* Form** *Is/Are* linking verbs and helping verbs not always necessary Examples AAVE: *She going to the game with us.* SE: *She is going to the game with us.*	
Two Syllable Stress Patterns Examples: **Po**-lice **Ho**-tel			

Linguistic Contrastive Analysis Chart

The Consonants of English

IPA	ENGLISH	SPANISH	VIETNAMESE	CANTONESE
p	*pit* Aspirated at the start of a word or stressed syllable	*pato* (duck) Never aspirated	*pin* (battery)	*pʰa (to lie prone)* Always aspirated
b	*bit*	*barco* (boat) Substitute voiced bilabial fricative/ɞ/ in between vowels	*ba* (three) Implosive (air moves into the mouth during articulation)	**NO EQUIVALENT** Substitute /p/
m	*man*	*mundo* (world)	*mot* (one)	*ma* (mother)
w	*win*	*agua* (water)	**NO EQUIVALENT** Substitute word-initial /u/	*wa* (frog)
f	*fun*	*flor* (flower)	*phư̛ơ̛ng* (phoenix) Substitute sound made with both lips, rather than with the upper lip and the teeth like English /f/	*fa* (flower) Only occurs at the beginning of syllables
v	*very*	**NO EQUIVALENT** Learners can use correct sound	*Việt Nam* (Vietnam)	**NO EQUIVALENT** Substitute /f/
θ	*thing* Rare in other languages. When done correctly, the tongue will stick out between the teeth.	**NO EQUIVALENT** Learners can use correct sound	**NO EQUIVALENT** Substitute /tʰ/ or /f/	**NO EQUIVALENT** Substitute /tʰ/ or /f/
ð	*there* Rare in other languages. When done correctly, the tongue will stick out between the teeth.	*cada* (every) Sound exists in Spanish only between vowels; sometimes substitute voiceless /θ/.	**NO EQUIVALENT** Substitute /d/	**NO EQUIVALENT** Substitute /t/ or /f/
t	*time* Aspirated at the start of a word or stressed syllable English tongue-touch. Is a little farther back in the mouth than the other languages.	*tocar* (touch) Never aspirated	*tám* (eight) Distinguishes aspirated and non-aspirated	*tʰa* (he/she) Distinguishes aspirated and non-aspirated
d	*dime* English tongue-touch is a little farther back in the mouth than the other languages.	*dos* (two)	*Đōng* (Dong = unit of currency) Vietnamese /d/ is implosive (air moves into the mouth during articulation)	**NO EQUIVALENT** Substitute /t/
n	*name* English tongue-touch is a little farther back in the mouth than the other languages.	*nube* (cloud)	*nam* (south)	*na* (take)
s	*soy*	*seco* (dry)	*xem* (to see)	*sa* (sand) Substitute *sh*– sound before /u/ Difficult at ends of syllables and words
z	*zeal*	**NO EQUIVALENT** Learners can use correct sound	*rồi* (already) In northern dialect only Southern dialect, substitute /y/	**NO EQUIVALENT** Substitute /s/
ɾ	*butter* Written 't' and 'd' are pronounced with a quick tongue-tip tap.	*rana* (toad) Written as single *r* and thought of as an /r/ sound.	**NO EQUIVALENT** Substitute /t/	**NO EQUIVALENT** Substitute /t/
l	*loop* English tongue-touch is a little farther back in the mouth than the other languages. At the ends of syllables, the /l/ bunches up the back of the tongue, becoming velarized /ɫ/ or dark-l as in the word *ball*.	*libro* (book)	*cú lao* (island) /l/ does not occur at the ends of syllables	*lau* (angry) /l/ does not occur at the ends of syllables

HMONG	FILIPINO	KOREAN	MANDARIN
peb (we/us/our) Distinguishes aspirated and non-aspirated	*paalam* (goodbye) Never aspirated	*pal* (sucking)	*pʰei* (cape) Always aspirated
NO EQUIVALENT Substitute /p/	*baka* (beef)	NO EQUIVALENT /b/ said between vowels Substitute /p/ elsewhere	NO EQUIVALENT
mus (to go)	*mabuti* (good)	*mal* (horse)	*mei* (rose)
NO EQUIVALENT Substitute word-initial /u/	*walo* (eight)	*gwe* (box)	*wen* (mosquito)
faib (to divide)	NO EQUIVALENT Substitute /p/	NO EQUIVALENT Substitute /p/	*fa* (issue)
Vaj ('Vang' clan name)	NO EQUIVALENT Substitute /b/	NO EQUIVALENT Substitute /b/	NO EQUIVALENT Substitute /w/ or /f/
NO EQUIVALENT Substitute /tʰ/ or /f/	NO EQUIVALENT Learners can use correct sound, but sometimes mispronounce voiced /ð/.	NO EQUIVALENT Substitute /t/	NO EQUIVALENT Substitute /t/ or /s/
NO EQUIVALENT Substitute /d/	NO EQUIVALENT Learners can use correct sound	NO EQUIVALENT Substitute /d/	NO EQUIVALENT Substitute /t/ or /s/
them (to pay) Distinguishes aspirated and non-aspirated	*takbo* (run) Never aspirated	*tal* (daughter)	*ta* (wet) Distinguishes aspirated and non-aspirated
dev (dog)	*deretso* (straight)	NO EQUIVALENT Substitute /d/ when said between vowels and /t/ elsewhere.	NO EQUIVALENT Substitute /t/
noj (to eat)	*naman* (too)	*nal* (day)	*ni* (you) May be confused with /l/
xa (to send)	*sila* (they)	*sal* (rice) Substitute *shi–* sound before /i/ and /z/ after a nasal consonant	*san* (three)
NO EQUIVALENT Learners can use correct sound	NO EQUIVALENT Learners can use correct sound	NO EQUIVALENT Learners can use correct sound	NO EQUIVALENT Substitute /ts/ or /tsʰ/
NO EQUIVALENT Substitute /t/	*rin/din* (too) Variant of the /d/ sound	Only occurs only between two vowels Considered an /l/ sound	NO EQUIVALENT
los (to come) /l/ does not occur at the ends of syllables	*salamat* (thank you)	*balam* (wind)	*lan* (blue) Can be confused and substituted with /r/

Linguistic Contrastive Analysis Chart

The Consonants of English (continued)

IPA	ENGLISH	SPANISH	VIETNAMESE	CANTONESE
ɹ	*red* Rare sound in the world Includes lip-rounding	**NO EQUIVALENT** Substitute /r/ sound such as the tap /ɾ/ or the trilled /r/	**NO EQUIVALENT** Substitute /l/	**NO EQUIVALENT** Substitute /l/
ʃ	***sh**allow* Often said with lip-rounding	**NO EQUIVALENT** Substitute /s/ or /ʧ/	*sieu thị* (supermarket) southern dialect only	**NO EQUIVALENT** Substitute /s/
ʒ	*vi**s**ion* rare sound in English	**NO EQUIVALENT** Substitute /z/ or /ʤ/	**NO EQUIVALENT** Substitute /s/	**NO EQUIVALENT** Substitute /s/
ʧ	***ch**irp*	***ch**ico* (boy)	***ch**ính phủ* (government) Pronounced harder than English *ch*	**NO EQUIVALENT** Substitute /ts/
ʤ	***j**oy*	**NO EQUIVALENT** Sometimes substituted with /ʃ/ sound Some dialects have this sound for the *ll* spelling as in *llamar*	**NO EQUIVALENT** Substitute /c/, the equivalent sound, but voiceless	**NO EQUIVALENT** Substitute /ts/ Only occurs at beginnings of syllables
j	***y**ou*	*cie**l**o* (sky) Often substitute /ʤ/	***y**eu* (to love)	***j**au* (worry)
k	***k**ite* Aspirated at the start of a word or stressed syllable	***c**asa* (house) Never aspirated	***c**om* (rice) Never aspirated	***k**ʰa* (family) Distinguishes aspirated and non-aspirated
g	***g**oat*	***g**ato* (cat)	**NO EQUIVALENT** Substitute /k/	**NO EQUIVALENT** Substitute /k/
ŋ	*ki**ng***	*ma**n**go* (mango)	***Ng**ũyen* (proper last name)	*pha**ŋ*** (to cook)
h	***h**ope*	***g**ente* (people) Sometimes substitute sound with friction higher in the vocal tract as velar /x/ or uvular /χ/	***h**oa* (flower)	***h**a* (shrimp)

HMONG	FILIPINO	KOREAN	MANDARIN
NO EQUIVALENT Substitute /l/	NO EQUIVALENT Substitute the tap /ɾ/	NO EQUIVALENT Substitute the tap or /ɾ/ confused with /l/	*ran* (caterpillar) Tongue tip curled further backward than for English /r/
sau (to write)	*siya* (s/he)	Only occurs before /i/; Considered an /s/ sound	*shi* (wet)
zos (village)	NO EQUIVALENT Learners can use correct sound	NO EQUIVALENT	NO EQUIVALENT Substitute palatal affricate /tþ/
cheb (to sweep)	*tsa* (tea)	*cʰal* (kicking)	*cheng* (red)
NO EQUIVALENT Substitute *ch* sound	*Dios* (God)	NO EQUIVALENT Substitute *ch* sound	NO EQUIVALENT Substitute /ts/
Yaj (Yang, clan name)	*tayo* (we)	*je:zan* (budget)	*yan* (eye)
Koo (Kong, clan name) Distinguishes aspirated and non-aspirated	*kalian* (when) Never aspirated	*kal* (spreading)	*ke* (nest) Distinguishes aspirated and non-aspirated
NO EQUIVALENT Substitute /k/	*gulay* (vegetable)	NO EQUIVALENT Substitute /k/ Learners use correct sound between two vowels	NO EQUIVALENT Substitute /k/
gus (goose)	*angaw* (one million)	*baŋ* (room)	*tang* (gong) Sometimes add /k/ sound to the end
hais (to speak)	*hindi* (no)	*hal* (doing)	NO EQUIVALENT Substitute velar fricative /x/

Linguistic Contrastive Analysis Chart

The Vowels of English

IPA	ENGLISH	SPANISH	VIETNAMESE	CANTONESE
i	*beat*	*hijo* (son)	*di* (to go)	*si* (silk)
ɪ	*bit* Rare in other languages Usually confused with /i/ (*meat* vs. *mit*)	**NO EQUIVALENT** Substitute /i/	**NO EQUIVALENT** Substitute /i/	*sik* (color) Only occurs before velars Substitute /i/
e	*bait* End of vowel diphthongized—tongue moves up to /i/ or /ɪ/ position	*eco* (echo)	*kê* (millet)	*se* (to lend)
ɛ	*bet* Rare in other languages Learners may have difficulty distinguishing /e/ and /ɛ/: pain vs. pen	**NO EQUIVALENT** Substitute /e/	**NO EQUIVALENT** Substitute /e/	*seŋ* (sound) Only occurs before velars; difficult to distinguish from /e/ in all positions
æ	*bat* Rare in other languages Learners may have trouble getting the tongue farther forward in the mouth	**NO EQUIVALENT** Substitute mid central /ʌ/ or low front tense /a/	*ghe* (boat)	**NO EQUIVALENT** Hard to distinguish between /æ/ and /e/
u	*boot*	*uva* (grape)	*mua* (to buy)	*fu* (husband)
ʊ	*could* Rare in other languages Learners may have difficulty distinguishing /u/ and /ʊ/; *wooed* vs. *wood*	**NO EQUIVALENT** Substitute /ù/	**NO EQUIVALENT** Substitute u' (high back unrounded)	*suk* (uncle) Only occurs before velars Difficult to distinguish from /u/ in all positions
o	*boat* End of vowel diphthongized – tongue moves up to /u/ or /ʊ/ position	*ojo* (eye)	*cô* (aunt)	*so* (comb)
ɔ	*law*	**NO EQUIVALENT** Substitute /o/ or /ɑ/ Substituting /o/ will cause confusion (*low* vs. *law*); substituting /ɑ/ will not	*cá* (fish)	*hok* (shell) Only occurs before velars Difficult to distinguish from /o/ in all positions
ɑ	*hot*	*mal* (bad)	*con* (child)	*sa* (sand)
ɑ ʊ	*house* Diphthong starts /ɑ/ and moves to /ʊ/	*pauta*	*dao* (knife)	*sau* (basket)
ɔ ɪ	*boy* Diphthong starts at /ɔ/ and moves to /ɪ/	*hoy* (today)	*rồi* (already)	*soi* (grill)
ɑ ɪ	*bite* Diphthong starts at /ɑ/ and moves to /ɪ/	*baile* (dance)	*hai* (two)	*sai* (to waste)
ə	*about* Most common vowel in English; only in unstressed syllables Learners may have difficulty keeping it very short	**NO EQUIVALENT** Substitute /ʌ/ or the full vowel from the word's spelling	*mua* (to buy)	**NO EQUIVALENT**
ʌ	*cut* very similar to schwa /ə/	**NO EQUIVALENT** Substitute /a/	*giờ* (time)	*san* (new)
ɝ	*bird* Difficult articulation, unusual in the world but common in American English Learners must bunch the tongue and constrict the throat	**NO EQUIVALENT** Substitute /ʌ/ or /ɛr/ with trill	**NO EQUIVALENT** Substitute /ɨ/	*hæ* (boot)

HMONG	FILIPINO	KOREAN	MANDARIN
ib (one)	zɩ:ʃaŋ (market)	zɩ:ʃaŋ (market)	*ti* (ladder) Sometimes English /i/ can be produced shorter
NO EQUIVALENT Substitute /i/	*limampu* (fifty) This vowel is interchangeable with /i/; hard for speakers to distinguish these	**NO EQUIVALENT** Substitute /i/	**NO EQUIVALENT**
tes (hand)	*sero* (zero)	*be:da* (to cut)	*te* (nervous) Sometimes substitute English schwa /ə/
NO EQUIVALENT Substitute /e/	*sero* (zero) This vowel interchanges with /e/ like *bait*; not difficult for speakers to learn	*thɛ:do* (attitude)	**NO EQUIVALENT**
NO EQUIVALENT Substitute /ɛ/	**NO EQUIVALENT** Substitute /ɑ/ as in *hot*	**NO EQUIVALENT**	**NO EQUIVALENT** Substitute /ə/ or /ʌ/
kub (hot or gold)	*tunay* (actual) This vowel interchanges with /ʊ/ like *could*; not difficult for speakers to learn	*zu:bag* (watermelon)	*lu* (hut) Sometimes English /u/ can be produced shorter
NO EQUIVALENT Substitute /ɨ/ (mid central with lips slightly rounded)	*gumawa* (act) This vowel interchanges with /u/ like *boot*; not difficult for speakers to learn	**NO EQUIVALENT**	**NO EQUIVALENT**
NO EQUIVALENT	*ubo* (cough)	*bo:zu* (salary)	*mo* (sword) This vowel is a little lower than English vowel
Yaj (Yang clan name)	**NO EQUIVALENT** Spoken as /ɑ/ as in *hot*	**NO EQUIVALENT**	**NO EQUIVALENT** Substitute /o/
mov (cooked rice)	*ikaw* (you)	*ma:l* (speech)	*ta* (he/she) Sometimes substitute back /o/ or /u/
plaub (four)	*apoy* (fire)	**NO EQUIVALENT**	**NO EQUIVALENT**
NO EQUIVALENT	*himatay* (faint)	**NO EQUIVALENT**	**NO EQUIVALENT**
qaib (chicken)	**NO EQUIVALENT** Spoken as /ɑ/ as in *hot*	**NO EQUIVALENT**	**NO EQUIVALENT**
NO EQUIVALENT	*rin/din* (too) Variant of the /d/ sound	**NO EQUIVALENT** Difficult sound for learners	**NO EQUIVALENT**
NO EQUIVALENT	**NO EQUIVALENT** Spoken as /ɑ/ as in *hot*	**NO EQUIVALENT**	**NO EQUIVALENT**
NO EQUIVALENT Substitute diphthong /əɨ/	**NO EQUIVALENT** Spoken as many different vowels (depending on English spelling) plus tongue tap /ɾ/	**NO EQUIVALENT**	**NO EQUIVALENT**

How to Use Cornerstone

Cornerstone is a research-based, standards-aligned program that ensures that students will master the academic skills necessary to be successful across the curriculum. The many resources of the program have been carefully designed to make lesson planning, pacing, teaching, and assessment easier.

Teaching the Unit

Each of the six units in a level focuses on a theme and is organized around a *Big Question*, which serves as the focal point for building students' understanding of concepts and developing their skills. The four readings in each unit were carefully chosen to give students experience reading both informational texts and classic and contemporary literature.

Each Unit Includes

The Big Question allows students to unite the readings and information in the unit under a general theme. The *Unit Opener* builds background on the theme and activates students' prior knowledge as they explore the *Big Question*.

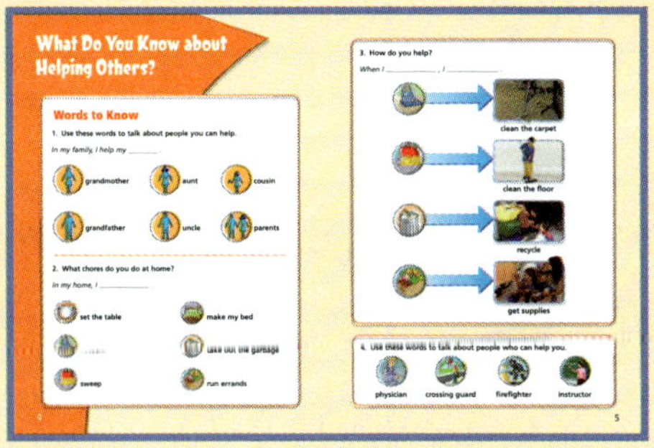

Words to Know introduces students to new vocabulary related to the unit theme and provides activities for language development.

Mini-Autobiographies help students learn about other cultures as they hear what other students say about the unit theme. *What About You* questions allow students to personalize the concepts.

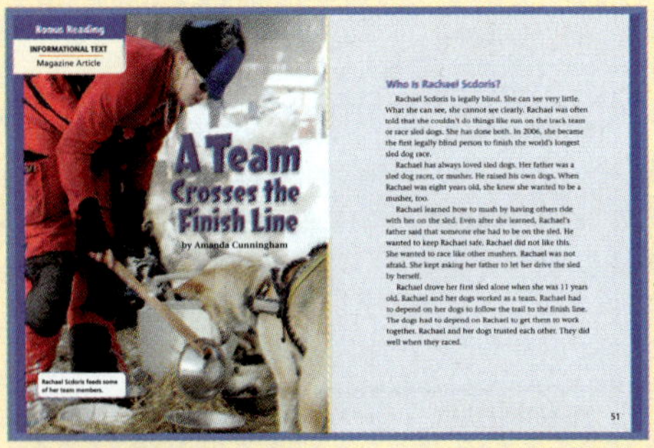

Bonus Reading concludes each unit and gives students an opportunity to build reading skills and read for pleasure.

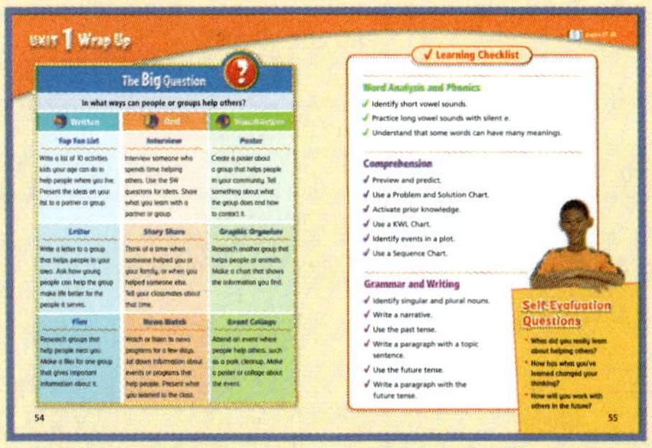

Unit Wrap Up provides assessment opportunities in multiple modalities. Students discuss the *Big Question* and select an *Assessment Project* to demonstrate their understanding.

Capture student interest with the engaging **Video Program DVD**, featuring background information about the theme.

Planning and Preparing to Teach

Start your planning with the **Teacher's Edition**. The *Longman Cornerstone* Teacher's Edition was specifically designed to provide easy-to-use, step-by-step lesson planning tools and includes a list of available teaching resources for every lesson. The program is organized in six-week instructional blocks so that thorough skills coverage is presented in manageable chunks. The standards covered in each lesson are listed on every left-hand page so that you and your students know what specific skills are being taught at any given point.

A ***Unit Planner*** introduces each unit and allows you to see all the readings, skills, resources, and assessment opportunities for the entire unit at a glance. Pacing suggestions are also included. A benchmark test is provided at the conclusion of each reading and unit so that you can effectively monitor student progress. This systematic, logical organization, with built-in progress monitoring, allows you to make sound instructional choices.

Use the **Teacher's Resource Book** for lesson plans, standards correlations, graphic organizers, selection summaries in multiple languages, and Parent/Guardian letters.

Use the **Teacher's CD-ROM** with **eBook** and **Exam*View*®** Test Generator to make lesson planning and testing easier. The **eBook** includes the entire Teacher's Edition, as well as all other print components, all available at a mouse click. The **Exam*View*®** electronic test generator lets you customize assessment to meet ever-changing classroom needs, and its powerful reporting functions allow you to get the most from your teaching.

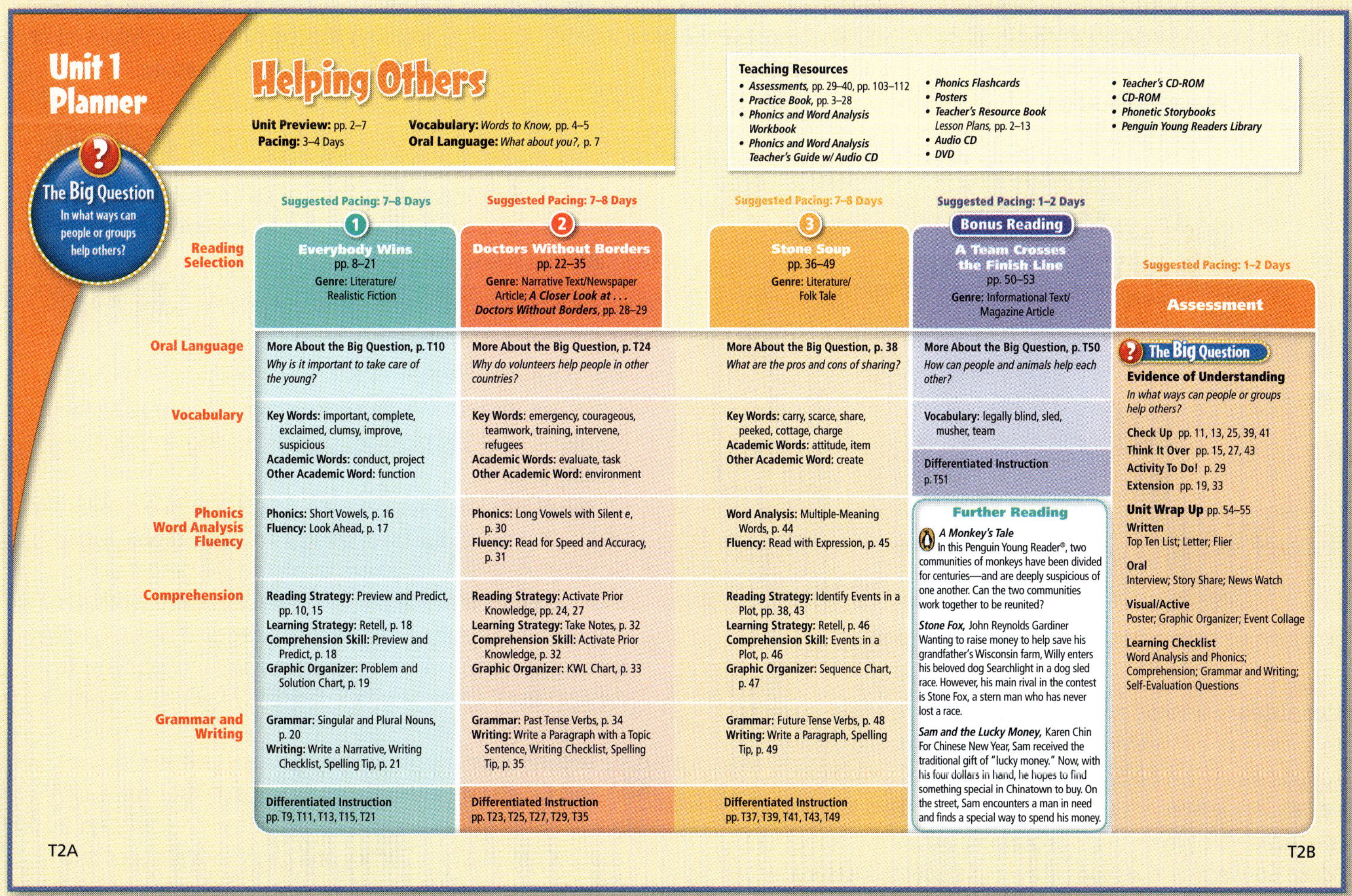

Unit 1 Planner

Helping Others

Unit Preview: pp. 2–7
Pacing: 3–4 Days
Vocabulary: *Words to Know*, pp. 4–5
Oral Language: *What about you?*, p. 7

The Big Question
In what ways can people or groups help others?

Teaching Resources
- *Assessments*, pp. 29–40, pp. 103–112
- *Practice Book*, pp. 3–28
- *Phonics and Word Analysis Workbook*
- *Phonics and Word Analysis Teacher's Guide w/ Audio CD*
- *Phonics Flashcards*
- *Posters*
- *Teacher's Resource Book* Lesson Plans, pp. 2–13
- *Audio CD*
- *DVD*
- *Teacher's CD-ROM*
- *CD-ROM*
- *Phonetic Storybooks*
- *Penguin Young Readers Library*

	Suggested Pacing: 7–8 Days	Suggested Pacing: 7–8 Days	Suggested Pacing: 7–8 Days	Suggested Pacing: 1–2 Days
Reading Selection	1 **Everybody Wins** pp. 8–21 **Genre:** Literature/ Realistic Fiction	2 **Doctors Without Borders** pp. 22–35 **Genre:** Narrative Text/Newspaper Article; ***A Closer Look at . . . Doctors Without Borders***, pp. 28–29	3 **Stone Soup** pp. 36–49 **Genre:** Literature/ Folk Tale	Bonus Reading **A Team Crosses the Finish Line** pp. 50–53 **Genre:** Informational Text/ Magazine Article
Oral Language	**More About the Big Question, p. T10** *Why is it important to take care of the young?*	**More About the Big Question, p. T24** *Why do volunteers help people in other countries?*	**More About the Big Question, p. 38** *What are the pros and cons of sharing?*	**More About the Big Question, p. T50** *How can people and animals help each other?*
Vocabulary	**Key Words:** important, complete, exclaimed, clumsy, improve, suspicious **Academic Words:** conduct, project **Other Academic Word:** function	**Key Words:** emergency, courageous, teamwork, training, intervene, refugees **Academic Words:** evaluate, task **Other Academic Word:** environment	**Key Words:** carry, scarce, share, peeked, cottage, charge **Academic Words:** attitude, item **Other Academic Word:** create	**Vocabulary:** legally blind, sled, musher, team **Differentiated Instruction** p. T51
Phonics Word Analysis Fluency	**Phonics:** Short Vowels, p. 16 **Fluency:** Look Ahead, p. 17	**Phonics:** Long Vowels with Silent *e*, p. 30 **Fluency:** Read for Speed and Accuracy, p. 31	**Word Analysis:** Multiple-Meaning Words, p. 44 **Fluency:** Read with Expression, p. 45	
Comprehension	**Reading Strategy:** Preview and Predict, pp. 10, 15 **Learning Strategy:** Retell, p. 18 **Comprehension Skill:** Preview and Predict, p. 18 **Graphic Organizer:** Problem and Solution Chart, p. 19	**Reading Strategy:** Activate Prior Knowledge, pp. 24, 27 **Learning Strategy:** Take Notes, p. 32 **Comprehension Skill:** Activate Prior Knowledge, p. 32 **Graphic Organizer:** KWL Chart, p. 33	**Reading Strategy:** Identify Events in a Plot, pp. 38, 43 **Learning Strategy:** Retell, p. 46 **Comprehension Skill:** Events in a Plot, p. 46 **Graphic Organizer:** Sequence Chart, p. 47	
Grammar and Writing	**Grammar:** Singular and Plural Nouns, p. 20 **Writing:** Write a Narrative, Writing Checklist, Spelling Tip, p. 21	**Grammar:** Past Tense Verbs, p. 34 **Writing:** Write a Paragraph with a Topic Sentence, Writing Checklist, Spelling Tip, p. 35	**Grammar:** Future Tense Verbs, p. 48 **Writing:** Write a Paragraph, Spelling Tip, p. 49	
	Differentiated Instruction pp. T9, T11, T13, T15, T21	**Differentiated Instruction** pp. T23, T25, T27, T29, T35	**Differentiated Instruction** pp. T37, T39, T41, T43, T49	

Further Reading

A Monkey's Tale
In this Penguin Young Reader®, two communities of monkeys have been divided for centuries—and are deeply suspicious of one another. Can the two communities work together to be reunited?

Stone Fox, John Reynolds Gardiner
Wanting to raise money to help save his grandfather's Wisconsin farm, Willy enters his beloved dog Searchlight in a dog sled race. However, his main rival in the contest is Stone Fox, a stern man who has never lost a race.

Sam and the Lucky Money, Karen Chin
For Chinese New Year, Sam received the traditional gift of "lucky money." Now, with his four dollars in hand, he hopes to find something special in Chinatown to buy. On the street, Sam encounters a man in need and finds a special way to spend his money.

Suggested Pacing: 1–2 Days

Assessment

The Big Question

Evidence of Understanding
In what ways can people or groups help others?

Check Up pp. 11, 13, 25, 39, 41
Think It Over pp. 15, 27, 43
Activity To Do! p. 29
Extension pp. 19, 33

Unit Wrap Up pp. 54–55
Written
Top Ten List; Letter; Flier

Oral
Interview; Story Share; News Watch

Visual/Active
Poster; Graphic Organizer; Event Collage

Learning Checklist
Word Analysis and Phonics; Comprehension; Grammar and Writing; Self-Evaluation Questions

T2A T2B

Teaching a Reading

Each reading is introduced with a *Big Question* for that reading to guide students' thoughts about the selection. Background building, vocabulary building, and a *Reading Strategy* are also provided to prepare students for a successful reading experience.

Each Reading Includes

Three readings include informational texts and fictional stories to engage students. Glossed words, which highlight potentially unfamiliar vocabulary, promote language acquisition.

Check-up questions at the bottom of every page and *Think It Over* questions at the end of every reading check comprehension.

The concluding *Reading Strategy* questions promote student use of the reading strategy that was introduced at the beginning of the reading.

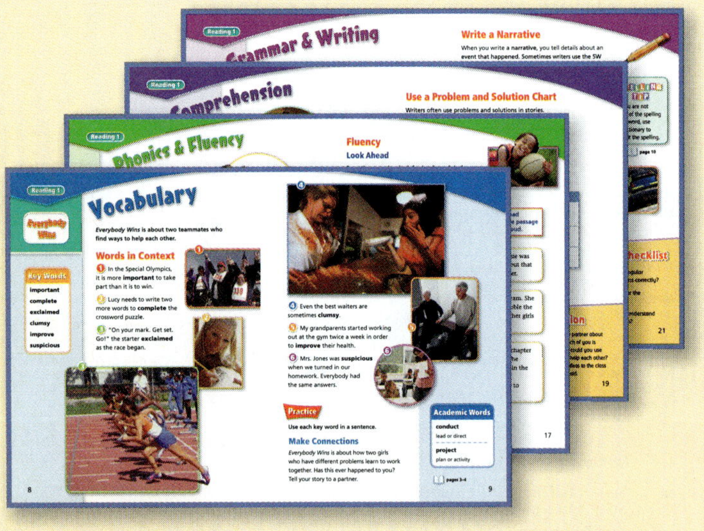

Vocabulary lessons precede each reading to allow students to encounter and learn new vocabulary in context with supportive visuals before they start the reading. These vocabulary lessons include both *Key Words* used in the reading and *Academic Words* that are portable across the curriculum. *Make Connection* questions draw out students' personal experiences related to the upcoming reading.

Practice Book references, at point of use, direct students and teachers to related activities that help students master foundational skills.

After each reading, students learn and practice a wealth of cross-curricular skills:

- **Word Analysis/Phonics & Fluency** pages teach how words are formed and give instruction in common phonetic elements. The Fluency pages provide practice in oral reading fluency.
- **Comprehension** pages teach a specific comprehension skill and then practice that skill using a related Graphic Organizer.
- **Grammar & Writing** pages teach specific grammar skills and then practice that skill in a structured writing assignment. Spelling Tips prompt students to check specific spelling patterns. A Writing Checklist prompts students to review their own writing independently and with a partner.

Technology The interactive **Student eBook** and **CD-ROM** make selections and activities come alive with audio support and interactivites for each reading. An *Audio CD* models oral reading fluency and gives critical support to English learners and struggling readers.

Monitoring Progress

Cornerstone makes it easy to monitor your students' progress with frequent opportunities to assess mastery and re-teach material.

- Use the **Placement Test** before students begin the program to ensure they are starting at the correct program level.
- Use the **Pretest** in the ***Assessment Book*** at the beginning of the school year to determine student readiness. You will find frequent checks and suggestions in the Teacher's Edition for monitoring student progress.
- After each Reading, use the **Reading Test** to assess understanding and mastery of the vocabulary, grammar, and comprehension skills taught with the Reading.
- After each Unit, use the **Unit Test** to assess student competency in vocabulary, oral reading fluency, word study, spelling, grammar, and writing.
- Use the **Midterm** and **Posttest** to gain more summative assessment information.
- Use the student score sheets in the ***Assessment Book*** to identify skills and standards that have been mastered, as well as those that need to be retaught.

Resources to Support Learning

- **Practice Book**
- **Graphic Organizers**
- **Reading Summaries**
- **Vocabulary Cards**
- **Daily Language Practice Transparencies**
- **Penguin Library**
- **Assessment**
- **Audio CD**
- **Video DVD**
- **Student eBook and CD-ROM**
- **Teacher eBook and CD-ROM**

- Use the **Exam*View*®** electronic test generator to customize assessment and provide powerful reporting tools to help tailor instruction to individual student needs.
- Use the **Exit Exam** to determine whether students are ready to join mainstream coursework or continue to the next level of the program.

Built-in Differentiated Instruction

Cornerstone gives unprecedented opportunities for reaching all students.

- **Teacher's Edition:** Use the strategies and techniques geared toward English learners (including standard English learners) and struggling readers. The CRI icon denotes suggestions that are appropriate for *Culturally Responsive Instruction*.
- **Practice Book:** This workbook gives students extra support in foundational skills and develops active reading habits, as the students interact with the text.
- **Transparencies:** *Daily Language Practice* gives students the chance to apply the language they learned in the previous lesson. *Graphic Organizers* give struggling readers and English learners a toolkit to organize their thoughts and writing with visual support.
- **Extension Activities:** Enriching activities in multiple modalities are provided at least twice in each unit to give students opportunities to expand on unit concepts.

Extension

Talk with your partner about things that each of you is good at. How could you use those skills to help each other? Present your ideas to the class using a visual aid.

- **Teacher's Resource Book:** *Reading Summaries* in English, Chinese, Cambodian, Hmong, Spanish, and Vietnamese give students a preview of each reading in their home language.

Using *Longman Cornerstone* with SIOP

Longman Cornerstone is designed to help English language learners develop English language skills and succeed in all content areas of academic studies. The recursive structure of the program aligns clearly with the components and features of the SIOP model.

Longman Cornerstone and SIOP

Preparation

- The Big Question (content objectives)
- Listening and Speaking (language objectives)
- Writing (language objectives)

Building Background

- What Do You Know About . . .
- Quick Write
- Vocabulary
- Your Stories About...

Comprehensible Input

- Photos, Pictures, Captions
- Charts and Graphic Organizers
- A Closer Look
- Glossed Words

Strategies

- Reading
- Check Up
- Word Analysis
- Phonics
- Fluency
- Learning Stategy

Interaction

- Work with a Partner
- Plays, Oral Reading, Poems
- Discuss

Practice and Application

- Word Analysis and Fluency
- Activity to Do
- Grammar and Writing
- Comprehension
- Think It Over

Lesson Delivery

- The Big Question
- Listening and Speaking
- Your Stories About . . .
- Writing
- What Do You Know About . . .

Review and Assessment

- Comprehension
- Extension
- Grammar and Writing
- Self-Evaluation Questions
- Unit Wrap Up (Learning Checklist)

For more information visit www.LongmanCornerstone.com

LONGMAN

CORNERSTONE

C

Anna Uhl Chamot

Jim Cummins

Sharroky Hollie

PEARSON
Longman

Longman Cornerstone C

Pearson Education, 10 Bank Street, White Plains, NY 10606

Staff credits: The people who made up the *Longman Cornerstone* team, representing editorial, production, design, manufacturing, and marketing, are John Ade, Rhea Banker, Liz Barker, Kenna Bourke, Jeffrey Buckner, Brandon Carda, Daniel Comstock, Martina Deignan, Gina DiLillo, Nancy Flaggman, Cate Foley, Patrice Fraccio, Tracy Grenier, Zach Halper, Henry Hild, Sarah Hughes, Karen Kawaguchi, Lucille Kennedy, Ed Lamprich, Jamie Lawrence, Niki Lee, Christopher Leonowicz, Tara Maceyak, Katrinka Moore, Linda Moser, Liza Pleva, Edie Pullman, Monica Rodriguez, Tara Rose, Tania Saiz-Sousa, Chris Siley, Heather St. Clair, Loretta Steeves, and Andrew Vaccaro.

Text design and composition: The Quarasan Group, Inc.
Illustration and photo credits: See page 363.

Library of Congress Cataloging-in-Publication Data
Chamot, Anna Uhl.
Longman Cornerstone / Anna Uhl Chamot, Jim Cummins, Sharroky Hollie.
p. cm.
Includes index.
Contents: 1. Level 1. —2. Level 2. — A. Level 3. — B. Level 4. — C. Level 5.
1. English language—Textbooks for foreign speakers. (1. English language—Textbooks for foreign speakers. 2. Readers.) I. Cummins, Jim. II. Hollie, Sharroky. III. Title.

ISBN-13: 978-0-13-514808-2
ISBN-10: 0-13-514808-1

PEARSON LONGMAN ON THE WEB

Pearsonlongman.com offers online resources for teachers and students. Access our Companion Websites, our online catalog, and our local offices around the world.

Visit us at **www.pearsonlongman.com**.

Printed in the United States of America

2 3 4 5 6 7 8 9 10–CRK–12 11 10 09 08

Dear Student,

Welcome to *Longman Cornerstone!*

We wrote *Longman Cornerstone* to help you succeed in all your school studies. This program will help you learn the English language you need to study language arts, social studies, math, and science. You will learn how to speak to family members, classmates, and teachers in English.

Cornerstone includes a mix of many subjects. Each unit has four different readings that include some fiction (made-up) and nonfiction (true) articles, stories, songs, and poems. The readings will give you some of the tools you need to do well in all your subjects in school.

As you use this program, you will build on what you already know, learn new words, new information and facts, and take part in creative activities. The activities will help you improve your English skills.

Learning a language takes time, but just like learning to skateboard or learning to swim, it is fun!

We hope you enjoy *Longman Cornerstone* as much as we enjoyed writing it for you!

Good luck!

Anna Uhl Chamot
Jim Cummins
Sharroky Hollie

A Cornerstone Unit Walkthrough

Your *Cornerstone* Unit!

Cornerstones are important for a building and important for learning, too.

Meet the program that will give you the cornerstones you need to improve in English and do better in all your subjects in school.

Kick Off Each Unit

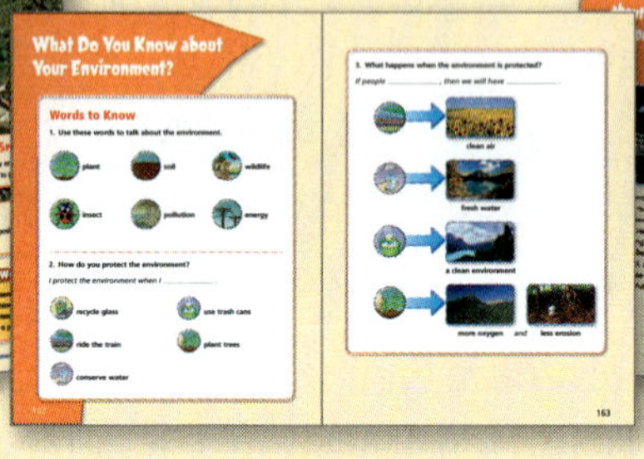

Big Question
The Big Question pulls all the readings together and helps you focus on big ideas.

Words to Know
Learn new vocabulary for the unit theme.

Mini-Autobiographies
Meet other students and hear what they say about the unit theme.

For Each Reading

Vocabulary
Get to know the words *before* you read.

Readings 1, 2, and 3
Read with success! Get help from glossed words and Check-Up questions.

After Each Reading

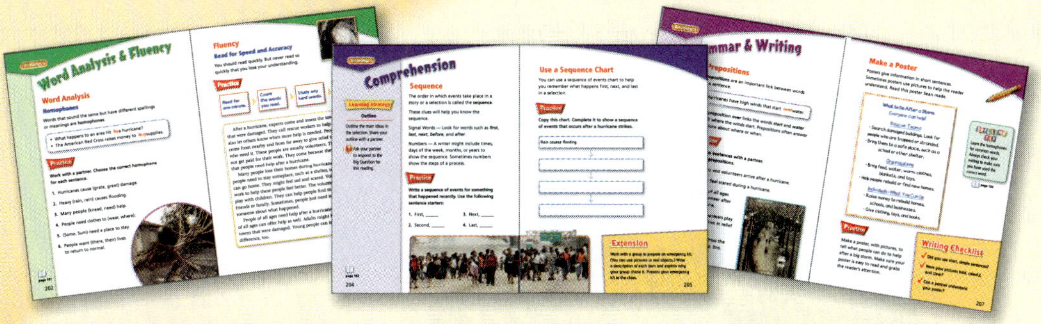

Word Analysis & Fluency
Become a better reader by learning about phonics and how words are formed. Then practice reading with ease on the fluency pages.

Comprehension
Focus on a comprehension skill and practice it using a graphic organizer.

Grammar & Writing
Learn rules of grammar to help you communicate. Then improve your writing skills.

Wrap Up Each Unit

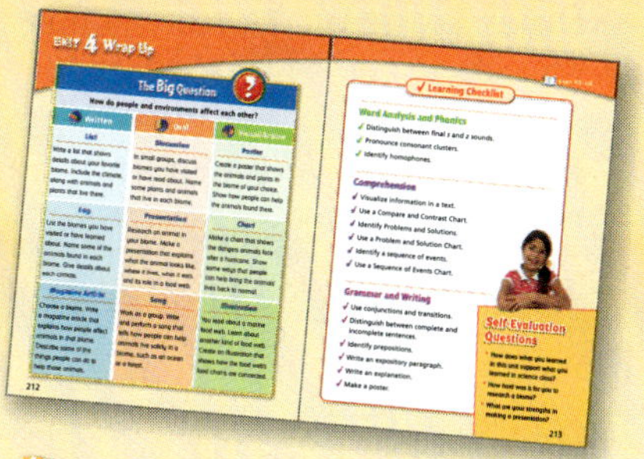

Bonus Reading
Take a break and read for fun.

Wrap up
Discuss the Big Question with your class. Choose an Assessment Project to show all you have learned.

Unit 1 Planner

Helping Others

Unit Preview: pp. 2–7
Pacing: 3–4 Days

Vocabulary: *Words to Know*, pp. 4–5
Oral Language: *What about you?*, p. 7

The Big Question
In what ways can people or groups help others?

	Suggested Pacing: 7–8 Days 1	Suggested Pacing: 7–8 Days 2
Reading Selection	**Everybody Wins** pp. 8–21 **Genre:** Literature/ Realistic Fiction	**Doctors Without Borders** pp. 22–35 **Genre:** Narrative Text/Newspaper Article; ***A Closer Look at . . . Doctors Without Borders***, pp. 28–29
Oral Language	**More About the Big Question, p. T10** *Why is it important to take care of the young?*	**More About the Big Question, p. T24** *Why do volunteers help people in other countries?*
Vocabulary	**Key Words:** important, complete, exclaimed, clumsy, improve, suspicious **Academic Words:** conduct, project **Other Academic Word:** function	**Key Words:** emergency, courageous, teamwork, training, intervene, refugees **Academic Words:** evaluate, task **Other Academic Word:** environment
Phonics Word Analysis Fluency	**Phonics:** Short Vowels, p. 16 **Fluency:** Look Ahead, p. 17	**Phonics:** Long Vowels with Silent *e*, p. 30 **Fluency:** Read for Speed and Accuracy, p. 31
Comprehension	**Reading Strategy:** Preview and Predict, pp. 10, 15 **Learning Strategy:** Retell, p. 18 **Comprehension Skill:** Preview and Predict, p. 18 **Graphic Organizer:** Problem and Solution Chart, p. 19	**Reading Strategy:** Activate Prior Knowledge, pp. 24, 27 **Learning Strategy:** Take Notes, p. 32 **Comprehension Skill:** Activate Prior Knowledge, p. 32 **Graphic Organizer:** KWL Chart, p. 33
Grammar and Writing	**Grammar:** Singular and Plural Nouns, p. 20 **Writing:** Write a Narrative, Writing Checklist, Spelling Tip, p. 21	**Grammar:** Past Tense Verbs, p. 34 **Writing:** Write a Paragraph with a Topic Sentence, Writing Checklist, Spelling Tip, p. 35
	Differentiated Instruction pp. T9, T11, T13, T15, T21	**Differentiated Instruction** pp. T23, T25, T27, T29, T35

Teaching Resources

- *Assessments,* pp. 29–40, pp. 103–112
- *Practice Book,* pp. 3–28
- *Phonics and Word Analysis Workbook*
- *Phonics and Word Analysis Teacher's Guide w/ Audio CD*
- *Phonics Flashcards*
- *Posters*
- *Teacher's Resource Book* Lesson Plans, pp. 2–13
- *Audio CD*
- *DVD*
- *Teacher's CD-ROM*
- *CD-ROM*
- *Phonetic Storybooks*
- *Penguin Young Readers Library*

Suggested Pacing: 7–8 Days

3 Stone Soup

pp. 36–49

Genre: Literature/ Folk Tale

More About the Big Question, p. 38
What are the pros and cons of sharing?

Key Words: carry, scarce, share, peeked, cottage, charge
Academic Words: attitude, item
Other Academic Word: create

Word Analysis: Multiple-Meaning Words, p. 44
Fluency: Read with Expression, p. 45

Reading Strategy: Identify Events in a Plot, pp. 38, 43
Learning Strategy: Retell, p. 46
Comprehension Skill: Events in a Plot, p. 46
Graphic Organizer: Sequence Chart, p. 47

Grammar: Future Tense Verbs, p. 48
Writing: Write a Paragraph, Spelling Tip, p. 49

Differentiated Instruction
pp. T37, T39, T41, T43, T49

Suggested Pacing: 1–2 Days

Bonus Reading

A Team Crosses the Finish Line

pp. 50–53

Genre: Informational Text/ Magazine Article

More About the Big Question, p. T50
How can people and animals help each other?

Vocabulary: legally blind, sled, musher, team

Differentiated Instruction
p. T51

Further Reading

A Monkey's Tale
In this Penguin Young Reader®, two communities of monkeys have been divided for centuries—and are deeply suspicious of one another. Can the two communities work together to be reunited?

Stone Fox, John Reynolds Gardiner
Wanting to raise money to help save his grandfather's Wisconsin farm, Willy enters his beloved dog Searchlight in a dog sled race. However, his main rival in the contest is Stone Fox, a stern man who has never lost a race.

Sam and the Lucky Money, Karen Chin
For Chinese New Year, Sam received the traditional gift of "lucky moncy." Now, with his four dollars in hand, he hopes to find something special in Chinatown to buy. On the street, Sam encounters a man in need and finds a special way to spend his money.

Suggested Pacing: 1–2 Days

Assessment

The Big Question

Evidence of Understanding
In what ways can people or groups help others?

Check Up pp. 11, 13, 25, 39, 41
Think It Over pp. 15, 27, 43
Activity To Do! p. 29
Extension pp. 19, 33

Unit Wrap Up pp. 54–55

Written
Top Ten List; Letter; Flier

Oral
Interview; Story Share; News Watch

Visual/Active
Poster; Graphic Organizer; Event Collage

Learning Checklist
Word Analysis and Phonics; Comprehension; Grammar and Writing; Self-Evaluation Questions

STEP 1: Introduce

Tell students that they will read about helping others in four different readings. Lead students in a discussion about helping others. Explain that helping others can mean helping family and friends and helping people you've never met before.

Unit Content Students practice reading and comprehension skills, such as preview and predict, activate prior knowledge, and identify events in a plot. They apply academic language strategies such as taking notes and retelling.

Visual Literacy

Labels Help students realize that each reading is numbered and that the title of the reading is below the picture. Have students read the titles and discuss what the people in the pictures may be doing to help each other.

STEP 2: Build Background

The Big Question

Explain that people can help others in a variety of ways, such as doing jobs for them, teaching them something new, or by working with them to achieve a common goal.

SAY *The Big Question is* In what ways can people or groups help others? *Think of different ways people can be affected by others who help.*

- *Why is it important to clean your room?*
- *What do students do to help others at your school?*
- *How could you help to improve the parks in your community?*

Have students make a chart like the one below to list ways to help people at home, at school, or in their community.

Chores at home	
Jobs at school	
Groups for volunteering	

UNIT 1 Helping Others

Teamwork can be hard sometimes, but when everyone pitches in, the results can be amazing.

READINGS

1

Everybody Wins

2

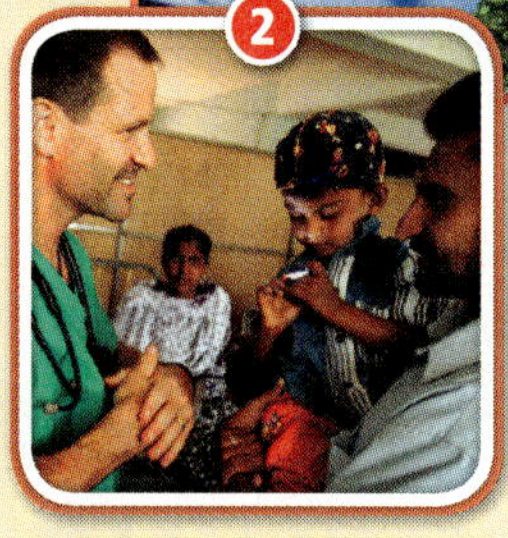

Doctors Without Borders

3

Stone Soup

TESOL Standards

Goal 1, Standard 2—To use English to communicate in social settings: Students will interact in, through, and with spoken and written English for personal expression and enjoyment.
Descriptors—Sharing social and cultural traditions and values; Expressing personal needs, feelings, and ideas.

The Big Question

In what ways can people or groups help others?

LISTENING AND SPEAKING

You will tell a story about people helping each other.

WRITING

You will write a story about a problem you had to solve.

Bonus Reading

A Team Crosses the Finish Line

Quick Write

What does cooperation mean to you? Write several sentences to explain your ideas.

Differentiated Instruction

Beginning	Read aloud the titles of the readings, listed on p. 2. Ask students to point to the pictures as you read and repeat each title.
Early Intermediate	Point to each inset picture on p. 2 and ask students to describe what they see. Elicit short answer responses such as *two girls*, *a doctor*, and *a boy and a girl*.
Intermediate	Ask students to guess which character in each inset picture is a helper. Have students explain what the character is doing to help.
Struggling Reader	Point to each picture on pp. 2–3. Say a word to describe the picture and have students repeat the words.

STEP 3: Connect

Listening and Speaking

Read the text in the box aloud. Ask students to think of people who have jobs that help others. Write a list of these jobs on the board and pronounce each one for students.

Possible Responses firefighter, doctor, nurse, teacher, lifeguard

Writing

Read the text in the Writing box aloud to students. Explain that their stories should be about how they worked with others to solve the problem.

SAY *Think of a time when you helped someone when they did not expect it.*

- *What did you do to cooperate?*
- *Did you have any problems?*
- *How were they resolved?*
- *What did you learn while helping?*

Have students describe an example of a problem they had problem to solve. Use a Sequence of Events Chart to help students describe ways to solve the conflict.

Adapt the Activity

Explain that *cooperation* means working together as a team. *Conflict* means disagreeing about what to do or how to do it. Have students write a list of ways they know to cooperate.

Quick Write

Have students write a definition of *cooperate* in their own words. Have them write a sentence to explain why it is important to learn more ways to cooperate.

Link to Social Studies

Ask students to write a short paragraph that describes an important event in history when people overcame a conflict and learned ways to cooperate with each other.

Visual Literacy

Graphic Organizer Introduce the Big Question transparency and use it throughout the unit to help students connect the readings to the Big Question.

STEP 1: Introduce

Unit Vocabulary

Use these pages to help students identify terms used to describe family members helping each other. Post your Words to Know poster for this unit in the classroom. As students read the unit, reinforce the unit vocabulary by using the Vocabulary Cards provided as a Blackline Master in the *Teacher's Resource Book* in memory games or as flash cards.

STEP 2: Teach

Words to Know

Say aloud each of the terms in section 1 for family members and encourage students to repeat the terms with you. Have students point to the correct icon for the family member as they say each term.

Direct students' attention to the question in section 2 about chores on p. 4. Have them complete the sentence stem using the words provided. Repeat this procedure with the question and sentence stem on p. 5.

Academic Words

Discuss the definitions for *proceed* and *estimate* with students. Share the following context sentences with students. Have students add the terms to their personal thesaurus.

> Before we could *proceed* to the next step of the instructions, we had to complete the first step.
>
> We had to *estimate* how many people attended the concert because we could not count each person.
>
> Challenge students to suggest synonyms for each of the two Academic Words.

Teaching Resources

- ***Teacher's Resource Book,*** pp. 89–90; 167
- ***Posters***
- ***Transparencies,*** pp. 1–6
- ***Assessments,*** pp. 3–10
- ***CD-ROM*** • ***Audio CD***

What Do You Know about Helping Others?

Words to Know

1. Use these words to talk about people you can help.

In my family, I help my ______ .

grandmother **aunt** **cousin**

grandfather **uncle** **parents**

2. What chores do you do at home?

In my home, I ____________ .

set the table **make my bed**

vacuum **take out the garbage**

sweep **run errands**

4

TESOL Standards

Goal 1, Standard 3—To use English to communicate in social settings: Students will use learning strategies to extend their communicative competence.
Descriptors—Testing hypotheses about language; Listening to and imitating how others use English; Exploring alternative ways of saying things; Using context to construct meaning.

3. How do you help?

When I ____________, I ____________.

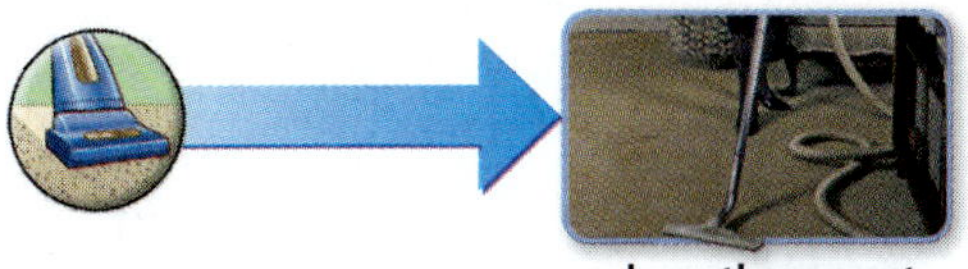

clean the carpet

clean the floor

recycle

get supplies

4. Use these words to talk about people who can help you.

physician

crossing guard

firefighter

instructor

5

Differentiated Instruction

Beginning	Read aloud the names of family members in random order. Ask students to point to the pictures as you read. Have students write each word.
Intermediate	Point to each picture on p. 4 and ask students what they see. Elicit short answer responses such as *uncle*, *aunt*, and *cousin*.
Greater Challenge	Ask students to work in pairs to discuss some responsibilities of the people in the pictures on p. 5.
Struggling Reader	Point to a picture of a family member and say the word. Have students repeat the word to describe the picture. Help students write each word.

Explain the Captions

Read the captions in section 3 aloud and have the class repeat them as they examine the pictures. Give students the following explanations of each caption.

vacuum use a machine that sucks up dirt

carpet large rug

broom floor brush with a long handle

sweep use a broom to clean the floor

recycle separate glass, paper and plastics from trash to be used again

errands jobs for the family you do away from home, like shopping at a store or going to the post office

supplies things that are needed

physician doctor

crossing guard person whose job is to help people cross the street safely

instructor teacher

Explain to students that the words *sweep* and *recycle* are used as verbs. Remind students that verbs are words that show action. Ask students which word in the list can be used as a verb or a noun.

STEP 3: Practice

Use Vocabulary

Writing Captions Ask students to create their own captions for each icon in section 4. Encourage them to draw pictures to illustrate the action that they have included in their labels. Display the captions and pictures in the classroom.

Build Discussion Ask students to brainstorm examples of more people who have jobs that help others. Encourage students to think of the different people they see each day. Write the following sentence on the board and have students fill in the blanks:

Today, when I ________, I saw ________ helping ________.

STEP 1: Introduce

Unit Background

On pp. 6–7, students read mini-autobiographies from peers around the world to learn about helping others. The peer mini-autobiographies and accompanying exercises are designed to increase comprehension. They are also designed to model how students can talk and write about helping others and working together. Use the exercises below to elicit students' prior knowledge, opinions, and ideas to help them tell their own helping stories.

STEP 2: Monitor Progress

Comprehension Check

Charlie

1. What does Charlie celebrate every year?
   He celebrates the Fourth of July.
2. How do the families celebrate the day?
   They celebrate with a potluck picnic.
3. How do the families cooperate?
   They bring food to share.

Clara

1. Where does Clara live?
   Clara lives in Spain.
2. What happened a few years ago where Clara lives?
   There was a huge oil spill.
3. Who came to help?
   People from all over the world came to help.

Link to Social Studies

Map Skills Draw students' attention to the map of the world in the background of these pages. Have students follow the lines from the photos of each student's home to the location on the map. Say the name of each location and have students repeat the locations aloud. Encourage students to use world maps in their social studies books to find the same locations.

Teaching Resources
- *Audio CD*

Your Stories about Helping

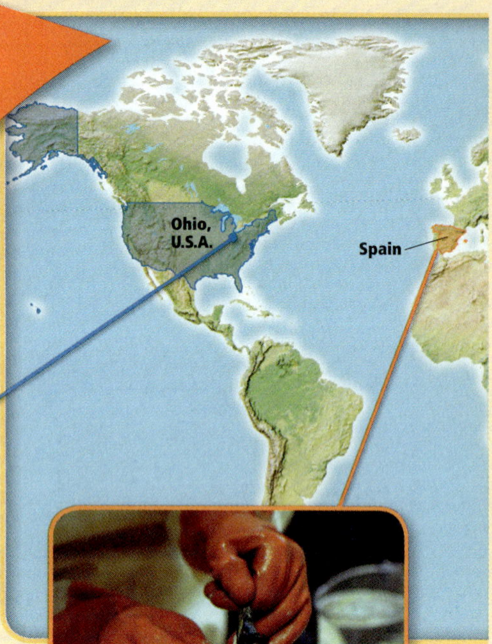

In my town in Ohio, we celebrate the Fourth of July every year with a potluck picnic. Every family brings a different dish, and we all share each other's food. There is always plenty of food to eat. We have a lot of fun.

I live in Spain. There was a huge oil spill a few years ago. The beaches were full of oil sludge. Many birds were covered with oil and were dying. People from all over the world came to help clean up after the oil spill.

6

TESOL Standards

Goal 1, Standard 1—To use English to communicate in social settings: Students will use English to participate in social interactions.
Descriptors—Using nonverbal communication in social interactions; Getting personal needs met; Engaging in conversations.

Goal 1, Standard 2—To use English to communicate in social settings: Students will interact in, through, and with spoken and written English for personal expression and enjoyment.
Descriptors—Sharing social and cultural traditions and values; Expressing personal needs, feelings, and ideas.

Sergei

An astronaut from my town of Batumi, Russia, is now in charge of the International Space Station. There, astronauts and engineers from many countries do research together to find out about Earth and the solar system. What they learn will help us make plans for a better future.

Mert

Archaeologists from all over the world have come to Egypt to participate in archaeological digs in the Valley of the Kings. A team of experts working together uncovered a tomb near the tomb of King Tutankhamen. By helping each other, experts learn more about ancient history.

What about you?

1. When have you worked with others?
2. How are these students' stories similar to yours?
3. Do you have a story about people helping each other? Tell your story!

7

Sharing Language and Culture

Global Perspective Have students share what they know about places around the world where people have come together to improve or rebuild their communities. Examples might include such things as building a road or irrigation system, or completely rebuilding a community, or region, following a natural disaster such as a tsunami or volcanic eruption.

Accelerate Language Development

Explain to students that writers use different points of view when writing or telling stories. When a writer tells a story in the first person, he or she is in the story. The writer will often use pronouns like *I* or *we* in the story. Have students find the personal pronouns used in the peer stories.

Mert

1. Who has come to Mert's country?
   Archaeologists from all over the world have come to her country, Egypt.
2. Why did they come?
   They came to participate in archaeological digs in the Valley of the Kings.
3. How does working together help experts?
   Working together helps experts learn more about ancient Egypt.

Sergei

1. Where does Sergei come from?
   Sergei comes from Russia.
2. Who is now in charge of the International Space Station?
   An astronaut from Sergei's town, Batumi.
3. How will the research help people?
   It will help us make plans for our future.

Study Skills

Internet Invite students to choose one of the countries in the stories on pp. 6–7. Have them research one fact about that country on the Internet.

STEP 3: Assess

What About You?

1. Have students describe their own experiences of helping others.
2. Have students try to get their listeners to imagine the experience their partners are describing.

Personal Story Have students write a mini-autobiography using the peer stories on pp. 6–7 as a model. Ask them to share their stories with their classmates. Encourage students to use a dictionary or thesaurus to find alternative words as needed.

STEP 1: Introduce

Key Words

Help students learn the skill of defining words by using context.

SAY *The vocabulary words from* Everybody Wins *are shown in the Words in Context selection. The pictures help us learn what the words mean.*

Explain that the red circled number 1 goes with the word *important* and the picture helps to explain the meaning of the word. Have students find each key word and connect it with its photograph.

STEP 2: Teach

Words in Context

Write the following sentences on the board. Have students complete this fill-in-the-blanks exercise using the key words and read the sentences aloud.

1. *If you want to win, it is* important *to play fairly.*
2. *When my homework is* complete, *I can visit my friend.*
3. *"What a beautiful day!" she* exclaimed.
4. *He was* clumsy *because he dropped his lunch tray.*
5. *More studying will help* improve *her grades.*
6. *My parents were* suspicious *when I said I did not have to study for my test.*

Ask students to work in groups to write additional sentences for each key word.

Study Skills

Dictionary Students can look up the vocabulary words in the dictionary to see if the Words in Context definitions are correct.

Online Dictionary Students can use an online dictionary or the CD that accompanies a learners' dictionary, such as the *Longman Basic Dictionary*.

www.LongmanCornerstone.com

Teaching Resources
- ***Practice Book***, pp. 3–4
- ***Transparencies***, p. 37
- ***CD-ROM*** • ***Audio CD***

Reading 1

Everybody Wins

Vocabulary

Everybody Wins **is about two teammates who find ways to help each other.**

Key Words
- important
- complete
- exclaimed
- clumsy
- improve
- suspicious

Words in Context

1. In the Special Olympics, it is more **important** to take part than it is to win.

2. Lucy needs to write two more words to **complete** the crossword puzzle.

3. "On your mark. Get set. Go!" the starter **exclaimed** as the race began.

8

TESOL Standards

Goal 1, Standard 3—To use English to communicate in social settings: Students will use learning strategies to extend their communicative competence.
Descriptors—Testing hypotheses about language; Listening to and imitating how others use English; Exploring alternative ways of saying things; Using context to construct meaning.

Goal 2, Standard 2—To use English to achieve academically in all content areas: Students will use English to obtain, process, construct, and provide subject matter information in spoken and written form.
Descriptors—Understanding and producing technical vocabulary and text features according to content area.

Goal 2, Standard 3—To use English to achieve academically in all content areas: Students will use appropriate learning strategies to construct and apply academic knowledge.
Descriptors—Using context to construct meaning.

4 Even the best servers are sometimes **clumsy**.

5 My grandparents started working out at the gym twice a week in order to **improve** their health.

6 Mrs. Jones was **suspicious** when we turned in our homework. Everybody had the same answers.

Practice

Use each key word in a sentence.

Make Connections

Everybody Wins is about how two girls who have different problems learn to work together. Has this ever happened to you? Tell your story to a partner.

Academic Words

conduct
lead or direct

project
plan or activity

Practice Book pages 3–4

Differentiated Instruction

Beginning	Have students point to the illustrations that correspond to each word and repeat the word. Then have students practice writing each word.
Early Intermediate	Have volunteers read the context sentences aloud. Then ask questions (both factual and inferential) based on the information contained in those sentences.
Greater Challenge	Have students reread pp. 8–9. Have them work with partners to write a short definition of these key words: *important*, *complete*, *suspicious*, and *exclaimed*.
Standard English Learner CRI	Reinforce the correct pronunciation of the words by pointing to the word in each context sentence and reading aloud a short phrase of the sentence that includes the key word. Have students repeat each phrase.

Visual Literacy

Photographs. Ask students to find the numbers in the story on pp. 8–9 that match the numbers in the pictures. Compare and contrast the activities people are doing in each photograph.

Academic Words

Discuss the definitions for *conduct* and *project* with students. Share the following context sentences with students. Have students add the terms to their personal thesaurus.

The band leader will *conduct* the orchestra for the school musical.

Planning has begun on the new *project* to add more seating to the sports arena.

Have students work in small groups to discuss how each academic word can be used as a noun or a verb. Ask students to write sentences using each term as a noun and a verb.

Other Academic Words

Write the following context sentences on the board and have students identify whether the word *function* is being used as a noun or verb.

We hope our computers will *function* correctly when we install new software. (verb)

They attended a *function* at the community center to help raise money for the animal shelter. (noun)

CRI Have students call out other words that can be used as nouns and verbs.

STEP 3: Practice

Flexible Grouping You may assign these exercises as a class discussion, partner activity, or an individual writing assignment.

Make Connections

Writing Fluency If students have difficulty telling a story for Make Connections, have them think of a time when they had a conflict while helping someone. Have students fill in a Story Map graphic organizer to describe their process for resolving the conflict. Encourage students to use a dictionary or thesaurus to find alternative words.

STEP 1: Introduce

More About The Big Question

The Big Question for this selection focuses on the theme of the story—that people who are good at different things can help each other.

SAY *As we read the story, pay attention to the ways teammates can help each other.*

- *Ask yourself "What is important about being a teammate?"*
- *Is winning always the most important thing?*

Encourage students to use the Sequence of Events Chart shown below to identify events in the plot for *Everybody Wins*.

Casey got a low score on her science test.
↓
Mr. Vega says she will have to quit the team.
↓
Casey asks Jessie for help.

STEP 2: Teach

Model the Reading Strategy

Preview and Predict Discuss with students how it is possible to predict what a story is about by looking at the title and the pictures and reading the word definitions at the bottom of the page.

SAY *What is the story is about?*

- *What do the pictures tell about the characters?*
- *Read the first and last paragraphs. What do you think happens?*

Understand Text Structure

Draw students' attention to the genre label. Tell students that realistic fiction is a made-up story, but it does describe something that could happen in real life.

Teaching Resources
- ***Teacher's Resource Book,*** pp. 103–104
- ***Practice Book,*** pp. 5–6
- ***CD-ROM*** • ***Audio CD***

Reading 1

LITERATURE

Realistic Fiction

The Big Question

How can people who are good at different things help each other?

Reading Strategy

Preview and Predict

- Read the title.
- Look at the illustrations.
- Read the words and the definitions at the bottom of each page.
- Read the first and last paragraph of the story.
- Predict what the story will be about.

Everybody Wins

by Pamela Walker
illustrated by Meredith Johnson

Casey was the best basketball player on the school team. She made more baskets than anyone else. She would dribble the ball past her teammates to the basket. Some of the other girls on the team called her a ball hog.

"Why didn't you pass the ball to Jessie?" Damaris asked after a game. "She was right under the basket."

"Because Jessie's too clumsy!" Casey exclaimed. "I wanted to win."

Carla said, "You're being mean. Jessie tries really hard. Besides, we're a team."

Winning was more important to Casey than working with her team.

---

dribble move a ball forward by bouncing it

ball hog someone who will not give the ball to other players on the team

pass throw

10

TESOL Standards

Goal 2, Standard 2—To use English to achieve academically in all content areas: Students will use English to obtain, process, construct, and provide subject matter information in spoken and written form.

Descriptors—Hypothesizing and predicting; Analyzing, synthesizing, and inferring from information; Demonstrating knowledge through application in a variety of contexts; Listening to, speaking, reading, and writing about subject matter information.

The next day, Mr. Vega asked to speak to Casey after class. He told Casey she got another low score on her science test.

"You're going to have to do much better," Mr. Vega said. "Unless your grades improve, you will have to quit the team."

"Quit the team!" Casey cried. "But I have to play basketball!"

"I'm sorry," Mr. Vega said. "These are the rules. You have three weeks to improve your science grade."

Casey couldn't believe what she was hearing! She would do anything to keep from being kicked off the team.

"Maybe you should ask Jessie to help you," Mr. Vega said. "She's one of my best science students."

Check Up How do you think Casey will react to Mr. Vega's idea?

11

Differentiated Instruction

Beginning	Have students work in pairs to use gestures and pantomime to act out winning a game. Have students identify each action being performed by saying a word or phrase.
Early Intermediate	Have students write short answers to these questions: *When have you played on a team? What did your teammates do to work together? What did you learn about being on a team?*
Intermediate	Have students reread pp. 10–11. Have them work with partners to discuss how people can work together when they are on a team.
Struggling Reader	Have students locate and read aloud the words in the text that answer these questions: *What ball game are the girls playing? In what subject must Casey improve her grades?*

Read Aloud

Have students take turns reading the paragraphs on pp. 10– 11 then describe what winning means to Casey in this story. Ask students to describe the action that is taking place in the two illustrations.

Build Vocabulary

Direct attention to the highlighted word in the text with a definition at the bottom of the page.

- Invite volunteers to read aloud the word and the definition.
- Have students write a context sentence using the word.
- Have students repeat this activity for each highlighted word as they read the selection.

STEP 3: Assess

Academic Words

Discuss the definitions for *structure* and *method* with students. Share the following context sentences with students. Have students add the terms to their personal thesaurus.

Every step of the plan for the *structure* of the bridge was written in the manual.

He used a very simple *method* to build the birdhouse.

Ask students to look up the terms in the dictionary and then write one complete sentence for each term.

Other Academic Words

Explain to students that terms like *structure* and *method* have meanings that are *similar*. Write the following definition on the board:

If two or more things are similar, *they have characteristics in common.*

Have students make a list of things that are *similar* about the girls on the basketball team.

Check Up

Have students work with partners to make predictions about how Casey will react to Mr. Vega's idea. Ask students to fill in a Prediction Chart.

STEP 1: Monitor Progress

Comprehension Check

Characters and Conflict After reading pp. 12–13 discuss with students what they have learned about Casey and Jessie.

SAY *Think of three words you would use to describe Casey. Now think of three words to describe Jessie.*

- *What about Casey's character caused her to need help?*
- *Why was Jessie reluctant to help Casey?*
- *Do you think Carla and Damaris were helpful? Why or why not?*

Explain to students that each question helps reveal details about the characters. Have students fill in a Cause and Effect Chart like the one below about how Casey and Jessie can resolve their conflict.

Casey did not pass the ball.	Winning is more important than her teammates.
Casey got a low score on a science test.	She may have to quit the team.
Casey needs help with science.	Jessie will help Casey with science; Casey will help Jessie with basketball.

Reteach

Have students work in small groups to read aloud the dialogue on pp. 12–13. After reading, ask students to make a list of words that describe each of the characters. Tell students they must hunt in the reading for clues about each character.

Possible Responses

Casey: competitive, determined, angry

Jessie: puzzled, willing to try

Damaris: concerned, optimistic

Carla: friendly, helpful

Casey was angry. The team's most important game of the year was in three weeks. She couldn't miss it. How could Mr. Vega be so mean? He knew the team wouldn't win if she didn't play.

Casey ran out of Mr. Vega's classroom. She did not look where she was going, and she crashed into Damaris and Carla.

"What's the matter?" asked Damaris.

"Mr. Vega said I am failing science. He said I can't play basketball if I don't get better grades," Casey said.

"Why don't you ask Jessie to help you?" asked Damaris.

"She's really good at science," said Carla.

"But she's angry with me," said Casey.

angry not happy

failing not doing well

12

TESOL Standards

Goal 2, Standard 2—To use English to achieve academically in all content areas: Students will use English to obtain, process, construct, and provide subject matter information in spoken and written form.

Descriptors—Hypothesizing and predicting; Analyzing, synthesizing, and inferring from information; Demonstrating knowledge through application in a variety of contexts.

Jessie came out of the art room as the other girls were talking.

"Hey, Jessie!" Carla said. "Casey wants to ask you something."

"I need your help," said Casey.

Jessie was puzzled. "Why should I help you?" she asked.

"I'm sorry I was mean to you. But, if you help me with science, I'll help you with basketball," said Casey.

"Why?" asked Jessie.

"Because if I don't do better in science class, I will be off the basketball team," Casey said.

"Come on," said Damaris. "You two can help each other. Everybody will win."

"It's worth a try," said Carla. "Okay?"

"Okay," said Jessie. "We can try to help each other."

Check Up Do you think the girls' plan will work? Why?

13

Differentiated Instruction

Beginning	Have students find the sentence that tells what Casey will do for Jessie if Jessie helps her. Have them describe what she will do.
Intermediate	Have students write a complete sentence to answer the following question: *How can Jessie and Casey help each other?*
Greater Challenge	Have students write a paragraph that explains what Damaris means when she says, "Everybody will win."
Standard English Learner CRI	Have students study the pictures of the girls, then work in pairs to describe to the class what is happening in the photos. Encourage students to describe many details using phrases or complete sentences.

STEP 2: Teach

Visual Literacy

Illustrations Draw students' attention to the illustrations on pp. 12 and 13. Point out that people's faces sometimes tell a lot about what they're thinking and feeling.

SAY *Look at the pictures of the girls on pages. 12 and 13. It is possible to draw a conclusion about a character by noticing his or her expression. A character's reaction is a clue to describing that character.*

- *What do you know about the setting of the story?*
- *What can you learn about the characters by knowing the action that takes place in each picture?*
- *What is Jessie's reaction when Casey asks her for help?*

Ask students to write one sentence to describe Casey and one sentence to describe Jessie.

Build Discussion

Context Clues Explain to students that authors add clues to a story to make it fun for readers to guess what will happen next. Have students describe to the class which clues in the story and in the pictures helped them draw conclusions about the two main characters in *Everybody Wins*.

Point of View

Explain to students that when a story is narrated in the first person, one of the characters is telling the story. *Everybody Wins* is narrated in the third person. This means that an outside observer is telling the story.

STEP 3: Assess

Check Up

Write the following prompt on the board. *Do you think the girls' plan will work?* Have students work in groups to write paragraphs in response to the prompt. Ask volunteers to read their responses to the class.

STEP 1: Monitor Progress

Comprehension Check

Main Idea and Details Direct students to read through to the end of the reading. Lead a class discussion about what they learned about the result of the girls' plan.

SAY *We looked for clues in the story to help us understand more about the characters. Clues also tell us about the plot of a story.*

- *What do you think was the most important event in the story?*
- *What clues in the story made the event seem important?*
- *If you were the author of* Everybody Wins, *how would you have ended the story?*

Have students fill in a Main Idea and Details Chart like the one below with information about the event they selected as the most important in the story. Suggest students work together if they picked the same event.

The girls have a plan.

Jessie helped Casey with science.	Casey often passed the ball to Jessie at practice.	Jessie scored the winning basket.

Build Discussion

Make Connections Invite students to relate the events in the story to their own experience with teamwork. Have them discuss what qualities a good teammate should have. Then have students describe things about themselves that make them good teammates.

Study Skills

Dictionary Have students work in pairs to look up the terms *compete* and *competition*. Ask them to compare the similarities in spelling and definitions.

Online Dictionary Students can use an online dictionary or the CD that accompanies a learners' dictionary, such as the *Longman Basic Dictionary*.

www.LongmanCornerstone.com

For the next three weeks, Jessie helped Casey with her science homework.

"When you study," Jessie told Casey, "first read the chapter all the way through. Then go back and write down the words you don't know. You can look up these words in the dictionary."

Jessie even made a practice science quiz for Casey to complete.

During basketball practice, Casey began to pass the ball to Jessie. At first the other girls were suspicious. Why was Casey being so helpful?

"Don't forget to bend your knees right before you shoot," Casey told Jessie during practice.

Casey's science grade improved, and she stayed on the team. Jessie began to improve in basketball, too.

14

TESOL Standards

Goal 2, Standard 2—To use English to achieve academically in all content areas: Students will use English to obtain, process, construct, and provide subject matter information in spoken and written form.

Descriptors—Hypothesizing and predicting; Analyzing, synthesizing, and inferring from information; Demonstrating knowledge through application in a variety of contexts; Listening to, speaking, reading, and writing about subject matter information.

Near the end of the next big game, Casey had the ball. The crowd was yelling and screaming. She was starting to dribble the ball toward the basket when she saw Jessie wave to her.

Jessie was wide open and right under the basket.

Casey passed the ball to her, and Jessie shot it into the basket!

"Great job, Jessie!" the team exclaimed. "We won! We won!"

"We won because Casey helped me," said Jessie.

"Great job, Casey!" the team said.

"No," said Casey. "We won because we're a team."

The girls laughed. "Great job, team!"

In the huddle after the game, the team shouted, "Everybody wins!"

---

wide open standing with nobody in the way

Practice Book pages 5–6

Reading Strategy

Preview and Predict

Before you read the story, you previewed it and made predictions.

- Were your predictions correct?
- Did making predictions help you to understand the story? How?

Think It Over

1. Who asks Jessie to help Casey?
2. How do Casey and Jessie help each other?
3. What have Casey and Jessie learned by the end of the story?

Differentiated Instruction	
Beginning	Have students complete the sentence frame about the picture on p. 15: The girls in the picture are _____ because _____.
Early Intermediate	Have students describe the action in the picture on p. 14. Tell students the sentence in the story that describes the action is on p. 15. Have students find and copy the sentence.
Intermediate	Jessie told Casey some things to improve Casey's science grade. Have students discuss with partners the two things that Jessie told her.
Struggling Reader	Point to the pictures on pp. 14–15 and say the word *team*. Say the following sentence and write it on the board: *A team works together. Have students copy the sentence.*

STEP 2: Teach

Visual Literacy

Illustrations Direct students to look at the picture on p. 15. Ask a volunteer to describe the action in the picture.

SAY *Pictures can help us understand a story better.*

- *What are the girls doing?*
- *Why are they so happy?*
- *Explain what they meant when they shouted "Everybody wins!"*

STEP 3: Assess

Reading Strategy

Preview and Predict Provide an example of making a prediction about this selection. Remind students that there are no wrong answers in making predictions.

SAY *Before I read this story, I wanted to know what it would be about.*

- *First, I previewed the title and the pictures. Then, I predicted what would happen.*
- *Some of my predictions were correct, and some were not.*
- *I predicted the story would be about basketball, but I didn't predict that Casey and Jessie would help each other.*
- *Making predictions made the story more interesting. I wanted to know what would happen next.*

Think It Over

Flexible Grouping You may assign this exercise as a whole class discussion, partner activity, or individual writing assignment.

Answer Key

1. Damaris asks Jessie to help Casey.
2. Casey helps Jessie with basketball, and Jessie helps Casey with science.
3. Casey and Jessie have learned that everybody wins when they help each other.

STEP 1: Introduce

Phonics

Short Vowels Help students understand that if a word has only one vowel, the sound of the vowel is short. Demonstrate the sound of a short vowel by saying the words *hid* and *hide*.

STEP 2: Teach

Review the pronunciation of short vowels with students. Write the words shown below on the board and ask students to say them aloud. Point out that each word is made up of vowels and consonants. Below each word, add the letters *C* for consonants and *V* for vowels as shown.

best CVCC	than CCVC	win CVC	as VC
class CCVCC	it VC	help CVCC	job CVC

Introduce the different spelling patterns. Point out that the spelling pattern of each word includes only one vowel. Review the rule about short vowel sounds.

SAY *This rule will help you pronounce words with one vowel:*

- *When a word has only one vowel, the vowel sound is usually short.*
- *All the words on the board have short vowel sounds.*

STEP 3: Practice

1. Have students work with partners. Tell them that some sentences in the Practice exercise will have more than one word with a short vowel sound.
2. For each word column, have partners take turns reading the words aloud. Have them work together to think of another word that has the same short vowel sound.

Teaching Resources
- ***Practice Book***, p. 7
- ***Phonics Workbook***
- ***Phonics Flashcards***
- ***CD-ROM*** • ***Audio CD***

Reading 1

Phonics & Fluency

Phonics

Short Vowels

The letters *a*, *e*, *i*, *o*, and *u* are **vowels**. Each word in the chart has one vowel.

Short Vowels

a	e	i	o	u
am can	Ed get	if win	on job	up but

Rule Box

When a word has a single vowel, the vowel sound is usually short.

Practice

Read the sentences with a partner. Look for short vowels.

- Will you let me join the team?
- Did you make the cut?
- Here is the game plan.
- Take your best shot.
- It's a slam dunk.

1. Make a short vowel chart like the one above.
2. Add the short vowel words you found to the chart.
3. Add one more word for each short vowel.

Practice Book page 7

16

TESOL Standards

Goal 2, Standard 3—To use English to achieve academically in all content areas: Students will use appropriate learning strategies to construct and apply academic knowledge.
Descriptors—Applying basic reading comprehension skills such as skimming, scanning, previewing, and reviewing text; Using context to construct meaning; Applying self-monitoring and self-corrective strategies to build and expand a knowledge base.

Goal 3, Standard 3—To use English in socially and culturally appropriate ways: Students will use appropriate learning strategies to extend their sociolinguistic and sociocultural competence.
Descriptors—Experimenting with variations of language in social and academic settings; Rehearsing variations of language use in different social and academic settings; Observing and modeling how others speak and behave in a particular situation or setting; Seeking information about appropriate language use and behavior.

Fluency

Look Ahead

Sometimes readers look for hard words before they read. They then try to figure them out.

Practice

Pick one passage. → Find any hard words. → Practice saying those words. → Read the passage aloud.

1 Casey was the best basketball player on the team. Jessie was an average player on the team. One day, they found out that they could both win if they learned to help each other.

2 Casey was the best basketball player on the school team. She made more baskets than anyone else. She would dribble the ball past her teammates to the basket. Some of the other girls on the team called her a ball hog.

3 "When you study," Jessie told Casey, "first read the chapter all the way through. Then go back and write down the words you don't know. You can look up these words in the dictionary."

Jessie even made a practice science quiz for Casey to complete.

17

Linguistic Note

Practice In the fluency exercise on p. 17, students encounter the word *practice*. Those who speak Spanish may recognize this word as being similar to *práctica* in their home language. Explain that the final *c* in *practice/práctica* have different pronunciations. In Spanish, the *c* in práctica has the /*k*/ sound; in English the *c in practice* has the /*s*/ sound.

Accelerate Language Development

Phonics In this lesson, students review the sounds of short vowels. Some languages do not have short vowel sounds and some students may not be familiar with this pronounciation.

STEP 1: Introduce

Fluency

Look Ahead Explain to students that fluent readers sometimes look ahead to find hard words. Finding and practicing these words can help students read more smoothly.

Play the audio CD for this reading to the class, asking students to listen for pacing, intonation, and expression.

STEP 2: Practice

Have students do the following exercise with partners:

- Assign one paragraph to each pair of students.
- Have students look for words that they think might be difficult to pronounce.
- Have students take turns reading the words aloud with their partners.

Students should make a list of the words that they consider difficult to pronounce and look up the definition of each word.

Possible Responses–Hard words

basketball, average, teammates, chapter, through, practice

Remind students to use appropriate verbal cues, facial expressions, and gestures while reading.

STEP 3: Extend

Study Skills

Thesaurus Explain to students that a thesaurus is a book of synonyms. Tell them that this is the place you look when you can't think of that one perfect word you need for what you are writing.

Write on the board the following list of words from the reading:

clumsy, improve, crashed, puzzled, suspicious

Have students look up each word in the thesaurus and find a synonym for each.

STEP 1: Monitor Progress

Learn Strategy

Retell Explain to students that retelling can help them understand the story when they finish reading it.

Before retelling *Everybody Wins*, have students review the Big Question for the reading. Then have students take turns retelling the story, emphasizing how the story begins and ends. After students have retold the story, have them take turns responding to the Big Question.

STEP 2: Teach

Preview and Predict

Students will review the predictions that they made when they previewed the story before they read it.

SAY *Sometimes when you preview a story, you discover that one or more of the characters has a problem. Use what you already know and what you learned from the preview to make a prediction about how that problem might be solved.*

STEP 3: Practice

Flexible Grouping You may assign the activity in the student book as a class discussion, partner activity, or individual written assignment.

Possible Responses

1. I learned it would be about a girls' basketball team.
2. I predicted the story was about a girls' basketball team and a big game. I was right.
3. I might look for diagrams, charts, or maps.
4. I think it is about doctors working all over the world.

Teaching Resources
- ***Practice Book,*** p. 8
- ***Transparencies,*** p. 63
- ***Teacher's Resource Book,*** p. 161
- ***CD-ROM***

Reading 1

Comprehension

Learning Strategy

Retell

Retell the story to a partner.

Ask your partner to respond to the Big Question for this reading.

Preview and Predict

After previewing, you can predict what you think the story will be about.

Practice

Answer the questions.

1. What did you learn from previewing the story?
2. What did you predict the story was about? Were you right?
3. The reading that starts on page 24 is nonfiction. What additional text features might you check as you preview the text?
4. Preview the next reading. What do you think it will be about?

Practice Book page 8

18

TESOL Standards

Goal 2, Standard 2—To use English to achieve academically in all content areas: Students will use English to obtain, process, construct, and provide subject matter information in spoken and written form.
Descriptors—Hypothesizing and predicting; Analyzing, synthesizing, and inferring from information; Demonstrating knowledge through application in a variety of contexts; Retelling information; Representing information visually and interpreting information presented visually

Goal 3, Standard 3—To use English in socially and culturally appropriate ways: Students will use appropriate learning strategies to extend their sociolinguistic and sociocultural competence.
Descriptors—Observing and modeling how others speak and behave in a particular situation or setting; Self-monitoring and self-evaluating language use according to setting and audience; Rehearsing variations of language use in different social and academic settings.

Use a Problem and Solution Chart

Writers often use problems and solutions in stories. Identifying the problems and solutions will help you better understand the story.

Practice

Copy this Problem and Solution Chart. Complete it to show each problem and solution from the story. Share your work with a partner.

Problem		Solution
The Team's Problem: Casey was not letting other players have the ball.	→	
Casey's Problem:	→	
Jessie's Problem:	→	

Extension

Talk with your partner about things that each of you is good at. How could you use those skills to help each other? Present your ideas to the class using a visual aid.

19

Accelerate Language Development

Development Conventions Not all rules of punctuation transfer from language to language. For example, in Spanish, questions begin with an inverted question mark and end with a question mark. Using the questions on p. 18, point out the correct punctuation of questions in English.

Linguistic Note

Problem For students who also speak Spanish, the word *problem* is a cognate of the Spanish word *problema* and may be familiar to them. Both words originated from the Greek word *problema*.

STEP 1: Teach

Use a Problem and Solution Chart

Ask students to think about three problems they had in the past that they solved. Have students write one sentence to describe each problem, then write one sentence to describe how each problem was solved. Have them mix up the problem and solution sentences and give them to their partners. Direct each partner to match the problem with its correct solution.

STEP 2: Practice

You may have students complete the graphic organizer provided as a Blackline Master in the *Teacher's Resource Book*. Have students discuss each problem and solution with partners.

Answer Key

- The Team's Solution: Casey learned to value teamwork as much as winning.
- Casey's Problem: She had to do better in science if she wanted to play basketball.
- Casey's Solution: Jessie helped her with science, and Casey improved her grade.
- Jessie's Problem: She was not good at basketball.
- Jessie's Solution: Casey showed Jessie ways to play better.

STEP 3: Extend

Oral Presentation Have students make up a simple story that tells how they help their partners and their partners help them. Students can choose to make a speech to the class or to present and describe a drawing or collage. Encourage students to fill in a Sequence of Events Chart to help them make up their stories. Remind students to use appropriate verbal cues, facial expressions, and gestures in their presentation.

STEP 1: Introduce

Help students understand that a singular noun names one person, place, or thing, and a plural noun names more than one person, place, or thing.

STEP 2: Teach

Singular and Plural Nouns

Have students read the Rule Box on p. 20. Copy onto the board the 3-column chart shown below and ask volunteers to fill in the blanks.

Rules	Singular	Plural
To form the plural of most nouns, add *-s*	player week, rule	players ________ ________
To form the plural of nouns ending in *s, ss, ch, sh, or x,* add *-es*.	bus pass bench	buses ________ ________
To form the plural of nouns ending in a consonant and *y*, change the y to *i* and add *-es*.	story city dictionary	stories ________ ________

STEP 3: Practice

Before students begin the Practice activity in their student books, have them write the singular form for the following plural nouns:

stores, houses, taxes, wishes, presses, carries

Encourage students to identify which rule for forming plurals applies to each of the plural nouns shown above.

Answer Key

1. months
2. classes
3. boxes
4. sandwiches
5. games
6. parties

Teaching Resources
- ***Practice Book***, pp. 9–10
- ***Transparencies***, pp. 69–80
- ***Assessements***, pp. 29–32
- ***CD-ROM***

Reading 1

Grammar & Writing

Singular and Plural Nouns

Singular nouns name one person, place, or thing. The words ***team***, ***basket***, and ***game*** are singular nouns. **Plural** nouns name more than one person, place, or thing. The words ***players***, ***teammates***, and ***rules*** are plural nouns.

Rule Box

To form the plural of most words, you simply add the letter **s**. To form the plural of nouns that end in *s, ss, ch, sh*, or *x*, you add **-es**. You form the plural of nouns that end in a consonant and *y* by changing the *y* to **i** and adding **-es**.

Practice

Copy each singular noun. Write the plural form.

1. month
2. class
3. box
4. sandwich
5. game
6. party

Practice Book page 9

20

TESOL Standards

Goal 1, Standard 3—To use English to communicate in social settings: Students will use learning strategies to extend their communicative competence.
Descriptors—Seeking support and feedback from others.

Goal 2, Standard 1—To use English to achieve academically in all content areas: Students will use English to interact in the classroom.
Descriptors—Following oral and written directions, implicit and explicit; Explaining actions; Expressing likes, dislikes, and needs.

Goal 2, Standard 3—To use English to achieve academically in all content areas: Students will use appropriate learning strategies to construct and apply academic knowledge.
Descriptors—Using context to construct meaning; Actively connecting new information to information previously learned; Imitating the behaviors of native English speakers to complete tasks successfully.

Goal 3, Standard 1—To use English in socially and culturally appropriate ways: Students will use the appropriate language variety, register, and genre according to audience, purpose, and setting.
Descriptors—Using a variety of writing styles appropriate for different audiences, purposes, and settings; Recognizing and using Standard English and vernacular dialects appropriately.

Write a Narrative

When you write a **narrative**, you tell details about an event that happened. Sometimes writers use the 5W questions to help see if they have included all the details in their narrative. The 5W question words are: ***who***, ***what***, ***where***, ***when***, and ***why***.

Read about Pedro's trip to a NASCAR race.

I love cars! My father took me to a NASCAR race in Daytona because I got straight A's on my report card. It was so exciting! I was amazed at all the colorful cars and the large crowd. The crowd started to scream as the race was about to begin. Then the starting flag came down, and the cars zoomed around the track. There was even a crash. Luckily, nobody was hurt. The cars went around the track many, many times. Finally, my favorite driver came in first. It was a great day!

SPELLING TIP

If you are not sure of the spelling of a word, use a dictionary to check the spelling.

Practice Book page 10

Practice

Write a paragraph about a sporting event you attended. If you have not been to one, you can make it up!

- Tell which sporting event you attended.
- Add enough details to explain what happened.
- Be sure to answer the 5W questions.

Writing Checklist

✓ Did you use singular and plural nouns correctly?

✓ Did you answer the 5W questions?

✓ Can a partner understand your paragraph?

21

Differentiated Instruction

Beginning	Point to the picture of the race cars on p. 21. Describe with words and gestures that Pedro's paragraph is about going to a car race. Have students find the word *cars*, then write all words in the paragraph that begin with the letter *c*.
Intermediate	Have students work in pairs to summarize what happened during Pedro's trip to the car race. Ask students to present their summaries to the class.
Greater Challenge	Have students read Pedro's narrative. Tell them to write each of the 5 W Questions about the information in the narrative.
Standard English Learner CRI	Have students tell the class their own narrative about attending a special event. Have students who are listening ask 5 W Questions about the event.

STEP 1: Introduce

Write a Narrative

Define a narrative for students.

SAY *A narrative is a story about an event that happened. A narrative can be one paragraph or many paragraphs.*

- *To understand a narrative, think about answering the 5 W Questions in your writing.*
- ***Who** is the story about?*
- ***What** happened?*
- ***Where** did the story happen?*
- ***When** did the story happen?*
- ***Why** did the characters do what they did?*

Stimulate class discussion and student questions by talking about the student-written narrative on p. 21.

SAY *Let's read Pedro's narrative on page 21. How does he answer the 5 W Questions?*

Spelling Tip Read the box to students. Have students make a list of words from Pedro's narrative that they want to check the spelling of in a dictionary.

STEP 2: Practice

Before students write their own narratives about attending a sporting event, have them answer 5 W Questions the event they chose.

STEP 3: Assess

Writing Checklist

✓ Have students circle all plural nouns in their narratives and check to see that they are spelled correctly.

✓ Have students find the parts of their narratives that answer the 5 W Questions.

✓ Ask students to read their narratives to partners. Then have the partners retell the stories to check for understanding.

The Five Step Writing Process in the Writing Handbook reference section of this book provides more writing instruction.

STEP 1: Introduce

Key Words

Help students define words by using context.

SAY *The vocabulary words from* Doctors Without Borders *are shown in the Words in Context selection. The pictures help us learn what the words mean.*

- *Find the highlighted vocabulary word in each sentence.*
- *What clues in the sentence help you learn the definition of the word?*

Have students find five numbered circles in the text and then find their corresponding numbered photos. Have students find each key word and connect it with its photograph.

STEP 2: Teach

Words in Context

Have students complete this fill-in-the-blanks exercise using the key words. Then have volunteers read the sentences aloud.

1. *During an* **emergency**, *you need help right away.*
2. *The hero who rescued the animal was a* **courageous** *person.*
3. *Winning requires good* **teamwork** *from everyone.*
4. *I finished my* **training** *course and now have a job.*
5. *The teacher will* **intervene** *to stop the fight.*
6. *During the war, many* **refugees** *left their homeland.*

Study Skills

Dictionary Students can look up the vocabulary words in the dictionary to see if the Words in Context definitions were correct.

Online Dictionary Students can use an online dictionary or the CD that accompanies a learners' dictionary, such as the *Longman Basic Dictionary*.

www.LongmanCornerstone.com

Teaching Resources

- *Practice Book*, pp. 11–12
- *Transparencies*, p. 38
- *CD-ROM*
- *Audio CD*

Reading 2

Doctors Without Borders

Vocabulary

Doctors Without Borders is about an organization that sends doctors to help people in need all over the world.

Key Words

- emergency
- courageous
- teamwork
- training
- intervene
- refugees

Words in Context

1 These operators answer the telephone when people call 911 to report an **emergency**.

2 Firefighters have to be **courageous**. They put their lives in danger so that we can be safe. They often work together to put out a fire. That is real **teamwork**.

22

TESOL Standards

Goal 1, Standard 3—To use English to communicate in social settings: Students will use learning strategies to extend their communicative competence.
Descriptors—Testing hypotheses about language; Listening to and imitating how others use English; Exploring alternative ways of saying things; Using context to construct meaning.

Goal 2, Standard 2—To use English to achieve academically in all content areas: Students will use English to obtain, process, construct, and provide subject matter information in spoken and written form.
Descriptors—Understanding and producing technical vocabulary and text features according to content area.

Goal 2, Standard 3—To use English to achieve academically in all content areas: Students will use appropriate learning strategies to construct and apply academic knowledge.
Descriptors—Using context to construct meaning.

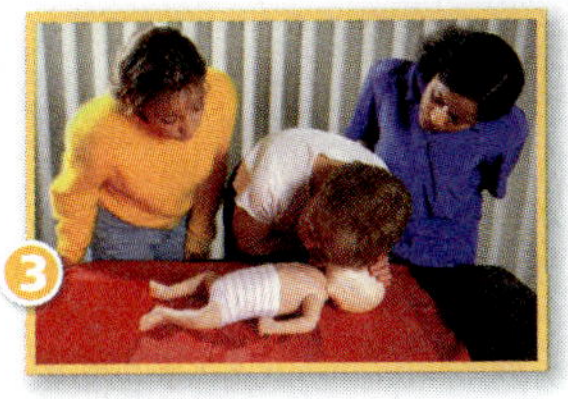

3 The local community center offers **training** to show people how to care for others who are sick or hurt.

4 Sometimes an adult has to **intervene** when students have problems.

5 **Refugees** are people who have to leave their countries because of war or food shortages.

Practice

Use each key word in a sentence.

Make Connections

Suppose you were asked to help others in another country. What help would you like to give? What supplies would you need to bring with you?

Academic Words

evaluate
look at something carefully

task
job to be done

Practice Book pages 11–12

Differentiated Instruction	
Beginning	Read the key words in random order from the list. As students repeat the words, have them point to the illustration for each key word, and then find the key word in the context sentence.
Early Intermediate	Have students tell what helpers they see in the photographs on pp. 22–23. Ask why the helpers in the pictures might be needed.
Intermediate	Have students reread pp. 22–23. Have them work with partners to write a definition for these key words: *emergency, courageous, intervene, refugees.*
Struggling Reader	Have students use gestures and simple props to demonstrate how people are helping each other in the photos on pp. 22–23.

Academic Words

Discuss the definitions for *evaluate* and *task* with students. Share the following context sentences with students:

The doctor can *evaluate* her patients by asking questions about their health.

Police officers know their *task* is to protect the people who live in the community.

Have students write their own context sentences for each word. Then ask students to take turns describing to partners something they would evaluate and a task they might do.

Other Academic Words

Remind students that some words can be used as verbs and nouns. Write two definitions of *challenge* on the board.

Challenge invite someone to fight or compete against you (verb); a demanding or stimulating situation (noun).

Write these context sentences on the board.

I *challenge* you to a checkers game. (verb)
It was a *challenge* to bring medical supplies to the village. (noun)

Ask students to identify which sentence is used as a noun and which sentence is used as a verb. Then have students write their own context sentences.

STEP 3: Practice

Flexible Grouping You may assign this exercise as a whole discussion, partner activity, or individual writing assignment.

Make Connections

Writing Fluency Begin a class discussion about people in other countries who might need help in emergency situations. Encourage students who were born outside the United States to share their own experiences. Encourage students to use a dictionary or thesaurus to find alternative words. Note that the answers can be related to the Big Question when you sum up the discussion.

STEP 1: Introduce

More About The Big Question

The Big Question for this selection focuses on the importance of helping people in other countries who are sick or hurt.

SAY *We are going to read about a group of doctors who help people all around the world.*

- *Who do Doctors Without Borders want to help?*
- *Why do you think the doctors want to volunteer to help others?*

Encourage students to fill in a K-W-L Chart like the one shown below to help them answer the Big Question.

K What I Know	W What I Want to Know	L What I Learned
Countries have war and natural emergencies.	Why do doctors want to go to other countries?	

STEP 2: Teach

Reading Strategy

Activate Prior Knowledge Help students use what they already know about doctors to make hypotheses about what Doctors With Borders does around the world. Discuss with students how activating prior knowledge will help them better understand what they read.

Understand Text Structure

Explain to students the importance of newspaper articles to learn about current events. Show students some of the features of a newspaper article, including the headline, byline, and captions. Many newspaper articles answer the 5 W Questions. Newspaper articles are nonfiction.

Teaching Resources

- ***Teacher's Resource Book,*** pp. 105–106
- ***Practice Book,*** pp. 13–14
- ***CD-ROM*** • ***Audio CD***

Reading 2

INFORMATIONAL TEXT

Newspaper Article

The Big Question

Why do volunteers help people in other countries?

Reading Strategy

Activate Prior Knowledge

Before you read, ask yourself:

- What do I already know about doctors?
- What do I want to find out about Doctors Without Borders?
- Copy the chart on page 33. Fill in the first two columns.

Doctors Without Borders

by Douglas Weisser

When we are sick or hurt, we go to the doctor. Some places in the world do not have enough doctors or supplies to help people. This is really true when there is a crisis in that place.

A group called Doctors Without Borders works to help people in need. If there is an emergency, these doctors volunteer to go where they are needed. The group gives medical care and other services. Doctors Without Borders has been helping people since 1971.

supplies things that people want or need

A member of Doctors Without Borders with refugees in Ethiopia.

24

TESOL Standards

Goal 2, Standard 1—To use English to achieve academically in all content areas: Students will use English to interact in the classroom.
Descriptors—Asking and answering questions.

Goal 2, Standard 2—To use English to achieve academically in all content areas: Students will use English to obtain, process, construct, and provide subject matter information in spoken and written form.
Descriptors—Hypothesizing and predicting; Analyzing, synthesizing, and inferring from information; Demonstrating knowledge through application in a variety of contexts; Listening to, speaking, reading, and writing about subject matter information.

Goal 2, Standard 3—To use English to achieve academically in all content areas: Students will use appropriate learning strategies to construct and apply academic knowledge.
Descriptors—Actively connecting new information to information previously learned.

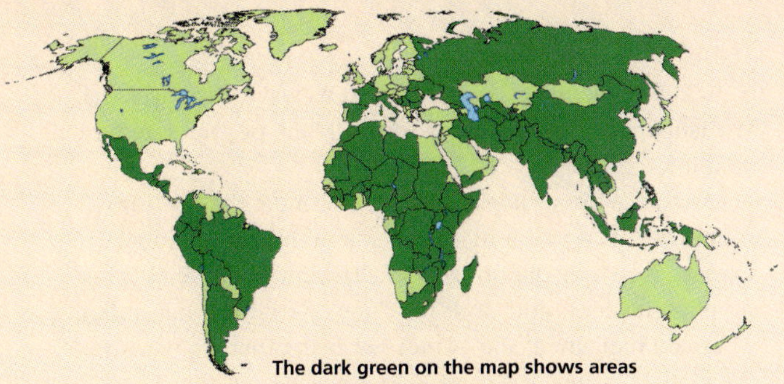

The dark green on the map shows areas where Doctors Without Borders works.

Bringing Help Where It Is Needed

The doctors bring their medical skills to places where they are needed. They also bring supplies like blankets and drinking water. Sometimes the doctors train other people so they can help, too.

Doctors Without Borders has worked in countries all over the world. If there is a war in a country, the people there need help. Refugees are people who have to leave their homes. They leave because there is no food or because fighting has made their homes unsafe.

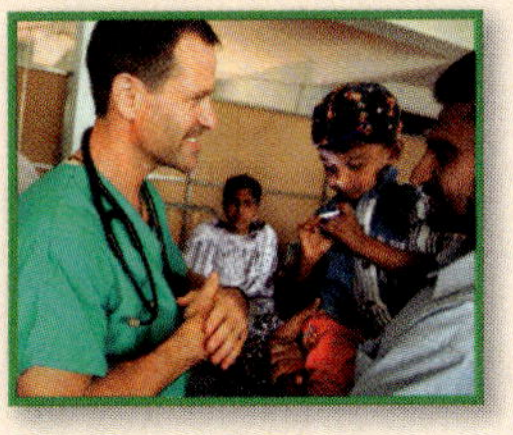

This doctor helped a child in Sri Lanka.

Doctors Without Borders can intervene to help refugees. Sometimes, refugees do not even have clean water. The volunteers come with water and medicine. They teach refugees how to eat better and stay healthy. They can show refugees how to make water safe for drinking.

skills something a person does well

medicine a substance used to treat sickness

healthy not sick

Check Up Where might Doctors Without Borders have gone recently to help?

25

Differentiated Instruction

Beginning	Direct students to the map on p. 25. Have them call out the names of the countries they know. Ask them if the dark green area shows where the doctors volunteer.
Intermediate	Ask students to discuss with partners why people might go to the doctor. What do they expect a doctor to do for them?
Greater Challenge	Have students write a paragraph to explain why Doctors Without Borders might be needed in so many places around the world.
Standard English Learner CRI	Choose a highlighted word and start a game of "Give One, Get One." Students can use a thesaurus to find synonyms for the chosen word. Have students take turns swapping words with each other until everyone has three new words for their personal thesaurus.

Read Aloud

Have students turn to pp. 24–25. Students should take turns reading aloud each paragraph. At the end of each paragraph, have the students who listened describe what was just read. Invite students to refer to the photos and illustrations as they talk about the reading.

Build Vocabulary

Direct attention to the highlighted word in the text with a definition at the bottom of the page.

- Invite volunteers to read aloud the word and the definition.
- Have students write a context sentence using the word.
- Have students repeat this activity for each highlighted word as they read the selection.

STEP 3: Assess

Check Up

Have students work with partners to think of places in the United States or around the world where doctors were needed recently because of an emergency or natural disaster.

Encourage students to use a T-chart like the one below to help them organize information about recent events that needed doctors.

Recent disasters and emergencies	
name of country or location of event	description of event, estimate of size of area affected, estimate of number of people affected

Link to Social Studies

Maps Some maps, like the one on p. 25, use colors and shading to give information. Areas in dark green indicate where Doctors Without Borders has worked. Areas in light green show where Doctors Without Borders does not operate. Have students use a world map to point to the regions of South and Central America, Africa, and Asia.

STEP 1: Monitor Progress

Comprehension Check

Main Idea and Details After reading p. 26 about the tsunami, discuss with students the main idea and supporting details.

SAY *We have just read about a* tsunami.

- *What is a synonym for a* tsunami?
- *Where did the event occur?*
- *What help did the people need?*

Tell students they can use the information just discussed to fill in a Main Idea and Details Chart.

The Tsunami in 2004

Many people in South Asia were hurt.	Doctors Without Borders gave medicine and supplies for more than a year.	The doctors also helped by listening to people say what happened.

Link to Science

Have students imagine they are going to study to be doctors. Have them work in small groups to brainstorm what classes they should take to become doctors. Ask volunteers to report their findings to the class.

Scaffolding

Direct students to look at the photograph on p. 26. Explain to students that many activities are taking place. Ask students to write one descriptive sentence for each activity they see in the picture.

Study Skills

Internet Invite students to use the Internet for their research. Have students make a list of words they cannot define.

Online Dictionary Students can use an online dictionary or the CD that accompanies a learners' dictionary, such as the *Longman Basic Dictionary*.
www.LongmanCornerstone.com

Tsunami!

In 2004 there was a tsunami, or tidal wave, in South Asia. The tsunami destroyed many towns. Many people were hurt or killed.

Doctors Without Borders worked for more than a year in countries that were hit by the tsunami. They gave people shots to make sure they did not get sick. The doctors gave people supplies like tents and clothing. They talked to people about what had happened. Sometimes just being there to listen to the victims helped the most.

---

tsunami huge wave that causes great destruction on land
destroyed damaged so that it cannot be used
victims people who have been affected by something bad

Workers unload supplies that doctors used to help the 2004 tsunami victims.

26

TESOL Standards

Goal 2, Standard 1—To use English to achieve academically in all content areas: Students will use English to interact in the classroom.
Descriptors—Asking and answering questions.

Goal 2, Standard 2—To use English to achieve academically in all content areas: Students will use English to obtain, process, construct, and provide subject matter information in spoken and written form.
Descriptors—Hypothesizing and predicting; Analyzing, synthesizing, and inferring from information; Demonstrating knowledge through application in a variety of contexts; Listening to, speaking, reading, and writing about subject matter information.

Goal 2, Standard 3—To use English to achieve academically in all content areas: Students will use appropriate learning strategies to construct and apply academic knowledge.
Descriptors—Actively connecting new information to information previously learned.

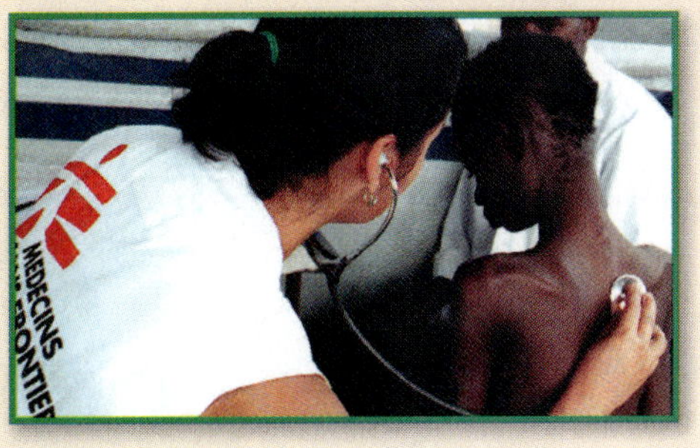

A doctor helps a boy in Sri Lanka after the 2004 tsunami.

Helping Others Help Themselves

Sometimes the volunteers help people in a town build new hospitals. That involves real teamwork!

Sometimes the best help the volunteers can give is training. It can be better for Doctors Without Borders to help train local doctors to take care of people after a crisis. The local doctors can give care to sick and hurt people after Doctors Without Borders leaves the area.

The volunteers who work for Doctors Without Borders travel all over the world to help people after emergencies. They are courageous, and borders do not stop them.

Practice Book pages 13–14

Reading Strategy

Activate Prior Knowledge

- How did your knowledge of doctors help you understand the reading?
- What have you learned about Doctors Without Borders?
- What else would you like to learn?

Think It Over

1. What is Doctors Without Borders?
2. How does Doctors Without Borders help people?
3. How did Doctors Without Borders help people after the tsunami in South Asia?

Differentiated Instruction

Beginning	Have students write the words for all the things they can identify in the photograph on p. 26.
Early Intermediate	Have students discuss with partners why it is important for Doctors Without Borders to train local doctors. Ask them to present their main ideas to the class.
Intermediate	Ask students to explain the meaning of the last sentence of the selection.
Struggling Reader	Sit with students and take turns reading sentences or paragraphs. This will reduce the size of the task for the student, making it less daunting and more manageable.

STEP 2: Teach

Visual Literacy

Captions Draw the students' attention to the captions for the photographs on pp. 26–27. Ask volunteers to read the captions aloud.

SAY *Think about the various activities you see happening in the photographs.*

- *What inferences can you make about the activities you see?*
- *Let's ask the 5 W Questions to learn more about the information in the photographs.*
- *Who is examining the boy on page 27?*
- *What was used to bring the supplies?*
- *Where are the volunteers unloading the supplies?*
- *When did the disaster occur?*
- *Why are some people wearing army uniforms?*

STEP 3: Assess

Reading Strategy

Activate Prior Knowledge Give students an example of ways to activate prior knowledge.

SAY *Before I read this story, I asked myself what I already knew about doctors and what I wanted to learn about Doctors Without Borders.*

- *I knew that doctors help people who are sick or hurt.*
- *I learned that Doctors Without Borders goes to places in the world where there are not enough doctors or supplies.*
- *I would like to know what other countries Doctors Without Borders is working in now.*

Think It Over

Flexible Grouping You may assign this exercise as a whole class discussion, partner activity, or individual writing assignment.

Answer Key

1. Doctors Without Borders is a group that visits different countries to help people who need doctors.
2. It helps people by giving them medicine, bringing them supplies, and training them.
3. The doctors gave shots for people who were sick, brought them supplies, and listened when people wanted to talk.

STEP 1: Introduce

More About The Big Question

Remind students of the Big Question for this reading.

SAY *The Big Question for the selection we just read asks: Why do volunteers help people in other countries?*

- *Why do you think groups like Doctors Without Borders have so many volunteers?*
- *If you were a doctor, would you want to volunteer with this group? Why or not?*
- *If a volunteer is not a doctor, in what ways can that person be helpful?*

Have students use a Venn Diagram like the one shown below to compare and contrast how doctors and other volunteers can be helpful to others. Lead a class discussion to help students fill in the details.

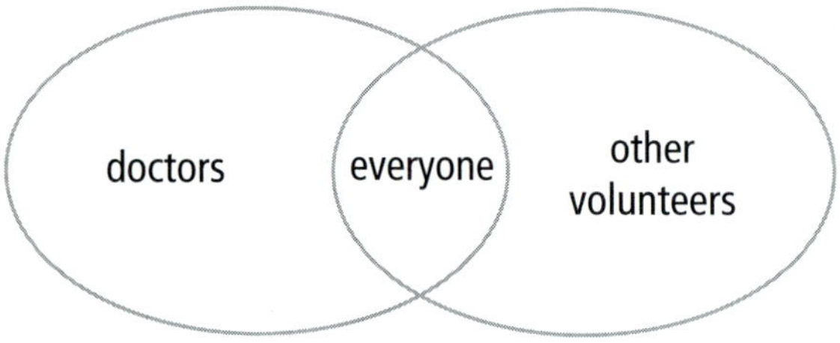

Link to Social Studies

Countries of the World Tell students that Angola, Rwanda, and Kenya are countries in Africa. Afghanistan is a country in Asia. Tibet is in Asia. Help students locate these places on a map or a globe.

Academic Words

Discuss the definitions for *indicate* and *identify* with students. Have students add the words to their personal thesaurus.

Indicate point out or point to something

identify reveal the name or identity of a person or thing

Explain to students that both terms relate to identification. Therefore the two words are synonyms. Tell students that even though words are synonyms, each word has a specific meaning in a specific context. Challenge students to write context sentences for each term, then read their sentences aloud to the class.

A Closer Look at... Doctors Without Borders

▲ **Angola**
Doctors Without Borders sets up centers to feed people who are hungry.

▲ **Tibet**
Doctors Without Borders works to help people in rural Tibet get clean drinking water.

▲ **Afghanistan**
This volunteer is training women in Afghanistan to provide care for the people in their village.

28

TESOL Standards

Goal 2, Standard 3—To use English to achieve academically in all content areas: Students will use appropriate learning strategies to construct and apply academic knowledge.
Descriptors—Focusing attention selectively; Applying basic reading comprehension skills such as skimming, scanning, previewing, and reviewing text; Using context to construct meaning; Taking notes to record important information and aid one's own learning; Imitating the behaviors of native English speakers to complete tasks successfully.

Goal 3, Standard 1—To use English in socially and culturally appropriate ways: Students will use the appropriate language variety, register, and genre according to audience, purpose, and setting.
Descriptors—Using a variety of writing styles appropriate for different audiences, purposes, and settings.

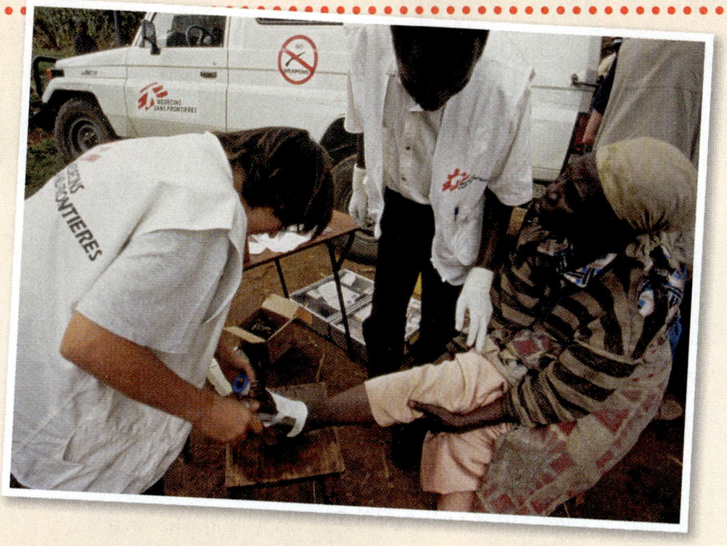

▲ **Rwanda**
These volunteers are taking care of a refugee's injured leg.

▲ **Kenya**
This doctor is giving a woman and her child checkups.

Activity to Do!

These pages use pictures and words to tell where Doctors Without Borders works.

- Research any country that interests you.
- Create two pages, using pictures and words, to tell about that country.

29

Differentiated Instruction

Beginning	Point to the name of each country or region shown on pp. 28–29. Direct students to a world map. Have students find each country or region on the world map.
Intermediate	Ask students to write descriptive sentences about what the doctor is doing for the woman and her child in Kenya. What do some people in rural Tibet need?
Greater Challenge	Have students draw a large map of the world and label each of the places that are mentioned on pp. 28–29.
Special Needs	Train students to slide their fingers along each line of text in order to track text visually and to see more than one word at a time, without being distracted by the next line.

STEP 2: Teach

Visual Literacy

Captions Draw the students' attention to the captions for the illustrations on pp. 28–29. Stimulate a discussion about the work Doctors Without Borders does.

SAY *Read the captions and look at the pictures on pages 28 and 29.*

- *What do the captions tell about Doctors Without Borders?*
- *Can you describe some of the ways people are being helped?*
- *Each caption has the name of a country or region.*
  Point to each place on a map.

Adapt the Activity

Tell students they are going to work in small groups to create a story about doctors helping after a disaster in another country. Have students imagine they volunteer for Doctors Without Borders. Using the Story Map, have students develop a plot and characters for their story. Encourage each group to present their story to the class.

STEP 3: Assess

Activity to Do!

Study Skills Ask students to use the Internet to research one of the places named in the photographs on pp. 28–29. Have students make a list of words they cannot define.

Online Dictionary Students can use an online dictionary or the CD that accompanies a learners' dictionary, such as the *Longman Basic Dictionary*.

www.LongmanCornerstone.com

SAY *As you learn about the country you want to research, you might want to find answers to these questions.*

- *Where is the country located?*
- *What is the land and weather of the country like?*
- *What kinds of challenges or emergencies do the people who live there face?*

STEP 1: Introduce

Phonics

Long Vowels with Silent *e* Review long vowels sounds with words that end with silent *e*. Write the following words on the board and ask students to say them aloud: *care*, *fine*, *home*, *sure*, *take*, *smile*, *globe*, and *cute.*

STEP 2: Teach

Point out that each word is spelled with consonants and vowels. Ask volunteers to label the vowels and consonants in each of the words as shown below. Tell students that in each word, the letter *e* is silent.

care	fine	home	globe
CVC*e*	CVC*e*	CVC*e*	CCVC*e*

Review the rule about long vowels with silent *e*.

SAY *The rule for the long vowel sound is if the first vowel in a one-syllable word is followed by a consonant and then an* e*, the vowel is usually long. The* e *at the end of a word is always silent.*

Point out the spelling patterns commonly used with long vowels with silent *e* are CVC*e* and CCVC*e*. Explain that some words do not follow the rule, such as *have*, *come*, and *none*.

STEP 3: Practice

1. Have students work with partners. Explain that they are making two lists because some of the words do not follow the long vowel rule.
2. Monitor students to see that they are placing their words into the correct lists.

Reteach Point out that plurals of long vowel words ending with a silent *e* are pronounced with the same vowel sound as the singular word. For example: *home/homes*, *smile/smiles*, *plane/planes*.

Teaching Resources
- ***Practice Book***, p. 15
- ***Phonics Workbook***
- ***Phonics Flashcards***
- ***CD-ROM*** • ***Audio CD***

Reading 2

Phonics & Fluency

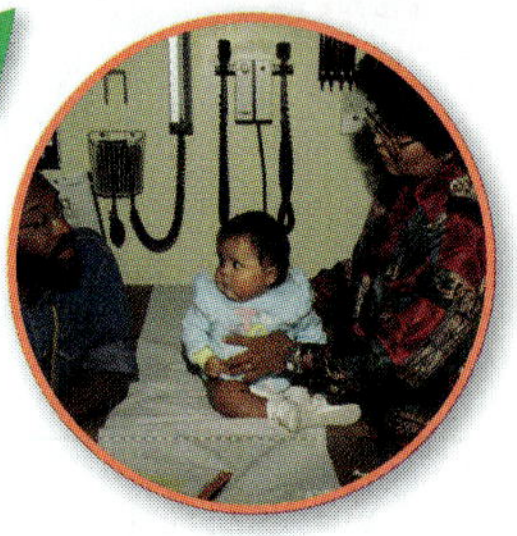

Phonics

Long Vowels with Silent e

Read the words on the chart. Which vowels say their names?

a_e	i_e	o_e	u_e
age take	ice fine	woke globe	use cube

Rule Box

When the first vowel (**V**) in a one-syllable word is followed by a consonant (**C**) and an **e**, the vowel is usually long. The final **e** is silent. This is the "silent **e** rule."

Some words that have a *v*, *m*, or *n* after the first vowel are exceptions to the rule.

Practice

With a partner, take turns reading the words below.

1. Use the words to make two lists.
   - Words that follow the silent e rule.
   - Exceptions to the silent e rule.
2. Read your list of words that follow the silent e rule to your partner. Point to and say the name of the long vowel in each word.

like	safe
gave	give
ate	line
gone	plane
make	move

Practice Book page 15

30

TESOL Standards

Goal 3, Standard 3—To use English in socially and culturally appropriate ways: Students will use appropriate learning strategies to extend their sociolinguistic and sociocultural competence.
Descriptors—Observing and modeling how others speak and behave in a particular situation or setting; Experimenting with variations of language in social and academic settings; Seeking information about appropriate language use and behavior.

Goal 1, Standard 3—To use English to communicate in social settings: Students will use learning strategies to extend their communicative competence.
Descriptors—Listening to and imitating how others use English; Self-monitoring and self-evaluating language development; Practicing new language; Focusing attention selectively.

Fluency

Read for Speed and Accuracy

You should read quickly. But never read so quickly that you lose your understanding.

Practice

Read for one minute. ▶ Count the words you read. ▶ Study any hard words. ▶ Read and count again.

When we are sick or hurt, we go to the doctor. Some places 13
in the world do not have enough doctors or supplies to help 25
people. This is really true when there is a crisis in that place. 38
A group called Doctors Without Borders works to help 47
people in need. If there is an emergency, these doctors 57
volunteer to go where they are needed. The group gives 67
medical care and other services. Doctors Without Borders 75
has been helping people since 1971. 81
The doctors bring their medical skills to places where 90
they are needed. They also bring supplies like blankets and 100
drinking water. Sometimes the doctors train other people so 109
that they can help, too. 113

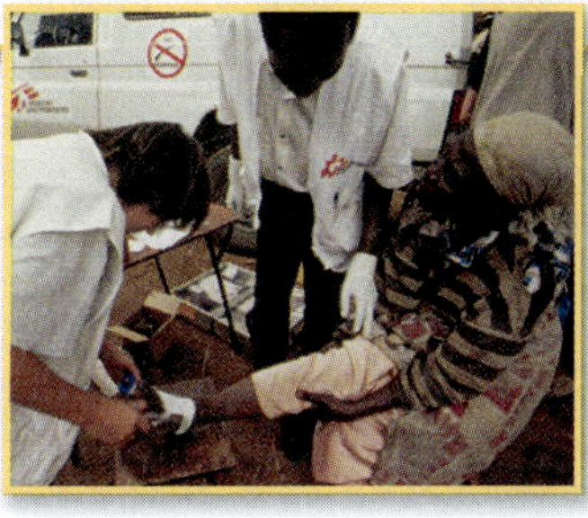

31

STEP 1: Introduce

Fluency

Read for Speed and Accuracy Explain to students that reading with accuracy will help them focus more closely on what they are reading. Explain that reading for speed does not mean reading too fast or too slow. It means reading at a normal, conversational speed.

Play the audio CD for this reading to the class, asking students to listen for pacing, intonation, and expression. Remind students to use appropriate verbal cues, facial expressions, and gestures while reading.

STEP 2: Practice

Have students look for any words that slowed them down while they were reading. Some words that might have caused difficulty are: *enough*, *supplies*, *crisis*, *emergency*, *volunteer*, *medical*, and *blankets*. Have students practice saying those words. Then have students complete the Practice activity.

- Divide the students in pairs.
- Provide each pair with a timer.
- Have one student read while the partner times him or her.
- Have students count the number of words they read.

STEP 3: Extend

Study Skills

Dictionary Have students work with partners to:

- write words that slowed them down
- look the words up in a dictionary
- read the sentences where the words appear
- define and pronounce the difficult words

Link to Math

Have students record the number of words they read in one minute. Then tell students to multiply that number by 60 to find the number of words they can read in an hour.

Linguistic Note

Phonics Students who speak Spanish or other Romance languages may have difficulty with the long *a* sound. Explain that the long *a* sound is similar to the sound they use for *e* in their home language. Write the words *leche* (*milk*) and *mesa* (*table*) on the board. Then write *age*, *take*, and *plane* on the board and pronounce each word. Guide students to recognize the similarity between the sound of *e* in *leche* and *mesa* and the sound of *a* in *age*, *take*, and *plane*.

Accelerate Language Development

Capitalization of Proper Nouns Explain to students that group names such as Doctors Without Borders are proper nouns. Remind them that all proper nouns begin with a capital letter. Share some examples of other proper nouns—Parent Teacher Association, United Nations, Boston Red Sox, Eagle Scouts. Ask students to share other group names they know of. Write each response on the board.

STEP 1: Monitor Progress

Learning Strategy

Take Notes Explain that taking notes helps readers remember important information. When you take notes, you only need to write down the words and phrases that will help you remember what you read.

STEP 2: Teach

Activate Prior Knowledge

Suggest that students use their skill for taking notes by quickly writing words or phrases to describe what they already know about how doctors help people.

SAY *Readers know many different things by reading about many subjects.*

- *When you start to read something that interests you, what do you hope to learn?*
- *As you read, what do you do when you read information you already know?*

Remind students they can use a KWL Chart to help them answer the questions.

STEP 3: Practice

Before they begin the Practice activity, have students make hypotheses about what they already know about natural disasters. They can use their ideas when they do the Practice activity.

Flexible Grouping You may assign the student book activity as a class discussion, partner activity, or individual written assignment.

Possible Responses

1. Tsunamis are tidal waves; they destroy buildings and towns; they happen suddenly.
2. How often do they occur? What was the size of the largest tidal wave? Are there any warnings before a tsunami occurs?

Teaching Resources

- *Practice Book*, p. 16
- *Transparencies*, p. 59
- *Teacher's Resource Book*, p. 157
- *CD-ROM*

Reading 2

Comprehension

Learning Strategy

Take Notes

Take notes on the reading. Share your notes with a partner.

Ask your partner to respond to the Big Question for this reading.

Practice Book page 16

32

Activate Prior Knowledge

When you **activate prior knowledge**, you use what you already know to learn more about something. For example, you can use what you already know about doctors to learn more about what doctors do in *Doctors Without Borders.*

Practice

Imagine that your next reading assignment is about tsunamis.

1. List three things you already know about tsunamis based on what you read in *Doctors Without Borders*.
2. List three things you want to learn about tsunamis.

TESOL Standards

Goal 2, Standard 2—To use English to achieve academically in all content areas: Students will use English to obtain, process, construct, and provide subject matter information in spoken and written form.
Descriptors—Listening to, speaking, reading, and writing about subject matter information; Gathering information orally and in writing; Retelling information; Selecting, connecting, and explaining information; Analyzing, synthesizing, and inferring from information; Responding to the work of peers and others; Representing information visually and interpreting information presented visually; Demonstrating knowledge through application in a variety of contexts.

Goal 2, Standard 3—To use English to achieve academically in all content areas: Students will use appropriate learning strategies to construct and apply academic knowledge.
Descriptors—Actively connecting new information to information previously learned; Taking notes to record important information and aid one's own learning.

Use a KWL Chart

A KWL Chart can be used to activate prior knowledge. It provides a plan for recording three kinds of information.

1. What you **know** about a topic before reading.
2. What you **want** to learn about the topic.
3. What you actually **learned** about the topic.

Practice

You completed the first two columns before. Now complete the final column. Reread the selection for facts to add.

Topic: Doctors Without Borders		
What I Know	What I Want to Know	What I Learned

1. What do you still want to learn about Doctors Without Borders?
2. Where can you look to find more information?

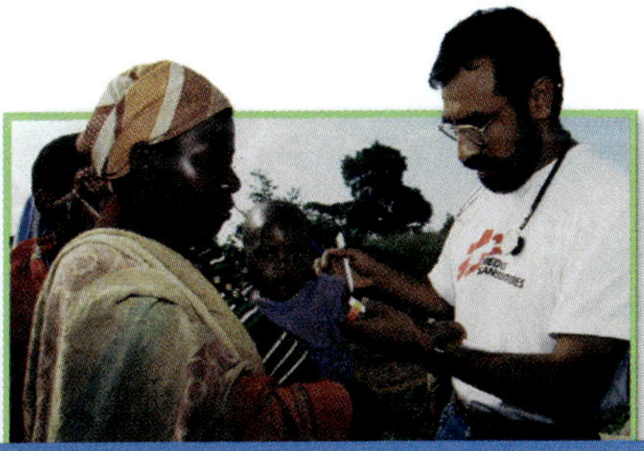

Extension

Imagine that your teacher asked you to be a volunteer in your community. What kind of work would you like to do? Discuss your ideas with a partner. Then present them to the class using a visual aid.

33

Accelerate Language Development

Acronyms Explain that some terms in English are formed from the first letters of words or parts of words. For example, the name *KWL Chart* is formed from the first letters of the words *know*, *want*, and *learned*. The letters *UN* are often used in writing and in speaking when referring to the United Nations.

For aural recognition of such terms, students need to know how to pronounce the names of letters in English. Work with beginners to recite the English alphabet.

STEP 1: Teach

Using a KWL Chart

Ask students to imagine they are going to read an informational article about the Statue of Liberty. Have them fill out the first two columns of a KWL Chart: What I Know, and What I Want to Know.

Possible Responses

What I Know

- It's tall.
- It's on an island.
- It's in New York Harbor.

What I Want to Know

- Why was it built?
- When was it built?
- Who built it?

STEP 2: Practice

You may have students complete the graphic organizer provided as a Blackline Master in the *Teacher's Resource Book*.

Possible Responses

What I Know

- Doctors help people who are sick or hurt.
- Doctors give you medicine and shots.
- Doctors have to go to school to learn how to help people.

What I Want to Know

- What is Doctors Without Borders?
- What do they do?
- Where do they work?

What I Learned

- Doctors Without Borders is a group of volunteer doctors that helps people all over the world. They take care of sick and hurt people and train other people to help in places where there are no doctors.

STEP 3: Extend

Oral Presentation Ask partners to draw or find illustrations representing jobs volunteers might do. Then have them show their pictures to the class and explain what the pictures show. Invite students to draw conclusions about their illustrations.

STEP 1: Introduce

Tell students that past tense verbs are about action in the past. Explain that many authors write about events in the past tense. Explain that the simple past is the most common form of the past tense. The past perfect tense explains something that was completed before an event in the past.

When I arrived home, he had already called.

STEP 2: Teach

Past Tense Verbs

Have students read the Rule box for past tense verbs on p. 34. Then copy the chart below onto the board and have volunteers fill in the missing words.

Rules	Present	Past
add *-ed.*	destroy work	destroyed ________
add *-d.*	save use	saved ________
change *y* to *i* and add *-ed.*	hurry worry	hurried ________
Double the consonant and add *-ed.*	stop grab	stopped ________

STEP 3: Practice

Have students write a short sentence using a past tense verb from the box above. Have students read their sentences aloud while others identify the past tense verbs.

Answer Key

1. needed
2. stepped
3. decided
4. carried
5. rubbed
6. placed
7. treated
8. dried

Teaching Resources

- ***Practice Book***, p. 17
- ***Transparencies***, pp. 69–80
- ***Assessments***, pp. 33–36
- ***CD-ROM*** • ***Teacher CD-ROM***

Reading 2

Grammar & Writing

Past Tense Verbs

Verbs are words that name actions.
Past tense verbs name actions that already happened.

The tsunami **destroyed** many towns.

Doctors Without Borders **worked** in countries hit by the tsunami.

Rule Box

To form the past tense of most verbs, add *-ed, -d,* or *-ied* to the end of the word.

destroy → destroyed   save → saved   hurry → hurried

For words ending in a consonant, double the consonant and add *-ed.*

stop → stopped

Irregular verbs do not follow these rules. ***Give***, ***teach***, and ***bring*** are examples of irregular verbs. Their past tense forms are ***gave***, ***taught***, and ***brought***.

Practice

Copy each verb. Write the past tense form.

1. need
2. step
3. decide
4. carry
5. rub
6. place
7. treat
8. dry

Practice Book page 17

TESOL Standards

Goal 3, Standard 1—To use English in socially and culturally appropriate ways: Students will use the appropriate language variety, register, and genre according to audience, purpose, and setting.
Descriptors—Recognizing and using Standard English and vernacular dialects appropriately.

Goal 2, Standard 3—To use English to achieve academically in all content areas: Students will use appropriate learning strategies to construct and apply academic knowledge.
Descriptors—Using context to construct meaning; Actively connecting new information-to-information previously learned; Imitating the behaviors of native English speakers to complete tasks successfully.

Write a Paragraph with a Topic Sentence

A **paragraph** is a group of sentences that have the same topic or idea. One sentence, called the **topic sentence,** gives the main idea of the paragraph. The other sentences are related to the topic sentence. They give more information about the main idea.

Read this paragraph about how Donna solved a problem.

SPELLING TIP

To form the plural of most nouns, just add an *-s*.

Practice Book page 18

I had a math test the following day, but I left my textbook at school. How was I going to study for the test? I was going out of my mind! My older brother saw that I was worried and decided to help me. He found his fifth grade math notes and made up math problems for me to practice. I was so ready for the test that I got an A!

Practice

Think about a problem that you had to solve. Write a paragraph about it.

- Start with a topic sentence that explains the problem.
- Add sentences to explain how you solved the problem.

Writing Checklist

✓ Did you write a clear topic sentence?

✓ Did you spell past tense verbs correctly?

✓ Can a partner understand both the problem and the solution?

35

Differentiated Instruction

Beginning	Have students fill in the word that answers the question: *Why couldn't Donna study for the test?* Donna left her ________ at school.
Early Intermediate	Have students write answers to these questions: *What did Donna need that she left at school? What finally happened when she took the test?*
Intermediate	Have students work with partners to find the past tense verbs in Donna's paragraph. Ask students to fill in a T-Chart with the past tense form and present tense form of each word they find.
Struggling Reader	Write the following words on the board: *test, textbook, study*. Have students find the words in Donna's paragraph and pronounce each word.

STEP 1: Introduce

Write a Paragraph with a Topic Sentence

Have students read aloud the definitions for a paragraph and for a topic sentence.

SAY *The topic of a paragraph is what the paragraph is about. The sentence that describes what the paragraph is about is called a topic sentence. It is usually the first sentence of the paragraph.*

Stimulate class discussion and student questions by talking about the student-written narrative on p. 35.

SAY *Which sentence of Donna's paragraph tells you what the paragraph is about?*

Spelling Tip Read the information in the Spelling Tip box to students. Then have students make a list of plural nouns they used in their paragraphs.

STEP 2: Practice

Have students write their own paragraphs with topic sentences. Discuss the parts of a paragraph:

- Did you begin your paragraph with a topic sentence that tells what the problem is?
- Did you add sentences to tell what you did?
- Did you explain how you solved your problem?

STEP 3: Assess

Writing Checklist

✓ Have students underline their topic sentences.

✓ Have students look at all past tense verbs and check them against the rules.

✓ Ask students to read their paragraphs to one another. Have listeners explain the problem and solution they heard.

The Five Step Writing Process in the Writing Handbook reference section of this book provides more writing instruction.

STEP 1: Introduce

Key Words

Help students learn the skill of defining words by using context.

SAY *The vocabulary words from Stone Soup are shown in the Words in Context selection. The pictures help us learn what the words mean.*

Explain that matching the pictures and the words helps to define the key words. Tell students to find each key word and connect it with the correct photograph.

STEP 2: Teach

Words in Context

Write the following sentences on the board. Have students complete this fill-in-the-blanks exercise using the key words. Ask students to read each sentence aloud.

1. *Every day I* carry *my textbooks home to study at night.*
2. *Our resources will become* scarce *unless we recycle and conserve energy.*
3. *At home, we* share *the work for the hosehold chores.*
4. *Do you think they* peeked *at the answer?*
5. *The* cottage *in the woods had a stone fireplace.*
6. *The runners* charge *ahead at the start of the race.*

Ask students to work in pairs to write one context sentence for each key word.

Study Skills

Dictionary Students can look up the vocabulary words in the dictionary to see if the Words in Context definitions are correct.

Online Dictionary Students can use an online dictionary or the CD that accompanies a learners' dictionary, such as the *Longman Basic Dictionary*.
www.LongmanCornerstone.com

Teaching Resources
- ***Practice Book,*** pp. 19–20
- ***Transparencies,*** p. 39
- ***CD-ROM*** • ***Audio CD***

Reading 3

Stone Soup

Vocabulary

Stone Soup **is about a boy who finds a clever way to feed some hungry villagers.**

Key Words
- carry
- scarce
- share
- peeked
- cottage
- charge

Words in Context

1 I helped Mom and Dad **carry** the groceries when we got back from the store.

2 When it gets cold in the winter, flowers growing outside become **scarce**.

3 It's always nice to **share**!

36

TESOL Standards

Goal 1, Standard 3—To use English to communicate in social settings: Students will use learning strategies to extend their communicative competence.
Descriptors—Testing hypotheses about language; Listening to and imitating how others use English; Exploring alternative ways of saying things; Using context to construct meaning.

Goal 2, Standard 2—To use English to achieve academically in all content areas: Students will use English to obtain, process, construct, and provide subject matter information in spoken and written form.
Descriptors—Understanding and producing technical vocabulary and text features according to content area.

Goal 2, Standard 3—To use English to achieve academically in all content areas: Students will use appropriate learning strategies to construct and apply academic knowledge.
Descriptors—Using context to construct meaning.

④ Jeffrey **peeked** out of the window to see if his mom's car was in the street.

⑤ The **cottage** was small but very cozy.

⑥ The elephants **charge** the lions at the watering hole.

Practice

Use each key word in a sentence.

Make Connections

The next story shows how everyone wins when people share. Do you have a story about sharing? Tell your story to a partner.

Academic Words

attitude
point of view; state of mind

item
single thing or piece

Practice Book pages 19–20

Differentiated Instruction	
Beginning	Ask students to point to sentences that use the key words. Then have students point to the pictures that illustrate the words.
Intermediate	Have students write a new context sentence for each of the following key words: *carry*, *scarce*, *share*, *peeked.*
Greater Challenge	Have students reread pp. 36–37. Have them work with partners to find synonyms for these key words: *scarce*, *share*, *charge*, *cottage*.
Standard English Learner (CRI)	Read aloud various context sentences on pp. 36–37. Have students shout out the key word in each sentence after you read it.

Visual Literacy

Illustrations Have students use their own words to compare and contrast what they see in each photograph on pp. 36–37.

Academic Words

Discuss the definitions for *attitude* and *item* with students. Share the following context sentences:

A person with a good *attitude* is a hard worker.

Be sure to buy every *item* on the shopping list.

Tell students that a synonym for *attitude* is *outlook*. Lead a class discussion about how these two terms can be used in the same context.

Have students describe how the noun *item* and the verb *itemize* are similar. Ask the following question: If an *item* is something on a list, what does it mean to *itemize*?

Other Academic Words

Have students work in small groups to discuss how new words are formed from root words. Give students the example of the word *create*. Challenge students to make a list of all the words they know that are variations of *create*.

STEP 3: Practice

Flexible Grouping You may assign these exercises as a whole discussion, partner activity, or individual writing assignment.

Make Connections

Writing Fluency Begin a class discussion about personal experiences with sharing. Note that the answers can be related to the Big Question when you sum up the discussion.

Reteach

Review with students how to use reference books such as a dictionary and a thesaurus. Provide students with a list of spelling words or vocabulary words. Have them look up the words, and then write down what guide words were at the top of the dictionary pages where they found each word.

STEP 1: Introduce

More About The Big Question

The Big Question for this selection focuses on the importance of sharing with others. Have students use a T-Chart like the one below to discuss the Big Question for this reading.

SAY *We have just discussed why sharing with others is important.*

- *Think about when you have shared something.*
- *How did it make you feel?*
- *Do you get something back when you share something?*

Pros of Sharing	Cons of Sharing
Help others Make friends	I get less People might not want it

STEP 2: Teach

Reading Strategy

Identify Events in a Plot Discuss with students how identifying events in a plot can help the reader better understand a story and help the reader become more involved.

As they read the story, encourage students to review what happens first, next, and last in the story. Remind students that the events in the story are the action that take place.

Understand Text Structure

Draw students' attention to the genre label. Explain to students that folktales are made-up stories that have been told many times for many years. Often the purpose of the folktale is to teach a moral in a fun way that is easy to remember.

Teaching Resources

- ***Teacher's Resource Book,*** pp. 107–108
- ***Practice Book,*** pp. 21–22
- ***CD-ROM*** • ***Audio CD***

Reading 3

LITERATURE

Folktale

The Big Question

What are the pros and cons of sharing?

Reading Strategy

Identify Events in a Plot

- Can you tell what happens first, next, and last in the story?
- How do you think the story ends?

Stone Soup

by P. J. Perkins
illustrated by Julie Downing

One of John's favorite things was a big iron pot. The pot had once belonged to his mother.

As much as he loved the pot, John was hungry. He decided to trade the pot for something to eat.

"I'm sorry," said the farmer's wife from her cottage door. "Food is scarce these days. I only have enough for my own family."

"Thank you, anyway," John said. "I will carry my pot to the next village."

John walked many miles.

"May I trade this nice iron pot for something to eat?" he asked everyone he saw.

But the people in this village were just as poor and hungry as John was.

belonged was owned

trade to give away for something else

village small town

38

TESOL Standards

Goal 2, Standard 2—To use English to achieve academically in all content areas: Students will use English to obtain, process, construct, and provide subject matter information in spoken and written form.

Descriptors—Listening to, speaking, reading, and writing about subject matter information; Gathering information orally and in writing; Retelling information; Selecting, connecting, and explaining information; Demonstrating knowledge through application in a variety of contexts.

As John started to leave the village, he saw a smooth, round stone in the road. If only this stone were something good to eat, he thought.

Then John got an idea. He filled his iron pot with water. He gathered sticks and dry wood and then built a blazing fire all around his pot.

As he waited for the water to get hot, he thought about how good his soup would taste. "This stone soup will be delicious!" he said to himself. "I can hardly wait to eat every drop!"

When the water began to bubble and boil, he dropped the stone into the pot.

---

gathered collected

blazing very bright

delicious tastes or smells very good

Check Up What event is happening on this page?

Differentiated Instruction

Beginning	Write the highlighted words on the board: *belonged*, *trade*, *village*, *gathered*, *blazing*, *delicious*. Have students use gestures and props to demonstrate the meaning of each word.
Early Intermediate	Have students explain to the class how John built a fire to heat water in his iron pot. Encourage students to describe each step of the process.
Intermediate	Have students look at the definitions for the words *belonged* and *trade*. Have them read the definitions aloud. Encourage them to write a comparison sentence using both words.
Struggling Reader	Have students work in pairs to name as many items as they can in the pictures on pp. 38–39. Write the words on the board and have students copy them.

Build Vocabulary

Direct attention to the highlighted word in the text with a definition at the bottom of the page.

- Invite volunteers to read aloud the word and the definition.
- Have students write a context sentence using the word.
- Have students repeat this activity for each highlighted word as they read the selection.

Academic Words

Discuss the definitions for *involved* and *required* with students. Share the following context sentences with students:

The music students are *involved* in planning the concert.

All students are *required* to take exams to pass each subject.

Challenge students to write more context sentences for each academic term. Suggest students write sentences that connect to the events in *Stone Soup*.

Character Qualities

Explain to students that the qualities of the characters in a story (courage, bravery, greed, etc.) influence the plot and the tone of a story. Have students write briefly about the qualities in John's character that they like or dislike and why.

STEP 3: Assess

Check Up

Have students work with partners to describe what event is happening on p. 39. Students should recognize that John boiled water in his pot and then dropped in the stone. Suggest to students that they use a Sequence of Events Chart to help them describe the action.

STEP 1: Monitor Progress

Comprehension Check

Make Inferences After reading pp. 40–41, lead a class discussion about the importance of making inferences to better understand the reading.

SAY *Making inferences about a reading is similar to the reading skill of previewing and predicting. When you make an inference, you guess what will happen without looking ahead in the reading.*

- *What is one inference we can make at this point in the story?*
- *Which detail in the story made you think of the inference?*

Have students fill in questions and answers in a 5 W Chart like the one shown below to help them make inferences about the story. Encourage students to complete the chart as they read the rest of the story.

Who helped John make soup?
What did the little girl put in the soup?
Where is John while he is cooking?
Why did John use stones for his soup?
When does this story take place?

Adapt the Activity

When students have finished reading pp. 40–41, explain that most of the story on these pages is written in dialogue. Have students imagine they are performing a play. Ask volunteers to read aloud and act out the dialogue. Remind students to use appropriate verbal cues, facial expressions, and gestures in their presentations.

"What are you doing?" asked a little girl, who had been watching him from a nearby garden.

"I'm making stone soup," John told her.

"Stone soup!" she cried. "Is it good?"

"You've never had stone soup?" he asked. "Stone soup is delicious!"

The little girl peeked into the pot of water. She saw the stone at the bottom of the pot.

"I have some extra potatoes," she told him. "Would potatoes be good in stone soup?"

"I like stone soup just as it is," John said. "But I think potatoes will make it even better."

The little girl smiled. "Let's put them in!" she said as she dropped the potatoes into the boiling water.

garden place where people grow fruit, vegetables, and flowers

40

TESOL Standards

Goal 2, Standard 2—To use English to achieve academically in all content areas: Students will use English to obtain, process, construct, and provide subject matter information in spoken and written form

Descriptors—Listening to, speaking, reading, and writing about subject matter information; Gathering information orally and in writing; Retelling information; Selecting, connecting, and explaining information; Demonstrating knowledge through application in a variety of contexts.

As the potatoes began to cook, wonderful smells floated through the village from cottage to cottage.

A young boy came over with some carrots. "Your soup smells so good," the boy said. "Would these carrots be good in the soup?"

"This stone soup will be delicious," John told him. "But carrots will make it even better."

The boy dropped the carrots into the pot.

John sniffed the delicious aroma coming from the pot. "This will be the best stone soup ever," he said to the boy and girl.

That's when John saw how hungry the children looked.

"Will you stay and share this soup with me?" he asked them.

"Will there be enough?" the little girl asked.

"More than enough!" John said.

---

floated traveled over air or water

aroma odor

Check Up What event happened on this page?

41

Differentiated Instruction

Beginning	Write the following sentences on the board and have students fill in the blanks: John wants to make ________. A ________ gives him ________.
Intermediate	Have students work in pairs to answer the following question: *What are some of the ways people have worked together to help each other in this story?*
Greater Challenge	Have students fill in a Sequence of Events Chart about the action so far in the story.
Standard English Learner (CRI)	Have students work in pairs to read aloud the dialogue on p. 40. Students can improvise words or use gestures but should tell the correct story.

STEP 2: Teach

Visual Literacy

Illustrations Draw the students' attention to the illustrations on pp. 40–41. Point out that the pictures help show how the characters feel and identify events in a plot.

SAY *Pictures often help us understand a story better.*

- *How do they show the characters cooperating with each other?*
- *What else do the pictures tell you about John and about the people he met?*

Have students work in pairs and describe to their partners what action is happening in each picture. Encourage students to include details they remember from the story and details of things they see in the picture that are not mentioned in the story.

STEP 3: Assess

Check Up

Lead a discussion about the events that happened before p. 41. Then ask what new event happened on p. 41. Ask students what they'd like to find out on the next page.

Scaffolding

Have students use a Story Map like the one shown below to fill in details about the folktale.

Explain to students that in the top two boxes, they should write the names of each character. As students read these pages have them fill in the conflict in the second box, and the outcome the third.

John | little girl, young boy

↓

John wants food.
John tells people he is making soup

↓

Two children bring vegetables to help John make soup.

STEP 1: Monitor Progress

Comprehension Check

Determine Character When students complete the reading, lead a class discussion about what they have learned about John's character.

SAY *Now that we have finished reading* Stone Soup, *think of words you would use to describe John.*

- *Is John a kind person or a mean person?*
- *If you met him, do you think you would like him? Why or why not?*
- *Do you believed John enjoyed having everyone help him make the soup? How do you know?*

Direct students to use a T-Chart like the one below to organize details for describing John's character. In the left column, use adjectives that describe his personality. In the right column, use phrases that describe his actions in the story.

John's character	
hard-working, smart, clever, friendly, hungry, young, hopeful, patient, a leader, generous, concerned	talks to people in the village; has an idea for making food; lets others help and share; is proud everyone worked together

Reteach

Review with students the rules for adjectives and adverbs. Write a list of nouns on the board that name items in the classroom or school and have students suggest adjectives to describe each item.

Study Skills

Dictionary Ask students to make a list of all the highlighted words from *Stone Soup* that are defined on pp. 38–43. Have students work in pairs to alphabetize the list of words.

Online Dictionary Students can use an online dictionary or the CD that accompanies a learners' dictionary, such as the *Longman Basic Dictionary*.

www.LongmanCornerstone.com

Soon, other people in the village began to charge toward John and his pot of stone soup.

"I've never heard of stone soup, but here is some meat," said a woman. "You may use it if you think it will be good in the soup."

"I have some onions," said another woman as she dropped them into the pot.

As the stone soup **simmered**, more and more people **lined up** to add something good to the pot.

John said to each person, "Please bring a bowl and spoon and share this soup with me. This is too much soup for me to eat alone."

Each person hurried home to get a bowl and spoon.

simmered cooked slowly

lined up stood one behind the other

42

TESOL Standards

Goal 2, Standard 2—To use English to achieve academically in all content areas: Students will use English to obtain, process, construct, and provide subject matter information in spoken and written form.

Descriptors—Listening to, speaking, reading, and writing about subject matter information; Gathering information orally and in writing; Retelling information; Selecting, connecting, and explaining information; Demonstrating knowledge through application in a variety of contexts.

When the soup had cooked, John looked at all the people who had gathered. Each person stood by the pot with a bowl and spoon. He wondered if there would be enough soup for everyone.

John looked into the pot of soup and saw the potatoes, carrots, onions, meat, and other good things. The pot was full!

John spooned the soup into everyone's bowls.

"This is the best soup ever!" exclaimed one person.

"I didn't know that stone soup could be so delicious!" said someone else.

After John finished his third bowl of soup, he called to the little girl who had given him potatoes. "This stone is for you," he said to her. "Now your village will never be hungry again."

Practice Book pages 21–22

Reading Strategy

Identify Events in a Plot

- What happened in the beginning of the story?
- How did the story end?
- Can you think of another ending to the story?

Think It Over

1. What is John's problem?
2. What event gives John his big idea?
3. How do the villagers react when they smell the soup?
4. What does John give the little girl at the end?

43

Differentiated Instruction

Beginning	Have students work in small groups to act out the story events that take place on pp. 42–43. Help them improvise dialogue as they perform their actions.
Early Intermediate	Have students write captions for each drawing on pp. 42–43. Remind students that a caption is a brief sentence that describes the main idea of the picture.
Intermediate	Ask students to imagine that they lived in the village in the story. What character would they want to be? Why?
Struggling Reader	Point to the pictures on pp. 42–43. Have students say words to describe the items in the pictures. Help students write the words.

STEP 2: Teach

Build Discussion

Context Clues Explain to students that authors add clues to a story to make it fun for readers to guess what will happen next. Have students describe to the class which clues in the story and in the pictures helped them draw conclusions about the main character in *Stone Soup*.

STEP 3: Assess

Reading Strategy

Identify Events in a Plot Give students suggestions for how to identify each action in a story and understand the sequence of events.

SAY *When you want to identify events in a plot for a story you are reading, ask yourself the following questions and write down your answers:*

- *Where does the action of the story take place?*
- *Does the action take place in more than one location?*
- *How many characters are in the story?*
- *Do all characters speak, or are some characters part of a crowd?*
- *Most stories have at least one problem and solution. What is the problem and solution in this story?*

Reteach

Have students review the reading strategy for taking notes. Remind students that the purpose of taking notes is to remember the most important details of what they are reading. Ask students if it is better to write whole sentences or to write words and phrases while taking notes.

Think It Over

Flexible Grouping You may assign this exercise as a class discussion, partner activity, or individual writing assignment.

Answer Key

1. John is hungry and has no food.
2. John sees a smooth, round stone in the road.
3. The villagers bring food to add to the soup.
4. John gives the little girl the stone from the soup.

STEP 1: Introduce

Word Analysis

Multiple-Meaning Words Help students understand that many words have more than one meaning. Tell students the word *drop* is used as a noun and as a verb.

Provide students with additional examples of words that can be used as nouns or a verbs. Have students practice writing context sentences for both parts of speech.

STEP 2: Teach

Review the rule about multiple-meaning words. Explain that only one meaning will usually make sense in a sentence.

SAY *Here's the rule. When you see a word that has more than one meaning, only one meaning for the word will make sense in that sentence.*

1. *John decided to* trade *the pot for something to eat.* to give away something for something else
2. *Before long, the people in the village began to* charge *toward John.* to run to or rush at
3. *John saw a smooth, round* stone *in the road.* a small piece of rock

STEP 3: Practice

1. Have students work with partners. If they find more than two meanings for a word, have them pick two that seem totally different.
2. Monitor students to see that they are writing definitions for two different meanings of each word.

Link to Science

Have students research how heat is transferred from a flame to an object and find out the temperature at which water will boil.

Teaching Resources
- ***Practice Book***, p. 23
- ***Phonics Workbook***
- *CD-ROM* • *Audio CD*

Reading 3

Word Analysis & Fluency

Word Analysis

Multiple-Meaning Words

Some words have more than one meaning.

John could hardly wait to eat every **drop** of the soup.

He waited for the water to boil to **drop** the stone into the pot.

A dictionary lists all the different meanings of a word.

Rule Box

You can look at how a word is used in a sentence to help you understand what it means.

- A drop of soup is a small amount of soup.
- Drop the stone into the pot means to let the stone fall.

Practice

Look up each word in the dictionary.
Write two different definitions for each word.

1. trade
2. charge
3. stone
4. fill
5. carry

Practice Book page 23

44

TESOL Standards

Goal 1, Standard 3—To use English to communicate in social settings: Students will use learning strategies to extend their communicative competence.
Descriptors—Listening to and imitating how others use English; Self-monitoring and self-evaluating language development; Practicing new language; Focusing attention selectively; Exploring alternative ways of saying things.

Goal 3, Standard 3—To use English in socially and culturally appropriate ways: Students will use appropriate learning strategies to extend their sociolinguistic and sociocultural competence.
Descriptors—Observing and modeling how others speak and behave in a particular situation or setting; Experimenting with variations of language in social and academic settings; Seeking information about appropriate language use and behavior.

Fluency

Read with Expression

When you read aloud, use your voice to show feelings.

Practice

Read silently. → Read aloud. → Get comments. → Read aloud again.

"What are you doing?" asked a little girl, who had been watching him from a nearby garden.

"I'm making stone soup," John told her.

"Stone soup!" she cried. "Is it good?"

"You've never had stone soup?" he asked. "Stone soup is delicious!"

The little girl peeked into the pot of water. She saw the stone at the bottom of the pot.

"I have some extra potatoes," she told him. "Would potatoes be good in stone soup?"

"I like stone soup just as it is," John said. "But I think potatoes will make it even better."

The little girl smiled. "Let's put them in!" she said as she dropped the potatoes into the boiling water.

45

Linguistic Note

Delicious Students who speak Spanish may recognize the English word *delicious*, since it is similar to the Spanish *delicioso*. Both words come from the Latin *deliciosus*. However, because *–cioso* is pronounced as three syllables in Spanish, students may have difficulty remembering to pronounce *–cious* as only one syllable in English.

STEP 1: Introduce

Fluency

Read with Expression Explain to students that reading with expression can help show the emotion intended in the selection. Some ways of showing feelings are reading louder or softer, faster or slower, and emphasizing certain words.

Play the audio CD for this reading to the class, asking students to listen for pacing, intonation, and expression. Remind students to use appropriate verbal cues, facial expressions, and gestures while reading.

STEP 2: Practice

Have students look for clues such as an exclamation mark, a question mark, the word *cried*, or the word *smiled*.

- Divide the students in pairs.
- Have one partner read the passage aloud to the other. Remind the reader to show feelings and use his or her voice to make the passage as interesting and exciting as possible.
- Have the listener give feedback. Then have the reader read the passage aloud again.
- Change roles and repeat the exercise.

Have partners list some tips for reading with expression.

STEP 3: Extend

Study Skills

Dictionary Point out that when a reader stumbles over a hard word, it's almost impossible to read that sentence with expression. Have each student

- write down three hard words that made it difficult to read with expression.
- look the words up in a dictionary.
- read the sentences from the reading in which the words appear.
- define and pronounce the hard words.

STEP 1: Monitor Progress

Learning Strategy

Retel As they retell the story, prompt students with transitional language such as: What happened first? Then what happened? What was the last thing that happened? Explain to students that retelling the story can help them remember and understand it. Have students take turns retelling the story to partners, emphasizing the beginning, one event in the middle, and the end of the story. Then have students take turns responding to the Big Question for this reading.

STEP 2: Teach

Events in a Plot

Students will learn how a plot is the sequence of events that happen in a story.

SAY *A plot is made up of the main events that happen in a story. An event is a major action that takes place.*

- *Every plot has a number of events.*
- *Events usually have details, which are things that happen but are not important events.*
- *When you retell the plot, you should mention all the important events.*
- *You don't have to retell every detail.*

When students work in pairs to retell the story, suggest that one student tell about one event. Have the partner tell about the next event. Encourage students to retell the story without looking in their books.

STEP 3: Practice

Flexible Grouping You may assign this activity as a class discussion, partner activity, or individual written assignment.

Answer Key

a, d, f - events   b, c, e, g - details

Teaching Resources

- *Practice Book*, pp. 24–25
- *Transparencies*, p. 46
- *Teacher's Resource Book*, p. 156
- *CD-ROM*

Reading 3

Comprehension

Learning Strategy

Retell

Retell the story to a partner.

Ask your partner to respond to the Big Question for this reading.

Practice Book page 24

Events in a Plot

The **plot** tells the events that happen in a story. The **events** are the major actions that take place.

Practice

Read this list of events and details from *Stone Soup*. Which ones are major events in the plot? Which ones are details?

a. John is hungry. He has a pot but no food.
b. The farmer's wife thinks John is a nice boy. She wishes she could help him.
c. John finds a smooth, round stone. The stone gives him an idea.
d. There were many other stones on the road, but none of them were as smooth or round.
e. John fills his pot with water and drops the stone in when the water is boiling.
f. The fire takes a long time to heat the water. John looks for more wood to burn.

46

TESOL Standards

Goal 2, Standard 2—To use English to achieve academically in all content areas: Students will use English to obtain, process, construct, and provide subject matter information in spoken and written form.
Descriptors—Listening to, speaking, reading, and writing about subject matter information; Gathering information orally and in writing; Retelling information; Selecting, connecting, and explaining information; Analyzing, synthesizing, and inferring from information; Responding to the work of peers and others; Representing information visually and interpreting information presented visually; demonstrating knowledge through application in a variety of contexts.

Use a Sequence Chart

Events in a story happen in order. That order is called the **sequence**. A Sequence Chart can help you put the events in order, from what happened first to what happened last.

Practice

Create a Sequence Chart for *Stone Soup*.

- Use the three major events you found on page 46.
- Add other events from the list below.
- Then answer the questions at the bottom.

John shares his soup with the villagers.
The villagers bring small bits of food to add to the soup.
A little girl sees John and offers to add potatoes to the stone soup.

Sequence Chart
1.
2.
3.
4.
5.
6.

1. What event in the story happened before line 1?
2. What event in the story happened after line 6?
3. If this story continued, what do you think would happen next?

Accelerate Language Development

Fruits and Vegetables Some fruits and vegetables like *tomato*, *lemon*, *banana*, and *potato* have similar names in Spanish and English, but are pronounced slightly differently. Some others, like *cereza* (Spanish)/*cherry* (English) and *espinaca* (Spanish)/*spinach* (English) come from the same root, but have quite different pronunciations. Spanish-speaking students may have difficulty remembering the differences in pronunciation. Provide photos of fruits and vegetables, and have students say the English words for each. For fun, ask all students to name the foods in their own languages.

STEP 1: Teach

Use a Sequence of Events Chart

Ask students to think about what they do each day. Ask them to create three sentences about what they do but NOT in order. Have them give their sentences to their partners, and have each partner number the sentences in the correct order.

Possible Responses
Out of order
I go to sleep.
I eat breakfast.
I take the bus home from school.

In order
1. I eat breakfast.
2. I take the bus home from school.
3. I go to sleep.

STEP 2: Practice

You may have the students complete the Sequence of Events Chart provided as a Blackline Master in the *Teacher's Resource Book*.

Possible Responses
1. John's mother died and he kept her pot.
2. John gave the soup stone to the little girl.
3. The people in the village would use the stone to make soup again.

STEP 3: Extend

Oral Presentation Ask students to fill in a Sequence of Events Chart that describes their daily routines. Divide the class into groups. Have students make a list of six things they do each day. Remind students to begin with the first thing they do each day and end with the last thing they do. Have students read the list to the class and remind students to listen without interruption.

Scaffolding

Explain to students that an author often rewrites a story before it is finished to add more details and events. Ask students to imagine they are authors and want to rewrite *Stone Soup*. Have students work in small groups before presenting their rewritten stories to the class.

STEP 1: Introduce

Help students understand that future tense verbs name an action that has not yet happened. These verbs require the helping verb *will*. Explain to students that the future perfect tense describes an event that is expected to happen before another event. I will have finished the paper next week.

STEP 2: Teach

Future Tense Verbs

Have students read the rule on p. 48. Then have them imagine what might happen to John after the ending of *Stone Soup*. Next, write the sentences below on the board. Ask students to look at the verb at the end of each sentence, and fill in the blank using the future tense.

1. *John ______ another soup tomorrow.* (cook)
2. *While he is cooking, the people ______ vegetables and meats to put in the soup.* (bring)
3. *Everyone ______ the soup again.* (share)
4. *The villagers ______ a good time. (have)*
5. *After that, the little girl ______ how to make stone soup herself.* (learn)
6. *Then she ______ her soup to everybody.* (give)

STEP 3: Practice

Before students begin the activity in their Student Books, have them write a short sentence for each future tense verb shown in the Rule Box.

Ask volunteers to read their sentences aloud. Then have students complete the Practice activity in their Student Books.

Answer Key

1. will cook	4. will bring
2. will share	5. will ask
3. will meet	6. will enjoy

Teaching Resources

- ***Practice Book,*** pp. 25–26
- ***Transparencies,*** pp. 69–80
- ***Assessments,*** pp. 37–40
- ***CD-ROM***

Reading 3

Grammar & Writing

Future Tense Verbs

In *Stone Soup*, John says to himself, "This soup will be delicious!" He also meets a girl and a boy and asks them, "Will you stay and share this soup with me?" In each of these sentences, John uses the future tense of a verb. **Future tense verbs** name an action that will happen in the future.

Rule Box

To form the future tense of a verb, use the helping verb ***will***.

be	→ will be	carry	→ will carry
stay	→ will stay	eat	→ will eat

Practice

Copy each verb. Write the future tense form.

Practice Book pages 25

1. cook	**3.** meet	**5.** ask
2. share	**4.** bring	**6.** enjoy

TESOL Standards

Goal 1, Standard 3—To use English to communicate in social settings: Students will use learning strategies to extend their communicative competence.
Descriptor—Seeking support and feedback from others.

Goal 2, Standard 1—To use English to achieve academically in all content areas: Students will use English to interact in the classroom.
Descriptors—Following oral and written directions, implicit and explicit; Explaining actions; Expressing likes, dislikes, and needs.

Goal 2, Standard 3—To use English to achieve academically in all content areas: Students will use appropriate learning strategies to construct and apply academic knowledge.
Descriptors—Using context to construct meaning; Actively connecting new information-to-information previously learned; Imitating the behaviors of native English speakers to complete tasks successfully.

Goal 3, Standard 1—To use English in socially and culturally appropriate ways: Students will use the appropriate language variety, register, and genre according to audience, purpose, and setting.
Descriptors—Recognizing and using Standard English and vernacular dialects appropriately; Using a variety of writing styles appropriate for different audiences, purposes, and settings.

Write a Paragraph

A paragraph contains a topic sentence that states the main idea. Supporting sentences give more information about the main idea. You can use the future tense to describe events that may happen in the future.

Read about how Lino described his uncle's upcoming visit.

I am very excited about next weekend. My uncle is going to come from London for a visit. He said he will take my whole family to Adventure Park for the weekend. We will fly in an airplane. That will be really fun. Then a car will pick us up and take us straight to the park. My sister, my uncle, and I will have a contest to see who can ride the scariest roller coaster. We are going to have a great time.

SPELLING TIP

When trying to spell compound words, look for a smaller word within the larger word:

every + thing = everything

Practice Book pages 26

Practice

Write a paragraph to describe a fun weekend you would like to have.

- Make sure your paragraph has a topic sentence and several supporting sentences.
- Your paragraph tells about the future, so you will use the future tense.
- Be sure to use the helping verb ***will*** in your writing.

Writing Checklist

- ✓ Is your topic sentence clear? Did you give supporting details?
- ✓ Did you use the future tense in your writing?
- ✓ Can your partner understand your paragraph?

49

STEP 1: Introduce

Write a Paragraph

Define a paragraph and a topic sentence.

SAY *A paragraph is a group of sentences that tells about one idea or event. The topic sentence states the main idea of the paragraph. In Lino's paragraph, for example, he tells us in the first sentence that the paragraph is about what will happen next weekend. The other sentences give details about what will happen next weekend, and why it will be exciting.*

Spelling Tip

Read the text in the box aloud to students. Tell students that they will find two compound words in Lino's paragraph. Have students find the words and write them down. Ask students what two smaller words are found in each compound word.

STEP 2: Practice

Have students write their own paragraphs about something that will happen in the future. Discuss the parts of a paragraph:

- Did you include a topic sentence that tells what the paragraph is about?
- Did you use the future tense to tell about things that will happen?
- Did you include supporting details?

STEP 3: Extend

Writing Checklist

- ✓ Have students underline or highlight their topic sentence.
- ✓ Have students make sure that verbs tell about future actions.
- ✓ Have students work with partners. Ask students to make sure their partners can understand what they have written.

Differentiated Instruction

Beginning	Have students point to the phrase in the paragraph that tells where Lino's uncle is going to take the whole family. Then have them find the sentence that tells who will have a contest.
Early Intermediate	Have students write short answers to these questions: *Where is Lino's uncle going to come from this weekend? How does Lino feel about flying in an airplane?*
Intermediate	Have students work with partners to find the future tense verbs in Lino's paragraph. Ask students to fill in a T-Chart with the future tense form and present tense form of each verb they find.
Struggling Reader	Point to a photo on p. 21. Have students say the correct word to describe the photo. Help students write the words as needed.

STEP 1: Introduce

More About The Big Question

Remind students of the Unit 1 Big Question. *In what ways can people or groups help others?*

SAY *The Big Question for this bonus reading is* How can people and animals help each other?

- *Read the title of the reading on page 50.*
- *Who do you think is on the team?*
- *Can you predict if Rachael will help the dogs or will the dogs help her?*

Visual Literacy

Photos Draw students' attention to the photograph on p. 50 and read the caption aloud.

SAY *Look at the photo on page 50.*

- *Who is the woman in the picture?*
- *What is she doing for the dogs?*
- *Where do you think they are?*
- *When during the year was this photo taken?*
- *Why is the dog wearing a harness?*

STEP 2: Teach

Understand Text Structure

Draw students' attention to the genre label. Explain that a magazine article has many of the same features as a newspaper article. Magazine articles usually examine small topics in depth. They may or may not describe current events.

Read Aloud

Tell students that an informational text often gets readers interested in the beginning by asking questions that will be answered later in the text. In this selection, the author asks a question at the top of the first p. Have students work in small groups to take turns reading paragraphs on p. 51.

Teaching Resources

- *Teacher's Resource Book,* p. 109
- *CD-ROM*
- *Audio CD*

Bonus Reading

INFORMATIONAL TEXT

Magazine Article

A Team Crosses the Finish Line

by Amanda Cunningham

Rachael Scdoris feeds some of her team members.

50

TESOL Standards

Goal 2, Standard 3—To use English to achieve academically in all content areas: Students will use appropriate learning strategies to construct and apply academic knowledge. **Descriptors**—Focusing attention selectively; Applying basic reading comprehension skills such as skimming, scanning, previewing, and reviewing text; Using context to construct meaning; Applying self-monitoring and self-corrective strategies to build and expand a knowledge base; Knowing when to use native language resources (human and material) to promote understanding.

Who Is Rachael Scdoris?

Rachael Scdoris is legally blind. She can see very little. What she can see, she cannot see clearly. Rachael was often told that she couldn't do things like run on the track team or race sled dogs. She has done both. In 2006, she became the first legally blind person to finish the world's longest sled dog race.

Rachael has always loved sled dogs. Her father was a sled dog racer, or musher. He raised his own dogs. When Rachael was eight years old, she knew she wanted to be a musher, too.

Rachael learned how to mush by having others ride with her on the sled. Even after she learned, Rachael's father said that someone else had to be on the sled. He wanted to keep Rachael safe. Rachael did not like this. She wanted to race like other mushers. Rachael was not afraid. She kept asking her father to let her drive the sled by herself.

Rachael drove her first sled alone when she was 11 years old. Rachael and her dogs worked as a team. Rachael had to depend on her dogs to follow the trail to the finish line. The dogs had to depend on Rachael to get them to work together. Rachael and her dogs trusted each other. They did well when they raced.

51

Vocabulary Definitions

The following vocabulary appears in *A Team Crosses the Finish Line* on p. 51. Definitions are provided for your convenience and are not meant for vocabulary acquisition or exercises.

legally blind able to see very little, even with eyeglasses or contact lenses

sled vehicle with two runners that goes over ice and snow

musher person who races sled dogs

team group of people and/or animals that work together

STEP 3: Extend

Ask students to think of other ways people and animals work together. Have them write a brief description of their ideas and present them to the class.

Make Connections

Writing Fluency Invite students to write an informational paragraph about an experience they may have had working with an animal or a team of animals. Encourage students to share their stories with the class. Have students discuss how they and the animals helped each other. Note that students' responses can be related to the Big Question.

Differentiated Instruction

Beginning	Have students point to the sentences that tell what Rachael's father did when she was a little girl.
Intermediate	Have students discuss the following questions with partners: *What happened when Rachael was eight years old? What happened when she was eleven years old?* Ask students to write a sentence to answer each question.
Greater Challenge	Have students write a paragraph that explains what Rachael did that no one was able to do before and why they think she could do it.
Standard English Learner CRI	Have students draw a picture of Rachael racing with her sled dogs. Write the following words on the board for things to include in the picture: *dog, sled, person, trees, snow, hills*.

FYI

The First Iditarod The Iditarod is the name of a trail that was used during the gold rush in Alaska during the 1880s and 1890s. In 1925, the people in Nome, Alaska, started getting sick with a disease known as diphtheria. There was no medicine in Nome to treat the disease. The closest city with the necessary medicine was on the other side of Alaska, in Anchorage. It was not certain that a plane could fly safely in Alaska's cold weather. So the medicine was taken as far as it could get by train, and then brought the rest of the way on dog sleds. About 2/3 of the 700-mile trip was along the old Iditarod trail. Fortunately, the medicine arrived in time to stop the disease from spreading.

STEP 1: Monitor Progress

Comprehension Check

Compare and Contrast Have students compare and contrast what they have learned so far about Rachael Scdoris and her sled dogs.

SAY *Rachael Scdoris is different from most people who enter a race, but in many ways she is also like others in the race.*

- *What is different about Rachael from most people who enter a race?*
- *What did she do in 2006 that no one had done before?*
- *In what way are Rachael and her father alike?*
- *After she learned to drive the sled, what did she and her father disagree about?*
- *To race well, what must Rachael and the dogs do together?*

Build Discussion

Remind students about the Big Question for this unit. Lead a class discussion about various ways people and animals work together.

SAY *The Big Question in this unit was about how individual people and groups can help each other. In this article, we read about a person and dogs who help each other.*

Have students discuss how humans and animals can help each other. Remind them that humans sometimes help pets and wild animals.

Ask the following questions for further class discussion:

Why might a human want to help an animal?

Why might an animal want to help a human?

Reteach

Sequence of Events Review with students the rules for listing events in a story in the order they happen. When students finish reading pp. 52–53, have them fill in a Sequence of Events Chart. Remind students to fill in the chart with the main events and not to include small details.

The Big Race

The Iditarod is a famous sled dog race in Alaska. The Iditarod is 1,150 miles long. A legally blind person had never finished it. Rachael wanted to try.

Rachael entered the Iditarod for the first time in 2005. A person on another sled went ahead of Rachael. He told her about obstacles that Rachael could not see. After 700 miles, Rachael had to quit. Some of her dogs were sick. It was hard for them to pull the sled. Rachael knew that she had to support her dogs because her dogs had supported her. She was sad to stop, but her dogs had to come first. They were a team.

52

TESOL Standards

Goal 2, Standard 3—To use English to achieve academically in all content areas: Students will use appropriate learning strategies to construct and apply academic knowledge. **Descriptors**—Focusing attention selectively; Applying basic reading comprehension skills such as skimming, scanning, previewing, and reviewing text; Using context to construct meaning; Applying self-monitoring and self-corrective strategies to build and expand a knowledge base; Knowing when to use native language resources (human and material) to promote understanding.

An Iditarod racer crosses the finish line with his team of dogs.

Rachael did not give up on her dream of finishing the Iditarod. She kept training herself and her dogs. In 2006, Rachael tried the Iditarod again. She raced for more than 12 days in very cold weather.

Rachael became the first legally blind person to finish the Iditarod. She could not see the finish line, but her dogs led the way. Rachael knew that she and her dogs were able to finish the Iditarod because they had worked together as a team. Rachael and her dogs showed what we can do when we work together.

53

FYI

Rachael Scdoris Even before Rachael finished the Iditarod in 2006, she had already set some records. In 2001, when she was 16 years old, she became the youngest person and the first legally blind person ever to complete a 500-mile sled dog race. The Women's Sports Foundation in New York named Rachael as one of the top female athletes in the United States..

Accelerate Language Development

Dream The first sentence on p. 53 says: "Rachael would not give up on her dream of finishing the Iditarod." Students may be familiar with the most common meaning of the word *dream*, the images you see in your mind while you're asleep. In English, though, *dream* is often used to mean "hope, wish, or goal for the future." It is this second meaning that is used in *A Team Crosses the Finish Line*.

STEP 2: Teach

Vocabulary Definitions

The following vocabulary appears in *A Team Crosses the Finish Line* on pp. 52–53. Definitions are provided for your convenience to share with your class if they require explanations of any words. They are not meant for vocabulary acquisition or exercises.

obstacles things that get in the way

quit stop or give up

support provide help or encouragement

STEP 3: Assess

Comprehension Check

1. What is the Iditarod?
   The Iditarod is a famous sled dog race in Alaska.
2. In what year did Rachael enter her first Iditarod?
   Rachael entered the Iditarod for the first time in 2005.
3. Did Rachael complete the Iditarod in 2005? If so, how did she do it? If not, why not?
   She did not complete the Iditarod because some of her dogs had gotten sick.
4. When did Rachael try the Iditarod again?
   in 2006
5. How long did it take her to race in 2006?
   more than 12 days.
6. Why was Rachael probably big news at the end of the 2006 Iditarod?
   She was the first legally blind person to finish the Iditarod.

Link to Math

Tell students that the total distance of the Iditarod race is 1,150 miles. Have students solve the following story problem: If Rachael finished the race in 12 days, how many miles did she go each day during the race?

STEP 1: Review

The Big Question

Evidence of Understanding

Read the Big Question for the unit with the students to focus students' attention on this unit's theme in a way that can be answered and assessed in a variety of modalities. The first tier is least challenging and the third tier is most challenging.

STEP 2: Transfer

Written

Top Ten List Discuss groups students might focus on, such as senior citizens, people with disabilities, the homeless, and the chronically ill.

Letter Suggest groups to write to, such as a hospital, senior citizen home, or mayor's office.

Flier Have students research groups and outreach services, such as food banks, soup kitchens, and after-school programs.

Oral

Interview Use a 5 W Chart to brainstorm some possible interview subjects, such as a health care professional, firefighter, police officer, or nanny.

Story Share Tell students to prepare an outline or a Sequence of Events Chart to arrange their story ideas.

News Watch Direct students to appropriate news programs on television, the radio, or online and learn their programming schedules.

Visual/Active

Poster Remind students to think of a name for their group and to design the poster so all the information is easy to read.

Graphic Organizer Review the different graphic organizers appropriate for the activity: webs, Main Idea and Details Charts, 5 W Chart, and KWL Charts.

Event Collage Display a community calendar or schedule about community events. Discuss what events students want to attend. Students can also make a collage or poster about a past community event.

UNIT 1 Wrap Up

The Big Question

In what ways can people or groups help others?

Written	Oral	Visual/Active
Top Ten List Write a list of 10 activities kids your age can do to help people where you live. Present the ideas on your list to a partner or group.	**Interview** Interview someone who spends time helping others. Use the 5W questions for ideas. Share what you learn with a partner or group.	**Poster** Create a poster about a group that helps people in your community. Tell something about what the group does and how to contact it.
Letter Write a letter to a group that helps people in your area. Ask how young people can help the group make life better for the people it serves.	**Story Share** Think of a time when someone helped you or your family, or when you helped someone else. Tell your classmates about that time.	**Graphic Organizer** Research another group that helps people or animals. Make a chart that shows the information you find.
Flier Research groups that help people near you. Make a flier for one group that gives important information about it.	**News Watch** Watch or listen to news programs for a few days. Jot down information about events or programs that help people. Present what you learned to the class.	**Event Collage** Attend an event where people help others, such as a park cleanup. Make a poster or collage about the event.

54

TESOL Standards

Goal 2, Standard 1—To use English to achieve academically in all content areas: Students will use English to interact in the classroom.
Descriptors—Negotiating and managing interaction to accomplish tasks; Elaborating and extending other people's ideas and words.

Goal 2, Standard 2—To use English to achieve academically in all content areas: Students will use English to obtain, process, construct, and provide subject matter information in spoken and written form.
Descriptors—Gathering information orally and in writing; Representing information visually and interpreting information presented visually; Understanding and producing technical vocabulary and text features according to content area; Demonstrating knowledge through application in a variety of contexts.

Goal 3, Standard 1—To use English in socially and culturally appropriate ways: Students will use the appropriate language variety, register, and genre according to audience, purpose, and setting.
Descriptors—Using the appropriate degree of formality with different audiences and settings; Recognizing and using Standard English and vernacular dialects appropriately; Using a variety of writing styles appropriate for different audiences, purposes, and settings; Responding to and using slang appropriately; Responding to and using idioms appropriately; Responding to and using humor appropriately; Determining when it is appropriate to use a language other than English; Determining appropriate topics for interaction.

Practice Book pages 27–28

✓ Learning Checklist

Word Analysis and Phonics

- ✓ Identify short vowel sounds.
- ✓ Practice long vowel sounds with silent *e*.
- ✓ Understand that some words can have many meanings.

Comprehension

- ✓ Preview and predict.
- ✓ Use a Problem and Solution Chart.
- ✓ Activate prior knowledge.
- ✓ Use a KWL Chart.
- ✓ Identify events in a plot.
- ✓ Use a Sequence Chart.

Grammar and Writing

- ✓ Identify singular and plural nouns.
- ✓ Write a narrative.
- ✓ Use the past tense.
- ✓ Write a paragraph with a topic sentence.
- ✓ Use the future tense.
- ✓ Write a paragraph with the future tense.

Self-Evaluation Questions

- What did you really learn about helping others?
- How has what you've learned changed your thinking?
- How will you work with others in the future?

Further Reading

A Monkey's Tale
In this Penguin Young Reader®, two communities of monkeys have been divided for centuries—and are deeply suspicious of one another. Can the two communities work together to be reunited?

Stone Fox, John Reynolds Gardiner
Wanting to raise money to help save his grandfather's Wisconsin farm, Willy enters his beloved dog Searchlight in a dog sled race. However, his main rival in the contest is Stone Fox, a stern man who has never lost a race.

Sam and the Lucky Money, Karen Chin
For Chinese New Year, Sam received the traditional gift of "lucky money." Now, with his four dollars in hand, he hopes to find something special in Chinatown to buy. On the street, Sam encounters a man in need and finds a special way to spend his money.

STEP 3: Assess

Learning Checklist

Word Analysis and Phonics

- ✓ Short vowels sounds: Reading 1, p. 16
- ✓ Long vowels sounds with silent *e*: Reading 2, p. 30
- ✓ Multiple-Meaning words: Reading 3, p. 44

Comprehension

- ✓ Preview and predict: Reading 1, p. 18
- ✓ Use a Problem and Solution Chart: Reading 1, p. 19
- ✓ Activate prior knowledge: Reading 2, p. 32
- ✓ Use a KWL Chart: Reading 2, p. 33
- ✓ Events in a plot: Reading 3, p. 46
- ✓ Use a Sequence of Events Chart: Reading 3, p. 47

Grammar and Writing

- ✓ Identify singular and plural nouns: Reading 1, p. 20
- ✓ Write a narrative: Reading 1, p. 21
- ✓ Use the past tense: Reading 2, p. 34
- ✓ Write a paragraph with a topic sentence: Reading 2, p. 35
- ✓ Use the future tense: Reading 3, p. 48
- ✓ Write a paragraph with the future tense: Reading 3, p. 49

Self-Evaluation Questions

The self-evaluation questions provide the teacher with important information about the students' learning processes as well as their self esteem.

- Have students review each reading to remember what they learned about helping others. Remind students of the Big Question.
- Tell students to consider the positive outcomes and effects of helping others as they respond.
- Remind students that even a simple gesture is valuable.

Teaching Resources

- ***Practice Book,*** pp. 27–28
- ***Transparencies,*** p. 81
- ***Assessment Book,*** pp. 103–112
- ***CD-ROM*** • ***Teacher's CD-ROM***

Unit 2 Planner

Heroes and Their Journeys

Unit Preview: pp. 56–61
Pacing: 3–4 Days
Vocabulary: *Words to Know,* pp. 58–59
Oral Language: *What about you?,* p. 61

The Big Question
What does it take to be a hero?

	Suggested Pacing: 7–8 Days	Suggested Pacing: 7–8 Days
Reading Selection	**1 The Three Gifts** pp. 62–75 **Genre:** Literature/ Folktale	**2 Brave Androcles!** pp. 76–85 **Genre:** Literature/ Poetry
Oral Language	**More About the Big Question, p. T64** *What gifts do heroes bring?*	**More About the Big Question, p. T78** *What is meant by "one good deed deserves another"?*
Vocabulary	**Key Words:** cooperate, bore, marvelous, millet, virtue, grateful **Academic Words:** assess, error **Other Academic Word:** hypothesis	**Key Words:** chased, arena, swollen, wander, criminal **Academic Words:** motive, principle **Other Academic Word:** principal
Phonics Word Analysis Fluency	**Phonics:** Long Vowel Pairs, p. 70 **Fluency:** Look Ahead, p. 71	**Phonics:** Vowel Pair: *ea*, p. 80 **Fluency:** Read with Expression, p. 81
Comprehension	**Reading Strategy:** Identify Characters and Plot, pp. 64, 69 **Learning Strategy:** Retell, p. 72 **Comprehension Skill:** Characters and Plot, p. 72 **Graphic Organizer:** Cause and Effect Chart, p. 73	**Reading Strategy:** Make Connections, pp. 78, 79 **Learning Strategy:** Retell, p. 82 **Comprehension Skill:** Make Connections, p. 82 **Graphic Organizer:** Story Map, p. 83
Grammar and Writing	**Grammar:** Adjectives and Adverbs, p. 74 **Writing:** Write about Causes and Effects, Writing Checklist, Spelling Tip, p. 75	**Grammar:** Pronouns, p. 90 **Writing:** Write a Poem, Writing Checklist, Spelling Tip, p. 91
	Differentiated Instruction pp. T63, T65, T69, T75	**Differentiated Instruction** pp. T77, T79

Teaching Resources

- *Assessments,* pp. 41–52, pp. 113–122
- *Practice Book,* pp. 29–54
- *Phonics and Word Analysis Workbook*
- *Phonics and Word Analysis Teacher's Guide w/ Audio CD*
- *Phonics Flashcards*
- *Posters*
- *Teacher's Resource Book* Lesson Plans, pp. 14–25
- *Audio CD*
- *DVD*
- *Teacher's CD-ROM*
- *CD-ROM*
- *Phonetic Storybooks*
- *Penguin Young Readers Library*

Suggested Pacing: 7–8 Days

3

The Wizard of Oz

pp. 86–99

Genre: Literature/ Fantasy

More About the Big Question, p. T94

Can ordinary people become heroes? How?

Key Words: blister, contained, broad, midst, merry, startle
Academic Words: distinct, interact
Other Academic Word: equation

Word Analysis: Word Origins, p. 94
Fluency: Read for Speed and Accuracy, p. 95

Reading Strategy: Identify Problems and Solutions, pp. 89, 93
Learning Strategy: Outline, p. 96
Comprehension Skill: Characters and Conflicts, p. 96
Graphic Organizer: Idea Web, p. 97

Grammar: Possessive Nouns, p. 98
Writing: Write a Descriptive Paragraph, Writing Checklist, Spelling Tip, p. 99

Differentiated Instruction
pp. T87, T89, T93, T99

Suggested Pacing: 1–2 Days

Bonus Reading

The Elephant Shepherd

pp. 100–103

Genre: Literature/ Short Story

More About the Big Question, p. T100

How can young people become heroes?

Vocabulary: shepherd, cattle, savanna, grazing, stomp, tusk, illegal, poachers, pasture, related, survive, herd

Differentiated Instruction
p. T101

Further Reading

The Road to El Dorado
This Penguin Young Reader® tells the story of two adventurers, Tulio and Miguel, who set out to seek fame and fortune. Then fate hands them a map to the place of their dreams: the city of gold El Dorado.

Ride Like the Wind: A Tale of the Pony Express, Bernie Fuchs
In the early 1860s, Pony Express riders used daring and courage to deliver the mail amid severe weather and harsh terrain. Here is the engaging story of rider Johnny Free and his pony JennySoo as they race to make their deliveries.

American Tall Tales, Mary Pope Osborne
This collection of nine adventurous legends includes stories about American folk heroes such as Sally Ann Thunder, Ann Whirlwind, Pecos Bill, and John Henry.

Suggested Pacing: 1–2 Days

Assessment

The Big Question

Evidence of Understanding

What does it take to be a hero?

Check Up pp. 65, 67, 89, 91
Think It Over pp. 69, 79, 83
Extension pp. 73, 83, 97

Unit Wrap Up pp. 104–105

Written
Definition; Story; Survey

Oral
Discussion; Reality Show; News Report

Visual/Active
Magazine Cover; Hero Cards; Awards Ceremony

Learning Checklist
Word Analysis and Phonics; Comprehension; Grammar and Writing; Self-Evaluation Questions

STEP 1: Introduce

Explain that the theme of this unit is about what it takes to be a hero. Ask students to brainstorm a list of heroes from films and literature. Have volunteers explain their choices.

Unit Content Students practice reading and comprehension skills such as identifying characters and plot, making connections between the reading and students' own experiences, and identifying problems and solutions. They apply academic language strategies such as retelling and outlining.

STEP 2: Build Background

The Big Question

Explain that heroes help people during a time that may be dangerous or difficult for those people.

SAY *The Big Question is* What does it take to be a hero? *Think about a person you believe is a hero.*

- *Who is a hero in your community? Why?*
- *Who is a hero in your family? Why?*
- *Has anyone ever called you a hero? Why?*

Have students fill out a Character Traits Web like the sample one shown below to describe someone they think is a hero.

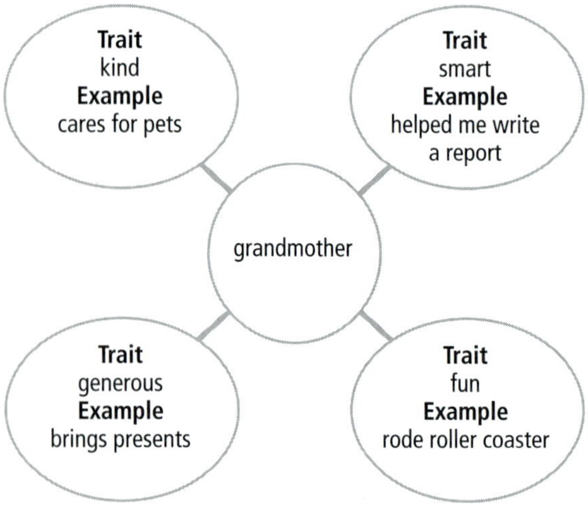

UNIT 2

Heroes and Their Journeys

There are many kinds of heroes. They always have interesting stories.

The Big Question

What does it take to be a hero?

READINGS

1 The Three Gifts

2 Brave Androcles

3 The Wizard of Oz

56

TESOL Standards

Goal 1, Standard 2—To use English to communicate in social settings: Students will interact in, through, and with spoken and written English for personal expression and enjoyment.

Descriptors—Sharing social and cultural traditions and values; Expressing personal needs, feelings, and ideas.

Goal 1, Standard 3—To use English to communicate in social settings: Students will use learning strategies to extend their communicative competence.

Descriptors—Testing hypotheses about language; Listening to and imitating how others use English; Exploring alternative ways of saying things; Using context to construct meaning.

Listening and Speaking

You will talk about your favorite heroes and what you think makes them heroes.

Writing

You will write a poem about your favorite hero.

Bonus Reading

The Elephant Shepherd

Quick Write

What does being a hero mean to you? Write down your ideas and share them with a partner.

Visit *LongmanCornerstone.com* 57

Differentiated Instruction	
Beginning	Read aloud the unit title, and ask students to repeat the title. Have students point to each title of the reading and say aloud what they see in each picture.
Early Intermediate	Have students look at the pictures for each reading. Then ask students to write one descriptive sentence for each picture.
Intermediate	Ask students to use the pictures and titles of the readings to predict who the hero will be in each reading.
Struggling Reader	Point to the Big Question and read it aloud. Then have students repeat the word *hero*. Ask: *Do you know a hero?* Help students draw and label pictures of their heroes.

STEP 3: Connect

Listening and Speaking

Read the text in the box aloud. Ask students to think of words that describe heroes and share them with the class. List the words on the board, and pronounce them for students.

Writing

Read the text in the Writing box aloud to students.

SAY *Imagine you are writing a poem about firefighters.*

- *How would you describe the firefighters?*
- *What do firefighters do?*
- *What tools do they use?*

Tell students they can write their poem about any hero they choose. Have students write 5 W questions and answers about that person. Explain to students that knowing more information makes it easier to add important details to creative writing.

Quick Write

Have students discuss with a partner what it means to be a hero, and ask them to take notes about what they say. Have them use their notes to write a paragraph with a topic sentence and supporting details.

Adapt the Activity

Tell students to imagine they are TV news reporters and their assignment is to interview a hero. Have students work in small groups to practice and perform the interview for the class. Remind students they should ask all the 5 W questions during the interview. Have students play various roles other than the hero and the interviewer such as the TV director, the camera person, and the sound person.

Visual Literacy

Graphic Organizer Introduce the Big Question transparency and use it throughout the unit to help students connect the readings to the Big Question.

STEP 1: Introduce

Unit Vocabulary

Use these pages to help students identify some terms used to describe heroes. Post your Words to Know poster for this unit in the classroom. As students read the unit, reinforce the unit vocabulary by using the Vocabulary cards provided as a Blackline Master in the *Teacher's Resource Book* as flash cards or by playing memory games.

STEP 2: Teach

Words to Know

Point to the pictures in section 1 that show the characteristics of heroes. Say each word aloud. Then have students say the word that names each picture.

Introduce the heroes in section 2 by pointing to each picture and naming the hero. Then have students complete the sentence stem by calling out their answers.

Academic Words

Discuss the definitions for *analyze* and *respond* with students. Share the following context sentences with students. Have students add the terms to their personal thesaurus.

analyze look at all parts and possibilities of a problem

respond react to something that is said or done

The doctors will *analyze* each symptom of the illness.

How does a hero *respond* to a call for help?

Have students write their own sentences using these academic words. Have them discuss their sentences in pairs or groups.

Teaching Resources

- ***Teacher's Resource Book,*** pp. 91–92, 168
- ***Transparencies,*** pp. 7–12
- ***Posters***
- ***CD-ROM*** • ***Audio CD***

What Do You Know about Heroes?

Words to Know

1. Use these words to talk about heroes.

creative — strong — wise

helpful — courageous — athletic

2. Who can be a hero?

A hero can be ______________ .

a paramedic — a firefighter

a service animal — me

a volunteer

58

TESOL Standards

Goal 1, Standard 3—To use English to communicate in social settings: Students will use learning strategies to extend their communicative competence.

Descriptors—Testing hypotheses about language; Listening to and imitating how others use English; Exploring alternative ways of saying things; Using context to construct meaning.

3. How can a hero help?

A ____________ can help by ____________ .

rescuing a cat

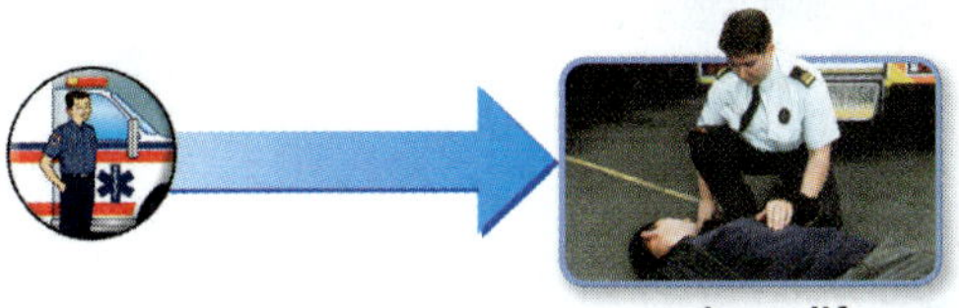

saving a life

guiding its owner

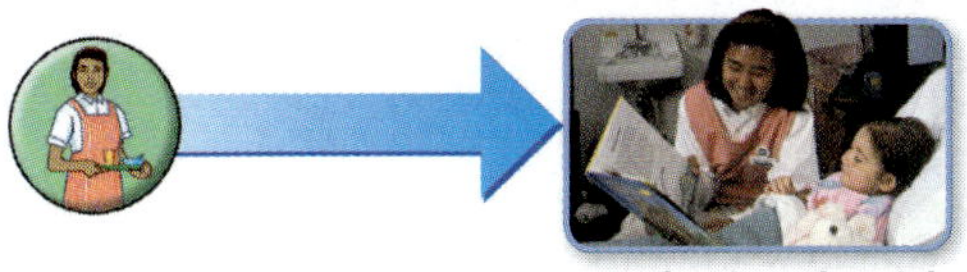

comforting the sick

Differentiated Instruction

Beginning	Say aloud, but out of order, the phrase for each action by a hero shown in the photos on p. 59. Have students point to the appropriate photo and repeat the phrase aloud.
Early Intermediate	Have students look at the pictures of heroes on p. 58. Ask students to find those pictures on p. 59 and say aloud the phrase beside it.
Intermediate	Ask students to look at the photographs on p. 59 of how heroes can help. Have students write a sentence to describe what they see in each picture.
Struggling Reader	Have students look at the pictures of heroes on p. 58 and then find those pictures on p. 59. Say the phrase for each hero as students point to the picture, and have them repeat the phrase.

Explain the Captions

Read the captions in section 3 aloud, and have the class repeat them as they examine the pictures. Read aloud the following context sentences for each caption.

We saw our neighbor *rescuing a cat* that could not climb down a tree.

If you are *saving a life* after an accident, you must work quickly.

The service dog was *guiding its owner* across the street.

I volunteer at the hospital because *comforting the sick* makes me feel good.

Have students write their own context sentences using the captions. Encourage students to write about something they experienced.

STEP 3: Practice

Use Vocabulary

Complete the Sentence Help students use the vocabulary words and the picture captions to complete the following sentence stems about heroes.

Write the following sentences on the board:

My favorite hero is ________ .

This hero helped people when ________ .

Invite students to read their sentences aloud. Lead a class discussion about heroes that focuses on why the heroes' actions were important and how people were helped. Avoid discussion about one hero being more important than another.

Scaffolding

Have students work in pairs to look through newspapers and magazines to find current event stories about heroes in other places in the United States or the world. Have pairs of students present their reports to the class.

STEP 1: Introduce

Unit Background

The peer mini-autobiographies and accompanying exercises are designed to increase comprehension and model how students can talk and write about heroes. Use the exercises below to elicit students' prior knowledge, opinions, and ideas to help them tell their own hero stories.

STEP 2: Monitor Progress

Comprehension Check

Charlene

1. Who is Charlene's hero?
   Charlene's hero is Binti.
2. Why is Binti an unusual hero?
   Binti is a female gorilla.
3. Where does Binti live?
   Binti lives in a zoo in Illinois.
4. Whom did Binti rescue?
   Binti rescued a three-year-old boy.

Sophie

1. Who is Sophie's hero?
   Sophie's hero is Ryan Hreljac.
2. Where are the people whom Ryan helped?
   The people Ryan helped are in Africa.
3. What did Ryan help the people get?
   Ryan helped them get clean water.
4. What is the name of Ryan's organization?
   The name of Ryan's organization is Ryan's Well.

Link to Social Studies

Map Skills Draw students' attention to the map of the world in the background of these pages. Have students follow the line from the photo of each child and his or her hero to the country in which he or she lives. Say the name of each country, and have students repeat the word after you. Encourage students to use world maps in their social studies books to find the locations.

Teaching Resources
- *Audio CD*

Your Stories about Heroes

Charlene

My hero is Binti. Binti is a female gorilla who lives in a zoo in Illinois. She rescued a three-year-old boy who fell from the railing into a zoo's gorilla exhibit. She carried the boy to an area where humans could take care of him. Binti is a very caring animal!

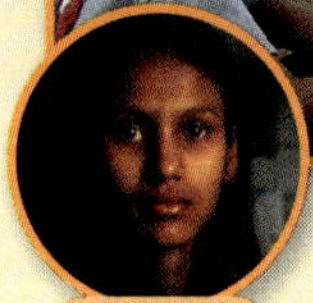

Sophie

My hero is Ryan Hreljac. Ryan wanted to help people in Africa get clean water. He saved enough money to build a well in Uganda. He was so happy with the result that he decided to help build more wells. His organization, Ryan's Well, raises money to build wells all over Africa.

60

TESOL Standards

Goal 1, Standard 2—To use English to communicate in social settings: Students will interact in, through, and with spoken and written English for personal expression and enjoyment.
Descriptors—Sharing social and cultural traditions and values; Expressing personal needs, feelings, and ideas.

Goal 1, Standard 3—To use English to communicate in social settings: Students will use learning strategies to extend their communicative competence.
Descriptors—Testing hypotheses about language; Listening to and imitating how others use English; Exploring alternative ways of saying things; Using context to construct meaning.

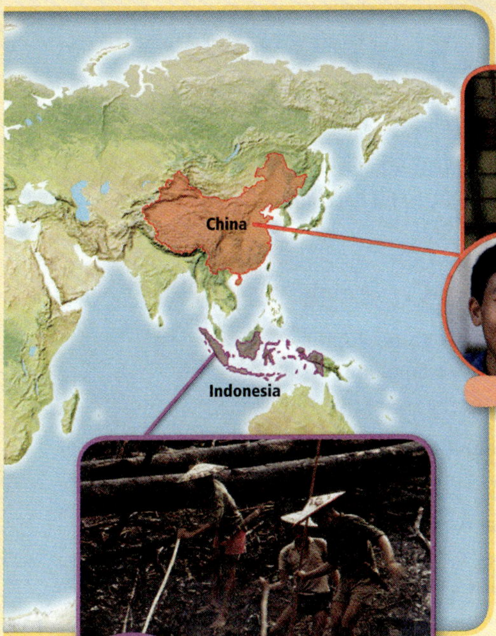

Dai

My hero is Jackie Chan. He stars in martial arts movies. We were both born in Hong Kong, an administrative region of China. He started the Jackie Chan Charitable Foundation in Hong Kong and Japan. This organization gives scholarships to needy students. He also has organizations to help the elderly and to give coats to homeless people. Jackie Chan is a great guy!

Panut

My hero is a woman from my country, Indonesia. Butet Manurung wanted to educate children who lived in the Jambi Forest. She volunteered to teach the Anak Dalam people how to read and write. Now Butet lives in the Jambi Forest. Butet's new goal is to teach people from other tribes, too.

What about you?

1. Who is a hero to you? Why?
2. How are these students' stories similar to yours?
3. Do you have a story about a hero? Tell your story!

Sharing Language and Culture

Global Perspective Students might know of heroes—both past and present—from other cultures or countries. Encourage students to talk about what these heroes did. Examples might include historical figures who fought for justice, or relatives who live and work overseas for an international aid organization.

Panut

1. Where does Panut live?
   Panut lives in Indonesia.
2. What is the name of Panut's hero?
   The name of Panut's hero is Butet Manurung.
3. What did Butet teach the Anak Dalam people?
   Butet taught the Anak Dalam people how to read and write.
4. Where does Butet live now?
   She lives in the Jambi Forest.

Dai

1. Where was Dai's hero born?
   Dai's hero was born in Hong Kong, as Dai was.
2. What does Dai's hero do for a living?
   Dai's hero stars in martial arts movies.
3. What does the Jackie Chan Charitable Foundation do?
   It gives scholarships to needy students.
4. How else does Jackie Chan help people?
   His organizations help the elderly and give coats to homeless people.

Study Skills

Internet Invite students to choose one of the heroes on pp. 60–61. Have them research one fact about that hero on the Internet.

STEP 3: Assess

What about you?

1. Tell students that a hero can be someone they know or someone they have read about in the news. Encourage them to fill in a Character Trait Web to help describe why the person is a hero.
2. To get students started, point out the one underlying similarity between their hero and the heroes written about on these pages—all the heroes have done something remarkable.
3. Have students use a Sequence of Events Chart to help tell their story.

Personal Story Have students write a story using the peer mini-autobiographies on pp. 60–61 as a model. Have students present their stories in small groups.

STEP 1: Introduce

Key Words

Help students learn the skill of defining words by using context.

SAY *The vocabulary words from* The Three Gifts *are shown in the Words in Context section. The pictures help us learn what the words mean.*

Have students connect the numbered circle beside each context sentence with the corresponding numbered photo.

STEP 2: Teach

Words in Context

Write the following sentences on the board. Have students complete this fill-in-the-blanks exercise using the key words. Then ask students to read the sentences aloud.

1. When two people cooperate, the work is easier to do.
2. The mother cat bore six kittens.
3. The museum has a marvelous new art exhibit.
4. My mother uses millet in her recipe for cornbread.
5. Her greatest virtue was her gentle voice.
6. I was so grateful when my brother fixed my bike.

Ask students to work in groups to write additional context sentences for each key word.

Study Skills

Dictionary Have students look up the key words in the dictionary to see whether the Words in Context definitions were correct.

Online Dictionary Look up words using an online dictionary or the CD that accompanies a learner's dictionary like the *Longman Basic Dictionary.*
www.LongmanCornerstone.com

Teaching Resources

- ***Practice Book,*** pp. 29–30
- ***Transparencies,*** pp. 41
- ***CD-ROM*** • ***Audio CD***

Reading 1

The Three Gifts

Vocabulary

The Three Gifts **is a folk tale about how an African leader and his children learn the gift of giving.**

Key Words

cooperate
bore
marvelous
millet
virtue
grateful

Words in Context

1. **A job gets done much faster when people cooperate.**
2. The apple tree **bore** a lot of fruit.
3. Lisa and her friends had a **marvelous** time at the party.

62

TESOL Standards

Goal 1, Standard 3—To use English to communicate in social settings: Students will use learning strategies to extend their communicative competence.
Descriptors—Testing hypotheses about language; Listening to and imitating how others use English; Exploring alternative ways of saying things; Using context to construct meaning.

Goal 2, Standard 2—To use English to achieve academically in all content areas: Students will use English to obtain, process, construct, and provide subject matter information in spoken and written form.
Descriptors—Understanding and producing technical vocabulary and text features according to content area.

Goal 2, Standard 3— To use English to achieve academically in all content areas: Students will use appropriate learning strategies to construct and apply academic knowledge.
Descriptors—Using context to construct meaning.

4 Have you ever tasted **millet?** It is a grain, like wheat and oats.

5 A **virtue** is something that is good about a person. Some people think neatness is a virtue.

6 People often show that they are **grateful,** or thankful, when having a feast with family and friends.

Academic Words

assess

evaluate; decide how good or significant something is

error

mistake

Practice

Use each key word in a sentence.

Make Connections

Think of one of your heroes. What do you admire, or like, about him or her? What do you dislike?

Practice Book pages 29–30

Differentiated Instruction

Beginning	Point to the word in each context sentence, and read aloud a short phrase that includes the key word. Have students repeat each phrase.
Intermediate	Have students read the context sentences aloud and write sentences using each key word.
Greater Challenge	Have students write a paragraph about what it takes to be a hero using each of the following key words: *cooperate, marvelous, virtue, grateful*.
Standard English Learner CRI	Select a key word that students can use for the activity "Give One Get One." Once a word is selected, have students call out synonyms. Make a list of the synonyms on the board. Encourage students to use dictionaries.

Visual Literacy

Illustrations Have students use their own words and the appropriate key word to describe what they see in each photo.

Academic Words

Discuss the definitions of *assess* and *error* with the students. Explain that *assess* is used to describe how we decide or measure things. Explain that checking your work is one way to prevent an *error*. Share the following context sentences with students.

After the storm, we went outside to *assess* the damage.

My answer was wrong because I made an *error* in the addition.

Have students work in pairs to discuss how the two academic terms can be used in the same sentence. Ask students to write context sentences using both academic terms.

Other Academic Words

Provide students with another example of a word that can be used in the process of making a decision. Tell students that a *hypothesis* is a guess based on fact. Write the following context sentences on the board.

The scientist made a *hypothesis* that dinosaurs lived 200 million years ago.

She learned new facts that proved that her *hypothesis* was correct.

STEP 3: Practice

Flexible Grouping

You may assign these exercises as a whole discussion, partner activity, or individual writing assignment.

Make Connections

Writing Fluency Have students use the questions in the activity to write a short paragraph about a hero they know of. Have volunteers share their paragraphs with the class.

STEP 1: Introduce

More About The Big Question

The Big Question for this selection focuses on how people benefit from acts of heroism.

SAY *We are going to read a folktale about how people who give gifts to others receive gifts in return. Gifts do not have to be objects. Kindness can be a gift. Time can be a gift. What are some gifts people can give?*

Discuss with students how giving to others in a time of need can be considered heroic. Have students fill in a Cause and Effect Chart like the one below to organize their ideas.

CAUSE	EFFECT
Too much rain causes a flood. People's homes are damaged.	Neighbors help them repair. They helped them find a place to stay.

STEP 2: Teach

Reading Strategy

Identify Characters and Plot Tell students that knowing and understanding the characters in a story and the plot of a story will help them get more involved in what they are reading as well as make the story more interesting.

Read aloud the bulleted items on p. 64. Have students predict what is going to happen in the story.

Understand Text Structure

Draw students' attention to the genre label. Tell them that folk tales are fiction that teach important lessons about life. The lesson is often the theme of the folktale.

Teaching Resources

- *Teacher's Resource Book*, pp. 111–112
- *Practice Book*, pp. 31–32
- *CD-ROM* • *Audio CD*

Reading 1

LITERATURE

Folktale

The Big Question

What gifts do heroes bring?

Reading Strategy

Identify Characters and Plot

Stories have a plot, or story line, that is usually a sequence of events. Stories also have characters, which are people or animals.

- Read the title.
- Look at the illustrations.
- Which characters are saying or doing something?
- What do you think is happening in the story?

The Three Gifts

by Shannon Doyne
illustrated by Soud

In Africa, there once was a leader named Jelani. He was a just leader. He cared about his people very much. The people in the village were happy and peaceful.

Jelani had three daughters and four sons. At school, Jelani's children learned about other places in Africa. In some villages, people were hungry. Crops did not grow well. Trees bore no fruit. In other villages, groups of people did not cooperate. They fought fiercely with each other.

Jelani's oldest daughter was named Ada. One night she said, "People in this village have marvelous lives. I want to travel to other places and do what I can to help others."

Jelani looked at her proudly. He said, "Finish school. Then you can help others."

That is just what Ada did.

---

just treating people the same, no matter who they are

fiercely hard

TESOL Standards

Goal 2, Standard 2—To use English to achieve academically in all content areas: Students will use English to obtain, process, construct, and provide subject matter information in spoken and written form.

Descriptors—Listening to, speaking, reading, and writing about subject matter information; Selecting, connecting, and explaining information; Formulating and asking questions; Understanding and producing technical vocabulary and text features according to content area; Demonstrating knowledge through application in a variety of contexts.

When Ada finished school, she went to other villages where she worked hard to help people. Ada's brothers and sisters admired her. She sent drawings of the school she helped to build. Ada wrote that it was a big job, but lots of fun.

One by one, Ada's brothers and sisters finished school. They all asked Jelani if they could go and help people. Jelani's eyes filled with joy each time, and he said, "Yes, you can help people."

In time, only the youngest son remained at home. His name was Kofi. Kofi loved to receive his siblings' letters. One brother helped dig wells for fresh water. Another brother helped farmers plant better crops. A sister helped a village hold an election to choose a better leader.

All of the letters were alike in one way. They all invited Kofi and Jelani to visit their villages.

---

admired looked up to

siblings brothers and sisters

election contest won by the person who gets the most votes

Check Up Why did Jelani's children want to help people?

Build Vocabulary

Help students recognize how to use the highlighted words that have are defined at the bottom of each page.

- Invite a volunteer to read one term and its definition aloud.
- Read the sentence with the highlighted word to the class. Then have students write a context sentence for the highlighted word.
- Have students repeat this activity for each highlighted word.

Multiple-Meaning Words Explain that the words *fair* and *well* have more than one meaning. Meanings for the word *fair* include "according to the rule," "light in color," and "an outdoor festival." Meanings for the word *well* include "a hole dug in the ground to find water" and "in a right or skilled way."

Have students choose one of the words, write a sentence for each meaning, and share their sentences with the class. Explain that the context in which a word is used in a sentence will help a reader determine which meaning the author has used. Encourage students to look for other multiple-meaning words in the reading.

Read

Have students take turns reading aloud the paragraphs on pp. 64–65. After the reading, have students describe what action in the story is shown in the two illustrations.

Link to Social Studies

Jelani Jelani means "mighty" in Swahili. Swahili is a language spoken in some African countries including Kenya, Uganda, Tanzania, Rwanda, Burundi, and parts of Zaire, Somalia, and Mozambique. Have students draw the continent of Africa and label these countries.

STEP 3: Assess

Check Up

Have students work with partners. Students should understand that the children wanted people in other villages to have good lives just as they do. Ask them to write a complete sentence to answer the question.

Differentiated Instruction

Beginning	Point to the highlighted word *admired* on p. 65. Have students draw a picture of someone they admire.
Early Intermediate	Have students write captions based on their answers to the following questions: *Who are the two people talking to each other? Who sent the letters?*
Intermediate	Have students work in pairs to discuss why Kofi received so many letters. Then have students explain their reasons to the class.
Struggling Reader	Have students point to the picture on p. 64 and say "father and daughter." Have students draw and label a picture with a father, three daughters, and four sons.

STEP 1: Monitor Progress

Comprehension Check

Sequence of Events After reading pp. 66–67, discuss the sequence of events with students. Use the following questions to guide students in their discussion.

SAY *You can understand the events of the story better if you remember their order.*

- *At what time of day did Kofi and Jelani set out on their trip?*
- *When did they stop to rest?*
- *What did they do before they finally rested?*
- *What did they do the next day?*
- *How long did Jelani and Kofi stay in Sekou's village?*

Have students use a Sequence of Events Chart like the one below to fill in the events in the story that have taken place so far.

Jelani's children want to help people in other villages.

↓

Ada finishes school and goes to another village.

↓

Other brothers and sisters finish school and leave home to help others.

↓

They all write letters home.

↓

Jelani and Kofi visit the brothers and sisters.

↓

Jelani gives millet to villagers.

↓

They visit Sekou and leave clothing for villagers.

Scaffolding

Have students work in small groups to read aloud the paragraphs on pp. 66–67. Ask volunteers to each read one speaking part, and ask a narrator to read the paragraphs that are not dialogue. Tell students to read with expression as if they were performing a play. Encourage each group to do something unique in their performances.

Kofi and Jelani decided to visit their family. Early one morning, they set out on their horses. They brought with them many of Jelani's advisors.

Late in the first day, they stopped to rest. Some people came out to meet them. They took a great interest in the horses. But their eyes looked sad. "What's wrong?" Kofi asked.

A woman replied, "We have horses, too. But we can't grow the right grains for them. Our horses' health is poor."

"Bring some sacks of millet," Jelani called to his men. "We can feed your horses and leave some sacks for you."

"We are so grateful," the people said. "Someday, we will repay this favor. Just call on us."

advisors people who help others decide what to do

grains crops such as wheat and oats

favor kind or helpful act

66

TESOL Standards

Goal 2, Standard 2—To use English to achieve academically in all content areas: Students will use English to obtain, process, construct, and provide subject matter information in spoken and written form.

Descriptors—Listening to, speaking, reading, and writing about subject matter information; Selecting, connecting, and explaining information; Formulating and asking questions; Understanding and producing technical vocabulary and text features according to content area; Demonstrating knowledge through application in a variety of contexts.

The next day, the group went to the village of Kofi's older brother. His name was Sekou. Sekou hugged Jelani and Kofi tightly. "I have missed you so much!" he said.

Sekou showed Jelani and Kofi the **well** he had helped to dig. "Another problem is the **harsh** sun," Sekou said. "Many people do not have the right clothing to protect them. I gave away all of my extra clothes. But so many people still need clothes."

When Jelani and Kofi **departed** a few days later, they left behind all the extra clothing they had. The villagers told Sekou, "One day, we will find a way to thank them. Please tell this to your father and brother. All they have to do is ask."

well deep hole in the ground where water is found

harsh strong or painful

departed left

Check Up How did Kofi and Jelani help the people in Sekou's village?

67

STEP 2: Teach

Academic Words

Discuss the definitions for *concept* and *research* with students. Share the following context sentences with students.

Her *concept* of the project was different from mine.

At the library, she finished the *research* for her report.

Explain to students that the academic words in these sentences are nouns. Then share the following context sentence with students, and explain that the academic word is a verb.

Use the Internet to *research* your report.

Tell students that in the last sentence, the academic word is used as a verb. Have students work in small groups to discuss other words that can be used as nouns or verbs.

STEP 3: Assess

Check Up

Have students work with partners to quickly write notes about what they remember. Have students exchange papers and then compare and contrast their answers.

Accelerate Language Development

Village Spanish speakers may recognize the word *village* through its Spanish cognate, *villa*. However, in the Spanish word *villa*, the double *l* is pronounced similarly to an English *y*. Model for students the correct pronunciation of the letters *ll* in *village* by reading aloud sentences from the text that include the word. Have students repeat each sentence after you. To reinforce the sound, write the following words on the board and have students pronounce each one after you: *millet, chilly, hello, pillow*, and *balloon*.

FYI

Millet Millet is one of many different kinds of grass that produce small seeds. Many types of millet can be grown in places where the weather is hot and dry and the soil is poor. For this reason, millet seeds are an important food for the people of Africa and Asia. Millet seeds are used to make cereals. When ground, the flour from millet is used to make breads. In the United States, millet is used to feed farm animals.

STEP 1: Monitor Progress

Comprehension Check

Identify Characters Explain to students that authors add clues to a story to make it fun for readers to guess what will happen next. Have students describe to the class which clues in the story and in the pictures helped them draw conclusions about the main characters in *The Three Gifts*.

SAY *Sometimes you have to look for clues in a story to help you figure out what the characters are like.*

- *How do you know Jelani was a kind man?*
- *What information tells you people in other villages were unhappy?*
- *In Kofi's letters, what do you learn about his siblings?*
- *Why do you think Jelani has advisors?*
- *What did you learn about Sekou when you read that he gave his clothes away?*
- *How did Ada feel when she said, "Everyone's homes are gone"?*

CRI Have students work in small groups to brainstorm a list of words to describe each character in the story. Tell students that some words can describe more than one character, but each character should have at least one word that describes only that character.

Adapt the Activity

Have students think of a favorite movie or novel and guide them to draw conclusions about the main characters. Ask students to describe the characters in their own words, and then explain what action in the story caused them to draw their conclusions about each character.

Study Skills

Dictionary Ask students to make a list of all the highlighted words from *The Three Gifts* that are defined on pp. 64–69. With the help of a partner, have students alphabetize the list of words.

Online Dictionary Students can use an online dictionary or the CD that accompanies a learner's dictionary like the *Longman Basic Dictionary*.

www.LongmanCornerstone.com

The next day, Kofi told his father, "I want to help people, too." Once again, Jelani felt great joy. All of Jelani's children shared the virtue of caring for others.

Just then, they passed several people. They were building a wood house, but they were having a difficult time. "Father," Kofi asked, "many of our men have learned to work with wood. Can we help them?"

Jelani called out, "Stop, everyone!" Jelani's advisors were soon teaching the others how to build a wood house. The people said, "You have helped us with this house. Now we can use these skills to build a whole village. One day, you will call on us, and we will return this favor."

The last stop was Ada's village. But something seemed very wrong. Kofi and Jelani saw there were piles of wood and mud and rocks where houses had once been. Kofi found Ada. "We had a terrible mudslide," Ada said. "Everyone's homes are gone."

---

several many
difficult hard
terrible very bad

68

TESOL Standards

Goal 2, Standard 2—To use English to achieve academically in all content areas: Students will use English to obtain, process, construct, and provide subject matter information in spoken and written form.
Descriptors—Listening to, speaking, reading, and writing about subject matter information; Selecting, connecting, and explaining information; Formulating and asking questions; Understanding and producing technical vocabulary and text features according to content area; Demonstrating knowledge through application in a variety of contexts.

Kofi, Jelani, Ada, the advisors, and people from the village started to work. They rebuilt houses. Everyone was very tired and hot. They were also out of supplies. Jelani sent his advisors for help.

Soon, 20 horses appeared. All of the horses had riders. Many of the horses also carried bags of supplies.

"You helped us when we had no food for our horses," one of the riders called. "We came to help you carry supplies."

Many more people appeared. One called out, "You taught us to build houses. Now we can help you."

People from Sekou's village put up a large tent. "You gave us your extra clothes. We stitched them together. You can live in this tent until the new houses are ready."

And together, they rebuilt Ada's village.

supplies things that are needed

stitched sewed

Practice Book pages 31–32

Reading Strategy

Identify Characters and Plot

- Who are the main characters in the story?
- What are three events in the plot?

Think It Over

1. What do Jelani's children learn in school?
2. What does Kofi receive that makes him want to visit his brothers and sisters?
3. How do the people in the other villages help Ada's village?

69

Differentiated Instruction	
Beginning	Write the following sentence on the board: *They saw [several/two] people building a house in the village.* Ask students to copy the sentence using the correct answer.
Intermediate	Have students present a summary to the class that describes the action in the illustrations.
Greater Challenge	Have students write a short paragraph to answer the following question: *Why do you think the story is called* The Three Gifts?
Standard English Learner CRI	Have students discuss the action in the illustration, and then do a short skit about the story events. Encourage students to improvise dialogue between the characters.

STEP 2: Teach

Visual Literacy

Illustrations

SAY *Think about the various activities you see happening in the illustrations. Look back at each of the pictures.*

- *Who is traveling to other villages?*
- *What did Kofi receive from his siblings while he was at home?*
- *Where did the villagers get the clothing?*
- *When did they begin to rebuild the homes in Ada's village?*
- *Why are the siblings smiling in the last picture?*

Have students fill in a 5 W Organizer Chart as they answer the questions.

STEP 3: Assess

Reading Strategy

Identify Characters and Plot Remind students of the importance of understanding the characters and knowing the events of a plot.

Read the following sentences aloud, and have students call out the answers to fill in the blanks.

- Jelani told Ada she could help people after she finished school.
- Jelani and Kofi went to visit Sekou and gave away clothes.
- The villagers were taught how to build a wood house.
- There was a mudslide in Ada's village.

Think It Over

Flexible Grouping You may assign this exercise as a whole class discussion, partner activity, or individual writing assignment.

Answer Key

1. Jelani's children learn about other places in Africa.
2. Kofi receives letters from his brothers and sisters about how they are helping people.
3. The people in other villages carry supplies, build houses, and put up a tent.

STEP 1: Introduce

Phonics

Long Vowel Pairs Help students understand that long vowel sounds are often spelled with two letters, and some can be spelled two ways. For example, the long vowel *a* can be spelled *ai* as in *main* or *ay* as in *may*.

STEP 2: Teach

Review the Long Vowel Pairs Chart on p. 70 with students. For each word, ask students to identify the vowels that spell the long vowel sound. Remind them that in some instances, the consonant *y* acts as a vowel. Draw students' attention to the Rule Box.

SAY *Here's the rule. When there are two vowels together, the first vowel is usually long, and the second vowel is silent.*

- *What are the vowel pairs with the long vowel sounds?*
- *Can the consonant* y *be in a long vowel pair with every vowel?*
- *What other words have the long vowel pair* ay*?*
- *Can you think of any words with vowel pairs that are an exception to this rule?* they, prey

CRI Have students work with partners to brainstorm as many words as possible with long vowel pairs. Provide students with a timer to see how many words they can write down in one minute.

STEP 3: Practice

1. Have students work with a partner. Make sure that both partners take part in the activity.
2. Monitor students to see that their charts are organized by long vowel sounds.
3. Have students share their new examples of words with each long vowel sound with the class.

Teaching Resources

- *Practice Book*, p. 33
- *Phonics Workbook*
- *Phonics Flashcards*
- *CD-ROM* • *Audio CD*

Reading 1

Phonics & Fluency

Phonics

Long Vowel Pairs

Long vowel sounds can be spelled in different ways.

Long Vowel Pairs

Long *a*	Long *e*	Long *i*	Long *o*	Long *u*
day	meet	lie	oats	cue
grain	seat		doe	fruit

Did you notice that each word has two vowels together? Which one of the vowels says its name?

Rule Box

When there are two vowels together, the first vowel is usually long, and the second vowel is silent. The vowel pairs below usually have long vowel sounds.

ay, ai	ee, ea	ie	oa, oe	ue, ui

Practice

Work with a partner. Take turns reading the words in the box.

need	pay	three
tried	coast	say
fail	tie	plain
road	due	fruit
clue		

1. Make a chart like the one above.
2. List the words from this box in the chart.
3. Add two more words for each long vowel sound.

Practice Book page 33

TESOL Standards

Goal 2, Standard 3—To use English to achieve academically in all content areas: Students will use appropriate learning strategies to construct and apply academic knowledge.
Descriptors—Applying basic reading comprehension skills such as skimming, scanning, previewing, and reviewing text; Using context to construct meaning; Applying self-monitoring and self-corrective strategies to build and expand a knowledge base

Goal 3, Standard 3—To use English in socially and culturally appropriate ways: Students will use appropriate learning strategies to extend their sociolinguistic and sociocultural competence.
Descriptors—Observing and modeling how others speak and behave in a particular situation or setting; Experimenting with variations of language in social and academic settings; Seeking information about appropriate language use and behavior; Rehearsing variations of language use in different social and academic settings.

Fluency

Look Ahead

Sometimes readers look for hard words before they read. They then try to figure them out.

Practice

Pick one passage. ▸ Find any hard words. ▸ Practice saying those words. ▸ Read the passage aloud.

1 Jelani's children decide to help people in other villages when they grow up. Later, when one of them needs help, they receive help in return.

2 One by one, Ada's brothers and sisters finished school. They all asked Jelani if they could go and help people. Jelani's eyes filled with joy each time, and he said, "Yes, you can help people."

In time, only the youngest son remained at home. His name was Kofi. Kofi loved to receive his siblings' letters.

3 "Father," Kofi asked, "many of our men have learned to work with wood. Can we help them?"

Jelani called out, "Stop, everyone!" Jelani's advisors were soon teaching the others how to build a wood house. The people said, "You have helped us with this house. Now we can use these skills to build a whole village. One day, you will call on us, and we will return this favor."

71

Linguistic Note

Possessives with Apostrophes Many languages do not feature possessives with apostrophes. In these languages, an English phrase like *the ruler's children* would be written as the equivalent of "the children of the ruler." Students who speak such a language may have difficulty recognizing the subject of the sentence. For example, in a clause such as *the ruler's children need help*, it may not be apparent to all readers that the sentence is about the children, not the ruler.

STEP 1: Introduce

Fluency

Look Ahead Remind students that the pronunciation for a word can be found in a dictionary.

Explain to students that fluent readers sometimes look ahead to find and practice hard words.

Play the Audio CD for this reading to the class, asking students to listen for pacing, intonation, and expression.

STEP 2: Practice

Have students do the following exercise with partners. You may want to assign each student a passage based on difficulty level (1—easy, 2—intermediate, 3—more difficult) or let students select their own passages.

- Have one partner look through the passage to find any hard words and practice saying those words.
- Then have that student read the passage to his or her partner.
- Have students change roles.

Possible Responses—Hard words

children	village	youngest
receive	several	advisors

STEP 3: Extend

Study Skills

Dictionary Have students work with partners to write down three words from the readings that were hard to pronounce. Ask them to look up the definitions in a dictionary, and practice pronouncing the words.

Reteach

Have students review *The Three Gifts* to find examples of words that follow the long vowel spelling patterns. Explain to students that words with more than one syllable can also include the long vowel spelling pattern. (remained, repay, rescue) Have students add the examples to their charts of Long Vowel Pairs.

STEP 1: Monitor Progress

Learning Strategy

Retell Retelling the story is a way for students to refresh their memories of the story. Have students work in pairs to retell the story and respond to the Big Question.

STEP 2: Teach

Characters and Plot

As they read a story, students will learn to identify what happens to a character as well as what events are caused by the character's action.

SAY *Knowing what happens to the characters and how those events cause other events is another way to remember the story.*

- *What is the first main event in* The Three Gifts?
- *What happened in the first event that caused the second event?*

Have students review the events in *The Three Gifts*. Ask them to work in small groups to fill in a Sequence of Events Chart and discuss what caused each event.

STEP 3: Practice

Flexible Grouping You may assign this activity as a class discussion, partner activity, or individual writing assignment.

Answer Key

1. People say their horses are underfed. Jelani and Kofi leave them millet. The villagers carry supplies to Ada's village.
2. People are having trouble building a house. Kofi, Jelani, and the advisors show the villagers how to build a house.
3. Ada helps her village build a school. The village is hit by a mudslide. People come to help her village rebuild.

Teaching Resources

- *Practice Book*, p. 34
- *Transparencies*, p. 62
- *Teacher's Resource Book*, p. 160
- *CD-ROM*

Reading 1

Comprehension

Learning Strategy

Retell

Retell the story to a partner.

Ask your partner to respond to the Big Question for this reading.

Characters and Plot

Every story has **characters**. The characters are the people, or sometimes animals, in the story. Every story also has a **plot**. The plot is the series of events that take place in the story.

Practice

Work with a partner. Make a chart like the one below.

1. Reread the story. Pay attention to the characters and events.
2. List characters and events in the chart. Follow the examples given.
3. Write a short summary of the story.

Character	What Happens	The Result
Jelani	Ada asks him if she can leave.	Jelani tells her to finish school.
Kofi	Gets letters from siblings to visit	Visits siblings with Jelani
Sekou	Gives away clothes	Jelani and Kofi give villagers extra clothing.

Practice Book page 34

TESOL Standards

Goal 2, Standard 2—To use English to achieve academically in all content areas: Students will use English to obtain, process, construct, and provide subject matter information in spoken and written form.

Descriptors—Listening to, speaking, reading, and writing about subject matter information; Selecting, connecting, and explaining information; Formulating and asking questions; Understanding and producing technical vocabulary and text features according to content area; Demonstrating knowledge through application in a variety of contexts; Retelling information; Gathering information orally and in writing; Responding to the work of peers and others; Representing information visually and interpreting information presented visually.

Use a Cause and Effect Chart

When one thing happens, it causes other things to happen. A Cause and Effect Chart helps you see how events in a plot are related.

Practice

Work with a partner. Copy this Cause and Effect Chart.

1. Add one more effect to the chart.
2. List two more causes.
3. Show what effects those events caused.

Causes		Effects
Jelani feeds the villagers' horses.	→	The villagers bring the horses to help carry supplies.
Jelani and Kofi give villagers extra clothing.	→	
	→	
	→	

Extension

Some people say it is better to give than to receive. Think about causes and effects in terms of something you have done for someone else. What was the effect of what you did? Why did you decide to do what you did? Present your experience to the class using a visual aid.

73

Accelerate Language Development

Signal Words You can help speakers of other languages identify cause and effect by reminding them of the English word *because*. The part of a sentence or phrase that comes after the word *because* is almost always a cause. Ask them to find the causes in the following short sentences: *The baby was crying because she was hungry. The boy ran to school because he was late. The bird flew away because it heard a loud noise*. Other signal words for cause-and-effect relationships include *since, due to, as a result of*, and *when.*

Linguistic Note

Cause For students who speak Spanish, the word *cause* is a cognate of the Spanish word *causa* and may be familiar to them.

STEP 1: Teach

Use a Cause and Effect Chart

Remind students that one action or event can cause another action or event to take place. Explain that the first action is called a cause and the resulting action is called an effect.

SAY *Think about it this way—Your alarm clock goes off in the morning. That is a cause. The action you take when you hear the alarm is the effect.*

- *What is the effect when you hear your alarm?*
- *You turn on a water faucet. What is the effect?*
- *A glass falls off a table. What is the effect?*

Have students make a list of other simple examples of cause and effect that they experience every day.

STEP 2: Practice

Review the Cause and Effect Chart with students. Remind them that the *cause* is what happens first. The *effect* is the result of that cause.

Answer Key

CAUSE		EFFECT
Jelani and Kofi give villagers extra clothing.	→	Villagers make a tent.
Jelani's men gave villagers sacks of millet.	→	Villagers' horses are healthy and can carry supplies.
Jelani helped villagers on the way to Ada's village.	→	Everyone helped build new homes for Ada's village.

STEP 3: Extend

Oral Presentation Ask partners to think of things they've done for others. What did the other people do next? Have students create a Cause and Effect Chart as a visual aid in telling the class about their experiences.

STEP 1: Introduce

Help students understand that adjectives give more information about nouns, and adverbs give more information about verbs. Some adjectives can be turned into adverbs by adding *-ly* at the end. Explain that the ending *-ly* is often—but not always—a sign that a word is an adverb. Exceptions include *silly, lonely, friendly,* and *lovely*, all of which are actually adjectives.

STEP 2: Teach

Adjectives and Adverbs

Write the following sentences on the board. Have students look at the underlined word in each sentence. Have volunteers explain whether the word tells more about a noun or a verb. Then write *adjective* or *adverb* after each sentence.

1. The horses were strong and beautiful. adjective
2. He walked quickly to get the bags of millet. adverb
3. There was a terrible mudslide in the town. adjective
4. Can you leave behind your extra clothing? adverb
5. They waved good-bye and slowly departed. adverb
6. We dug a well to find fresh water. adjective

STEP 3: Practice

Before students begin the Practice activity, write on the board the following adjectives and adverbs from *The Three Gifts:*

happy	fiercely	proudly
youngest	harsh	soon

Ask students to identify the word as an adjective or adverb. Have them write their own sentences using each word.

Answer Key

Adjectives: fair, strong, tired
Adverbs: fiercely, gladly

Teaching Resources

- ***Practice Book***, pp. 35–36
- ***Transparencies***, pp. 69–80
- ***Assessments***, pp. 41–44
- ***CD-ROM***

Reading 1

Grammar & Writing

Adjectives and Adverbs

Adjectives and adverbs tell more about other words. **Adjectives** tell more about nouns. They can tell what someone or something is like.

In some villages, the people were **hungry**.

Adverbs describe verbs. They can tell how something happens or is done.

Jelani looked at her **proudly**.

Practice

Read the sentences. Find the adjectives and adverbs. List them in two labeled columns.

1. Jelani was a fair man.
2. The strong people fought fiercely.
3. The tired villagers thanked Kofi and Jelani.
4. The villagers gladly helped Ada at the end.

Practice Book page 35

TESOL Standards

Goal 1, Standard 3—To use English to communicate in social settings: Students will use learning strategies to extend their communicative competence.
Descriptor—Seeking support and feedback from others.

Goal 2, Standard 3—To use English to achieve academically in all content areas: Students will use appropriate learning strategies to construct and apply academic knowledge.
Descriptors—Using context to construct meaning; Actively connecting new information to information previously learned; Imitating the behaviors of native English speakers to complete tasks successfully.

Goal 3, Standard 1—To use English in socially and culturally appropriate ways: Students will use the appropriate language variety, register, and genre according to audience, purpose, and setting.
Descriptors—Use the appropriate degree of formality with different audiences and settings; Recognizing and using Standard English and vernacular dialects appropriately; Using a variety of writing styles appropriate for different audiences, purposes, and settings.

Write about Causes and Effects

When you write about causes and effects, it is important to describe both the cause and the effect. Read how Zaheda described one cause and effect in *The Three Gifts*.

Kofi and his family wanted to help people who were not as lucky as they were. On their way to visit Ada, Kofi and Jelani met some villagers who were having a hard time building a house. Kofi and Jelani stopped to help. They taught the people in the village how to build houses. Later, when Ada's village was destroyed in a mudslide, the villagers remembered. They helped Ada rebuild her village.

SPELLING TIP

When the letters *c* and *h* or *s* and *h* are together in a word, they make one sound.

Practice Book page 36

Practice

Write your own cause and effect paragraph.

1. Think about a situation.
2. Write what you think caused the situation.
3. Write one good or bad effect of that cause.
4. Write a concluding sentence that summarizes the cause and effect.

Writing Checklist

✓ Did you describe the situation?

✓ Did you identify one cause of the situation?

✓ Did you describe one effect from that cause?

✓ Can a partner understand your paragraph?

75

Differentiated Instruction

Beginning	Direct students to copy the sentence in Zaheda's paragraph that tells what Kofi and Jelani taught the villagers.
Early Intermediate	Have students write short phrases to fill in the blanks for the following either/or camparison. *When they saw villagers needed help, Kofi and his family could ________ or ________ .*
Intermediate	Have students identify a cause and effect in *The Three Gifts and* then give a verbal summary.
Struggling Reader	Write the following sentences on the board: *The flowers bloomed because it was sunny. When the sun rose, the birds began to sing.* Have students draw a picture of the flowers blooming and the birds singing.

STEP 1: Introduce

Write about Causes and Effects

Review cause and effect with students.

SAY *When you write about a cause and effect, you have to describe both the cause and the effect.*

Stimulate class discussion and encourage student questions by talking about how Zaheda describes cause and effect in her written narrative on p. 75.

SAY

- *What is the cause described in the narrative?*
- *What is the effect?*
- *Did the cause have more than one effect? What was it?*

Spelling Tip

Read the box to students. Then ask students to think of words that have the /sh/ or /ch/ sounds. Share some examples to help students get started: *chair, bench, pitched, shoe, fish*, and *cushion*. List students' /ch/ and /sh/ words on the board.

STEP 2: Practice

Before students write their own cause and effect narratives, use Zaheda's paragraph to show what students should include in their writing:

1. a description of the scene or setting (lines 1–3)
2. a clearly stated cause (line 4)
3. an effect that is a result of the stated cause (line 6)
4. a conclusion sentence that summarizes the cause and effect (line 5)

STEP 3: Assess

Writing Checklist

✓ Students may need help thinking of a cause and effect that are clearly related.

✓ Have students share their paragraph with partners. Have each student identify the cause and effect in his or her partner's paragraph.

The Five-Step Writing Process in the Writing Handbook reference section of this book provides more writing instruction.

STEP 1: Introduce

Key Words

Help students learn the skill of defining words by using them in context.

SAY *All the vocabulary words from* Brave Androcles *are used in the Words in Context sentences.*

Have students find each key word and connect it with its photograph.

Explain that many words in the English language come from other languages. For example, *arena* comes from the Latin word *harena*, which means "place of combat." *Chase* comes from the French word *chacier*, which means "to catch."

STEP 2: Teach

Words in Context

Write the following sentences on the board. Have students complete this fill-in-the-blanks exercise using the key words from the Words in Context passage.

1. The boys thought they were being chased when they heard footsteps.
2. We went to a football game at the new arena.
3. The river was swollen after the heavy rainstorm.
4. Don't wander away from the crowd!
5. The criminal tried to steal the cash register.

Have students rewrite each context sentence by using a synonym for each vocabulary word.

Study Skills

Dictionary Have students look up the key words to see whether the Words in Context definitions were correct.

Online Dictionary Students can use an online dictionary or the CD that accompanies a learner's dictionary, like the *Longman Basic Dictionary*.
www.LongmanCornerstone.com

Teaching Resources

- *Practice Book,* pp. 37-38
- *Transparencies,* pp. 41
- *CD-ROM* • *Audio CD*

Reading 2

Brave Androcles

Vocabulary

Brave Androcles **is a poem about a boy and a lion who become heroes to each other.**

Key Words

- chased
- arena
- swollen
- wander
- criminal

Words in Context

1 The lion **chased** the warthog.

2 This **arena** was built almost 2,000 years ago in Rome.

76

TESOL Standards

Goal 1, Standard 3—To use English to communicate in social settings: Students will use learning strategies to extend their communicative competence.
Descriptors—Testing hypotheses about language; Listening to and imitating how others use English; Exploring alternative ways of saying things; Using context to construct meaning.

Goal 2, Standard 2—To use English to achieve academically in all content areas: Students will use English to obtain, process, construct, and provide subject matter information in spoken and written form.
Descriptor—Understanding and producing technical vocabulary and text features according to content area.

Goal 2, Standard 3—To use English to achieve academically in all content areas: Students will use appropriate learning strategies to construct and apply academic knowledge.
Descriptor—Using context to construct meaning.

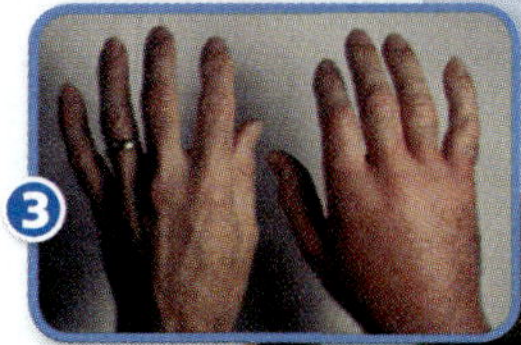

3 The bee sting made his hand **swollen.**

4 It is fun to **wander** down by a stream on a nice summer's day.

5 The police officer arrested the **criminal.**

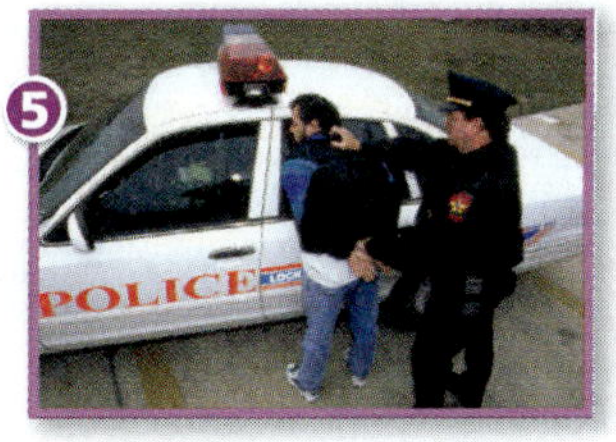

Practice

Use each key word in a sentence.

Make Connections

The place where the early Romans went to watch sports and games was called an arena. What are the names of other places where sports and games are played?

Academic Words

motive
underlying reason

principle
basic truth; rule

Practice Book pages 37–38

Differentiated Instruction	
Beginning	Point to each picture. Ask *What key word goes with this picture?* Have students point to and say the correct word.
Intermediate	Have students say the key word that answers each context question. For example, *What did the lion do to the warthog?*
Greater Challenge	Have students select three key words and write new context sentences for each word.
Standard English Learner CRI	Have students develop their personal thesaurus by playing the "Give One, Get One game." For each key word, ask students to call out a synonym.

Visual Literacy

Labels Ask students to look at the photos and think about what action is happening or could possibly happen. Have students select one photo and write a descriptive paragraph about the setting and the action.

Academic Words

Discuss the definitions for *motive* and *principle* with students. Share the following context sentences with students.

His *motive* for working hard is to get a promotion.

He believes in the *principle* that hard work has rewards.

Other Academic Words

Remind students that words that sound alike but have different meanings are homonyms. Write the homonyms *principle* and *principal* and their definitions on the board.

principal main item or element, person in a leading position, a school *principal*

Tell students that one easy way to remember the correct word usage is to think, *the principal is your pal,* to remember the correct spelling of the last three letters.

STEP 3: Practice

Flexible Grouping

You may assign this exercise as a class discussion, partner activity, or individual writing assignment.

Make Connections

Writing Fluency Have students write briefly about their own experiences of attending sporting events. Have them describe the place where the event took place. They can answer the 5 W questions to fill in more details about the event.

STEP 1: Introduce

More About The Big Question

The Big Question for this selection focuses on doing good deeds for others.

SAY *We are going to read a poem about a person who risks his safety by stopping to offer help.*

Have students use a chart to organize their stories about helping.

My dog Bennie was lost.
↓
Someone found him injured in a park.
↓
We offered the finder a reward.

STEP 2: Teach

Reading Strategy

Make Connections Help students relate the poem to their own lives.

SAY *Describe how you helped someone.*

- *Why did you do it?*
- *Why is it important to do good deeds?*

Have students write a paragraph that explains whether they think one good deed deserves another.

Understand Text Structure

Tell students that the purpose of a poem is to create a picture we can see in our imaginations, with lines and verses that have different rhythms.

Read

Have students take turns reading lines of the poem aloud. Remind them to read with expression by following clues in the punctuation.

Teaching Resources

- *Teacher's Resource Book*, pp. 113–114
- *Practice Book*, pp. 39–40
- *CD-ROM* • *Audio CD*

Reading 2

LITERATURE

Poetry

The Big Question

What is meant by "one good deed deserves another"?

Reading Strategy

Make Connections

- As you read the poem, think of moments in your own life when you have felt like Androcles.

Brave Androcles

by Miguel Rivera

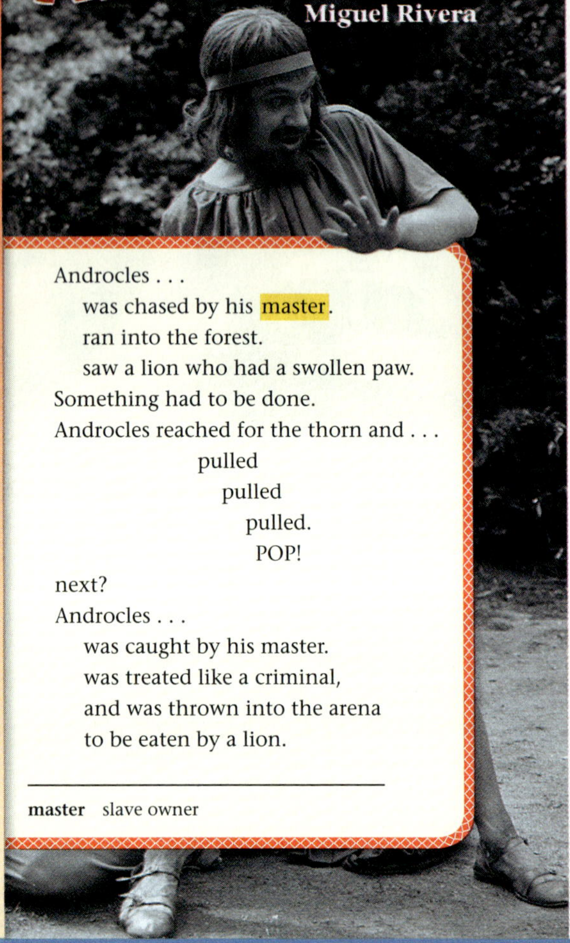

Androcles . . .
was chased by his master.
ran into the forest.
saw a lion who had a swollen paw.
Something had to be done.
Androcles reached for the thorn and . . .
pulled
pulled
pulled.
POP!
next?
Androcles . . .
was caught by his master.
was treated like a criminal,
and was thrown into the arena
to be eaten by a lion.

master slave owner

78

TESOL Standards

Goal 2, Standard 1—To use English to achieve academically in all content areas: Students will use English to interact in the classroom.
Descriptors—Participating in full-class, group, and pair discussions; Asking and answering questions.

Goal 2, Standard 2—To use English to achieve academically in all content areas: Students will use English to obtain, process, construct, and provide subject matter information in spoken and written form.
Descriptors—Retelling information; Selecting, connecting, and explaining information; Listening to, speaking, reading, and writing about subject matter information; Demonstrating knowledge through application in a variety of contexts.

Not just any ordinary lion, his friend.
The lion was as sweet as sugar.
He was as quiet as a mouse.
All he did was wander around the arena.
He did not . . .
bite.
eat.
growl.
next?
Master was . . .
shocked.
amazed
confused.
And Androcles was a hero.
Never bothered again,
WHEW!

ordinary average
amazed surprised
confused unable to think clearly

Practice Book pages 39–40

Reading Strategy

Make Connections

- When have you done something even though you were scared to do it?
- In what ways are you like Androcles?

Think It Over

1. Who is Androcles?
2. What problem does the lion have?
3. Why does the lion help Androcles?
4. How are Androcles and the lion alike?

79

Build Vocabulary

Help students use the highlighted vocabulary words in context sentences.

- Invite volunteers to read a vocabulary word and its definition.
- Have students use a thesaurus to find at least one synonym for each word.
- Have students copy the lines from the poem that include the vocabulary words and replace them with the synonyms.

STEP 3: Assess

Build Discussion

Explain that writers (especially poets) often use literary devices such as simile, metaphor, and personification to make their writing more interesting. Explain that similes can often be identified by the words *like* or *as*. Have students find and discuss the similes used in the poem.

Link to Literature

Brave Androcles is based on the Aesop's fable *Androcles and the Lion.* Experts believe Aesop's fables actually came from a variety of sources. The story of *Androcles and the Lion* has been retold in many different ways, including as a play by George Bernard Shaw and in several movies and television programs. Have students research and discuss another version of the fable.

Think It Over

Flexible Grouping You may assign this exercise as a class discussion, partner activity, or individual writing assignment.

Answer Key

1. Androcles is a slave.
2. The lion has a thorn in his paw.
3. The lion helps Androcles because Androcles helped him.
4. Androcles and the lion are alike because they both had a problem and each was helped by the other.

Differentiated Instruction

Beginning	Read the poem aloud with students, and help them work in pairs to demonstrate what action occurs in the poem.
Early Intermediate	Have students work in pairs to read aloud the stanzas on pp. 78–79. Students should alternate reading the lines. Ask students to summarize each stanza when they finish reading it.
Intermediate	Ask students to look at the three defined words on p. 79. Have them write a sentence about what happens in the poem using all three words.
Special Needs	Have students listen to the audio recording. Encourage them to read along as they listen to the poem.

STEP 1: Introduce

Phonics

Vowel Pairs *ea* Help students understand that in some words the vowel pair *ea* stands for the short *e* sound; in other words *ea* stands for the long *e* sound.

STEP 2: Teach

Review the Vowel Pairs Chart on p. 80 with students. Ask students to pronounce the words that have the long *e* vowel sound and then pronounce the words that have the short *e* vowel sound.

Write the following words on the board as shown:

neat	*heat*	*bean*	*team*
breath	*sweat*	*thread*	*bread*

Have students indicate whether the word has a short or long *e* vowel sound.

Draw students' attention to the Rule Box.

SAY *Here's the rule. The vowel pair* ea *can have a long* e *sound as in* eat *or a short* e *sound as in* head. *If you come across a word you do not know, try reading it both ways!*

STEP 3: Practice

1. Have students work with partners. Remind them to say the words aloud when they're unsure of the pronunciation. read, reach
2. Monitor students to see that they are placing their words into the correct lists. ahead, deadly
3. Possible Responses

long *e* spelled *ea*: heal, clean, please
short *e* spelled *ea*: health, meant, deaf

Teaching Resources

- ***Practice Book,*** p. 41
- ***Phonics Workbook***
- ***Phonics Flashcards***
- ***CD-ROM*** • ***Audio CD***

Reading 2

Phonics & Fluency

Phonics

Vowel Pair: *ea*

Each word in the chart has the vowel pair *ea*.

Vowel Pair *ea*			
Long *e*		**Short *e***	
eat	plead	head	sweat
sea	speak	bread	death
teach		spread	

The vowel pair *ea* can stand for two sounds.

Rule Box

The vowel pair *ea* can have the long *e* sound, as in ***eat,*** or the short *e* sound, as in ***head***. If you come across a word you do not know, try reading it both ways!

Practice

Read the sentences in the box with a partner.

1. List the words in which *ea* has the long *e* sound.
2. List the words in which *ea* has the short *e* sound.
3. Add two more words to each list.

- I can read about heroes.
- Some heroes reach out to others.
- Some heroes work hard to get ahead.
- Some heroes fight in deadly battles.

Practice Book page 41

TESOL Standards

Goal 1, Standard 3—To use English to communicate in social settings: Students will use learning strategies to extend their communicative competence.
Descriptors—Listening to and imitating how others use English; Self-monitoring and self-evaluating language development; Practicing new language; Focusing attention selectively.

Goal 3, Standard 3—To use English in socially and culturally appropriate ways: Students will use appropriate learning strategies to extend their sociolinguistic and sociocultural competence.
Descriptors—Observing and modeling how others speak and behave in a particular situation or setting; Experimenting with variations of language in social and academic settings; Seeking information about appropriate language use and behavior.

Fluency

Read with Expression

When you read aloud, use your voice to show feelings.

Practice

Read silently. → Read aloud. → Get comments. → Read aloud again.

1 Androcles . . .
was chased by his master.
ran into the forest.
saw a lion who had a swollen paw.
Something had to be done.
Androcles reached for the thorn and . . .
pulled
pulled
pulled.
POP!

Accelerate Language Development

Punctuation Students who speak other languages at home may not be familiar with the onomatopoeic word *POP!* Explain to students that *POP!* in this poem is a word that imitates a sound —the noise of the thorn finally bursting out of the lion's paw. Say *POP!* loudly and have students repeat it. Ask students to think of other words they know of that imitate sounds, such as *boom! bang!* and *whoosh!*

Linguistic Note

Homographs Write the word pairs *read/read* and *lead/lead* on the board. Tell students that the words are homographs: they are spelled alike but have different meanings and pronunciations. Help them recognize that in these words, the vowel pair *ea* can have a long *e* or a short *e* sound but that the pronunciation depends on how the word is used in a sentence.

STEP 1: Introduce

Fluency

Read with Expression Explain to students that reading with expression can help show the emotion intended in the selection. Some ways of showing feelings are reading louder or softer, reading faster or slower, and emphasizing certain words.

Play the Audio CD for this reading to the class, asking students to listen for pacing, intonation, and expression.

Remind students to use appropriate verbal cues, facial expressions, and gestures while reading.

STEP 2: Practice

Have students work with partners and take turns reading aloud the passage in the Practice activity. Tell students to listen closely to the way their partner reads the words.

- Have students first read the verse silently, thinking about the author's purpose and the character's feelings.
- Tell students to look for clues in the punctuation for words to emphasize.
- Have one partner read the verse aloud, focusing on reading with expression.
- Have the listener comment on the reading by describing any feelings they had from words that were emphasized.
- Then have partners reverse roles.

STEP 3: Extend

Study Skills

Dictionary Have students work with partners to reread the lines from the verse, focusing on pronunciation and expression as they read. After reading, ask students to do the following:

- write down three words to emphasize while reading aloud
- look the words up in a dictionary to make sure they are pronouncing the words correctly

STEP 1: Monitor Progress

Learning Strategy

Retell Retelling the story is a way for students to refresh their memories of the story. Have students work in pairs. One student should retell the story, and the other student should respond to the Big Question. Encourage pairs of students to present their retelling and response to the Big Question to the class.

STEP 2: Teach

Make Connections

Discuss with the class some of the ways readers can connect a reading to their own lives.

SAY *When we are reading, there are ways we can connect the events in the story to our own experiences.*

- *What people do you know who are like the characters you are reading about?*
- *Can you think of time when you were in a similar situation?*
- *What other stories have you read that have similar characters, settings, or plots?*
- *What do you already know about the topic or events that you are reading about?*

STEP 3: Practice

Flexible Grouping You may assign this activity as a class discussion, partner activity, or individual writing assignment.

Possible Responses

1. I was scared when I had to tell my mother I dropped a good glass and it broke.
2. I wanted to tell her, but I was too afraid.
3. I told my sister, and she helped me tell my mother.
4. My older sister helped me.

Teaching Resources

- ***Practice Book,*** p. 42
- ***Transparencies,*** p. 66
- ***Teacher's Resource Book,*** p. 163
- ***CD-ROM***

Reading 2

Comprehension

Learning Strategy

Retell

Retell the poem to a partner.

Ask your partner to respond to the Big Question for this reading.

Practice Book page 42

Make Connections

One way to understand a text is to make connections between what happens in the text and your life.

Practice

- Read the first column. It tells about situations in the story.
- Answer the questions in the second column to tell about similar situations in your life.

Situations in the Story	Situations in Your Life
1. Androcles was chased by his master.	1. When have you been scared?
2. The lion has a problem.	2. What kinds of problems have you had?
3. Androcles and the lion become friends.	3. What happened afterward?
4. Androcles gets helps from the lion to solve his problem.	4. Who helped you with your problem?

TESOL Standards

Goal 2, Standard 2—To use English to achieve academically in all content areas: Students will use English to obtain, process, construct, and provide subject matter information in spoken and written form.

Descriptors—Retelling information; Selecting, connecting, and explaining information; Listening to, speaking, reading, and writing about subject matter information; Demonstrating knowledge through application in a variety of contexts; Representing information visually and interpreting information presented visually.

Use a Story Map

You can use a Story Map to help you better understand a story or poem.

Practice

Copy this Story Map. Complete it to show the main characters, the setting, and what happens in *Brave Androcles*.

Characters | Setting

Beginning

Middle
1.
2.
3.

End

Extension

Take turns talking about good deeds you have done with a partner. Then describe something that happened as a result of your good deed.

83

Linguistic Note

Situation Spanish-speakers may be familiar with the Spanish word *situación*, which is a cognate of the English *situation*. Those students who do know the Spanish word may have difficulty pronouncing the English word correctly. Model the pronunciation of *situation*, stressing the long *a* sound.

STEP 1: Teach

Use a Story Map

To prepare students for completing the Story Map, ask them to imagine that they are going to tell someone a story they have read before. Have students write down the characters, the setting, and the plot of their stories. Then have partners tell their stories to one another. Remind students to use the words *next*, *then*, and *finally*.

Scaffolding

Encourge students to expand their storytelling skills by completing a Story Map for an original story. Ask students to invent characters and a plot for a story they would like to tell. Have students fill in a Story Map and write their stories. Then ask volunteers to tell their stories to the class.

STEP 2: Practice

Have students fill in the Story Map on p. 83.

You may have students complete the graphic organizer provided as a Blackline Master in the *Teacher's Resource Book.*

Answer Key

Characters: Androcles, lion, master

Setting: a forest and an arena

Beginning: Androcles is running away from his master when he takes a thorn out of the lion's paw.

Middle: Androcles is caught by his master and thrown into the arena to be eaten by the lion.

End: It is the same lion Androcles helped, so the lion does not eat Androcles.

STEP 3: Extend

Oral Presentation Have students discuss with a partner the good deeds that they have done. Ask students to take notes as they discuss their experiences. Encourage students to use a Cause and Effect Chart to explain the good deed they did and what happened as a result. Have students describe the cause and effect to the class.

STEP 1: Introduce

Help students understand that pronouns take the place of nouns. Explain that there are two types of pronouns: subject pronouns and object pronouns. A subject pronoun is the subject of the sentence that performs the action. An object pronoun is the person or thing that receives the action in the sentence. Review the table of pronouns with students.

STEP 2: Teach

Pronouns

Direct students to the Rule Box, and have volunteers read aloud the definitions of subject pronouns and object pronouns. Write the following sentences on the board. Have students identify the subject pronouns and object pronouns. Remind students to ask themselves who in the sentences performs the action and who receives it.

- The teacher read us a story. us-object pronoun
- I like to read poetry. I-subject pronoun
- Arthur helped him understand the hard words. him-object pronoun
- Have you read the poem? you-subject pronoun
- Yesterday, we wrote a poem together. we-subject pronoun
- My mother gave me a new book. me-object pronoun

STEP 3: Practice

Have students work with a partner to complete the activity. Tell them to write the subject and object pronouns for each sentence.

Answer Key

1. them-object pronoun
2. We-subject pronoun
3. I, subject pronoun, him-object pronoun
4. she-subject pronoun
5. It-subject pronoun

Teaching Resources

- ***Practice Book***, pp. 43–44
- ***Transparencies***, pp. 69–80
- ***Assessments***, pp. 45–48
- ***CD-ROM***

Reading 2

Grammar & Writing

Pronouns

Pronouns take the place of nouns. In these sentences, the pronouns are in red.

Androcles is a young boy. **He** is very courageous. Nothing scares **him**.

Rule Box

Subject pronouns refer to the subject of a sentence. → **We** are *brave*.

Object pronouns receive the action of the verb. → *The hero saved* **us**.

Subject Pronouns	Object Pronouns
I, you, he, she, it, we, they	me, you, him, her, it, us, them

Practice

List the subject and object pronouns in each sentence.

1. Heroes are courageous and nothing can scare them.
2. We helped each other and became friends.
3. I helped him.
4. Padma said she enjoyed the poem.
5. It is a poem about a young hero!

Practice Book page 43

84

TESOL Standards

Goal 1, Standard 2—To use English to communicate in social settings: Students will interact in, through, and with spoken and written English for personal expression and enjoyment.
Descriptors—Describing, reading about, or participating in a favorite activity; Sharing social and cultural traditions and values; Expressing personal needs, feelings, and ideas; Participating in popular culture.

Goal 2, Standard 3—To use English to achieve academically in all content areas: Students will use appropriate learning strategies to construct and apply academic knowledge.
Descriptors—Using context to construct meaning; Actively connecting new information-to-information previously learned; Imitating the behaviors of native English speakers to complete tasks successfully.

Goal 3, Standard 1—To use English in socially and culturally appropriate ways: Students will use the appropriate language variety, register, and genre according to audience, purpose, and setting.
Descriptors—Using the appropriate degree of formality with different audiences and settings; Recognizing and using standard English and vernacular dialects appropriately; Using a variety of writing styles appropriate for different audiences, purposes, and settings; Responding to and using slang appropriately; Responding to and using idioms appropriately; Responding to and using humor appropriately.

Write a Poem

Poems use patterns and sounds to express ideas and emotions. Some poems have lines that rhyme, and some poems don't. Groups of lines, called **verses**, give the poem a nice rhythm.

Read Michael's poem:

He walks through flames.
He climbs high-rises.
He puts out fires
Without surprises!

He can help rescue
Your cat from a tree,
Or he can show the firehouse
To you and to me!

SPELLING TIP

When the letter *c* is followed by *a, o,* or *u,* as in *cat, cone,* or *cub,* it stands for the sound /k/.

Practice Book page 44

Practice

1. Who is the hero of this poem?
2. How many verses does the poem have?
3. Write a poem about your favorite hero. Remember to use a capital letter to start each verse.

Writing Checklist

✓ Did you use pronouns in your poem? Underline them.

✓ Did all your verses start with a capital letter?

✓ Can a partner understand your poem?

85

Accelerate Language Development

Pronouns In many languages other than English, most nouns have a gender. Students who speak other languages at home may have difficulty knowing when to use the neuter *it*. Explain that in English, the pronouns *he*, *him*, *she*, and *her* are most commonly used only for people and animals that are either male or female.

STEP 1: Introduce

Write a Poem

Define the elements of a poem for students.

SAY *When you write a poem, pay attention to the rhythm, or beat, and the sounds of the words. You can make lines rhyme, or you can choose not to.*

You can write lines and verses any way you want. Express what you want the reader to understand. Let's read Michael's poem on page 85.

- *Do any of the lines rhyme?*
- *What are the words that rhyme?*
- *Does the poem have a rhythm, or beat?*
- *How would you describe it?*

Spelling Tip

Read the box aloud to students. Then have students make a list of words they know that have the /k/ sound and are spelled with the letter *c*.

STEP 2: Practice

Have students work with partners to discuss their answers to the first two questions.

Encourage students to use the sample poem as a guide for their own writing. You may want to have students brainstorm a list of rhyming word pairs to use in their poems.

STEP 3: Assess

Writing Checklist

✓ Students might need help identifying the pronouns in their writing.

✓ Be sure students capitalize the first word in each verse.

✓ Ask students to read their poems to one another. If the poem was hard to understand, have partners work together to make it more clear.

✓ Encourage students to use a dictionary or thesaurus to find alternative words.

The Five-Step Writing Process in the Writing Handbook reference section of this book provides more writing instruction.

STEP 1: Introduce

Key Words

Help students learn the skill of defining words by using context.

SAY *The pictures help us learn what the words mean.*

- *What is the vocabulary word in each sentence?*
- *What clues in the sentence help you understand the definition of the word?*

Have volunteers pronounce the key words and describe each photograph.

STEP 2: Teach

Words in Context

Write the following sentences on the board. Have students complete this fill-in-the-blanks exercise using the key words. Then have volunteers read the sentences aloud.

1. His skin will blister if he gets a sunburn.
2. The letter contained the information we needed.
3. The Mississippi is a broad river.
4. We were in the midst of dinner when the phone rang.
5. I always feel merry when I sing.
6. The hikers might startle the sleeping bear cubs.

Have students work in groups to write more context sentences for each key word.

Study Skills

Dictionary Have students look up the key words in the dictionary to see whether the Words in Context sentences were correct.

Online Dictionary Students can use an online dictionary or the CD that accompanies a learner's dictionary like the *Longman Basic Dictionary*.
www.LongmanCornerstone.com

Teaching Resources
- *Practice Book,* pp. 45–46
- *Transparencies,* p. 42
- *CD-ROM* • *Audio CD*

Reading 3

The Wizard of Oz

Vocabulary

In this retelling of *The Wizard of Oz*, Dorothy falls asleep at home on the farm and wakes up in a strange place.

Key Words
- blister
- contained
- broad
- midst
- merry
- startle

Words in Context

1 The paint was so old that it started to **blister.**

2 Jake took out a book about his favorite artist. It **contained** many pretty illustrations of the artist's work.

3 Many people can drive cars on this **broad** avenue at the same time.

86

TESOL Standards

Goal 1, Standard 3—To use English to communicate in social settings: Students will use learning strategies to extend their communicative competence.
Descriptors—Testing hypotheses about language; Listening to and imitating how others use English; Exploring alternative ways of saying things; Using context to construct meaning.

Goal 2, Standard 2—To use English to achieve academically in all content areas: Students will use English to obtain, process, construct, and provide subject matter information in spoken and written form.
Descriptors—Understanding and producing technical vocabulary and text features according to content area.

Goal 2, Standard 3—To use English to achieve academically in all content areas: Students will use appropriate learning strategies to construct and apply academic knowledge.
Descriptors—Using context to construct meaning.

4 Grandma Elizabeth loved sitting in the **midst** of her family.

5 Mr. Smith is a **merry** man. He is always laughing and smiling.

6 I can **startle** the cat by turning on the vacuum cleaner.

Practice

Use each key word in a sentence.

Make Connections

Is being in a strange situation scary, exciting, or both? Describe a time you were in a strange situation.

Academic Words

distinct
separate; different from others

interact
act upon or with another

Practice Book pages 45–46

87

Differentiated Instruction

Beginning	Read the key words out of order, and ask students to repeat each word. Have students point to the sentence and the photograph for each word.
Intermediate	Ask students to use the appropriate key word to describe each photograph.
Greater Challenge	Have students look up the key words in the dictionary to find the parts of speech for each word. Then have students fill in a two-column chart and list the verbs and adjectives.
Standard English Learner CRI	Challenge students to create a new context sentence for each key word. Have one student start the sentence, and have others call out words to complete the sentence.

Visual Literacy

Photographs Have students compare and contrast the photographs shown on pp. 86–87.

SAY *Photographs give us information about people, places, and events.*

- *What do you see in each of the photographs?*
- *How did the photographs help you understand the meanings of the key words?*

Academic Words

Discuss the definitions for *distinct* and *interact* with students. Share the following context sentences with students.

The special sauce gives this dish a *distinct* flavor.

When you *interact* with others, you can share ideas.

Explain to students that both academic words can be changed to nouns by adding the same suffix. Help students determine that the suffix is *-ion*. Have students look up *distinction* and *interaction* and write context sentences.

Other Academic Words

Provide students with another example of a word that can be changed to a noun by adding the suffix *-ion*. Write the following context sentences on the board, and have students identify which term is a verb and which is a noun.

It may be a mistake to *equate* criticism with blame.

She solved the *equation* by knowing each factor.

Have students make a list of other words that can be changed to nouns by adding the suffix *-ion*.

STEP 3: Practice

Flexible Grouping

You may assign these exercises as a whole discussion, partner activity, or individual writing assignment.

Make Connections

Writing Fluency Have students write about an exciting or strange situation that required that they do a good deed or that someone do a good deed for them.

STEP 1: Introduce

More About The Big Question

The Big Question for this selection focuses on ordinary people who become heroes.

SAY *In* The Wizard of Oz, *some unexpected things happen to an ordinary girl.*

- *Have you ever felt bored and wished for something new to happen?*
- *How can new things be exciting or scary?*

Have students use a chart to identify a main idea and details about an exciting or scary experience.

I was in my first school play.

It was the first time I had to say lines.	I was scared that I would forget what to say.	It was exciting when the audience clapped.

STEP 2: Teach

Reading Strategy

Identify Problems and Solutions

Discuss with students how identifying problems and solutions in a reading can help the reader get more involved. Read aloud the bulleted questions on p. 88, and have students discuss the answers.

Understand Text Structure

Tell students that fantasy stories often have strange characters and unusual settings, and the story couldn't happen in real life.

Read

Have students take turns reading aloud the selection. At the end of each page, have the students take turns describing events.

Teaching Resources

- ***Teacher's Resource Book,*** pp. 115–116
- ***Practice Book,*** pp. 47–48
- ***CD-ROM*** • ***Audio CD***

Reading 3

LITERATURE

Fantasy

The Big Question

Can ordinary people become heroes? How?

Reading Strategy

Identify Problems and Solutions

You may know the story of *The Wizard of Oz*. Look through this reading.

- What problem do you think Dorothy has?
- What solutions might she find?

The Wizard of Oz

adapted by Leonard Pringle

Dorothy's life was good, but boring. She lived on a farm in Kansas with her Uncle Henry and Aunt Em. "There's nothing to do here," she said to herself many times a day. She stared and stared at the broad, gray fields. She waited for something to happen.

The sun came up every day. It often got hot enough to blister the paint on the house's walls. Then the sun set. Dorothy didn't notice. Each day was like the other.

Dorothy loved her aunt and uncle. They were kind to her. Uncle Henry and Aunt Em just did not know how to help a bored and lonely young girl.

notice pay attention to

88

TESOL Standards

Goal 2, Standard 2—To use English to achieve academically in all content areas: Students will use English to obtain, process, construct, and provide subject matter information in spoken and written form.

Descriptors—Listening to, speaking, reading, and writing about subject matter information; Gathering information orally and in writing; Retelling information; Selecting, connecting, and explaining information; Listening to, speaking, reading, and writing about subject matter information; Demonstrating knowledge through application in a variety of contexts; Formulating and asking questions.

It was a good thing that Dorothy had Toto, her little, black dog. Toto had merry eyes and funny, little teeth. It always looked like he was smiling. Dorothy would laugh at her silly, little dog. She would say, "Oh, Toto, you are my only friend in the world."

During one boring day, the wind started to howl. Uncle Henry came running from the field. He yelled, "There's a **tornado** coming! Em! Dorothy! Let's get in the **cellar**!"

Uncle Henry's voice was loud enough to startle Toto. He jumped out of Dorothy's arms and hid under the bed. She ran after him.

"Hurry, Dorothy!" Aunt Em called from the cellar stairs. Her voice sounded quiet in the midst of the windy storm.

tornado powerful wind storm with funnel-shaped clouds

cellar basement

Dorothy thought life on the farm in Kansas was boring.

Check Up Why is Dorothy bored?

Build Vocabulary

Direct attention to the highlighted word in the text with a definition at the bottom of the page.

- Invite volunteers to read aloud the word and the definition.
- Have students write a context sentence using the word.
- Have students repeat this activity for each highlighted word as they read the selection.

Irregular Plurals Explain to students that to make a plural of most nouns you add the letter *s*. Tell students that some plurals are irregular. Have students find the word *teeth* on p. 89. Explain that *teeth* is the plural of *tooth*. Write on the board the following examples of other irregular plural nouns:

foot/feet; mouse/mice;
goose/geese; woman/women

Adapt the Activity

The story of The Wizard of Oz has been made into several films, television programs, and stage productions. Ask students to write briefly about which type of adaptation they think would tell the story best. Have students explain their reasoning.

STEP 3: Assess

Check Up

Have students work with partners to explain why Dorothy is bored. Encourage students to reread pp. 88–89 to use specific details from the story for their explanations.

Link to Literature

The story of the Wizard of Oz began as a book called *The Wonderful Wizard of Oz*. It was written by L. Frank Baum in 1900. Before he died in 1919, Baum wrote 14 full-length books and six short stories that take place in Oz. The character of Dorothy only appears in some of them.

Differentiated Instruction

Beginning	Have students draw a picture of this scene: Dorothy lives on a farm with her aunt and uncle and small dog. One day they see a tornado coming toward the house.
Early Intermediate	Have students work with a partner to find the paragraph in the story that describes why everyone had to run to the cellar.
Intermediate	Have students work in pairs to read aloud pp. 88–89. Encourage students to read with feeling.
Struggling Reader	Read aloud the definitions located at the bottom of the page. Have students identify the word you defined. Then have them read the sentences in which the words appear.

STEP 1: Monitor Progress

Literary Devices Explain to students that writers often use metaphors to make their writing more interesting and to help the reader visualize. Explain that a metaphor is an expression of understanding of one concept in terms of something else.

SAY *A metaphor is basically an explanation of one concept in terms of something else.*

- *The expression, "time is running out" compares time to a natural resource.*
- *In the sentence, "Jeremy's anger burned for days," the anger is being compared to a fire.*
- *In the reading, "only the howling wind answered" might be compared to a storm or a monster.*

Have students find items in the reading that could be described in terms of other items. Have students use a T-Chart like the one below to develop their ideas. Then have students try writing their own metaphors.

Item	What it might describe
spinning house howling wind	time machine, spaceship storm, monster

Build Discussion

Have students discuss the author's purpose for writing a fantasy story.

- What details of the story should we believe and not believe?
- What do you think the author wants us to learn by reading the story?
- What can we learn from a story we know cannot happen?

Dorothy crawled under the bed and grabbed Toto. As she was standing up, the house seemed to shake. She fell down. Something seemed to keep her from standing up. "Oh!" Dorothy cried. "Aunt Em!"

Only the howling wind answered. Under the house, the strong storm winds met with a crash. Dorothy knew that she, Toto, and the house were in the center of the tornado. As the winds grew stronger, they lifted up the house like a balloon.

A second later, the house started to spin around. Once, twice, three times, it went around in a circle!

Dorothy stayed on the floor. The house was carried far away from Kansas. Soon, Dorothy felt like she was being rocked to sleep. In time, she did fall asleep.

center middle

A tornado lifted Dorothy's house up, up, and away!

90

TESOL Standards

Goal 2, Standard 2—To use English to achieve academically in all content areas: Students will use English to obtain, process, construct, and provide subject matter information in spoken and written form.

Descriptors—Listening to, speaking, reading, and writing about subject matter information; Gathering information orally and in writing; Retelling information; Selecting, connecting, and explaining information; Listening to, speaking, reading, and writing about subject matter information; Demonstrating knowledge through application in a variety of contexts; Formulating and asking questions.

Dorothy was startled when she woke up. The house had landed gently on the ground. Bright sunshine poured through the windows' unbroken panes.

A beautiful new world appeared. There were huge flowers, tall trees, and a small, sparkling brook.

It was nothing like the farm in Kansas.

A group of people walked toward Dorothy. They were all very small. Their clothes contained every color of the rainbow. Dorothy thought they were children. Then she saw that some of the people had long beards. Some of the people had white hair and wrinkled faces.

"Welcome to Oz, brave witch," a woman said. "We are so grateful to you for killing the Wicked Witch of the East. Now the Munchkins are free!"

Dorothy meets the Munchkins.

gently softly

panes pieces of glass

brook small stream

Check Up How did the Munchkins react to Dorothy?

91

STEP 2: Teach

Academic Words

Discuss the definitions for *conclude* and *deduce* with students. Share the following context sentences with students.

conclude make a decision; bring an idea or a task to an end

deduce find an answer or solve a problem using a step-by-step procedure

She was able to *conclude* that her answer was correct.

After many experiments, the scientist could *deduce* that the data was correct.

Explain to students that both vocabulary words relate to completing a thought process. Therefore the two words are synonyms. Tell students that even though words are synonyms, each word has a specific meaning in a specific context. Challenge students to write context sentences for each word, and then read their sentences aloud to the class.

Link to Science

Explain to students that it is unlikely for a tornado to lift a house without destroying it. Have students research facts about tornadoes and write a short report on what they learn. Encourage students to discuss wind speed and what causes a tornado to form.

Accelerate Language Development

Pronouncing Possessive Plurals Students who know something about English syntax but are not completely familiar with it, may not know how to pronounce the phrase *the windows' unbroken panes.* Because singular possessives add an *s* sound at the end of a noun, students may think that a similar rule applies for plurals and say what sounds like "windows-es." Point out that the plural possessive is pronounced without adding an extra *s* sound at the end. Write the following on the board for students to pronounce: *the girls' pets; the boys' games; the dogs' food*.

STEP 3: Assess

Check Up

Have students work with partners. Tell each student to quickly write notes for what they remember about the Munchkins' reaction without rereading the pages. Have students exchange papers with their partners and then compare and contrast their answers.

Reteach

Remind students that when using the reading skill compare and contrast, they should discuss how their answers are similar and how they are different from their partners' answers.

STEP 1: Monitor Progress

Comprehension Check

Sequence of Events Discuss the sequence of events in the story. Use the following questions to guide students in their discussion.

SAY *You can understand the events of the story better if you remember their order.*

- *How did Dorothy and Toto get to Oz?*
- *What was the first thing they saw when they arrived?*
- *Whom did they meet first?*
- *Why did the Munchkins say she killed someone?*
- *Who is Glinda?*
- *What did Glinda give to Dorothy?*
- *What does Dorothy want to do at the end of the reading?*

Have students use a Sequence of Events Chart like the one below to fill in the events in the story that have taken place so far.

A tornado carries Dorothy and Toto to a strange place.

↓

The first thing they see is a beautiful new world.

↓

The Munchkins welcome Dorothy to Oz.

↓

Dorothy learns that the house has landed on the Wicked Witch of the West.

↓

Dorothy meets Glinda, the Witch of the North.

↓

Glinda gives Dorothy red slippers.

↓

Dorothy asks Glinda to help her go home.

Scaffolding

Have students work in small groups to read aloud the paragraphs on pp. 92–93. Ask volunteers to each read one speaking part, and ask a narrator to read the paragraphs that are not dialogue. Tell students to read with expression as if they were performing a play.

"You are very kind," Dorothy said, "but I'm afraid you are mistaken. I didn't kill anyone."

The woman smiled and said, "Well, your house killed someone. Come and look."

Dorothy looked down. Sure enough, two feet stuck out from under the house. The feet wore red shoes.

"Oh, dear," Dorothy cried. "The house must have fallen on her. What can we do to help her?"

"Nothing," the woman replied. "I'm afraid it is too late."

A new person appeared. She wore a pretty gown, and she was much taller than the Munchkins.

"Hello, Dorothy. I am Glinda, the Witch of the North," the new woman said. "I came to tell you that those shoes now belong to you."

Dorothy looked down at the red shoes. Then she looked back at the Witch of the North. "Really?" Dorothy said.

---

mistaken wrong

gown long dress

Dorothy gets red shoes from the Witch of the North.

92

TESOL Standards

Goal 2, Standard 2—To use English to achieve academically in all content areas: Students will use English to obtain, process, construct, and provide subject matter information in spoken and written form.

Descriptors—Listening to, speaking, reading, and writing about subject matter information; Gathering information orally and in writing; Retelling information; Selecting, connecting, and explaining information; Listening to, speaking, reading, and writing about subject matter information; Demonstrating knowledge through application in a variety of contexts; Formulating and asking questions

Just then, Glinda waved her long, silver wand in a circle around the shoes. There was a puff of smoke. Dorothy blinked. Suddenly, she was wearing the red shoes.

"Thank you," Dorothy said. "I have to go home now. Can you tell me how to get back to Kansas? I am sure I am late for supper."

"You will have to find that out for yourself," Glinda said.

This was the beginning of Dorothy's adventures in Oz.

blinked opened and closed quickly

Dorothy meets the Wicked Witch of the West, the Scarecrow, the Tin Man, and the Cowardly Lion in Oz.

Practice Book pages 47–48

Reading Strategy

Identify Problems and Solutions

Before you read the story, you thought about the problems that Dorothy might face.

- What problems are solved in the story?
- What new problems does Dorothy find?

Think It Over

1. What does Dorothy think of her life in Kansas?
2. How does Toto make Dorothy's life happier?
3. Where does the tornado take Dorothy?
4. What adventures do you think Dorothy will have?

93

STEP 2: TEACH

Visual Literacy

Illustrations Have students use their own words to write a description of the event they see taking place in each picture in the story. Encourage students to think of the following questions when writing their descriptions.

- What clues do you look for in a picture to find out how a character may feel?
- What clues do you look for to know what action is taking place in the picture?
- How important are the pictures to telling the story?
- Would it be possible to understand this story without pictures? Why or why not?

STEP 3: ASSESS

Reading Strategy

Identify Problems and Solutions Explain to students how defining the problem and solution in a story can make reading more interesting.

SAY *Identifying problems and solutions as you read is a good way to get more involved in what you are reading. When you discover a problem, you will read more closely to see how the problem is solved.*

- *What was Dorothy's first problem?*
- *How did the author solve that problem?*
- *What other problems and solutions can you find in the story?*

Have students use a Cause and Effect Chart to list each problem and solution in the story.

Think It Over

Flexible Grouping You may assign this exercise as a class discussion, partner activity, or individual writing assignment.

Answer Key

1. Dorothy thinks her life in Kansas is boring.
2. Toto is Dorothy's only friend. He makes her laugh.
3. The tornado takes Dorothy to Oz.
4. Dorothy will have to find someone to help her get home to Kansas.

Differentiated Instruction

Beginning	Have students work in pairs to use gestures and pantomime to act out the events on pp. 92–93. Ask students to say aloud the character's name as they show the action.
Intermediate	Have student write short answers to the following questions: *Whom did Dorothy tell was mistaken? Who appeared in a pretty gown? What happened after Dorothy blinked?*
Greater Challenge	Have students describe each picture and which event in the plot it shows.
Standard English Learner CRI	Have students retell the most important events that happened on pp. 92–93. Encourage students to add more details about the story.

STEP 1: Introduce

Word Analysis

Word Origins Tell students that languages change as time passes, and new words come into use while other words are used less and less. Explain to students that many of the words or phrases they use every day probably did not exist when their parents or grandparents were young.

STEP 2: Teach

Direct students' attention to the paragraph that explains word origins. Help them understand that people who speak one language often borrow many words and phrases from other languages. Encourage students to share examples of words and phrases that are common in English that they know come from another language.

SAY *We have discussed that a language is always changing. New words appear, and other words get dropped. Many languages are related to one or more languages that people spoke many years ago.*

- *What are some common words we use that are borrowed from another language?*
- *The word tele is Greek. It means "distant." Can you think of any words we use today that come from this very old Greek word?*

STEP 3: Practice

Explain to students that it is not important to correctly pronounce the words in bold, but to focus on matching them with the vocabulary words.

Answer Key

1. cellar
2. notice
3. pane
4. mistaken
5. gown

Teaching Resources

- ***Practice Book***, p. 49
- ***Phonics Workbook***
- ***CD-ROM***

Reading 3

Word Analysis & Fluency

Word Analysis

Word Origins

Like many words in English, the word ***tornado*** comes from another language. ***Tornado*** is a form of the Spanish word ***tronada***, which means thunderstorm. What do you know about tornadoes?

Practice

Read the clues below. Match each clue with a word from the box.

mistaken
cellar
pane
gown
notice

1. This word is taken from the Latin word ***cella***, which means "small room" or "storeroom."
2. This word can be traced back to the Latin word ***noscere***, which means "to get to know."
3. This word for "a piece of glass" is from the French word ***pan***, meaning "piece."
4. This word is a form of the Norse word ***mistaka***, which means "to take in error."
5. This word for "long dress" is from the French word ***goune***, which means "long coat."

Practice Book page 49

94

TESOL Standards

Goal 1, Standard 3—To use English to communicate in social settings: Students will use learning strategies to extend their communicative competence.
Descriptors—Testing hypotheses about language; Listening to and imitating how others use English; Exploring alternative ways of saying things; Practicing new language; Using context to construct meaning; Learning and using word "chunks"; Using primary language to ask for clarification; Self-monitoring and self-evaluating language development.

Goal 3, Standard 3—To use English in socially and culturally appropriate ways: Students will use appropriate learning strategies to extend their sociolinguistic and sociocultural competence.
Descriptors—Experimenting with variations of language in social and academic settings; Seeking information about appropriate language use and behavior.

Fluency

Read for Speed and Accuracy

You should read quickly. But never read so quickly that you lose your understanding.

Practice

Read for one minute. → Count the words you read. → Study any hard words. → Read and count again.

Dorothy's life was good, but boring. She lived on a farm in 12
Kansas with her Uncle Henry and Aunt Em. 20
"There's nothing to do here," she said to herself many 30
times a day. She stared and stared at the broad, gray fields. She 43
waited for something to happen. 48
The sun came up every day. It often got hot enough to 60
blister the paint on the house's walls. Then the sun set. Dorothy 72
didn't notice. Each day was like the other. 80
Dorothy loved her aunt and uncle. They were always kind 90
to her. Uncle Henry and Aunt Em just did not know how to 103
help a bored and lonely young girl. 110
It was a good thing that Dorothy had Toto, her little, black 122
dog. Toto had merry eyes and funny, little teeth. It always looked 134
like he was smiling. Dorothy would laugh at her silly, little dog. 146
She would say, "Oh, Toto, you are my only friend in the world." 159

95

Linguistic Note

Tornado As explained on p. 94, the English word *tornado* comes from *tronada*, a Spanish word meaning *thunderstorm*. However, the Spanish language now has a word for tornado, too. That word is *tornado*, which is spelled exactly the same as it is in English.

STEP 1: Introduce

Fluency

Read for Speed and Accuracy Discuss with students how reading for speed and accuracy can help them understand what they read. Emphasize that if they read too slowly they might forget what they are reading about; if they read too quickly they might also lose track of the story.

Play the Audio CD for this reading to the class, asking students to listen for pacing, intonation, and expression.

STEP 2: Practice

Have students complete the exercise with partners.

- Provide pairs of students with a timer.
- Have one partner read while the other student times the student who is reading.
- Have students look at the number next to the last line they completed reading. If they stopped in the middle of a line, have them count the words up to that point.

Students should write down their speed after the first time they read the passage.

Have students look for any words that slowed their reading speed. After students have practiced those words and reread the passage, have them determine whether their speed improved.

STEP 3: Extend

Study Skills

Dictionary Have students work with partners to make a list of words that slowed their reading. Have each student write down three words, and ask them to look the words up in a dictionary. Have them define and pronounce the words in their lists.

Remind students that they can use this study skill anywhere, in social studies or science class, or when they read at home.

STEP 1: Monitor Progress

Learning Strategy

Outline Explain that when you outline, you organize the main idea and details in order.

After students have completed their outlines, have them discuss how the Big Question relates to Dorothy's experience.

STEP 2: Teach

Characters and Conflicts

Students will learn how to identify whether one or more than one character faces a specific conflict.

SAY *In the story we just read, the characters experienced conflicts they did not expect.*

- *What problems did each of them face?*
- *How did the different conflicts affect each character in the story?*
- *How were the conflicts finally resolved?*
- *How do the settings of the story influence the conflict?*

STEP 3: Practice

Tell students to think about the characters and the events in the story as they begin the activity.

Flexible Grouping You may assign this activity as a class discussion, partner activity, or individual written assignment.

Answer Key

1. within Dorothy
2. between characters
3. between a character and an event; between characters
4. between characters; between a character and an event
5. within Dorothy

Teaching Resources

- *Practice Book*, p. 50
- *Transparencies*, p. 67
- *Teacher's Resource Book*, p. 165
- *CD-ROM*

Reading 3

Comprehension

Learning Strategy

Outline

Make an outline of the main characters and events in the story.

Share your outline with a partner.

Ask your partner to respond to the Big Question for this reading.

Practice Book page 50

Characters and Conflicts

A **conflict** is a disagreement. A story can have more than one conflict. A conflict can be within the character, between different characters, or between a character and an event.

Practice

Tell whether the conflict is within one character, between characters, or between a character and an event. Sometimes there is more than one correct answer.

1. Dorothy had a good life on the farm, but she was bored.
2. Uncle Henry and Aunt Em did not know how to help Dorothy.
3. Aunt Em tried to get Dorothy to go to the cellar.
4. Dorothy tried to keep Toto safe from the tornado.
5. Dorothy wants to explore Oz, but she also wants to go home.

TESOL Standards

Goal 2, Standard 2—To use English to achieve academically in all content areas: Students will use English to obtain, process, construct, and provide subject matter information in spoken and written form.
Descriptors—Listening to, speaking, reading, and writing about subject matter information; Gathering information orally and in writing; Retelling information; Selecting, connecting, and explaining information; Listening to, speaking, reading, and writing about subject matter information; Demonstrating knowledge through application in a variety of contexts; Formulating and asking questions

Goal 3, Standard 3—To use English in socially and culturally appropriate ways: Students will use appropriate learning strategies to extend their sociolinguistic and sociocultural competence
Descriptors—Observing and modeling how others speak and behave in a particular situation or setting; Self-monitoring and self-evaluating language use according to setting and audience; Rehearsing variations of language use in different social and academic settings; Analyzing the social content to determine appropriate language use; Deciding when use of slang is appropriate.

Use an Idea Web

An Idea Web can help you see how different ideas in a story are connected.

Practice

Copy this Idea Web. Complete it to show what you know about Dorothy's conflicts.

- Share your work with a partner.
- Discuss how you think Dorothy will solve the conflicts she faces.

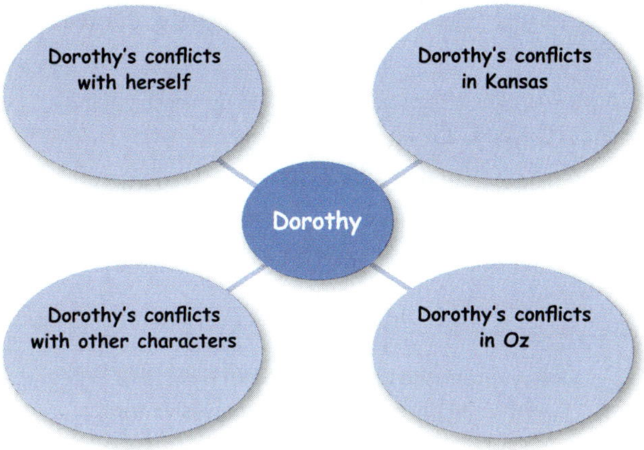

Extension

Describe a strange situation or place you found yourself in. Draw a picture of your experience. Then share what you drew with the class.

97

Accelerate Language Development

The *ph* Combination The *ph* letter combination does not occur in Spanish. Speakers of that language may have difficulty remembering that this consonant combination stands for the /f/ sound. The English word *graphic* has a cognate in Spanish: *gráfico*. Spanish-speaking students may find it easier to remember the *ph* sound by thinking about the sound of the word from their own language.

STEP 1: Teach

Use an Idea Web

Tell students that everyone has conflicts. Ask them to think about some conflicts in their own lives. Have them decide whether the conflicts are with themselves, with one person, or with more than one person. Ask them to write sentences about three conflicts they have. Then have them give their sentences to a partner and have the partner guess what kind of conflict each sentence discusses.

Possible Responses

Conflicts

1. My parents ask me to do chores, but I don't want to.
2. My sister borrows my clothes without asking.
3. I can't decide which TV show to watch.

Kinds of Conflict

1. more than one person
2. one person
3. with myself

STEP 2: Practice

You may have students complete the graphic organizer provided as a Blackline Master in the *Teacher's Resource Book*.

Answer Key

Dorothy's conflicts with herself: She's bored.

Dorothy's conflicts with other characters: She wants Glinda to tell her how to get home.

Dorothy's conflicts in Kansas: Nothing interesting ever happens.

Dorothy's conflicts in Oz: She thinks Oz is interesting, but she wants to go home.

STEP 3: Extend

Oral Presentation Have students consider the conflicts of other characters in the story. Ask students to use an Idea Web to list the conflicts for Aunt Em, Glinda, or the Munchkins. Have volunteers present to the class the information in the Idea Web for the character they selected.

STEP 1: Introduce

Help students understand that possessive nouns are used to show that someone or something owns or "possesses" something else.

STEP 2: Teach

Possessive Nouns

Have students read aloud the rules shown in the Rule Box on p. 98. Then write the following sentences from *The Wizard of Oz* on the board. Have volunteers complete the sentences with the correct possessive noun.

1. The heat from the sun made the paint blister. The sun's heat made the paint blister.
2. The Munchkins live in Oz. Oz is the Munchkins' home.
3. Some of the men had beards. The men's beards were white.
4. The witch had red shoes on her feet. The witch's shoes were red.
5. The wand belongs to Glinda. It is Glinda's wand.

STEP 3: Practice

Have partners take turns identifying whether the underlined noun is singular or plural and rewriting the possessive form of the noun.

Answer Key

1. Amy's dog
2. Mrs. Smith's hat
3. houses' roofs
4. women's meeting

Reading 3

Grammar & Writing

Possessive Nouns

When you use **possessive nouns**, you are saying something belongs to a person. If you want to talk about shoes that belong to your sister, you might say, "my sister's shoes."

Rule Box

To make a singular noun possessive, add an apostrophe (') and **s**. Example: **girl's** dog

To make a plural noun possessive, you add an apostrophe (') after the **s**. Example: the **boys'** lunchboxes.

To make a plural noun that does not end in *s* possessive, add an apostrophe and *s*. Example: **children's** toys.

Practice

Tell whether the underlined noun is singular or plural. Rewrite the phrase, using the possessive form.

1. the dog belonging to Amy
2. the hat belonging to Mrs. Smith
3. the roofs belonging to the houses
4. the meeting the women went to

Practice Book page 51

98

TESOL Standards

Goal 1, Standard 3—To use English to communicate in social settings: Students will use learning strategies to extend their communicative competence.
Descriptor—Seeking support and feedback from others.

Goal 2, Standard 1—To use English to achieve academically in all content areas: Students will use English to interact in the classroom.
Descriptors—Following oral and written directions, implicit and explicit; Expressing likes, dislikes, and needs.

Goal 2, Standard 3—To use English to achieve academically in all content areas: Students will use appropriate learning strategies to construct and apply academic knowledge.
Descriptors—Using context to construct meaning; Actively connecting new information to information previously learned; Imitating the behaviors of native English speakers to complete tasks successfully.

Goal 3, Standard 1—To use English in socially and culturally appropriate ways: Students will use the appropriate language variety, register, and genre according to audience, purpose, and setting.
Descriptors—Recognizing and using standard English and vernacular dialects appropriately; Using a variety of writing styles appropriate for different audiences, purposes, and settings.

Teaching Resources

- *Practice Book*, pp. 51–52
- *Transparencies*, pp. 69–80
- *Assessments*, pp. 49–52
- *CD-ROM*

Write a Descriptive Paragraph

Look. Sniff. Feel. Use your senses to help you write. What does a thing look like? Smell or taste like? What does it feel like when you touch it? What sounds do you hear if you tap it?

Notice the words Sophia used to describe a room in her home.

The best thing in my dad's house is the giant playroom. My brother and I use our imaginations and become whatever we want. I can be a fearless superhero. I can swing from tall buildings and onto dark rooftops, where I step into slick, wet puddles.

My brother likes to paint bright, colorful paintings. He painted a slick, silver race car with a black roof. He says it's his dream car. I said that I don't need a car. I'll just use my speedy, sturdy wings to fly as fast as a rocket ship.

What's that? I can smell something sweet. Time to become me again and have some of the hot, fresh cookies Dad baked. Mmm!

SPELLING TIP

An apostrophe (') takes the place of letters left out in words like ***don't***.

Practice Book page 52

Practice

Write about a room in your home.

- Choose a room.
- Explore it with all your senses.
- List things you see, feel, smell, and hear. Then write your description.

Writing Checklist

- ✓ Did you describe what you saw, smelled, touched, or tasted?
- ✓ Can a partner see what you are describing?

99

Differentiated Instruction

Differentiated Instruction	
Beginning	Have students point to the phrase in Sophia's paragraph that tells what Sophia pretends to be in the giant playroom. Have them find the sentence that describes what her brother likes to paint. Help students repeat the sentences aloud.
Early Intermediate	Have students repeat the descriptive words from Sophia's paragraphs as they take turns reading each sentence aloud.
Intermediate	Have students reread Sophia's descriptive paragraphs and make a list of as many descriptive words as they can find.
Struggling Reader	Have students point to and say aloud the descriptive words in the following sentence: *The loud wind felt cold on my red face.*

STEP 1: Teach

Write a Descriptive Paragraph

Define a descriptive paragraph for students.

SAY *A descriptive paragraph helps readers more clearly imagine the scene or object. When you write a descriptive paragraph, you choose words that tell the reader what something looks like, sounds like, smells like, feels like, and tastes like.*

- *How does Sophia describe the puddles?*
- *What does she write about the race car?*
- *What other descriptive words and phrases Sophia use?*

Spelling Tip

Read the box to students. Then have students tell what letters were replaced by the apostrophe in the following words:

can't	wouldn't	couldn't
I'm	she's	aren't
we're	they're	isn't

STEP 2: Practice

Have students refer to their lists of descriptive words as they write their paragraphs. Remind students they should use sensory words that help readers hear, see, taste, smell, and feel what they are describing.

STEP 3: Assess

Writing Checklist

- ✓ Have students underline the name of each thing they describe.
- ✓ Have students circle all sensory words they used.
- ✓ Have students work as partners—one reader and one listener. Have listeners tell their partners three things they remember about what they just heard.
- ✓ Encourage students to use a dictionary or thesaurus to find alternative words.

The Five-Step Writing Process in the Writing Handbook reference section of this book provides more writing instruction.

STEP 1: Introduce

More About The Big Question

Tell students the Big Question for this reading is: *How can young people become heroes?* Ask students to brainstorm names of young people who have become heroes.

SAY *The title of this reading is* The Elephant Shepherd.

- *Look at the illustration on this page. What can you tell about a shepherd from this picture?*
- *Do you think the shepherd or the elephants will be heroes in this story?*
- *How do you think the young shepherd might become a hero?*

Visual Literacy

Illustrations Lead a class discussion about drawing conclusions from what is shown in the illustrations. Have students fill in a KWL Chart with information from the discussion. Ask students to continue to complete the chart as they read the short story.

STEP 2: Teach

Understand Text Structure

Draw students' attention to the genre label. Tell them that a short story is fiction with characters, setting, and a plot, and is told in a few pages. Have students compare and contrast how a novel and a short story are alike and different.

Read

Direct students to the information below the title of the story indicating that the story is retold. Ask students to explain what they think it means if a story is retold. Have students take turns reading the paragraphs in the story aloud.

Teaching Resources

- *Teacher's Resource Book*, pp. 117–118
- *CD-ROM* • *Audio CD*

Bonus Reading

LITERATURE
Short Story

The Elephant Shepherd

retold by Abdoul Tafari
illustrated by Gary Torrisi

Ousmane was finally old enough to watch the cattle by himself. He loved spending his days on top of the hill looking over the savanna. He knew he had an important job to do. Ousmane's father, Amadou, told him that the family needed the cattle to survive.

One hot, sunny day, Ousmane was standing on the hill watching the cattle. The cattle were grazing calmly. Then Ousmane heard loud stomping noises. He thought a giant was coming. The cattle looked up.

Ousmane saw what was making the noise. It was a herd of elephants. Ousmane was so excited. His father had told him about elephants, but he had never seen one. Ousmane liked watching the baby elephant with its mother the best.

100

TESOL Standards

Goal 2, Standard 3—To use English to achieve academically in all content areas: Students will use appropriate learning strategies to construct and apply academic knowledge. **Descriptors**—Focusing attention selectively; Applying basic reading comprehension skills such as skimming, scanning, previewing, and reviewing text; Using context to construct meaning; Applying self-monitoring and self-corrective strategies to build and expand a knowledge base; Knowing when to use native language resources (human and material) to promote understanding.

"Ousmane!"

Suddenly, Ousmane saw his father, Amadou, running toward the elephants. "Shoo!" "Shoo!" Amadou yelled at the elephants. The elephants started to move away. The baby elephant looked scared and walked close to its mother.

"Why did you scare the elephants away?" asked Ousmane.

"I like the elephants, too. But we need the grass for our cattle," Amadou replied. "If the elephants stomp on the grass, the cattle will have nothing to eat."

Ousmane was sad. That night at supper, Ousmane told Amadou that he hoped the mother and baby elephant would come back to visit when there was more grass for the cattle.

Ousmane dreamed about the mother and baby elephant that night.

101

Differentiated Instruction

Beginning	Have students point to the sentence that tells what Ousmane said to Amadou about the mother and baby elephant. Then have them point to the sentence that tells about Ousmane's dream.
Intermediate	Have students write captions for each of the pictures on pp. 100–101.
Greater Challenge	Have students think about Ousmane's dream and write a paragraph that answers the following questions: *What do they think he dreamed about the elephants? Why?*
Standard English Learner CRI	Read aloud various sentences from pp. 100–101 that describe what is happening in the pictures. Then have students describe the action in the story in their own words.

Vocabulary Definitions

The following vocabulary appears in *The Elephant Shepherd*. Definitions are provided to share with the class if students require definitions for any of the words. They are not meant for vocabulary acquisition or exercises.

shepherd person who watches over animals

cattle cows and other animals like them

grazing eating grass or other growing plants

tusks horns or bone-like structures that stick out from above an elephant's mouth

illegal against the law

poachers people who break the law that protects animals from being hunted and killed

survive stay alive

Build Vocabulary

Help students recognize the nouns in the short story that name a person, place, or thing.

- Have students create a 3-Column Chart with columns for person, place, and thing.
- Review pp. 100–101 for nouns to write in the chart.
- Exchange lists with partners to compare and contrast the nouns they found.

STEP 3: Extend

Context Clues

Have students answer the following questions based on what they read on pp. 100–101. Remind students to look for context clues when the author does not tell all the information.

- Who is the main character of the story?
- What is his job?
- What caused the stomping he heard?
- Why did Amadou scare away the elephants?

Have students write a short answer that explains how Ousmane and Amadou feel about the elephants.

STEP 1: Monitor Progress

Comprehension Check

Summarize Tell students that a summary is a short explanation of the main characters and most important events in a story.

SAY *You can better understand the events of a story if you remember the order in which they occurred. Let's discuss what events have happened in this story.*

- *What was Ousmane doing on top of the hill?*
- *What happened next?*
- *What did Amadou do when he saw the elephants?*
- *What did the elephants do?*

Have students use a Sequence of Events Chart like the one below to fill in the events in the story just discussed. Have students complete the chart as they continue to read the story.

Ousame was watching cattle on the hill.

↓

He heard stomping noises.

↓

He saw a herd of elephants.

↓

Amadou scared the herd away.

Build Discussion

Have students discuss the author's purpose for writing a short story. Encourage students to discuss answers to the following questions:

- What details of the setting are different from where we live?
- How does Ousmane spend his time differently than we do?
- Why should we read about things we may never experience ourselves?

Adapt the Activity

Have students choose another way to tell this story, like a poem, novel, newspaper article, etc. Ask students to choose the medium they would use to retell the story and to write a short paragraph explaining their choice.

Early the next day, Ousmane and Amadou set out to find good grass for their cattle. They came across an elephant on the ground. They were shocked to see that the elephant's tusks had been sawed off.

"Poachers," said Amadou. "They take the tusks and sell them for money. It is against the law, but some people don't care."

"Why would someone want to hurt the elephants?" Ousmane asked sadly.

Ousmane and Amadou walked on and came upon the rest of the elephant herd. They watched the elephants for a little while and then went back to tend their cattle.

Ousmane thought about the elephants all day. He wished he could stop the poachers.

102

TESOL Standards

Goal 2, Standard 3—To use English to achieve academically in all content areas: Students will use appropriate learning strategies to construct and apply academic knowledge.
Descriptors—Focusing attention selectively; Applying basic reading comprehension skills such as skimming, scanning, previewing, and reviewing text; Using context to construct meaning; Applying self-monitoring and self-corrective strategies to build and expand a knowledge base; Knowing when to use native language resources (human and material) to promote understanding.

Ousmane and Amadou took their cattle to a pasture near the elephants the next day. The elephants were eating leaves off some trees. Ousmane and Amadou stopped to watch.

"They are such beautiful, strong creatures," Amadou said. "Look how nicely the baby elephant and the adults are getting along."

"Do you think they are related?" Ousmane asked.

"Probably," replied Amadou. "Elephants have families like we do."

When he returned to school the following week, Ousmane decided to ask his teacher if his classmates could do something to protect the elephants. After school the next day, Ousmane and his classmates started to tell the other villagers why it was important to protect the elephants from poachers.

103

STEP 2: Teach

Building Vocabulary

The Suffix *-er* Explain to students that many words ending in *-er* name a person who does or performs a certain action or job.

SAY *Look at the word* poachers *on page 102. A poacher is a person who breaks the law and hunts animals. The word comes from the verb* poach *which means "to hunt illegally." When you add -er to the verb* poach, *the new word is a noun that names the person that does the poaching.*

Write the following nouns on the board:

teach	*play*	*hunt*	*farm*
travel	*lead*	*work*	

Have students work on their own or with a partner to add the suffix *-er* to each noun to form a verb that names the person performing each action. When students have completed the activity, have them share the words with the class.

STEP 3: Extend

Have students work with a partner to think of things the villagers can do to protect the elephants. Ask students to discuss whether they think someone who protects elephants is a hero.

FYI

The Elephant Poaching Ban Elephant tusks are composed of a hard white material called ivory, which has always been considered valuable. From 1979 to 1989, the African elephant population dropped from approximately 1.3 million animals to about 600,000. This drop was mainly due to ivory poachers. In 1989, an international organization called CITES (Convention on International Trade in Endangered Species) banned the sale of any elephant parts, including ivory, throughout the world. Although a few African countries are once again allowed to sell ivory, it is still illegal to import it into the United States.

Linguistic Note

The Word *elephant* Spanish-speaking students should recognize the English word *elephant* from the Spanish *elefante*. In the Spanish pronunciation, however, the syllable *-fan-* is stressed. Model the English pronunciation for students who have difficulty.

FYI

Elephant Families Elephants live in big families, led by the oldest female. A family cooperates to protect and teach the young. If the family senses danger, the elephants get close together, pushing the babies and young into the center of the group where they are safe. The oldest female faces the direction of the threat and decides whether the family should fight or run away. If one member of the family is hurt, the other elephants often come to help it.

STEP 1: Review

The Big Question

Evidence of Understanding

Read the Big Question with students to focus students' attention on this unit's theme. The first tier of projects is least challenging, and the third tier is most challenging.

STEP 2: Transfer

Written

Definition Allow students to use a student's dictionary or an online source, if necessary, to help them write their definitions.

Story Encourage students to use new words they have learned in their stories. Remind them to include a problem and solution in the plot.

Survey Suggest that students think of as many questions as they can about heroes and then select their ten favorites for the survey.

Oral

Discussion Have students review the list of descriptive words on p. 58 and think of other abilities or traits for a hero.

Reality Show You may choose to have students take the roles of their heroes and describe "their own" experiences.

News Report Discuss features of a TV news report. What kinds of things does the anchor say? Does the reporter use visual aids?

Visual/Active

Magazine Cover Bring in an assortment of magazine covers for students to look at.

Hero Cards Students may create their cards with the visuals on the front and the descriptions on the back.

Awards Ceremony Encourage students to picture each nominee's activities as if they were scenes in a movie.

All projects can be assessed on the basis of content and presentation. A rubric delineating standards for assessment can be helpful and is available as a Blackline Master in the *Teacher's Resource Book*.

UNIT 2 Wrap Up

The Big Question

What does it take to be a hero?

Written	Oral	Visual/Active
Definition Write your own dictionary definition for the word ***hero***. List five people who would fit your definition.	**Discussion** Have a discussion asking: What is the most important quality a hero needs? Give examples to support your choice.	**Magazine Cover** Create a magazine cover that shows one of your heroes and words that describe him or her. Give the magazine a special title.
Story Write a story about a character who becomes a hero. Use the 5 W Questions to describe your hero. Be sure the plot shows how your character becomes a hero.	**Reality Show** Work with a group. Have each student describe a hero from real life or from stories. Ask questions, and vote for the most heroic character.	**Hero Cards** Create a set of cards about heroes. One set of cards should show pictures of heroes. The set of matching cards should describe what the heroes did.
Survey Write a 10-question survey about heroes. Ask your classmates to complete the survey as it relates to their favorite heroes. Report your results to the class.	**News Report** Create a news story titled *Three More Gifts* in which character A helps character B, who helps character C, and so on. Present your story as a news report.	**Awards Ceremony** Design awards for heroes. Create a storyboard for each nominee that tells about the event that made him or her a hero.

104

TESOL Standards

Goal 3, Standard 1—To use English in socially and culturally appropriate ways: Students will use the appropriate language variety, register, and genre according to audience, purpose, and setting.
Descriptors—Using the appropriate degree of formality with different audiences and settings; Recognizing and using Standard English and vernacular dialects appropriately; Using a variety of writing styles appropriate for different audiences, purposes, and settings; Responding to and using slang appropriately; Responding to and using idioms appropriately; Responding to and using humor appropriately; Determining when it is appropriate to use a language other than English; Determining appropriate topics for interaction; Greet and take leave appropriately in a variety of settings.

Goal 3, Standard 2—To use English in socially and culturally appropriate ways: Students will use nonverbal communication appropriate to audience, purpose, and setting.
Descriptors—Interpreting and responding appropriately to nonverbal cues and body language; Demonstrating knowledge of acceptable nonverbal classroom behaviors; Using acceptable tone, volume, stress, and intonation, in various social settings; Recognizing and adjusting behavior in response to nonverbal cues.

Practice Book pages 53–54

✓ Learning Checklist

Word Analysis and Phonics

- ✓ Pronounce long vowel pairs correctly.
- ✓ Pronounce the vowel pair *ea* correctly.
- ✓ Use word origins to determine the meanings of unknown words.

Comprehension

- ✓ Identify characters and plot.
- ✓ Use a Cause and Effect Chart.
- ✓ Make connections between text and self.
- ✓ Use a Story Map.
- ✓ Identify characters and conflicts.
- ✓ Use an Idea Web.

Grammar and Writing

- ✓ Identify adjectives and adverbs.
- ✓ Use pronouns correctly.
- ✓ Use apostrophes to make singular and plural possessives.
- ✓ Describe causes and effects.
- ✓ Write a poem.
- ✓ Write a descriptive paragraph.

Self-Evaluation Questions

- How is a hero similar to or different from other people?
- How does what you've learned connect to other learning?
- How could you learn more about what makes a person a hero?

105

Further Reading

The Road to El Dorado
This Penguin Young Reader® tells the story of two adventurers, Tulio and Miguel, who set out to seek fame and fortune. Then fate hands them a map to the city of gold, El Dorado.

Ride Like the Wind: A Tale of the Pony Express,
Bernie Fuchs
In the early 1860s, Pony Express riders used daring and courage to deliver the mail amid severe weather and harsh terrain. Here is the engaging story of rider Johnny Free and his pony JennySoo as they race to make their deliveries.

American Tall Tales, Mary Pope Osborne
This collection of nine adventurous legends includes stories about American folk heroes such as Sally Ann Thunder, Ann Whirlwind, Pecos Bill, and John Henry.

STEP 3: Assess

Learning Checklist

Word Analysis and Phonics

- ✓ Vowel pairs: Reading 1, p. 70
- ✓ Vowel pair *ea*: Reading 2, p. 80
- ✓ Word origins: Reading 3, p. 94

Comprehension

- ✓ Identify characters and plot: Reading 1, p. 72
- ✓ Use a Cause and Effect Chart: Reading 1, p. 73
- ✓ Make connections between text and self: Reading 2, p. 82
- ✓ Use a Story Map: Reading 2, p. 83
- ✓ Identify characters and conflict: Reading 3, p. 96
- ✓ Use an Idea Web: Reading 3, p. 97

Grammar and Writing

- ✓ Identify adjectives and adverbs: Reading 1, p. 74
- ✓ Describe causes and effects: Reading 1, p. 75
- ✓ Use pronouns correctly: Reading 2, p. 84
- ✓ Write a poem: Reading 2, p. 85
- ✓ Use apostrophes to make singular and plural possessives: Reading 3, p. 98
- ✓ Write a descriptive paragraph: Reading 3, p. 99

Self Evaluation Questions

The self-evaluation questions provide the teacher with important information about the students' learning progress as well as their self-esteem.

- A hero is just like other people because he wants to help others. A hero is different because he is braver, stronger, or luckier.
- What I learned connects to social studies because I read about Africa.
- I could read about other heroes.

Teaching Resources

- *Practice Book,* pp. 53–54
- *Transparencies,* p. 82
- *Assessments,* pp. 123–131
- *CD-ROM* • *Teacher CD-ROM*

Unit 3 Planner

Building a New Country

Unit Preview: pp. 106–111
Pacing: 3–4 Days
Vocabulary: *Words to Know*, pp. 108–109
Oral Language: *What about you?*, p. 111

The Big Question
How do people create new countries?

	Suggested Pacing: 7–8 Days	Suggested Pacing: 7–8 Days
Reading Selection	1 **Writing a Great Speech** pp. 112–125 **Genre:** Informational Text/Speeches ***A Closer Look at . . .*** *Great American Speakers*, pp. 118–119	2 **One Hot Summer in Philadelphia** pp. 126–137 **Genre:** Informational Text/ Social Studies
Oral Language	**More About the Big Question, p. T114** *Why do people make speeches when new countries are being formed?*	**More About the Big Question, p. T128** *Why was life so hard in the early days of our country?*
Vocabulary	**Key Words:** colonies, crown, adversary, taxes, liberty, representation **Academic Words:** contract, compensate **Other Academic Word:** document	**Key Words:** delegates, confidential, privy, secrecy, merchants, tailors, cobblestone, curious **Academic Words:** individual; legal **Other Academic Word:** evidence
Phonics Word Analysis Fluency	**Phonics:** *R*-Controlled: *ar*, *or*, *ore*, p. 120 **Fluency:** Read for Speed and Accuracy, p. 121	**Phonics:** Consonant Diagraphs: *ch*, *sh*, and *th*, p. 132 **Fluency:** Look Ahead, p. 133
Comprehension	**Reading Strategy:** Compare and Contrast, pp. 114, 117 **Learning Strategy:** Outline, p. 122 **Comprehension Skill:** Compare and Contrast, p. 122 **Graphic Organizer:** Venn Diagram, p. 123	**Reading Strategy:** Identify Main Idea and Details, pp. 128, 131 **Learning Strategy:** Summarize, p. 134 **Comprehension Skill:** Main Idea and Details, p. 134 **Graphic Organizer:** Main Idea and Details Chart, p. 135
Grammar and Writing	**Grammar:** Subject-Verb Agreement, p. 124 **Writing:** Write a Persuasive Speech, Writing Checklist, Spelling Tip, p. 125	**Grammar:** Letters, p. 136 **Writing:** Write a Persuasive Letter, Writing Checklist, Spelling Tip, p. 137
	Differentiated Instruction pp. T113, T115, T117, T119, T125	**Differentiated Instruction** pp. T127, T129, T131, T137

Teaching Resources

- *Assessments*, pp. 53–64, pp. 123–132
- *Practice Book*, pp. 55–80
- *Phonics and Word Analysis Workbook*
- *Phonics and Word Analysis Teacher's Guide w/Audio CD*
- *Phonics Flashcards*
- *Posters*
- *Teacher's Resource Book* Lesson Plans, pp. 26–37
- *Audio CD*
- *DVD*
- *Teacher's CD-ROM*
- *CD-ROM*
- *Phonetic Storybooks*
- *Penguin Young Readers Library*

Suggested Pacing: 7–8 Days

3 One Out of Many

pp. 138–151

Genre: Literature/Play

More About the Big Question, p. 140

How did we create one country out of many colonies?

Key Words: surrender, veteran, republic, federal, separate, legislature
Academic Words: convention, debate
Other Academic Word: issue

Word Analysis: Synonyms and Antonyms, p. 146
Fluency: Read with Expression, p. 147

Reading Strategy: Make Inferences, pp. 140, 145
Learning Strategy: Retell, p. 148
Comprehension Skill: Make Inferences, p. 148
Graphic Organizer: 5 W Chart, p. 149

Grammar: Commas in a Series, p. 150
Writing: Write a Historical Speech, Writing Checklist, Spelling Tip, p. 151

Differentiated Instruction
pp. T139, T141, T143, T145, T151

Suggested Pacing: 1–2 Days

Bonus Reading

The Real Soldier

pp. 152–157

Genre: Literature/Historical Fiction

More About the Big Question, p. T152

What can young people do to help a new country?

Vocabulary: colony, rule, militia, Minutemen, Redcoats, camp, relieved, proud

Differentiated Instruction
p. T153

Further Reading

The Swiss Family Robinson, Johann Wyss
In this Penguin Young Reader® adaptation of the classic story, a shipwrecked family builds a new home on a tropical island and learns how to live in a new land.

The First Thanksgiving, Jean Craighead George
From the formation of Plymouth Rock to the Pilgrims' friendship with Squanto, readers learn about the first Thanksgiving.

Ben and Me: A New and Astonishing Life of Benjamin Franklin as Written by His Good Mouse Amos, Robert Lawson
This tale of Ben Franklin told by his mouse friend, Amos, tells of the patriot's great contributions to the American people.

Suggested Pacing: 1–2 Days

Assessment

The Big Question

Evidence of Understanding

How do people create new countries?

Check Up pp. 115, 129, 141, 143
Think It Over pp. 117, 131, 145
Activity To Do! p. 119
Extension pp. 123, 135, 149

Unit Wrap Up pp. 158–159

Written
Biography; Letter; Report

Oral
Speech; Skit; Presentation

Visual/Active
Collage; Brochure; Diorama

Learning Checklist
Word Analysis and Phonics; Comprehension; Grammar and Writing; Self-Evaluation Questions

STEP 1: Introduce

Students will learn about building a new country. Lead a class discussion to brainstorm a list of things a new country needs.

Unit Content Students practice reading and comprehension skills, such as compare and contrast, identifying main idea and details, summarizing, and making inferences. They apply academic language strategies such as retelling, outlining, and summarizing.

Visual Literacy

Illustrations Tell students that the illustrations on these pages give clues for three stories they will read about how our government began. Ask about their prior knowledge of government.

STEP 2: Build Background

The Big Question

Explain to students that the United States was formed over 200 years ago when government leaders wrote new laws, called a constitution, that the original 13 colonies agreed to follow.

SAY *The Big Question is* How do people create new countries? *You can look at forming a new country in the same way you look at forming a new group.*

- *Have you ever joined a group? Did you have to set up rules for the group?*
- *What rules do you think helped the group the most?*
- *If you were in favor of a particular rule, how did you get others to agree with you?*

Have students fill out a Predictions Chart and use their prior knowledge of government and famous leaders.

What I Predict	What Happens
Leaders give speeches about how to improve the country.	People decide to seek independence.
People meet at a convention to make laws.	
All the leaders agree on the new constitution.	

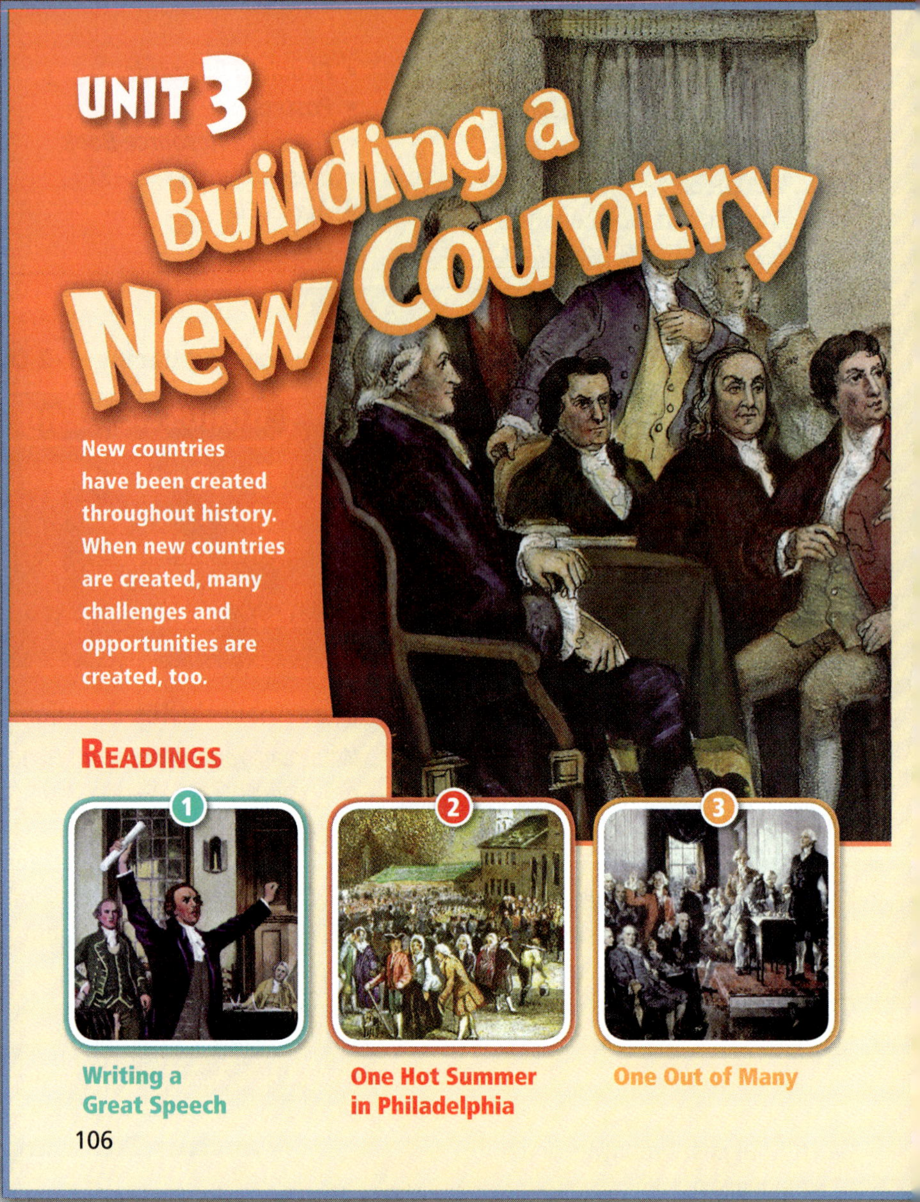

UNIT 3

Building a New Country

New countries have been created throughout history. When new countries are created, many challenges and opportunities are created, too.

READINGS

1 Writing a Great Speech

2 One Hot Summer in Philadelphia

3 One Out of Many

106

TESOL Standards

Goal 1, Standard 2 —To use English to communicate in social settings: Students will interact in, through, and with spoken and written English for personal expression and enjoyment.

Descriptors—Sharing social and cultural traditions and values; Expressing personal needs, feelings, and ideas.

The Big Question

How do people create new countries?

Listening and Speaking

You will talk about how people celebrate the creation of a new country.

Writing

You will write a speech that persuades someone to agree with you or to take action.

Bonus Reading

The Real Soldier

Quick Write

What do you know about the early history of the United States or your home country? Write down five facts.

Differentiated Instruction	
Beginning	Have students find the words *new country* in the unit title. Ask them to write down the Big Question.
Early Intermediate	Point to a picture of each of the readings on p. 106 and ask students what they see: *speech*, *meeting*, *leader*, *crowd of people*.
Intermediate	Encourage students to look at the pictures and make inferences about the content of the readings. Have them discuss with partners and present a short summary to the class.
Struggling Reader	Ask students to look at the picture on p. 107 and point to the man standing. Write the name *George Washington* on the board. Have students repeat the name and write it down.

STEP 3: Connect

Listening and Speaking

Have volunteers describe the traditions or activities that take place when people celebrate the creation of their home countries.

Writing

Read the text in the Writing box aloud to students.

SAY *Imagine that you have complained to a neighbor about his dog that barks at night.*

- *How can you convince the dog owner that the barking is unfair to the neighbors?*
- *How could you work with other neighbors to talk to the dog owner?*

Have students write a speech to convince the dog owner to do something about the barking.

Quick Write

Have students look at the illustrations on pp. 106–107 and write five facts they know about the early history of United States or their home countries. Ask students to write a complete sentence for each fact.

Possible Responses

- George Washington was the first president of United States.
- Philadelphia was an important city.
- People came from many countries to settle in the American colonies.

Adapt the Activity

Have students pick one of the five facts they listed in the Quick Write activity and write a paragraph with a main idea and supporting details about the fact. Encourage students to research more about the topic to complete their paragraphs.

Visual Literacy

Graphic Organizer Introduce the Big Question transparency and use it throughout the unit to help students connect the readings to the Big Question.

STEP 1: Introduce

Unit Vocabulary

Use these pages to help students identify some terms used to describe the building of a new country. Post your Words to Know poster for this unit in the classroom. As students read the unit, reinforce the unit vocabulary by using the Vocabulary Cards provided as a Blackline Master in the *Teacher's Resource Book* as flash cards or in memory games.

STEP 2: Teach

Words to Know

Point to the pictures in section 1 that show the things needed for a new country. Say each word aloud. Point to each icon again and have students say the word that names each picture.

Introduce the names of countries in section 2 by pointing to each picture of a flag and and having volunteers find each country on a world map.

Academic Words

Discuss the definitions for *culture* and *immigrate* with students. Share the following context sentences with students. Have students add the terms to their personal thesaurus.

culture customs and beliefs of people who live in the same area or practice the same religion

immigrate permanently move from the country where you were born to live in another country

We learned more about the *culture* of the country when we lived there.

People from all over the world *immigrate* to the United States every day.

Have students discuss prior knowledge of other cultures and describe how they learned about them.

Teaching Resources

- ***Teacher's Resource Book,*** pp. 93–94, 169
- ***Posters***
- ***Transparencies,*** pp. 13–18
- ***CD-ROM*** • ***Audio CD***

What Do You Know about Building a New Country?

Words to Know

1. Use these words to talk about a new country.

 laws
 currency
 flag
 government
 citizens
 language

2. Where do people come from?

People come from ______________ .

 India
 Mexico
 China
 Nigeria
 Ireland
 Colombia

108

TESOL Standards

Goal 1, Standard 3—To use English to communicate in social settings: Students will use learning strategies to extend their communicative competence.
Descriptors—Testing hypotheses about language; Listening to and imitating how others use English; Exploring alternative ways of saying things; Using context to construct meaning; Comparing verbal and nonverbal cues.

3. What does a new country need?

A new country needs ____________ to ____________ .

control traffic

trade

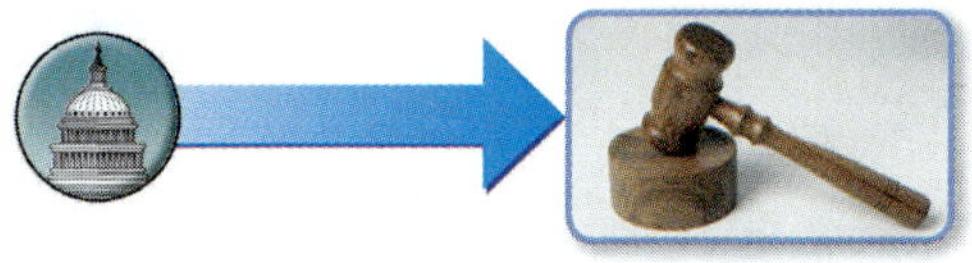

make laws

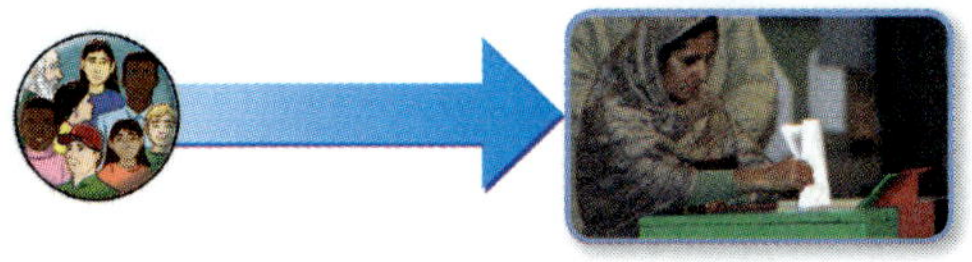

vote

4. Use these words to talk about country symbols.

bird | national anthem | flower | landmarks

Differentiated Instruction

Beginning	Say aloud, but out of order, the words in section 1 that describe a new country. Have students point to the appropriate picture and pronounce each word.
Early Intermediate	Have students look at the words for a new country on p. 108. Ask students to find the matching picture on p. 109, then write the word and the phrase as a short sentence.
Intermediate	Ask students to look at the words in section 1 and match them with the correct phrase on p. 109. Have students write the four complete sentences using the correct word and phrase.
Struggling Reader	Have students look at the pictures on p. 108 of flags of different countries. Have students find the country of each flag on a world map.

Explain the Captions

Read the captions in section 3 aloud and have the class repeat them as they examine the pictures. Have students complete the sentence stem with the word from section 1 and the correct caption.

Have students write their own sentences using the words from section 1 with a different ending to the sentence.

STEP 3: Practice

Use Vocabulary

Build Discussion Help students use the words and pictures in section 4 to learn more about other countries. Discuss what other things could be symbols, such as flags. Have students select two countries from section 2 and compare and contrast important symbols for each country. Encourage students to use the Internet for their research. Have students fill in a Venn Diagram like the one shown below.

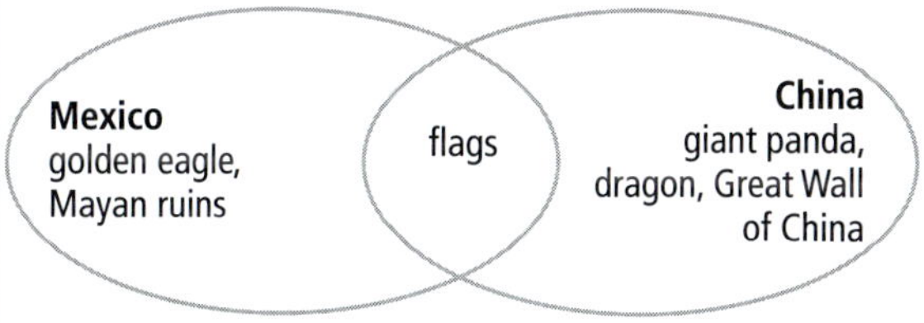

Scaffolding

Lead a class discussion about the historical landmarks they have visited. Explain the landmark can be something famous like the Statue of Liberty or a local historical landmark. Have students work in small groups to research one landmark and write a brief report.

Link to Social Studies

The Star Spangled Banner Many people think the Star Spangled Banner was written during the American Revolution. It was actually written during the War of 1812. Francis Scott Key wrote the words for the song in one day after a fierce battle with the British. Find the lyrics to the song, and ask students to discuss the symbolism used to describe the American flag.

STEP 1: Introduce

Unit Background

The peer mini-autobiographies and accompanying exercises are designed to model how students can talk and write about celebrations in other countries. Use the exercises below to elicit students' prior knowledge, opinions, and ideas to help them tell their own stories about independence celebrations.

STEP 2: Monitor Progress

Comprehension Check

Diego

1. Where is Diego from? Diego is from Mexico City, Mexico.
2. What is *El Grito*? *El Grito* is the celebration of Mexican independence from Spain.
3. How do people in Mexico celebrate this day? People decorate every plaza in Mexico City with beautiful lights. They sell flags, sombreros and food in the streets.

Trinidad

1. In which country does Trinidad live? Trinidad lives in Trinidad.
2. What does her country celebrate on this day? Her country celebrates its independence from the United Kingdom.
3. What happens on Independence Day in Trinidad? There are many parades and street festivals.

Link to Social Studies

Map Skills Draw students' attention to the map of the world in the background of these pages. Have students follow the lines from the photos of each student and the celebration they enjoy to the location on the map. Ask students to say the name of each country aloud.

Teaching Resources
- *Audio CD*

Your Stories about Building a New Country

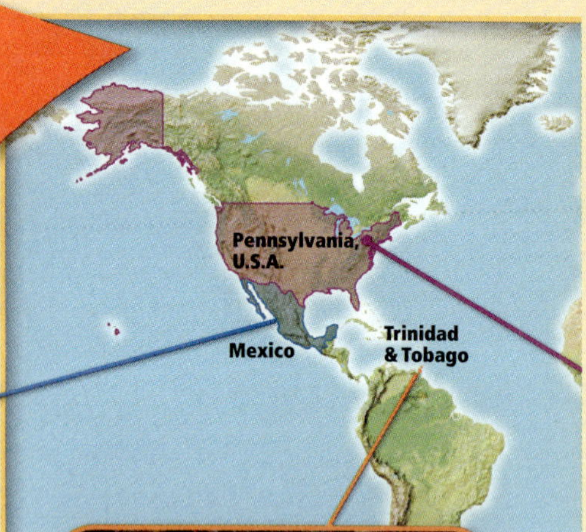

I live in Mexico City, Mexico. I love to walk around the plazas on El Grito, which is September 16. El Grito is the celebration of Mexico's independence from Spain. People decorate every plaza in Mexico City with beautiful lights. They sell flags, sombreros, and food in the streets.

I live in Trinidad. My parents named me Trinidad because I was born on August 31. That's the day that my country celebrates its independence from the United Kingdom. There are many parades and street festivals on Independence Day. It feels as if the whole country is celebrating my birthday!

110

TESOL Standards

Goal 1, Standard 2—To use English to communicate in social settings: Students will interact in, through, and with spoken and written English for personal expression and enjoyment.

Descriptors—Sharing social and cultural traditions and values; Expressing personal needs, feelings, and ideas.

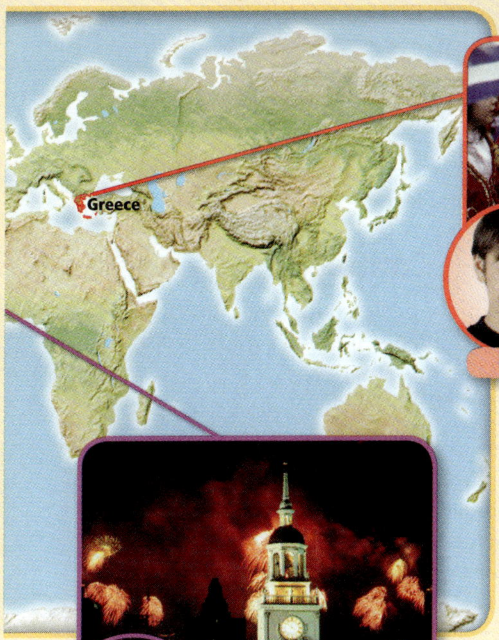

Ezio

In Greece, we celebrate Independence Day on March 25. Greece became an independent country on March 25, 1821. I am learning traditional Greek dances at school so that I can join the Independence Day festival in my town next year. I am excited to help my community celebrate this special day!

Andie

I live in Philadelphia, Pennsylvania. My city is sometimes called the birthplace of the United States because the U.S. Declaration of Independence was signed here in 1776. Each year on July 4, we have parades and fireworks to celebrate this special day.

What about you?

1. Does your home country celebrate its independence? How do you celebrate?
2. How are these students' stories similar to yours?
3. Do you have a story to tell about your country's independence day? Tell your story!

111

Sharing Language and Culture

Global Perspective Students might have knowledge of other national celebrations in the United States or in other countries. Encourage students to talk about these celebrations and what happens on these days. Encourage students to discuss the meaning of the ceremonies and symbolic objects used in those celebrations.

Accelerate Language Development

Idioms Students may be unfamiliar with words that often go together in English. For instance, *to give a speech*, *to make a law* and *to wave a flag* would be similar if we translated these terms into Spanish: *dar un discurso*, *hacer una ley*, and *ondear una bandera*. However, *to pass a law* in Spanish would be *aprobar una ley* ("approve" a law).

Andie

1. Where does Andie live? Andie lives in Philadelphia, Pennsylvania.
2. Why is her city also called the birthplace of the United States? The Declaration of Independence was signed there in 1776.
3. How do people in Pennsylvania celebrate July 4? They have parades and fireworks to celebrate Independence Day.

Ezio

1. Where is Ezio from? He is from Greece.
2. When do Greek people celebrate Independence Day? They celebrate Independence Day on March 25.
3. Why is Ezio learning traditional Greek dances? He is learning traditional Greek dances to join the Independence Day festival in his town next year.
4. Why is he excited? He is excited about helping his community celebrate this special day.

Study Skills

Internet Invite students to choose one of the countries in the stories on pp. 110–111. Have them research one fact about that country on the Internet.

STEP 3: Assess

What About You?

1. Have students discuss how they celebrate Independence Day.
2. Have students talk about the stories on these pages. Ask them to talk about similarities and differences as they compare the stories to their own experiences.
3. Have students tell about the country they are from or research another country's Independence Day.

Writing Fluency Ask students to write a story using the peer stories in pp. 110–111 as models. Have students present their stories in small groups.

STEP 1: Introduce

Key Words

Help students learn the skill of defining words by using context.

SAY *The vocabulary words for* Writing a Great Speech *are shown in the Words in Context selection. The pictures help us learn what the words mean.*

Have students find each key word and connect it with its photograph.

STEP 2: Teach

Words in Context

Write the following sentences on the board. Have students complete this fill-in-the-blanks exercise using the key words.

1. *Many artists'* colonies *will offer lessons in painting and drawing.*
2. *A* crown *can be a word for a government or for the top of your head.*
3. *During the war, we knew an* adversary *was spying on us.*
4. *We pay* taxes *so the government can improve the country.*
5. *People in the United States have the* liberty *to pursue their dreams.*
6. *People want honest* representation *when they elect someone to the government.*

Study Skills

Dictionary Have students look up their words in the dictionary to see if the Words in Context definitions were correct.

Online Dictionary Students can look up words using an online dictionary or the CD that accompanies a learner's dictionary, like the *Longman Basic Dictionary*.

www.LongmanCornerstone.com

Teaching Resources

- ***Practice Book***, pp. 55–56
- ***Transparencies***, pp. 43–45
- ***CD-ROM*** • ***Audio CD***

Reading 1

Writing a Great Speech

Vocabulary

Writing a Great Speech **is about great speakers and great speeches.**

Key Words

- colonies
- crown
- adversary
- taxes
- liberty
- representation

Words in Context

1 Some of the earliest British **colonies** in North America were Virginia, Massachusetts, New Hampshire, and Maryland.

1
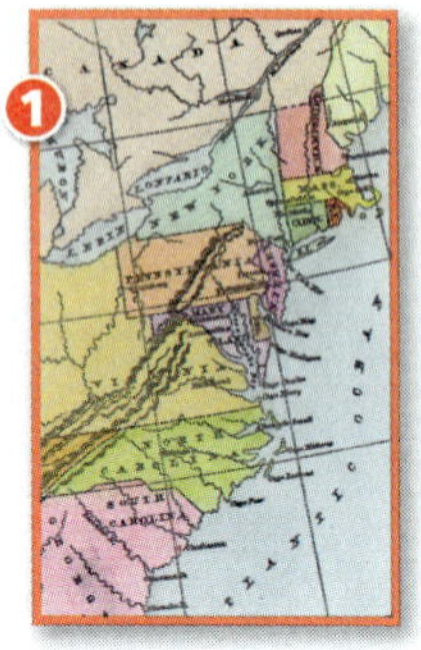

2 American colonists often spoke of the British **crown**. They used this word to mean the British government — not just what kings and queens wore on their heads!

2

3 Bruce was not worried, even though his **adversary** in the boxing ring was much taller than he was.

3

112

TESOL Standards

Goal 1, Standard 3—To use English to communicate in social settings: Students will use learning strategies to extend their communicative competence.
Descriptors—Testing hypotheses about language; Listening to and imitating how others use English; Exploring alternative ways of saying things; Using context to construct meaning.

Goal 2, Standard 2—To use English to achieve academically in all content areas: Students will use English to obtain, process, construct, and provide subject matter information in spoken and written form.
Descriptor—Understanding and producing technical vocabulary and text features according to content area.

Goal 2, Standard 3—To use English to achieve academically in all content areas: Students will use appropriate learning strategies to construct and apply academic knowledge.
Descriptor—Using context to construct meaning.

④ April 15 is the day Americans must pay their income **taxes** to the U.S. government and their state governments.

⑤ This statue is a symbol of **liberty**, or freedom, all over the world.

⑥ In the United States, the voters elect people to give them **representation** in the government.

Practice

Use each key word in a sentence.

Make Connections

People pay taxes to provide money for the government. What are some kinds of taxes that people pay? What does the government do with the money?

Academic Words

contract
legal agreement between two or more people

compensate
pay or reward

Practice Book pages 55–56

Differentiated Instruction

Beginning	Lead students in pronouncing each key word. Read aloud a short phrase from the context sentence that includes the key word and have students repeat the phrase.
Intermediate	Ask students to complete the following sentence: *The phrase* British crown *can mean the* ________ *or what kings and queens* ________.
Greater Challenge	Have volunteers write a new context sentence for each key word. Ask them to read aloud their sentences leaving out the key word, and ask a partner to fill in the key word.
Standard English Learner CRI	Choose a key word to use for a game of "Give One, Get One." Then have students swap synonyms with each other until they have at least three new words.

Visual Literacy

Illustrations Have students use their own words and the appropriate key word to describe what they see in each photo.

Academic Words

Discuss the definitions of *contract* and *compensate* with the students. Explain that a *contract* is a promise. Explain that *compensate* means to reward someone for work that was completed. Share the following context sentences with students:

> When she signed the *contract*, she became the new president of the company.
>
> She will *compensate* her employees for their help with the new project.

Have students work in pairs to discuss how the two academic words have meanings that are important in government and making laws.

Other Academic Words

Provide students with another example of a word that is important in law and government. Tell students that a *document* is written proof or information about something. A contract is one type of document. Explain to students that the word can be used as a noun or a verb.

> The *document* explained all the steps for creating a music library.
>
> The best way to *document* the event is to use a video camera.

STEP 3: Practice

Flexible Grouping You may assign these exercises as a whole class discussion, partner activity, or individual writing assignment.

Make Connections

Writing Fluency Have students write a paragraph that explains why paying taxes is important. Have students connect their writing to the Big Question for this unit by explaining how taxes help people create new countries. Encourage them to mention that the government uses tax money to pay for education, medical assistance, and new roads.

STEP 1: Introduce

More About The Big Question

The Big Question for this selection is designed to stress the importance of speeches that help form a new country.

SAY *We are going to learn why people make speeches. Think of a speech you may have heard before.*

- *What was the purpose of the speech?*
- *Who was listening to the speech?*
- *What did you learn from the speech?*

Have students fill in a Main Idea and Details Chart like the one shown below about a speech they gave or heard before.

The soldiers who died at Gettysburg

Our government believes all men are created equal.	The Civil War may end our government.	The government must continue to honor the soldiers.

STEP 2: Teach

Reading Strategy

Compare and Contrast Students should compare and contrast their own opinions with those of the speaker before they agree or disagree with the speech.

Read aloud the bulleted questions on p. 114. Have students preview the speeches on pp. 116–117 then discuss what they think they are about.

Understand Text Structure

Draw students' attention to the genre label for informational text. The first part of the reading explains how to make a great speech. The second part shows two speeches from the American Revolution.

Teaching Resources

- *Teacher's Resource Book*, pp. 115–116
- *Practice Book*, pp. 57–58
- *CD-ROM*
- *Audio CD*

Reading 1

INFORMATIONAL TEXT

Speeches

The Big Question

Why do people make speeches when new countries are being formed?

Reading Strategy

Compare and Contrast

When you compare, you look for ways in which things are similar. When you contrast, you look for ways in which things are different.

- How are the themes of the speeches similar or different?
- What do the two speeches want their audiences to do?

Writing a Great Speech

by Dan Ahearn

Dr. Martin Luther King, Jr.'s *I Have a Dream* speech was one of the most famous speeches in U.S. history. The theme of King's speech spoke for itself.

First, pick a theme you care about. Be specific. The theme "freedom" is too general. "What freedom means to me" is more specific. Then, think about why you want to give the speech. Do you want people to take action? Do you want people to agree with you? Look for true stories about your theme. These stories will show how your ideas work in real life.

Finally, learn about your audience. What do they already know? What would you like them to learn?

theme main idea

specific detailed and exact

audience people listening or watching

Dr. Martin Luther King, Jr. gave one of the most famous speeches in U.S. history.

114

TESOL Standards

Goal 2, Standard 2—To use English to achieve academically in all content areas: Students will use English to obtain, process, construct, and provide subject matter information in spoken and written form.

Descriptors—Comparing and contrasting information; Listening to, speaking, reading, and writing about subject matter information; Selecting, connecting, and explaining information; Analyzing, synthesizing, and inferring from information

A speech should have a beginning, a middle, and an end. Make sure each part helps the audience follow your ideas.

The beginning is important. A good beginning gives the speech's theme. The beginning of the speech should also fit the theme. A joke at the start of a speech may not go with a serious theme. A good beginning makes people interested in what you have to say. It will stay in a listener's mind.

The middle of the speech explains your theme. It gives reasons and facts. It should have a true story or a real-life example of your theme.

The ending tells your theme again in a new way. In a few words, connect the theme to your facts. Keep your purpose in mind. End your speech by asking the audience to take action or agree with your ideas.

---

example something that helps explain or support a general idea

purpose goal or result

A good speech keeps your audience interested.

Check Up What is one difference between a good speech and a bad speech?

115

Build Vocabulary

Direct attention to the highlighted words in the text with definitions at the bottom of the page.

- Invite volunteers to read aloud the word and the definition.
- Have students write a context sentence using the word.
- Have students repeat this activity for each highlighted word as they read the selection.

Link to Literature Dr. Martin Luther King, Jr.'s *I Have A Dream* speech used many of the same literary devices that great writing does. He compared Abraham Lincoln's Emancipation Proclamation to "a great beacon light of hope". Encourage students to read all or part of King's speech. Discuss the metaphors and figurative language King used to communicate his ideas.

Read Aloud

Have volunteers take turns reading aloud each paragraph on pp. 114–115. Explain to students that the quality of speech depends on how well the audience understands it and if they remain interested. Tell them the purpose of the speech is to convince the audience to agree with the speaker's opinion.

STEP 3: Assess

Check Up

Before reading the two speeches on pp. 116–117, tell students to make a list of all the things necessary for a good speech that they just learned.

Differentiated Instruction

Beginning	Have students look at the photo on p. 114. Tell students this is a photo of a very famous man. Help students read the name aloud from the caption.
Early Intermediate	Have students fill in the blanks: *Martin Luther King, Jr. gave a famous ________, and it was called ________.*
Intermediate	Ask students to reread pp. 114–115. Have them work with partners to make a list of all the elements that a good speech should have.
Struggling Reader	Have students repeat the following words: *great leader, famous speech.* Demonstrate a person giving a speech. Have students draw and label a picture of a person giving a speech.

STEP 1: Monitor Progress

Comprehension Check

Prepare for a Speech After students have read the speech *Independence Now . . . or Never,* guide students in a class discussion to learn more about the speech using the 5 W Questions:

- *Who wrote the speech?*
- *What is the theme of the speech?*
- *When does the author want independence?*
- *Why did the author want to give this speech?*
- *Why are the taxes paid to King George unfair?*
- *What does the author want the audience to do?*

Structure of a Speech Discuss the structure of the speech by helping students identify the *beginning, middle, and ending*. Ask students to explain how they know which part of the speech they have identified. Then ask:

- *Which sentence expresses the theme of the speech ?* The colonies must be free of the British Crown.
- *What part of the beginning of the speech got you interested?* Taxes are not fair.
- *Which sentences form the middle part of the speech?* The sentences that list the complaints about taxes and troops.
- *What lines are the ending of the text?* The last three sentences in which the speechwriter tells people what to do.

Link to Social Studies

Patrick Henry and the American Revolution During the late 18th century, American colonists began to demand independence from the British crown. Some prominent colonists like Patrick Henry and Samuel Adams gave important speeches against King George, who was the head of the British government.

Have students research speeches by these two men, select an important part of one speech that expresses its theme, and present it to the class.

Speeches

Boston, Massachusetts, July 1776

INDEPENDENCE NOW . . . OR NEVER!

by Abigail Smith

The colonies must be free of the British crown. Why? The taxes we pay to King George are not fair. He taxes everything, even the news! We do not get anything for what we pay! The king takes away our liberty. We have no representation in England. The king will not even let us pick our own leaders in America. He sends troops to make us do as we are told. You and your family must let these armed men live in your house. Under this king, even your life is not yours. King George is making war against us. British soldiers killed unarmed people in Boston. They might kill you next time. Take action! We do not need a king! We want independence now!

---

troops soldiers

unarmed without weapons

independence freedom of action and choice

Patrick Henry said, "Give me liberty or give me death" in his famous speech.

116

TESOL Standards

Goal 2, Standard 2—To use English to achieve academically in all content areas: Students will use English to obtain, process, construct, and provide subject matter information in spoken and written form

Descriptors—Comparing and contrasting information; Listening to, speaking, reading, and writing about subject matter information; Selecting, connecting, and explaining information; Analyzing, synthesizing, and inferring from information.

WE ARE PART OF THE EMPIRE

by Nathan Powell

We need to stay with England. King George is our only chance. The king is not your adversary. We need him. We are British. The taxes we pay are fair. They pay for our defense. Yes, there have been mistakes. But King George took care of these problems. We no longer pay a tax on our papers. We need British troops to protect us. They protect us from people like the Sons of Liberty. The Sons of Liberty were wrong to throw tea into the sea. If things quiet down, we will be left alone. With King George, our lives are safe. Without him, our lives will be very dangerous. Do not do something you will be sorry for. Believe in King George. He believes in us.

---

defense protection from invaders

Practice Book pages 57–58

Reading Strategy

Compare and Contrast

- In what ways are the two speeches similar?
- How are the two speeches different?

Think It Over

1. What is the purpose of a good speech?
2. What was the purpose of Abigail Smith's speech?
3. What is the theme of Nathan Powell's speech?
4. What do you need to know in order to write a good speech?

Differentiated Instruction

Beginning	Have students point to and pronounce the highlighted words on pp. 116–117. Have them copy each sentence with a highlighted word.
Intermediate	Have students read aloud the title of each speech and identify which speech favors, and which speech opposes, independence.
Greater Challenge	Have students write a short paragraph that explains why independence was a good idea for some colonists and a bad idea for other colonists.
Standard English Learner CRI	Tell students the picture on p. 116 shows a leader giving a famous speech. Have students select a current topic and improvise a speech to get people to take an action.

STEP 2: Teach

Visual Literacy

Captions Draw students' attention to the illustrations on pp. 116–117. Have students read the caption on p. 116. Lead a class discussion about drawing conclusions from the illustration. Have students fill in a KWL Chart with information from the discussion and then complete the chart as they read the speeches.

STEP 3: Assess

Reading Strategy

Compare and Contrast

Explain to students that the purpose of a speech is to express an opinion and have people take action based on the opinion. Have students compare and contrast the opinions and the actions each speaker wanted the people to take.

SAY *Let's compare and contrast the ways the speakers get their audiences to agree with them or to take action.*

- *Abigail Smith asks* Why? *at the beginning of her speech. She then answers her own question.*
- *Nathan Powell tries to explain the positive things King George has done.*
- *Both speeches persuade the audience to agree or to do something, but they use different strategies.*

Think It Over

Flexible Grouping You may assign this activity as a class discussion, partner activity or individual writing assignment.

Answer Key

1. A good speech should persuade people or make them take action.
2. She asked people to take action and fight for independence.
3. He explained the reasons colonists needed to stay with King George.
4. You must pick a specific theme, decide why you want to give the speech, and learn about the people who will hear it.

STEP 1: Introduce

A Closer Look

The photos on these pages are intended to demonstrate the variety of themes in famous speeches and the people who have contributed important ideas.

More About The Big Question

The Big Question for the A Closer Look selection also focuses on the reasons people want to give speeches. Have students examine the visuals and read the captions on pp. 118–119. Lead a class discussion on giving speeches.

SAY *Think about the different speeches you have heard in the past. They may have been speeches by classmates, leaders of the community, or our government leaders.*

- *What kinds of speeches have you heard?*
- *Did a speech ever convince you to take action for a cause?*
- *What topic could inspire you to make a speech?*

Have students select two speakers and write a paragraph that describes what each speaker intended when making their speeches. Have students compare and contrast the topics for each speaker.

Make Connections

Writing Fluency Have students think about a topic that interests them and ask them to write a short speech. Encourage them to pick a topic they think is important, think about who they are giving the speech to, and what they want people to learn or do.

A Closer Look at...

Great American Speakers and Speeches

Abraham Lincoln ▶
Abraham Lincoln gave his *Gettysburg Address* on November 19, 1863. It remains one of the greatest speeches in American history.

▲ Frederick Douglass
Frederick Douglass was a prominent African American author and speaker. His speech, *What to the Slave is the 4th of July?* inspired many people to question their beliefs about equality.

César Chávez ▶
César Chávez was a Mexican American labor leader and civil rights activist. His speeches inspired thousands to work for the fair treatment of migrant workers.

▲ Maya Angelou
Poet Maya Angelou moved many people when she read her poem *On the Pulse of the Morning* during President Bill Clinton's inauguration in 1993.

118

TESOL Standards

Goal 2, Standard 3—To use English to achieve academically in all content areas: Students will use appropriate learning strategies to construct and apply academic knowledge.

Descriptors—Focusing attention selectively; Applying basic reading comprehension skills such as skimming, scanning, previewing, and reviewing text; Using context to construct meaning; Taking notes to record important information and aid one's own learning; Applying self-monitoring and self-corrective strategies to build and expand a knowledge base; Planning how and when to use cognitive strategies and applying them appropriately to a learning task.

Goal 3, Standard 1—To use English in socially and culturally appropriate ways: Students will use the appropriate language variety, register, and genre according to audience, purpose, and setting.

Descriptors—Recognizing and using standard English and vernacular dialects appropriately; Using a variety of writing styles appropriate for different audiences, purposes, and settings.

Sojourner Truth
A former slave, Sojourner Truth became a civil rights activist. Her most famous speech, *Ain't I a Woman?*, was delivered in 1851 at a women's rights convention in Akron, OH.

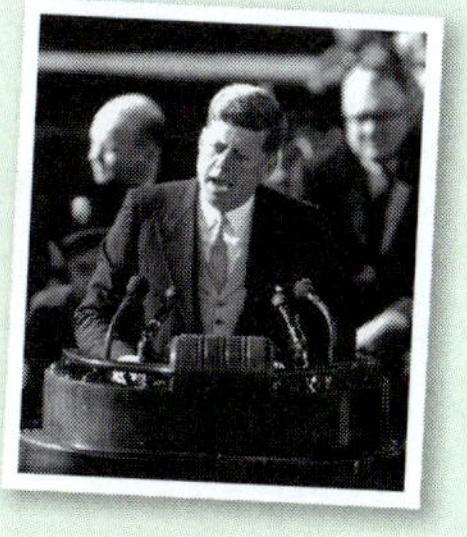

John F. Kennedy
In his inaugural speech in 1961, President John F. Kennedy inspired Americans to become active citizens. He said, "Ask not what your country can do for you; ask what you can do for your country."

Eleanor Roosevelt
Eleanor Roosevelt was a delegate to the United Nations General Assembly. She chaired the committee that wrote and approved the Universal Declaration of Human Rights.

Barack Obama
Barack Obama gave an important speech at the 2004 Democratic National Convention. The speech made him one of the most popular politicians in the nation.

Activity to Do!

On these pages, you learned about great speakers in American history.

- Choose a speaker.
- Research the speaker.
- Create two pages, using pictures and words, to tell about that speaker.

119

Differentiated Instruction

Beginning	Ask students to find the name of a famous person in the captions and say each name in this sentence stem: ________ *gave a famous speech.*
Early Intermediate	Have students make a two-column list of men and women from the pictures on pp. 118–119.
Intermediate	Have students work in pairs to look up the meaning of these caption words: *inauguration*, *delegate*, *activist*, *prominent*, *migrant workers*.
Struggling Reader	Ask students to point to the photograph of each famous person as you say the name aloud. Have students repeat each name and the phrase *is a leader*.

STEP 2: Teach

Visual Literacy

Illustrations and Captions Ask students to look at the photos of famous speakers. Have them discuss what can be learned about what topics were important at the time the they gave their speeches.

SAY *Look at the photos on pages 118 and 119 and read each caption.*

- *Do you recognize any of the speakers and have any prior knowledge about them?*
- *What do the speakers shown on these pages all have in common?*
- *Which speakers gave speeches that were related to human rights and equality?*
- *Which speaker made one of the greatest speeches in American history, and what was the purpose of the speech?*

Have students select one speaker and write a descriptive paragraph about the purpose of his or her speech. Encourage students to use their prior knowledge and their answers to the previous questions when they write their descriptions.

STEP 3: Assess

Activity to Do!

Study Skills Ask students to choose one of the people shown on pp. 118–119 and use the Internet to find out more about that person. Tell them to imagine they are planning to write an article about the speaker and should answer the following questions about the speaker they chose:

- When did this person live?
- Where did this person live?
- Why did this person want to give a speech?
- What fact about this person's life is interesting to you?

Ask volunteers to take turns reporting aloud to the class what they found out about the person they chose.

STEP 1: Introduce

Phonics

R*-controlled words *ar, or, ore Explain to students that the letters *ar, or,* and *ore* have a special sound when pronounced together in a word.

STEP 2: Teach

Ask students to look at the list of words on p. 120 that shows how the sound of each word changes when the vowel is followed with an *r.* Ask students to say aloud each word in the second box.

Draw students' attention to the Rule Box on the page.

SAY *The letters* ar *usually have the vowel sound in* arm. *The letters* or *and* ore *usually have the vowel sound in* torn. *When an* r *follows a vowel, the vowel is pronounced as a soft vowel.*

STEP 3: Practice

Answer Key

1. same
2. same
3. different
4. different
5. different
6. same

Reteach

Have students work with partners. Ask them to take turns reading the list of words below and discuss whether the words have the same vowel sound. Have students review the examples of each vowel followed by *-r.* Ask students to suggest other words that use the /ar/, /or/, and /ore/ sounds.

- farm, alarm, harm, swarm
- born, storm
- sore, core

Teaching Resources
- ***Practice Book,*** p. 59
- ***Phonics Workbook***
- ***Phonics Flashcards***
- ***CD-ROM*** • ***Audio CD***

Reading 1

Phonics & Fluency

Phonics

R-controlled: *ar, or, ore*

Read each pair of words. Notice how the letter *r* changes the vowel sound.

am	ton	toe
arm	torn	tore

Here are more words with an *r* after a vowel. Read them aloud.

far	or
hard	for
dark	more

Rule Box

The letters ***ar*** usually have the vowel sound in ***arm***.
The letters ***or*** and ***ore*** usually have the vowel sound in ***torn***.

Practice

Work with a partner. Take turns.

- Read each pair of words.
- Tell whether the words have the same vowel sound.

1. arm, park
2. more, form
3. car, rack
4. care, George
5. sure, soar
6. bore, floor

Practice Book page 59

120

TESOL Standards

Goal 1, Standard 3 —To use English to communicate in social settings: Students will use learning strategies to extend their communicative competence.

Descriptors—Listening to and imitating how others use English; Self-monitoring and self-evaluating language development; Practicing new language; Focusing attention selectively.

Goal 3, Standard 3—To use English in socially and culturally appropriate ways: Students will use appropriate learning strategies to extend their sociolinguistic and sociocultural competence.

Descriptors—Observing and modeling how others speak and behave in a particular situation or setting; Experimenting with variations of language in social and academic settings; Seeking information about appropriate language use and behavior.

Fluency

Read for Speed and Accuracy

You should read quickly. But never read so quickly that you lose your understanding.

Practice

Read for one minute.	Count the words you read.	Study any hard words.	Read and count again.

We need to stay with England. King George is our only 11
chance. The king is not your adversary. We need him. 21
We are British. The taxes we pay are fair. They pay for our 34
defense. Yes, there have been mistakes. But King George 43
took care of these problems. We no longer pay a tax on our 56
papers. We need British troops to protect us. They protect 66
us from people like the Sons of Liberty. The Sons of Liberty 78
were wrong to throw tea into the sea. If things quiet down, 90
we will be left alone. With King George, our lives are safe. 102
Without him, our lives will be very dangerous. Do not do 113
something you will be sorry for. Believe in King George. He 124
believes in us. 127

121

Linguistic Note

Pronunciation of the consonant *r* in *ar, or,* and *ore*. In this lesson, students study the sounds of the vowel *a* and *o* in the groups *ar, or,* and *ore*. Some regional dialects of English do not have the same pronunciation of the consonant *r* when it appears in these groups of letters. Give students an example of the way of saying the *r* in several dialects, such as a Boston accent, which substitutes an *ah* sound for *ar*.

STEP 1: Introduce

Fluency

Read for Speed and Accuracy Explain to students that when reading aloud, they should read at an appropriate speed—not too slow, or too fast. Tell students that they should also carefully pronounce each word in a sentence.

Play the audio CD for this reading to the class, asking students to listen for pacing, intonation, and expression.

STEP 2: Practice

Have students complete the exercise with partners.

- Provide pairs of students with a timer.
- Have one partner read while the other student times the student who is reading.
- Have students look at the number next to the line they last completed reading.

Students should write down their speed after the first time they read the passage.

Have students practice the words that slowed their reading speed, then reread the passage.

Link to Math

Explain to students that articles and essays for newspapers and magazines are often written to a specific word count. Tell students to use their word count number from the Practice activity and determine how long it will take them to read a 1500-word article and a 5000-word article.

STEP 3: Extend

Study Skills

Dictionary Have students work with partners to complete the following activity:

- Write down three words that were hard to pronounce from the readings.
- Look the words up in a dictionary.
- Read the sentences from the reading in which the hard words appeared, and define the difficult words
- Write new context sentences for each word.

STEP 1: Monitor Progress

Learning Strategy

Outline Explain that making an outline of a speech before you write it is the best way to organize your thoughts, focus on the main idea, and think of supporting details. Have students make an outline of one of the speeches on pp. 116–117.

STEP 2: Teach

Compare and Contrast

Tell students that when they compare, they tell how things are alike; when contrasting, they tell how things are different.

SAY *Comparing and contrasting can help you learn more about what you are reading. To start writing an outline, list ways in which two or more things are alike and different.*

- *How would you compare and contrast an orange and an apple?*
- *Why is it necessary to compare and contrast ideas in a speech?*

STEP 3: Practice

Flexible Grouping You may assign this activity as a class discussion, partner activity, or individual written assignment.

Answer Key

1. Both are vehicles, but are different sizes.
2. Both are fruits, but they have different tastes and colors.
3. Both are sports, but they have different rules and equipment.
4. Both are animals, but they have different appearances and behaviors.

Teaching Resources

- *Practice Book,* p. 60
- *Transparencies,* p. 56
- *Teacher's Resource Book,* p. 154
- *CD-ROM*

Reading 1

Comprehension

Learning Strategy

Outline

Make an outline of one of the speeches. Show your outline to a partner.

Ask your partner to respond to the Big Question for this reading.

Compare and Contrast

One way to understand the ideas you read about is to compare and contrast them. When you **compare**, you tell how two or more things are similar. When you **contrast**, you tell how two or more things are different.

Practice

Compare and contrast the items described in each pair of words.

1. car and bus
2. apple and orange
3. soccer and football
4. dog and horse

Practice Book page 60

122

TESOL Standards

Goal 2, Standard 2—To use English to achieve academically in all content areas: Students will use English to obtain, process, construct, and provide subject matter information in spoken and written form.
Descriptors—Comparing and contrasting information; Listening to, speaking, reading, and writing about subject matter information; Selecting, connecting, and explaining information; Analyzing, synthesizing, and inferring from information; Representing information visually and interpreting information presented visually.

Use a Venn Diagram

You can use a Venn Diagram to compare and contrast events or characters. Circle A represents one item. Circle B represents another. The part that overlaps represents things that are true for both.

Practice

Create a Venn Diagram to compare the speeches.

- Reread the speeches.
- Show how the speeches are similar and different.

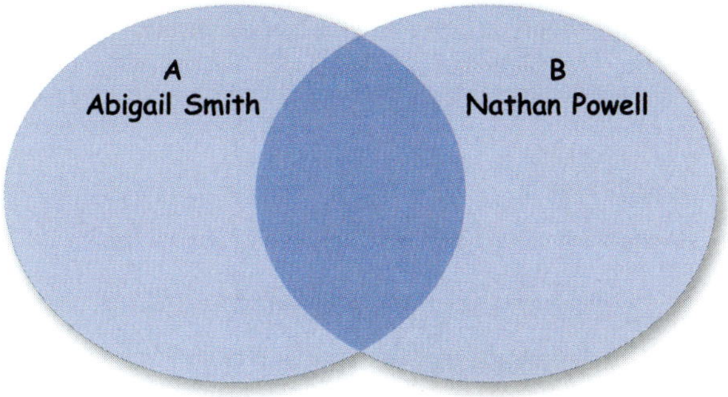

Extension

Think about a speech you have heard. Answer the 5 W Questions about the speech. Present your answers to the class using part of the speech or a visual aid.

STEP 1: Teach

Use a Venn Diagram

Ask students to make a list of things they like, such as sports, food, music, or movies. Then tell them to compare and contrast their likes with partners. Next draw a Venn Diagram on the board. Have two volunteers to come to the board and contrast and compare their likes by writing them in the diagram.

STEP 2: Practice

You may have students complete the graphic organizer provided as a Blackline Master in the *Teacher's Resource Book*.

Answer Key

A. Abigail Smith
- asks people to fight for their independence.
- says taxes are unfair and the king even taxes the news.
- says the king is sending troops to force them to do as they are told.

B. Nathan Powell
- explains the need to stay with the British Crown.
- says taxes are fair, and says the king does not tax papers any more.
- says the king sends troops to protect them.

Alike
- Both talk about taxes and troops.
- Both address the American colonists.
- Both ask people to think about the problem and make a choice.

STEP 3: Extend

Oral Presentation Ask groups of students to make speeches about an unfair situation that could involve the whole class. Ask them to review what they learned about speeches. Have students then write the 5 W Questions about the information they want to include in their speeches. Then have them prepare an outline for their speeches.

Accelerate Language Development

Adjectives of nationality

When you are talking about the nationality of a person or group of people, you should capitalize the adjective describing their nationality, such as *American*, *British*, *Chinese*, and so on. In Spanish, these adjectives are not capitalized, for example *americano, británico, chino,* and so on. The same thing happens when these words refer to a language, so English (the language) is written in lower-case in Spanish, *inglés*.

Linguistic Note

Respond For students who also speak Spanish, the word *respond* is a cognate of the Spanish word *responder* and may be familiar to them.

STEP 1: Introduce

Help students understand that all verb forms should agree with noun forms that are sentence subjects. Therefore, singular subjects need singular verbs and plural subjects need plural verbs. Remind students that every complete sentence must have a subject and a verb.

Before students begin the Practice activity, read aloud the rules and the examples on p. 124.

STEP 2: Teach

Subject-Verb Agreement

Write the following sentences on the board. Explain that when the subject is a singular noun or one of the pronouns *he*, *she*, or *it*, we should add *-s* or *-es* to the verb. Have volunteers select the correct verb in each sentence.

1. We want/wants independence.
2. He tax/taxes everything.
3. The king send/sends troops.
4. They pay/pays for our defense.
5. George take/takes care of our problems.
6. Colonialists need/needs to stay with England.

STEP 3: Practice

Before beginning the Practice activity, have students write a sentence about how they get to school each day. Ask them to underline the subject and the verb and check to see if the subject and verb are in agreement.

Answer Key

1. prepare
2. help
3. tells
4. restates
5. moves

Teaching Resources

- *Transparencies*, pp. 69–80
- *Practice Book*, pp. 61–62
- *Assessments*, pp. 53–56
- *CD-ROM*

Reading 1

Grammar & Writing

Subject-Verb Agreement

Singular subjects need singular verbs. Plural subjects need plural verbs.

Singular	A good speech **gives** the theme of the speech.
Plural	Good speeches **keep** people interested.

Rules	Examples
When the subject is a singular noun or ***he, she,*** or ***it,*** add *-s* to the verb.	The student **makes** a speech. She **makes** a speech.
When the subject is a plural noun or ***I, we, you,*** or ***they,*** do not add *-s* to the verb.	Her classmates **listen.** They **listen.**

Practice

Write each sentence. Use the correct form of the verb.

1. I ______ my speech carefully. (prepare)
2. You ______ me with the ending. (help)
3. A speech's ending ______ the theme again in a different way. (tell)
4. It ______ the theme once again. (restate)
5. A good speech ______ the audience to action. (move)

Practice Book page 61

124

TESOL Standards

Goal 2, Standard 2—To use English to achieve academically in all content areas: Students will use English to obtain, process, construct, and provide subject matter information in spoken and written form.
Descriptor—Persuading, arguing, negotiating, evaluating, and justifying.

Goal 2, Standard 3—To use English to achieve academically in all content areas: Students will use appropriate learning strategies to construct and apply academic knowledge.
Descriptors—Using context to construct meaning; Actively connecting new information-to-information previously learned; Imitating the behaviors of native English speakers to complete tasks successfully.

Goal 3, Standard 1—To use English in socially and culturally appropriate ways: Students will use the appropriate language variety, register, and genre according to audience, purpose, and setting.
Descriptors—Recognizing and using standard English and vernacular dialects appropriately; Using a variety of writing styles appropriate for different audiences, purposes, and settings; Responding to and using slang appropriately; Responding to and using idioms appropriately; Responding to and using humor appropriately; Determining when it is appropriate to use a language other than English; Determining appropriate topics for interaction.

Write a Persuasive Speech

When you write a persuasive speech, you want the audience to agree with you or to do something. Read Jose's speech. Think about the ways Jose's speech persuades.

Freedom of speech is an important right in the United States. Freedom of speech means that you have a right to say you don't like the government, and you won't be punished. It means that you can say what you think and not be afraid.

To keep freedom of speech, we need to practice it. Say what you think. Let other people say what they think. Freedom of speech is important. Keep it alive!

SPELLING TIP

When *i* and *e* appear together in a word, *i* is usually before *e*. But watch out, the exceptions can be tricky!

Practice Book page 62

Practice

Choose a theme and write a persuasive speech.

- What real-life examples might help your audience understand your theme?
- Remember, your purpose is to persuade people to do something or to agree with you.
- Give your speech a beginning, a middle, and an end.
- Read your speech aloud to a partner.

Writing Checklist

✓ Did you state your theme at the beginning of your speech?

✓ Did you use real-life examples?

✓ Did your speech persuade your partner?

125

Differentiated Instruction

Beginning	Have students choose the correct answer for the following sentences: *I exercise/exercises everyday. They learn/learns about history.*
Intermediate	Have students write two complete sentences using the correct singular or plural verb.
Greater Challenge	Make a two-column chart and write these following verbs in column 2: *learn, reads, writes, speak, runs, study*. Have students write a correct pronoun for each verb in column 1.
Standard English Learner CRI	Write the word *verb* on the board and ask students to copy it. Say *I walk*, have students repeat it, then demonstrate walking.

STEP 1: Teach

Write a Persuasive Speech

Define a persuasive speech for students.

SAY *When you want the audience to agree with you or to do something, you need to write a persuasive speech. Let's review what Jose wrote about freedom of speech.*

- *What do you think is the purpose of his speech?*
- *How did he explain clearly to the audience what he wanted them to believe?*

Spelling Tip

Write these words on the board without the underlining beneath the vowels. Ask a volunteer to come to the board and underline all the *ei* words. Then ask another volunteer to come to the board and underline all the *ie* words.

neighbor	*ceiling*	*weird*	*brief*
friend	*cashier*	*receipt*	*piece*

STEP 2: Practice

Before students write their own persuasive speeches, remind them of the importance of making an outline and using the 5 W Questions.

- Do you have a clear opening statement?
- Are you providing examples to explain the purpose of your speech?
- Do you know how to end the speech?

STEP 3: Assess

Writing Checklist

✓ Help students develop phrases that express their themes.

✓ Be sure students' speeches are based on their own lives or something they know about.

✓ Have students work in pairs to listen to each other's speeches. Remind them to be respectful of one another's efforts.

The Five Step Writing Process in the Writing Handbook reference section of this book provides more student writing instruction.

STEP 1: Introduce

Key Words

Help students define words by using context.

SAY *All the vocabulary words from* One Hot Summer in Philadelphia *are illustrated in the Words in Context selection. Let's read the passages that introduce these words and find the pictures.*

Have students find the numbered circles for each context sentence, then find the corresponding numbered photos.

STEP 2: Teach

Words in Context

Write the following sentences on the board. Have students complete this fill-in-the-blanks exercise using the key words from the Words in Context passage.

1. *Two* delegates *at the state convention live in my neighborhood.*
2. *I promised to not tell anyone the* confidential *information.*
3. *My great-grandfather built the* privy *for his family.*
4. *The club was known for its* secrecy.
5. *The* merchants *at the mall offer holiday discounts.*
6. *The* tailors *made the tuxedoes for the wedding.*
7. *Along the* cobblestone *street were oil lanterns.*
8. *My parents were* curious *about my grades.*

Study Skills

Word Roots Remind students that many English words come from Greek and Latin. *Delegate* comes from the Latin word *delegatus,* which means "to send as a representative." *Confidential* comes from the Latin word *confidentia,* which means "to trust."

Online Dictionary Students can use an online dictionary or the CD that accompanies a learners' dictionary, such as the *Longman Basic Dictionary.*

www.LongmanCornerstone.com

Teaching Resources
- ***Practice Book,*** pp. 63–64
- ***Transparencies,*** p. 44
- ***CD-ROM*** • ***Audio CD***

Reading 2

One Hot Summer in Philadelphia

Vocabulary

One Hot Summer in Philadelphia **describes what life was like in Philadelphia during the Constitutional Convention.**

Key Words
- delegates
- confidential
- privy
- secrecy
- merchants
- tailors
- cobblestone
- curious

Words in Context

1. States sent several **delegates** to represent them at the Constitutional Convention.

2. Shredding papers is one way to keep information **confidential**.

3. Long ago, most houses did not have bathrooms inside. Many people had a **privy** in their backyards.

4. Jane swore Amanda to **secrecy** about the surprise party.

126

TESOL Standards

Goal 1, Standard 3—To use English to communicate in social settings: Students will use learning strategies to extend their communicative competence.
Descriptors—Testing hypotheses about language; Listening to and imitating how others use English; Exploring alternative ways of saying things; Using context to construct meaning.

Goal 2, Standard 2—To use English to achieve academically in all content areas: Students will use English to obtain, process, construct, and provide subject matter information in spoken and written form.
Descriptor—Understanding and producing technical vocabulary and text features according to content area.

5 Some **merchants** sell their goods in street markets.

6 **Tailors** work hard to make sure people's clothes fit well.

7 **Cobblestone** streets seem bumpy compared to most streets today.

8 Sam and Sasha were **curious** about the goldfish in the bowl.

Practice

Use each key word in a sentence.

Make Connections

Have you ever visited a historical village or house? What surprised you there? What would you miss from modern life if you were sent back to live in colonial times?

Academic Words

individual
separate from others in the same group

legal
allowed by law

Practice Book pages 63–64

Differentiated Instruction

Beginning	Have students find the sentence that describes what they see in picture 5. Then have them find two key words that describe someone who sells something.
Early Intermediate	Tell students to find three key words that describe people who do a job. Ask students to make a list of these three key words.
Intermediate	Have students write new context sentences for each of the three key words that describe people who do a job.
Struggling Reader	Say the following context words aloud and have students point to the sentence with the key word and the correct picture: *delegates, merchants, tailors.*

Visual Literacy

Labels Discuss the photos and drawings on these pages.

SAY *Look at each picture and find the correct number next to each sentence.*

- *Who are the people shown in picture 1?*
- *In picture 2, what does it show you can do to keep things confidential?*
- *If you swear to secrecy, what do you promise?*

Academic Words

Discuss the definitions of *individual* and *legal* with students. Share the following context sentences:

Her *individual* test score was higher than the group's test score.

We must always be aware of what is *legal* so we can properly follow the law.

Have students work in pairs to discuss how the two academic terms can be used in the same sentence. Ask students to write sentences using both terms.

Other Academic Words

Explain that *evidence* is a fact that can be proven to help tell the truth of a situation. It is a term that is often used in law and government.

Ask students to describe *evidence* that proves what the weather is today.

STEP 3: Practice

Flexible Grouping

You may assign these exercises as a partner activity or individual writing assignment.

Make Connections

Writing Fluency Have students write a paragraph about how life is different today from how it was in 1787. Students may choose to write their paragraphs in the form of a letter, newspaper article, or journal entry. Have students read aloud their paragraphs to the class.

STEP 1: Introduce

More About The Big Question

The Big Question in this selection is designed to help students think about how life was different in 1787 when leaders were creating a new country.

SAY *Life today is very different from life in 1787. Let's think of differences between life now and then.*

Have students fill in a Venn Diagram like the one shown below to compare and contrast life today with life in 1787.

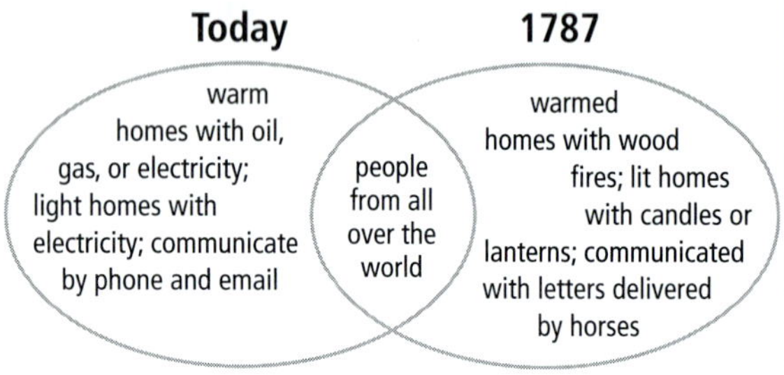

STEP 2: Teach

Reading Strategy

Identify Main Idea and Details Discuss how to recognize the main idea of a paragraph and supporting details. Review the bulleted items in the side column on p. 128.

Understand Text Structure

Draw students' attention to the genre label. Explain that informational text gives details and facts about a specific topic.

Read Aloud

Have students take turns reading the paragraphs in pairs or groups. Have them stop and discuss what they learned at the end of each paragraph. They can use the illustrations to aid their discussion.

Teaching Resources

- *Teacher's Resource Book*, pp. 121–122
- *Practice Book*, pp. 65–66
- *CD-ROM* • *Audio CD*

Reading 2

INFORMATIONAL TEXT

Social Studies

The Big Question

Why was life so hard in the early days of our country?

Reading Strategy

Identify Main Idea and Details

The **main idea** of a selection tells you what the story is about. The **details** give you information about the main idea.

- What is this selection about?
- What is the most important thing the author wants to tell you?

One Hot Summer in Philadelphia

by Ann Ponti

Delegates from every state except Rhode Island went to Philadelphia in 1787 for the Constitutional Convention. There were no railroads or airplanes. Some delegates traveled for many days over dirt and cobblestone roads.

The weather was very hot that summer. Men and women dressed more formally in those days. Women wore one or more petticoats under long dresses or skirts. Men often wore suits made of wool. People buttoned their shirts all the way up, even in the summer. There was no air conditioning. People did not take off or loosen their clothing when they were hot.

---

formally dressed up

petticoats long skirts worn under skirts or dresses

Crowds gathered outside Independence Hall in Philadelphia.

128

TESOL Standards

Goal 2, Standard 2 —To use English to achieve academically in all content areas: Students will use English to obtain, process, construct, and provide subject matter information in spoken and written form.

Descriptors—Listening to, speaking, reading, and writing about subject matter information; Gathering information orally and in writing; Retelling information; Selecting, connecting, and explaining information; Understanding and producing technical vocabulary and text features according to content area; Demonstrating knowledge through application in a variety of contexts.

It was hard to get medical care in the past.

The meetings in the State House were confidential. It was hot that summer, but the windows were kept closed. Guards kept watch to make sure that no one heard any secrets from the people in the State House. The delegates promised not to tell anyone what happened in their meetings.

The secrecy did not stop people from gathering in front of the State House. They knew important work was taking place. The locked windows and doors made the people curious.

The delegates had to be tough to get through the long, hot summer. If any of the delegates got sick or fainted from the heat, people called a doctor. It was important for the delegates to stay healthy.

Long ago, most people didn't go to the doctor unless they were very sick. There weren't a lot of medicines. People often drank herbal teas to feel better when they were sick. They also made some medicines from plants. Sometimes people didn't get better. Many people died from illnesses that are easy to treat today.

---

tough able to deal with hard times

fainted lost consciousness

Check Up How did the heat affect people at the convention?

129

Differentiated Instruction

Beginning	Ask students to complete the sentences: *The delegates had to be ________ to get through the long, hot summer. Men and women dressed more ________ in those days.*
Intermediate	Have students write three short sentences with each including one fact about the Constitutional Convention.
Greater Challenge	Have students write a paragraph that summarizes the description on pp. 128–129 of Philadelphia during the summer of 1787.
Standard English Learner CRI	Write the following sentence on the board: *Leaders make laws for a new country.* Have students role play leaders making laws and citizens asking questions.

Build Vocabulary

Direct attention to the highlighted words in the text with definitions at the bottom of the page.

- Invite volunteers to read aloud a word and its definition.
- Have students write a context sentence using each word.
- Have students repeat this activity for each highlighted word as they read the selection.

Two-Word Phrases Explain that sometimes when two words are combined they have a different meaning. For example, combining the words *take* and *place*, results in *take place*, which means *happen*. In the text, *They knew important work was taking place* means *They knew important work was happening*.

Link to Social Studies

The Constitutional Convention of 1787 The Constitutional Convention took place from May 25 to September 17, 1787. It was held to address problems following the colonists' victory in the American Revolution. Before the Constitution was written, the nation operated under laws called the Articles of Confederation, which did not clearly define the rights and responsibilities of each state. This led to disagreements between states about how to raise money and run the country.

STEP 3: Assess

Check Up

Discuss with students that the meetings in the selection took place long before buildings were cooled by air conditioning. Ask students if the delegates made the right decision to keep the windows closed. Have students explain why the delegates wore heavy clothing and why people were afraid to faint or get sick.

STEP 1: Monitor Progress

Comprehension Check

Text Details Explain that this text has many details about life in 1787 in Philadelphia. After reading pp. 130–131, have the class decide if the following are main ideas or details.

1. *People drank tea or coffee rather than water.*
2. *A whole family would bathe in the same tub, using the same water.*
3. *Rich and poor people lived in the same types of houses.*
4. *Bakers and tailors sold their goods from their homes.*

Discuss how these details help the reader decide what the main idea is. Encourage students to keep a list of facts, or details, as they read.

***Would* in the Past** Explain that the modal verb *would* is sometimes used with a verb to describe a routine that took place in the past. It often has the same meaning as the past tense of the verb. Write these examples on the board and point out that the two sentences have the same meaning:

- A whole family *would bathe* in the same tub.
- A whole family *bathed* in the same tub.
- Poor people *lived* in houses on the side alleys.
- Poor people *would live* in houses on the side alleys.

Ask volunteers to come to the board to underline the verbs in each sentence.

Link to Social Studies

Fact and Opinion Explain to students that it is sometimes difficult to tell the difference between fact and opinion, even in informational text. Have a volunteer read this sentence: *The person who went last didn't get very clean!* Have students discuss whether they think this sentence is a fact or the writer's opinion. Have students explain their reasoning.

Water sometimes made people sick in the 1780s. People had no way of knowing if their drinking water was clean. To be safe, people didn't drink much plain water. They drank cider, milk, tea, and coffee. They could boil water for tea and coffee.

Houses did not have bathrooms. People used buckets to carry water from nearby wells to their houses. They filled washbowls and pitchers with water to clean their hands and faces. People didn't take baths very often. When they did, they would set a big wooden tub in front of the kitchen fire. After they filled the tub, a whole family would bathe in the same water. The person who went last didn't get very clean!

Like the well, the toilet was outside. It was in a separate building called a privy.

People used washbowls and pitchers to wash their hands and faces.

130

TESOL Standards

Goal 2, Standard 2—To use English to achieve academically in all content areas: Students will use English to obtain, process, construct, and provide subject matter information in spoken and written form.
Descriptors—Listening to, speaking, reading, and writing about subject matter information; Gathering information orally and in writing; Retelling information; Selecting, connecting, and explaining information; Understanding and producing technical vocabulary and text features according to content area; Demonstrating knowledge through application in a variety of contexts.

The 40,000 people who lived in Philadelphia in 1787 had come to the United States from all over the world. People from England and Germany lived next to people from Africa.

People in Philadelphia worked as bakers, teachers, merchants, tailors, and carpenters. They made bread, soap, furniture, and clothing. Their houses were small and close together. Rich people lived in large houses at the ends of the blocks. Poor people lived in houses on the side alleys.

People from all over the world lived as neighbors in Philadelphia.

Bakers and tailors sold their goods from their homes. Farmers used horses and wagons to drive their goods to market from farms around the city.

Life was harder in 1787 than it is today. But the people who lived in Philadelphia witnessed one of the most exciting times in U.S. history.

---

alleys narrow streets

witnessed saw

Practice Book pages 65–66

Reading Strategy

Identify Main Idea and Details

- What was the main idea?
- What were some details?
- How did thinking about the main idea and details help you?

Think It Over

1. Why did delegates meet in Philadelphia in 1787?
2. How many people lived in Philadelphia in 1787?
3. Name three kinds of jobs that people in Philadelphia had.
4. Why was water the cause of many health problems?

Differentiated Instruction

Beginning	Ask students to work in pairs to find the number that tells how many people lived in Philadelphia in 1787.
Early Intermediate	Ask students to fill in the blanks: *People used ________ to carry ________ from ________ near their ________ .*
Intermediate	Have students write three complete sentences that each state one fact about life in Philadelphia in 1787.
Special Needs	Ask students closed questions about the text as they read. Closed questions help students focus their attention. Students may not be ready for the critical thinking skills that are called for in open questions.

STEP 2: Teach

Visual Literacy

Captions Draw students' attention to the captions on pp. 130–131. Ask volunteers to read the captions aloud.

SAY *Illustrations and captions tell us more about the text.*

- *What did you learn about Philadelphia from the caption of the washbowl?*
- *What did you learn about Philadelphia from reading the caption on page 131?*

STEP 3: Assess

Reading Strategy

Identify Main Idea and Details Help students complete a Main Idea and Details Chart like the one below.

Main Idea

Life in Philadelphia in 1787

Supporting Details

- Water sometimes made people sick; to be safe, people drank cider, milk, tea and coffee.
- Houses lacked bathrooms; people used washbowls to wash themselves; people used a privy.
- People from all over the world lived in Philadelphia.
- People worked as merchants, tailors and carpenters; bakers sold their goods from their homes.

Think It Over

Flexible Grouping You may assign this activity as a class discussion, partner activity or individual writing assignment.

Answer Key

1. Delegates met in Philadelphia to write a new set of rules for governing the United States. These rules became the U.S. Constitution.
2. In 1787, there were 40,000 people living in Philadelphia.
3. People worked as bakers, teachers, merchants, tailors, or carpenters.
4. People had no way of telling if their drinking water was clean.

STEP 1: Introduce

Phonics

Consonant Digraphs *ch, sh,* and *th*

Help students understand that when two consonants are combined in a digraph, the pronunciation is different from the sound of the separate letters.

STEP 2: Teach

Read the words in the box aloud. Tell students they will learn about pronouncing the digraphs *ch, sh,* and *th*.

SAY *The letters* ch *stand for one sound, as in the words* charm *and* merchant*; The letters* sh *stand for another sound, as in* ship *and* shut*; and the letters* th *stand for another sound, as in* than.

Write the following words on the board and ask students to pronounce them with you. Mark the digraphs in each word as you read them.

bathtub	*change*	*cash*
another	*thunder*	*shock*
cherish	*dishcloth*	

STEP 3: Practice

Have students work with partners. Encourage students who have finished to look through books or magazines to find other words with the same digraphs.

Answer Key

1. both, Martha, Washington, there
2. merchant, ships, there
3. teachers, butchers, shoemakers, there
4. the, fathers, there
5. the, cheese

Teaching Resources

- *Practice Book*, p. 67
- *Phonics Workbook*
- *Phonics Flashcards*
- *CD-ROM* • *Audio CD*

Reading 2

Phonics & Fluency

Phonics

Consonant Digraphs: *ch, sh,* and *th*

Read the words in the chart aloud. Listen for the sounds of the letters.

ch	sh	th
charm	ship	than
merchants	shut	gathered

Rule Box

The letters *ch* blend together to make one sound. So do the letters *sh* and the letters *th*. These digraphs can be at the beginning, in the middle, or at the end of a word.

Practice

Read the sentences below with a partner.

- List each word with *ch*, *sh*, or *th*.
- List six other words spelled with *ch, sh,* or *th*.

Facts about Philadelphia

1. Both George and Martha Washington slept there.
2. Many merchant ships docked there.
3. Teachers, butchers, and shoemakers lived there.
4. The Founding Fathers met there.
5. It's the home of cheese steaks and hoagies.

Practice Book page 67

132

TESOL Standards

Goal 2, Standard 3—To use English to achieve academically in all content areas: Students will use appropriate learning strategies to construct and apply academic knowledge.
Descriptors—Applying basic reading comprehension skills such as skimming, scanning, previewing, and reviewing text; Using context to construct meaning; Applying self-monitoring and self-corrective strategies to build and expand a knowledge base.

Goal 3, Standard 3—To use English in socially and culturally appropriate ways: Students will use appropriate learning strategies to extend their sociolinguistic and sociocultural competence.
Descriptors—Experimenting with variations of language in social and academic settings; Rehearsing variations of language use in different social and academic settings; Observing and modeling how others speak and behave in a particular situation or setting; Seeking information about appropriate language use and behavior.

Fluency

Look Ahead

Sometimes readers look for hard words before they read. Then they try to figure them out.

Practice

Pick one passage. → Find any hard words. → Practice saying those words. → Read the passage aloud.

1 Life in Philadelphia was hard in 1787. Many delegates had to travel a long way on cobblestone roads. The delegates went to Philadelphia because they had an important job to do.

2 The meetings in the State House were confidential. It was hot that summer, but the windows were kept closed. Some of the windows were nailed shut! Guards kept watch to make sure that no one heard any secrets from the people in the State House.

3 Water sometimes made people sick in the 1780s. People had no way of knowing if their drinking water was clean. To be safe, people didn't drink much plain water. They drank cider, milk, tea, and coffee. They could boil water for tea and coffee.

Houses did not have bathrooms. People used buckets to carry water from nearby wells to their houses. They filled washbowls and pitchers with water to clean their hands and faces. People didn't take baths very often. When they did, they would set a big wooden tub in front of the kitchen fire.

133

Linguistic Note

Remind students that difficult words can often be taken apart to make them easier to understand. For example, *wooden* contains *wood* and *cobblestone* contains *stone*.

Accelerate Language Development

Explain that keeping a list of hard words and reviewing them every week can help students develop a larger vocabulary in English that they can use in their everyday lives.

STEP 1: Introduce

Fluency

Look Ahead Explain that finding the meanings of hard words can help students read with more understanding. Tell them that sometimes readers look for hard words before they read.

Play the audio CD for this reading to the class, asking students to listen for pacing, rhythm, intonation, and expression.

STEP 2: Practice

Have students do the following exercise with partners.

- Assign one passage to each pair of students.
- Have them look for words that are difficult.
- Tell them to practice pronouncing the hard words.
- Then have students read their passage aloud to each other.

Have each pair of students list the words they had difficulty pronouncing, and repeat the activity if necessary.

Possible Responses–Hard Words

Philadelphia	delegates	cobblestone
confidential	guards	cider
buckets	nearby	wooden

STEP 3: Extend

Study Skills

Thesaurus Have students work with partners to write down three words that were hard to understand from the reading. Ask them to use a thesaurus to look for words with a similar meaning.

- Have students write a context sentence for each difficult word.
- Then, using the similar words they found in the thesaurus, have them replace the words, and rewrite the sentence.
- Have students check to be sure the meaning of the sentence is the same.

STEP 1: Monitor Progress

Learning Strategy

Summarize Summarizing the story is a way to briefly retell the most important points of the story. Have students work in pairs to review the reading. After students have summarized the reading, have them take turns responding to the Big Question for this reading. Ask students if they believe that people living in Philadelphia in 1787 witnessed an important part of history. Have them explain their reasoning.

STEP 2: Teach

Main Idea and Details

Encourage students to share the main idea from their summaries and discuss some of the details that support the main idea.

SAY *Identifying the main idea will help you understand what you read. Use your summary to identify the main idea of the reading.*

STEP 3: Practice

Flexible Grouping You may assign this activity as a class discussion, partner activity or individual writing assignment.

Possible Responses

1. People traveled on dirt and cobblestone roads to get to Philadelphia. (detail)
2. Many people in Philadelphia got sick from drinking dirty water. (detail)
3. There was very hot weather during the summer of 1787. (detail)
4. The Constitutional Convention took place in Philadelphia in 1787. (main idea)
5. The closed windows of the State House made people curious. (detail)

Teaching Resources

- ***Practice Book,*** p. 68
- ***Transparencies,*** p. 55
- ***Teacher's Resource Book,*** p. 153
- ***CD-ROM***

Reading 2

Comprehension

Learning Strategy

Summarize

Summarize the reading for a partner.

Ask your partner to respond to the Big Question for this reading.

Practice Book page 68

Main Idea and Details

Identifying the **main idea and details** can help you understand what you read. Ask yourself, "What was the reading about?" Your answer to the question is the main idea of the selection.

Practice

Write a sentence about each of the phrases. Then state whether if your sentence tells about a detail or the main idea of the selection.

1. cobblestone roads
2. dirty water
3. hot weather
4. Constitutional Convention
5. closed windows

TESOL Standards

Goal 2, Standard 2—To use English to achieve academically in all content areas: Students will use English to obtain, process, construct, and provide subject matter information in spoken and written form.

Descriptors—Listening to, speaking, reading, and writing about subject matter information; Gathering information orally and in writing; Retelling information; Selecting, connecting, and explaining information; Understanding and producing technical vocabulary and text features according to content area; Demonstrating knowledge through application in a variety of contexts.

Use a Main Idea and Details Chart

You can use a Main Idea and Details Chart to help you understand what you read.

Practice

Copy this Main Idea and Details Chart. Fill in the chart to show the main idea of the selection and some details that support it.

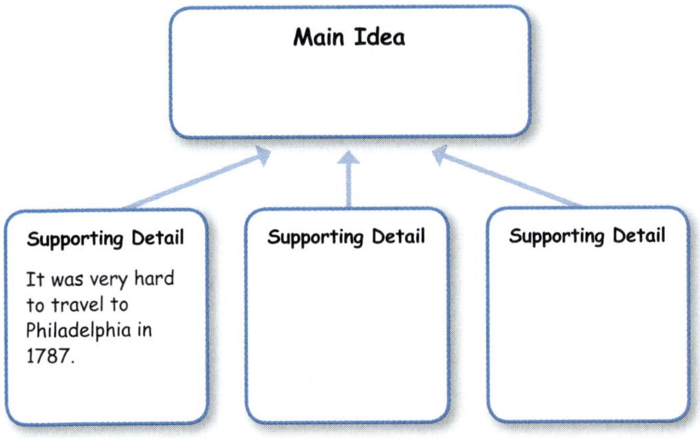

Extension

Choose one supporting detail from your chart. Write your ideas about how that detail is different today. For example, today it is easy to travel to Philadelphia by car, bus, train, or airplane. Share your work with a partner or group.

135

Accelerate Language Development

Dramatization Have small groups of students use the oral presentation about life today to create a brief sketch with students playing themselves in their everyday lives. Encourage groups to create speaking roles for several students using the supporting details they wrote.

Linguistic Note

Tell students that the word *Philadelphia* comes from the Greek words *philos* (brotherly love) and *delphia* (city) that together mean "city of brotherly love."

STEP 1: Teach

Use a Main Idea and Details Chart

Ask students to think about their own lives, specifically the different activities and responsibilities they have. Explain to them that a Main Idea and Details Chart can help them organize their thoughts and ideas. Have them complete a Main Idea and Details Chart, writing details for the following main idea: My life is very busy.

Possible Responses

Main Idea

My life is very busy.

Supporting Detail

I have softball practice on Tuesday and Thursday.

Supporting Detail

On Wednesday, I have dinner with my dad.

Supporting Detail

On the weekends, I do my homework, watch my younger sister, and spend time with my friends.

Have students share their charts in small groups.

STEP 2: Practice

Have students refer to the reading to complete this activity. You may have students complete the graphic organizer provided as a Blackline Master in the *Teacher's Resource Book*.

STEP 3: Extend

Oral Presentation Have students prepare a presentation about what life is like for them today and to compare and contrast it with the way people lived in 1787. Remind them to use a main idea as a starting point and then add details. Let students take turns presenting their information.

STEP 1: Introduce

Help students understand how being able to write letters will help them in many different situations, such as applying for a job. Ask the class to think about different situations where they might need to write a letter.

Possible Responses

- to request information about a product or event
- to write a letter to a government official
- to apply to an after school program

STEP 2: Teach

Letters

Have students look at the sample letter on p. 136. Identify the different parts of the letter: address, date, salutation, body, closing, and signature. Have the class discuss the role and importance of each part.

SAY *Each part of a letter is important.*

- *Why are these parts important?*
- *What would happen if we did not include these parts?*

STEP 3: Practice

Before students begin the Practice activity, have them work in groups to compose a simple letter. The letters can be a request for information about an upcoming event in their school or community. Have students use the sample letter on p. 136 as a guide and to include all the parts of the letter. When students have completed their letters, have volunteers read their letters aloud. Then ask students to complete the Practice activity.

Answer Key

1. Main Street
2. Miami, FL
3. April 28, 2008
4. Dear Mr. Singh,
5. Sincerely,

Teaching Resources

- ***Practice Book***, pp. 69–70
- ***Transparencies***, pp. 69–80
- ***Assessment***, pp. 57–60
- ***CD-ROM***

Reading 2

Grammar & Writing

Letters

Steve wrote a letter to a teacher to ask her for information about Philadelphia. This is a formal letter.

address — 984 Clearview Avenue
Sunnyville, CA 90012

date — October 20, 2010

salutation — Dear Ms. Johnson,

body — Please send me information about Philadelphia. I am interested in places that are important in the city's early history. I plan to share the information with my class.

Thank you for your help.

closing — Sincerely,

signature — Steve Cho

Practice

Write each item correctly. Use the sample letter as a guide.

1. main street
2. miami fl
3. april 28 2008
4. dear mr singh
5. sincerely

Practice Book page 69

TESOL Standards

Goal 2, Standard 3—To use English to achieve academically in all content areas: Students will use appropriate learning strategies to construct and apply academic knowledge.
Descriptors—Using context to construct meaning; Actively connecting new information-to-information previously learned; Imitating the behaviors of native English speakers to complete tasks successfully; Recognizing the need for seeking assistance appropriately from others (e.g. teachers, peers, specialists, community members).

Goal 3, Standard 1—To use English in socially and culturally appropriate ways: Students will use the appropriate language variety, register, and genre according to audience, purpose, and setting.
Descriptors—Using the appropriate degree of formality with different audiences and settings; Recognizing and using standard English and vernacular dialects appropriately; Using a variety of writing styles appropriate for different audiences, purposes, and settings.

Write a Persuasive Letter

Read this letter from Jake to his friend, Tracy. He wants her to visit Philidelphia. This is an example of a friendly letter.

January 5, 2009

Dear Tracy,

You have to go to Philadelphia. I went on a weekend trip with my family, and it was awesome.

I visited Independence Hall. That is where the Declaration of Independence was written. It was great to imagine myself signing that important piece of paper.

I also ate a cheesesteak. Philadelphia is famous for that messy sandwich. It was delicious! You have to go to there and try it.

Your friend,
Jake

SPELLING TIP

If the vowel sound is short, there must be two consonants between the ending and *-le*. If the vowel is long, one consonant is enough.

little table

Practice Book page 70

Practice

Write a letter to persuade someone to help you solve a problem.

- Identify yourself and explain what you want.
- Give good reasons why the person should help you.
- Read your letter aloud to a partner.

Writing Checklist

✓ Did your letter explain your point of view?

✓ Did you ask the reader to think about your idea?

✓ Can a partner understand your letter?

137

Differentiated Instruction	
Beginning	Ask students to look at the parts of a letter on p. 136. Then have students look at the letter on p. 137 and point to the address, the greeting, and the body of the letter.
Intermediate	Have students read the letter on p. 137 and write a one sentence summary of the reasons explained in the letter for visiting Philadelphia..
Greater Challenge	Have students work with partners to make a list of three or more persuasive arguments to add to the letter on p. 137.
Standard English Learner CRI	Read parts of the letter on p. 137 out of order. Have students locate and point to that part of the letter. Then have them say the name of that part.

STEP 1: Introduce

Write a Persuasive Letter

Define a persuasive letter. Have volunteers point out and read aloud the different parts of the letter: address, date, salutation, body, closing and signature.

SAY *When you write a persuasive letter, you want to convince the person you're writing to do something.*

Now let's read this letter from Jake, to his friend, Tracy.

- *What does Jake want Tracy to do?*
- *What does Jake say in his letter to persuade Tracy?*
- *After you read Jake's letter, do you want to visit Philadelphia? Why or why not?*

Spelling Tip

Read the box aloud to students. Review the pronunciation of short vowels and long vowels for each of the five vowels. Write a list on the board of words with two consonants and one consonant for words ending in *-le*.

STEP 2: Practice

Before students write their persuasive letters, have them discuss the following questions with a partner:

- Who are you writing this letter to?
- What do you want from this person?
- What are your reasons?
- How are you going to organize the letter?

STEP 3: Assess

Writing Checklist

✓ Students might need help understanding that a point of view is an opinion or feeling about something.

✓ Be sure students' ideas are clearly stated in their letters.

✓ Ask students to read their partner's letters. Remind students to be respectful of their partner's work and constructive in their feedback.

The Five Step Writing Process in the Writing Handbook reference section of this book provides more student writing instruction.

STEP 1: Introduce

Key Words Help students learn the skill of defining words by using context.

SAY *The vocabulary words from the reading are used in the Words in Context selection. Let's figure out the definition for each vocabulary word.*

Have students find the numbered circles for each context sentence, then find the corresponding numbered photos.

STEP 2: Teach

Words in Context

Write the following sentences on the board. Have students complete this fill-in-the-blanks exercise using key words.

1. *The enemy soldiers will* surrender *to the general at dawn.*
2. *My grandfather was a* veteran *of the World War II.*
3. *The United States is a* republic *because our leader is a president, not a king.*
4. *Many* federal *employees work in Washington, D.C.*
5. *I do homework in one room and listen to music in a* separate *room.*
6. *All members of the* legislature *are elected.*

Have students read the paragraphs with the words in context and explain how the pictures help them understand the words.

Study Skills

Dictionary Have students look up key words in the dictionary to see if the context definitions are correct.

Online Dictionary Students can look up words using an online dictionary or the CD from a learner's dictionary, like the *Longman Basic Dictionary*.

www.LongmanCornerstone.com

Teaching Resources
- *Practice Book,* pp. 71–72
- *Transparencies,* p. 45
- *CD-ROM* • *Audio CD*

Reading 3

One Out of Many

Vocabulary

One Out of Many **is about some of the things people discussed at the Constitutional Convention in 1787.**

Key Words
- **surrender**
- **veteran**
- **republic**
- **federal**
- **separate**
- **legislature**

Words in Context

1 A white flag is the universal symbol of **surrender**. It means you want to stop fighting.

2 This **veteran** was a soldier in the Vietnam War.

3 George Washington was the first president of the new **republic** called the United States.

1

2

3

138

TESOL Standards

Goal 1, Standard 3—To use English to communicate in social settings: Students will use learning strategies to extend their communicative competence.
Descriptors—Testing hypotheses about language; Listening to and imitating how others use English; Exploring alternative ways of saying things; Using context to construct meaning.

Goal 2, Standard 2—To use English to achieve academically in all content areas: Students will use English to obtain, process, construct, and provide subject matter information in spoken and written form.
Descriptor—Understanding and producing technical vocabulary and text features according to content area.

4

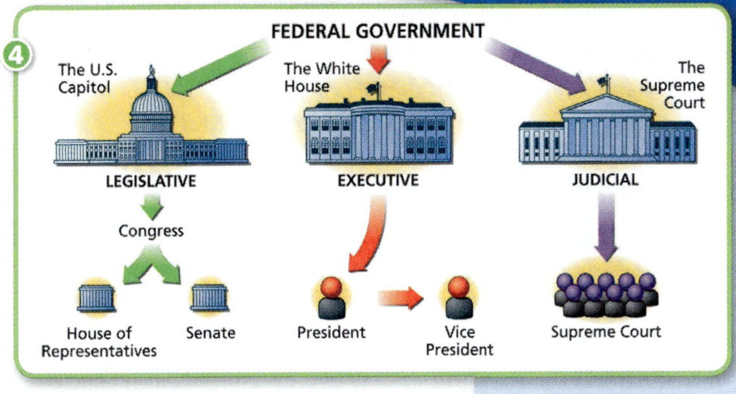

4 The United States has a **federal** government that has three **separate** branches: the executive branch, the legislative branch, and the judicial branch.

5 The **legislature** of the U.S. government is also called Congress. It has two parts: the Senate and the House of Representatives.

5

Practice

Use each key word in a sentence.

Make Connections

Congress has two senators from every state. The number of representatives from each state depends on the number of people in the state. Find out the names of your state's senators and representatives.

Academic Words

convention
formal meeting for a specific purpose

debate
formal discussion

Practice Book pages 71–72

Differentiated Instruction

Beginning	Ask students to work in pairs to demonstrate *surrender*. Have students hand each other something that represents a white flag and say, "I surrender," then shake hands.
Early Intermediate	Ask students to make a list of the names of the three branches of the federal government, then point to each name in the picture on p. 139.
Intermediate	Ask students to make a 3-column chart for the branches of the federal government. Add information in picture 4 for each branch.
Struggling Reader	Read the key words out of order. Have students point to the word and illustration for each key word as you read. Have students find the word *government* in the picture on p. 139.

Visual Literacy

Charts Discuss the chart about the federal government on p. 139. Explain that sometimes writers use charts to help a reader understand difficult or important information.

SAY *This chart makes it easier to learn about and remember the three branches of government.*

- *What is shown in the pictures?*
- *How do the pictures in the top row relate to the ones on the bottom?*

Academic Words

Discuss the definitions for *convention* and *debate* with students. Share the following context sentences with students.

We will attend a political *convention* in Chicago next week.

Twelve candidates will *debate* the freedom of speech on television tonight.

Other Academic Words

Provide students with another example of a word that can be used in the discussion of government. Write the following definition and context sentence on the board:

issue a situation or topic that can affect many people

The candidates will debate each *issue* that concerns the voters.

STEP 3: Practice

Flexible Grouping You may assign these exercises as a partner activity or individual research assignment.

Make Connections

Writing Fluency Encourage students to write a brief report on what they would do to get elected to Congress. You may want to get students started by discussing some of the things candidates do: give speeches, appear on television, and participate in debates. Encourage students to think of different things they might do to get people's votes.

STEP 1: Introduce

More About The Big Question

The Big Question for this selection is designed to make students think about how the United States was formed as one country from 13 separate colonies.

SAY *In our school, students, teachers and administrators make up our school community.*

- *How is our school government similar to the federal government?*
- *Why is it necessary for a government to enforce rules?*

Have students fill in a KWL Chart with what they know and what they want to learn about government. Tell them to fill in the *What I Learned* column as they continue to read the play.

STEP 2: Teach

Reading Strategy

Make Inferences Tell students that when you make inferences, you use what you read and your prior knowledge to determine what the author does not tell you directly. Read aloud the bulleted question and have students make inferences about what they think they will learn when they read the play.

Understand Text Structure

Have students discuss what they know about plays. Have students read aloud the cast of characters and scene description.

Read Aloud

Ask volunteers to choose a character and read the play aloud. Have another volunteer read the narrator's part (italic text). Have students stop at the end of each page and discuss what is happening.

Teaching Resources

- ***Teacher's Resource Book***, pp. 123–124
- ***Practice Book***, pp. 73–74
- ***CD-ROM*** • ***Audio CD***

Reading 3

LITERATURE

Play

The Big Question

How did we create one country out of many colonies?

Reading Strategy

Make Inferences

You make inferences when you use clues from the story to figure out something that the author doesn't tell you.

- Why was the constitutional convention held in 1787?

One Out Of Many

by Bob McCall

Cast of Characters:

Benjamin Franklin	famous statesman and scientist
George Washington	general in the American Revolution
Alexander Hamilton	army officer and statesman
Bob	boy, 10
Ned	boy, 10

Scene: May, 1787. Philadelphia. Outside the State House. Benjamin Franklin and George Washington are sitting on a bench.

The Pennsylvania State House in 1787.

TESOL Standards

Goal 2, Standard 2—To use English to achieve academically in all content areas: Students will use English to obtain, process, construct, and provide subject matter information in spoken and written form.

Descriptors—Listening to, speaking, reading, and writing about subject matter information; Gathering information orally and in writing; Retelling information; Selecting, connecting, and explaining information; Analyzing, synthesizing, and inferring from information; Understanding and producing technical vocabulary and text features according to content area.

Franklin: It's too hot, Washington. Make them open the windows in there.
Washington: They don't want rumors to start. (*He sighs.*) This is going to be a very long summer.

Bob and his friend Ned enter. They give the men glasses of water.

George Washington was at the convention.

Washington: Thank you, Bob.
Franklin: Thanks, Ned.
Bob: General Washington, what is this convention all about?
Washington: It's a kind of meeting.
Ned: But what is the meeting *for*?
Washington: We are here to write a constitution for the United States.
Ned: Oh, a constitution! (*pause*) What's that?
Franklin: A constitution is a set of rules for a government.
Bob: I thought that we already had rules.
Franklin: We do. But they don't work.
Ned: Why not?
Washington: We are the United States. What does the word "united" mean?
Ned: It means "all together."
Washington: How many states do we have, Ned?
Ned: Thirteen.
Washington: It's like we have 13 separate countries. Does that sound united to you?

rumors information passed between people that may or may not be true

Check Up Why did the delegates want to write a constitution?

141

Differentiated Instruction

Beginning	Have students find and say aloud the sentence in which Washington explains the purpose of the meeting. We are here to write a constitution for the United States.
Intermediate	Have students write a short answer to the following question: *What is a constitution?*
Greater Challenge	Ask students to write a two-sentence summary of the events in the play that have happened on pp. 140–141.
Standard English Learner CRI	Assign roles to students who will role play the dialogue on pp. 140–141 as you read each line aloud. Direct students to accurately role play the action and to have them improvise some of the dialogue.

Build Vocabulary

Remind students to look for the definition of the highlighted word at the bottom of the page.

- Invite a volunteer to read the term and its definition aloud.
- Ask another volunteer to read the sentence with that highlighted word aloud.
- Then let another volunteer write on the board a new context sentence for the word.

Nouns Ending in *-ing* Write the word *meeting* on the board. Ask students to look at the word *meet* in this word. Explain that sometimes you can make a noun out of a verb by adding the ending *–ing*. If you know the meaning of the verb, it will help you understand the noun. Write the following examples and discuss their meanings.

Verb	Noun	Example
meet	meeting	We have a meeting.
skate	skating	Skating is fun!

STEP 3: Assess

Check Up

Have students work with partners to review p. 141. They should tell each other why he or she thinks the delegates wanted to write a new constitution.

Scaffolding

Have pairs of students select a topic for a speech about something they would like to change in their school government. Ask students to work together to improvise a speech for the class.

Link to Social Studies

George Washington (1732–1799) was a key figure in the founding of the United States. Washington led the Continental Army to victory over Britain in the Revolutionary War (1775–1783). Washington presided over the Constitutional Convention and was elected the first President of the United States of America in 1789.

STEP 1: Monitor Progress

Comprehension Check

Make Inferences Before students read pp. 142–143, point out the italics in the text that gives them extra information about what the characters are doing or how they are feeling. Discuss the meaning of *upset, stiffly* and *laughing*. As students read these pages, make sure they look for these clues.

After reading these pages, ask students if they thought this meeting was easy or difficult for Washington, Hamilton, and Franklin. Have them explain which clues helped them infer their answer.

Possible Responses

It was a difficult meeting. Some of the clues are:

- Ned complains it is very hot; he asks a lot of questions; he seems frustrated.
- Hamilton speaks stiffly and groans; he questions Mr. Gerry's statement.
- Franklin is afraid of a new war; he is concerned about money; he complains that people are afraid of a new government.

Link to Social Studies

Explain to students that Washington, Franklin, and Hamilton were leaders who attended this convention when our nation was being formed. Have students research one of the leaders and write a short report about how that leader contributed to forming the federal government.

Adapt the Activity

Have students write about one of the issues the characters in the play discussed during the Constitutional Convention. Have them explain whether they think the issue they chose was resolved in the play. They should use examples from the play to explain their reasoning.

Bob and Ned: No, sir.

Ned: It's so hot! Why are the windows closed? Do you want to make King George's son the king of the United States? People say that's why the room is closed up tight.

Franklin: Washington, tell the boys we won't let that happen. I told you the windows should be open.

Alexander Hamilton opens the door. He's very upset.

Hamilton: Washington, you must stop Mr. Gerry from talking!

Franklin: That's why we're here, Hamilton, to talk.

Washington: Bob and Ned, this is Alexander Hamilton.

Hamilton: (*stiffly*) Oh. Good day, children.

Ned and Bob: Pleased to meet you!

Hamilton: Gerry says that a federal government will take power from the states.

Franklin: That's true.

Hamilton: But who cares about that?

Franklin: (*laughing*) Mr. Gerry, I guess.

Hamilton groans and goes back into the convention.

Bob: I hope Mr. Gerry talks for a week. I need this job.

Washington: Don't worry, Bob. The convention might last all summer.

Ned: All summer! You really think it will take them that long?

Alexander Hamilton wanted a strong federal government.

142

TESOL Standards

Goal 2, Standard 2—To use English to achieve academically in all content areas: Students will use English to obtain, process, construct, and provide subject matter information in spoken and written form.

Descriptors—Listening to, speaking, reading, and writing about subject matter information; Gathering information orally and in writing; Retelling information; Selecting, connecting, and explaining information; Analyzing, synthesizing, and inferring from information; Understanding and producing technical vocabulary and text features according to content area.

The British surrendered to George Washington at Yorktown.

Franklin: Yes. People are afraid of government. They think it will take away their liberty.

Ned: We don't want that!

Bob: Make the government weak!

Franklin: What if we have to fight the British again?

Bob: Didn't they surrender?

Washington: Yes. But they might come back.

Ned: We just need a strong army then.

Franklin: Armies cost money. Yesterday, I saw an army veteran in great need. We must take care of the soldiers who fought in the war. France gave us a loan. We should pay them back. Where will we get the money?

Bob: Oh. Is that the only problem?

Franklin: No! There are many things to figure out. But first, we need a strong federal government.

Washington: But not so strong that we lose our freedom. Understand?

---

loan something, usually money, that is borrowed and then returned

Check Up What are some reasons for having a strong government?

Differentiated Instruction

Beginning	Ask students to complete the following sentence: *The ________ might last all summer.*
Early Intermediate	Ask students to complete the following sentence: *Either people were ________ of the government, or they wanted a ________ government.*
Intermediate	Have students work in pairs to read aloud the dialogue between Franklin and Hamilton, then present to the class a short summary about the main idea of the dialogue.
Struggling Reader	Have students point to the picture of Alexander Hamilton. Read aloud the caption next to his picture on p. 142 and have students repeat the caption with you.

STEP 2: Teach

Visual Literacy

Pictures Refer students to the pictures on pp. 142–143.

SAY *Paintings and portraits from the past can tell us a lot about people who lived during those times.*

- *What does the picture of Alexander Hamilton tell us about the way men dressed long ago?* They wore very dark clothes that were plain and looked heavy. They wore ties that were different from the ties men wear today.
- *What does the picture on page 143 tell you about soldiers and war long ago?* Soldiers wore very formal uniforms. Many soldiers carried swords and rode horses.

Academic Words

Discuss the definitions of *final* and *impact* with students. Write the following definitions and context sentences on the board:

final end or conclusion of something

impact effect that an event or situation has on someone or something

Congress has taken the *final* vote on the new law.

His speech had a significant *impact* on the audience.

Explain to students that the academic word *impact* can be a noun or a verb. Have students write a context sentence with *impact* used as a verb.

STEP 3: Assess

Check Up

Have students work in small groups. Ask them to discuss some of the reasons people want a strong government. Encourage groups to write a list of reasons and share it with the class.

STEP 1: Monitor Progress

Comprehension Check

Sequence of Events Draw students' attention to clues in the play that indicate a passage of time.

SAY *Look at the information after the word* Scene *on page 144. How much time has passed since the first* Scene*?*

Factual Data After reading pp. 144–145, read aloud the statements shown below. Ask students to say whether each statement is true or false. Have volunteers read aloud the sections of the text they used to respond to each statement.

1. *The new government is called a republic.* true
2. *The new government will have a king* false
3. *The government will have three branches: the legislative, the judicial, and the executive.* true
4. *Franklin believes the government will take away people's rights.* false
5. *The new government unifies the states.* true

Adapt the Activity

Have students work in groups of three to role-play the scene on pp. 144–145. Encourage students to read with expression and clearly pronounce the words. After their presentations, have students retell in their own words what happened in the scene.

Link to Social Studies

Out of Many, One is a translation of the Latin *E Pluribus Unum*. It refers to the different colonies coming together as the United States. This expression is included on most U.S. currency. Have students find the phrase on different coins.

Scene: About three months later. July 1787. Outside the State House.

Ned: What is the new government called?

Franklin: It's called a republic. The people who live in each state vote for representatives to run things. People will elect representatives every two years. The government will have three parts: The first branch is the legislature, or Congress—

Bob: The legislature makes the laws.

Franklin: Right. The second branch is the Supreme Court or judicial branch. This court will tell us what the laws mean if there are any questions. The third branch is the president or executive branch. He will make sure that people follow the laws.

Ned: He's like a king.

Franklin: No. He will only be president for four years. Then people will elect a new president.

Bob: So everything got done after all.

Franklin: There's still a lot to figure out.

Bob: Like what?

---

representatives people chosen to speak or act for others

Benjamin Franklin was a statesman and scientist.

144

TESOL Standards

Goal 2, Standard 2—To use English to achieve academically in all content areas: Students will use English to obtain, process, construct, and provide subject matter information in spoken and written form.

Descriptors—Listening to, speaking, reading, and writing about subject matter information; Gathering information orally and in writing; Retelling information; Selecting, connecting, and explaining information; Analyzing, synthesizing, and inferring from information; Understanding and producing technical vocabulary and text features according to content area.

Franklin: We need a list of rights. People's rights are things the government can't take away, like freedom to say what you think. Then each state has to agree on the list.

Ned: Are you happy with the new government, sir?

Delegates sign the U.S. Constitution.

Franklin: People make governments, Ned. If the people do the right thing, our government will be fine. We still have big problems, such as slavery and rights for women. But you young people will have to figure those things out. We did the best we could.

Ned: Mr. Franklin, you did one very good thing.

Franklin: What was that?

Ned: When you came to Philadelphia, we had 13 separate states. But when you leave, we will have one country.

Franklin: "Out of many, one." That's good. We should put that on a coin.

Reading Strategy

Make Inferences

- Why was the constitutional convention held in 1787?
- Why did the convention divide the government into three parts?
- What helps you make inferences about things the author doesn't tell you about?

Practice Book pages 73–74

Think It Over

1. Who are the characters in this play?
2. What problems do the characters want to solve?
3. What problems still needed to be solved at the end of the play?

145

Differentiated Instruction

Beginning	Have students look at the photo on p. 145, then draw a picture of a delegate speaking to a crowd.
Intermediate	Have students write a short answer to the following question: *What two problems had to be solved after the Constitution was signed?*
Greater Challenge	Have students write a summary paragraph about the events that occur during the scene on pp. 144–145.
Standard English Learner CRI	Have students play a version of "Back, Back, Back it Up." Have students retell the events in the play as if they were news reporters reporting on the Constitutional Convention as if it just happened. Students can use information from the play to back up their news reports.

STEP 2: Teach

Build Vocabulary

Guide students how to use the highlighted word in the text that is defined at the bottom the page.

- Invite a volunteer to read the term and its definition aloud.
- Ask another volunteer to read the sentence with the highlighted word aloud to the class.
- Then let another volunteer make another sentence using the highlighted term.

STEP 3: Assess

SAY *From reading the conversation between Franklin, Bob and Ned, we can tell that Franklin cared about what he was doing. He participated in creating a new government and pointed out that the work was not done, as people, in particular slaves and women, needed more rights.*

Encourage students to write their own answers to the Reading Strategy questions, then compare their answers with partners.

Make Connections

Writing Fluency Have students write a brief report on what they learned about the U.S. Constitution from reading this play.

Think It Over

Flexible Grouping You may assign this activity as a class discussion, partner activity, or individual writing assignment.

Answer Key

1. Bob and Ned are two 10-year-old boys, Benjamin Franklin is a famous statesman and scientist, George Washington is a general in the American Revolution, and Alexander Hamilton is an army officer and a statesman.
2. They want to write a new constitution that will unify the different states and build a strong federal government.
3. Some of the problems that still need to be solved are people's rights, slavery, and women's rights.

STEP 1: Introduce

Word Analysis

Synonyms and Antonyms Explain to students that synonyms are words with the same or similar meanings, and antonyms are words with opposite meanings. Write the following word pairs on the board. Have students identify the synonyms and antonyms.

large/huge	*long/short*
talk/speak	*loud/quiet*
funny/amusing	*big/small*

STEP 2: Teach

Direct students to review *One Out of Many* to look for synonyms and antonyms.

Write the following words on a chart with space for synonyms and antonyms and ask students to share examples. Have a volunteer write them in the appropriate column.

famous	*afraid*	*care*
weak	*surrender*	*agree*

STEP 3: Practice

Have students work individually and then share their answers with a small group. If the activity is too challenging, have students work with a thesaurus.

Answer Key

1. heat—synonym: warmth; antonym: coldness
2. closed—synonym: shut; antonym: open
3. strong—synonym: dependable; antonym: weak

Reteach

Ask students to search other books and magazines to find three words that have both a synonym and an antonym. Have students use reference sources such as a dictionary and a thesaurus to help them complete the activity.

Teaching Resources
- ***Practice Book***, p. 75
- ***Phonics Workbook***
- ***CD-ROM*** • ***Audio CD***

Reading 3

Word Analysis & Fluency

Word Analysis

Synonyms and Antonyms

Read these sentences.

Washington: It's like we have 13 **separate** countries. Does that sound **united** to you?

The word ***separate*** means "divided or not joined."
The word ***united*** means "joined together."
Separate and ***united*** have opposite meanings.
They are **antonyms.**

Synonyms have the same meaning. What is a synonym for ***separate***?

Word	Synonym Same Meaning	Antonym Opposite Meaning
separate	divided	united

Practice

Give one synonym and one antonym for each underlined word.

1. Ben Franklin suffered from the heat.
2. He complained because the windows in the State House were kept closed.
3. Some people at the convention wanted a strong federal government.

Practice Book
page 75

146

TESOL Standards

Goal 1, Standard 3—To use English to communicate in social settings: Students will use learning strategies to extend their communicative competence.
Descriptors—Listening to and imitating how others use English; Self-monitoring and self-evaluating language development; Practicing new language; Focusing attention selectively.

Goal 3, Standard 3 —To use English in socially and culturally appropriate ways: Students will use appropriate learning strategies to extend their sociolinguistic and sociocultural competence.
Descriptors—Observing and modeling how others speak and behave in a particular situation or setting; Experimenting with variations of language in social and academic settings; Seeking information about appropriate language use and behavior.

Fluency

Read with Expression

When you read aloud, use your voice to show feelings.

Practice

Read silently. → Read aloud. → Get comments. → Read aloud again.

Ned: He's like a king.
Franklin: No. He will only be president for four years. Then people will elect a new president.
Bob: So everything got done after all.
Franklin: There's still a lot to figure out.
Bob: Like what?
Franklin: We need a list of rights. People's rights are things the government can't take away, like freedom to say what you think. Then each state has to agree on the list.
Ned: Are you happy with the new government, sir?
Franklin: People make governments, Ned. If the people do the right thing, our government will be fine. We still have big problems, such as slavery and rights for women. But you young people will have to figure those things out. We did the best we could.
Ned: Mr. Franklin, you did one very good thing.
Franklin: What was that?
Ned: When you came to Philadelphia, we had 13 separate states. But when you leave, we will have one country.
Franklin: "Out of many, one." That's good. We should put that on a coin.

147

Linguistic Note

Cognates Encourage students to use cognates that can help them understand the text. Help them make connections between these words: *separate*: *separado* (Spanish, Portuguese), *séparé* (French); *veteran*: *veterano* (Spanish, Portuguese), *vétéran* (French) *weteran* (Polish); *federal*: *federal* (Spanish, Portuguese), *federal* (French); *federalny* (Polish); *convention*: *convención* (Spanish), *convenção* (Portuguese), *convention* (French); *debate*: *debate* (Spanish, Portuguese), *débat* (French).

Accelerate Language Development

Expression Some speakers of Asian languages may have difficulty with the concept of reading with expression in English. Chinese words can change meaning depending on intonation. In Mandarin, *Ma* can mean four different things: *Mā* (mother), *Má* (hemp), *Ma* (horse), and *Mà* (curse).

STEP 1: Introduce

Fluency

Read with Expression Discuss with students that reading with expression will help them enjoy what they are reading and become better readers. Write the following sentences on the board:

I love their music!

What is that?

This movie is amazing!

I'm really tired.

Read the sentences without expression the first time. Then, ask volunteers to read the sentences with expression. Have the class discuss how the punctuation is a clue to the type of expression.

Play the audio CD for this reading to the class, asking students to listen for pacing, rhythm, intonation, and expression.

STEP 2: Practice

Have students do the following exercise with partners:

- Have each student silently read the text on p. 147. Encourage them to think about how they are going to read aloud with expression.
- Tell them to look for words and phrases they might say with emphasis.
- Have pairs read the whole text to each other. Encourage students to listen closely to their partners' reading for ideas on words to emphasize.

Have each student underline a sentence where they read with expression and read it aloud for the class. Have them describe the expression they used.

STEP 3: Extend

Readers' Theater

Have students work in groups of three to make the dialogue in the Practice activity into a Readers' Theater. Encourage groups to continue reading with expression and add movement and gestures to their readings. Encourage volunteer groups to present their efforts to the class.

STEP 1: Monitor Progress

Learning Strategy

Retell Retelling is a comprehension skill used to organize information about a story or reading. Have students complete a Story Map that summarizes the characters, setting, and plot for *One Out of Many.* After students work with partners to retell, lead a class discussion on how the leaders united the colonies into one country. Have students share their responses to the Big Question for this reading.

STEP 2: Teach

Make Inferences

Remind students they can make inferences by using their prior knowledge and what they read.

SAY *Making inferences helps readers get more out of a story when the author doesn't tell the reader everything about their characters.*

STEP 3: Practice

Flexible Grouping You may assign this activity as a class discussion, partner activity, or individual written assignment.

Answer Key

1. George Washington helped write a new constitution; he cared because he answered the boys' questions.
2. Benjamin Franklin helped write a new constitution; he did not believe in a monarchy; he cared because he wanted rights for all people.
3. The United States is a country that was formed by uniting many different states.
4. The 13 colonies had different ways of governing themselves. Slavery existed in some of these colonies.

Teaching Resources

- *Practice Book,* p. 76
- *Transparencies,* p. 61
- *Teacher's Resource Book,* p. 159
- *CD-ROM*

Reading 3

Comprehension

Learning Strategy

Retell

Retell what happened in the play to a partner.

Ask your partner to respond to the Big Question for this reading.

Make Inferences

When you make inferences, you use what you already know to make guesses about things the author does not directly tell you. Thinking about what you already know will help you make inferences.

Practice

Tell what you know about the following characters and places in the play.

1. George Washington
2. Benjamin Franklin
3. The United States
4. The 13 colonies

Practice Book page 76

148

TESOL Standards

Goal 2, Standard 2—To use English to achieve academically in all content areas: Students will use English to obtain, process, construct, and provide subject matter information in spoken and written form.

Descriptors—Listening to, speaking, reading, and writing about subject matter information; Gathering information orally and in writing; Retelling information; Selecting, connecting, and explaining information; Analyzing, synthesizing, and inferring from information; Understanding and producing technical vocabulary and text features according to content area.

Use a 5 W Chart

You can ask the 5 W Questions to help get information about an event.

Who? **What?** **Where?** **When?** **Why?**

When you answer these questions, you are giving most of the needed information.

Practice

Copy the Chart. Write a question for each of the 5 Ws. Have a partner answer your questions.

Who?	Who attended the convention?
What?	
Where?	
When?	
Why?	

Extension

With a group, make a time capsule of objects that you would like people to find in the future. Write a description of each object. Present your work to the class.

149

Linguistic Note

Question Formation Non-English speakers may have difficulty when formulating questions with correct word order. Speakers of Arabic, for instance, may tend to invert subject and verb: *Where the meeting was?* instead of *Where was the meeting?* Other students may have difficulty with auxiliary verbs such as *do* or *did*, since these do not exist in their languages. Spanish-speakers, for instance, may tend to omit the auxiliary verb when formulating a question and say *What they did?* instead of *What did they do?* Be conscious of these differences among languages and provide extra practice when necessary.

Accelerate Language Development

Students can reorganize the information in their oral presentations in the form of questions and answers to reinforce their understanding of using the 5 W Questions to tell about something.

STEP 1: Teach

Use a 5 W Chart

Ask students to think about where they are right now. To describe this event, have them write one question for each of the 5 W Questions.

Possible Responses

Who is sitting next to me in this class?

What are we learning today?

Where is this classroom located in this school?

When does the school day end?

Why do we sit at desks?

Scaffolding

Have students use the information from the answers to their questions to write a paragraph that describes where they are right now.

STEP 2: Practice

You may have students complete the graphic organizer provided as a Blackline Master in the *Teacher's Resource Book*.

Answer Key

1. **Who** attended the convention?
   George Washington, Benjamin Franklin, Alexander Hamilton, and two boys, Ned and Bob.
2. **What** did they do at the meeting?
   They formed a new federal government.
3. **Where** did the convention take place?
   In the State House in Philadelphia
4. **When** did the convention take place?
   In the summer of 1787
5. **Why** was the convention important?
   A new country was formed; this decision affected a lot of people and was made to improve their lives.

STEP 3: Extend

Oral Presentation Ask students to prepare an oral presentation to share their time capsules with the rest of the class. Encourage students to bring the objects they would like to put in the time capsule to the presentation.

STEP 1: Introduce

Help students understand that commas are used to separate, or set items apart, in a list or group. Explain that when used this way, commas help a reader keep track of information in lists or groups.

STEP 2: Teach

Commas in a Series

Have students read the information below the boxed text. Then write the following sentences on the board and have students fill in the missing commas:

1. *We read a play about Washington Hamilton and Franklin.*
2. *Virginia Georgia and New York were colonies.*

STEP 3: Practice

Before completing the activity, have students rewrite each sentence in the box by adding information to each one. In the first sentence have them add the names *Ned* and *Bob*. In the second sentence, have them add *the soldiers* and *the colonies*.

Answer Key

1. Franklin, Washington, and Hamilton were in Philadelphia.
2. Philadelphia, Boston, and New York were three important cities.
3. Pennsylvania, Massachusetts, and New York were three of the first states.

Reteach

Remind students of the difference between nouns and verbs. Explain that nouns name a person, place, or thing, and verbs describe actions. Tell students when they have a list in their writing, the words in the list must be the same part of speech. Nouns and verbs cannot be in the same list.

Teaching Resources
- ***Practice Book,*** pp. 77–78
- ***Transparencies,*** pp. 69–80
- ***Assessment,*** pp. 61–64
- ***CD-ROM***

Reading 3

Grammar & Writing

Commas in a Series

Sometimes, you need to list many different people, things, or ideas in a sentence. When you list three or more items in a series, you need to use commas.

Here are two examples of commas used in a series.

> Benjamin Franklin, George Washington, and Alexander Hamilton were talking.
>
> They discussed the army, the government, and the king.

The commas separate the items. Notice that one comma comes before the word ***and***. You do not use a comma after the last item.

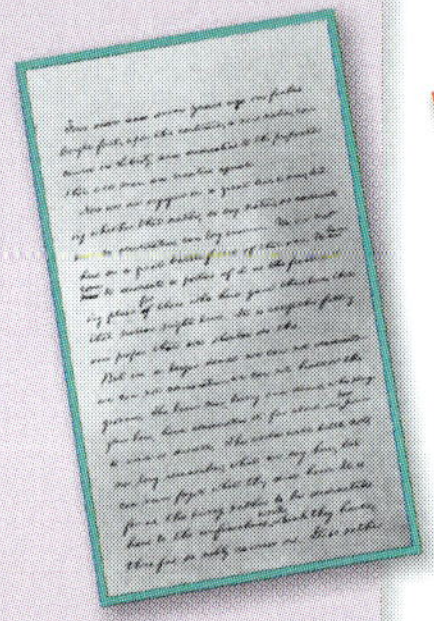

Practice

Write each sentence. Use commas to separate the items in each series.

1. Franklin Washington and Hamilton were in Philadelphia.
2. Philadelphia Boston and New York were three important cities.
3. Pennsylvania Massachusetts and New York were three of the first states.

Practice Book page 77

150

TESOL Standards

Goal 2, Standard 2—To use English to achieve academically in all content areas: Students will use English to obtain, process, construct, and provide subject matter information in spoken and written form.
Descriptor—Persuading, arguing, negotiating, evaluating, and justifying.

Goal 2, Standard 3—To use English to achieve academically in all content areas: Students will use appropriate learning strategies to construct and apply academic knowledge.
Descriptors—Using context to construct meaning; Actively connecting new information to information previously learned; Imitating the behaviors of native English speakers to complete tasks successfully.

Goal 3, Standard 1 —To use English in socially and culturally appropriate ways: Students will use the appropriate language variety, register, and genre according to audience, purpose, and setting.
Descriptors—Using the appropriate degree of formality with different audiences and settings; Recognizing and using standard English and vernacular dialects appropriately; Using a variety of writing styles appropriate for different audiences, purposes, and settings.

Write a Historical Speech

William stood outside the State House during the Constitutional Convention. Here is a speech he might have written. He wanted to persuade people to accept the Constitution.

We must now come together to form a strong government. We need to be able to defend our country. We need a government that can collect taxes and pay for things. We have written a Constitution for this new government, called a republic. The people elect representatives, who make laws. The president serves for only four years. He never will be a king. This new government will protect the rights of its citizens. It will act for the good of all 13 states. I urge you to accept this new Constitution that will make "one out of many."

SPELLING TIP

Some words have silent letters. In words like ***might*** and ***daughter***, the *gh* is silent. You will have to memorize these words.

Practice Book page 78

Practice

Write a short speech that a historical person might have made.

- Write one or two points you think the person would want to make.
- Think about the words the person would have used.

Writing Checklist

✓ Did your speech have a beginning, a middle, and an end?

✓ Did you choose a historical theme?

✓ Can a partner understand your speech?

151

Differentiated Instruction

Beginning	Write the following sentence on the board: *The soldiers were brave smart and strong.* Have students copy the sentence and add the correct commas.
Early Intermediate	Have students work in pairs to discuss the following question about William's speech: *What are three reasons William gives for accepting the Constitution?*
Intermediate	Based on facts in the reading, have students write a short speech that is either for or against accepting the Constitution.
Struggling Reader	Have students draw a picture of William giving his speech while others listen to him.

STEP 1: Teach

Write a Historical Speech

Define a historical speech for students.

SAY *Let's read the historical speech that William wrote to the people in 1787.*

- *Why did William give this speech?*
- *What words or ideas in the speech helped you to know that it was a historical speech?*
- *How well did William communicate his ideas?*
- *What strategies did William use to persuade people to accept the Constitution?*

Spelling Tip

Read aloud the box to students. Have them review the speech to find words that contain silent letters. Ask them to circle the silent letters in each word.

STEP 2: Practice

Before students write their own historical speeches, have students brainstorm a list of historical figures and their accomplishments. As they write their speeches, tell students to focus on one topic, use words that show emotion or try to persuade, and use the correct punctuation, including commas in a series.

STEP 3: Assess

Writing Checklist

✓ Guide students to begin their speeches with a statement that explains the reason for the speech.

✓ If students are having trouble coming up with an idea or topic, encourage them to choose one of the ideas the class came up with.

✓ Have students work with partners. Remind them to be respectful of one another's work and be constructive in any feedback or questions they might have.

The Five Step Writing Process in the Writing Handbook reference section of this book provides more student writing instruction.

STEP 1: Introduce

More About The Big Question

Remind students of the Unit 3 Big Question.

SAY *We will read about a boy who lived during the Revolutionary War. The Big Question for this Bonus Reading is* What can young people do to help a new country?

- *How do young people help in the making of the new nation?*
- *Why is it important for young people to be involved in a new country?*
- *Describe some of the activities young people have participated in throughout this unit.*

Have students fill in a Word Web to help them brainstorm ideas.

Visual Literacy

Pictures Use the pictures to help you preview the story.

SAY *Look at the pictures on pages 152 to 157.*

- *How do you think the boy is feeling at the beginning of the story? Why?*
- *Why is the boy looking out the barndoor?*
- *How do you think he feels at the end of the story? Why?*

STEP 2: Teach

Understand Text Structure

Refer students' attention to the genre box. Tell them that historical fiction is fiction, but the story is about a true event in history. Have students compare and contrast fiction and historical fiction.

Teaching Resources

- *Teacher's Resource Book,* pp. 125–126
- *CD-ROM*
- *Audio CD*

Bonus Reading

LITERATURE

Historical Fiction

The Real Soldier

by Laurie Calkhoven
illustrations by Doris Ettlinger

"Star, someday we'll ride in front of an army, just like General Washington," Jacob said, rubbing the horse's nose.

"You're too young," said his sister Emily.

"I said someday." Jacob was tired of being told he was too young. He and his father believed the colonies should be free from British rule. Two days ago, Jacob and his father had watched the local militia ride by his family's farm. They were called Minutemen.

Jacob wanted to be a soldier. He wanted to join the Minutemen, like his father. His father and other farmers in the area had promised to join General George Washington if he needed help.

152

TESOL Standards

Goal 2, Standard 3 —To use English to achieve academically in all content areas: Students will use appropriate learning strategies to construct and apply academic knowledge. **Descriptors**—Focusing attention selectively; Applying basic reading comprehension skills such as skimming, scanning, previewing, and reviewing text; Using context to construct meaning; Applying self-monitoring and self-corrective strategies to build and expand a knowledge base; Knowing when to use native language resources (human and material) to promote understanding.

Jacob was getting some wood to bring into the house when his mother rushed into the barn.

"Redcoats are here," she whispered.

Jacob was scared. He wondered if the British soldiers knew that his father and the other farmers were Minutemen.

Emily was scared, too. She ran and hid in Star's stall. Jacob wanted to hide with her, but his mother needed him. Together, they walked into the yard to face the British soldiers.

Jacob was relieved when he heard what the Redcoats wanted. This time, they only wanted food and supplies.

Jacob chose his words carefully. "My father has gone to the market," he said. "We don't have anything here." Jacob didn't tell the soldiers that the "market" was General Washington's camp!

When Jacob's father got home, he was proud. "Good thinking," he said. "You fooled them."

153

Differentiated Instruction	
Beginning	Have students complete the following sentences: *The British soldiers are called ________ . Jacob wants to join the ________ .*
Intermediate	Have students write a sentence that explains why Jacob wanted to be a soldier.
Greater Challenge	Ask students to make a list of the names of the characters in the story on pp. 152–153. Then have students write a description of the setting.
Standard English Learner CRI	Have students work in pairs to describe the action in the pictures on pp. 152–153.

Vocabulary Definitions

The following vocabulary appears in the text of *The Real Soldier*. You may share with your class if they require explanations of any words. They are not meant for vocabulary acquisition or exercises.

colony territory ruled by or belonging to another nation

rule act of governing or controlling

militia group of citizens that receive military training but are not part of the country's official army

Minutemen men who fought in the colonies' militia during the Revolutionary War

Redcoats British soldiers

camp outdoor area with temporary shelter such as tents

relieved feeling less anxiety or fear

proud pleased with oneself or someone else because of something that was done

Build Vocabulary

Remind students of the correct use of adjectives and adverbs. Tell students that adjectives give more information about nouns, and adverbs give more information about verbs. Explain that adjectives and adverbs can appear anywhere in a sentence—next to the word they describe or elsewhere in a sentence. Have students do the following:

- Create a two-column chart for adjectives and adverbs.
- Have students work in pairs to find these words in the story.
- Encourage students to fill in the chart as they read through the story.

STEP 3: Extend

Author's Purpose Remind students that authors write an article, play, or short story for one or more reasons. Discuss why the author wrote *The Real Soldier.* Guide students to recognize that the author wrote the story to inform readers. Point out, however, that because the text is fiction, it is also entertaining.

STEP 1: Monitor Progress

Comprehension Check

Sequence of Events After students finish reading pp. 154–155, have partners work together to fill in a Sequence of Events Chart like the one shown below. Ask them to list the main events that have happened up to this point in the story. Remind students that identifying the sequence of events will help them to better understand what they have read, recognize how one event may lead to the next, and remember what they have read.

Jacob and Emily are talking in the barn because Jacob wants to be a Minuteman.

↓

Jacob's mother tells him the British soldiers were there.

↓

Jacob talks to the soldiers and fools them.

↓

Jacob's father comes home and says he is proud of him.

↓

Minutemen come to the house to make plans.

"I want to help you fight the Redcoats," Jacob said.

"I know," his father said. "But you have work to do here, too. It is important to make sure everything at home looks as if nothing unusual is going on. Your job is to take care of your mother and Emily."

Later that night, Jacob heard a knock at the door. He was scared. What if the British soldiers had come back? He walked slowly to the door.

Jacob opened the door and saw three men. They were carrying guns. Jacob knew the men. They often visited his father. They were some of the Minutemen he had seen two days ago.

"Hi, Jacob," one of the men said.

"My father isn't here," Jacob said.

"We know. Your father said we could meet here. He said you would keep watch and that your mother had food for us."

FYI

Minutemen is a name given to the colonial militias that fought the British during the American Revolutionary War (1775–1783). This name was first given to the Massachusetts militia that vowed to be ready for battle "in a minute's notice." Minutemen were made up of such people as farmers, shop owners, and teachers who trained as soldiers in order to protect their rural communities.

TESOL Standards

Goal 2, Standard 3—To use English to achieve academically in all content areas: Students will use appropriate learning strategies to construct and apply academic knowledge.
Descriptors—Focusing attention selectively; Applying basic reading comprehension skills such as skimming, scanning, previewing, and reviewing text; Using context to construct meaning; Applying self-monitoring and self-corrective strategies to build and expand a knowledge base; Knowing when to use native language resources (human and material) to promote understanding.

Jacob kept watch while the men made their plans. Jacob's mother served the men stew and bread.

Jacob listened to their plans, his eyes wide. "May I come with you?" he asked.

"Your job is here," one of the men replied.

"But my father said I was brave today. I can be brave again," Jacob said. "Star is ready for battle, and so am I."

The men laughed.

"What if the Redcoats come back?" one of the men asked. "We need you here." The men grabbed their guns and hats. "Look after your mother and sister," they said as they went out into the night.

There was a loud knock at the door a few hours later.

155

Linguistic Note

Some speakers of other languages may have difficulty understanding and producing the possessive/genitive case as in *Washington's army*. Speakers of Spanish and Arabic, for instance, may tend to say "the army of Washington" instead, which is a direct translation of how this construction is used in their own languages. Arabic speakers may tend to simply omit the *'s* and say *Washington army*. If necessary, review this case, providing opportunity to practice.

Accelerate Language Development

Pronunciation You may have noticed that some Russian speakers may have difficulty pronouncing the /w/ in "Washington." There is no /w/ sound in Russian. Speakers typically substitute it with /v/ and may have trouble perceiving the difference between the two sounds. Be conscious of this and provide plenty of opportunity for practice.

STEP 2: Teach

Visual Literacy

Illustrations Have students look over the illustrations on pp. 153–155. Explain to students that fiction often has pictures to help readers follow the story and see the characters and setting. Have students work in small groups to fill in a Story Map up to this point using only information from the illustrations.

Academic Words

Discuss the definitions for *period* and *occur* with students. Write the following definitions and context sentences on the board:

period portion of time involving significant related events

occur begin in existence, happen

During the Revolutionary War *period*, people lived in colonies.

The colonists knew the war would *occur* and men would volunteer to be soldiers.

Have students discuss prior knowledge of other important periods in history and describe how they learned about them. Lead a class discussion about how the two academic words can be used in one sentence to describe the building of a new country. Have students suggest context sentences.

Study Skills

Internet Tell students that the Internet can be a great resource for accessing historical images. If possible, conduct a computer search to find images of items referenced in the text, including muskets, British Redcoats, and colonial Minutemen. Studying such images will reinforce the meanings of new vocabulary, and help students visualize the action of the story.

STEP 3: Assess

Make Predictions

Organize students into small groups. Have students discuss the events of the story up to this point. Encourage them to make predictions about what they think may happen next.

STEP 1: Monitor Progress

Comprehension Check

Identifying Details Have students discuss the answers to the following questions after they read pp. 156–157:

- Two more British soldiers come to Jacob's house. What are they looking for? They are looking for Jacob's father. They are also looking for Minutemen.
- What does Jacob tell the soldier about the Minutemen? He tells them they have not seen any Minutemen today.
- What did the British soldiers do? They searched the house.
- What did Jacob's father tell him when he came home? He said that Jacob had helped his family, because he had fooled the soldiers.

Context Clues

Explain to students that often a writer does not tell the reader all the details about the characters and the plot. Tell them readers must be able to figure out some of the information themselves.

SAY *To figure out the details that an author has not described, you must find context clues and make predictions.*

- *What do we know about Jacob up to this point in the story?*
- *What context clues suggest how he is feeling?*
- *What unexpected situation has happened to Jacob?*
- *How do you think Jacob will react?*

Have students fill in a Predictions Chart using the information from the answers to the questions. Explain to students that they should add information to the chart as they finish reading the story.

Scaffolding

Read aloud the last sentence on p. 157. Lead a class discussion about why Jacob believes he is a real soldier. Guide students to realize Jacob protected his family, which is the same reason his father is fighting with the Minutemen.

Jacob opened the door a tiny bit. Two British soldiers pushed the door open and marched into the room.

"Where is your husband?" a soldier shouted to Jacob's mother.

"He went to the market," she said.

Emily held on to her mother's skirts. She hugged her doll tightly.

Jacob knew he had to be brave. He put his hands in his pockets and tried to act calm. He tried to act like a soldier.

"We haven't seen any Minutemen today," Jacob said in a strong voice. Like his mother, he chose his words carefully. The Minutemen left his house a few hours ago.

The soldier narrowed his eyes and stared at Jacob.

Jacob did not move. He looked directly at the man. "British soldiers were here earlier today," he said. "But no Minutemen."

156

TESOL Standards

Goal 2, Standard 3 —To use English to achieve academically in all content areas: Students will use appropriate learning strategies to construct and apply academic knowledge. **Descriptors—**Focusing attention selectively; Applying basic reading comprehension skills such as skimming, scanning, previewing, and reviewing text; Using context to construct meaning; Applying self-monitoring and self-corrective strategies to build and expand a knowledge base; Knowing when to use native language resources (human and material) to promote understanding.

The Redcoats searched the house. They did not find any Minutemen. The Redcoats were angry, but they left. Jacob, Emily, and their mother sighed with relief. They hoped that they would not see any more British soldiers.

The next morning, Jacob's father came home. He said that the British soldiers had been driven out of the area.

"You helped us by fooling the Redcoats," Jacob's father said to him. "We were able to surprise them."

Jacob knew his father had gone to fight the war, but he was a real soldier at home.

157

STEP 2: Teach

Vocabulary Definitions

The following definitions are provided to share with your class if they require explanations of any words.

tiny very small

narrowed made small, less wide

stared looked with a steady gaze

searched looked thoroughly and carefully

sighed with relief let out a long deep breath, feeling better

fooled tricked or deceived

Build Vocabulary

Write the vocabulary words listed above on the board. Lead the class in a group effort to write a long sentence using all of the vocabulary words. Tell students the sentence should be fiction and can be a run-on sentence with many details.

Make Connections

Writing Fluency Invite students to write a story about an experience they have had working with a club or group when everyone had to agree on a decision. Tell students the story can be about a group at school or a group in the community. Encourage students to share their stories with the class. Have students discuss how the group members worked together to reach an agreement. Remind students their stories can be related to the Unit 3 Big Question.

STEP 3: Extend

Reader's Theater

Organize students into small groups. Have each group present a dramatization of one of the scenes from the story. After each group has presented their performances, have students consider how acting out the selection helped them to further understand the story and its importance.

Differentiated Instruction

Beginning	Have students look at the picture on p. 156. Ask students to decide by looking at the picture if the soldiers are friendly or mean.
Early Intermediate	Have students work in pairs to demonstrate what happened when the Redcoats came to Jacob's house.
Intermediate	Have students work in pairs to discuss details of a scene of the story. Ask volunteers to make oral presentations to describe the scene of the story.
Struggling Reader	Have students draw a picture of Jacob and label it.

STEP 1: Review

The Big Question

Evidence of Understanding

Read the Big Question with the students to focus students' attention on this unit's theme in a way that can be answered and assessed in a variety of modalities. The first tier is the least challenging and the third tier is the most challenging.

STEP 2: Transfer

Written

Biography Help students identify a suitable historical figure and access sources on the Internet or in the school library for information.

Letter Have students share what they remember about Philadelphia in 1787 from the readings. List their ideas on the board.

Report Guide students in using the Internet to conduct searches on the Constitutional Convention and the leaders who attended it.

Oral

Speech Help students use the Internet to locate a famous speech. Encourage them to practice reading speeches to a partner before reading them aloud to the class.

Skit Have students discuss who the Redcoats and the Minutemen were, and how the colonists felt about King George.

Presentation To prepare, have students review and list facts from the readings about the United States government.

Visual/Active

Collage Tell students to bring in old newspapers and magazines to use in their collages.

Brochure Bring in sample brochures or download them from the Internet to give students an idea of how to make their own brochures.

Diorama To give them ideas for their dioramas have students review the photographs and pictures from the readings before they get started.

UNIT 3 Wrap Up

The Big Question

How do people create new countries?

Written	Oral	Visual/Active
Biography Research one of the people who helped form our country. Write a short biography of his of her life.	**Speech** Find the text of a famous speech. Practice reading part of the speech. Then deliver it to the class.	**Collage** Use drawings, photos, and magazine clippings to create a collage that shows what freedom means to you.
Letter Suppose you lived in Philadelphia in 1787. Write a letter to a friend, telling about the events in this unit. Be sure to tell about everyday life, too.	**Skit** Write and perform a skit about a family during the American Revolution. Include details about the Minutemen, the Redcoats, and people's opinions about King George.	**Brochure** Design a brochure that tells about the historical sites in Philadelphia. Include illustrations and captions.
Report Learn more about the Constitutional Convention. Choose one topic and write a short report about it.	**Presentation** Work as a group. Create a program that explains one feature of the new U.S. government. Present your program to younger students.	**Diorama** Create a diorama that shows an important scene from U.S. history. Include important people and events in your scene.

158

TESOL Standards

Goal 2, Standard 2—To use English to achieve academically in all content areas: Students will use English to obtain, process, construct, and provide subject matter information in spoken and written form.
Descriptors—Gathering information orally and in writing; Representing information visually and interpreting information presented visually; Understanding and producing technical vocabulary and text features according to content area; Demonstrating knowledge through application in a variety of contexts.

Goal 3, Standard 1—To use English in socially and culturally appropriate ways: Students will use the appropriate language variety, register, and genre according to audience, purpose, and setting.
Descriptors—Using the appropriate degree of formality with different audiences and settings; Recognizing and using Standard English and vernacular dialects appropriately; Using a variety of writing styles appropriate for different audiences, purposes, and settings; Responding to and using slang appropriately; Responding to and using idioms appropriately; Responding to and using humor appropriately; Determining when it is appropriate to use a language other than English; Determining appropriate topics for interaction.

Practice Book pages 79–80

✓ Learning Checklist

Word Analysis and Phonics

- ✓ Pronounce *r*-controlled words that contain *ar*, *or*, and *ore*.
- ✓ Recognize consonant digraphs *ch, sh,* and *th*.
- ✓ Use synonyms and antonyms.

Comprehension

- ✓ Compare and contrast information.
- ✓ Use a Venn Diagram.
- ✓ Identify main idea and details.
- ✓ Use a Main Idea and Details Chart.
- ✓ Make inferences.
- ✓ Use a 5W Chart.

Grammar and Writing

- ✓ Practice subject-verb agreement.
- ✓ Use correct punctuation and capitalization in letters.
- ✓ Use commas in a series correctly.
- ✓ Write a persuasive speech.
- ✓ Write a persuasive letter.
- ✓ Write a historical speech.

Self-Evaluation Questions

- How does what you've learned in this unit support what you've learned in social studies class?
- How does what you've learned in this unit relate to the present or the future?
- What grade do you deserve on your project? Why?

159

Further Reading

The Swiss Family Robinson, Johann Wyss
In this Penguin Young Reader® adaptation of the classic story, a shipwrecked family works together to build a new home on a tropical island and learns how to live in a strange new land.

The First Thanksgiving, Jean Craighead George
From the formation of Plymouth Rock eons ago, to the Pilgrims' friendship with Squanto, readers learn rich details about the first Thanksgiving.

Ben and Me: A New and Astonishing Life of Benjamin Franklin as Written by His Good Mouse Amos, Robert Lawson This whimsical tale of Ben Franklin is told from the perspective of the famous patriot's mouse friend, Amos. Many highlights of Franklin's life are depicted, including the Revolutionary War and invention of the Franklin stove.

STEP 3: Assess

Learning Checklist

Word Analysis and Phonics

- ✓ *r*-controlled words that contain *ar, or,* and *ore*: Reading 1, p. 120
- ✓ Consonant digraphs *ch, sh*, and *th*: Reading 2, p. 132
- ✓ Synonyms and antonyms: Reading 3, p. 146

Comprehension

- ✓ Compare and contrast: Reading 1, p. 122
- ✓ Venn Diagram: Reading 1, p. 123
- ✓ Main idea and details: Reading 2, p. 134
- ✓ Main Idea and Details Chart: Reading 2, p. 135
- ✓ Make inferences: Reading 3, p. 148
- ✓ 5 W Chart: Reading 3, p. 149

Grammar and Writing

- ✓ Subject-verb agreement: Reading 1, p. 124
- ✓ Write a persuasive speech: Reading 1, p. 125
- ✓ Letters: Reading 2, p. 136
- ✓ Write a persuasive letter: Reading 2, p. 137
- ✓ Commas in a series: Reading 3, p. 150
- ✓ Write a historical speech: Reading 3, p. 151

Self-Evaluation Questions

The self-evaluation questions provide the teacher with important information about the students' learning processes as well as their self-esteem.

- Students should know the difference between historical fiction and nonfiction.
- Students should be able to draw from the readings that individuals can make a difference.
- Students should fairly assess their progress, giving examples of growth and areas where improvement is needed.

Teaching Resources

- ***Practice Book,*** pp. 79–80
- ***Transparencies,*** p. 83
- ***Assessment,*** pp. 11–18, pp. 123–131
- ***CD-ROM*** • ***Audio CD***

Unit 4 Planner

Your Environment

Unit Preview: pp. 160–165
Pacing: 3–4 Days
Vocabulary: *Words to Know*, pp. 162–163
Oral Language: *What about you?*, pp. 164–165

The Big Question

How do people and environments affect each other?

	Suggested Pacing: 7–8 Days 1	Suggested Pacing: 7–8 Days 2
Reading Selection	**Biomes All Over the World** pp. 166–181 **Genre:** Informational Text/Science ***A Closer Look at . . .*** ***Animals and Their Biomes***, pp. 174–175	**Springer Goes Home** pp. 182–193 **Genre:** Informational Text/ Magazine Article
Oral Language	**More About the Big Question, p. T168** *Why does Earth have so many different biomes?*	**More About the Big Question, p. T184** *How can humans protect wild animals in their environment?*
Vocabulary	**Key Words:** biome, tundra, equator, desert, tropical, grasslands, ocean **Academic Words:** adapt, classify **Other Academic Word:** role	**Key Words:** pods, orphan, migrated, predator, reunite, starvation **Academic Words:** consume, goal **Other Academic Word:** respond
Phonics Word Analysis Fluency	**Phonics:** Final Sound: *s*, *z*, p. 176 **Fluency:** Look Ahead, p. 177	**Phonics:** Consonant Clusters, p. 188 **Fluency:** Read with Expression, p. 189
Comprehension	**Reading Strategy:** Visualize, pp. 168, 173 **Learning Strategy:** Take Notes, p. 178 **Comprehension Skill:** Visualize, p. 178 **Graphic Organizer:** Compare and Contrast Chart, p. 179	**Reading Strategy:** Make Predictions, pp. 184, 187 **Learning Strategy:** Summarize, p. 190 **Comprehension Skill:** Problem and Solution, p. 190 **Graphic Organizer:** Problem and Solution Chart, p. 191
Grammar and Writing	**Grammar:** Conjunctions and Transitions, p. 180 **Writing:** Write an Expository Paragraph, Writing Checklist, Spelling Tip, p. 181	**Grammar:** Complete and Incomplete Sentences, p. 192 **Writing:** Write an Explanation, Writing Checklist, Spelling Tip, p. 193
	Differentiated Instruction pp. T161, T163, T167, T169, T173, T181	**Differentiated Instruction** pp. T183, T185, T187, T193

Teaching Resources

- *Assessments*, pp. 65–76, pp. 133–142
- *Practice Book*, pp. 81–106
- *Phonics and Word Analysis Workbook*
- *Phonics and Word Analysis Teacher's Guide w/Audio CD*
- *Phonics Flashcards*
- *Posters*
- *Teacher's Resource Book* Lesson Plans, pp. 38–49
- *Audio CD*
- *DVD*
- *Teacher's CD-ROM*
- *CD-ROM*
- *Phonetic Storybooks*
- *Penguin Young Readers Library*

Suggested Pacing: 7–8 Days

3

After the Hurricane

pp. 194–207

Genre: Informational Text/ Social Studies

More About the Big Question, p. T196
How does a community recover from an environmental disaster?

Key Words: assistance, handle, damage, stranded, relief
Academic Words: authorities, establish
Other Academic Word: define

Word Analysis: Homophones, p. 202
Fluency: Read for Speed and Accuracy, p. 203

Reading Strategy: Ask Questions, pp. 196, 201
Learning Strategy: Outline, p. 204
Comprehension Skill: Sequence, p. 204
Graphic Organizer: Sequence Chart, p. 205

Grammar: Prepositions, p. 206
Writing: Make a Poster, Writing Checklist, Spelling Tip, p. 207

Differentiated Instruction
pp. T195, T197, T201, T207

Suggested Pacing: 1–2 Days

Bonus Reading

Marine Food Web

pp. 208–211

Genre: Informational Text/ Science

More About the Big Question, p. T208
How do humans affect food webs?

Vocabulary: producers, consumers, decomposers, organism, overfishing, phytoplankton, drift, zooplankton

Differentiated Instruction
p. T209

Further Reading

The Crane's Gift, Steve and Megumi Biddle
This Penguin Young Reader® is a beautiful and moving tale set in Japan. An old man rescues an injured crane and his kindness changes his life.

Welcome to the Sea of Sand, Jane Yolen
Arizona's Sonoran Desert, the picturesque "sea of sand" habitat of a wide variety of animals, is described in engaging verse form with vivid illustrations.

Dive: My Adventures in the Deep Frontier, Sylvia A. Earle
Here, the world's oceans come alive, as the author, a marine biologist, takes readers on an underwater journey, exploring the fascinating world within the sea.

Suggested Pacing: 1–2 Days

Assessment

The Big Question

Evidence of Understanding
How do people and environments affect each other?

Check Up pp. 169, 171, 185, 197, 199
Think It Over pp. 173, 187, 201
Activity To Do! p. 175
Extension pp. 179, 191, 205

Unit Wrap Up pp. 212–213
Written
List; Log; Magazine Article

Oral
Discussion; Presentation; Song

Visual/Active
Poster; Chart; Illustration

Learning Checklist
Word Analysis and Phonics; Comprehension; Grammar and Writing; Self-Evaluation Questions

STEP 1: Introduce

Tell students they will learn about the environment and how they affect it. Have students work in groups to discuss the various environments they have experienced or heard about. Then ask students about the people, animals, and plants they would expect to find in those environments.

Unit Content Students practice reading and comprehension skills such as visualizing, making predictions, and asking questions. They apply academic learning strategies such as taking notes, summarizing, and outlining.

Visual Literacy

Photographs Have students look at the photographs for the readings in this unit. Point out that each reading is numbered, and the title of the reading appears below the photograph. Read aloud each title, and discuss students' prior knowledge about their environment.

STEP 2: Build Background

The Big Question

Read aloud the Big Question.

SAY *Let's think about the environment where we live.*

- *How would you describe our environment?*
- *What plants and wild animals are there?*
- *What experiences have you had in your environment?*

Have students fill in a Cause and Effect Chart like the one shown below that describes ways they interact with the environment.

CAUSE	EFFECT
I saw a lot of litter on the beach.	I joined a volunteer group that cleans the beach on weekends.
I heard that our town is experiencing a drought.	I take quick showers.
Our City Council bought trees to plant on Earth Day.	I planted trees in the park.

UNIT 4

Your Environment

Deserts, mountaintops, tropical rain forests, and grasslands are all places where people live. Animals and plants live in these places, too.

READINGS

1 Biomes All Over the World

2 Springer Goes Home

3 After the Hurricane

160

TESOL Standards

Goal 1, Standard 2—To use English to communicate in social settings: Students will interact in, through, and with spoken and written English for personal expression and enjoyment

Descriptors— Sharing social and cultural traditions and values; Expressing personal needs, feelings, and ideas.

The Big Question

How do people and environments affect each other?

Listening and Speaking

You will talk about your environment and things you can do to protect it.

Writing

You will write an expository paragraph about a biome.

Bonus Reading

Marine Food Web

Quick Write

Write several sentences describing one thing you do to protect your environment. Share your work with a partner.

Visit *LongmanCornerstone.com* 161

Differentiated Instruction

Beginning	Say the difficult words in the names of the readings, but not in the order they appear on pp. 160–161: *biomes, Springer, hurricane, marine*. Ask students to point to the appropriate picture, and say the word aloud.
Intermediate	Ask students to use the pictures and titles to guess what each reading will be about. Have them explain their guesses.
Greater Challenge	Ask students to write a descriptive sentence for each of the three pictures for the readings shown on p. 160.
Struggling Reader	Point to the photo on pp. 160–161. Have students name some of the things they see in the photo. Write their responses on the board, and have students read them aloud.

STEP 3: Connect

Listening and Speaking

Read the text in the box aloud. Ask students to suggest words that describe an environment. Write the list of words on the board, and model their pronunciation for students.

Possible Responses dry, hot, humid, wet, grassy, freezing, forest, mountains, desert

Writing

Read the text in the Writing box aloud to students.

SAY *A biome is an environment where animals and plants live together. Every kind of biome has its own animals and plants.*

- *What kinds of animals and plants would you find in a forest?*
- *What kinds of animals and plants would you find in the ocean?*

Tell students that an expository paragraph explains facts or important information about one topic. Encourage students to use a 5W Chart to find out more about the biome they live in and organize their information.

Quick Write

Before students begin writing their sentences, have students brainstorm ways they and their families protect the environment. Tell students to explain in the sentences they write what they do to help the environment and how they do it.

Adapt the Activity

Have students work in groups to draw a large mural of people in the community working together to protect the environment. Explain that the mural can show things they have already done or things they think should be done to help the environment.

Visual Literacy

Graphic Organizer Introduce the Big Question transparency and use it throughout the unit to help students connect the readings to the Big Question.

STEP 1: Introduce

Unit Vocabulary

Use these pages to help students identify terms used to describe the environment. Post your Words to Know poster for this unit in the classroom. As students read the unit, reinforce the unit vocabulary by using the Vocabulary Cards provided as a Blackline Master in the *Teacher's Resource Book* as flash cards or in memory games.

STEP 2: Teach

Words to Know

Point to the pictures in section 1 of things in the environment. Say each term aloud and have students point to the correct icon.

Draw students' attention to the question and sentence stem in section 2. Have them complete the sentence stem with the words provided. Repeat the procedure with the questions and sentence stem on p. 163.

Academic Words

Discuss the definitions for *consist of* and *data* with students. Share the following context sentences with students. Have students add the terms to their personal thesaurus.

consist of contain or be composed of something

data collection of facts used for planning or calculating

Environments *consist of* people, animals, and plants.

The *data* on energy use shows we must learn to conserve our resources.

Challenge students to use both academic words in the same sentence about environments. Students can use a thesaurus to find words with similar meanings.

Teaching Resources

- ***Teacher's Resource Book,*** pp. 95–96, 170
- ***Posters***
- ***Transparencies,*** pp. 19–24
- ***CD-ROM*** • ***Audio CD***

What Do You Know about Your Environment?

Words to Know

1. Use these words to talk about the environment.

 **plant**

 **soil**

 **wildlife**

 **insect**

 **pollution**

 **energy**

2. How do you protect the environment?

I protect the environment when I ____________ .

 **recycle glass**

 **use trash cans**

 **ride the train**

 **plant trees**

 **conserve water**

162

TESOL Standards

Goal 1, Standard 3—To use English to communicate in social settings: Students will use learning strategies to extend their communicative competence.

Descriptors—Testing hypotheses about language; Listening to and imitating how others use English; Exploring alternative ways of saying things; Using context to construct meaning.

3. **What happens when the environment is protected?**

If people ____________ *, then we will have* ____________ .

clean air

fresh water

a clean environment

more oxygen *and* less erosion

163

Explain the Captions

Read the captions in section 3 aloud, and have the class repeat them as they examine the pictures. After they complete the sentence stem, have students write their own context sentences using the words from section 1 and the captions.

STEP 3: Practice

Build Discussion

Help students use the vocabulary words to write about protecting the environment.

Write the following sentences on the board:

I recycle glass bottles and cans.

You can conserve water by using less of it.

Ask students to write similar sentences for the phrases *ride the train*, *use trash cans*, and *plant trees*. Have students share their sentences, and discuss each one with the class.

Scaffolding

Word Origins Explain to students that many words in English come from other languages. *Conserve* comes from the Latin word *conservare*, which means "to keep."

Differentiated Instruction

Beginning	Direct students to the icons for activities to protect the environment shown on p. 162. Have students work in pairs to demonstrate each activity.
Early Intermediate	Have students look at the icons on p. 162. Ask them to work in pairs, and select one icon to describe to the class.
Intermediate	Ask students to select a photo on p. 163 of a biome that looks like a place they have visited. Have students write a short description of where they visited.
Standard English Learner CRI	Have students work in pairs, and make a list of descriptive words for the things they see in the photos on p. 163. Ask them to add the list to their personal thesaurus.

FYI

Earth Day In 1969, U.S. Senator Gaylord Nelson decided we needed one special day a year when everyone went outside and did something important to improve the environment. That day officially became Earth Day on April 22, 1970. On that first Earth Day, people from many different countries promised to get involved and help keep the environment clean. Earth Team volunteers lead groups year-round to protect the soil, water, and wildlife in their communities. Earth Day is a day for everyone in the world to celebrate all that has been done to protect our planet.

STEP 1: Introduce

Unit Background

The peer mini-autobiographies and accompanying exercises are designed to increase comprehension and to model how students can talk and write about the environment. Use the exercises below to elicit student prior knowledge and ideas to help them tell their own stories.

STEP 2: Monitor Progress

Comprehension Check

Roth

1. What country does Roth live in?
   Germany.
2. What do the people there think about recycling?
   They take it very seriously.
3. What do Roth's neighbors do with plastic and glass bottles?
   They put them in bins to be used again.
4. What do the people hope protecting the environment will mean?
   They hope it means a better future for everyone.

Sharma

1. What country is Sharma from?
   Sharma is from Bangladesh.
2. What is Dhaka?
   Dhaka is a large city in Bangladesh.
3. What are some things that cause pollution in Bangladesh?
   Cars and factories cause pollution there.
4. What might happen if Bangladesh has more modern cars and factories?
   The air might get cleaner.

Link to Social Studies

Map Skills Draw students' attention to the map of the world in the background of these pages. Have students say the names of each location aloud, and use other world maps or globes to find the locations.

Teaching Resources

- *Audio CD*

Your Stories about Your Environment

Roth

In Germany, we take recycling very seriously. Every city and town has bins where people can bring their used plastic and glass bottles, newspapers, cardboard, and aluminum cans. We hope this will mean a better future for everyone.

Sharma

Air pollution is a big problem in Bangladesh. In large cities, like Dhaka, we are just beginning to measure pollution that comes from cars and factories. We hope modern cars and factories will mean cleaner air for everyone.

164

TESOL Standards

Goal 1, Standard 2—To use English to communicate in social settings: Students will interact in, through, and with spoken and written English for personal expression and enjoyment.
Descriptors—Sharing social and cultural traditions and values; Expressing personal needs, feelings, and ideas.

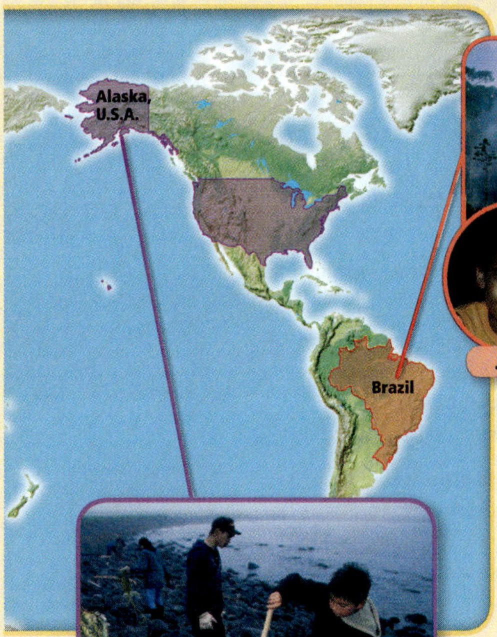

João

In Brazil, where I live, rain forests grow along the Amazon River. Rain forests are home to many animals. The trees give off oxygen, which we all need to live. Some people have cut down trees to build homes or have cleared the land for farming. We need to stop cutting down trees. The whole world needs them.

Ama

I live on St. Paul's Island in Alaska. Our rocky beaches get lots of garbage from boats that pass by. We get together and pick up trash, bottles, and cans. In September, children and adults from around the world do the same thing. It's called the International Coastal Cleanup.

What about you?

1. What have you done to help your environment?
2. How are these students' stories similar to yours?
3. Do you have your own stories about how you helped your environment? Tell your story!

Sharing Language and Culture

Global Perspective Students might have a story about a family member, friend, or neighbor who helped protect the environment in another country. Encourage students to describe the environment these people helped protect.

Ama

1. Where does Ama live?
   Ama lives on St. Paul's Island in Alaska.
2. What does Ama see when she goes to the rocky beach near her home?
   She sees garbage from boats.
3. What does Ama do on the beach to help the environment?
   Ama picks up trash, bottles, and cans.
4. What happens during the International Coastal Cleanup?
   People from around the world pick up trash, bottles, and cans on their beaches.

João

1. Where does João live?
   João lives in Brazil.
2. What kind of environment would you find along the Amazon River where João lives?
   You would find rain forests along the Amazon River.
3. Why do people in Brazil cut down trees?
   People in Brazil cut down trees to build homes or to clear the land for farming.
4. Does João think it's good to cut down trees? Why or why not?
   He does not think it's good to cut down trees because the whole world needs them.

Study Skills

Internet Invite students to choose one of the countries from the stories on pp. 164–165. Have them research one fact about that country on the Internet.

STEP 3: Assess

What About You?

1. Have students tell about their own experiences picking up litter, recycling, conserving water, or planting trees.
2. Have students look for similarities not only in what the writers did, but in how they feel about the environment.
3. **Personal Stories** Have students write a description of something they did to help the environment that turned out to be a lot of fun.

STEP 1: Introduce

Key Words

Help students learn the skill of defining words by using context.

SAY *All the vocabulary words from* Biomes All Over the World *are defined in the Words in Context selection.*

- *What kind of place is a desert?*
- *What kind of place is tropical?*
- *What kind of place is a grassland?*

Have students find three sentences in the passage that contain key words.

STEP 2: Teach

Words in Context

Write the following sentences on the board. Have students complete this fill in the blanks exercise using the key words from the Words in Context passage.

1. In the ocean biome, you will find the deepest spot on the planet.
2. The explorers crossed the tundra wearing snow shoes.
3. The hottest temperatures occur at the equator.
4. If you live in the desert, it doesn't rain often.
5. On a tropical island, you pick fruit from the trees.
6. Grasslands can have wet and humid tall-grass or dry short-grass.
7. The ocean is made of saltwater that people cannot drink.

Study Skills

Dictionary Students can use the dictionary to see if the Words in Context definitions are correct.

Online Dictionary Students can use an online dictionary or the CD that accompanies a learner's dictionary, like the *Longman Basic Dictionary*.

www.LongmanCornerstone.com

Teaching Resources

- *Practice Book*, pp. 81–82
- *Transparencies*, p. 46
- *CD-ROM* • *Audio CD*

Reading 1

Biomes All Over the World

Vocabulary

Biomes All Over the World **describes the major biomes on Earth.**

Key Words

biome
tundra
equator
desert
tropical
grasslands
ocean

Words in Context

1 The Eden Project in Cornwall, England, has several man-made biomes. A **biome** is a group of plants and animals in a geographic area.

2 The **tundra** is found at the North and South Poles. Plants do not grow very tall, because the ground is often frozen or covered with snow.

3 The **equator** is an imaginary line that runs around the middle of our planet. It divides Earth in half.

4 A **desert** is usually dry and hot.

166

TESOL Standards

Goal 1, Standard 3—To use English to communicate in social settings: Students will use learning strategies to extend their communicative competence.
Descriptors—Testing hypotheses about language; Listening to and imitating how others use English; Exploring alternative ways of saying things; Using context to construct meaning.

Goal 2, Standard 2—To use English to achieve academically in all content areas: Students will use English to obtain, process, construct, and provide subject matter information in spoken and written form.
Descriptor—Understanding and producing technical vocabulary and text features according to content area.

Goal 2, Standard 3—To use English to achieve academically in all content areas: Students will use appropriate learning strategies to construct and apply academic knowledge
Descriptor—Using context to construct meaning.

5

5 Most **tropical** rain forests are near the equator. They are usually hot and humid!

6 **Grasslands** are large areas covered with grasses. Savannas and prairies are two types of grasslands.

6

7 The **ocean** is the largest biome in the world. Oceans cover more than 70 percent of Earth's surface.

7

Practice

Use each key word in a sentence.

Make Connections

What kind of biome do you live in? Describe the plants and animals that live around your home.

Academic Words

adapt
change to fit a new situation

classify
put into groups

Practice Book pages 81–82

Differentiated Instruction	
Beginning	Read the list of key words aloud, and ask students to repeat each word. Have students find each key word in the context sentences.
Intermediate	Have students work in pairs to discuss details about each biome and select one biome to describe to the class.
Greater Challenge	Have students complete a two-column chart. In column one, list the following biomes: *tundra*, *desert*, *grassland*, *ocean*. In column two, include all details for each biome found on pp. 166–167.
Struggling Reader	Ask students to write and repeat the word *tundra*. Have them draw a picture of the tundra shown in picture 2, and label it *cold tundra*. Repeat the exercise for picture 4.

Visual Literacy

Photographs Have students look at the photographs on pp. 166–167. Ask them to select one photo and describe what they see.

Academic Words

Discuss the definitions for *adapt* and *classify* with students. Share the following context sentences with students:

Some desert plants *adapt* to their environment by growing needles instead of leaves.

Knowing about biomes helps you *classify* wild animals.

Point out that the word *classify* contains the word *class*. Point out that to classify is to put things into classes, or groups. It comes from the French word *classifier*.

Other Academic Words

Provide students with another example of a word that can be used in the discussion of protecting the environment. Tell students that a *role* is a character played by an actor, but it can also be what someone does as a member of a group.

Her *role* was the leader of the volunteer group.

The *role* of a leader is to encourage others.

Students can use a thesaurus to find words with similar meanings.

STEP 3: Practice

Flexible Grouping You may assign these exercises as a class discussion, partner activity, or individual writing assignment.

Make Connections

Writing Fluency Have students work in pairs to write descriptions of their biome. Invite a class discussion by asking students about the climate in their biome, the features of the land, and the wild animals and plants they see. Ask students to discuss whether or not they think their biome is a comfortable place for people to live. Relate their opinions to the Big Question when you sum up the discussion.

STEP 1: Introduce

More About The Big Question

The Big Question for this selection is designed to get students thinking about the different biomes in the world and the animals and plants that live in them.

SAY *In a biome, plants and animals must be able to adapt to survive.*

- *What lives in the ocean?*
- *What lives in the forest?*
- *What lives in the desert?*

Have students determine which biome they live in and fill in a Word Web similar to the one below.

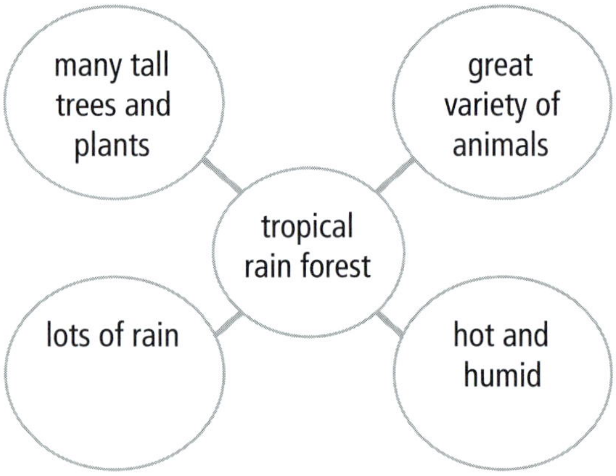

STEP 2: Teach

Reading Strategy

Visualize Explain that mental pictures help readers remember and understand what they read. Descriptions in a text tell readers what to "draw" in their minds.

Understand Text Structure

Draw students' attention to the genre label. Tell them that informational text about science is nonfiction because it is based on facts. This nonfiction text teaches readers about places in the natural world.

Teaching Resources

- ***Teacher's Resource Book***, pp. 127–128
- ***Practice Book***, pp. 83–84
- ***CD-ROM*** • ***Audio CD***

Reading 1

INFORMATIONAL TEXT

Science

The Big Question

Why does Earth have so many different biomes?

Reading Strategy

Visualize

Good readers often try to visualize, or see in their minds, what they are reading about.

- Use the descriptions in the text and the photos to create a mental picture of what you read.

168

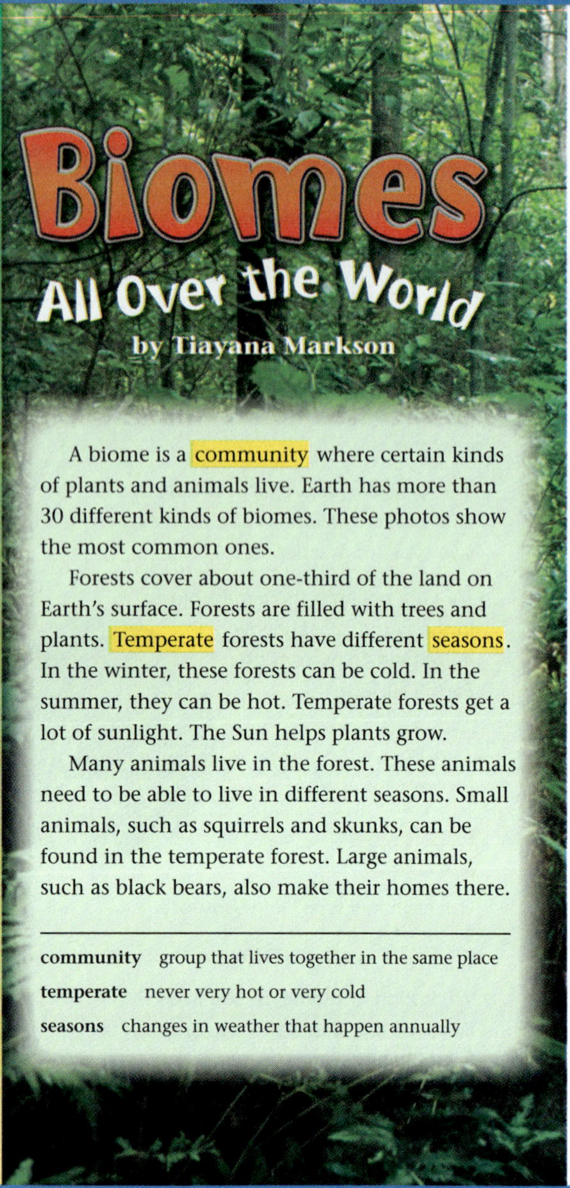

Biomes All Over the World

by Tiayana Markson

A biome is a community where certain kinds of plants and animals live. Earth has more than 30 different kinds of biomes. These photos show the most common ones.

Forests cover about one-third of the land on Earth's surface. Forests are filled with trees and plants. Temperate forests have different seasons. In the winter, these forests can be cold. In the summer, they can be hot. Temperate forests get a lot of sunlight. The Sun helps plants grow.

Many animals live in the forest. These animals need to be able to live in different seasons. Small animals, such as squirrels and skunks, can be found in the temperate forest. Large animals, such as black bears, also make their homes there.

community group that lives together in the same place

temperate never very hot or very cold

seasons changes in weather that happen annually

TESOL Standards

Goal 2, Standard 3—To use English to achieve academically in all content areas: Students will use appropriate learning strategies to construct and apply academic knowledge. **Descriptors**—Focusing attention selectively; Using context to construct meaning; Planning how and when to use cognitive strategies and applying them appropriately to a learning task; Imitating the behaviors of native English speakers to complete tasks successfully; Knowing when to use native language resources (human and material) to promote understanding.

A temperate forest is one kind of biome on Earth.

This tropical rain forest is located in South America.

Another kind of forest is the tropical rain forest. Tropical rain forests are in areas near the equator. All rain forests get a lot of rain every year. The rain helps plants grow. In fact, rain forests have more kinds of plants than any other biome. The trees grow so well that very little sunlight can get through the canopy of leaves. This makes the ground in the rain forest wet and dark.

The darkness inside the rain forest makes it a perfect home for animals such as bats and small insects. Many exotic birds, reptiles, and mammals live in rain forests.

canopy cover

exotic unusual and exciting

Check Up What do trees in the tropical rain forest look like?

169

Differentiated Instruction

Beginning	Read the captions and ask students to look at the photographs, then draw a picture of a rain forest with many plants and animals.
Early Intermediate	Ask students to fill in the blanks: *Temperate forests are ________ in summer.* *Temperate forests are ________ in winter.*
Intermediate	Ask students to write a paragraph describing in their own words what they would expect to find in the forest during winter and summer.
Standard English Learner (CRI)	Have students participate in a "Jump-In" activity. Explain to students that you will begin reading, and they are to jump in and read when they want, for as long as they want.

Build Vocabulary

Help students recognize how to use the highlighted words defined at the bottom of the page.

- Invite a volunteer to read one term and its definition aloud.
- Read the line with that highlighted word aloud to the class. Then read the line again replacing the term with a synonym from the definition. Example: *Many unusual and exciting birds, reptiles, and mammals live in the rain forests.*

Adjectives Have students review the paragraphs on pp. 168 and 169 and make a list of the adjectives they find. Remind students that an adjective describes or gives more information about a person, place, or thing.

Read Aloud

Have students take turns reading the paragraphs aloud on pp. 168–169. At the end of each paragraph, have the reader ask the listeners a question about what he or she just read. Invite the listeners to make up other questions about each paragraph.

STEP 3: Assess

Check Up

Have students work in pairs. Ask each partner to look at the photo and the text on p. 169 to help them describe trees in the tropical rain forest. Have students describe what it might feel like to walk in a tropical rain forest.

Link to Social Studies

Tropical Rain Forests Tropical rain forests can be found in Central and South America, Africa, Asia, and Australia. These forests account for over 1.5 million species of plants and animals, which is more species than the rest of the world combined. Give students a world map outline and have students indicate on the map the location of each of these continents. Then have students research to find three species of plants and animals for each continent and list the information on their maps.

STEP 1: Monitor Progress

Comprehension Check

Compare and Contrast After students read pp. 170–171, ask them to answer the following questions to compare and contrast biomes:

- How is the top of a mountain similar to the tundra? It is cold and windy, and both have ice and snow.
- For plants, how are deserts different from the tundra in summer? Plants and flowers grow in the tundra, but most plants cannot grow in the desert.
- Think about trees. How is the bottom of a mountain different from both the tundra and the desert? The bottoms of mountains have forests, but the tundra and deserts do not.

Author's Purpose Tell students that authors have various reasons for writing. They may want to

- entertain readers.
- persuade readers.
- express their feelings.
- teach readers about something.

Ask students why they think the author of *Biomes All Over the World* wrote this selection. Have students explain their answers.

Scaffolding

Ask volunteers to read aloud the paragraphs on page 170. Then have students write a short paragraph that describes which author's purpose from the list above they think applies to the paragraphs and explain why they chose that purpose.

Link to Math

Have students research the average temperature in January and July for three cities in three different biomes. Have students calculate the variation in temperature between the two months for each city, then determine which city has the greatest variation in temperature.

The arctic tundra is the coldest biome on Earth. Trees do not grow in the tundra. Winds are very strong. Ice covers the ground, and water freezes. Animals such as polar bears must be able to live in the cold. Most animals that live in the tundra have extra fat to keep them warm. Many birds and other animals migrate, or move, to a warmer climate for the winter.

In the summer, the weather is warm enough in the tundra for things to grow. Plants and flowers appear. These plants and flowers can live in colder temperatures. Animals that eat plants and grass can find more food during the summer.

---

arctic very cold

climate typical weather in an area

Flowers appear on the tundra in the warmer months.

Polar bears like the snow and cold weather in the tundra.

170

TESOL Standards

Goal 2, Standard 3—To use English to achieve academically in all content areas: Students will use appropriate learning strategies to construct and apply academic knowledge. **Descriptors**—Focusing attention selectively; Using context to construct meaning; Planning how and when to use cognitive strategies and applying them appropriately to a learning task; Imitating the behaviors of native English speakers to complete tasks successfully; Knowing when to use native language resources (human and material) to promote understanding.

Mountains are on every continent on Earth. Most mountains have forests at the bottom of them. The higher you go up a mountain, the colder and windier it gets. The tops of very high mountains look like the tundra. Only small plants and flowers grow in these areas. The plants usually grow close to the ground, so the wind cannot knock them over. Animals that live on mountains, such as mountain goats and mountain lions, must be strong climbers.

Desert biomes have very little rain. Most plants cannot grow there. Deserts are either very hot or very cold. These climates make it hard for anything to live there. Plants and animals that live in the desert have adapted to live with very little water.

---

continent one of the main masses of land on Earth

The tops of many tall mountains are very cold and snowy.

Very little grass grows in the desert.

Check Up What kind of climate does the tundra have?

Linguistic Note

Cognate Mountain Students whose home language is Spanish may recognize the Spanish cognate *montaña*. If they are very familiar with that Spanish word, they may have difficulty pronouncing the first vowel sound /ow/ in the English word *mountain.* Model the correct pronunciation of the *ou* vowel pair in these words: *mountain, round, bounce, sound*.

Accelerate Language Development

Comparative Endings Students who speak Spanish will be used to forming the comparative of adjectives by inserting the word *más* before the adjective. Explain that in English, we add the suffix -*er* to compare two things. Have students look at p. 170 to find two different words that compare temperatures. (*warmer, colder*)

STEP 2: Teach

Visual Literacy

Photographs and Captions Ask students to look at the photos on pp. 170–171 of three biomes. Have students discuss their prior knowledge of mountains, deserts, and the tundra.

SAY *The photos on pages 170 and 171 show you scenes from some biomes and the captions tell us some important facts.*

- *If you were visiting the tundra in the summer, what might you see?*
- *If you were a polar bear, why would you like the tundra in the winter?*
- *What might you need to hike to the top of a mountain?*
- *What plants do you know that grow in the desert?*

Academic Words

Write the following definitions and context sentences for *source* and *category* on the board.

source where something begins

category one division or group in a classification system

The *source* of the river is a lake in the north woods.

There is more than one *category* of plants and animals in a biome.

Explain to students that both academic words can be used when explaining facts about things that survive in nature. Have students write their own context sentences for each academic word.

Shades of Meaning Explain that in English, we often use the suffix –*er* to describe something that is more than something else. *It is colder on top of a mountain than it is at the bottom.* We often use the suffix –*est* to compare more than two items. *The top of a mountain is the coldest of all the biomes.*

STEP 3: Assess

Check Up

Have students reread p. 170, which describes the tundra. Then have students write one sentence in their own words that describes the tundra.

STEP 1: Monitor Progress

Comprehension Check

Cause and Effect Explain that identifying cause and effect can help a reader understand a selection. Have students fill in the effect for each of the causes listed in the Cause and Effect Chart shown below. Remind students that one cause and effect can lead to another cause and effect.

CAUSE	EFFECT
People have turned grasslands into farms.	There are fewer grasslands today than long ago.
The soil is good for planting crops, and animals can graze on the grass.	People have turned most prairies into farms.
Ocean water is salty.	Ocean animals are able to drink salt water.

Types of Sentences Explain that in informational articles, the author may ask a question. Draw students' attention to the last sentence in the selection. Have students discuss why the author asks this question.

Link to Science

Ocean Mammals Most ocean creatures, like fish and crabs, breathe underwater. Mammals, though, must come to the surface to breathe air. Whales, dolphins, and porpoises are some of the air-breathing mammals that live in the ocean. Have students research and write a short report on how the various ocean creatures and mammals breathe. Ask students to describe the difference between lungs and gills and explain how they each function.

Bison eat in this grassland in South Dakota.

Grasslands, like deserts, get very little rain. The plants and animals that live on grasslands do not need a lot of water. Enough rain falls to help grasses and some plants grow. They have rain in the summer, but they do not have rain in the winter.

Animals such as zebras and buffalo live on savannas. Many small animals and insects also make their homes on grasslands.

Prairies and savannas are two types of grasslands. Savannas are located near the equator. Prairies are in more temperate areas. Many small animals and insects also make their homes on grasslands. Large animals, like bison, elephants, and zebra, live in grasslands, too.

People have turned most prairies into farms. The soil is good for planting crops. Farm animals can graze on the grass. But this means that there are not as many grasslands on Earth as there used to be.

crops plants grown by a farmer and used for food

graze feed on grass

172

TESOL Standards

Goal 2, Standard 3—To use English to achieve academically in all content areas: Students will use appropriate learning strategies to construct and apply academic knowledge. **Descriptors**—Focusing attention selectively; Using context to construct meaning; Planning how and when to use cognitive strategies and applying them appropriately to a learning task; Imitating the behaviors of native English speakers to complete tasks successfully; Knowing when to use native language resources (human and material) to promote understanding.

The ocean biome is the largest biome on Earth. Oceans are huge bodies of water. They make up 70 percent of Earth's surface. Many kinds of animals and plants live in oceans. Fish, crabs, and clams spend their lives under water. Larger animals, such as whales, sharks, and dolphins, also live in the ocean. Blue whales live in the ocean. They are the largest known mammals on Earth. Ocean water is very salty. Animals that live in the ocean must be able to drink salt water.

Earth has many different biomes with a variety of plants and animals. Look around you. Which biome is most like the place where you live?

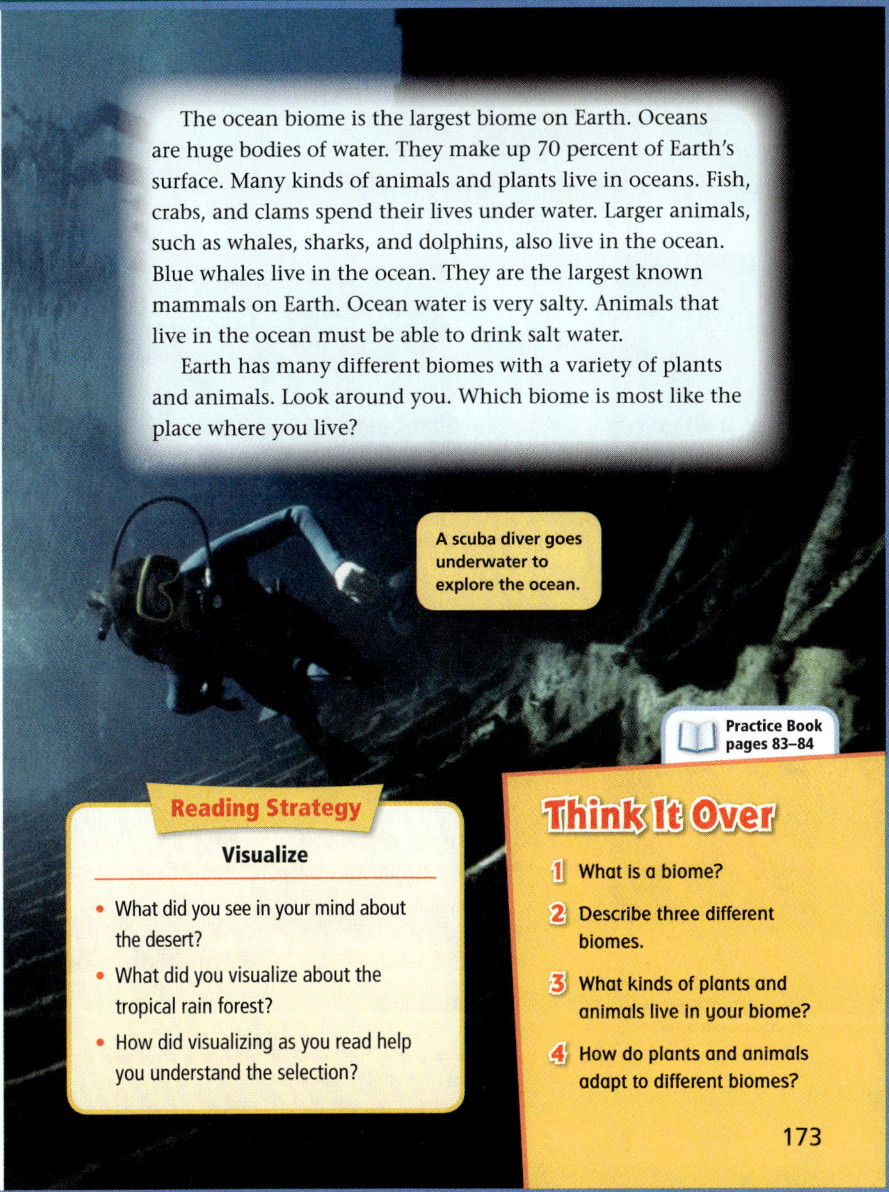

A scuba diver goes underwater to explore the ocean.

Practice Book pages 83–84

Reading Strategy

Visualize

- What did you see in your mind about the desert?
- What did you visualize about the tropical rain forest?
- How did visualizing as you read help you understand the selection?

Think It Over

1. What is a biome?
2. Describe three different biomes.
3. What kinds of plants and animals live in your biome?
4. How do plants and animals adapt to different biomes?

Differentiated Instruction

Beginning	Have students find the caption that includes the word *grassland*. Ask them to copy the sentence, then answer the following question: *What word in the sentence names an animal?*
Intermediate	Have students pretend that they are one of the large animals mentioned on pp. 172–173. Ask volunteers to describe to the class what their life is like in their biome.
Greater Challenge	Have students work in small groups to draw a large picture of all the fish and animals found in the ocean that are mentioned on p. 173.
Struggling Reader	Have students look at a map or globe, and find all the places on Earth that are part of the ocean biome. Ask them to write down the name of each ocean they find.

STEP 2: Teach

Build Discussion

Have students select one of the biomes they learned about in this reading, then tell what facts they learned about the biome, and discuss what it might be like for humans to live in that biome. Have students write a paragraph about the biome that answers the following questions:

How would people dress in that biome?
What kinds of shelter would people build?
What kinds of food could people find?

STEP 3: Assess

Reading Strategy

Visualize Give students an example of how to visualize.

SAY *Let's use the details in the selection to help us visualize different biomes.*

- *When you visualize the desert, how would you describe a very dry place that has no grass?*
- *When you visualize a tropical rain forest, how would you describe a hot place with tall trees.*
- *How does visualizing help you understand the selection?*

Think It Over

Flexible Grouping You may assign this activity as a class discussion, partner activity, or individual writing assignment.

Answer Key

1. A biome is a group of plants and animals in a certain kind of area.
2. The tundra is cold and windy. Tropical rain forests are hot and humid and have lots of tall trees. The ocean is a large body of very salty water.
3. Students should name some plants and animals that they see locally in the wild.
4. Plants and animals adapt to different biomes by learning how to survive in that particular climate.

STEP 1: Introduce

A Closer Look

The photos on these pages are designed to serve as visuals to expand vocabulary related to *Biomes All Over the World*.

More About The Big Question

The A Closer Look focuses on why the earth has so many different biomes.

SAY *Let's talk about different kinds of wild animals you have read about or have seen at a zoo or on TV.*

- *How do wild animals find food?*
- *Why do many of them have camouflage that helps them blend in with their surroundings?*
- *Why would a fish not be able to survive on land?*
- *Why would a polar bear not be able to survive in the desert?*

Make Connections

Writing Fluency Have students pick one of the biomes they learned about. Have them imagine that they spent a day in that biome, and write a short description of what they did and how they felt.

A Closer Look at...

Animals and Their Biomes

▲ **Temperate Forest**
Squirrels are one of the many kinds of animals that live in temperate forests.

▲ **Desert**
This roadrunner lives in the desert. It had to run very fast to catch its dinner!

▲ **Tundra**
The arctic fox lives in the tundra. Its fur coat changes color with the seasons.

▲ **Mountain**
These llamas live in the Andes Mountains. Some llamas are wild, but people in the Andes also raise llamas for their fur and meat.

FYI

Adaptation Adaptation does not happen all of a sudden. It's not a conscious decision by a plant or animal species to change because it would rather live somewhere else. Animals adapt because of changes in their environments, changes that have happened many times throughout Earth's long history. As an environment slowly changes, some plants and animals slowly change with it; over many generations, they become new species and survive. Plants and animals that do not make the right kinds of changes become extinct.

TESOL Standards

Goal 2, Standard 3—To use English to achieve academically in all content areas: Students will use appropriate learning strategies to construct and apply academic knowledge.
Descriptors—Focusing attention selectively; Using context to construct meaning; Planning how and when to use cognitive strategies and applying them appropriately to a learning task; Imitating the behaviors of native English speakers to complete tasks successfully; Knowing when to use native language resources (human and material) to promote understanding.

▲ **Tropical Rain Forest**
This poison arrow frog lives in the tropical rain forests of South America.

▲ **Ocean**
Sharks live in the ocean. They are an important part of the marine food web.

◀ **Savanna**
The rhinoceros is one of many animals that live on the savanna. People hunt rhinoceroses for their meat and horns.

▲ **Prairie**
Prairie dogs are very social animals. They live in underground burrows called towns.

Activity to Do!

These pages use pictures and words to tell about animals and biomes.

- Pick any animal that interests you.
- Research that animal and its biome.
- Create two pages, using pictures and words, to describe that animal and its biome.

175

Linguistic Note

Savanna The word *savanna* comes from the Taino word *zabana*. The Taino were native Americans who lived in the Caribbean islands before Europeans arrived. Spanish speakers took the word and changed it slightly, so that it became *sabana*. The English word derives from that.

Accelerate Language Development

Consonants *b* and *v* Spanish speakers pronounce certain *b's* and *v's* inside words with the same sound, which can be compared to an English *b* pronounced with the lips slightly open. At beginnings of Spanish words, *v* is usually pronounced almost identically to an English *b*. Students who come from homes in which Spanish is the primary language may have difficulty pronouncing certain English words, like *savanna*, *very*, and *variety*.

STEP 2: Teach

Visual Literacy

Photographs and Captions

SAY *Read the captions as we study the pictures.*

- *What do the large boldface words tell about each picture?*
- *How can you find out the kind of animal in each picture?*
- *Would you expect to find any of these animals in a different biome than the one they're in? Why or why not?*
- *Which animals on the page have you seen? Where?*
- *Which animal on the page seems the most dangerous to you? Why?*

Have students write a paragraph about an encounter they have had with a bird or animal in nature. Tell students it can be an experience like spotting an unusual bird or seeing a deer in the woods.

Adapt the Activity

Have students select one of the biomes listed on pp. 174–175, and draw a picture of that biome. Tell students to include plants and animals that live in the biome and any other details they know about the biome.

STEP 3: Assess

Activity to Do!

Study Skills Ask students to select an animal they see on these two pages or another animal they would like to know about. Have them use the Internet, books, or magazines to do their research.

SAY *Remember to include specific details about your animal and its biome.*

- *What biome does your animal live in?*
- *What does your animal eat?*
- *What does your animal look like? Why is its body shaped the way it is?*
- *What must it do to survive?*

STEP 1: Introduce

Phonics

Final sound: *s, z* Help students understand that words ending in *s* don't all have the same final sound. Sometimes the *s* sounds like the /s/ in *yes*, sometimes it sounds like /z/ as in *men's*, and sometimes like /iz/ as in *wages*.

STEP 2: Teach

Review the three sounds of words ending in *s*. Read aloud the words in the box at the top of p. 176. Have students repeat only the final *s* sound in each word.

Write the following words on the board, and ask students to pronounce them, and say which sound comes at the end:

dogs	*miss*	*ages*	*toes*
glass	*senses*	*faces*	*things*

Draw students' attention to the Rule Box.

SAY *Remember: a word that ends in s might have three different sounds.*

- *Which sound is at the end of cages?*
- *Which sound is at the end of pens?*
- *Which sound is at the end of bus?*

STEP 3: Practice

Flexible Grouping

You may assign this activity as a class discussion, partner activity, or individual writing assignment.

Answer Key

1. class s	**2.** rings z	**3.** mixes iz
4. was z	**5.** always z	**6.** faxes iz
7. pages iz	**8.** goes z	**9.** walks s

Reteach

Have students review some of the selections they've read in their textbooks to find six words with a final *s* sound. Have them say the words and tell which final *s* sound they're using.

Teaching Resources

- ***Practice Book***, p. 85
- ***Phonics Workbook***
- ***Phonics Flashcards***
- ***CD-ROM*** • ***Audio CD***

Reading 1

Phonics & Fluency

Phonics

Final sound: *s, z*

Read these words that end in *s*.

mountains	biomes	pages	tops

What is the final *s* sound of each word?

Rule Box

Voiceless **s** sounds like a snake hissing, sssss. Voiced **s** sounds like *z*. Think of the sound a bee makes, buzzz.

Practice

Work with a partner.

- Read each word aloud.
- Tell whether the final *s* sounds like *s* or *z*.

1. class	**6.** faxes
2. rings	**7.** pages
3. mixes	**8.** goes
4. was	**9.** walks
5. always	

Practice Book page 85

176

TESOL Standards

Goal 2, Standard 3—To use English to achieve academically in all content areas: Students will use appropriate learning strategies to construct and apply academic knowledge.
Descriptors—Applying basic reading comprehension skills such as skimming, scanning, previewing, and reviewing text; Using context to construct meaning; Applying self-monitoring and self-corrective strategies to build and expand a knowledge base.

Goal 3, Standard 3—To use English in socially and culturally appropriate ways: Students will use appropriate learning strategies to extend their sociolinguistic and sociocultural competence.
Descriptors—Observing and modeling how others speak and behave in a particular situation or setting; Experimenting with variations of language in social and academic settings; Seeking information about appropriate language use and behavior. understanding.

Fluency

Look Ahead

Sometimes readers look for hard words before they read. They then try to figure them out.

Practice

Pick one passage. → Find any hard words. → Practice saying those words. → Read the passage aloud.

1. A biome is a community where certain kinds of plants and animals live. Earth has more than 30 different kinds of biomes. The most common biomes are tropical rain forests, tundra, mountains, grasslands, deserts, and oceans.

2. Mountains are on every continent on Earth. Most mountains have forests at the bottom of them. The higher you go up a mountain, the colder and windier it gets. The tops of very high mountains look like the tundra. Only small plants and flowers grow in these areas.

3. The ocean biome is the largest biome on Earth. Oceans are huge bodies of water. They make up 70 percent of Earth's surface. Many kinds of animals and plants live in oceans. Fish, crabs, and clams spend their lives under water. Larger animals, such as whales, sharks, and dolphins, also live in the ocean. Blue whales live in the ocean. They are the largest known mammals on Earth.

177

Accelerate Language Development

Dropped final *s* Some students whose home language is Spanish, particularly those who come from the Caribbean, may be accustomed to dropping the final *s* sound entirely. This dropping of the final /s/ is also common in many regional and local American dialects. Be aware that students may understand that a word is a plural or present-tense verb in the third person singular and still drop the final *s* sound. Model the standard English pronunciations for students when appropriate.

STEP 1: Introduce

Fluency

Look Ahead Explain to students that sometimes readers look ahead to find hard words. Identifying hard words and practicing them can help students read more smoothly.

Play the Audio CD for this reading and ask students to listen for pacing, intonation, and expression.

STEP 2: Practice

Have students do the exercise with partners. You may want to assign each student a passage based on difficulty level (1–easy, 2–intermediate, 3–more difficult), or let students select their own passages.

- Have one partner look through the passage to find any hard words, and practice saying those words. Students may ask partners for help in pronouncing the hard words.
- Have the student read the passage to his or her partner, then have students change roles.

Possible Responses–Hard words

community	certain	continent
windier	areas	huge
dolphins		

STEP 3: Extend

Study Skills

Thesaurus Have students work with partners to:

- write down three words from the reading that were hard to pronounce;
- look up the words in a thesaurus to find synonyms the author might have used;
- read the sentences from the reading in which the hard words appear, substituting a synonym for each hard word.

Remind students that they can use this study skill anywhere. In social studies or science class, or when they read at home, they can find the hard words and write them down. Students can then look up synonyms in an online or print thesaurus.

STEP 1: Monitor Progress

Learning Strategy

Take Notes Taking notes is a way for students to remember important details in any selection they read. Have students work in pairs to review the reading, and take notes on three of the biomes. Explain that notes can be full sentences, phrases, or single words—anything that helps them remember.

STEP 2: Teach

Visualize

Students will learn how to visualize, making mental pictures from the details they find in their reading.

SAY *Visualizing helps you picture in your mind the details of what you read.*

- *What kinds of details help you visualize a person?*
- *What kinds of details help you visualize a place?*
- *What kinds of details help you visualize an object?*

Have students select an animal, place, or object that does not appear in any of the photos, but that the author described. Have students draw a picture of what they visualize from the description, then explain their drawings to the class.

STEP 3: Practice

Flexible Grouping You may assign this activity as a class discussion, partner activity, or individual written assignment.

Build Discussion

Have students make a list of the details that helped them visualize their partners' object, person, or place. Have students share their favorite details with the rest of the class. Discuss why these details were helpful.

Teaching Resources

- ***Practice Book,*** p. 86
- ***Transparencies,*** p. 63
- ***Teacher's Resource Book,*** p. 50
- ***CD-ROM***

Reading 1

Comprehension

Learning Strategy

Take Notes

Take notes on the different biomes. Share your notes with a partner.

Ask your partner to respond to the Big Question for this reading.

Practice Book page 86

Visualize

Writers use words to help readers visualize what they are reading about. As you read, look for words that describe. These words will help you visualize what you are reading about.

Practice

Describe an object, a person, or a place to a partner by telling only a few details.

- Have your partner guess what you are describing.
- After your partner guesses the object, ask your partner to tell which details helped the most.
- Switch roles.

TESOL Standards

Goal 2, Standard 3—To use English to achieve academically in all content areas: Students will use appropriate learning strategies to construct and apply academic knowledge. **Descriptors**—Focusing attention selectively; Using context to construct meaning; Planning how and when to use cognitive strategies and applying them appropriately to a learning task; Imitating the behaviors of native English speakers to complete tasks successfully; Knowing when to use native language resources (human and material) to promote understanding.

Use a Compare and Contrast Chart

When you **compare**, you tell how two or more things are similar. When you **contrast**, you tell how two or more things are different. You can use a T-Chart like this one to help you identify things that are alike and different.

Practice

Copy this chart. Compare and contrast the desert and grassland biomes. One example has been given.

How grasslands and deserts are similar	How grasslands and deserts are different
Both deserts and grass lands get very little water.	

Extension

Make a brochure that shows things people need when they visit your biome. Use photos or drawings to show the items. Write a brief description of each item and explain why you chose it. Show your brochure to the class.

Accelerate Language Development

T-Chart Beginning students who have not mastered the pronunciation of the names of English letters may not understand what you are saying when you speak about a T-Chart. Write a large capital letter *T* on the board, say its name, and have students repeat it. Then, using the *T* that you drew, create a T-Chart. Say the word *T-Chart*, emphasizing the name of the letter and using your finger to trace its outline. Use a similar technique to teach them how to pronounce *T-shirt* and *T-bone* (steak).

Linguistic Note

Cognates *Compare and Contrast* Students who also speak Spanish may be familiar with the Spanish words *comparar* and *contrastar*, which are cognates of the English words *compare* and *contrast*. As in English, the word *comparar* is sometimes used in everyday speech to mean both *compare* and *contrast*.

STEP 1: Teach

Use a Compare and Contrast Chart

Ask students to think about two animals they would like to compare and contrast. Have students use a Compare and Contrast Chart to organize the information about how the animals are similar and different. Ask them to answer these questions:

- How do the animals look?
- What do the animals eat?
- Where do the animals live?

STEP 2: Practice

You may have students complete the graphic organizer provided as a Blackline Master in the *Teacher's Resource Book.*

Answer Key

How grasslands and deserts are similar	How grasslands and deserts are different
Both are biomes; both get very little rain; both can be found in the United States.	Grasslands have lots of grass. People turn grasslands into farms, but they do not turn deserts into farms; rhinoceroses live in grasslands, but never in deserts.

STEP 3: Extend

Oral Presentation Divide the class into groups, and assign one group for each biome. Bring in some sample travel brochures for students to look at as models. Have students work together to decide what illustrations they would like to include and what descriptions they want to write.

STEP 1: Introduce

Help students understand that a conjunction can be used to make one sentence by combining two related sentences. Transitions show a change in ideas between two sentences.

STEP 2: Teach

Conjunctions and Transitions

Write the following sentences on the board. Ask students to identify the conjunctions or transitions.

1. *I used to live on the prairie,* and *Sarah used to live in the desert.*
2. *Many fish live in the ocean.* But *some mammals live there, too.*
3. *Tropical rain forests are hot,* and *they also have many tall trees.*
4. *The tundra is a really cold biome.* But *some animals survive very well there.*

Link to Math

Help students visualize what "70 percent of Earth's surface" means. Show students a pie chart with 70 percent of the chart shaded. Have students solve the following calculations: *If there are 30 students in your class, how many students make up 70 percent of your class? How many students make up 70 percent of your school?*

STEP 3: Practice

Before students begin the Practice activity, have them write two short sentences about biomes, then use a conjunction to make one compound sentence.

Answer Key

1. conjunction
2. transition
3. conjunction
4. conjunction

Teaching Resources

- ***Practice Book***, pp. 87–88
- ***Transparencies***, pp. 69–80
- ***Assessments***, pp. 65–68
- ***CD-ROM***

Reading 1

Grammar & Writing

Conjunctions and Transitions

Conjunctions join two related sentences together to form a compound sentence.

Ice covers the ground, **and** water freezes in the tundra.

Transitions show a change in ideas from one sentence to another.

Grasslands, like deserts, get very little rain. **But** enough rain falls to help grasses and some plants grow.

Practice

Read the sentences. Tell whether *and* or *but* are conjunctions or transitions.

1. Many kinds of plants grow in a forest, and many kinds of animals live there.
2. Most of the animals, such as squirrels and chipmunks, are small. But larger animals also live in forests.
3. Oceans are huge bodies of water, and they make up 70 percent of Earth's surface.
4. Some animals that live in the ocean eat plants, and some hunt other animals for food.

Practice Book page 87

180

TESOL Standards

Goal 1, Standard 3—To use English to communicate in social settings; Students will use learning strategies to extend their communicative competence.
Descriptors—Seeking support and feedback from others; Requesting and providing clarification; Requesting information and assistance.

Goal 2, Standard 1—To use English to achieve academically in all content areas: Students will use English to interact in the classroom.
Descriptor—Asking and answering questions.

Goal 2, Standard 2—To use English to achieve academically in all content areas: Students will use English to obtain, process, construct, and provide subject matter information in spoken and written form.
Descriptor—Selecting, connecting, and explaining information.

Goal 2, Standard 3—To use English to achieve academically in all content areas: Students will use appropriate learning strategies to construct and apply academic knowledge.
Descriptor—Using context to construct meaning.

Goal 3, Standard 1—To use English in socially and culturally appropriate ways: Students will use the appropriate language variety, register, and genre according to audience, purpose, and setting.
Descriptors—Using the appropriate degree of formality with different audiences and settings; Recognizing and using standard English and vernacular dialects appropriately.

Write an Expository Paragraph

Expository writing answers a question or explains something. Read Yukiko's answer to a science question.

Why are there no trees on mountaintops? Trees cannot live on mountaintops. The weather is too cold. Lower down, mountains do have trees. But as you go up a mountain, the air gets colder and windier. As you go higher, only small plants, grasses, and flowers can grow. No plants can grow at the very tops of mountains.

SPELLING TIP

When a one-syllable word ends with a short vowel and the /ch/ sound, that sound is spelled *ch* or *tch*. Check a dictionary to get the correct spelling.

Practice Book page 88

Practice

Write a paragraph that explains one feature of a biome.

- Think of a question to answer or decide what you want to explain.
- What is the most important thing you want to say? Write that.
- Write facts that support that statement.

Writing Checklist

✓ Did you answer a question or explain something about a biome?

✓ Did you support your answer with facts from the selection?

✓ Can a partner understand your paragraph?

Differentiated Instruction

Beginning	Ask students to point to words in Yukiko's paragaph that describe the weather, then use those words in short sentences.
Early Intermediate	Have students discuss what happens to the air as you go up a mountain, then write a short answer to describe what happens to plants at the top of a mountain.
Intermediate	Have students work with partners to find places where they could use conjunctions or transitions in Yukiko's paragraph.
Standard English Learner CRI	Read Yukiko's paragraph aloud and add *why* to the beginning of every sentence. Have students shout out answers to each question.

STEP 1: Introduce

Write an Expository Paragraph

Define an expository paragraph for students.

SAY *When you write an expository paragraph, you answer a question you think the reader might have, or you explain something the reader probably doesn't know. Let's read Yukiko's expository paragraph.*

- *What question did she answer?*
- *What did you learn from her answer?*
- *Do you think she answered the question well? Why or why not?*

Spelling Tip

Read the box aloud to students. Have students call out words they know that end with the *-ch* sound. Have students use a dictionary to look up each word they suggest to see if the final sound is spelled *-ch* or *-tch*.

STEP 2: Practice

Before students begin to write, discuss the purpose of expository paragraphs:

- Will you answer a question or explain something?
- What details do you need to include?
- How can you use descriptions to help the reader visualize?

STEP 3: Assess

Writing Checklist

✓ Students may need help phrasing questions that they would like to answer.

✓ Review the main ideas of each biome with students before they write their expository paragraphs.

✓ Have students work with partners. Ask students to exchange their paragraphs with their partners. Remind students to visualize as they read their partner's explanation.

The Five Step Writing Process in the Writing Handbook reference section of this book provides more student writing instruction.

STEP 1: Introduce

Key Words

Help students learn the skill of defining words by using context.

Have students find the numbered circles for each context sentence, then find the corresponding numbered photos.

STEP 2: Teach

Words in Context

Write the following sentences on the board. Have students complete this fill-in-the-blanks exercise using the key words from the Words in Context passage.

1. When we went whale watching, we saw two large pods of whales.
2. Our parents let us adopt the puppy that is an orphan.
3. The monarch butterflies migrated to the same place every year.
4. The killer whale is a predator that eats other animals.
5. The mother duck was happy to reunite with her chicks.
6. In many countries, starvation is a daily struggle for many families.

Study Skills

Dictionary Students can use the dictionary to see if the Words in Context definitions are correct.

Online Dictionary Students can use an online dictionary or the CD that accompanies a learner's dictionary, such as the *Longman Basic Dictionary*.

www.LongmanCornerstone.com

Teaching Resources

- *Practice Book*, pp. 89–90
- *Transparencies*, p. 47
- *CD-ROM* • *Audio CD*

Reading 2

Springer Goes Home

Vocabulary

Springer Goes Home **is about an orca, or killer whale, who is reunited with her pod.**

Key Words

pods
orphan
migrated
predator
reunite
starvation

Words in Context

1 Groups of the same kind of animal have special names. Groups of orcas, or killer whales, are called **pods**.

2 This elephant has lost its mother. It is an **orphan**.

3 These geese **migrated** to their spring breeding grounds.

1

2

3

182

TESOL Standards

Goal 1, Standard 3—To use English to communicate in social settings: Students will use learning strategies to extend their communicative competence.
Descriptors—Testing hypotheses about language; Listening to and imitating how others use English; Exploring alternative ways of saying things; Using context to construct meaning.

Goal 2, Standard 2—To use English to achieve academically in all content areas: Students will use English to obtain, process, construct, and provide subject matter information in spoken and written form.
Descriptor—Understanding and producing technical vocabulary and text features according to content area.

Goal 2, Standard 3—To use English to achieve academically in all content areas: Students will use appropriate learning strategies to construct and apply academic knowledge.
Descriptor—Using context to construct meaning.

4 An owl is a **predator**. It hunts at night for mice and other small animals.

5 Tom was happy to **reunite** with his dog, Max.

6 These people are giving away food so that others don't suffer from **starvation**.

Practice

Use each key word in a sentence.

Make Connections

If you find a wild animal that is an orphan, should you try to help it? Why or why not?

Academic Words

consume
eat

goal
something you want to achieve

Practice Book pages 89–90

Visual Literacy

Photos Have students look at the photos on pp. 182–183. Ask them to think about what is happening or could possibly happen. Have students select one photo, and write a descriptive paragraph about the setting and the action.

Academic Words

Discuss the definitions for *consume* and *goal* with students. Share the following context sentences with students:

An adult elephant can *consume* 400 pounds of grass and leaves every day.

My *goal* is to be a doctor when I grow up.

Explain to students that many words in English come from older English words, or even from other languages. *Consume* comes from the Latin word *consumere*, which means "use up." *Goal* comes from the old English word *gal*, which means "barrier."

Other Academic Words

Provide students with another example of a word that can be used in the discussion of animals living in the wild.

respond react or answer to something

Tell students that animals can *respond* to each other with affection and *respond* when others need help, just as people can.

STEP 3: Practice

Flexible Grouping You may assign these exercises as a class discussion, partner activity, or individual writing assignment.

Make Connections

Writing Fluency Have students write a description of an orphan wild animal they might find. Have them consider these questions:

Do you know how to take care of a wild animal? Are there people who know how to take care of a wild animal? How could you find a person who knows how to take care of a wild animal?

Have students relate their answers to the Big Question when they sum up their paragraphs.

Differentiated Instruction

Beginning	Tell students that in each context sentence, they can find one word for a bird or animal. Have students write down each word in their personal thesaurus.
Intermediate	Have students write a new context sentence for each of the following key words: *pods*, *migrated*, *predator*, *starvation*.
Greater Challenge	Challenge students to write one paragraph that contains all of the key words. Explain to students that the paragraph must have one topic sentence, and the other sentences must contain supporting details.
Struggling Reader	Say each context word aloud, and have students point to the correct picture. Ask students to repeat each key word aloud.

STEP 1: Introduce

More About The Big Question

The Big Question for this selection is designed to get students thinking about what humans can do to protect wild animals.

SAY *We will read about people who helped an animal.*

- *Have you ever helped a wild animal?*
- *What can people do to protect wild animals?*

Have students fill in a Sequence of Events Chart like the one below about an experience they may have had helping animals.

My dad taught me how to build a bird feeder.
↓
We hung it from a branch where we could see it.
↓
I saw a bluejay eating birdseed there.

STEP 2: Teach

Reading Strategy

Make Predictions Have students follow the bulleted steps on p. 184 and fill in a Make Predictions Chart for information about predicting what is on each page of the reading.

Understand Text Structure

Draw students' attention to the genre label. Tell them that a magazine article often tells a true story about something interesting that happened. A good magazine article teaches while it entertains.

Read Aloud

Have students take turns reading aloud the paragraphs on p. 184. At the end of each paragraph, have the listeners discuss what they learned.

Teaching Resources

- ***Teacher's Resource Book***, pp. 129–130
- ***Practice Book***, pp. 91–92
- ***CD-ROM*** • ***Audio CD***

Reading 2

INFORMATIONAL TEXT

Magazine Article

The Big Question

How can humans protect wild animals in their environment?

Reading Strategy

Make Predictions

- Read the title.
- Look at the pictures and read the captions.
- Read the words and definitions at the bottom of the page.
- Read the first and last paragraph.
- Predict what the selection is about.

Springer Goes Home

by Matt Kachur

People traveling to work on the ferry in Puget Sound, near Seattle, Washington, got a surprise one morning in 2002. A baby orca was swimming alone in the water. Orcas are sometimes called killer whales. They are not whales at all. They are dolphins.

People were **delighted** to watch the baby orca. She played with floating logs and rubbed against boats. They called her Springer. Scientists gave her the name A-73. They were very **concerned**. Orcas live in family groups called pods. It is rare to see an orca traveling alone. Scientists also worried about Springer's smell because they thought she might be starving to death. Mammals, like Springer, sometimes have bad breath when they are breaking down their own body fat instead of eating.

delighted very pleased

concerned worried

184

TESOL Standards

Goal 2, Standard 2—To use English to achieve academically in all content areas: Students will use English to obtain, process, construct, and provide subject matter information in spoken and written form.

Descriptors—Listening to, speaking, reading, and writing about subject matter information; Gathering information orally and in writing; Selecting, connecting, and explaining information; Analyzing, synthesizing, and inferring from information; Hypothesizing and predicting.

Scientists could tell which pod Springer belonged to by the sounds she made. The scientists believed Springer's mother died in 2000, leaving her an orphan.

After six months, scientists had to decide what to do with Springer. They had three choices. First, they could leave Springer alone. They were afraid she would face starvation. Second, the scientists could capture Springer. They could bring her to a marine park to live. She would be well taken care of in a marine park, but scientists thought she would be unhappy. Third, scientists could try to reunite Springer with her pod.

Scientists and environmentalists both liked the third idea. No one had ever reunited an orca with its pod before. What would happen to Springer if her pod did not accept her? Scientists and environmentalists also knew that Springer could be hurt or killed when they tried to capture her.

---

capture catch

environmentalists people concerned about the environment

Orcas, or killer whales, usually live in groups called pods.

Check Up How will the scientists try to help Springer?

185

Build Vocabulary

Help students use the highlighted words that are defined at the bottom of each page.

- Invite a volunteer to read one of the terms and its definition aloud.
- Read the line with that highlighted word aloud to the class. Then read the line again replacing the term with a synonym from the definition. Example: *People were very pleased to watch the baby orca*.

Could The word *could* is used four times in the first paragraph on p. 185. Make sure that students understand *could* has a similar meaning to *can*, but shows that the author wants the reader to be unsure about something. In the paragraph on p. 185, all three choices are possible, but the author doesn't want the reader to know yet which choice the scientists will pick.

Word Study Explain to students that many words in English come from other languages. Science comes from the Latin word *scientia*, which means "knowledge." When you add the suffix *-ist*, which means "one who practices," you get *scientist*, or "one who practices science."

STEP 3: Assess

Check Up

Tell students that to make a prediction, they will need to think about what they already know and what they have read in the selection. Point out that predictions may or may not turn out to be true, but a good prediction *could* be right. Ask pairs to share their predictions with the class.

Link to Science

Orcas Orcas can be found in oceans all over the world. They are the largest members of the dolphin family—and the fastest. Orcas can eat almost any creature they find in the water: fish, squids, seabirds, seals, and even other species of dolphins. Ask students to imagine they are marine biologists who are studying a pod of orcas near the Hawaiian islands. Have students research the behavior of orcas and write a report on what it would be like to watch and study orcas.

Differentiated Instruction

Beginning	Have students find the key word in the caption p. 185. Then point to the word that describes the animal.
Early Intermediate	Have students look at the definitions for the words *delighted* and *concerned*. Have them write a comparison sentence using both words.
Intermediate	Have students write a paragraph that describes the choices scientists had for helping Springer.
Standard English Learner (CRI)	Choose one key word for a game of "Give One, Get One". Have students call out synonyms for the word. Then have them swap synonyms with each other until they each have three new words.

STEP 1: Monitor Progress

Comprehension Check

Main Idea and Details Explain that a well-written paragraph has a main idea. To find the main idea, readers should ask themselves: *What is this paragraph about?* Sometimes, but not always, the main idea is clearly stated in a sentence in the paragraph. Ask the following questions about the paragraphs on p. 186:

- Look at the first paragraph on p. 186. Which sentence states the main idea? Scientists decided to reunite Springer with her pod.
- The main idea of the second paragraph is not stated by the author. What is the paragraph about? Scientists made Springer healthy again.
- Which sentence in the third paragraph tells readers the main idea? When she was healthy and eating enough food, it was time to take her to her pod.

Context Clues Point out that the author does not define *net pen* for readers. But from its name and from the photo on p. 186, readers should be able to figure out what a *net pen* is. Explain that a *pen* is an enclosed space to keep animals in. *Net* is a kind of material with spaces that allows water to flow in and out. Have a volunteer tell what context clues helped define *net pen*.

Adapt the Activity

If students have difficulty identifying the main idea in the third paragraph, have them write a sentence to answer each of the following questions:

- In the first paragraph, the author tells you what the scientists decided to do. What did they decide to do?
- The second paragraph tells you why the scientists needed to take care of Springer before they could do that. Why did they need to take care of her?
- Which sentence in the third paragraph tells you what happened after the scientists took care of Springer?

Springer gets medical attention in her net pen.

Scientists decided to reunite Springer with her pod. They acted quickly. Springer was already rubbing against boats in Puget Sound. It was easy for scientists to coax Springer into letting them touch her and put a net around her. Then they lifted Springer onto a barge. They transported her to a special net pen where she would have freedom to swim, and scientists could care for her.

Scientists examined Springer. They found she was starving. Her skin had many open sores. Scientists fed Springer salmon that had been treated with antibiotics. They fed Springer through a tube so she would not learn to connect the scientists with her food.

Springer lived in the net pen for about a month. When she was healthy and eating enough food, it was time to take her to her pod.

---

coax gently persuade

examined studied something to find out more about it

antibiotics drugs that kill bacteria and cure infections

186

TESOL Standards

Goal 2, Standard 2—To use English to achieve academically in all content areas: Students will use English to obtain, process, construct, and provide subject matter information in spoken and written form.

Descriptors—Listening to, speaking, reading, and writing about subject matter information; Gathering information orally and in writing; Selecting, connecting, and explaining information; Analyzing, synthesizing, and inferring from information; Hypothesizing and predicting.

Orcas are predators. They eat other animals. Scientists knew that Springer's pod had migrated to a place near British Columbia to feed on salmon.

Scientists took Springer to the area where her pod was feeding. They placed microphones in the water to try to hear the calls of her pod. It wasn't long before Springer heard the squeaks and squeals of her pod. She got very excited!

The scientists put a monitoring device on Springer so they could check on her health. They set her free the next morning.

The next summer, scientists were happy to see Springer swimming with her pod. They believe a relative taught her how to hunt and stay away from boats.

Practice Book pages 91–92

Reading Strategy

Make Predictions

- Were your predictions about this reading correct?
- Did making predictions help you to understand the story? How?

Think It Over

1. Why was Springer swimming alone?
2. What decisions did the scientists need to make about Springer?
3. How did the reading end?
4. Describe how the scientists helped Springer.

187

STEP 2: Teach

Visual Literacy

Maps Have students look at the map on p. 187. Have them reread the first sentence of the selection to find out where people found Springer. Ask them to locate that place on the map. Then have them read p. 187 to find out where Springer's pod went. Ask them to locate that place on the map. Ask: *In what country is Seattle, Washington? In what country is British Columbia?*

STEP 3: Assess

Reading Strategy

Make Predictions Give students an example of how to make predictions.

SAY *Making predictions before you read a selection is a good way to stay interested in what you are reading.*

- *How can you make a prediction about something you are about to read?*
- *What prior knowledge did you use to make predictions about this selection?*
- *Where did you learn that prior knowledge?*

Have students work in small groups to read aloud the predictions from their Make Predictions Charts. Have students compare and contrast all the predictions from the group.

Think It Over

Flexible Grouping You may assign this activity as a class discussion, partner activity, or individual writing assignment.

Answer Key

1. She was an orphan and got separated from her pod.
2. They needed to decide the best way to help her.
3. At the end, Springer found her pod and learned to be a normal orca.
4. The scientists brought Springer to a net pen. They fed her and made her healthy. Then they took her to her pod.

Differentiated Instruction

Beginning	Have students fill in the blanks: *The* ________ *moved Springer to a* ________ *to help her get* ________ *so she could return to her* ________ *.*
Intermediate	Have students write a brief report about ways orcas protect each other when they are migrating in pods.
Greater Challenge	Have students research careers in marine biology. Ask students to create a chart that shows the name of the career, a brief description, and a list of the skills needed to do the job.
Special Needs	Check students' powers of recall by stopping periodically and asking students to tell you what they learned from the text. Monitor and praise students.

STEP 1: Introduce

Phonics

Consonant Clusters Help students understand that when two consonants are together, their sounds often blend together.

STEP 2: Teach

Review the consonant blends with students. Model the pronunciation of the words on p. 188 and have students repeat after you. Direct students' attention to the Rule Box.

SAY *Sometimes two consonants together in a word blend together when you pronounce that word. Consonants that often blend with others are* l, r, *and* s.

- *Which two consonants blend in* swim?
- *Which two consonants blend in* predator?
- *Which two consonants blend in* black?

Write the following words on the board. Ask students to pronounce each word, then have them copy the words and circle the consonant blend.

skip	*bread*	*play*	*spell*
prize	*swing*	*from*	*flat*

STEP 3: Practice

Answer Key

1. *r*-blend: orcas, predators, British, try; free; from; *l*-blend: place, placed; *s*-blend: Springer, squeaks, squeals, swimming, stay
2. **a.** predator **c.** spectator
   b. floating **d.** swim

Reteach

Have students find more words in the reading with *r*-blend , *l*-blend, and *s*-blend consonant clusters, then list the words in a 3-column chart.

Teaching Resources

- ***Practice Book***, pp. 93
- ***Phonics Workbook***
- ***Phonics Flashcards***
- ***CD-ROM*** • ***Audio CD***

Reading 2

Phonics & Fluency

Phonics

Consonant Clusters

Read the words in the chart. Pay attention to the beginning consonant sounds.

r-blends	*l*-blends	*s*-blends
bring	black	skin
free	floating	spectator
predator	pleased	swim

Rule Box

When **r**, **l**, or **s** come together with another consonant at the beginning of a word, the sounds of both letters usually blend together.

Practice

1. Read the first paragraph on page 187. Make a list of any *r*-blends, *l*-blends, and *s*-blends that you find.
2. Use the words in the box above to answer these clues.
   a. This word begins with an *r*-blend. It's an animal that hunts other animals.
   b. This word begins with an *l*-blend. It means "resting on top of water."
   c. This word begins with an *s*-blend. It's someone who watches something.
   d. This word begins with an *s*-blend. It's something to do in hot weather.

Practice Book page 93

188

TESOL Standards

Goal 1, Standard 3—To use English to communicate in social settings: Students will use learning strategies to extend their communicative competence.
Descriptors—Listening to and imitating how others use English; Self-monitoring and self-evaluating language development; Practicing new language; Focusing attention selectively.

Goal 3, Standard 3—To use English in socially and culturally appropriate ways: Students will use appropriate learning strategies to extend their sociolinguistic and sociocultural competence.
Descriptors—Observing and modeling how others speak and behave in a particular situation or setting; Experimenting with variations of language in social and academic settings; Seeking information about appropriate language use and behavior.

Fluency

Read with Expression

When you read aloud, use your voice to show feelings.

Practice

Read silently. ▶ Read aloud. ▶ Get comments. ▶ Read aloud again.

Orcas are predators. They eat other animals. Scientists knew that Springer's pod had migrated to a place near British Columbia to feed on salmon.

Scientists took Springer to the area where her pod was feeding. They placed microphones in the water to try to hear the calls of her pod. It wasn't long before Springer heard the squeaks and squeals of her pod. She got very excited!

The scientists put a monitoring device on Springer so they could check on her health. They set her free the next morning.

The next summer, scientists were happy to see Springer swimming with her pod. They believe a relative taught her how to hunt and to stay away from boats.

Linguistic Note

Orca Spanish-speaking students may be interested to know that the Spanish word for *orca* is exactly the same as the English word: *orca*. This is because both Spanish and English took the word from Latin. Be aware, though, that in Spanish the word itself is feminine, regardless of the gender of the particular killer whale a student may be talking about. Since Springer is a female, you may not notice when a student refers to a non-specific orca as *she*.

Accelerate Language Development

Consonant Clusters Students whose home language is Spanish may have difficulty with the pronunciations of words that begin with *s*-blend consonant clusters. In Spanish, words do not begin with an *s*-blend. Spanish words in which the *s*-blend is the first consonantal sound always start with a vowel, most commonly *e*.

STEP 1: Introduce

Fluency

Read with Expression Explain to students that reading with expression means showing emotion with your voice, which can help your listeners understand what they hear. Some ways of showing expression are: reading slowly or quickly, loudly or softly, and emphasizing certain words.

Play the Audio CD for this reading to the class, asking students to listen for pacing, intonation, and expression.

STEP 2: Practice

Have students do the following exercise with partners. You may want to assign only one or two paragraphs, depending on the students' abilities. If you prefer, let students select their own passages.

- Have one partner look through the passage to find any words that he or she wants to emphasize.
- Then have that student read the passage to his or her partner.
- Have the listeners describe what emotions they heard during the reading. Then have students change roles.

Possible Words to Emphasize

predators	eat	microphones
family	very	free

STEP 3: Extend

Study Skills

Dictionary Have students work with partners to:

- write down three words from the reading that they want to emphasize;
- look up the words in a dictionary to check their correct pronunciation;
- read the words in context in the reading and pronounce them correctly.

Remind students that they can use this study skill anywhere. In social studies, science class, or when they read at home, students can find out how to pronounce the words by looking them up online or in the dictionary.

STEP 1: Monitor Progress

Learning Strategy

Summarize Summarizing is a way to briefly retell the most important points of the story. Have students work in pairs to summarize *Springer Goes Home*. Remind them that a summary includes only the main idea and the most important details. Have students review the selection to help them include details in their summaries about what people can do to protect wild animals.

STEP 2: Teach

Problem and Solution

Draw students' attention to the definitions for problem and solution at the top of p. 190. Explain that identifying problems and solutions when they read will help them summarize the important details.

SAY *Identifying the problems and solutions in this magazine article will help you summarize the important details.*

- *Did the scientists have more than one problem to solve to help Springer?*
- *If you were the scientist in charge of helping Springer, what would your solution be?*

STEP 3: Practice

Flexible Grouping You may assign this activity as a class discussion, partner activity, or individual writing assignment.

Answer Key

1. They knew which pod Springer came from by the sounds she made.
2. Scientists took Springer to the area where her pod was feeding.
3. Scientists could tell if Springer was healthy by examining her.
4. Scientists put a monitoring device on Springer.

Teaching Resources

- ***Practice Book,*** p. 94
- ***Transparencies,*** p. 63
- ***Teacher's Resource Book,*** p. 161
- ***CD-ROM***

Reading 2

Comprehension

Learning Strategy

Summarize

Summarize the reading for a partner.

Ask your partner to respond to the Big Question for this reading.

Problem and Solution

The **problem** is the main conflict the characters face. The **solution** is how the characters solve the problem.

- What problems did Springer and the scientists have?
- What were some solutions to those problems?
- How were the problems solved?

Practice

These problems are posed as questions. Write a solution for each.

1. How did scientists know which pod was Springer's pod?
2. How did scientists help Springer find her pod?
3. How could scientists tell if Springer was healthy?
4. How did scientists keep track of Springer?

Practice Book page 94

190

TESOL Standards

Goal 2, Standard 2—To use English to achieve academically in all content areas: Students will use English to obtain, process, construct, and provide subject matter information in spoken and written form.
Descriptors—Listening to, speaking, reading, and writing about subject matter information; Gathering information orally and in writing; Retelling information; Selecting, connecting, and explaining information; Demonstrating knowledge through application in a variety of contexts.

Use a Problem and Solution Chart

You can use a Problem and Solution Chart to help you record problems and solutions as you read.

Practice

Copy this Problem and Solution Chart. Show the main problems and solutions in *Springer Goes Home*.

Problem
Who? ______
What? ______
Why? ______

↓

Solution
Who? ______
What? ______
Why? ______

↓

Result
______
______
______

Extension

Find a problem in your classroom. Work with a group to come up with different solutions. Decide which one is best. Present the problem and your solution to the class.

191

Accelerate Language Development

Noun to Verb: *Summary* to *Summarize* Students who are not used to hearing spoken English may not notice the relationship between the words *summary* and *summarize*. Explain that a *summary* is a very short version of the most important points in a story or article. *Summary* is a thing, a noun. When you write a summary, you *summarize*. *Summarize* is a verb, telling what you do. Write both words on the board and have students find the letters that they share in common. If you wish to give another example, show how *alphabet* is the root of *alphabetize*.

Linguistic Note

Cognate Problem Students whose home language is Spanish may recognize the cognate *problema*. Some of these students may have difficulty pronouncing *problem* as they may accent the second syllable. Pronounce *problem*, exaggerating the accented first syllable.

STEP 1: Teach

Use a Problem and Solution Chart

Ask students to think about a problem at school they once had. Have them copy the graphic organizer on this page, write the answer to each question for the problem and solution, and write the result. Have students exchange graphic organizers with partners. Then have each student explain their partner's problem and solution.

STEP 2: Practice

You may have students complete the graphic organizer provided as a Blackline Master in the *Teacher's Resource Book*.

Problem
Who? Springer
What? She was all alone.
Why? Her mother had died.

↓

Solution
Who? Scientists
What? They moved Springer to where her pod was feeding.
Why? They wanted to reunite her with her pod.

↓

Result
Springer lived as a normal orca with her pod.

STEP 3: Extend

Oral Presentation

To make this exercise even more interesting, have students work in small groups to come up with a different solution to Springer's problem. Have students present each of the different solutions. Have the entire class discuss which solution would work best.

STEP 1: Introduce

Help students understand that complete sentences should express a complete thought, which includes a subject and a predicate, or verb. A sentence that does not express a complete thought is incomplete. An incomplete sentence is missing a subject or a verb, either at the end or the beginning. Explain that the length of the sentence does not indicate whether it is complete. For example, a very short complete sentence is:

Springer got better.

STEP 2: Teach

Complete and Incomplete Sentences

Write the following sentences on the board. Ask students to decide whether each is complete or incomplete.

1. *Springer rubbed against boats.* complete
2. *She played with.* incomplete
3. *To watch the baby orca.* incomplete
4. *Orcas live in family groups.* complete
5. *Scientists could tell which pod Springer.* incomplete
6. *They had to decide what to.* incomplete
7. *Had ever reunited an orca with her pod.* incomplete
8. *Environmentalists liked the third idea.* complete

STEP 3: Practice

Before students begin the Practice activity, have them work with partners to write three short complete sentences about the reading.

Answer Key

1. Incomplete; A baby orca was all alone.
2. Complete Sentence
3. Complete Sentence
4. Incomplete; Springer was swimming with boats.

Teaching Resources

- ***Practice Book***, p. 95
- ***Transparencies***, pp. 69–80
- ***Assessments***, pp. 69–72
- ***CD-ROM***

Reading 2

Grammar & Writing

Complete and Incomplete Sentences

Look at each group of words.

People traveling to work near Seattle

People traveling to work near Seattle got a surprise one morning.

The first group of words describes some people. It does not tell what they did. It does not express a complete thought, so it is not a complete sentence. It is **incomplete**.

The second group of words tells what the people did. It expresses a complete thought, so it is a **complete** sentence.

Practice

Read each group of words. If the words make a complete sentence, write *Complete Sentence*. If it is not a complete sentence, add words to make it complete.

1. A baby orca.
2. Scientists saw a baby orca.
3. People in the area called her Springer.
4. Swimming with boats.

Practice Book page 95

TESOL Standards

Goal 2, Standard 2—To use English to achieve academically in all content areas: Students will use English to obtain, process, construct, and provide subject matter information in spoken and written form.
Descriptors—Listening to, speaking, reading, and writing about subject matter information; Gathering information orally and in writing; Retelling information; Selecting, connecting, and explaining information.

Goal 2, Standard 3—To use English to achieve academically in all content areas: Students will use appropriate learning strategies to construct and apply academic knowledge.
Descriptors—Using context to construct meaning; Actively connecting new information to information previously learned; Imitating the behaviors of native English speakers to complete tasks successfully.

Goal 3, Standard 1—To use English in socially and culturally appropriate ways: Students will use the appropriate language variety, register, and genre according to audience, purpose, and setting.
Descriptors—Using the appropriate degree of formality with different audiences and settings; Recognizing and using standard English and vernacular dialects appropriately; Using a variety of writing styles appropriate for different audiences, purposes, and settings.

Write an Explanation

Katrinka thought of one decision scientists made about Springer. She reread the text to find facts. Then she wrote an explanation.

Why did scientists decide to help Springer? They watched her carefully for a long time. First, they saw that she was swimming alone. The scientists knew that orcas usually travel in pods. They could tell Springer was a baby. She probably didn't know how to take care of herself. Next, Springer didn't smell right. The scientists thought it might mean she was starving. They were also afraid Springer might get hurt or killed by a passing boat. She needed help!

SPELLING TIP

You can simply add *-ed* or *-ing* to many one-syllable verbs. However, with some one-syllable verbs, you will need to double the final consonant, as in ***swimming***.

Practice Book page 96

Practice

Think about a time when you had to make an important decision. Tell about the decision you had to make. Write about some of the choices you had. Then write to explain your decision.

Writing Checklist

- ✓ Did you identify the problem?
- ✓ Did you write about the choices you had?
- ✓ Can a partner understand why you made your decision?

Differentiated Instruction	
Beginning	Have students find the sentence in Katrinka's explanation that describes the first reason scientists wanted to help Springer.
Early Intermediate	Ask students to write two fact questions based on the information in Katrinka's explanation. Then have them work with partners to answer the questions.
Intermediate	Have students write three incomplete sentences about how the scientists helped Springer. Have them exchange sentences with partners. Have students add words to complete the sentences.
Standard English Learner CRI	Read aloud Katrinka's explanation then ask students to write and perform a short skit that shows what the scientists did to help Springer.

STEP 1: Introduce

Write an Explanation

Define an explanation for students.

SAY *An explanation often tells why a fact is true or why a person does something.*

- *How does thinking of questions help you understand an explanation?*
- *What can you do to answer questions you have about something?*

Fill in a Main Idea and Details Chart for Katrinka's explanation.

Scientists decide to help Springer.

- She was swimming alone.
- She might be starving.
- She might be killed by a passing boat.

Spelling Tip

Have students make a list of words with double consonants and *-ed* or *-ing* endings.

STEP 2: Practice

Review the purpose of an explanation:

- What do you want to explain?
- What facts do you need to use?
- Will a reader understand your explanation?

STEP 3: Assess

Writing Checklist

- ✓ Point out that Katrinka begins her explanation with a question.
- ✓ Students may find it helpful before writing to make a list of the choices they had to make.
- ✓ Have students exchange their work with partners. Have students see if they understand their partners' explanations.

The Five Step Writing Process in the Writing Handbook reference of this book provides more student writing instruction.

STEP 1: Introduce

Key Words

Help students learn the skill of defining words by using context.

SAY *All the vocabulary words from* After the Hurricane *are defined in the Words in Context section. Let's figure out the definition of each by reading the context sentences.*

Have volunteers pronounce each key word, and then describe each photograph.

STEP 2: Teach

Words in Context

Write the following sentences on the board and have students fill in the blanks using key words from the Words in Context passage.

1. People need assistance in an emergency.
2. It is difficult to handle living without electricity after a storm.
3. After the tornado, we saw the damage to the house.
4. The skiers were stranded during the blizzard.
5. Volunteers quickly formed a relief team to help people caught in the flood.

Have students work in pairs to write more context sentences for each key word.

Study Skills

Dictionary Have students look up the key words to see if their Words in Context definitions are correct.

Online Dictionary Students can use an online dictionary or the CD that accompanies a learner's dictionary, like the *Longman Basic Dictionary*.

www.LongmanCornerstone.com

Teaching Resources

- ***Practice Book***, pp. 97–98
- ***Transparencies***, p. 48
- ***CD-ROM*** • ***Audio CD***

Reading 3

After the Hurricane

Vocabulary

After the Hurricane **describes how people recover from hurricanes and other big storms.**

Key Words

assistance
handle
damage
stranded
relief

Words in Context

1 Volunteers gave **assistance**. They helped people find food, housing, and first aid.

2 The worker at the emergency center could not **handle** all the calls that came in during the storm.

3 The flood caused a lot of **damage** inside the house.

194

TESOL Standards

Goal 1, Standard 3—To use English to communicate in social settings: Students will use learning strategies to extend their communicative competence.
Descriptors—Testing hypotheses about language; Listening to and imitating how others use English; Exploring alternative ways of saying things; Using context to construct meaning.

Goal 2, Standard 2—To use English to achieve academically in all content areas: Students will use English to obtain, process, construct, and provide subject matter information in spoken and written form.
Descriptor—Understanding and producing technical vocabulary and text features according to content area.

4 During the flood, many people were **stranded** in trees or on rooftops, with no way to get to safety.

5 The volunteers handed out **relief** supplies, including soap, toothpaste, toothbrushes, and food.

Practice

Use each key word in a sentence.

Make Connections

Have you ever been in a bad storm? What happened? Was there any damage? What did you do to clean up after the storm?

Academic Words

authorities
people who are in charge of an area

establish
bring into existence

Practice Book pages 97–98

Differentiated Instruction	
Beginning	Have students work in small groups to demonstrate how people help others during a hurricane. Encourage students to use strong verbal statements during the role playing.
Intermediate	Have students imagine one of the photos is a scene in a movie or TV show. Ask them to use key words to describe to the class what might happen as the scene continues.
Greater Challenge	Ask students to think of other situations when volunteers are asked to give assistance. Have students work in pairs to create a large poster entitled *Volunteers Are Needed*.
Struggling Reader	Have students repeat each key word, and point to the key word in its context sentence. Have students copy each key word into their personal thesaurus.

Visual Literacy

Photographs Have students select a photograph from pp. 194–195. Have them name as many things as they can that they see in the photograph. For fun, you may choose to make this a contest between teams. Have teams take turns naming things. Teams get a point for each thing they name.

Academic Words

Discuss the definitions for *authorities* and *establish*. Share the following context sentences with students:

When the forest fire was burning, the *authorities* directed people to a shelter.

Whose idea was it to *establish* the American Red Cross?

You may want to point out that the word *authorities* has the same root as the Spanish word *autoridad*. Spanish-speaking students who are familiar with that word may have difficulty pronouncing *th* instead of *t*. Model the pronunciation for them.

Other Academic Words

Explain to students that the term *define* can be used in contexts other than defining a word. Write the following context sentences on the board:

The firefighters will *define* the boundary of the forest fire.

Before beginning the game, we will *define* the rules.

Have students use a thesaurus to write three context sentences for *define* with a different use of the word for each sentence.

STEP 3: Practice

Flexible Grouping You may assign these exercises as a class discussion, partner activity, or individual writing assignment.

Make Connections

Writing Fluency Invite students to write a story about their experiences in a bad storm. Have them share their stories with the class. Have students discuss how they and their neighbors helped each other. Note that students' responses can be related to the Big Question when you sum up the discussion.

STEP 1: Introduce

More About The Big Question

The Big Question is designed to get students thinking about how authorities and organizations in a community help others after a disaster.

SAY *You can sometimes prepare for disasters. Other disasters happen without warning.*

- *What environmental disasters have happened in our community?*
- *How did the community respond?*

Have students fill in a Main Idea and Supporting Details Chart about their own or other people's experiences.

Rain flooded our area.

Stores could not open and lost income.	Firefighters volunteered to repair the damage.	Restaurants donated food for the volunteers.

STEP 2: Teach

Reading Strategy

Ask Questions Have students fill in a 5W Chart with questions about the selection.

Understand Text Structure

Tell students that an informational text about social studies is nonfiction because it teaches about events that already happened or continue to happen.

Read Aloud

Have a volunteer read aloud the first paragraph on p. 196. Ask students what questions they could ask about the information in that paragraph.

Teaching Resources

- *Teacher's Resource Book*, pp. 131–132
- *Practice Book*, pp. 99–100
- *CD-ROM* • *Audio CD*

Reading 3

INFORMATIONAL TEXT

Social Studies

The Big Question

How does a community recover from an environmental disaster?

Reading Strategy

Ask Questions

Good readers ask themselves questions as they read. Here are some questions to consider:

- What are you learning?
- What are you having trouble understanding?
- What are you wondering about?
- What other questions do you have?

After the Hurricane

by Ryan Hunter

When a hurricane happens, it may seem like you are in a very bad **rainstorm**. Hurricanes are severe tropical storms. They form in the southern Atlantic Ocean, the Caribbean Sea, the Gulf of Mexico, and the eastern Pacific Ocean.

Hurricanes form when winds mix with warm water to make **energy**. The winds begin to move in a circle. The center of the storm is called an eye, which is a very calm place. As the energy builds, the hurricane grows bigger and more dangerous.

Hurricanes get stronger when they are over the water. Sometimes, hurricanes make big waves. Hurricanes lose energy when they move over land. But the waves might crash onto land and **destroy** nearby homes.

---

rainstorm sudden, heavy downpour

energy power

destroy damage something so badly it cannot be fixed

196

TESOL Standards

Goal 2, Standard 1—To use English to achieve academically in all content areas: Students will use English to interact in the classroom.
Descriptor—Asking and answering questions.

Goal 2, Standard 2—To use English to achieve academically in all content areas: Students will use English to obtain, process, construct, and provide subject matter information in spoken and written form.
Descriptor—Formulating and asking questions.

Goal 2, Standard 3—To use English to achieve academically in all content areas: Students will use appropriate learning strategies to construct and apply academic knowledge.
Descriptors—Focusing attention selectively; Applying basic reading comprehension skills such as skimming, scanning, previewing, and reviewing text.

Hurricanes may cause great damage. Sometimes, the strong winds pick up cars or street signs. People who live near the ocean have the hardest time during a hurricane. Big waves and heavy rain can knock down or damage things. Hurricanes can cause floods that destroy homes and cars.

Hurricanes often leave people stranded. Cars might not work. This makes it hard for people to get out of the area. People who can help might not be able to get into the area. Cars and trucks break down because of the wind and water. This makes it hard for rescue workers to get supplies into an area where they can help people.

Hurricanes usually begin over oceans and then move to land.

floods large amounts of water that cover an area

break down stop working

Check Up What kinds of help do people need after a hurricane?

Differentiated Instruction

Differentiated Instruction	
Beginning	Write the following sentence on the board: *The eye of a hurricane is a very calm/noisy place.* Ask students to copy the sentence using the correct answer.
Early Intermediate	Ask students to write a short caption for the photo at the bottom of p. 197. and include one fact from the photo.
Intermediate	Have students imagine that they're watching a news program about the effects of a hurricane. Have them work in pairs to discuss what a news reporter might say.
Standard English Learner CRI	Ask students what they predict they will learn about hurricanes. Students should shout out as many answers as possible. Write their responses on the board.

Build Vocabulary

Direct attention to the first highlighted word in the text with a definition at the bottom of the page.

- Invite volunteers to read aloud the word and the definition.
- Have students write a context sentence using the word.

Have students repeat this activity for each highlighted word as they read the selection.

Multiple Meaning Words Tell students that some words have more than one meaning. For example, the word *heavy* means *having a lot of weight; hard to lift*. But in the first paragraph on p. 197, a sentence says:

Big waves and heavy rain can knock down or damage things.

In that sentence, *heavy* means *strong, powerful.* Have students look for the word *can* in the last sentence on p. 197. Tell them *can* might mean *a container for food* or *are able to*. Which meaning fits in that sentence?

Idioms An idiom is a word or group of words that has a special meaning that is different from the regular usage of the words. Tell students that people often say "it is raining cats and dogs" when it is raining heavily. A "can do" person is someone who gets a job done well and quickly. Ask students to share idioms in their own languages to describe a heavy rain.

Link to Science

Storm Photos Draw students' attention to the photo of the hurricane on p. 197. Explain to students that photos like these are used by professional meteorologists who study weather patterns. Have students research how meteorologists predict where and when a hurricane will occur.

STEP 3: Assess

Check Up

Have students work with partners. Have partners brainstorm reasons why people might need help after a hurricane. Then have them think of ways to help.

STEP 1: Monitor Progress

Comprehension Check

Make Inferences After students read p. 198, explain that sometimes a reader must make inferences about information in the story that the author does not explain.

SAY *Sometimes you have to use what you know from your own experiences to help you figure something out.*

- *Do you think there are usually fires in an area right after a hurricane? Why or why not?*
- *If there are no fires, why would firefighters be good helpers in a place that just had a hurricane?*
- *Why might people need to be rescued from their homes after a hurricane?*

Link to Math

Describe the following possible situation to students: During the hurricane, the books on the top floor of the library were knocked off the shelves. The librarian estimated 18,000 books had to be put back. If each volunteer can shelve 25 books an hour, how many volunteers does the library need to complete the job in 8 hours? One volunteer shelves 200 books in 8 hours, therefore 90 volunteers can shelve 18,000 books.

Making Hypotheses Explain that a hypothesis is an explanation of something but is not proven. Have students make a hypothesis about why so much water flooded a street during a hurricane. Then have students discuss how they might prove their hypotheses.

Link to Social Studies

Hurricane Names Every tropical storm, which may or may not become a hurricane, is given a name. Because there is often more than one tropical storm happening at the same time, the names help meteorologists easily talk about specific storms. The names are assigned in alphabetical order. The first hurricane of the year has a name that begins with the letter *A*, the second with *B*, and so on. A name may be reused six years later unless the storm caused so much damage that people want to remember it forever.

People might need firefighters or the police to help them during a hurricane.

In an emergency, people in the damaged towns cannot handle all the work that needs to be done. They need help rebuilding homes and roads. They also need basic things, such as food and water. People come from all over to offer assistance. They do what they can to help.

Firefighters and police come quickly. These people go into dangerous places to make sure that everyone is safe. A firefighter might need to go into a damaged home to make sure that no one is left inside. Streets might be flooded. Rescue workers will need to help people get through the water to safety. The workers must act quickly to help people and save lives.

---

emergency an unexpected and dangerous event

dangerous likely to harm or kill

Hurricanes can destroy houses.

198

TESOL Standards

Goal 2, Standard 1—To use English to achieve academically in all content areas: Students will use English to interact in the classroom.
Descriptor—Asking and answering questions.

Goal 2, Standard 2—To use English to achieve academically in all content areas: Students will use English to obtain, process, construct, and provide subject matter information in spoken and written form.
Descriptor—Formulating and asking questions.

Goal 2, Standard 3—To use English to achieve academically in all content areas: Students will use appropriate learning strategies to construct and apply academic knowledge.
Descriptors—Focusing attention selectively; Applying basic reading comprehension skills such as skimming, scanning, previewing, and reviewing text.

This woman has come from far away. She is helping children who lost their homes after a hurricane.

After a hurricane, experts come and assess the towns that were damaged. They call rescue workers to help. They also let others know when more help is needed. People come from nearby and from far away to give relief to those who need it. These people are usually volunteers. They do not get paid for their work. They come because they know that people need help after a hurricane.

Many people lose their homes during hurricanes. These people need to stay someplace, such as a shelter, until they can go home. They might feel sad and scared. Volunteers work to help these people feel better. The volunteers can play with children. They can help people find missing friends or family. Sometimes, people just need to talk to someone about what happened.

---

experts people with special skills and knowledge

Check Up What work needs to be done after a hurricane?

199

Linguistic Note

Cognate Hurricane Spanish-speaking students who have experienced hurricanes in their home countries may recognize the Spanish cognate *huracán*. The English word comes from the Spanish one, which was adopted by Spanish explorers from the Taino Indians of the Caribbean. Note that Spanish speakers may have difficulty pronouncing the English word, which is accented on the first syllable rather than the last and features different vowel sounds.

Accelerate Language Development

The /sh/ sound The Spanish language does not have the /sh/ sound. The closest Spanish language comes to that sound is /ch/. Be aware that students whose first language is Spanish may have difficulty pronouncing words such as *shelter* (p. 199), *ocean* (p. 197), and even *she*. Model the pronunciation of these words for students who have difficulty with them. For fun and practice, you might teach them the old tongue twister: *She sells seashells by the seashore.*

STEP 2: Teach

Visual Literacy

Photographs Draw the students' attention to the photographs on pp. 198–199.

SAY *The photographs on pages 198 and 199 show scenes after a hurricane. Let's look at the pictures and make inferences about what is happening or could be happening in each photo.*

- *What is the fireman probably doing in the photo at the top of page 198?* rescuing a baby
- *What does the photo at the bottom of page 198 show?* a house that was destroyed
- *In the photo at the top of page 199, how is the volunteer helping the children?* She's playing with them so they are not afraid of being away from home.

Academic Words

Discuss the definitions for *major* and *significant* with students. Write the following definitions and context sentences on the board:

major having an important meaning or lasting effect

significant having important power or influence

The weather report indicates a *major* storm will occur tomorrow.

The president is a *significant* world leader.

Explain to students that both academic words are synonyms for *important*. Ask students to use the thesaurus to look up *important* and find the listings for the two academic words. Have students explain the specific definitions for the two words.

STEP 3: Assess

CRI Check Up

Have students work in groups. Have them brainstorm the kinds of damage a hurricane might cause. Then ask them how the things that are damaged might be fixed or replaced. Ask them to create a list of their thoughts and read it to the class.

STEP 1: Monitor Progress

Comprehension Check

Literary Elements Explain to students that authors will sometimes use repetition for emphasis.

SAY *Authors sometimes repeat words or phrases at the beginning of sentences to emphasize ideas, or make them sound important. Let's reread the first paragraph on page 200.*

- *What four-word phrase starts two sentences in a row?*
- *Why does the author add* of all ages *instead of just saying* people?
- *Why do you think the author repeated the phrase in this selection for young readers?*

Context Clues Ask students to look at the word *raise* in the first sentence of the second paragraph on p. 200. Write the following three definitions of *raise* on the board and have students write context sentences based on each definition.

raise lift higher; help children grow up; increase in size or number

Build Discussion

Have students brainstorm ways they might raise money to help people who have recently experienced a disaster in their community. Have students work in small groups to write a short speech that will convince people to donate money to help the community. Remind students to answer the 5W questions in their speeches. Review how to use persuasive language.

Fact or Opinion Remind students that informational text can contain facts, opinions, or both. Have students discuss whether the reading is based on fact or opinion. Ask students to explain their responses using information from the reading.

Make Connections

Writing Fluency Ask students to imagine they have volunteered with the Red Cross to help after a hurricane and they are assigned to be team leaders. Have students decide what their team is going to do to help, then write a plan of how to do it. Tell students it might be helpful to use a Sequence Chart to help organize the steps in their plans.

The American Red Cross helps people after emergencies.

People of all ages need help after a hurricane. People of all ages can offer help as well. Adults might help in towns that were damaged. Young people can make a difference, too.

Some young people try to raise money to send to people who need it. Students at schools might have bake sales or car washes to earn money. They send this money to people who have lost their homes because of a hurricane.

People might donate their own money or money they have raised. Organizations such as the American Red Cross use this money to buy supplies. For example, the money might buy new books for schools that were flooded. Money also helps the Red Cross build shelters where people can stay until their homes are rebuilt.

---

bake sales events where members of a group sell food to raise money

donate give something useful to people who need help

supplies goods that people need or want

200

TESOL Standards

Goal 2, Standard 1— To use English to achieve academically in all content areas: Students will use English to interact in the classroom.
Descriptor—Asking and answering questions.

Goal 2, Standard 2—To use English to achieve academically in all content areas: Students will use English to obtain, process, construct, and provide subject matter information in spoken and written form.
Descriptor—Formulating and asking questions.

Goal 2, Standard 3—To use English to achieve academically in all content areas: Students will use appropriate learning strategies to construct and apply academic knowledge.
Descriptors—Focusing attention selectively; Applying basic reading comprehension skills such as skimming, scanning, previewing, and reviewing text.

People come from other places to help build houses after a hurricane.

There are many ways to help after a hurricane. Think about what people might need if their homes were lost or damaged. People will not have clothes to wear or food to eat. Children will not have books to read or toys to play with. These are all things that can be sent to people after a hurricane.

We cannot stop these scary storms from happening. But we can try to help people after the storms. Even from far away, volunteers can help people whose lives have been changed by a hurricane.

Practice Book pages 99–100

Reading Strategy

Ask Questions

- What questions did you ask yourself as you read?
- How did asking questions help you understand what you read?

Think It Over

1. What kinds of damage can hurricanes cause?
2. What do experts assess after a hurricane?
3. Why are floods dangerous?
4. Name two things the American Red Cross does in areas affected by a hurricane.

201

Differentiated Instruction

Beginning	Have students look at the pictures on pp. 200–201. Ask students to draw a large picture of ways to help others after a hurricane.
Early Intermediate	Have students discuss with a partner different ways to help people after a hurricane. Ask students to make a list of their ideas, then read their lists aloud to the class.
Intermediate	Have students imagine they are Red Cross workers helping after a hurricane. Ask them to role play how to organize volunteers to help as many people as possible.
Standard English Learner CRI	Have students recall their predictions about the information in the reading. Have students say whether they were right or wrong. Then have students tell what they learned from the reading.

STEP 2: Teach

Visual Literacy

Photos Draw students' attention to the photos on pp. 200–201. Explain that both photos show people working together to help others. Have students work in groups to create a poster that shows people working together to help a community.

STEP 3: Assess

Think It Over

Flexible Grouping You may assign this activity as a class discussion, partner activity, or individual writing assignment.

Answer Key

1. Hurricanes bring strong winds, big waves, and heavy rain. They can pick up cars and street signs. They often cause floods that destroy homes and cars.
2. Experts assess the damage and call for rescue workers and other help.
3. Floods are dangerous because they can destroy homes, leave people stranded, and make cars break down.
4. The Red Cross buys supplies and builds shelters.

Reading Strategy

Ask Questions Give students an example of how to ask questions.

SAY *As we read this article, we asked ourselves who can help, and how can they help, after a hurricane.*

- *Why is it important to ask questions before you begin to read?*
- *Did the author answer all the questions you would ask?*
- *What information did you learn that was not from a question you asked?*
- *How does asking questions keep you more interested in what you are reading?*

Critique Remind students of the Big Question for this reading. Ask students if they think the author provided enough information for the students to respond to the question. Ask them what information they think the selection needs.

STEP 1: Introduce

Word Analysis

Homophones Help students understand that sometimes two different words, with different meanings, can sound exactly the same.

STEP 2: Teach

Ask students to read the sentences in the box. Have the class find the words that are homophones.

SAY *Words that sound the same may have different meanings and different spellings.*

- *How do you spell two different words that sound like* by*?*
- *How do you spell two different words that sound like* rode*?*
- *What are the definitions for* new *and* knew*? Can you use each one in a sentence?*

Write the following sentences on the board and ask students to select the right homophone.

1. *The (hare/hair) had fluffy white (hare/hair).*
2. *Nobody (nose/knows) that my (nose/knows) itches.*
3. *When you (toe/tow) that car, please don't run it over my (toe/tow)!*
4. *We (rode/road) our bikes on the (rode/road).*
5. *There are just (to, two, too) apples, but I want (to, two, too) have one. Do you want one, (to, two, too)?*

STEP 3: Practice

Answer Key

1. great
2. rain
3. need
4. wear
5. Some
6. their

Scaffolding

Have students look up the following words that were not chosen in the exercise: *grate*, *rein*, *knead*, *where*, *sum*, *there* and write a definition for each.

Teaching Resources

- ***Practice Book,*** p.101
- ***CD-ROM*** • ***Audio CD***

Reading 3

Word Analysis & Fluency

Word Analysis

Homophones

Words that sound the same but have different spellings or meanings are **homophones**.

- What happens to an area hit **by** a hurricane?
- The American Red Cross raises money to **buy** supplies.

Practice

Work with a partner. Choose the correct homophone for each sentence.

1. Hurricanes cause (grate, great) damage.
2. Heavy (rain, rein) causes flooding.
3. Many people (knead, need) help.
4. People need clothes to (wear, where).
5. (Some, Sum) need a place to stay.
6. People want (there, their) lives to return to normal.

Practice Book page 101

TESOL Standards

Goal 1, Standard 3—To use English to communicate in social settings: Students will use learning strategies to extend their communicative competence.
Descriptors—Listening to and imitating how others use English; Self-monitoring and self-evaluating language development.

Goal 3, Standard 3—To use English in socially and culturally appropriate ways: Students will use appropriate learning strategies to extend their sociolinguistic and sociocultural competence.
Descriptors—Observing and modeling how others speak and behave in a particular situation or setting; Experimenting with variations of language in social and academic settings; Seeking information about appropriate language use and behavior.

Fluency

Read for Speed and Accuracy

You should read quickly. But never read so quickly that you lose your understanding.

Practice

Read for one minute. → Count the words you read. → Study any hard words. → Read and count again.

After a hurricane, experts come and assess the towns 9
that were damaged. They call rescue workers to help. They 19
also let others know when more help is needed. People 29
come from nearby and from far away to give relief to those 41
who need it. These people are usually volunteers. They do 51
not get paid for their work. They come because they know 62
that people need help after a hurricane. 69
Many people lose their homes during hurricanes. These 77
people need to stay someplace, such as a shelter, until they 88
can go home. They might feel sad and scared. Volunteers 98
work to help these people feel better. The volunteers can 108
play with children. They can help people find missing 117
friends or family. Sometimes, people just need to talk to 127
someone about what happened. 131
People of all ages need help after a hurricane. People 141
of all ages can offer help as well. Adults might help in 153
towns that were damaged. Young people can make a 162
difference, too. 164

Linguistic Note

Cognate Volunteer Students whose home language is Spanish may recognize the Spanish cognate *voluntario*. The same Spanish word is an adjective meaning *voluntary*, the opposite of *compulsary*.

Accelerate Language Development

Someone Spanish-speaking students will most likely be familiar with the way the Spanish language forms terms such as *someplace* and *sometimes* (which both appear in the reading on p. 203). In Spanish, the words *algún/alguna* correspond with *some* and is often used to precede the Spanish words for *place, times,* and so on. For example: *sometimes* = *algunas veces; someplace* = *alguna parte*.

STEP 1: Introduce

Fluency

Read for Speed and Accuracy Explain to students that reading for speed and accuracy will help them improve their concentration as they read. Emphasize that students should not read so quickly that they miss information in the selection.

Play the Audio CD for this reading to the class, asking students to listen for pacing, intonation, and expression.

STEP 2: Practice

Have students work with partners to do the following exercise. Before they begin reading for speed and accuracy, they should find the hard words that will slow them down and practice saying them. When both partners feel that they are ready, have them begin the exercise.

- Have one partner read while the other acts as the timer. When the reader has read for one minute, have the timer say stop.
- Have partners look at the end of the last complete line the reader read, and make a note of the number.
- Have partners repeat the process. Then have partners change roles.

Possible Responses–Hard words

assess	rescue	volunteers
nearby	someplace	shelter

STEP 3: Extend

Study Skills

Dictionary Have students work with partners to:

- write three words from the reading that slowed them down;
- look up the words in a dictionary;
- read the sentences from the reading in which the hard words appear and define the hard words.

Remind students that they can use this study skill anywhere. In social studies or science class, or when they read at home, they can find the hard words and write them down. Students can then look them up online or in the dictionary.

STEP 1: Monitor Progress

Learning Strategy

Outline Making an outline is a way to help students remember the main ideas and most important details in a selection. Have students work in pairs, with one student selecting the main ideas and the other explaining how they help answer the Big Question. Encourage students to use a Main Idea and Supporting Details Chart to record their information.

STEP 2: Teach

Sequence of Events

Students will learn to put events in sequence.

SAY *When you talk about a sequence of events, you take a trip through time. You start at the time that was longest ago, and you travel forward in a sequence. At the beginning, you should say* first*. Words that help direct the sequence are called* order words.

- *What order word might be on the sign right after* first? second, next, then
- *What other order words on the signs will you want to include?* third, next, then, later
- *What are some good order words for the sign at the end of the trip?* last, finally

STEP 3: Practice

Flexible Grouping You may assign this activity as a class discussion, partner activity, or individual written assignment.

Possible Responses

1. First, it started to rain.
2. Second, the rain became very heavy.
3. Next, our street flooded.
4. Last, we had to wear boots to walk to school.

Teaching Resources

- *Practice Book*, p. 102
- *Transparencies*, p. 58
- *Teacher's Resource Book*, p. 156
- *CD-ROM*

Reading 3

Comprehension

Learning Strategy

Outline

Outline the main ideas in the selection. Share your outline with a partner.

Ask your partner to respond to the Big Question for this reading.

Practice Book page 102

Sequence

The order in which events take place in a story or a selection is called the **sequence**.

These clues will help you know the sequence.

Signal Words — Look for words such as ***first***, ***last***, ***next***, ***before***, and ***after***.

Numbers — A writer might include times, days of the week, months, or years to show the sequence. Sometimes numbers show the steps of a process.

Practice

Write a sequence of events for something that happened recently. Use the following sentence starters:

1. First, ______

2. Second, ______

3. Next, ______

4. Last, ______

TESOL Standards

Goal 2, Standard 2—To use English to achieve academically in all content areas: Students will use English to obtain, process, construct, and provide subject matter information in spoken and written form.

Descriptors—Listening to, speaking, reading, and writing about subject matter information; Gathering information orally and in writing; Retelling information; Selecting, connecting, and explaining information; Demonstrating knowledge through application in a variety of contexts.

Use a Sequence Chart

You can use a sequence chart to help you remember what happens first, next, and last in a selection.

Practice

Copy this chart. Complete it to show a sequence of events that occurs after a hurricane strikes.

Rain causes flooding.
↓
↓
↓

Extension

Work with a group to prepare an emergency kit. (You can use pictures or real objects.) Write a description of each item and explain why your group chose it. Present your emergency kit to the class.

205

Accelerate Language Development

Ordinal numbers

Students whose families speak languages other than English at home may not be familiar with the ordinal numbers in English. This may make it difficult for them to talk about a sequence of events or a series of steps in directions. Write the numbers one through five on the board, and next to each number, write its ordinal: *first, second, third, fourth, fifth*. Have students say each number and then read the ordinal that goes with it. For a further challenge, write the numbers scrambled in one column and the ordinals scrambled in another, and have students play a matching game.

STEP 1: Teach

Use a Sequence Chart

Ask students to think about something they've made or built. Ask them to think about three steps they followed in order. Then have them write the steps, but NOT in order. Have students trade their lists of steps with partners, and have partners try to number the steps in the correct order.

Possible Responses

Out of order

I pasted the pictures on a poster.

I wrote captions under the pictures.

I cut out pictures from a magazine.

In order

I cut out pictures from a magazine.

I pasted the pictures on a poster.

I wrote captions under the pictures.

STEP 2: Practice

You may have students complete the graphic organizer provided as a Blackline Master in the *Teacher's Resource Book*.

Answer Key

Rain causes flooding.
↓
People get stranded.
↓
Firefighters and police come to help them.
↓
Volunteers bring supplies.

STEP 3: Extend

Oral Presentation Ask students to think of things they might need for an emergency kit (for example: flashlight, batteries, water, band-aids). Students can use pictures instead of real objects, and they can use a box as their kit. Have them show each item to the class and explain what it is and why it's in their emergency kit.

STEP 1: Introduce

Help students understand that prepositions are words that function as important links between words and phrases in a sentence.

STEP 2: Teach

Prepositions

Read aloud the definition of prepositions on p. 206. Write the following sentences on the board. Ask students to fill in each blank with an appropriate preposition. Ask students to describe the where or when that the preposition explains in each sentence.

1. *I went* to *the movies.*
2. *David got an email* from *Lucy.*
3. *The dog stepped* in *a puddle.*
4. *When it rains, I take an umbrella* with *me.*
5. *Did you learn* about *hurricanes today?*
6. *My eyes are* on *my face.*
7. *Can you make a list* of *your favorite songs?*

STEP 3: Practice

Before students begin the Practice activity, have them work in pairs to make a list of the prepositions they used to fill in the blanks in the classroom exercise. Then have them pick any three and write a sentence using each one.

Answer Key

1. after
2. during
3. of, after
4. with, in
5. across

Teaching Resources

- ***Practice Book***, pp. 103–104
- ***Transparencies***, pp. 69–80
- ***Assessments***, pp. 73–76
- ***CD-ROM***

Reading 3

Grammar & Writing

Prepositions

Prepositions are an important link between words in a sentence.

Hurricanes have high winds that start over water.

The preposition ***over*** links the words ***start*** and ***water*** to tell where the winds start. Prepositions often answer questions about where or when.

Practice

Read the sentences with a partner.
List the prepositions.

1. Experts and volunteers arrive after a hurricane.
2. People feel scared during a hurricane.
3. People of all ages can volunteer after a hurricane.
4. Some volunteers play with children in relief centers.
5. Students across the country help, too.

Practice Book page 103

TESOL Standards

Goal 2, Standard 2—To use English to achieve academically in all content areas: Students will use English to obtain, process, construct, and provide subject matter information in spoken and written form.
Descriptor—Representing information visually and interpreting information presented visually.

Goal 2, Standard 3—To use English to achieve academically in all content areas: Students will use appropriate learning strategies to construct and apply academic knowledge.
Descriptors—Using context to construct meaning; Actively connecting new information to information previously learned; Imitating the behaviors of native English speakers to complete tasks successfully.

Goal 3, Standard 1—To use English in socially and culturally appropriate ways: Students will use the appropriate language variety, register, and genre according to audience, purpose, and setting.
Descriptors—Using the appropriate degree of formality with different audiences and settings; Recognizing and using standard English and vernacular dialects appropriately; Using a variety of writing styles appropriate for different audiences, purposes, and settings; Ask for assistance with a task.

Make a Poster

Posters give information in short sentences. Sometimes posters use pictures to help the reader understand. Read this poster Sean made.

> **What to Do After a Storm**
> Everyone can help!
>
> <u>Rescue Teams</u>
> • Search damaged buildings. Look for people who are trapped or stranded.
> • Bring them to a safe place, such as a school or other shelter.
>
> <u>Organizations</u>
> • Bring food, water, warm clothes, blankets, and toys.
> • Help people rebuild or find new homes.
>
> <u>Individuals–What You Can Do</u>
> • Raise money to rebuild homes, schools, and businesses.
> • Give clothing, toys, and books.

SPELLING TIP

Learn the homophones for common words. Always check your writing to make sure you have used the correct word.

Practice Book page 104

Practice

Make a poster, with pictures, to tell what people can do to help after a big storm. Make sure your poster is easy to read and grabs the reader's attention.

Writing Checklist

✓ Did you use short, simple sentences?

✓ Were your pictures bold, colorful, and clear?

✓ Can a partner understand your poster?

Differentiated Instruction

Beginning	Ask students to copy the following statement and fill in the blanks: *Rescue teams ______ buildings. Organizations ______ food and water. People ______ clothing and toys.*
Intermediate	Ask students to work in pairs to find the nouns and verbs on Sean's poster.
Greater Challenge	Have students work in pairs to identify and make a list of the prepositions on Sean's poster.
Struggling Reader	Write the following words on the board: *Teams, people, school, food, water, homes.* Ask students to find the words on the poster and repeat them.

STEP 1: Introduce

Make a Poster

Explain that a poster has pictures and information about something that's going to happen. You hang a poster up to advertise an event.

SAY *Let's read Sean's poster. He is offering information about how to help after the storm.*

- *What sections did Sean show on his poster?*
- *What other important information does his poster provide?*
- *Do you think Sean's poster would inspire you to volunteer? Why or why not?*

Spelling Tip

Remind students that homophones are often spelled differently. Write the following on the board, and have students spell a homophone for each word:

by	*too*	*eight*	*knew*
rowed	*deer*	*sea*	*beet*

STEP 2: Practice

Before students write their own posters, have them discuss the following parts of a poster:

- How can you make your words look interesting?
- What pictures can you include?
- What will you advertise with your poster?

STEP 3: Assess

Writing Checklist

✓ Tell students that their sentences should be short, but the poster should also include all the important details.

✓ Students who are not comfortable drawing may cut out pictures from magazines.

✓ Have students exchange posters with partners. Ask students to tell whether they understand their partner's poster. Remind partners to be respectful to one another as they share their work.

The Five Step Writing Process in the Writing Handbook reference of this book provides more student writing instruction.

STEP 1: Introduce

More About The Big Question

A Big Question for this reading could be: *How do humans affect food webs?* Lead a discussion about what might happen to a food web if humans consumed all of the animals or plants in one part of it.

SAY *Remember that the Unit 4 Big Question asked how people and environments affect each other. In this Bonus Reading, we're going to learn why there are so many kinds of animals in the ocean.*

- *What big mammals live or hunt in the ocean?*
- *Can you think of any birds that hunt in the ocean?*
- *What about animals with shells? Can you think of any that live or hunt in the ocean?*

Visual Literacy

Diagrams Draw students' attention to the diagram on p. 208.

SAY *Look at the diagram with pictures of various creatures in the ocean.*

- *What does the diagram show?*
- *What kinds of pictures do you see in the diagram?*
- *What do the lines show?*

STEP 2: Teach

Understand Text Structure

Draw students' attention to the genre label. Remind them that the selection in this unit *Biomes All Over the World* is also informational text. Ask them what they remember about the structure of that selection.

Teaching Resources

- *Teacher Resource Book*, pp. 133–134
- *CD-ROM* • *Audio CD*

Bonus Reading

INFORMATIONAL TEXT

Science

Marine Food Web

by Hiro Ishida

This diagram shows a basic marine food web.

What is the difference between a food chain and a food web? A food chain shows one way that energy travels between producers, consumers, and decomposers. A food web shows many food chains that are connected to one another.

The diagram shows a marine food web. The word *marine* means anything that has to do with the oceans or seas.

Food webs are very important to humans. Any change to one organism in a food web affects all the other organisms in the food web. Natural events, such as hurricanes and earthquakes, cause some major changes to food webs. Humans cause changes to marine food webs by overfishing or pollution. It is important to learn about food webs so that you can help to keep them balanced.

TESOL Standards

Goal 2, Standard 3—To use English to achieve academically in all content areas: Students will use appropriate learning strategies to construct and apply academic knowledge. **Descriptors**—Focusing attention selectively; Applying basic reading comprehension skills such as skimming, scanning, previewing, and reviewing text; Using context to construct meaning; Applying self-monitoring and self-corrective strategies to build and expand a knowledge base; Knowing when to use native language resources (human and material) to promote understanding.

The marine food web starts with the Sun. The Sun gives energy for all life on Earth. Tiny plants called phytoplankton live in water. They capture the Sun's energy and use it to make food. Most phytoplankton cannot move around. They drift in the water. Yet everything in the marine food web that lives depends on them.

Zooplankton are very small animals. They move through the water and eat phytoplankton. This makes zooplankton the second connection in the marine food web. Small jellyfish, worms, and krill are examples of zooplankton.

Many small fish feed on plankton. These fish often swim in schools or groups. This makes it harder for predators to hunt them.

Humpback whales feed on small fish and plankton.

209

Differentiated Instruction

Beginning	Have students find the photo of zooplankton. Ask them to look at the text next to the photo, and point to the names of three different kinds of zooplankton.
Intermediate	Have students write a short answer to explain why everything in the marine food web depends on phytoplankton.
Greater Challenge	Have students work in small groups to draw a picture of the Marine Food Web that includes the Sun, photoplankton, zooplankton, plankton, small fish, and whales.
Standard English Learner CRI	Have students select one of the photos on p. 209. Ask them to make a drawing based on what the photo makes them think about or how it makes them feel.

Vocabulary Definitions

The following vocabulary appears on pp. 208–209 of *Marine Food Web*. Definitions are provided for your convenience to share with your class if they require explanations of any words. They are not meant for vocabulary acquisition or exercises.

producers makers of food

consumers eaters

decomposers organisms that eat waste

organism living thing

overfishing fishing too much

phytoplankton tiny plants that live in water

drift get moved along by the flow of water

zooplankton tiny animals that live in water

Build Vocabulary

Have students use a Venn Diagram to compare and contrast one of the following pairs of terms:

producers and consumers
phytoplankton and zooplankton

Link to Science

Explain to students that plankton is the most abundant life form on Earth and it can be as small as a microbe or as large as a jellyfish. Have students research plankton and write a short report on why it is a critical part of the marine food web.

STEP 3: Extend

Make sure students are following the logical sequence in this selection. Explain to students that the sequence in this selection is determined by connections in a food web that repeat a cycle. It is not a sequence of events that happen one after the other.

SAY *Usually when we talk about sequence, we mean events in time order. With the marine food web, we can trace the sequence in the food web to show who eats who!*

- *What's the first thing that happens in the marine food web?* Phytoplankton capture the Sun's energy and use it to make food.
- *Then what happens?* Zooplankton eat phytoplankton.
- *What happens next?* Small fish eat plankton.

STEP 1: Monitor Progress

Comprehension Check

Compare and Contrast Help students identify similarities and differences between certain marine animals. Use Venn Diagrams on the board to organize information from the discussion.

SAY *Marine animals have some ways in which they're similar and some ways in which they're different. Let's compare and contrast some marine animals.*

- *How are sharks and elephant seals similar? How are they different?* Sharks and elephant seals are similar because they both eat fish in the ocean. They are different because sharks spend their whole lives in the water but elephant seals do not.
- *How are orcas and penguins similar? How are they different?* They are similar because they both eat fish. They are different because orcas are at the top of the marine food web, but penguins are in the middle.

Adapt the Activity

Students may enjoy learning more about marine animals. Have students find information about a local aquarium and write a short report about what marine animals can be found there. In their report, have them include a description of what they saw if they have visited an aquarium.

Large fish, such as sharks and tuna, eat smaller fish. Other animals that do not spend their entire lives in the water are also part of the marine food web. Penguins and elephant seals also eat fish.

210

FYI

Penguins Penguins are birds that can't fly, but they need their wings anyway—to use as paddles to help them move through ocean waters. There are 17 species of penguins, all of which live below the equator. Some species live in or near the Antarctic region, but more of them live in temperate zones. One species, the Galapagos Penguin, lives on the equator. All penguins have white bellies and black backs for protection. To a predator below, the white belly looks like light on the surface of the water. To a predatory bird flying above, the black back blends with the ocean.

TESOL Standards

Goal 2, Standard 3—To use English to achieve academically in all content areas: Students will use appropriate learning strategies to construct and apply academic knowledge. **Descriptors**— Focusing attention selectively; Applying basic reading comprehension skills such as skimming, scanning, previewing, and reviewing text; Using context to construct meaning; Applying self-monitoring and self-corrective strategies to build and expand a knowledge base; Knowing when to use native language resources (human and material) to promote understanding.

Polar bears and orcas are at the top of the marine food web. This means they have no predators. They live on fish and other marine mammals.

Decomposers in the marine food web include bacteria and scavengers, such as lobsters. Decomposers eat the waste products of other organisms in the marine food web. They also eat dead animals and plants.

211

Linguistic Note

Cognate Tuna Students whose home language is Spanish will most likely be familiar with the word *atún*, from which the English word *tuna* is derived. Note that the syllables are flipped in the two languages. Be aware, that *tuno/a* has several meanings in Spanish. It can mean *rascal* or it can describe a university musical group.

STEP 2: Teach

Vocabulary Definitions

The following vocabulary appears on pp. 210–211 of *Marine Food Web*. Definitions are provided for your convenience to share with your class if they require explanations of any words. They are not meant for vocabulary acquisition or exercises.

polar having to do with either the North Pole or the South Pole.

bacteria microscopic organisms

scavengers animals that eat dead organisms

Visual Literacy

Photographs Draw students' attention to the photos on pp. 210–211.

SAY *The photos on pages 210 and 211 show different kinds of animals that live or hunt in the water.*

- *If you could be any animal on page 210 or 211, which would you want to be?*
- *Why would you want to be that animal?*
- *What do you think your life would be like?*

Have students write a description of a day in the life of the animal they would like to be.

STEP 3: Extend

Explain to students that a food web is balanced if there is enough food for everyone in it. If there is too little food for a particular species, it may die out. If there is too much food, the species will most likely do well and it may have too many healthy babies—eventually there would not be enough food. Ask students to explain why people should work to protect the oceans and the animals in them.

STEP 1: Review

The Big Question

Evidence of Understanding

Read the Big Question for the unit with students to focus their attention on this unit's theme in a way that can be answered and assessed in a variety of modalities. The first tier is least challenging, and the third tier is most challenging.

STEP 2: Transfer

Written

List Suggest that students use a dictionary if they're unsure how to spell the names of animals or plants.

Log Encourage students to record in their logs as journal or diary entries.

Magazine Article Make some children's science magazines available to help give students ideas for how to organize their articles.

Oral

Discussion Have each student think of one or two descriptive words that will help others picture the plants and animals they describe.

Presentation Urge students to use illustrations, photos, charts, or maps in their presentations.

Song Point out that students can take a familiar song and set different words to it.

Visual/Active

Poster Remind students to include illustrations and words on their posters and to use vivid colors.

Chart Allow students to work in small groups. Have them brainstorm ways that hurricanes can change animals' lives.

Illustration Have students work in pairs. You may want to make encyclopedias, reference books, or safe Internet access available.

All projects can be assessed on the basis of content and presentation. A rubric delineating standards for assessment can be helpful and is available as a Blackline Master in your *Teacher's Resource Book*.

UNIT 4 Wrap Up

The Big Question

How do people and environments affect each other?

Written	Oral	Visual/Active
List Write a list that shows details about your favorite biome. Include the climate, along with animals and plants that live there.	**Discussion** In small groups, discuss biomes you have visited or have read about. Name some plants and animals that live in each biome.	**Poster** Create a poster that shows the animals and plants in the biome of your choice. Show how people can help the animals found there.
Log List the biomes you have visited or have learned about. Name some of the animals found in each biome. Give details about each climate.	**Presentation** Research an animal in your biome. Make a presentation that explains what the animal looks like, where it lives, what it eats, and its role in a food web.	**Chart** Make a chart that shows the dangers animals face after a hurricane. Show some ways that people can help bring the animals' lives back to normal.
Magazine Article Choose a biome. Write a magazine article that explains how people affect animals in that biome. Describe some of the things people can do to help those animals.	**Song** Work as a group. Write and perform a song that tells how people can help animals live safely in a biome, such as an ocean or a forest.	**Illustration** You read about a marine food web. Learn about another kind of food web. Create an illustration that shows how the food web's food chains are connected.

212

TESOL Standards

Goal 1, Standard 3—To use English to communicate in social settings: Students will use learning strategies to extend their communicative competence.
Descriptors—Testing hypotheses about language; Selecting different media to help understand language.

Goal 2, Standard 2—To use English to achieve academically in all content areas: Students will use English to obtain, process, construct, and provide subject matter information in spoken and written form.
Descriptors—Gathering information orally and in writing; Representing information visually and interpreting information presented visually; Understanding and producing technical vocabulary and text features according to content area; Demonstrating knowledge through application in a variety of contexts.

Goal 3, Standard 1—To use English in socially and culturally appropriate ways: Students will use the appropriate language variety, register, and genre according to audience, purpose, and setting.
Descriptors—Using the appropriate degree of formality with different audiences and settings; Recognizing and using Standard English and vernacular dialects appropriately; Using a variety of writing styles appropriate for different audiences, purposes, and settings; Responding to and using slang appropriately; Responding to and using idioms appropriately; Responding to and using humor appropriately; Determining when it is appropriate to use a language other than English; Determining appropriate topics for interaction.

Practice Book pages 105–106

✓ Learning Checklist

Word Analysis and Phonics

- ✓ Distinguish between final *s* and *z* sounds.
- ✓ Pronounce consonant clusters.
- ✓ Identify homophones.

Comprehension

- ✓ Visualize information in a text.
- ✓ Use a Compare and Contrast Chart.
- ✓ Identify Problems and Solutions.
- ✓ Use a Problem and Solution Chart.
- ✓ Identify a sequence of events.
- ✓ Use a Sequence Chart.

Grammar and Writing

- ✓ Use conjunctions and transitions.
- ✓ Distinguish between complete and incomplete sentences.
- ✓ Identify prepositions.
- ✓ Write an expository paragraph.
- ✓ Write an explanation.
- ✓ Make a poster.

Self-Evaluation Questions

- How does what you learned in this unit support what you learned in science class?
- How hard was it for you to research a biome?
- What are your strengths in making a presentation?

213

Further Reading

The Crane's Gift, Steve and Megumi Biddle
This Penguin Young Reader® is a beautiful and moving tale set in Japan. An old man rescues an injured crane, and the crane's kindness changes his life.

Welcome to the Sea of Sand, Jane Yolen
Arizona's Sonoran Desert, the picturesque "sea of sand" habitat of a wide variety of animals, is described in engaging verse form with vivid illustrations.

Dive: My Adventures in the Deep Frontier, Sylvia A. Earle
Here, the world's oceans come alive as the author, a marine biologist, takes readers on an underwater journey, exploring the fascinating world within the sea.

STEP 3: Assess

Learning Checklist

Word Analysis and Phonics

- ✓ Final *s* and *z* sounds: Reading 1, p. 176
- ✓ Consonant clusters: Reading 2, p. 188
- ✓ Homophones: Reading 3, p. 202

Comprehension

- ✓ Visualize: Reading 1, p. 178
- ✓ Use a Compare and Contrast Chart: Reading 1, p. 179
- ✓ Problems and Solutions: Reading 2, p. 190
- ✓ Use a Problem and Solution Chart : Reading 2, p. 191
- ✓ Sequence of Events: Reading 3, p. 204
- ✓ Use a Sequence of Events Chart: Reading 3, p. 205

Grammar and Writing

- ✓ Conjunctions and Transitions: Reading 1, p. 180
- ✓ Write an Expository paragraph: Reading 1, p. 181
- ✓ Complete and incomplete sentences: Reading 2, p. 192
- ✓ Write an Explanation: Reading 2, p. 193
- ✓ Prepositions: Reading 3, p. 206
- ✓ Make a Poster: Reading 3, p. 207

Self-Evaluation Questions

The self-evaluation questions provide the teacher with important information about the students' learning progress, as well as their self esteem.

- Have students explain other facts about the environment that they have learned in science class.
- Have students describe the easiest and hardest tasks they had to do during their research.

Teaching Resources

- ***Practice Book,*** pp. 105–106
- ***Transparencies,*** p. 84
- ***Assessments,*** pp. 133–141
- ***CD-ROM*** • ***Teacher's CD-ROM***

Unit 5 Planner

Sounds and Music

Unit Preview: pp. 214–219
Pacing: 3–4 Days
Vocabulary: *Words to Know*, pp. 216–217
Oral Language: *What about you?*, p. 219

The Big Question
How do people make and use music?

	Suggested Pacing: 7–8 Days 1	Suggested Pacing: 7–8 Days 2
Reading Selection	**Touching Sound with Evelyn Glennie** pp. 220–231 **Genre:** Informational Text/ Internet Article	**A Song Map** pp. 232–243 **Genre:** Literature/ Song
Oral Language	**More About the Big Question, p. T222** *How can you hear without using your ears?*	**More About the Big Question, p. T234** *What messages can songs carry?*
Vocabulary	**Key Words:** musicians, instruments, percussion, sounds, vibrations, hearing **Academic Words:** context, demonstrate **Other Academic Word:** range	**Key Words:** code, escape, landmarks, secret, riverbank, tracks **Academic Words:** assist, accompany **Other Academic Word:** alternative
Phonics Word Analysis Fluency	**Phonics:** Endings: *-ed*, p. 226 **Fluency:** Look Ahead, p. 227	**Word Analysis:** Figurative Language, p. 238 **Fluency:** Read with Expression, p. 239
Comprehension	**Reading Strategy:** Identify Main Idea and Details, pp. 222, 225 **Learning Strategy:** Summarize, p. 228 **Comprehension Skill:** Main Idea and Details, p. 228 **Graphic Organizer:** Main Idea and Details Chart, p. 229	**Reading Strategy:** Summarize, pp. 234, 237 **Learning Strategy:** Summarize, p. 240 **Comprehension Skill:** Make Inferences, p. 240 **Graphic Organizer:** Inference Chart, p. 241
Grammar and Writing	**Grammar:** Appositives and Prepositional Phrases, p. 230 **Writing:** Write an Introductory Paragraph, Writing Checklist, Spelling Tip, p. 231	**Grammar:** Dependent and Independent Clauses, p. 242 **Writing:** Write a Compare and Contrast Essay, Writing Checklist, Spelling Tip, p. 243
	Differentiated Instruction pp. T221, T225, T231	**Differentiated Instruction** pp. T233, T235, T237, T243

Teaching Resources

- *Assessments*, pp. 77–88, pp. 143–152
- *Practice Book*, pp. 107–132
- *Phonics and Word Analysis Workbook*
- *Phonics and Word Analysis Teacher's Guide w/Audio CD*
- *Phonics Flashcards*
- *Posters*
- *Teacher's Resource Book* *Lesson Plans*, pp. 50–61
- *Audio CD*
- *DVD*
- *Teacher's CD-ROM*
- *CD-ROM*
- *Phonetic Storybooks*
- *Penguin Young Readers Library*

Suggested Pacing: 7–8 Days

3

Homemade Music

pp. 244–257

Genre: Informational Text/Music

A Closer Look at . . .
Homemade Instruments, pp. 250–251

More About the Big Question, p. T246
How do people make musical instruments?

Key Words: rhythms, kazoo, harmonies, flea market, improvisation
Academic Words: complexity, variety
Other Academic Word: consist

Phonics: Words with: *ow*, *ou*, p. 252
Fluency: Read for Speed and Accuracy, p. 253

Reading Strategy: Identify Author's Purpose, pp. 246, 249
Learning Strategy: Take Notes, p. 254
Comprehension Skill: Author's Purpose, p. 254
Graphic Organizer: Compare and Contrast Chart, p. 255

Grammar: Commonly Misused Verbs, p. 256
Writing: Write a Descriptive Paragraph, Writing Checklist, Spelling Tip, p. 257

Differentiated Instruction
pp. T245, T247, T249, T251, T257

Suggested Pacing: 1–2 Days

Bonus Reading

The Radio Storm

pp. 258–261

Genre: Literature/ Realistic Fiction

More About the Big Question, p. T258
How can we make great sound effects?

Vocabulary: radio station, sound effects, galloping, blasting off

Differentiated Instruction
p. T259

Further Reading

Rumpelstiltskin
In this Penguin Young Reader® adaptation of the classic Grimm's fairy tale, a queen must find out the name of a mysterious little man in time to save her family.

What Charlie Heard, Mordicai Gerstein
Here is the engaging story of twentieth-century composer Charles Ives. As a child, Charlie was fascinated by sounds of all kinds. Later, as an adult, he tried to re-create those sounds in his music.

The Philharmonic Gets Dressed,
Karla Kuskin
When all 105 members of the Philharmonic Orchestra come together, they make beautiful music. Readers meet the musicians first as individuals before they become a coordinated group.

Suggested Pacing: 1–2 Days

Assessment

The Big Question

Evidence of Understanding
How do people make and use music?

Check Up pp. 223, 235, 247
Think It Over pp. 225, 237, 249
Activity To Do! p. 251
Extension pp. 229, 241, 255

Unit Wrap Up pp. 262–263

Written
Slogans; Outline; Report

Oral
Game; Song; Radio Play

Visual/Active
Demonstration; Mural; Catalog

Learning Checklist
Word Analysis and Phonics; Comprehension; Grammar and Writing; Self-Evaluation Questions

STEP 1: Introduce

Have students work in pairs or groups to brainstorm kinds of music they have heard. Ask them what kinds of music they have made themselves and what they did to make the music.

Unit Content Students will practice reading and comprehension skills, including identifying the main idea and details and author's purpose and summarizing. They will also apply language strategies such as taking notes and summarizing.

Visual Literacy

Photographs Have students look at the photographs on pp. 214–215. Encourage them to describe what the students are doing in the pictures.

STEP 2: Build Background

The Big Question

Tell students that they will be reading about different people who make music. Encourage students to discuss their experiences making music.

SAY *The Big Question for Unit 5 is* How do people make and use music? *Think about the kinds of music you make and listen to.*

- *When do you like to listen to music?*
- *When do you like to make music yourself?*

Guide the class to fill in a Story Map to help them tell a story about a musical experience they may have had.

My family
↓
Our neighborhood park
↓
We went to a July 4th picnic.
↓
We heard loud drumming.
↓
A marching band came into the park and played music for the crowd.

UNIT 5 Sounds and Music

Playing instruments, listening, singing, and dancing are all ways we can appreciate sounds and music.

READINGS

1 

Touching Sound with Evelyn Glennie

2 

A Song Map

3 

Homemade Music

214

TESOL Standards

Goal 1, Standard 2—To use English to communicate in social settings: Students will interact in, through, and with spoken and written English for personal expression and enjoyment.
Descriptor—Sharing social and cultural traditions and values; Expressing personal needs, feelings, and ideas.

The Big Question
How do people make and use music?

LISTENING AND SPEAKING

You will talk about the different ways people make music.

WRITING

You will compare two musical instruments and two types of music.

Bonus Reading

The Radio Storm

Quick Write

Write about your favorite kind of music. Why do you like it?

Differentiated Instruction	
Beginning	The pictures on pp. 214–215 explain that people enjoy music. Have students work in pairs to demonstrate people playing instruments and singing.
Intermediate	Ask students to read aloud the titles of the readings. Then have them write a title for a story about singing or playing an instrument and draw a picture that illustrates the title.
Greater Challenge	Ask students to write three descriptive sentences that describe the action in the three pictures for the readings shown on p. 214.
Struggling Reader	Point to the Big Question and read it aloud. Then ask students to draw a picture showing people singing and playing music. Have them label some of the items in their pictures.

STEP 3: Connect

Listening and Speaking

Read the text in the box aloud. Ask students to suggest words that have to do with making music. Write a list of these words on the board and model their pronunciation for students.

Possible Responses sing, dance, hum, band, piano, melody, rhythm

Writing

Read the text in the Writing box aloud to students.

SAY *Imagine you are the conductor of an orchestra and you want to have a concert.*

- *What two types of music would you select?*
- *How are classical music and jazz similar?*
- *How are they different?*
- *What instruments do you need for each?*

Remind students of the difference between comparing and contrasting. In this unit, they will write about how two types of music are similar and different.

Quick Write

Before they begin writing, have students work in pairs to describe the kinds of music they like. Then ask them why they like that music and how it makes them feel when they hear it. Encourage students to write their descriptions like a speech. They can present their speeches to the class.

Adapt the Activity

Have students research the history of a type of music they like. They can use the 5W questions to guide their research. Have them prepare brief reports about the types of music they have chosen and present their reports to the class.

Visual Literacy

Graphic Organizer Introduce the Big Question Transparency and use it throughout the unit to help students connect the readings to the Big Question.

STEP 1: Introduce

Unit Vocabulary

Use these pages to help students identify some terms used to describe music. Post your Words to Know Poster for this unit in the classroom. As students read the unit, reinforce the unit vocabulary by using the Vocabulary Cards provided as a Blackline Master in the *Teacher's Resource Book* as flash cards or in memory games.

STEP 2: Teach

Words to Know

Point to the pictures in section 1 and say each of the terms aloud. Encourage students to repeat the terms with you. Have students point to the correct icon as they say each term.

Draw students' attention to the question in section 2. Have them complete the sentence stem with the words provided. Ask volunteers to demonstrate the motion of playing each type of instrument.

Academic Words

Discuss the definitions for *theory* and *design* with students. Share the following context sentences with students. Have students add the terms to their personal thesaurus.

theory idea that explains facts or events

design a plan or sketch

You must understand music *theory* to be a composer.

She presented her *design* for a new instrument.

Have students discuss their prior knowledge of musical instruments. Lead a class discussion about musical instruments that students play or would like to play. Encourage students to think of ideas for inventing a new instrument. Have students brainstorm different items that can be used to make musical sounds.

Teaching Resources

- ***Teacher's Resource Book***, pp. 97–98; 171
- ***Posters***
- ***Transparencies***, pp. 25–30
- ***CD ROM*** • ***Audio CD***

What Do You Know about Sounds and Music?

Words to Know

1. Use these words to talk about music.

 **band**
 **orchestra**
 **conductor**
 **notes**
 **concert**
 **instruments**

2. What are some different types of instruments?

A ______________ is an instrument.

 **violin**
 **guitar**
 **drum**
 **trumpet**
 **flute**
 **cello**

216

TESOL Standards

Goal 1, Standard 3—To use English to communicate in social settings: Students will use learning strategies to extend their communicative competence.
Descriptors—Testing hypotheses about language; Listening to and imitating how others use English; Exploring alternative ways of saying things; Using context to construct meaning.

3. How do you use instruments to make music?

You make music on a _____________ by _____________.

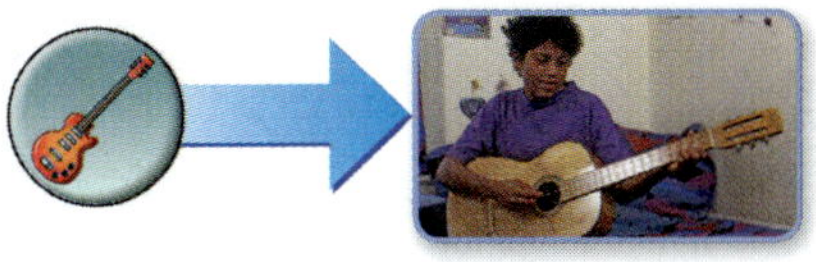

strumming

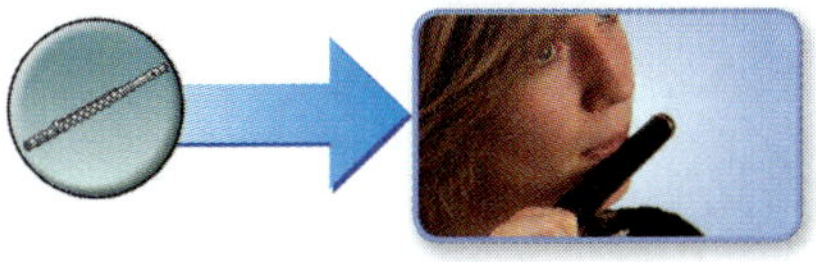

blowing

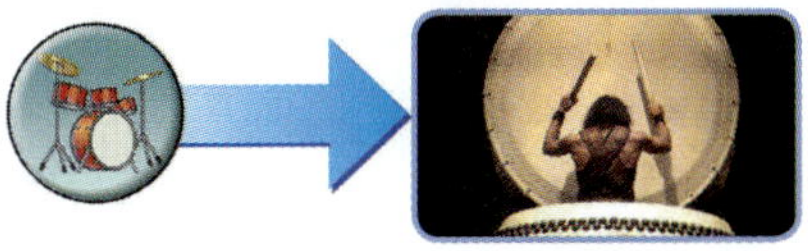

striking

bowing *and* **plucking**

4. Use these words to talk about other instruments.

bagpipes

bongos

tambourine

harp

Differentiated Instruction

Beginning	Say aloud, but out of order, the names of each instrument shown on pp. 216–217. Have students point to the appropriate icon for each instrument and repeat the word aloud.
Early Intermediate	Tell students there are ten musical instruments shown on pp. 216–217. Ask them to make a list of all the musical instruments.
Intermediate	Ask students to explain how the musical instruments shown on pp. 216–217 are played. Have them make a three-column chart for instruments played by striking, plucking, and blowing.
Standard English Learner CRI	Have student draw a picture of people playing musical instruments, then label their drawings with the names of the instruments.

Visual Literacy

Photographs and Captions Have students look at the icons and photographs in section 3 on p. 217. Point out that they may recognize some of the musical instruments in the pictures. Write the sentence stems on the board and have volunteers fill in the blanks.

Have students write a paragraph that describes what happens when an orchestra is playing music. Have students research what instruments are in an orchestra and what sounds those instruments make. Then have students describe how each instrument is played.

STEP 3: Practice

Use Vocabulary

Context Sentences Help students use the vocabulary to write about different instruments and where they are played. Write the following sentences on the board with the names of the instruments left out, and have students fill in the blanks.

My brother plays the guitar in a rock band.

Lisa plays the flute in an orchestra.

I heard a trumpet when I went to a concert.

Lead a class discussion about playing in a band or orchestra. Have students explain how they think the instruments can play at the same time and still sound beautiful or exciting.

Scaffolding

Play a recording of a well-known piece of music that you can easily stop and rewind. Ask students to listen carefully to identify what instruments they hear. As students identify an instrument, write its name on the board.

Link to Social Studies

The Guitar People have been playing some form of guitar for 5,000 years, but the acoustic guitar that we know has been played since the Renaissance periods or about 500 years. Have students research the development of different types of guitars.

STEP 1: Introduce

Unit Background

The peer mini-autobiographies and accompanying exercises are designed to increase comprehension and model how students can talk and write about their own musical experiences. Use the exercises below to elicit students' prior knowledge, opinions, and ideas to help them tell their own music stories.

STEP 2: Monitor Progress

Comprehension Check

Janak

1. Where does Janak live?
   Janak lives in Varanasi, India.
2. What kind of instrument is the *tabla*?
   The *tabla* is two drums.
3. How are the *daya* and the baya different?
   The *daya* makes high sounds and the *baya* makes low sounds.
4. Do you think Janak will play the *tabla* well? Why or why not?
   I think Janak will play the *tabla* well, because he loves the sounds it makes.

Peiti

1. Where does Peiti live?
   Peiti lives in Taiwan.
2. Where do Peiti's parents play musical instruments?
   Peiti's parents play musical instruments in the orchestra of the Ho-Lo Opera Troupe.
3. Which of Peiti's parents plays in the *Wen Cheng*?
   Peiti's mother plays in the *Wen Cheng*.
4. What does Peiti's father play?
   Peiti's father plays the drums.

Link to Social Studies

Map Skills Draw students' attention to the map in the background of these pages. Have students follow the lines from the photo of each student's home to its location on the map.

Teaching Resources
- *Audio CD*

Your Stories about Sounds and Music

Janak

Varanasi, India, is famous for its beautiful music. I am learning to play the *tabla* at school. One drum of the tabla is called the *daya*. It makes high sounds. The *baya* makes low sounds. These drums make the most beautiful sounds in Indian music.

Peiti

I live in Taiwan. My parents play in the orchestra of the Ho-Lo Opera Troupe. In Taiwanese opera, the orchestra is divided into two parts. My mother plays the violin in the part of the orchestra called the *Wen Cheng*. My father plays the drums in the *Wu Cheng*. When I grow up, I hope to join the orchestra, too!

218

TESOL Standards

Goal 1, Standard 2—To use English to communicate in social settings: Students will interact in, through, and with spoken and written English for personal expression and enjoyment.
Descriptors—Sharing social and cultural traditions and values; Expressing personal needs, feelings, and ideas.

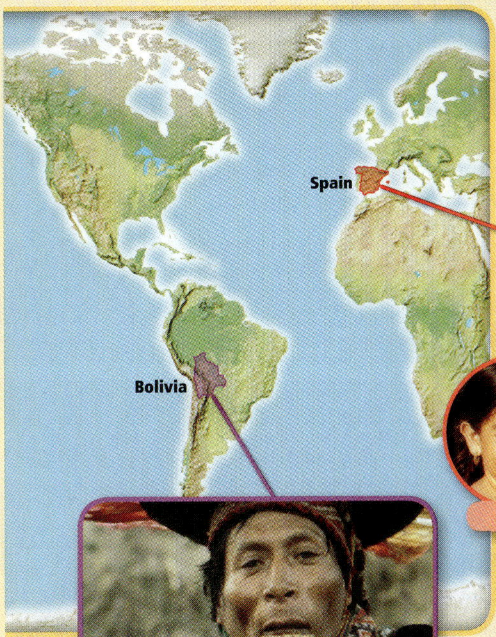

Inez

I live in Antequera, the heart of flamenco in Spain! I am going to school to be a flamenco singer. I am learning to dance. I am also learning to play the guitar and the *palillos*, or castanets. I want to share the rhythms of flamenco with the world.

Kory

I live in Bolivia. We play our flutes when we celebrate Carnival and other festivals. We carve the flutes carefully from wood. They make such beautiful sounds that people all over the world play them.

What about you?

1. Do you play an instrument?
2. How are these students' stories similar to yours?
3. Do you have stories about music where you are from? Tell your story!

Sharing Language and Culture

Global Perspective Students might have a story about an unusual instrument, song, or dance they have seen or heard in another city, state, or country. Encourage students to describe what they are sharing so that everyone in the class can draw a mental picture.

Kory

1. Where does Kory live?
   Kory lives in Bolivia.
2. What kinds of instruments does Kory write about?
   Kory writes about flutes.
3. What are those instruments made out of?
   Those instruments are made out of wood.
4. Kory's instrument is played in his country. Where else is it played?
   It is played all over the world.

Inez

1. Where does Inez live?
   Inez lives in Antequera, Spain.
2. What is Inez learning to be?
   She is learning to be a flamenco singer.
3. What else is Inez learning?
   She's learning to dance and to play the guitar and the *palillos*.
4. What is the English word for *palillos*?
   The English word for *palillos* is *castanets*.

Study Skills

Internet Invite students to choose one of the countries from the stories on pp. 218–219. Have them research one fact about that country on the Internet.

STEP 3: Assess

What about you?

1. Have students name and describe the instrument they play and tell how they learned to play it.
2. Students who do not play an instrument or have someone in their family who plays an instrument may have difficulty identifying with one of their peers. Have students describe an instrument they would like to learn to play or a type of instrument they like to listen to.
3. Allow students to write about a song or dance their families share at home.

Personal Story Have students write a story using the peer mini-autobiographies on pp. 218–219 as a model. Have students present their stories in small groups.

STEP 1: Introduce

Key Words

Help students learn the skill of defining words by using context.

SAY *All the key words from* Touching Sound with Evelyn Glennie *are defined in the Words in Context selection.*

- *What do you need for a band?*
- *What are four types of percussion instruments?*
- *Which of your five senses can you use to experience music other than your hearing?*

Have students connect the visuals with the key words.

STEP 2: Teach

Words in Context

Have students complete this fill-in-the-blanks exercise using the key words from the Words in Context passages.

1. Many musicians start playing music when they are young.
2. I want to learn to play many instruments.
3. The percussion instruments carry the beat of the music.
4. What sounds do you like to hear at a concert?
5. I could feel the vibrations from the loud drumming.
6. What famous composer lost his hearing?

Study Skills

Dictionary Students can look up words to see if the Words in Context definitions are correct.

Online Dictionary Students can look up words using an online dictionary or the CD that accompanies a learner's dictionary like the *Longman Basic Dictionary*.

www.LongmanCornerstone.com

Teaching Resources

- *Practice Book*, pp. 107–108
- *Transparencies*, p. 49
- *CD-ROM* • *Audio CD*

Reading 1

Vocabulary

Touching Sound with Evelyn Glennie

Touching Sound with Evelyn Glennie is about a world-famous percussionist.

Key Words

musicians
instruments
percussion
sounds
vibrations
hearing

Words in Context

1 A band is made up of **musicians** playing many different **instruments**.

220

TESOL Standards

Goal 1, Standard 3—To use English to communicate in social settings: Students will use learning strategies to extend their communicative competence.
Descriptors—Testing hypotheses about language; Listening to and imitating how others use English; Exploring alternative ways of saying things; Using context to construct meaning.

Goal 2, Standard 2—To use English to achieve academically in all content areas: Students will use English to obtain, process, construct, and provide subject matter information in spoken and written form.
Descriptor—Understanding and producing technical vocabulary and text features according to content area.

2 Percussion instruments make sounds when they are hit, shaken, rubbed, or scraped. Snare and bass drums, cymbals, timpani, and marimbas are percussion instruments.

3 Sounds travel as **vibrations** in the air. These vibrations are called sound waves. The sound waves enter the ear so you can hear the sounds. **Hearing** is one of the five senses.

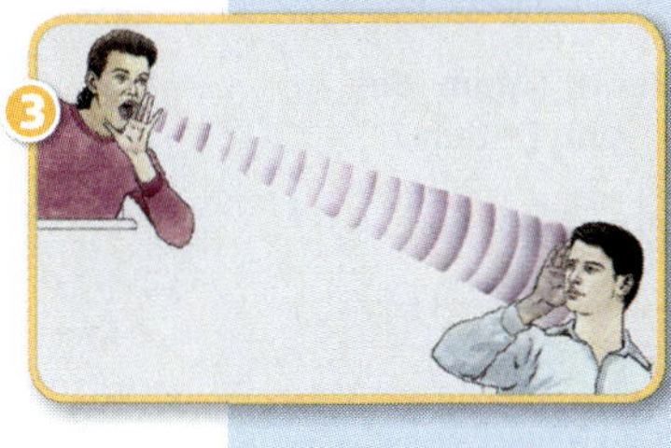

Practice

Use each key word in a sentence.

Make Connections

Sit silently for one minute with your eyes closed. Then write a list of the different sounds you heard.

Academic Words

context
situation, events, or information related to something

demonstrate
show

Practice Book pages 107–108

Differentiated Instruction	
Beginning	Read the list of key words aloud and have students find each key word in the context sentences, then act out the meaning.
Intermediate	Ask students to name three different percussion instruments. Then challenge them to name an instrument that is not a percussion instrument.
Greater Challenge	Have students discuss why people all over the world love music. Ask students to make notes of their discussion then make a short report to the class using as many key words as possible.
Struggling Reader	Have students work together to perform a percussion piece. They may use tongue clicks, finger snaps, claps, and foot stomps as their instruments.

Visual Literacy

Illustrations Have students look at the illustration of sound waves on p. 221. Have them explain what the illustration shows.

Academic Words

Discuss the definitions for *context* and *demonstrate* with students. Share the following context sentences with students.

The music provided *context* for the words in the song.

Can you *demonstrate* how to play your violin?

Explain to students that they may already have learned the word *context* when they were taught to look for *context* clues to a word's meaning. To look for a context clue is to think about the situation in which the word appears.

Other Academic Words

Provide students with another word that can be used in the discussion of making music. Tell students that musicians play within a *range*, which is the lowest note up to the highest note that they can play. Explain that the word can be a verb or a noun. Write the following context sentences on the board:

She could play a *range* of notes over four octaves.

Her talents *range* from playing the violin to conducting the orchestra.

STEP 3: Practice

Flexible Grouping You may assign this exercise as a class discussion, partner activity, or individual writing assignment.

Make Connections

Writing Fluency Remind students that most people are not aware of many of the sounds around them. When they close their eyes, they can concentrate on their sense of hearing and listen closely. Could any of the sounds they hear be used in music? Note that students' lists can be related to the Big Question when you sum up the discussion.

STEP 1: Introduce

More About The Big Question

The Big Question for this selection focuses on how a deaf person can sense and make music.

SAY *The Big Question for this selection is* How can you hear without using your ears?

- *Have you ever felt music in your body? What kind of music? What did it feel like?*
- *Can you hear a song in your head? How do you think you can do that?*
- *If you watch people playing instruments, can you see music? Explain your answer.*

Have students fill in a Word Web to describe ways to experience music without hearing it.

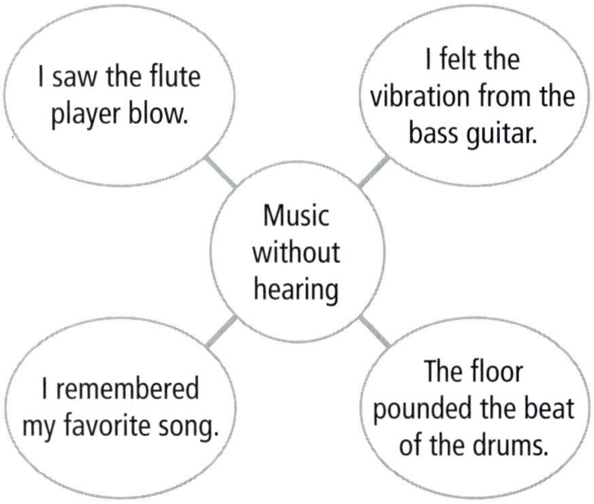

STEP 2: Teach

Reading Strategy

Identify Main Idea and Details Discuss with students that identifying the main idea and details can help them better remember information.

Review the bulleted items on p. 222 with students. Have students fill in a Main Idea and Details Chart as they read the selection.

Teaching Resources
- *Teacher's Resource Book*, pp. 135–136
- *Practice Book*, pp. 109–110
- *CD-ROM* • *Audio CD*

Reading 1

INFORMATIONAL TEXT
Internet Article

The Big Question
How can you hear without using your ears?

Reading Strategy

Identify Main Idea and Details

As you read, ask yourself:
- What is the selection about?
- What is the most important idea?
- What details help support the main idea?

Touching Sound with Evelyn Glennie

by Trish Marx

People walking through Grand Central Station in New York City often hear musicians performing. Musicians like to play there because of the large crowds.

One day, people gathered in the main **concourse** to hear Evelyn Glennie play her snare drum. She is the first percussionist in the world who made a career of performing as a **soloist**. Evelyn's performance was filmed for a **documentary** called *Touch the Sound*. The audience applauded when she finished playing.

Many people watching Evelyn did not know she couldn't hear the music she played. She is almost completely deaf.

concourse large hallway
soloist musician who performs alone
documentary movie about real people and events

The marimbas are one of many instruments Evelyn Glennie plays.

222

TESOL Standards

Goal 2, Standard 2—To use English to achieve academically in all content areas: Students will use English to obtain, process, construct, and provide subject matter information in spoken and written form.
Descriptors—Listening to, speaking, reading, and writing about subject matter information; Gathering information orally and in writing ; Retelling information; Selecting, connecting, and explaining information; Understanding and producing technical vocabulary and text features according to content area; Demonstrating knowledge through application in a variety of contexts.

Evelyn grew up on a farm in Scotland. There was a piano in her home. As a young child, she asked her parents to let her take piano lessons. They let her take lessons when she was eight years old. Evelyn soon found out she had what musicians call "perfect pitch." She could hear the notes perfectly in her mind. This was good, because she was slowly losing her hearing.

Evelyn found that hearing aids kept her from being able to perceive sounds with the rest of her body. She stopped wearing them when she was 12 years old. Evelyn knew she could hear the correct music notes in her mind. She also used her body to feel the vibrations the instruments made. She learned to play many percussion instruments. This surprised her teachers, who thought Evelyn would not be able to play music once she lost her hearing.

---

perceive experience

Kettle drums are also called timpani.

Check Up How does Evelyn hear sounds?

223

Understand Text Structure

Draw students' attention to the genre label. Tell them that an Internet article is like a magazine article, except you read it on a screen instead of from a page.

Build Vocabulary

Direct attention to the highlighted word in the text with a definition at the bottom of the page.

- Invite volunteers to read aloud the word and the definition.
- Have students write a context sentence using the word.
- Have students repeat this activity for each highlighted word as they read the selection.

Link to Math

Writing Numbers Students may be confused because the number eight is spelled out while 12 is written in numerals. Explain that the common style in books is to spell out numbers from one to ten, but to use numerals for all other numbers.

Read Aloud

Have students take turns reading the paragraphs in the selection aloud. Have each reader make up a question about what he or she just read, and ask the listeners to answer.

Build Discussion

Percussion Instruments Lead a class discussion about the two types of percussion instruments: those that are tuned, and those that aren't. Tuned percussion, like the piano, marimbas and steel drums, play notes and can make a melody. Untuned percussion, like bass drums, tom-toms, gongs, and crash cymbals, are only used for rhythm.

Accelerate Language Development

Names of Countries Students who speak languages other than English at home may have difficulties with the English names of foreign countries. For example, in Spanish, Evelyn Glennie's home country of Scotland is *Escocia*, and the United Kingdom is *Reino Unido*. It might be helpful if you can get maps labeled in English, as well as maps labeled in the home languages of your students. Have them compare the names of countries in the two maps.

Linguistic Note

Cognate—*Musician* Students familiar with Spanish may recognize the cognate *músico*. Be aware that the female version of this noun, *música*, is also the Spanish word for *music*. Write the word *musician* and the word *músico* on the board and ask students to find the English word that appears in both (*music*).

STEP 3: Assess

Check Up

Have students work in pairs. Remind them that they can find the answer to the Check Up question in the text. Encourage them to answer the question using their own words.

STEP 1: Monitor Progress

Comprehension Check

Make Inferences Explain that authors don't always tell readers everything they need to know. Sometimes readers have to figure out information themselves.

SAY *There's some information in **Touching Sound with Evelyn Glennie** that the author doesn't write.*

- *What kind of school is the Royal Academy of Music?*
- *What do you think Evelyn Glennie studied there?*
- *Why does Evelyn perform barefoot?*
- *Why do you think many musicians have written compositions for Evelyn to play?*

Figurative Language Explain that words are sometimes used to mean something that they don't normally mean. In the first sentence, the writer says that music made Evelyn feel "sometimes happy, sometimes sad, but always alive." Ask students what the author meant by saying that music made Evelyn feel alive.

Scaffolding

Metaphors Remind students that metaphors make a comparison between two seemingly unrelated things. Have students read the quote from Evelyn's website, "Hearing is a special form of touch." Remind students that the documentary about Evelyn is called *Touch the Sound.* Lead a discussion about how students think they can touch sounds.

Link to Science

Have students research how sound waves are created and how they travel. Have students create a poster with a large chart that explains this. Also have students explain what can stop sound waves from traveling.

Evelyn loved the way music made her feel — sometimes happy, sometimes sad, but always alive.

She studied at the Royal Academy of Music after high school. She has had a successful career as a musician ever since.

On her Web site, Evelyn says, "Hearing is a special form of touch. Deafness does not mean that you can't hear. It only means that there is something wrong with the ears."

Evelyn uses her whole body to feel sounds. She often performs barefoot.

"Anything you can pick can create a sound," says Evelyn.

Evelyn plays well-known percussion instruments such as the snare, kettle, and bass drums. She also plays marimbas, xylophones, gongs, and the water drums pictured below. She has been filmed creating music using common objects, such as plates, pots and pans, bottles, pipes, and glasses filled with water.

career job or profession

These are water drums.

224

TESOL Standards

Goal 2, Standard 2—To use English to achieve academically in all content areas: Students will use English to obtain, process, construct, and provide subject matter information in spoken and written form.

Descriptors—Listening to, speaking, reading, and writing about subject matter information; Gathering information orally and in writing; Retelling information; Selecting, connecting, and explaining information; Understanding and producing technical vocabulary and text features according to content area; Demonstrating knowledge through application in a variety of contexts.

Evelyn performs in more than 100 concerts each year. She has won many awards for her music, including several Grammy Awards. These awards recognize high achievement in making and recording music. Evelyn has performed with some of the world's most famous musicians and orchestras. She writes and produces her own music. Many musicians have written compositions for her to play.

When she is not performing or writing music, Evelyn works hard to improve music education in schools in the United Kingdom. She also enjoys riding her motorcycle and making jewelry.

If you are inspired by Evelyn's life and music, learn more about your favorite instrument, and make your own music.

Evelyn performs more than 100 concerts each year.

achievement accomplishment

compositions pieces of music

inspired given energy to do something

Practice Book pages 109–110

Reading Strategy

Identify Main Idea and Details

- What is the main idea of the selection?
- What details told you about the main idea?
- How did finding the main idea and details help you understand the selection?

Think It Over

1. What kinds of instruments does Evelyn play?
2. What does perfect pitch mean?
3. What does Evelyn say about hearing?
4. Why did Evelyn win several Grammy Awards?

225

STEP 2: Teach

Build Discussion

Explain that many common objects can be used as percussion instruments. Have students read the objects mentioned in the last sentence on p. 224. Have students suggest other common items they might use as percussion instruments. Have them explain how they would play the items.

Link to Social Studies

Touch the Sound (2004) was directed by German filmmaker Thomas Riedelsheimer. One goal he had in making the film was to have the audience see the sounds as Evelyn Glennie created them. Consider showing all or part of the film to students, and ask students to decide whether they think Riedelsheimer succeeded.

STEP 3: Assess

Reading Strategy

Main Idea and Details Give students an example of how to identify the main idea and details of a reading selection.

SAY *The main idea is what the selection is about, and the details help you understand the main idea.*

- *I think the main idea is that Evelyn Glennie is a special musician.*
- *There are many details in the selection that show how she is special. For example, she won several Grammy Awards and performs in more than 100 concerts each year.*

Think It Over

Flexible Grouping You may assign this activity as a class discussion, partner activity, or individual writing assignment.

Answer Key

1. Evelyn plays percussion instruments.
2. *Perfect pitch* means that you can hear the notes perfectly in your mind.
3. Evelyn says that hearing is a special form of touch.
4. Evelyn won several Grammy Awards because of her high achievement in making and recording music.

Differentiated Instruction

Beginning	Have students point to the words on p. 224 that tell how music makes Evelyn feel. Have them define the words by saying a word, making a facial expression, or gesturing.
Early Intermediate	Have students write a short answer for the following: *If Evelyn cannot hear with her ears, how does she hear the music she plays?*
Intermediate	Have students write a short paragraph that explains how Evelyn Glennie can hear her music without using hearing aids.
Standard English Learner (CRI)	Have students study the photographs of Evelyn Glennie and then work in pairs to describe to the class what is happening in the photos.

STEP 1: Introduce

Phonics

Ending: *-ed* Help students understand that many past tense verbs end in *-ed*. Sometimes *-ed* is pronounced as a separate syllable, and sometimes it isn't.

STEP 2: Teach

Review how adding *-ed* changes many verbs to the past tense. Draw students' attention to the information about pronunciation of *-ed* in the Rule Box.

SAY *If the letter* d *or the letter* t *comes before the* -ed *ending, then* -ed *is pronounced as a separate syllable.*

Write the following words on the board and ask students to add *-ed* to put them into the past tense.

worked	started	watched
learned	performed	handed
corrected	minded	

Ask a volunteer to read the sentences in the box. Then ask students to find the present tense of the words to which *-ed* was added.

STEP 3: Practice

- Have students work with partners. Encourage partners to read the words aloud, first in the present tense without the *-ed*, and then in the past tense with the *-ed*. Have them count the syllables each time they read the word.
- Monitor students to see that they are pronouncing the words correctly. If not, model the pronunciations for them while they count syllables.

Teaching Resources

- ***Practice Book***, pp. 111
- ***Phonics Workbook***
- ***Phonics Flashcards***
- ***CD-ROM*** • ***Audio CD***

Reading 1

Phonics & Fluency

Phonics

Ending: *-ed*

The ending *-ed* is often part of past tense verbs. Pay attention to how the *-ed* ending is pronounced.

> Evelyn's performance was filmed for a documentary called *Touch the Sound*. The audience applauded when she finished playing.

The *-ed* in ***applauded*** is a separate syllable. The *-ed* in ***filmed*** and ***finished*** is not a separate syllable.

Why is the *-ed* ending a separate syllable in some words and not in others?

Rule Box

If the letter *d* or the letter *t* comes before the *-ed* ending, then *-ed* is pronounced as a separate syllable.

Practice

Work with a partner. Take turns.

- Write five other words with the ending *-ed*.
- Ask your partner to read each word and tell whether the *-ed* is a separate syllable.

Practice Book page 111

TESOL Standards

Goal 2, Standard 3—To use English to achieve academically in all content areas: Students will use appropriate learning strategies to construct and apply academic knowledge.
Descriptors—Applying basic reading comprehension skills such as skimming, scanning, previewing, and reviewing text; Using context to construct meaning; Applying self-monitoring and self-corrective strategies to build and expand a knowledge base.

Goal 3, Standard 3—To use English in socially and culturally appropriate ways: Students will use appropriate learning strategies to extend their sociolinguistic and sociocultural competence.
Descriptors—Observing and modeling how others speak and behave in a particular situation or setting; Experimenting with variations of language in social and academic settings; Seeking information about appropriate language use and behavior.

Fluency

Look Ahead

Sometimes readers look for hard words before they read. They then try to figure them out.

Practice

Pick one passage.	Find any hard words.	Practice saying those words.	Read the passage aloud.

1 Evelyn Glennie is the world's first solo percussionist. She has never let deafness stop her from playing music. Evelyn travels around the world, playing with many famous musicians and orchestras.

2 One day, people gathered in the main concourse to hear Evelyn Glennie play her snare drum. She is the first percussionist in the world who made a career of performing as a soloist. Evelyn's performance was filmed for a documentary called *Touch the Sound*. The audience applauded when she finished playing.

3 Evelyn found that hearing aids kept her from being able to perceive sounds with the rest of her body. She stopped wearing them when she was 12 years old. Evelyn knew she could hear the correct music notes in her mind. She also used her body to feel the vibrations the instruments made. She learned to play many percussion instruments.

227

Accelerate Language Development

Italics Students unfamiliar with written English may wonder why certain words and phrases, like *Touch the Sound*, referred to in the Phonics lesson, are printed in slanting letters. Explain that these kinds of letters are called *italics*. Italics are used when printing the title of a book or a movie. Ask students whether *Touch the Sound* is the title of a book or a movie. a movie How do they know? The text says that it's a documentary. Would they know that *Touch the Sound* was a title even if the text didn't say so? Why or why not? They would know because it's printed in italics.

STEP 1: Introduce

Fluency

Look Ahead Explain to students that fluent readers sometimes look ahead to find hard words. Finding and practicing these words can help students read more smoothly.

Play the Audio CD for this reading to the class, asking students to listen for pacing, intonation, and expression.

STEP 2: Practice

Have students do the exercise with a partner. You may want to assign each student a passage based on difficulty level (1–easy, 2–intermediate, 3–more difficult) or let students select their own passages.

- Have one partner look through the passage to find any hard words and practice saying those words. Students may ask partners for help in pronouncing the hard words.
- Then have each student read the passage to his or her partner.
- Have students change roles.

Possible Responses–Hard Words

percussionist	deafness	concourse
audience	documentary	perceive

STEP 3: Extend

Study Skills

Dictionary Have students work with partners to:

- write down three words that were hard to understand from the readings;
- look the words up in a dictionary;
- read the sentences from the reading in which the hard words appear and ask them to define the words.

Remind students that they can use this study skill anywhere. In social studies or science class, or when they read at home, they can find the hard words and write them down. Students can then look them up online or in the dictionary.

STEP 1: Monitor Progress

Learning Strategy

Summarize Remind students that a summary includes only the most important details. Have the students work in pairs. Have one student summarize *Touching Sound with Evelyn Glennie* and the other student respond to the Big Question. You may then have one pair present their summary and response to the Big Question to the class.

STEP 2: Teach

Main Idea and Details

Students will learn how to identify the main idea and details. Prompt students as they think about the main idea and details with the following discussion.

SAY *Identifying the main idea and details helps you understand what you've read. To summarize well, you have to decide which details are important.*

- *What is the selection about?*
- *What details give information about the main idea?*
- *Which details do you think are the most important ones to use in a summary?*

STEP 3: Practice

Flexible Grouping You may assign this activity as a class discussion, partner activity, or individual written assignment.

Answer Key

1. The last sentence tells the main idea.
2. The first three sentences provide important details that support the main idea.

Teaching Resources

- *Practice Book*, pp. 112
- *Transparencies*, p. 55
- *Teachers Resource Book*, pp. 153
- *CD-ROM*

Reading 1

Comprehension

Learning Strategy

Summarize

Summarize the selection for a partner.

Ask your partner to respond to the Big Question for this reading.

Practice Book page 112

Main Idea and Details

The **main idea** is the most important idea in a selection. **Details** give information about the main idea. The details support the main idea by telling important facts.

Practice

Read the sentences below.

- Evelyn says hearing is a special form of touch.
- Evelyn could feel the vibrations the instruments made.
- Musicians play in Grand Central Station because of the large crowds.
- Evelyn Glennie's story proves that people can overcome challenges.

1. Which sentence tells the main idea?
2. Which two sentences tell important details to support the main idea?

228

TESOL Standards

Goal 2, Standard 2—To use English to achieve academically in all content areas: Students will use English to obtain, process, construct, and provide subject matter information in spoken and written form.
Descriptors—Listening to, speaking, reading, and writing about subject matter information; Gathering information orally and in writing; Retelling information; Selecting, connecting, and explaining information; Understanding and producing technical vocabulary and text features according to content area; Demonstrating knowledge through application in a variety of contexts.

Goal 2, Standard 2—To use English to achieve academically in all content areas: Students will use English to obtain, process, construct, and provide subject matter information in spoken and written form.
Descriptor—Representing information visually and interpreting information presented visually.

Use a Main Idea and Details Chart

Writers use details to help explain the main idea. A Main Idea and Details Chart can help you see a writer's plan.

Practice

Copy this Main Idea and Details Chart. Add the main idea from the previous page. Then reread the selection and add at least two more details.

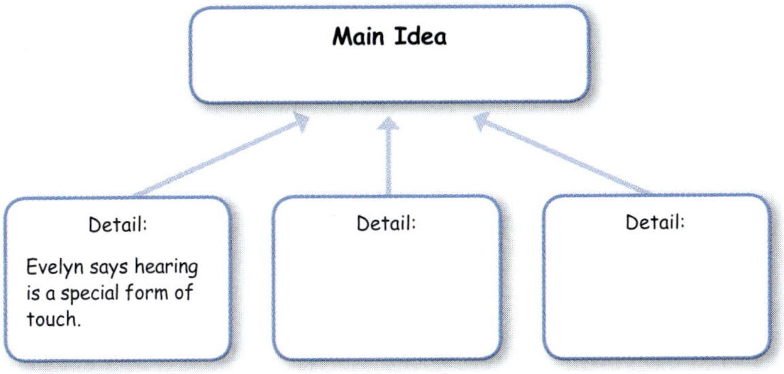

Extension

Make a brochure of different percussion instruments from around the world. Use pictures, photos, and text to describe the instruments. Share your brochure with the class.

229

Linguistic Note

Brochure Many students may not pronounce *brochure* correctly. For one thing, they may be fooled by the spelling and pronounce a */ch/* sound rather than a */sh/* sound. Those students who come from Spanish-speaking homes may not be able to say the */sh/* sound, since it is not a phoneme used in Spanish. For these students, you might offer the following tongue-twister as an entertaining practice: *She showed me a brochure from a shirt shop.*

STEP 1: Teach

Use a Main Idea and Details Chart

Ask students to think of something they'd like to tell about an object they own. Have them write a sentence that tells the main idea about the object and three other sentences that give details. Have them write their sentences out of order and exchange papers with a partner. Then have partners try to guess which sentence describes the main idea and which sentences describe the details.

Possible Responses
They look really great.
I never had sneakers that felt so comfortable.
My new sneakers are the best ones I ever had.
They help me run faster and jump higher.

Main Idea:
My new sneakers are the best ones I ever had.

Details:
They look really great.
I never had sneakers that felt so comfortable.
They help me run faster and jump higher.

STEP 2: Practice

You may have students complete the graphic organizer provided as a Blackline Master in the *Teacher's Resource Book*.

Answer Key
Main Idea: Evelyn Glennie's story proves that people can overcome challenges.

Possible Responses Details: Evelyn has won many awards, including several Grammy Awards; Evelyn studied at the Royal Academy of Music; Evelyn performs in more than 100 concerts a year.

STEP 3: Extend

Oral Presentation Provide books, magazines, and, if possible, Internet access to help students find text and pictures of percussion instruments. Ask them to include at least one detail for each instrument they show on their brochure. Then have students describe their brochures to the class.

STEP 1: Introduce

Help students understand that an *appositive* usually explains the noun that comes right before it. An *appositive* is placed between commas. A prepositional phrase begins with a preposition and links nouns, pronouns, and phrases to other words in a sentence.

STEP 2: Teach

Appositives and Prepositional Phrases

Write the following on the board. Ask students to identify the appositives and prepositional phrases.

Our new kitten, Tiger, is yellow. appositive

Tomas, my best friend, lives down the street. appositive

We found my baseball under a parked car. prepositional phrase

The teacher gave a good grade to Annie and Arnie, the Smith twins. appositive

My uncle's plane arrived at the airport before the rainstorm. prepositional phrase

STEP 3: Practice

Before students begin the Practice activity, have them work with partners. Have each pair of students make up a sentence that uses an appositive and another sentence that uses a prepositional phrase.

Answer Key

1. Bonnie (appositive); during the trip (prepositional phrase)
2. Alex (appositive); at school (prepositional phrase)
3. my older brother (appositive); in the bushes (prepositional phrase)

Teaching Resources

- ***Practice Book***, pp. 113–114
- ***Assessments***, pp. 77–80
- ***Transparencies***, pp. 69–80
- ***CD-ROM***

Reading 1

Grammar & Writing

Appositives and Prepositional Phrases

An **appositive** is a noun or noun phrase that is placed beside another noun to help explain it.

My neighbor, **Elsa**, is in my dance class.

Sometimes, an appositive can include more than one word.

Rocky, **the smallest puppy**, loves to run and play.

A **prepositional phrase** begins with a preposition, such as ***after*** or ***in***, and ends with a noun.

preposition ↓ noun ↓
We told spooky stories **during the thunderstorm**.

Practice

Read each sentence. List each appositive. Then list each prepositional phrase.

1. My sister, Bonnie, slept during the trip.
2. A great singer, Alex, won the contest at school.
3. José, my older brother, hid the ball in the bushes.

Practice Book page 113

TESOL Standards

Goal 1, Standard 1—To use English to communicate in social settings: Students will use English to participate in social interactions.
Descriptor—Expressing needs, feelings, and ideas.

Goal 1, Standard 3—To use English to communicate in social settings: Students will use learning strategies to extend their communicative competence.
Descriptor—Seeking support and feedback from others.

Goal 2, Standard 1—To use English to achieve academically in all content areas: Students will use English to interact in the classroom.
Descriptors—Following oral and written directions, implicit and explicit; Explaining actions; Expressing likes, dislikes, and needs.

Goal 2, Standard 3—To use English to achieve academically in all content areas: Students will use appropriate learning strategies to construct and apply academic knowledge.
Descriptors—Using context to construct meaning; Actively connecting new information to information previously learned; Imitating the behaviors of native English speakers to complete tasks successfully.

Goal 3, Standard 1—To use English in socially and culturally appropriate ways: Students will use the appropriate language variety, register, and genre according to audience, purpose, and setting.
Descriptor—Using a variety of writing styles appropriate for different audiences, purposes, and settings.

Write an Introductory Paragraph

When you write a long essay, it is important to write a paragraph that introduces the topic. Muna wrote this paragraph to introduce her essay about two artists in her class.

There are many artists in my class. They use different themes in their art. Today, I am going to write about art made by two of my classmates, Olivia and Ron. Both Olivia and Ron are excellent artists, but their art is very different. Olivia likes to paint scenes of castles, princes, and dragons. Ron uses the same themes in his art, but he draws cartoons. Olivia's art has a long-ago feeling. Ron's art is more modern. Both types of art tell wonderful stories, which I will describe in this essay.

SPELLING TIP

Thinking of a related word will help you spell a word you don't know. For example, remembering ***crumble*** can help you spell ***crumb*** correctly.

Practice Book page 114

Practice

Write an introductory paragraph in which you compare two instruments.

- Give some basic information to introduce your topic, but save the details for paragraphs that will follow.
- Read your paragraph aloud to a partner.

Writing Checklist

✓ Did you indent the first sentence of your paragraph?

✓ Did your paragraph introduce your topic?

✓ Did your paragraph give some basic information?

✓ Can a partner identify the two items you were comparing?

231

Differentiated Instruction	
Beginning	Have students fill in the blanks: *Olivia painted scenes of* ________, ________, *and* ________. *Ron draws* ________.
Intermediate	Have students draw or paint a picture in Ron's or Olivia's style, then present and describe their drawing to the class.
Greater Challenge	Have students work in pairs to draw a picture in a long-ago style and draw a cartoon in a modern style. Ask students to explain to the class the two different styles of drawings.
Struggling Reader	Direct students to Muna's paragraph. Write the following words on the board: *artists*, *art*, *scenes*, and *cartoons*. Have students find them in the paragraph, then copy the words.

STEP 1: Teach

Write an Introductory Paragraph

Explain that the introductory paragraph comes at the very beginning of a long essay. It tells the topic of the essay and features a sentence that states the main idea and grabs the readers' attention.

SAY *The purpose of an introductory paragraph is to introduce the topic of the essay.*

- *What does Muna say her essay will be about?*
- *According to Muna, how are Olivia's art and Ron's art alike?*
- *According to Muna, how is the art different?*

Spelling Tip

Read the box to students. Then have students say how the following pairs of words are related:

music–musician *study–students*
active–activity *summary–summarize*

STEP 2: Practice

Before students begin to write, discuss the parts of an introductory paragraph.

- What two things do you compare?
- What basic information do you need to introduce your topic?

STEP 3: Assess

Writing Checklist

✓ Remind students that an introductory paragraph should not contain too many details; it should tell a reader what will come next.

✓ Help students understand the difference between basic information and details they may want to save for later in their essay.

✓ Have students exchange their paragraphs with partners and tell what they think their partner's essay will be about.

The Five Step Writing Process in the Writing Handbook reference section of this book provides more student writing instruction.

STEP 1: Introduce

Key Words

Help students learn the skill of defining words by using context.

SAY *Read the passages to find the meaning of the key words.*

- *What do some baseball players use to communicate with their teammates?*
- *Why do you think a big old tree is often one of the landmarks in an area?*
- *What might you find beside a riverbank?*
- *Have you ever left tracks? When?*

Have students use a dictionary to write the definitions for three of the key words.

STEP 2: Teach

Words in Context

Write the following sentences on the board.

Have students complete this fill-in-the-blanks exercise using the key words.

1. The thief tried to figure out the alarm code.
2. Would you like to escape to a deserted island?
3. The one-room schoolhouse was named a historical landmark by the city council.
4. I promised not to tell anyone her secret.
5. Along the riverbank you can find many small marine creatures.
6. As we hiked in the snow, we saw deer tracks.

Study Skills

Dictionary Have students see if the Words in Context definitions are correct.

Online Dictionary Students can look up words using an online dictionary or the CD that accompanies a learner's dictionary, like the *Longman Basic Dictionary*.
www.LongmanCornerstone.com

Teaching Resources

- *Practice Book*, pp. 115–116
- *Transparencies*, p. 50
- *CD-ROM* • *Audio CD*

A Song Map

Vocabulary

A Song Map is about a song called *Follow the Drinking Gourd.*

Key Words

- code
- escape
- landmarks
- secret
- riverbank
- tracks

Words in Context

1. The baseball player used a **code** to communicate with his teammates during a game.

2. The boy opened the cage because he thought the bird wanted to **escape**.

3. The big, old tree is one of the well-known **landmarks** in our area.

TESOL Standards

Goal 1, Standard 3—To use English to communicate in social settings: Students will use learning strategies to extend their communicative competence.
Descriptors—Testing hypotheses about language; Listening to and imitating how others use English; Exploring alternative ways of saying things; Using context to construct meaning.

Goal 2, Standard 2—To use English to achieve academically in all content areas: Students will use English to obtain, process, construct, and provide subject matter information in spoken and written form.
Descriptor—Understanding and producing technical vocabulary and text features according to content area.

4 Dan told his friend a **secret**.

5 In spring, wildflowers cover the **riverbank**. They grow right up to the edge of the water.

6 When people or animals walk in the dirt or mud, they leave **tracks**. Can you guess who or what left these tracks?

Practice

Use each key word in a sentence.

Make Connections

Can you make up a secret code? With a partner, pick signals or sounds to use in place of words. Then talk to each other using only your secret code.

Academic Words

assist
help

accompany
go with

Practice Book pages 115–116

Differentiated Instruction

Beginning	Have students point to the illustration for each key word, then find the key word in the context sentence.
Early Intermediate	Ask volunteers to repeat each context word as you read aloud each sentence. Have students write a short answer to the question in item 6.
Intermediate	Have students select one photo and imagine it's an illustration for a short story. Have them describe the plot.
Standard English Learner CRI	Choose one of the key words for a game of *Give One, Get One.* Have students go around the class swapping synonyms for the word with each other until each student has three new words. Encourage students to use dictionaries to check definitions.

Visual Literacy

Photos Have students look at the photo on p. 233 of the wildflowers on the riverbank. Ask them to guess what helps the wildflowers grow there.

Academic Words

Discuss the definitions for *assist* and *accompany* with students. Share the following context sentences with students.

The student could not find a book she wanted, so the librarian offered to *assist* her.

Would you like to *accompany* me to the movies on Saturday?

Students whose home language is Spanish may be confused by *assist*. The Spanish cognate, *asistir*, can sometimes mean *to help*, but it also means *to attend* or *go*. Point out that the word *accompany* includes the word *company* in it.

Other Academic Words

Provide students with another example of a word that can be used to discuss of music. Ask students if they are familiar with the term *alternative* music. Explain that in this context, *alternative* means different. Explain that *alternative* can be used as an adjective or a noun. Have students write context sentences for both parts of speech.

There is no *alternative* but to study for the test.

An *alternative* plan is to study for the test before soccer practice.

STEP 3: Practice

Flexible Grouping You may assign these exercises as a class discussion, partner activity, or individual writing assignment.

Make Connections

Writing Fluency After students have made up their code, have them work together to write a simple set of rules so other people can use it, too. If students use sounds in their code, have them describe those sounds and demonstrate them. Note that the answers to these questions can be related to the Big Question when you sum up the discussion.

STEP 1: Introduce

More About The Big Question

The Big Question for this selection focuses on how songs can carry messages with meanings that can be helpful to all of us.

SAY *The Big Question for this selection is* What messages can songs carry? *Sometimes songs carry messages.*

- *Can you think of a song that has taught you something? What did it teach you?*
- *If you were going to write a song what message would you like it to tell?*

Have students think of an important message they would like to write a song about. Have them fill in a Main Idea and Supporting Details Chart to explain the message in their songs.

Our Freedoms		
We can make a speech about our ideas.	We can express our opinions.	We can write about any topic we choose.

STEP 2: Teach

Reading Strategy

Summarize Tell students that when you summarize, you include a sentence telling what the selection is mainly about. Have students fill in a Sequence Chart as they read the selection.

Understand Text Structure

Draw students' attention to the genre label. Tell them that a song is a poem set to music. All songs have rhythm and many songs use rhyme.

Teaching Resources

- *Teacher's Resource Book*, pp. 137–138
- *Practice Book*, pp. 117–118
- *CD-ROM* • *Audio CD*

Reading 2

LITERATURE

Song

The Big Question

What messages can songs carry?

Reading Strategy

Summarize

Summarizing a selection or a song can help you understand it.

- As you read this selection, think about what it is mainly about.

A Song Map

by Ben McKenzie

Can a song also be a map? Some people think the song *Follow the Drinking Gourd* was really a secret code. Did the words in the song give instructions to slaves who were trying to escape? Did the song point the slaves toward freedom?

Follow the Drinking Gourd

Stanza 1

When the sun comes back and the first
quail calls,
Follow the drinking gourd.
For the old man is waiting for to carry
you to freedom
If you follow the drinking gourd.

The Big Dipper is a pattern of stars, or constellation, that points north. Could that be the drinking gourd? The sun comes back in the spring. Quail are birds that begin to call in the spring. Did this stanza tell slaves to leave when spring began and to follow the Big Dipper to the north?

instructions directions

234

TESOL Standards

Goal 2, Standard 2—To use English to achieve academically in all content areas: Students will use English to obtain, process, construct, and provide subject matter information in spoken and written form.

Descriptors—Persuading, arguing, negotiating, evaluating, and justifying; Listening to, speaking, reading, and writing about subject matter information; Gathering information orally and in writing; Retelling information; Selecting, connecting, and explaining information.

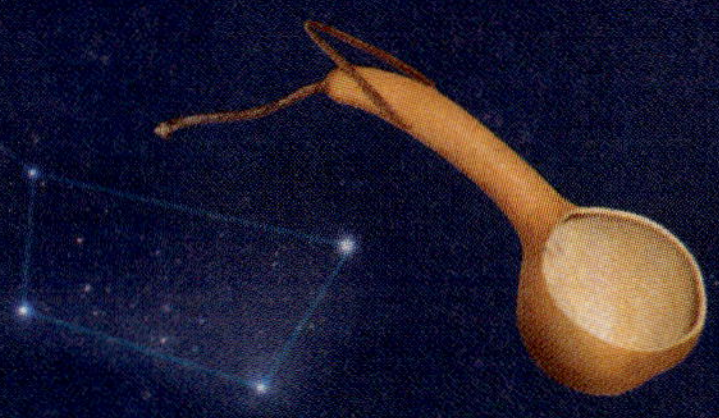

In the past, people used gourds to drink water. The Big Dipper looks like a drinking gourd.

Who was the old man waiting to carry them to freedom? Some people believe he was Peg Leg Joe, a former sailor who helped slaves. Peg Leg Joe used a wooden leg.

Chorus
Follow the drinking gourd!
Follow the drinking gourd!
For the old man is waiting for to carry you to freedom
If you follow the drinking gourd.
Stanza 2
The riverbank makes a very good road,
The dead trees will show you the way,
Left foot, peg foot traveling on,
Following the drinking gourd.

Some people say Peg Leg Joe marked trees and other landmarks along the riverbank. This helped the slaves make sure they were going in the right direction. These tracks, or marks, were often a mud or charcoal outline of a human left foot and another mark. Some people believe the other mark was Peg Leg Joe's wooden leg.

---

charcoal black substance made of burned wood

Check Up What did the song tell the slaves to do?

235

Differentiated Instruction

Beginning	Have students find and point to the phrase "Follow the drinking gourd". Read the song aloud, having the students repeat the phrase when you come to those words.
Intermediate	Have students read aloud the stanzas on pp. 234–235. Encourage students to read with feeling to emphasize meaning.
Greater Challenge	Challenge students to write one stanza for the song. Direct students to use descriptive language that is a secret code for instructions.
Special Needs	Choose one sentence from the text. Write each word of the sentence on individual cards. Mix up the cards. Then have students put the words in the correct order.

Build Vocabulary

Direct attention to the highlighted word in the text with a definition at the bottom of the page.

- Invite volunteers to read aloud the word and the definition.
- Have students write a context sentence using the word.
- Have students repeat this activity for each highlighted word as they read the selection.

Reading Songs Explain to students that songs have stanzas and a chorus. Each stanza contains different words from the previous stanza, but the chorus repeats the same words. It is often sung after each stanza or after every other stanza. Point out to students that the first two lines of the chorus are the same, and the last line is nearly the same. Ask them how the last line differs from the first two. It starts with the words *If you*, and doesn't have an exclamation mark at the end.

Read Aloud

Have students take turns reading aloud the words to the song *Follow the Drinking Gourd*. Ask them to pay attention to the spacing of the lines on the page. They should read with expression to make their reading rhythmic and attractive for the listener.

Link to Science

Explain to students that there are hundreds of species of gourds. They are vines, which bear some of the most unusual fruits in the world. Some of the gourds familiar to Americans include pumpkins, squash, melons, and cucumbers. Have students research some of the types of musical instruments that are made from gourds.

STEP 3: Assess

Check Up

Lead a class discussion to help students understand the slaves were told to follow a trail. Ask students to point to the words in the song that explain how the slaves were able to follow the trail and why they could only travel at night.

STEP 1: Monitor Progress

Comprehension Check

Make Inferences Explain to students that when authors don't include every detail in the selection, they want the reader to be more involved by figuring out some details on their own. Sometimes readers have to use their prior knowledge and clues in the text to figure things out.

SAY *There are a few details that the author of* A Song Map *doesn't tell readers. But you can use your own prior knowledge and clues in the text to figure these details out.*

- *The slaves followed the stars when they ran away. Why do you think they traveled at night?* So they couldn't be seen and captured.
- *Why were the slaves heading north?* Because the states where they could be free were in the North.
- *Why do you think the Ohio River is important in the song?* On one side of the river was Kentucky, a slave state. On the other side of the river was Illinois, a free state.

Main Idea and Details. After students read the selection, write the following four statements on the board. Have volunteers read the statements aloud. Then ask students to decide which is the main idea of *A Song Map*, and explain their reasoning.

1. *Follow the Drinking Gourd* is a song that slaves liked to sing and dance to.
2. Some people like to draw maps while they listen to beautiful music.
3. The words to *Follow the Drinking Gourd* were used as a map by slaves trying to escape.
4. An old man named Peg Leg Joe wrote the song.

Possible Responses Number 3 is correct. *A Song Map* tells how slaves could use the words of *Follow the Drinking Gourd* to make a map. Number 1 is wrong because the selection doesn't say anything about singing and dancing. Number 2 is wrong because the selection is not about people who draw maps while listening to music. Number 4 is wrong because the text does not say that Peg Leg Joe wrote the song.

Stanza 3
The river ends between two hills,
Follow the drinking gourd.
There's another river on the other side,
Follow the drinking gourd.

As the slaves walked north, they were told to look for the place where the river ends between two hills. Many people think Woodhall Mountain in Mississippi is this landmark.

The Tennessee River is on the other side of the mountain. If slaves kept following the drinking gourd, they went north. They were closer to the states where they could be free.

Slaves found shelter across the river.

236

TESOL Standards

Goal 2, Standard 2—To use English to achieve academically in all content areas: Students will use English to obtain, process, construct, and provide subject matter information in spoken and written form.

Descriptors—Persuading, arguing, negotiating, evaluating, and justifying; Listening to, speaking, reading, and writing about subject matter information; Gathering information orally and in writing; Retelling information; Selecting, connecting, and explaining information.

(Repeat Chorus)

Stanza 4

Where the great big river
meets the little river,
Follow the drinking gourd.
The old man is waiting for to
carry you to freedom,
If you follow the drinking gourd.

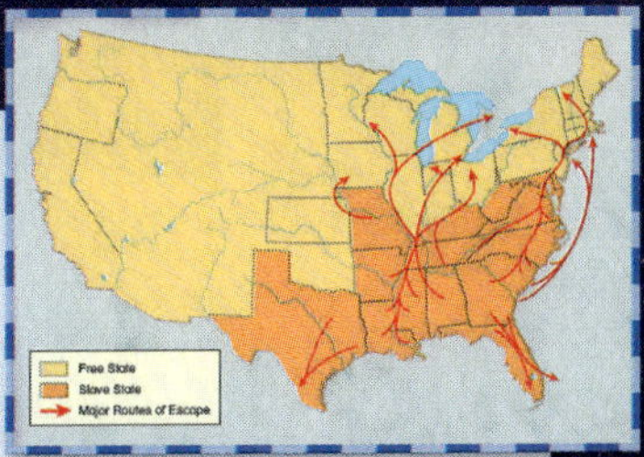

This map shows the directions in which slaves traveled.

The Ohio River is a big river that meets the Tennessee River on the border between Kentucky and Illinois. The song told slaves that the old man was waiting for them on the banks of the Ohio River. Some people believe Peg Leg Joe was there himself to lead the slaves to freedom.

What do you believe? Is *Follow the Drinking Gourd* just a song? Or is it a secret map?

border official line that separates two areas

Practice Book pages 117–118

Reading Strategy

Summarize

- Summarize the directions in Stanza 2 of *Follow the Drinking Gourd.*
- Summarize the directions in Stanza 4 of the song.
- Did summarizing help you understand what you read? How?

Think It Over

1. What is the Big Dipper? What does it look like?
2. Who was Peg Leg Joe?
3. What clues did slaves get from *Follow the Drinking Gourd?*
4. What was one location identified in the reading?

237

Differentiated Instruction

Beginning	Read aloud stanzas 3 and 4. Have students work in small groups to draw a large picture of what the words describe.
Early Intermediate	Ask students to work in pairs to write the words for the things they see in the picture on p. 236.
Intermediate	Have students work in a group to write a short poem or song that people could use as directions to go from the school to their house.
Standard English Learner CRI	Have students work together in a large group to read aloud and perform all four stanzas of the poem. Encourage students to use simple musical instruments and sing the words.

STEP 2: Teach

Visual Literacy

Maps Have students look at the map at the top of p. 237. Ask them to explain what the yellow and orange areas are. Provide a U.S. map so they can name some of the states marked in either yellow or orange. Then have them explain what the arrows mean.

STEP 3: Assess

Reading Strategy

Summarize Give students a concrete example of how to summarize.

SAY *Summarizing is a good way to help you understand the main idea and details of a selection.*

- *What does Stanza 2 say that slaves should find if they follow the riverbank?*
- *Why does Stanza 4 tell slaves to go north across the Ohio River?*
- *What other details in the song are clues for the slaves to follow?*

Link to Social Studies

Have students work in large groups to draw a map of the actual places that the selection describes where the slaves traveled. Ask students to label the states on the map and any other places described in the selection.

Think It Over

Flexible Grouping You may assign this activity as a class discussion, partner activity, or individual writing assignment.

Answer Key

1. The Big Dipper is a constellation. It looks like a drinking gourd.
2. Peg Leg Joe was a former sailor with a wooden leg. He helped slaves escape.
3. The words to *Follow the Drinking Gourd* gave slaves directions on how to get to places where they would be free.
4. The reading said that Woodall Mountain in Mississippi may be the place where the river ends between two hills.

STEP 1: Introduce

Word Analysis

Figurative Language Help students understand that authors sometimes use words in unusual ways to help paint a word picture.

STEP 2: Teach

Review the purpose of figurative language.

SAY *When authors use figurative language, they paint a picture in their readers' minds.*

- *Why would an author want to paint a picture in readers' minds?*
- *Why do many readers like to see pictures in their minds?*
- *Do you like language that helps you paint a picture in your mind? Why or why not?*

Make a list of the following topics on the board and ask students to suggest figurative language to describe each topic.

cat's tongue	*baking bread*
rainfall	*mountain range*
field of wildflowers	

STEP 3: Practice

1. Have students work with partners. Have one partner read the first sentence of a pair aloud, then have the other partner read the second sentence aloud. Have partners discuss which sentence helped them paint a mental picture.
2. Monitor students to see that they are understanding the word pictures that are being painted. If they're not, discuss the sentence pairs with them.

Answer Key

1. a **2.** b **3.** b

Teaching Resources

- *Practice Book*, p. 119
- *Phonics Workbook*
- *CD-ROM* • *Audio CD*

Word Analysis & Fluency

Word Analysis

Figurative Language

Figurative language helps you see in your mind what the author is describing.

When the sun comes back and the first quail calls, follow the drinking gourd.

The "drinking gourd" is a symbol for the Big Dipper. "When the sun comes back," it is spring, when days begin to get warmer. That line could be rewritten as:

At the first sign of spring, follow the Big Dipper north.

Figurative language does not mean exactly what it says. It paints a word picture.

Practice

Work with a partner. Read each pair of sentences. Tell which sentence creates a better word picture.

1. **a.** The leaves danced in the wind.
   b. The wind blew the leaves around.
2. **a.** At night, there are stars in the sky.
   b. The night sky wears a necklace of diamonds.
3. **a.** The sun provides light for Earth.
   b. The sun lights the world with its flame.

Practice Book page 119

TESOL Standards

Goal 1, Standard 3—To use English to communicate in social settings: Students will use learning strategies to extend their communicative competence.
Descriptors—Testing hypotheses about language; Listening to and imitating how others use English; Exploring alternative ways of saying things; Focusing attention selectively; Practicing new language; Using context to construct meaning.

Goal 3, Standard 1—To use English in socially and culturally appropriate ways: Students will use the appropriate language variety, register, and genre according to audience, purpose, and setting.
Descriptors—Using the appropriate degree of formality with different audiences and settings; Recognizing and using standard English and vernacular dialects appropriately; Responding to and using idioms appropriately.

Fluency

Read with Expression

When you read aloud, use your voice to show feelings.

Practice

Read silently. → Read aloud. → Get comments. → Read aloud again.

Stanza 1

When the sun comes back and the first quail calls,
Follow the drinking gourd.
For the old man is waiting for to carry you to freedom
If you follow the drinking gourd.

Chorus

Follow the drinking gourd!
Follow the drinking gourd!
For the old man is waiting for to carry you to freedom
If you follow the drinking gourd.

239

Linguistic Note

Cognate—*Expression* Students who come from Spanish-speaking homes may recognize the cognate *expresión* and its adjectival form *expresivo* (meaning *expressive*). Be aware that some Spanish-speakers pronounce the *x* as an *s*. Some Spanish-speaking students may have difficulty pronouncing their English equivalents.

Accelerate Language Development

Reading Poetry and Songs Students may have difficulty reading poetry and songs expressively. In general, readers should take a short pause at the end of each line. Students may better remember to do this if you encourage them to take a breath when they come to the end of a line. Point out, though, that normal punctuation is also used. The pause at the end of a line should be a little bit longer if there's a comma than if there isn't. If there's a period or an exclamation mark, the pause should be even longer.

STEP 1: Introduce

Fluency

Read with Expression Explain to students that reading with expression can help show the emotion intended in the selection. Some ways of showing feelings are reading louder or softer, faster or slower, and emphasizing certain words or phrases.

Play the Audio CD for this reading to the class, asking students to listen for pacing, intonation, and expression.

STEP 2: Practice

Have students do the following exercise in small groups. You may want to assign only the stanza or the chorus, depending on the student's proficiency. If you prefer, let students select their own stanzas from the song.

- Have one partner look through the passage to find any words or phrases that he or she wants to emphasize. Remind students that phrases before exclamation marks are often emphasized.
- Then have that student read the passage to his or her partner. Encourage the partner to give constructive comments.
- Have the students change roles.

Possible Responses

sun	first quail	old man
waiting	freedom	drinking gourd

STEP 3: Extend

Study Skills

Thesaurus Have students write the line from the song: *For the old man is waiting for to carry you to freedom*. Then have them work with partners to:

- pick three words and look them up in a thesaurus to find synonyms or words with similar meanings;
- replace each word they looked up with a synonym;
- read their new line to the class.

STEP 1: Monitor Progress

Learning Strategy

Summarize Have students work in pairs to summarize *A Song Map*. You may then have volunteers share their summaries and their responses to the Big Question with the class.

STEP 2: Teach

Make Inferences

Making inferences will help students identify with the slaves who made inferences while listening to *Follow the Drinking Gourd*. Draw students' attention to the text at the top of p. 240.

SAY *Sometimes you have to find clues and use information you already know if you want to figure out what the author is trying to say.*

- *What are some of the differences between daytime and nighttime?*
- *What are some of the differences between summer and winter?*
- *If you are going someplace you've never visited before, what could help you find your way?*

Adapt the Activity

Ask students to read the three questions at the end of the story on p. 237 and write a paragraph based on their answers.

STEP 3: Practice

Flexible Grouping You may assign this activity as a class discussion, partner activity, or individual written assignment.

Answer Key

1. c. 2. a. 3. b

Teaching Resources

- *Practice Book*, p. 120
- *Transparencies*, p. 59
- *Teacher's Resource Book*, p. 157
- *CD-ROM*

Reading 2

Comprehension

Learning Strategy

Summarize

Summarize the song for a partner.

Ask your partner to respond to the Big Question for this reading.

Make Inferences

The slaves who used the song *Follow the Drinking Gourd* had to make inferences. They put the words of the song together with things they already knew to figure out what the clues meant.

Practice

Write the letter of the inference that can be made from each statement.

a. The slaves crossed the Tennessee River in winter when it froze.
b. The song was like a map.
c. The slaves did not want to be seen.

1. People escaping slavery often traveled at night.
2. The Tennessee River was hard to cross in the summer.
3. The slaves sang the song as they traveled.

Practice Book page 120

TESOL Standards

Goal 2, Standard 2—To use English to achieve academically in all content areas: Students will use English to obtain, process, construct, and provide subject matter information in spoken and written form.
Descriptors—Persuading, arguing, negotiating, evaluating, and justifying; Listening to, speaking, reading, and writing about subject matter information; Selecting, connecting, and explaining information; Analyzing, synthesizing, and inferring from information; Representing information visually and interpreting information presented visually.

Use an Inference Chart

An Inference Chart can help you use what you know to make inferences.

Practice

We often make inferences based on what we hear. Name a sound. Tell what you know about that sound. Make an inference. One has been done for you.

Sound	What I Know	Inference
song playing over microphone	ice cream truck plays that song	ice cream truck is coming

Extension

Find the words to one or more verses of *The Star Spangled Banner*. Discuss the meaning of the words with a partner. Use a visual aid to present your interpretation to the class.

Accelerate Language Development

Idiom: *Come up with* The text explaining Make Inferences on page 240 uses the phrase *come up with*. Students unfamiliar with English may not understand that this phrase is an idiom. It has nothing to do with the usual meaning of *come* or the usual meaning of *up*. *Come up with* means *think of*. To test their understanding of this phrase, ask students: *Can you come up with a word used in the song* Follow the Drinking Gourd? *Can you come up with the name of a food you like to eat?*

Linguistic Note

Cognate—Chart Students whose home language is Spanish may be confused with the false cognate *carta*. In English, *chart* is a visual aid using a table or a graph. In Spanish, however, *carta* means *letter*.

STEP 1: Teach

Use an Inference Chart

Share the following scenario with students. You hear a loud crashing noise in your kitchen in the middle of the night. You know that you left some dinner dishes on the table. You also know that you have a clumsy cat who loves to lick dinner dishes on the table. Ask them what inference they could make about the crash. Then have them fill out another line of the chart, showing what they know and the inference they made.

Possible Responses

Sound: loud crash in the kitchen
What I Know: I left dinner dishes in the kitchen, and my cat loves to lick dinner dishes.
Inference: My cat knocked over a dish and it broke.

STEP 2: Practice

You may have students complete the graphic organizer provided as a Blackline Master in the *Teacher's Resource Book*.

Possible Responses

Sound: car door closing outside the house
What I Know: My father comes home from work every day around this time.
Inference: My father is home.
Sound: barking in the house
What I Know: My dog barks when he wants to go for a walk.
Inference: My dog wants to go for a walk.

STEP 3: Extend

Oral Presentation Encourage partners to discuss the meaning of difficult words and phrases. Remind students to look at the context to help them figure out the meanings. Then have them create a visual aid showing what the sense of the song means. Have them label their drawings with the appropriate lyrics.

STEP 1: Introduce

Help students understand that independent clauses can stand alone as complete sentences. Dependent clauses, need more words or another clause to make a complete sentence.

STEP 2: Teach

Dependent and Independent Clauses

Write the following clauses on the board. Ask students to decide whether each clause is independent or dependent. Point out to students that there are certain clue words that commonly begin dependent clauses. Some of these words are *after*, *before*, *while*, *until*, *when*, and *where*.

after we got to the park
Samantha ate her lunch.
The children played tag.
Before it started to rain
Until my parents told me
I didn't know my aunt's last name.

STEP 3: Practice

Before students begin the Practice activity, have them work with a partner to write three dependent clauses. Then have them use those dependent clauses in sentences.

Answer Key

1. Independent: Gael likes applesauce
   Dependent: before he goes to bed.
2. Dependent: When the doorbell rang
   Independent: we knew it was time to go.
3. Independent: Soula stretches
   Dependent: before every workout
4. Dependent: After going to the movies
   Independent: Nina and I went home
   Dependent: where we ate lunch

Teaching Resources

- ***Practice Book,*** pp. 121–122
- ***Transparencies,*** pp. 69–80
- ***Assessments,*** pp. 81–84
- ***CD-ROM***

Grammar & Writing

Dependent and Independent Clauses

A **clause** is a group of words that has both a subject and a verb. The verb can be called a **predicate**.

An **independent clause** can stand alone as a sentence. A **dependent clause** has a subject and verb, but it cannot stand alone as a sentence.

Independent	Dependent
Clay went to the park	before he did his homework.

Practice

Copy each sentence. Label each dependent and independent clause.

1. Gael likes applesauce before he goes to bed.
2. When the doorbell rang, we knew it was time to go.
3. Soula stretches before every workout.
4. After going to the movies, Nina and I went home, where we ate lunch.

Practice Book page 121

TESOL Standards

Goal 2, Standard 2—To use English to achieve academically in all content areas: Students will use English to obtain, process, construct, and provide subject matter information in spoken and written form.
Descriptors—Comparing and contrasting information; Persuading, arguing, negotiating, evaluating, and justifying; Listening to, speaking, reading, and writing about subject matter information.

Goal 2, Standard 3—To use English to achieve academically in all content areas: Students will use appropriate learning strategies to construct and apply academic knowledge.
Descriptors—Using context to construct meaning; Actively connecting new information to information previously learned; Imitating the behaviors of native English speakers to complete tasks successfully.

Goal 3, Standard 1—To use English in socially and culturally appropriate ways: Students will use the appropriate language variety, register, and genre according to audience, purpose, and setting.
Descriptor—Using a variety of writing styles appropriate for different audiences, purposes, and settings.

Write a Compare and Contrast Essay

Charlie thought about two different types of music. Read how he compared blues music to rap music.

One of my favorite types of music is blues music. I like the way people sing blues songs, as if they are speaking the melody. The voice is like one of the instruments.

Rap music is very different from blues. It's more spoken. Rap is almost like a drum, with a sharp rhythm that doesn't stop.

Both kinds of music have a lot of feeling in them. The melody seems more important in blues music, and the beat seems more important in rap.

SPELLING TIP

When the /j/ sound is spelled with a *g*, the *g* is followed by *i*, *e*, or *y*, as in ***giant***, ***gentle***, and ***gym***.

Practice Book page 122

Practice

Compare two types of music.

- Describe each type of music. Write all the adjectives you can think of for each one.
- Discuss the musical instruments each type of music uses.
- First tell how the two types of music are different.
- Then tell how they are similar.

Writing Checklist

✓ Did you use at least two or three adjectives to describe each type of music?

✓ Did you talk about the sound and the feeling in the music?

✓ Can a partner understand your comparison?

243

Differentiated Instruction

Beginning	Read aloud Charlie's essay and have students point to all instances of the word *blues*. Then read it again and have them find all instances of the word *rap*.
Intermediate	Have students work in pairs to discuss if they agree with Charlie about blues and rap, then explain their opinions to the class.
Greater Challenge	Challenge students to write their own paragraph comparing and contrasting blues and rap. Encourage students to research information on the Internet.
Struggling Reader	Have students use gestures and sounds to demonstrate the differences between blues and rap that Charlie mentions in his essay.

STEP 1: Introduce

Write a Compare and Contrast Essay

Define a Compare and Contrast Essay for students. Explain that a Compare and Contrast Essay shows how two things are different and also how they are alike.

SAY *Let's read Charlie's essay.*

- *What two things is he comparing?*
- *According to Charlie, what is one way that blues music and rap music are alike?*
- *What is one important way that blues music is different from rap music.*

Spelling Tip

Read the box to students. Then have students pronounce the following words:

gesture	*gem*	*generous*
geography	*ginger*	*Egypt*

STEP 2: Practice

Before students write their own essays, discuss the parts of a Compare and Contrast Essay:

- Which two types of music will you compare?
- What makes them different?
- How do you think they are similar?

STEP 3: Monitor Progress

Writing Checklist

✓ Point out that using descriptive adjectives helps readers understand what you are writing about.

✓ Remind students that people listen to the words and the sounds in music. They also think about how the music makes them feel. These are all things that might be similar or different in the two kinds of music they picked.

✓ Have partners exchange essays and discuss what they wrote.

The Five Step Writing Process in the Writing Handbook reference section of this book provides more student writing instruction.

STEP 1: Introduce

Key Words

Help students learn the skill of defining words by using context.

SAY *All the vocabulary words from* Homemade Music *are defined in the Words in Context selection.*

- *What words in the sentence help you to understand the meaning of* rhythm*?*
- *How would you use those clues to define the word?*

Repeat a similar line of questioning for each of the remaining key words.

STEP 2: Teach

Words in Context

Write the following sentences on the board.

Have students complete this fill-in-the-blanks exercise using the key words from the Words in Context passage.

1. Musicians can play different rhythms in the same song.
2. The first instrument I played was a kazoo.
3. The chorus sang the harmonies beautifully.
4. We shop every weekend at the flea market.
5. To be good at improvisation , you have to listen closely.

Study Skills

Dictionary Have students look up their words in the dictionary to see if their Words in Context definitions are correct.

Online Dictionary Students can look up their words using an online dictionary or the CD that accompanies a learner's dictionary like the *Longman Basic Dictionary*.

www.LongmanCornerstone.com

Teaching Resources

- ***Practice Book,*** pp. 123—124
- ***Transparencies,*** p. 51
- ***CD-ROM*** • ***Audio CD***

Reading 3

Homemade MUSIC

Vocabulary

Homemade Music explains how to make instruments out of household items.

Key Words

- rhythms
- kazoo
- harmonies
- flea market
- improvisation

Words in Context

1 You can beat many different **rhythms** on a drum.

2 A **kazoo** is an instrument that's easy to play.

3 Groups of singers often sing different **harmonies**. Some singers may sing high notes. Others sing low notes.

244

TESOL Standards

Goal 1, Standard 3—To use English to communicate in social settings: Students will use learning strategies to extend their communicative competence.
Descriptors—Testing hypotheses about language; Listening to and imitating how others use English; Exploring alternative ways of saying things; Using context to construct meaning.

Goal 2, Standard 2—To use English to achieve academically in all content areas: Students will use English to obtain, process, construct, and provide subject matter information in spoken and written form.
Descriptor—Understanding and producing technical vocabulary and text features according to content area.

4

4 You can buy many interesting and unusual things at a **flea market**.

5 **Improvisation** is doing something without having an exact plan. Jazz musicians are good at improvisation.

5

Academic Words

complexity
quality of being complicated or detailed

variety
difference or range

Practice

Use each key word in a sentence.

Make Connections

Have you ever played an instrument? If you could play any instrument, which one would you choose? Explain your choice.

Practice Book pages 123–124

Visual Literacy

Photographs Have students look at the photos on pp. 244–245. Ask them to select the photo they find most interesting, then describe what they see in it, using as many descriptive words as possible.

Academic Words

Discuss the definitions for *complexity* and *variety*. Share the following context sentences with students.

Songs have different levels of *complexity*. Some songs are easy to play, but others are hard.

I enjoy listening to a *variety* of instruments.

You might want to point out the difference in spelling at the ends of these two words. *Complexity* ends in *-ity*. But *variety* ends in *-ety*. Students may notice the same root in *variety* as in *various*, which means *different*. Explain that *variety* is a noun, while *various* is an adjective. Students from Spanish-speaking homes may recognize the cognates *variedad* and *varios*.

Other Academic Words

Write the word *consist* on the board and share the meaning "to be made up of." Tell students they can use the word to talk about orchestras: "What instruments does the orchestra *consist* of?" "The orchestra *consists* of drums, horns, and a harp." Have students work with partners to write a sentence using the word based on the topic of homemade music.

Differentiated Instruction

Beginning	Have students draw and label a picture of a musical instrument. Then have them use the name of the instrument in a sentence.
Early Intermediate	Have students use gestures and expressions to act out one of the scenes depicted in the photographs.
Intermediate	Have students work with partners to write a caption for each of the photographs. Encourage them to use key words in their writing.
Standard English Learner CRI	Challenge students to create a sentence using each key word. Have one student start the sentence then have others call out one word at a time to complete the sentence.

STEP 3: Practice

Flexible Grouping You may assign these exercises as a class discussion, partner activity, or individual writing assignment.

Make Connections

Writing Fluency Even though some students may have learned to play an instrument, they may want to learn to play something else. Have students write their paragraphs based on what instrument they would like to learn. Have them describe why the instrument interests them and how they feel when they hear the sound of the instrument.

STEP 1: Introduce

More About The Big Question

The Big Question for this selection focuses on how musical instruments are made.

SAY *Think about a time you may have made a musical instrument.*

- *What did you make?*
- *How did you make it?*
- *What type of music did you play?*

Invite students to share ways they like to make music on their own without using a traditional instrument, such as whistling, or using their hands and a table top to mimic the beat of drums.

STEP 2: Teach

Reading Strategy

Identify Author's Purpose Explain that an author has a purpose for writing—to inform, to persuade, or to entertain. Lead a class discussion on the types of writing and whether some types of writing have two or all three purposes.

Understand Text Structure

Draw students' attention to the genre label. Tell them that informational text teaches the reader facts about something. This selection teaches them about music. It is nonfiction.

Read Aloud

Tell students that the beginning of an informational text often gets readers interested by asking questions that will be answered in the rest of the text. In this selection, the author asks questions in the first two paragraphs. Have students work in small groups to read the questions aloud and make predictions about what they may learn in the selection.

Teaching Resources

- *Teacher's Resource Book*, pp. 139–140
- *Practice Book*, pp. 125–126
- *CD-ROM* • *Audio CD*

Reading 3

INFORMATIONAL TEXT

Music

The Big Question

How do people make musical instruments?

Reading Strategy

Identify Author's Purpose

- Look at the pictures and captions.
- Do you think the author wrote the selection to inform, to persuade, or to entertain?
- Read the selection to see if you are right.

Homemade MUSIC

by Nicky Simser

What do a comb, a washboard, bells, and a glass bottle have in common?

You can make each of them into an instrument. A comb becomes a kazoo. Bells make musical bracelets. A bottle sounds like a flute when you blow into it. And washboards? Keep reading to find out! Invite your friends over. You will soon have a band.

People made music long before instruments were invented. They used sticks to beat rhythms. Pieces of wood became whistles. People used objects they found around them every day. It just took some imagination to make music.

flute musical instrument shaped like a pipe
imagination ability to form ideas in your mind

Steel pan drums are made from barrels that once contained oil.

246

TESOL Standards

Goal 2, Standard 2—To use English to achieve academically in all content areas: Students will use English to obtain, process, construct, and provide subject matter information in spoken and written form.
Descriptors—Understanding and producing technical vocabulary and text features according to content area; Demonstrating knowledge through application in a variety of contexts.

A kazoo is a tube with a hole in the middle. You play a kazoo by singing or humming into one end of the tube. You can use your hand or finger to control how sound moves through the other end. It makes your voice sound different. Kazoos are fun to play. You can make different harmonies with a kazoo.

It is easy to make a kazoo out of a comb. Use any comb. Cut a piece of wax paper. The paper should be twice the size of the comb. Hold the comb with the teeth down. Fold the paper over the comb. Make a crease at the top. Hold the paper close to the sides of the comb, and then sing or hum into the open end. Try not to press on the paper with your lips. When you sing or hum, the paper vibrates against the comb. Does it sound like your voice?

---

crease sharp edge where something has been folded

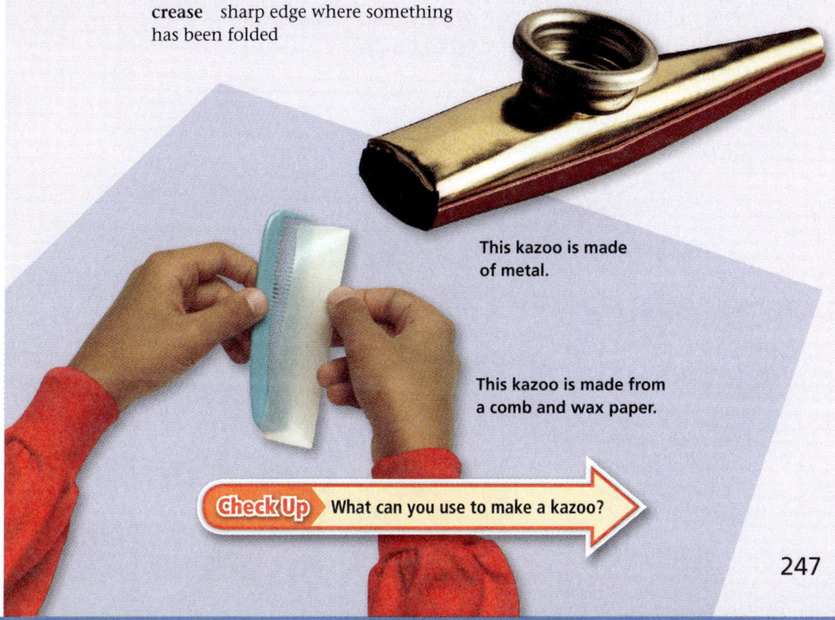

This kazoo is made of metal.

This kazoo is made from a comb and wax paper.

Check Up What can you use to make a kazoo?

Differentiated Instruction

Beginning	Have students make a vibration noise similar to that of a kazoo. Then fold a piece of paper in two to demonstrate of *crease* and *vibrate*.
Intermediate	Have students demonstrate to the class how to make a kazoo from a comb. Encourage students to have fun and use big gestures.
Greater Challenge	Have students think of other "homemade" ways to make music. Have them demonstrate how their homemade instrument works and sounds.
Struggling Reader	Have students make the comb kazoo, then practice humming into it. Demonstrate each highlighted word with gestures.

Build Vocabulary

Direct attention to the highlighted word in the text with a definition at the bottom of the page.

- Invite volunteers to read aloud the word and the definition.
- Have students write a context sentence using the word.
- Have students repeat this activity for each highlighted word as they read the selection.

Silent Letters Tell students that some common words in English are spelled with other letters that are not pronounced. On pp. 246–247 are *rhythms*, which has a silent *h* after the *r*, and *comb*, which has a silent *b*. Point out that students may know some other words with a silent *h* or a silent *b*. Write these words on the board: *ghost*, *rhyme*, *climb*, *thumb*. Ask students to name the silent letters. ghost, rhyme = h; climb, thumb = b

STEP 3: Assess

Check Up

Ask students to write a description of the steps involved in making a kazoo from a comb.

Adapt the Activity

Make a Kazoo from a Comb Have students reread the text on p. 247 and use the information to make a kazoo from a comb. As they are making their kazoos, have students talk about what they are doing. For example, *I am cutting the wax paper. The paper is twice the size of the comb. I'm making a crease at the top.* When students have completed their kazoos, invite them to practice making different types of sounds.

Link to Social Studies

The musical saw is one of the world's most popular homemade instruments. Most saw players use an ordinary saw used for cutting wood. The musician holds the handle of the saw between his or her legs and either uses a bow or a mallet on the blade. The musician then moves the blade of the saw with his or her free hand to make different notes. Have students research the musical saw or other unusual instruments.

STEP 1: Monitor Progress

Comprehension Check

Identify Cause and Effect Have students discuss various ways to make musical sounds. Help students recognize there are many objects to use and ways to make musical sounds. Have students fill in a Cause and Effect Chart like the one shown below to describe the sounds.

CAUSE	EFFECT
Cover a comb with wax paper and sing or hum into it	vibrating sound like a kazoo
Place bells loosely on an elastic band and shake them	jingling sounds based on the type of movement
Stroke ridges of a washboard	percussion sound based on the object used on it

Scaffolding

You're in the Band Help students organize themselves to stand in rows and play in a classroom band. They may use the kazoos they made on p. 247 or create other instruments that are simple to make, such as drums and cymbals.

Link to Science

Explain to students that different sound waves travel at different speeds. Have students research the basic principles of how sounds travel to our ears. Have students write a short report on the information they find.

Build Discussion

Explain to students that authors sometimes expect readers to come up with ideas of their own. On p. 249, the author talks about washboards: *You can stroke the ridges with almost anything.* Then she lists a few examples. Have students brainstorm to think of other things they could use to make music on a washboard. Have them describe what they think the sounds would be like and tie the discussion to the Big Question for the selection.

Jingle bracelets sound like their name – they jingle! Use thread to tie four or five jingle bells onto an elastic hair band. Leave a space between each bell. Mix the sizes of bells. Each size will have a different sound. Make as many jingle bracelets as you want to wear.

These are Indian jingle bracelets. You can make your own with things from a craft store or flea market.

Practice moving with the bracelets. How do they sound when you shake your arms? How do they sound when you sway your arms? Put the bracelets on your ankles. How do they sound when you march? Do they sound different when you dance?

Jingle bells can be played alone, or they can be part of a band or orchestra. They will add a delicate sound to your group, unless you shake and rattle them!

---

sway move slowly from one side to the other

delicate pleasant and not too strong

You can play in your own band using homemade instruments.

248

TESOL Standards

Goal 2, Standard 2—To use English to achieve academically in all content areas: Students will use English to obtain, process, construct, and provide subject matter information in spoken and written form.

Descriptors—Understanding and producing technical vocabulary and text features according to content area; Demonstrating knowledge through application in a variety of contexts.

A washboard is a piece of wood or metal with ridges. Many years ago, people used washboards to wash clothes. The ridges helped to get out the dirt. Now, people play music on washboards. You can stroke the ridges with almost anything. Some players use thimbles. Other players use wooden spoons, can openers, or their fingers. Each object will make a different sound. If you go to a local flea market, you may find a washboard!

You have your instruments. Your band is ready to go! Have each of your friends pick an instrument. Let them practice on their own. Then get together and play. Now it is time for some improvisation. Improvisation can also be called jamming. Jam with your friends on your homemade instruments!

Many people play washboards.

thimbles metal or plastic caps used to protect fingers while sewing

Practice Book pages 125–126

Reading Strategy

Identify Author's Purpose

- Did this author write to inform, to entertain, or to persuade? Explain.
- How did thinking about the author's purpose help you to understand the selection?

Think It Over

1. What object sounds like a flute when you blow into it?
2. What is the first step in making a kazoo from a comb?
3. What musical instruments can you make using bells?
4. What do some people use to play washboards?

249

Differentiated Instruction

Beginning	Help students say the names of the items used for instruments in the photo on p. 248, then use gestures to show how to play each instrument.
Early Intermediate	Have students work in a group to draw a large picture of household items and items in the classroom that could be used as instruments.
Intermediate	Have students work with the class to create a comb-kazoo band and to improvise a melody and a harmony.
Standard English Learner (CRI)	Have students assemble their comb kazoos and any other possible instruments in the classroom. Have them participate in an activity using the instruments.

STEP 2: Teach

Visual Literacy

Photographs Ask students to look at the photograph at the bottom of p. 248. Have students identify the different musical instruments and speculate about how each might sound. Encourage them to use objects from class to perform their ideas about how the instruments sound.

STEP 3: Assess

Reading Strategy

Identify Author's Purpose Give students an example of how to identify author's purpose.

SAY *As you read a selection, you should try to decide why the author wrote it.*

- *Were you entertained by some of the instruments the author wrote about?*
- *Do you think the author's main purpose was to entertain the reader?*
- *What do you think the author was trying to persuade the reader to do?*
- *What opinion did the author share with the reader?*

Have students write a paragraph about how they were entertained, what they were persuaded to do, and the author's opinion.

Think It Over

Flexible Grouping You may assign this activity as a class discussion, partner activity, or individual writing assignment.

Answer Key

1. A bottle sounds like a flute when you blow into it.
2. The first step is to cut a piece of wax paper.
3. You can make jingle bracelets using bells.
4. Some people use thimbles to play washboards.

Make Connections

Writing Fluency Ask students to imagine that they want to form a band. Have them write a short essay answering these questions: *What kinds of instruments would you like to have in your band? Why would you like those instruments? What kind of music do you want to play?*

STEP 1: Introduce

A Closer Look

The photos on these pages are designed to serve as visuals to expand vocabulary related to *Homemade Instruments*.

More About The Big Question

The Big Question for this selection also focuses on how people make homemade musical instruments. Have students try to imagine how musical instruments were first discovered.

SAY *Some of the earliest instruments were probably not that different from the simple ones you see on pages 250 and 251. No one is certain how the first simple musical instruments were invented, but it is possible to guess.*

- *What do you think the first drums might have looked like?*
- *What did people use to make them?*
- *What do you think people used to make the first flutes?*
- *What might people have used to make the strings on stringed instruments?*

Link to Social Studies

Prehistoric Stringed Instruments It's likely that the first stringed instruments were monochords, single strings stretched over a sound box of some kind. No one knows how humans first noticed that strings could make interesting sounds, but one theory is that ancient hunters noticed the interesting sounds strings made when they hunted with bows and arrows. Some historians believe that prehistoric musicians placed one end of the bow in their mouths, and tapped the string sharply to make it "sing." By changing the position of their jaws and cheeks, these ancient musicians could produce different notes.

A Closer Look at... Homemade Instruments

Bells from bottles
Put a different amount of water in each bottle. Then tap on the side of each bottle with a spoon. Soon you will know what sound each bottle makes.

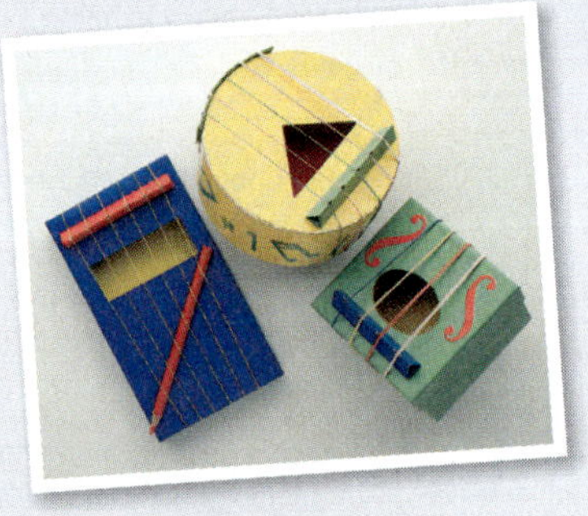

Cardboard harps
This zither, guitar, and harp are made from cardboard boxes and rubber bands.

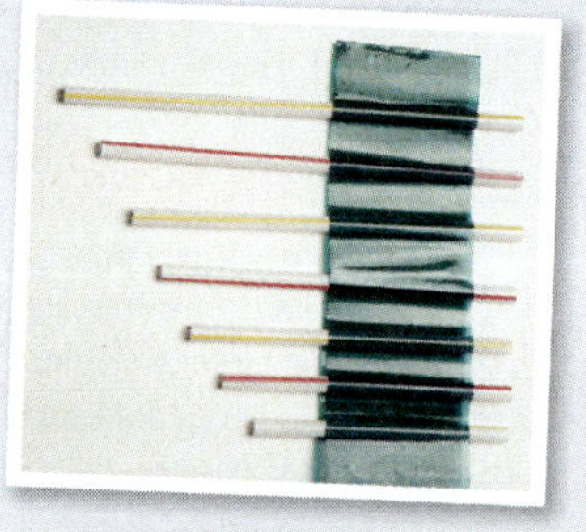

Straw flute
These pan pipes are made from drinking straws and sticky-backed plastic. You can change the pitch of the notes by changing the lengths of the straws.

250

TESOL Standards

Goal 2, Standard 3—To use English to achieve academically in all content areas: Students will use appropriate learning strategies to construct and apply academic knowledge.
Descriptors—Focusing attention selectively; Applying basic reading comprehension skills such as skimming, scanning, previewing, and reviewing text; Using context to construct meaning; Taking notes to record important information and aid one's own learning; Applying self-monitoring and self-corrective strategies to build and expand a knowledge base; Planning how and when to use cognitive strategies and applying them appropriately to a learning task.

Goal 3, Standard 1—To use English in socially and culturally appropriate ways: Students will use the appropriate language variety, register, and genre according to audience, purpose, and setting.
Descriptors—Recognizing and using standard English and vernacular dialects appropriately; using a variety of writing styles appropriate for different audiences, purposes, and settings.

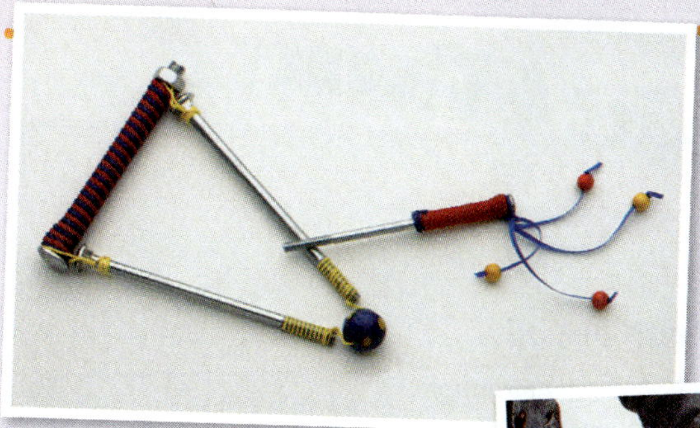

▲ **Triangle of nails**
The triangle is a popular percussion instrument. This one is made from nails, bolts, and twine.

▲ **Spoons**
This person is playing spoons. Hit the spoons between your hand and your knee. They will make a clicking sound.

▼ **Bottle flutes**
Put your upper lip over your lower one and blow into the bottle. You will hear a sound like a flute.

Activity to Do!

- Choose an instrument.
- Find out how to make that instrument.
- Create two pages to tell about that instrument.
- Present your work to the class.

251

Differentiated Instruction	
Beginning	Read a caption aloud and have students point to the picture it describes. Then ask them to use their own words to tell what they see.
Intermediate	Have students describe which standard instruments are played by strumming, blowing, or drumming.
Greater Challenge	Provide students with tall glass bottles of various sizes, each filled with a different amount of water. Have students play a tune for the class by tapping with a spoon or blowing across the top.
Struggling Reader	Read the captions for each picture and have students point to the correct photo. Encourage students to write a caption for one of the photos.

STEP 2: Teach

Visual Literacy

Illustrations and Captions Have students look at the captions on pp. 250–251.

SAY *Read the captions and look at the pictures.*

- *How do you make different sounds with the bottles?* You put a different amount of water in each one.
- *If you make a cardboard harp, what do you use for strings?* You use rubber bands.
- *What would you do to change the pitch of the notes on a straw flute?* I'd cut the straws to change their length.
- *Why do you think spoons are better for making a clicking sound than forks are?* A spoon has no spaces between the metal.

Adapt the Activity

Have students practice making sounds with the bells from bottles and the bottle flutes. Tell students to practice with different sound levels until they can play what they consider to be a complete melody. Have students perform their melody for the class.

STEP 3: Assess

Activity to Do!

Study Skills Ask students to select one of the instruments they read about on pp. 246–251, or to choose another simple instrument they know. Suggest that they use the Internet to find out how to make the instrument they've chosen. Have students share their work with the class. If enough students want to follow through and create instruments, you may consider having an in-class concert.

SAY *When you choose an instrument you'd like to make, ask yourself these questions:*

- *What items do I need to make this instrument?*
- *Do I need any tools, like scissors?*
- *What steps should I follow to make this instrument?*
- *How will I decorate my instrument?*

STEP 1: Introduce

Phonics

Words with *ow, ou* Help students understand that the sound of the blend in the diphthong /ou/ can sound the same if it is spelled *ou* or *ow*, as in *loud* and *how*. Sometimes the long *o* sound is also spelled *ow* as in *low*.

STEP 2: Teach

Draw students' attention to the Rule Box. Have a volunteer read the rule aloud.

SAY *Let's look at some words with* ou *or* ow.

- *Write the word* round. *How do you spell the /ou/ sound?*
- *Write the word* now. *How do you spell the /ou/ sound?*
- *Write the word* show. *How do you spell the long* o *sound?*

Write the following words on the board. Ask students to read them aloud and tell how the *ou* or *ow* is pronounced in each word.

ground	*slow*	*owl*
cow	*sound*	*grow*
throw	*town*	*mouth*

Then ask volunteers to read the words in the boxes. Then have them say just vowel sound.

STEP 3: Practice

Have students work with partners. Encourage partners to take turns reading aloud the words in the chart. Have the other students listen carefully, and say the vowel sound they hear in each word.

1. know, known , owner
2. about, amount, around, how, powerful, prowl

Teaching Resources

- *Practice Book*, p. 127
- *Phonics Workbook*
- *Phonics Flashcards*
- *CD-ROM* • *Audio CD*

Reading 3

Phonics & Fluency

Phonics

Words with *ow, ou*

Read these words. Pay attention to the vowel sounds.

how loud low

Which words have the same letters? Which words have the same vowel sound?

Rule Box

The diphthong /ou/ can be spelled as either *ow* or *ou*.
The long /ō/ sound is sometimes spelled with *ow*.

Each word in the chart has the letters *ou* or *ow*. Read the words. If one sound doesn't make sense, try the other.

about	how	owner
amount	know	powerful
around	known	prowl

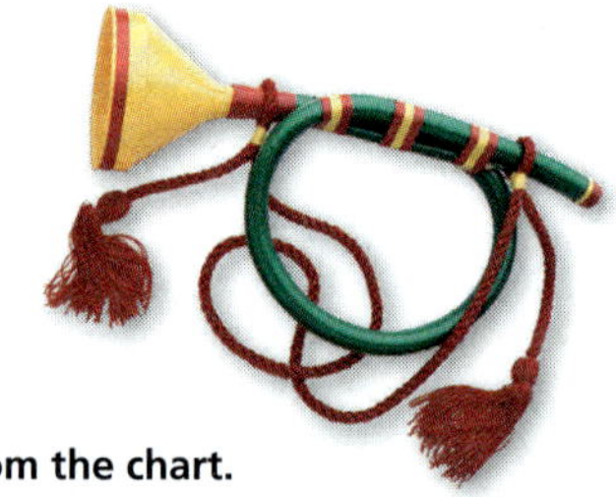

Practice

Work with a partner. Use the words from the chart.

1. List the words in which *ow* has the long /ō/ sound.
2. List the words in which *ow* or *ou* has the vowel sound in ***how***.
3. Add three more words to each list.

Practice Book page 127

TESOL Standards

Goal 1, Standard 3—To use English to communicate in social settings: Students will use learning strategies to extend their communicative competence.
Descriptors—Listening to and imitating how others use English; Self-monitoring and self-evaluating language development; Practicing new language; Focusing attention selectively.

Goal 3, Standard 3—To use English in socially and culturally appropriate ways: Students will use appropriate learning strategies to extend their sociolinguistic and sociocultural competence.
Descriptors—Observing and modeling how others speak and behave in a particular situation or setting; Experimenting with variations of language in social and academic settings; Seeking information about appropriate language use and behavior.

Fluency

Read for Speed and Accuracy

You should read quickly. But never read so quickly that you lose your understanding.

Practice

Read for one minute. → Count the words you read. → Study any hard words. → Read and count again.

What do a comb, a washboard, bells, and a glass bottle 11
have in common? 14
You can make each of them into an instrument. A 24
comb becomes a kazoo. Bells make musical bracelets. 32
A bottle sounds like a flute when you blow into it. And 44
washboards? Keep reading to find out! Invite your friends 53
over. You will soon have a band. 60
People made music long before instruments were 67
invented. They used sticks to beat rhythms. Pieces of 76
wood became whistles. People used objects they found 84
around them every day. It just took some imagination to 94
make music. 96
Look around you. Do you see anything that could 105
make music? Your hands can. Tap them on a table. Tap 116
a little harder. Tap a little faster. You are making music! 127

Accelerate Language Development

Compound Words Remind students that a compound word is a word that is made up of two or more smaller words. Write the word *washboard* on the board. Have students identify and explain the meaning of the smaller words—*wash* and *board*. Help them use the word's meanings to formulate a definition for *washboard*—"a board used for washing." Have students follow the strategy to figure out the meanings for these compound words—*homemade*, *moonlight*, *schoolhouse*, *thunderstorm*, *dishwasher*.

Linguistic Note

music/música Spanish-speaking students will recognize the word *music*, which is close in spelling to the Spanish word that has the same meaning *música*. Review the pronunciation of the word *music* with students. Spanish speakers may have a tendency to add a third syllable to the word, as its Spanish counterpart has three syllables.

STEP 1: Introduce

Fluency

Read for Speed and Accuracy Explain to students that reading with accuracy will improve their understanding because they will focus more closely on what they are reading. Help students understand that reading for speed does not mean reading too fast or too slow; instead, reading for speed means reading at a normal, conversational speed.

Play the Audio CD for this reading to the class, asking students to listen for pacing, intonation, and expression.

STEP 2: Practice

Have students work with partners to do the following exercise. Before they begin reading for speed and accuracy, they should find the hard words that will slow them down and practice saying them. When both partners feel that they are ready, have them begin the exercise.

- Have one partner read while the other acts as the timer. When the reader has read for a minute, have the timer say, "Stop."
- Have the partners look at the end of the last complete line the reader read, and make a note of the number.
- Have partners change roles.

Possible Response

Words that will slow me down

comb	washboard	instrument
bracelet	rhythms	whistles
imagination		

STEP 3: Extend

Study Skills

Dictionary Have students work with partners to:

- write down three words from the reading that slowed them down;
- look up the words in a dictionary;
- read the sentences from the reading in which the hard words appear and define the hard words.

STEP 1: Monitor Progress

Learning Strategy

Take Notes Taking notes helps readers remember the most important details in a selection. When taking notes, readers jot down whatever they want to remember from the selection without having to reread it. Have students work in pairs, with one student taking notes and the other formulating a response to the Big Question.

STEP 2: Teach

Author's Purpose

Knowing the author's purpose will help students take notes about the reading.

- If the author's purpose was to inform, students will look for facts.
- If the author's purpose was to persuade, students will look for persuasive language or specific promises or claims.
- If the author's purpose was to entertain, students will look for things they found entertaining.

SAY *Knowing an author's purpose helps you to know what kinds of information to look for when taking notes. Sometimes an author might write to inform you of how two or more things are alike and different. Your notes should include details that compare and contrast these things.*

STEP 3: Practice

Flexible Grouping You may assign this activity as a class discussion, partner activity, or individual written assignment.

Teaching Resources

- *Practice Book*, p. 128
- *Transparencies*, pp. 59 or 63
- *Teacher's Resource Book*, pp. 157 or 161
- *CD-ROM*

Reading 3

Comprehension

Learning Strategy

Take Notes

Take notes on the different homemade instruments. Share your notes with a partner.

Ask your partner to respond to the Big Question for this reading.

Practice Book pages 128

254

Author's Purpose

Authors write to inform or give information to their readers. Authors also write to entertain. Sometimes, authors write to persuade or change the reader's mind.

In *Homemade Music*, the author's purpose was to inform. You learned how people make instruments using everyday objects. The author also informed you about how the instruments are alike and different.

Practice

In the next reading, a class puts on a play. Write sentences about a made-up play. Follow the directions below.

1. Write a sentence to persuade.
2. Write a sentence to inform.
3. Write a sentence to entertain.

TESOL Standards

Goal 2, Standard 2—To use English to achieve academically in all content areas: Students will use English to obtain, process, construct, and provide subject matter information in spoken and written form.
Descriptors—Understanding and producing technical vocabulary and text features according to content area; Demonstrating knowledge through application in a variety of contexts; Representing information visually and interpreting information presented visually.

Use a Compare and Contrast Chart

A Compare and Contrast Chart can help you tell how instruments are similar and different.

Practice

Reread *Homemade Music* including *A Closer Look*. Complete this Compare and Contrast Chart.

Instruments	Compare	Contrast
spoons and washboard	both are percussion instruments	Spoons make sounds when they are hit. A washboard makes sounds when you rub something on it.

Extension

Find information about your favorite type of music. Make a presentation to the class using samples of music and visual aids. Tell about the history of the music, the kinds of instruments used, and some of the music's performers.

Accelerate Language Development

The Word *music* Write the word *music* on the board. Tell students that many nouns in English are root words and can be used to form other words or terms. Ask students to think of other words they can make with the word *music*—*musical*, *musician*, *music box*, *musical chairs*. Write the words on the board. Have students explain how the meaning of each word relates to *music*.

Linguistic Note

history Spanish-speaking students may have difficulty understanding the word *history*. The Spanish word *historia* means the same as the English word *history*—past events. However, *historia* also means "a story." Guide students to recognize that when they see the English word *history*, the text is referring to something relating to past events, not "a story."

STEP 1: Teach

Use a Compare and Contrast Chart

Have students think about two rooms in their home. Have them make a 3-column chart similar to the one shown on p. 255 to show how the rooms are alike and different.

Scaffolding

Have students complete a compare and contrast exercise using a Venn Diagram. Ask students to think of different times of the day when they listen to music. Have them compare and contrast what they listen to at two different times, such as in the morning, after school, at night during the week, or at night on the weekend.

STEP 2: Practice

You may have students complete the graphic organizer provided as a Blackline Master in the *Teacher's Resource Book*.

To help students get started, provide the pairs of instruments listed below to compare and contrast.

Flute and kazoo

Jingle bracelets and washboard

Straw flutes and bell bottles

STEP 3: Extend

Oral Presentation Students can use reference books or the Internet to learn more about their favorite kinds of music. Encourage them to copy, trace, photocopy, or download images to use in their oral presentations. Students can make their presentations to a partner, in small groups, or to the class. You may want to collect the visuals and add them to a music bulletin board display. Use the visuals to build vocabulary relating to the performing arts, music, and musical instruments.

STEP 1: Introduce

Write the verbs *lie, lay, sit, set, raise,* and *rise* on the board. Explain that people often use these verbs incorrectly. *Lie, sit,* and *rise* are intransitive verbs. They describe actions taken by the subject of the sentence. *Lay, set,* and *raise* are transitive verbs and describe actions that are done to something else.

STEP 2: Teach

Commonly Misused Verbs

Write the following sentences on the board. Ask students to select the correct verb to complete each sentence then tell if the verb is transitive or intransitive.

It was my turn to (deal/dealt) in the card game. intransitive

Yesterday we (ride/rode) our bikes to school. transitive

I like to (take/took) walks during the sunset. transitive

The mother (sing/sang) to her children. intransitive

STEP 3: Practice

Before students begin the Practice activity, lead a class discussion on the irregular verbs *lie*, *lay*, *rise*, and *raise*. List all four verbs on the board and the past tense of each. Explain to students that the past tense of *lie* (to recline) is *lay*, and the past tense of *lay* (to place on something) is *laid*.

Answer Key

1. lie
2. lay
3. lie

Possible Responses

I watched the sun *rise* this morning.
I asked my parents to *raise* my allowance.

Teaching Resources

- ***Practice Book***, pp. 129–130
- ***Teacher's Resource Book***, pp. 69–80
- ***Posters***

Reading 3

Grammar & Writing

Commonly Misused Verbs

Pay attention to the difference between **set** and **sit**.

Set means to place, adjust, or arrange something.
Sit means to rest, or to put your bottom in a chair.

Please set the plates on the table.	Please sit in that chair.

Set is a **transitive** verb.
It must act on an object, like ***plates***.

Sit is an **intransitive** verb.
It does not need to act on an object.

Rule Box

Transitive verbs have to act on objects. Intransitive verbs never have to act on objects.

Practice

Look up the words *lay* and *lie*. Then complete the sentences below. Look up *raise* and *rise*. Write your own sentences.

1. I am going to ____ on the couch.
2. Anna will ____ the bowls on the table.
3. Do not ____ around doing nothing all afternoon!

Practice Book page 129

256

TESOL Standards

Goal 1, Standard 3—To use English to communicate in social settings: Students will use learning strategies to extend their communicative competence.
Descriptor—Seeking support and feedback from others.

Goal 2, Standard 1—To use English to achieve academically in all content areas: Students will use English to interact in the classroom.
Descriptors—Following oral and written directions, implicit and explicit; Expressing likes, dislikes, and needs.

Goal 2, Standard 3—To use English to achieve academically in all content areas: Students will use appropriate learning strategies to construct and apply academic knowledge.
Descriptors—Using context to construct meaning; Actively connecting new information to information previously learned; Imitating the behaviors of native English speakers to complete tasks successfully.

Goal 3, Standard 1—To use English in socially and culturally appropriate ways: Students will use the appropriate language variety, register, and genre according to audience, purpose, and setting.
Descriptors—Recognizing and using standard English and vernacular dialects appropriately; Using a variety of writing styles appropriate for different audiences, purposes, and settings.

Write a Descriptive Paragraph

Read how Juanita described a violin.

The violin is made mostly of wood. Most of it is hollow. It has four strings. The violinist holds the violin under the chin and makes sounds by pulling and pushing a bow across the strings. Violinists can also make sounds by plucking the strings. The violin sounds beautiful, almost like a person singing. The violin can play all kinds of music, from classical, to jazz, to rock and roll. I like listening to classical music the best.

SPELLING TIP

Learn to spell words with silent letters and hard spellings by saying them aloud exactly as they are spelled.

tom—or—row

Practice Book page 130

Practice

Write a paragraph that describes a musical instrument.

- Choose an instrument.
- Find out what the instrument is made of, what it looks like, how someone plays it, and what kind of sound it makes.
- Read your paragarph aloud to a partner.

Writing Checklist

✓ Did you use adjectives to describe the instrument?

✓ Did you describe what the instrument looks and sounds like?

✓ Did you describe what the instrument is made of?

✓ Can a partner understand your description?

257

Differentiated Instruction	
Beginning	Write the following words on the board: *guitar*, *violin*. Have students draw pictures of the instruments and demonstrate the sounds of each.
Intermediate	Have students write short answers to these factual questions: What material is used to make violins? How many strings are on a violin? What are two ways to make sounds on a violin?
Greater Challenge	Have each student choose a musical instrument and write a descriptive paragraph about how it is played and the sound it makes.
Standard English Learner CRI	Have students brainstorm a list of words they might use to describe the sounds made by different musical instruments. Have them work with partners to make a list of the words.

STEP 1: Introduce

Write a Descriptive Paragraph

Define a descriptive paragraph for students.

SAY *In a descriptive paragraph, you use adjectives and other descriptive words to help readers draw a mental picture of what you're describing.*

- *What is Juanita describing?*
- *Does Juanita tell readers what the instrument looks like? What does she say?*
- *Does Juanita tell readers how to make sounds on the violin? What does she say?*

Spelling Tip

Read the box to students. Write the following words on the board. Have students identify the silent letters.

know	name	light
comb	knife	school

STEP 2: Practice

Before students write their own paragraphs, discuss the important parts of a descriptive paragraph.

- What do you want to describe?
- Can you picture what it looks like and hear its sounds in your head?
- What modifiers can you think of that will help the reader draw a mental picture?

STEP 3: Monitor Progress

Writing Checklist

✓ Tell students that adjectives will help readers see and hear the instrument in their minds.

✓ Help students find pictures and recordings of the instrument they choose.

✓ Explain that some individual instruments may be made from materials that are unusual.

✓ Remind readers to look for descriptions of what the instrument looks like and sounds like in thier partner's paragraph.

The Five Step Writing Process in the Writing Handbook reference section of this book provides more student writing instruction.

STEP 1: Introduce

More About The Big Question

The Big Question for this reading is *How can we make great sound effects?* Explain to students that people use sound effects in film, television, and radio. Sound effects are often used in commercials, too.

SAY *We hear sounds every day, but we may not think about them because they seem so ordinary.*

- *What kinds of sounds do cars, trucks, and buses make?*
- *What kinds of sounds do you hear when it rains?*
- *How can we make those sounds for a radio or television program?*

Visual Literacy

Illustrations Draw students' attention to the picture at the top of p. 259.

SAY *Look at the picture closely. The students are visualizing what they would like the play to be about.*

- *Besides the students, what else do you see in this picture?*
- *Is that white space a big cloud in the room with the students? Are those things really in the cloud?*
- *What do you think the picture means?*

STEP 2: Teach

Understand Text Structure

Draw students' attention to the genre label. Tell them that realistic fiction has characters and settings that seem like real people and places, however they are not actual.

Teaching Resources

- *Teacher's Resource Book*, pp. 141–142
- *CD-ROM* • *Audio CD*

Bonus Reading

LITERATURE

Realistic Fiction

The Radio Storm

by Zaman Ahmed
illustrated by Jennifer Emery

On Monday morning, Mr. Parker told our class we were going to put on a play.

"There's just one thing," he said. "It must be a radio play."

"A radio play?" Maria asked. "What's that?"

Mr. Parker explained that the play would be a story. We would act out the parts.

"But you won't act on a stage where people can see you," he said. "The radio station will come here to record your play. People at home can listen to your play on their radios."

"You mean they can't see us?" I asked. "Then how will they know what's going on?"

I looked at my best friend, Marco.

"A *radio* play?" I whispered.

258

TESOL Standards

Goal 2, Standard 3—To use English to achieve academically in all content areas: Students will use appropriate learning strategies to construct and apply academic knowledge.
Descriptors— Focusing attention selectively; Applying basic reading comprehension skills such as skimming, scanning, previewing, and reviewing text; Using context to construct meaning; Applying self-monitoring and self-corrective strategies to build and expand a knowledge base; Knowing when to use native language resources (human and material) to promote understanding.

The next day, Mr. Parker asked us what we would like our play to be about.

"Remember," he said. "This is a radio play. You need to think of something that has great sound effects."

"Maybe a play about a noisy, galloping horse?" Maria asked.

"Or a play about a rocket ship blasting off?" I asked.

"How about a play with a loud helicopter that makes a whump, whump, whump sound?" asked Bradley.

"Now you're thinking," said Mr. Parker. "Think about things that make noise."

Maria began to tap on her desk. "Here's a galloping horse, Mr. Parker," she said.

Then we all began to make galloping sounds by tapping on our desks.

"Whoa!" said Mr. Parker. "All horses back to the barn!"

259

Differentiated Instruction

Beginning	Have students say aloud the name of each item shown in the cloud on p. 259. Find the words for the sounds of the horse, rocket, and helicopter.
Early Intermediate	Have students work with a partner to find the three sentences that describe the sounds of the horse, rocket ship, and helicopter.
Intermediate	Have students describe the action in the illustrations and discuss whether the drawings show something that helps tell the story.
Struggling Reader	Tell students that the author uses a word three times in a row to imitate the sound of a helicopter. Have students find that word and then use it to imitate a helicopter.

Vocabulary Definitions

The following vocabulary appears on pp. 258–259 of *The Radio Storm*. Definitions are provided for your convenience to share with your class if they require explanations of any words. They are not meant for vocabulary acquisition or exercises.

radio station place where radio broadcasts are made.

sound effects sounds used in plays or movies to remind the audience of real noises

galloping running fast

blasting off making a loud noise or explosion while taking off into space

Point of View

The Radio Storm uses first person narration. When a story is told in the first person, one of the characters in the story tells the story. Have students compare the narrative style of *The Radio Storm* with another story in the book that is told in the third person, or by someone who is not a character in the story.

Read Aloud

Have students review pp. 258–259 to prepare for reading aloud the narration and dialogue on the two pages. Ask volunteers to read one paragraph at a time. Remind students to look for clues that tell what expression to use while reading aloud.

STEP 3: Extend

Draw Conclusions

Have students answer the following factual and inferential questions about the text on pp. 258–259.

SAY *Authors don't always tell you everything. Sometimes you have to look at the text and think about what you know. Then you can figure things out for yourself.*

- *Will the students need costumes for their radio play? Why or why not?*
- *Why does Mr. Parker want his students to think of things that make noise?*
- *If you wanted to make people hear the sounds of a horse, would you need a real horse for a radio play? Why or why not?*

STEP 1: Monitor Progress

Comprehension Check

Literary Element: Onomatopoeia Help students understand that some words are spelled like they sound. As students answer the following questions, have them try making the sounds themselves.

SAY *Some English words are used to describe sounds. The words imitate the sounds.*

- *Which words does the author use to describe the sounds of people running?* clop, clop
- *Which word does the author use to imitate the sound of wind?* SHHHHHH
- *Which words does the author use to describe the sounds of water pouring from a bucket?* Splash, split, splat, splash!
- *Which word does the author use to describe the sound of thunder?* Boom!

Make Connections

Invite students to write their own radio play using various sound effects. Encourage students to write about something they experienced. Have students fill in a Story Map to plan the details of their play. Remind students the radio audience cannot see the performance, so students should use their sound effects effectively.

We started naming all the noisy things we could think of.

Finally, Mr. Parker said, "Remember, this is going to be a play. That means you need to tell a story, too."

Kaleed raised his hand. "I have an idea for a good story that can be noisy," he said.

"What is it?" Marco asked.

"Okay, it starts like this: It was a dark and stormy night."

"A scary story!" I said. "But can we make storm noises?"

"Easy," said Kaleed. "We wave sheets of metal through the air to make thunder. We all say 'SHHHHHH' at the same time to make the sound of wind. And we can pour water from a watering can to make the sound of rain. We can use coconuts to make the sound of feet running!"

We all loved Kaleed's ideas for the story and the sound effects.

"That sounds like a dark and stormy night to me," said Mr. Parker. "Thank you, Kaleed."

260

FYI

Radio Sound Effects Here are some sound effects used in old-time radio:

A person walking in snow was made by squeezing a box of cornstarch. A bird flapping its wings was made by waving a pair of gloves. A door opening on a science fiction rocket ship was made by pulling a piece of paper out of an envelope. A person crunching through leaves or grass was made by balling up tape. The sound of breaking eggs was made by squeezing a folded piece of sandpaper. And two people kissing each other was made by the sound effects person kissing his or her own hand! Share these ideas with students. If possible, try them out with your students.

TESOL Standards

Goal 2, Standard 3—To use English to achieve academically in all content areas: Students will use appropriate learning strategies to construct and apply academic knowledge. **Descriptors**—Focusing attention selectively; Applying basic reading comprehension skills such as skimming, scanning, previewing, and reviewing text; Using context to construct meaning; Applying self-monitoring and self-corrective strategies to build and expand a knowledge base; Knowing when to use native language resources (human and material) to promote understanding.

We couldn't wait to perform our play. Mr. Parker let Kaleed choose the sound effect he wanted to make. He said, "I want to make the sound of feet running!"

Kaleed practiced making the sounds of people running. He clapped the coconuts together in different ways. First, he tried tapping them together. Then, he tried tapping them on the table. He liked the way they sounded on the table best. *Clop clop*. The coconuts sounded just like people running.

Maria and I made sounds of thunder by shaking metal sheets. We made the thunder sound like it was crashing right next to us. We all said "SHHHHHH" to make the sound of wind. When it was time for the rain to start, we poured water from the watering can into a bucket. *Splash, split, splat, splash!*

After Marco finished reading the last page of the play, we put down the coconuts, metal sheets, and watering can. But we still heard the sounds of rain and thunder. *Boom! Splash, split, splat, splash!*

We were confused. Then Mr. Parker pointed at the window. There was a real storm outside!

261

STEP 2: Teach

Vocabulary Definitions

The following vocabulary appears on pp. 260–261 of *The Radio Storm*. Definitions are provided for your convenience to share with your class if they require explanations of any words. They are not meant for vocabulary acquisition or exercises.

stormy rainy or snowy, often with strong winds and lightning

sheets of metal long pieces of metal, shaped like sheets

coconuts large round nuts with hard shells that grow on palm trees Their shells can be cut in half and used for sound effects.

watering can a pitcher with a long spout for sprinkling water on plants

Visual Literacy

Illustrations Draw students' attention to the illustration on the bottom of p. 261. Have students describe what all the items on the table are used for, and what the students are doing.

Adapt the Activity

Plan a Radio Play Explain to students that radio plays are fun to put on and fun to listen to because they require a lot of imagination. Ask them to think of an idea for a radio play that the whole class can perform. Have students write one or two paragraphs telling what their play will be about. Remind them to include information about the sound effects they would use.

STEP 3: Extend

Write a Radio Play

Have the entire class work together to write a script for the radio play they planned in the previous exercise. Remind students to keep in mind the Big Question for this and to use homemade instruments and their voices for sound effects. Tell students when they rehearse their play, they can also improvise dialogue and sound effects along with what they have written to help make the play more fun and interesting.

Differentiated Instruction

Beginning	Read pp. 260–261 aloud, or ask for volunteers. After hearing the paragraphs read aloud, have students find as many words on the page as possible that are words that describe sounds.
Intermediate	Have students describe the sounds that the various characters made during the radio play.
Greater Challenge	Make a radio play available to students, either in script form or in a recording. Have students read or listen to the radio play, then perform sections of the play for class.
Standard English Learner CRI	Have students improvise their own radio play about a dark and stormy night. Encourage students to present a story that has a beginning, middle, and end.

STEP 1: Review

The Big Question

Evidence of Understanding

Lead a discussion of the Big Question. Encourage students to give concrete examples from the readings or from their own lives.

STEP 2: Transfer

Written

Slogans Tell students that a slogan is a short statement telling why something is good or important.

Outline You may have to remind students how to create an outline. Use one of the instruments from Unit 5 as your model.

Report Help students brainstorm the names of some musicians they know who are physically challenged.

Oral

Game It may help students if you first play recordings of various instruments for them.

Song Allow students to write their own melodies or put new words to songs they already know.

Radio Play Provide students with appropriate props for making sound effects.

Visual/Active

Demonstration You may choose to have students form a "band" with their homemade instruments and perform two or three songs together.

Mural Have students add labels to their mural. Encourage them to incorporate the words into their design.

Catalog Recommend that students organize their catalogs by putting the instruments in alphabetical order, size order, or in order of difficulty to make.

All projects can be assessed on the basis of content and presentation. A rubric delineating standards for assessment can be helpful, and is available as a Blackline Master in the *Teacher's Resource Book*.

UNIT 5 Wrap Up

The Big Question

How do people make and use music?

Written	Oral	Visual/Active
Slogans Write a few slogans that tell what is good about being able to make music.	**Game** With a partner, listen to a piece of music played by an orchestra. Take turns naming instruments that you hear.	**Demonstration** Make one of the instruments described in *Homemade Music*. Show a group how the instrument is played.
Outline Skim all the selections in this unit. Look for each musical instrument named. Write an outline that shows each instrument and what it is made of.	**Song** Write a song that gives instructions. Use *Follow the Drinking Gourd* as an example. Show your teacher the words. Then perform the song for your class.	**Mural** Work with a group. Create a mural that shows how slaves might have used the Big Dipper and the song *Follow the Drinking Gourd* to guide them to freedom.
Report Research and write a report about the life of a musician who faces physical challenges.	**Radio Play** With a small group, write and record a radio play. Use some sound effects. Play the recording. Ask listeners to identify the source of each sound.	**Catalog** Make a catalog that shows drawings and descriptions of homemade instruments. Include the instruments you read about and make up some of your own.

262

TESOL Standards

Goal 2, Standard 2—To use English to achieve academically in all content areas: Students will use English to obtain, process, construct, and provide subject matter information in spoken and written form.
Descriptors—Gathering information orally and in writing; Representing information visually and interpreting information presented visually; Understanding and producing technical vocabulary and text features according to content area; Demonstrating knowledge through application in a variety of contexts.

Goal 3, Standard 1—To use English in socially and culturally appropriate ways: Students will use the appropriate language variety, register, and genre according to audience, purpose, and setting.
Descriptors—Using the appropriate degree of formality with different audiences and settings; Recognizing and using Standard English and vernacular dialects appropriately; Using a variety of writing styles appropriate for different audiences, purposes, and settings; Responding to and using slang appropriately; Responding to and using idioms appropriately; Responding to and using humor appropriately; Determining when it is appropriate to use a language other than English; Determining appropriate topics for interaction.

Practice Book pages 131–132

✓ Learning Checklist

Word Analysis and Phonics

- ✓ Identify final *-ed* sounds.
- ✓ Understand figurative language.
- ✓ Distinguish between *ow* and *ou* sounds.

Comprehension

- ✓ Identify the main idea and details.
- ✓ Use a Main Idea and Details Chart.
- ✓ Make inferences.
- ✓ Use an Inference Chart.
- ✓ Identify author's purpose.
- ✓ Use a Compare and Contrast Chart.

Grammar and Writing

- ✓ Use appositives and prepositional phrases.
- ✓ Distinguish between dependent and independent clauses.
- ✓ Identify commonly confused verbs.
- ✓ Write an introductory paragraph.
- ✓ Write a compare and contrast essay.
- ✓ Write a descriptive paragraph.

Self-Evaluation Questions

- How have the activities affected your feelings about music?
- How does what you have learned apply to other classes?
- How can you share your interest in music with other students?

263

Further Reading

Rumpelstiltskin
In this Penguin Young Reader® adaptation of the classic Grimms fairytale, a queen must find out the name of a mysterious little man in time to save her family. Could the song he sings hold the clue to his name?

What Charlie Heard, Mordicai Gerstein
Here is the engaging story of twentieth-century composer Charles Ives. As a child, Charlie was fascinated by sounds of all kinds. Later, as an adult, he tried to re-create those sounds in his music.

The Philharmonic Gets Dressed, Karla Kuskin
When all 105 members of the Philharmonic Orchestra come together, they make beautiful music. In this intriguing book, readers meet the musicians first as individuals before they become a coordinated group.

STEP 3: Assess

Learning Checklist

Word Analysis and Phonics

- ✓ The ending *-ed*: p. 226
- ✓ Figurative Language: p. 238
- ✓ Words with *ow, ou*: p. 252

Comprehension

- ✓ Main Idea and Details: p. 228
- ✓ Use a Main Idea and Details Chart: p. 229
- ✓ Make Inferences: p. 240
- ✓ Use an Inference Chart: p. 241
- ✓ Author's Purpose: p. 254
- ✓ Use a Compare and Contrast Chart: p. 255

Grammar and Writing

- ✓ Appositives and Prepositional Phrases: p. 230
- ✓ Dependent and Independent Clauses: p. 242
- ✓ Commonly Misused Verbs: p. 256
- ✓ Write an Introductory Paragraph: p. 231
- ✓ Write a Compare and Contrast Essay: p. 243
- ✓ Write a Descriptive Paragraph: p. 257

Self-Evaluation Questions

The self-evaluation questions provide the teacher with important information about the students' learning progress as well as their self-esteem.

- ✓ If students made instruments or performed in class, have them describe their experiences.
- ✓ Remind students to think about how they overcome challenges, figure out clues, or make things.
- ✓ Suggest that students imagine they are talking to friends or relatives who are in different schools or different grades.

Teaching Resources

- *Practice Book*, pp. 131–132
- *Transparencies*, p. 85
- *Assessments*, pp. 143–151
- *CD-ROM* • *Teacher CD-ROM*

Unit 6 Planner

Visiting National Parks

Unit Preview: pp. 264–269 **Vocabulary:** *Words to Know*, pp. 266–267
Pacing: 3–4 Days **Oral Language:** *What About You?*, p. 269

The Big Question
Why are national parks important?

	Suggested Pacing: 7–8 Days 1	Suggested Pacing: 7–8 Days 2
Reading Selection	**Yosemite National Park** pp. 270–281 **Genre:** Functional Writing/ Newspaper Article	**How to Prepare for a Trip to Yosemite** pp. 282–295 **Genre:** Functional Writing/E-mail, ***A Closer Look at . . . . . Things You Might Need On a Camping Trip***, pp. 288–289
Oral Language	**More About the Big Question, p. T272** *Why is it important to set aside land for national parks?*	**More About the Big Question, p. T284** *What can we learn from visiting national parks?*
Vocabulary	**Key Words:** tributaries, national parks, cliffs, sequoias, grove **Academic Words:** area, region **Other Academic Word:** site	**Key Words:** environment, ecosystem, alpine, landslide, conservation, secluded, scenic **Academic Words:** specific, features **Other Academic Words:** maintain, obtain
Phonics Word Analysis Fluency	**Phonics:** Words with *v* and *w*, p. 276 **Fluency:** Look Ahead, p. 277	**Phonics:** Variant Vowel: *oo*, p. 290 **Fluency:** Read with Expression, p. 291
Comprehension	**Reading Strategy:** Make Connections, pp. 272, 275 **Learning Strategy:** Notetaking, p. 278 **Comprehension Skill:** Connect Text to Self, p. 278 **Graphic Organizer:** 5W Chart, p. 279	**Reading Strategy:** Draw Conclusions, pp. 284, 287 **Learning Strategy:** Summarize, p. 292 **Comprehension Skill:** Draw Conclusions, p. 292 **Graphic Organizer:** KWL Chart, p. 293
Grammar and Writing	**Grammar:** Four Types of Sentences, p. 280 **Writing:** Write a Business Letter, Writing Checklist, Spelling Tip, p. 281	**Grammar:** Active and Passive Voice, p. 294 **Writing:** Write a Paragraph in the Active Voice, Writing Checklist, Spelling Tip, p. 295
	Differentiated Instruction pp. T271, T273, T275, T281	**Differentiated Instruction** pp. T283, T285, T287, T289, T295

Teaching Resources

- *Assessments,* pp. 89–100, pp. 153–162
- *Practice Book,* pp. 133–158
- *Phonics and Word Analysis Workbook*
- *Phonics and Word Analysis Teacher's Guide w/Audio CD*
- *Phonics Flashcards*
- *Posters*
- *Teacher's Resource Book* *Lesson Plans,* pp. 62–73
- *Audio CD*
- *DVD*
- *Teacher's CD-ROM*
- *CD-ROM*
- *Phonetic Storybooks*
- *Penguin Young Readers Library*

Suggested Pacing: 7–8 Days

3

My Trip to Yosemite

pp. 296–307

Genre: Functional Writing/ Scrapbook

More About the Big Question, p. T298

How could you share what you experienced at a national park with others?

Key Words: cascade, meadow, peak, ascend, forest, valley
Academic Words: comment, correspond
Other Academic Words: mountain, obtain

Word Analysis: Latin Word Roots, p. 302
Fluency: Read for Speed and Accuracy, p. 303

Reading Strategy: Review and Retell, pp. 298, 301
Learning Strategy: Retelling, p. 304
Comprehension Skill: Review and Retell, p. 304
Graphic Organizer: Main Idea and Details Chart, p. 305

Grammar: Articles, p. 306
Writing: Write a Concluding Paragraph, Writing Checklist, Spelling Tip, p. 307

Differentiated Instruction
pp. T297, T299, T307

Suggested Pacing: 1–2 Days

Bonus Reading

Jay Writes a Research Paper

pp. 308–313

Genre: Functional Writing/ E-mail

More About the Big Question, p. T308

Why do we need to know how to write a research paper?

Vocabulary: topic, bibliography

Differentiated Instruction
p. T309, T311, T313

Further Reading

Famous Sports, Cameron Fox
This Penguin Young Reader® is a collection of great stories, facts, and quizzes about American football, basketball, athletics, and more.

John Muir, America's Naturalist, Thomas Locker
Muir's study of nature in Yosemite National Park is highlighted in this biography of the famed naturalist.

Two Bear Cubs: A Miwok Legend from California's Yosemite Valley, Robert D. San Souci
In this story, based on a Miwok Native American legend, two grizzly bear cubs are stuck on the top of El Capitan rock. Their mother seeks the help of other members of the animal kingdom to rescue her cubs.

Suggested Pacing: 1–2 Days

Assessment

The Big Question

Evidence of Understanding

Why are national parks important?

Check Up pp. 273, 285, 299
Think It Over pp. 275, 287, 301
Activity To Do! p. 289
Extension pp. 279, 293, 305

Unit Wrap Up pp. 314–315

Written
Poem; Brochure; Newspaper Article

Oral
Conversation; Debate; Script

Visual/Active
Poster; Bumper Sticker; Blueprint

Learning Checklist
Word Analysis and Phonics; Comprehension; Grammar and Writing; Self-Evaluation Questions

STEP 1: Introduce

In this unit, students will learn about national parks. Have students work in groups to brainstorm about things they have done or would like to do outdoors. Ask each group to share their ideas with the class.

Unit Content Students practice reading and comprehension skills, such as making connections, drawing conclusions, and summarizing. They apply academic learning strategies, such as note-taking, reviewing, and retelling.

Visual Literacy

Photographs and Illustrations Read aloud the introductory text on p. 264 as students study the large photograph on pp. 264–265. Then have students look at the insets on p. 264 and read aloud the selection titles.

STEP 2: Build Background

The Big Question

Explain to students that they will be reading about our national parks and why they are important.

SAY *The Big Question is* Why are national parks important? *Think about national parks you have visited or seen in pictures.*

- *Is there something in nature you especially love, like mountains, rivers, or flowers?*
- *How might creating national parks help keep these things for everyone to enjoy?*
- *What rules should you follow when visiting a park?*

Have students fill in a Word Web like the one shown below about a national park or another place in nature that they visited. In each of the outer circles ask students to write a description of the important features they saw.

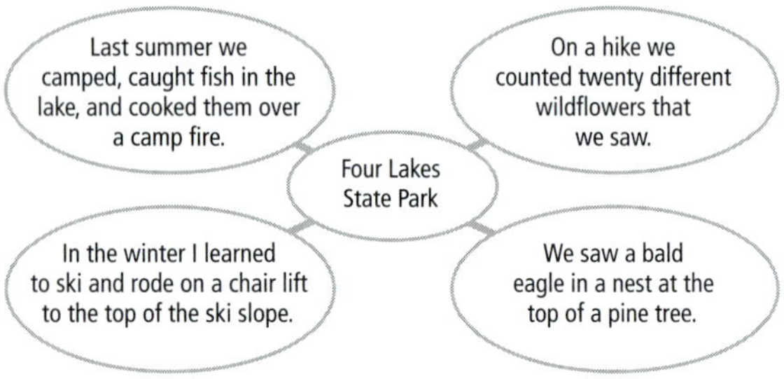

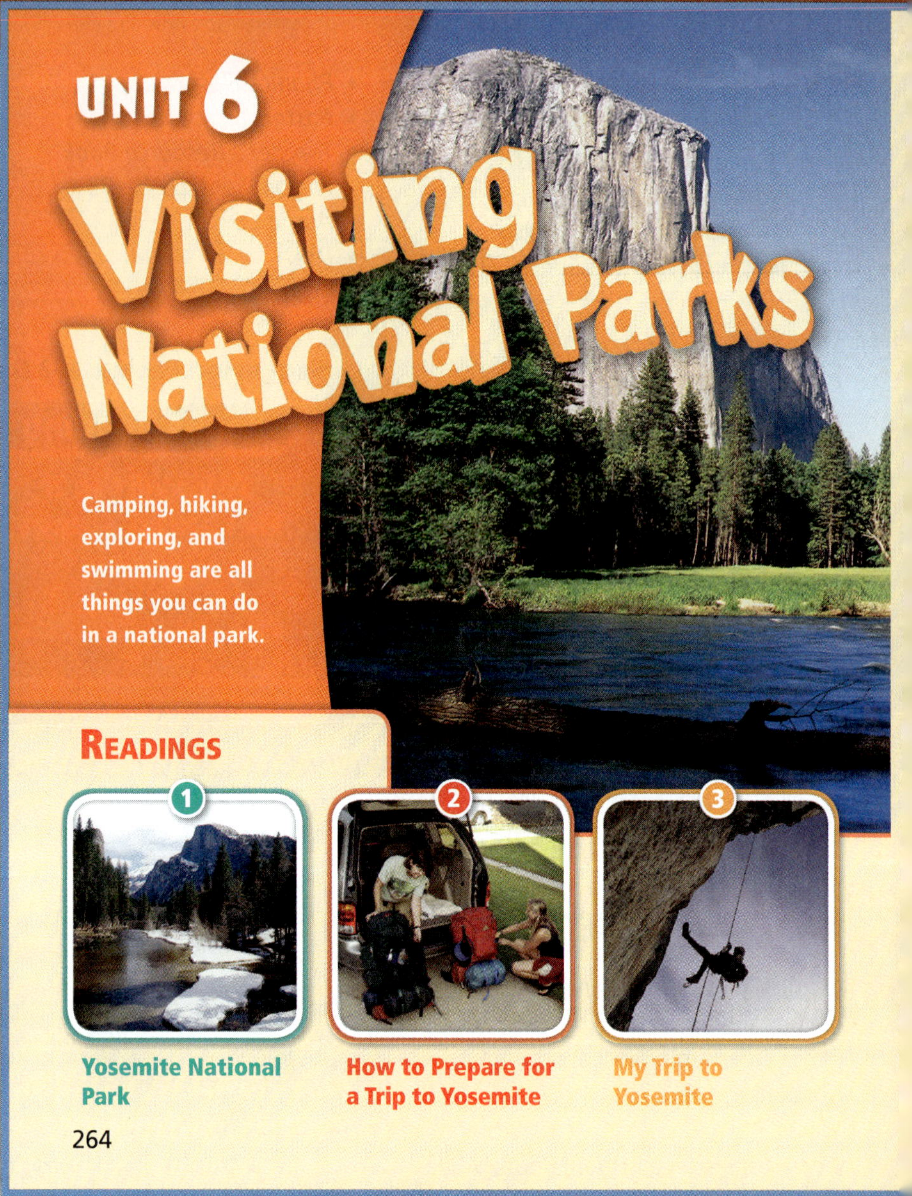

UNIT 6
Visiting National Parks

Camping, hiking, exploring, and swimming are all things you can do in a national park.

READINGS

1 Yosemite National Park

2 How to Prepare for a Trip to Yosemite

3 My Trip to Yosemite

264

TESOL Standards

Goal 1, Standard 2—To use English to communicate in social settings: Students will interact in, through, and with spoken and written English for personal expression and enjoyment.
Descriptors—Sharing social and cultural traditions and values; Expressing personal needs, feelings, and ideas.

The Big Question

Why are national parks important?

Listening and Speaking

You will talk about a place that you have visited or would like to visit.

Writing

You will write a research paper about a place you have visited or would like to visit.

Bonus Reading

Jay Writes a Research Paper

Quick Write

Write about an interesting place you have seen. Share what you wrote with a partner.

Visit *LongmanCornerstone.com* 265

Differentiated Instruction	
Beginning	Lead students in reading aloud the titles for each of the readings. Ask them to spell aloud the word that appears in all three titles. Guide them to correctly pronounce *Yosemite*.
Intermediate	Have students use words and phrases to describe what they see in each of the photographs on pp. 264–265.
Greater Challenge	Help students make inferences about the content of the readings from their titles and the photographs. Have them predict what kinds of things they might learn in each of the readings.
Struggling Reader	Point to the large photo on pp. 264–265. Have students name some of the things they see in the photo. Write their responses on the board, and have all students read them aloud.

STEP 3: Connect

Listening and Speaking

Read the text in the box aloud. Ask students if they have ever visited a national or state park. Ask what kinds of activities they did, or would like to do in the park. Prompt them to think of specific words for these activities. List the words they come up with on the board and lead students in pronouncing them aloud.

Writing

Read the text in the Writing box aloud to students.

SAY *There are many ways to experience the outdoors with fun activities in every season.*

- *Is there some place you would like to visit?*
- *What are some of the activities you can do in a national park?*
- *What kind of information would you like to have before your visit?*

Help students start brainstorming topics for their research papers by displaying pictures of national parks or other places students would like to visit. Explain that any questions the students ask about the pictures can be potential topics for their papers. Keep a list of the suggested topics for future reference.

Quick Write

Have students recall an interesting place they have visited, either in the United States or their home countries. Ask them to write several sentences about what they saw and why it interested them.

Visual Literacy

Graphic Organizer Introduce the Big Question transparency and use it throughout the unit to help students connect the readings to the Big Question.

STEP 1: Introduce

Unit Vocabulary

Use these pages to help students identify some terms that are related to national parks. Post your Words to Know poster for this unit in the classroom. As students read the unit, reinforce the unit vocabulary by using the Blackline Master Vocabulary Cards as flashcards or in memory games.

STEP 2: Teach

Words to Know

Say each of the terms aloud and encourage students to repeat the terms with you. Have students point to the correct picture as they say each term.

Direct students' attention to the question on p. 266. Have them complete the sentence stem using the words provided. Repeat this procedure with the question and sentence stem on p. 267.

Academic Words

Discuss the definitions for *locate* and *achieve* with students. Share the following context sentences with students. Have students add the terms to their personal thesaurus.

locate find the position of something

achieve accomplish with effort

You must *locate* the trail before hiking into the wilderness.

It takes hard work to *achieve* your goals.

Explain to students that the two vocabulary words are verbs, and both can be changed to nouns by adding a suffix. Have students determine what nouns can be formed from these words and write context sentences for those nouns.

What Do You Know about Visiting a National Park?

Words to Know

1. Use these words to talk about national parks.

 tent
 picnic table
 trail map
 pond
 mountain
 rowboat

2. What can you do in a national park?

I can go __________ at a national park.

 camping
 picnicking
 hiking
 climbing
 swimming
 boating

266

TESOL Standards

Goal 1, Standard 3—To use English to communicate in social settings: Students will use learning strategies to extend their communicative competence.
Descriptors—Testing hypotheses about language; Listening to and imitating how others use English; Exploring alternative ways of saying things; Using context to construct meaning.

Teaching Resources

- ***Teacher's Resource Book,*** pp. 99–100; 172
- ***Posters***
- ***Transparencies,*** pp. 31–36
- ***CD-ROM*** • ***Audio CD***

3. What do you need at a national park?

You need a ____________ *for* ____________ .

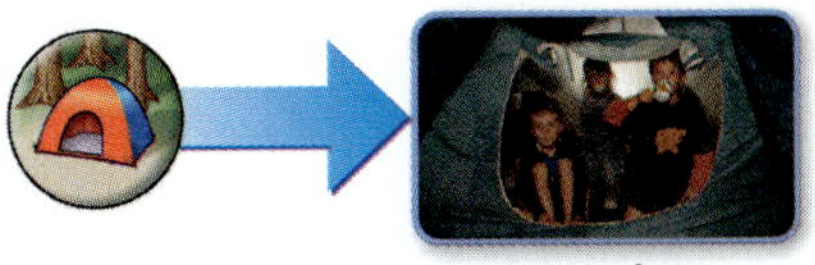

camping

hiking

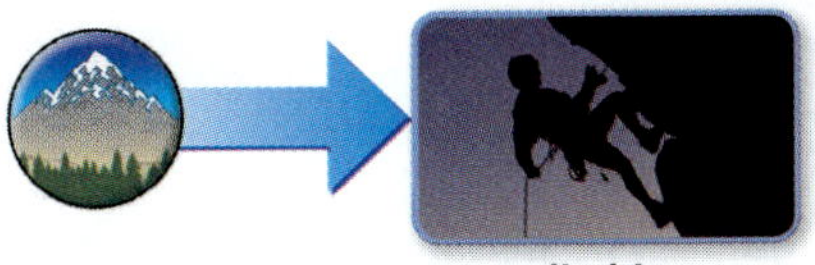

climbing

swimming *and* boating

4. Use these words to talk about other things in national parks.

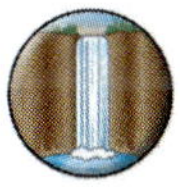

waterfall

tourists

wildflowers

267

Differentiated Instruction

Beginning	Read aloud the picture labels in random order. Have students find the word and picture, then say the word aloud. Then have students choose an action word and act it out.
Early Intermediate	Have students work with partners to select one photo on p. 267 and describe to the class what is happening.
Intermediate	Have students write a paragraph about visiting a national park using each of the Words to Know terms.
Standard English Learner CRI	Have students make a list of descriptive words for the things they see in the photos on p. 267 and add the list to their personal thesaurus.

Vocabulary Definitions

Read aloud the words for activities in section 3 and have students repeat them as they identify the pictures. Go over the definitions for each term.

camping living outdoors in tents

hiking walking great distances outdoors

climbing to go up a hill or steep incline, using your hands, feet, and sometimes, rope

swimming moving across water by stroking and kicking

boating traveling on water in a floating vehicle

Have students write their own context sentences using each of the words for an outdoor activity.

STEP 3: Practice

Use Vocabulary

Build Discussion Have students reread the unit Big Question: *Why are national parks important?* Encourage students to use ideas and vocabulary from pp. 266–267 to write a response. Students can also use ideas from things they may have read about or seen in news programs as the basis for their responses. Set aside time for students to share their answers to the Big Question with the class.

Adapt the Activity

Drawing Have students review the pictures on pp. 266–267. Ask students to draw and label a picture of a fun thing to do in a national park, or something parks help protect. Organize a bulletin board into two sections. Label them *Fun Things to Do* and *Natural Things to Protect*. Use the display to reinforce what students learned about national parks.

STEP 1: Introduce

Unit Background

The peer mini-autobiographies and accompanying exercises are designed to increase comprehension. Use the exercises below to elicit student prior knowledge, opinions, and impressions to help them share their own experiences in national parks.

STEP 2: Monitor Progress

Comprehension Check

Victor

1. Where does Victor live? Nuuk, Greenland
2. What does he say is special about the Northeast Greenland National Park? It is the largest in the world.
3. What else does he say is special about Greenland? It is the world's largest island.
4. What animals would you see in Victor's park? You would see musk ox, polar bears, and walruses.

Amaia

1. Where does Amaia live? Quito, Ecuador
2. What did the government set aside more than a million acres for? Galapagos National Park
3. Why do people visit this national park? They want to see the plants and animals you can't see anywhere else in the world.
4. What does Amaia say that you can only see in this park and nowhere else? frigates and giant tortoises

Link to Social Studies

Map Skills Draw students' attention to the map of the world in the background of these pages. Have students follow the lines from the photo of each student's home to its location on the map. Encourage students to use other world maps or globes to find the same locations.

Teaching Resources

- *Audio CD*

Your Stories about Visiting National Parks

Victor

I live in Nuuk, Greenland. Did you know that Greenland is the world's largest island? My country is also home to the Northeast Greenland National Park, the largest national park in the world. The park covers an area of 370,000 square miles. Musk ox, polar bears, and walruses live there.

Amaia

I live in Quito, Ecuador. My government set aside more than a million acres for the Galapagos National Park in 1959. People visit the Galapagos Islands to see birds and animals you can't find anywhere else in the world, such as frigates and giant tortoises.

268

TESOL Standards

Goal 1, Standard 2—To use English to communicate in social settings: Students will interact in, through, and with spoken and written English for personal expression and enjoyment.
Descriptors—Sharing social and cultural traditions and values; Expressing personal needs, feelings, and ideas.

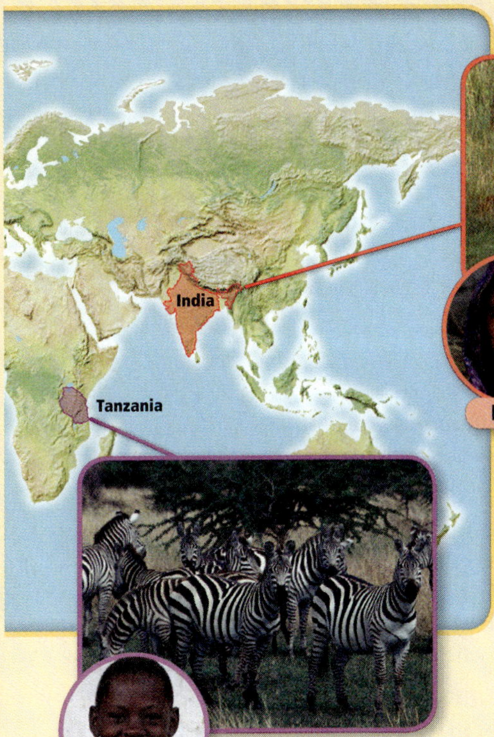

I live in India near the Jim Corbett National Park. The park was created more than 70 years ago. The wildlife there includes tigers, elephants, chital, sambar, king cobras, Indian wild boars, hedgehogs, flying foxes, and nearly 600 species of birds. The park helps keep these animals safe from hunters.

I live in Tanzania. The Serengeti National Park has one of the most diverse plant and animal collections in the world. These zebras are some of the many migratory animals that make their homes in the Serengeti. People come to study the plants and animals here.

What about you?

1. Which of these national parks would you like to visit? Why?
2. How are these students' stories similar to yours?
3. Have you visited a national park? Tell your story!

Sharing Language and Culture

Global Perspective While the Galapagos Islands are a part of Ecuador's national park system, they are also home to a worldwide legacy. When Charles Darwin visited in 1835, he discovered many new species of animals that were unique to the Galapagos. Discuss with students how the islands' isolation—they are about 600 miles from land—contributed to the uniqueness of their wild life. Encourage them to see the importance of preserving such a world treasure. Ask those of your students who were born or have lived outside the United States to share their memories of natural wonders they may have seen that cannot be found anywhere else.

Jojo

1. What country does Jojo come from? Tanzania
2. What park does he tell about? the Serengeti National Park
3. What is unique about this national park? It has a diverse plant and animal collection.
4. The zebras in the photo are part of what sort of animal group? migratory animals

Pooja

1. Where does Pooja live? India
2. Which national park does she live near? the Jim Corbett National Park
3. How many types of animals does Pooja say the park contains? She mentions eight kinds of animals and 600 kinds of birds.
4. What does the park do for all these animals? The park keeps them safe from hunters.

Study Skills

Internet Have student pairs use the Internet to locate a map of one of the places noted on the world map—Greenland, Ecuador, Tanzania, or India. Have students study the map and record three pieces of information about the place, such as its capital or important regions, bodies of water, or landforms. Have students share their results in small groups.

STEP 3: Assess

What about you?

1. Students can share their reasons for wanting to visit the park of their choice. Encourage them to cite specific reasons for their choices.
2. Have students compare their own stories to the stories of the students on these pages. Guide them to recognize ways that most parks preserve nature, but how some offer more activities than others.
3. **Personal Story** Have students write a story about a national park they know about—or maybe even have visited themselves—using the peer stories on pp. 268–269 as a model. Students can choose another scenic area if they cannot think of a national park. Have students present their stories in small groups or to the class.

STEP 1: Introduce

Key Words

Help students learn the skill of defining words by using context.

SAY *All the key words from Yosemite National Park are defined in the Words in Context sentences. Each sentence has context clues that will help you figure out the meaning of a key word. Look at the word* tributaries *in the first paragraph.*

- *What words in the paragraph help you understand the meaning of the word?*
- *How would you use these words to write your own definition of* tributaries*?*

Point to the key words at random, having students say and spell the word aloud.

STEP 2: Teach

Words in Context

Have students complete this fill-in-the-blanks exercise using the key words.

1. *The* tributaries *leading to the river help provide water for the farmlands.*
2. *I want to hike in all the* national parks *in the United States.*
3. *On the* cliffs*, we could see the entire valley.*
4. *The* sequoias *are more than 100 years old.*
5. *We camped in a* grove *of pine trees.*

Ask students to work in groups to write additional context sentences for each key word.

Study Skills

Dictionary Have students look up the key words in the dictionary to see if their Words in Context definitions are correct.

Online Dictionary Students can use an online dictionary or the CD that accompanies a learner's dictionary, like the *Longman Basic Dictionary*.

www.LongmanCornerstone.com

Teaching Resources

- *Practice Book*, pp. 133–134
- *Transparencies*, p. 52
- *CD-ROM* • *Audio CD*

Reading 1

Yosemite
National Park

Vocabulary

Yosemite National Park **describes one of the most popular national parks in the United States.**

Key Words

- **tributaries**
- **national parks**
- **cliffs**
- **sequoias**
- **grove**

Words in Context

1 A smaller river that joins a bigger river is called a tributary. The Missouri River has more than 50 **tributaries**. The Missouri River is a tributary of the Mississippi River.

2 Yellowstone National Park is one of many **national parks** around the world. Is there a national park near where you live?

3 It is exciting to walk along **cliffs**. But, be careful not to walk too close to the edge.

TESOL Standards

Goal 1, Standard 3—To use English to communicate in social settings: Students will use learning strategies to extend their communicative competence.
Descriptors—Testing hypotheses about language; Listening to and imitating how others use English; Exploring alternative ways of saying things; Using context to construct meaning.

Goal 2, Standard 2—To use English to achieve academically in all content areas: Students will use English to obtain, process, construct, and provide subject matter information in spoken and written form.
Descriptor—Understanding and producing technical vocabulary and text features according to content area.

4 **Sequoias** are some of the biggest trees in the world.

5 This **grove** of birch trees is in Acadia National Park in Maine.

Practice

Use each key word in a sentence.

Make Connections

What national parks are in your state? If you could visit any national park, which park would you choose? Why?

Academic Words

area
place, geographical region

region
location, large geographic area

Practice Book pages 133–134

Differentiated Instruction

Beginning	Have students draw and label their own pictures of one of the key words. Display the pictures in class and have students use them as a review tool.
Intermediate	Have students complete the following sentences: *When smaller rivers join larger ones, they are called ________. When the land drops away sharply, it is called a ________. A group of trees is called a ________.*
Greater Challenge	Have students select three of the key words and write a descriptive sentence for each of them. Direct students to include at least one fact in each sentence.
Struggling Reader	Lead students in pronouncing each of the key words aloud. Reinforce the words by pointing to the word in each context sentence and reading aloud a short phrase of the sentence that includes the key word.

Visual Literacy

Photographs Discuss with students how each photograph gives more information about a topic or idea. Guide students to recognize that photographs give information that is not included in the text, thus they are critical to reading and comprehension.

Academic Words

Discuss the definitions of *area* and *region* with students. Share the following context sentences with students:

The total *area* of the park is more than one hundred square miles.

In the United States, the *region* of the southwest is primarily desert.

Have students compare and contrast how the two vocabulary words are alike and different. Ask students to determine if the two words could be synonyms.

Other Academic Words

Provide students with another word that can be used in the discussion of national parks. Tell students that a *site* is the location of something or the place of an event or occurrence.

We picked the *site* next to the river to set up our tents.

The beach at sunset is a romantic *site* for a wedding.

STEP 3: Practice

Flexible Grouping You may assign these exercises as a class discussion, partner activity, or individual writing assignment.

Make Connections

Writing Fluency Tie the discussion to the Big Question by guiding students to recognize that national parks preserve beautiful parts of the country and give people a place to encounter nature. Have students write a paragraph that describes a geographical feature, plant, or animal found in a national park and how to preserve it.

STEP 1: Introduce

More About The Big Question

The Big Question is designed to help students understand why it is important to set aside land for national parks.

SAY *We are going to read about Yosemite National Park.*

- *Why do you think it is important to have national parks?*
- *How do national parks help improve the environment?*

Ask students to imagine they work in a national park. Have students fill in a Sequence of Events Chart that describes a day at work.

All the park guides meet at the lodge to start the day.
↓
Today, we led a group of first graders through the reptile exhibit.
↓
A few kids were afraid of the snakes, but we told them they were not in danger.
↓
We explained how to identify snakes by the markings on their skin.

STEP 2: Teach

Reading Strategy

Make Connections Read the bulleted items in the side column on p. 272. Encourage students to ask similar questions of themselves as they read the article to help them make connections.

Understand Text Structure

Draw students' attention to the genre label. Tell students this newspaper article might appear in the features section of a newspaper.

Teaching Resources

- ***Teacher's Resource Book***, pp. 143–144
- ***Practice Book***, pp. 135–136
- ***CD-ROM*** • ***Audio CD***

Reading 1

FUNCTIONAL WRITING

Newspaper Article

The Big Question

Why is it important to set aside land for national parks?

Reading Strategy

Make Connections

Think about your own life as you read.

- Have you visited places similar to Yosemite National Park?
- What plants and animals look familiar to you?
- Have you ever done any of the activities described in the article?

Yosemite National Park

by Vivian Ortiz

Whether climbing, camping, or hiking, Yosemite has something for everyone.

The Yosemite region of California takes up almost 1,200 square miles. It is known for its **mighty** waterfalls, deep valleys, and huge meadows. People have lived in the Yosemite region for 8,000 years. In the 1830s, people from other places visited. Some people built hotels and houses there. Environmentalists worried about this. They feared the land would be **ruined**.

mighty very big and amazing

ruined be spoiled or completely destroyed

The Merced River is a great place to visit any time of the year.

TESOL Standards

Goal 2, Standard 1—To use English to achieve academically in all content areas: Students will use English to interact in the classroom.
Descriptors—Participating in full-class, group, and pair discussions; Asking and answering questions.

Goal 2, Standard 2—To use English to achieve academically in all content areas: Students will use English to obtain, process, construct, and provide subject matter information in spoken and written form.
Descriptors—Retelling information; Selecting, connecting, and explaining information; Listening to, speaking, reading, and writing about subject matter information; Demonstrating knowledge through application in a variety of contexts.

Giant sequoias grow in Yosemite's Mariposa Grove.

The U.S. government stepped in to help. In 1890, the area became known as Yosemite National Park. Rules make sure the land is preserved for people to enjoy now and in the future. More than three million people visit the park each year.

Yosemite Valley is a popular destination for visitors. It has cliffs and rock forms. Many guests spend time gazing at its waterfalls. Yosemite Valley is open all year. People often travel to the valley by car.

Yosemite National Park is also famous for its trees. Giant sequoias seem to reach the sky. The biggest group of giant sequoias is found in Mariposa Grove. Between November and March, the road to Mariposa Grove is closed to cars because of snow. Can you think of other ways to reach the grove? You can hike or ski!

destination place someone is going to

gazing looking at something for a long time

Rafting is a fun thing to do on the Merced River.

Check Up What can people do at a national park?

273

Differentiated Instruction	
Beginning	Have students work in pairs to use gestures and pantomime to act out things they might do at Yosemite National Park.
Early Intermediate	Have students rewrite the three captions on pp. 272–273. Encourage students to use descriptive words, phrases, or complete sentences.
Intermediate	Have students work in pairs to make a list of facts about Yosemite National Park that they can find on pp. 272–273.
Standard English Learner CRI	Have students work in pairs to discuss the various things they see in the photos on pp. 272–273. Ask volunteers to describe one activity they would do at the park.

Build Vocabulary

Direct attention to the highlighted words in the text that are defined at the bottom of the page.

- Invite a volunteer to read the words and their definitions aloud.
- Read the sentence with that highlighted word aloud to the class.
- Then read the sentence again, replacing the term with a synonym from the definition. Example: *It is known for its very big and amazing waterfalls.*

Link to Math

Direct attention to the number 1,200 in the second line on p. 272. Tell students that there are two ways to read the number—*twelve hundred* and *one thousand two hundred*. Write these numbers on the board and have students say each number two different ways: 1,400, 2,600, 7,300.

Months of the Year

Have students find and read aloud the months noted on p. 273 (*November*, *March*). Then have volunteers say the months of the year, beginning with January and ending in December. Write each month on the board as students say them aloud. Then review the list with students, guiding them to carefully pronounce each month. To reinforce the months, you may want to have students talk about different things they do or special days they celebrate in each month.

Read Aloud

Have students read pp. 272–273. Students should take turns reading the paragraphs on the page. At the end of each paragraph, have students identify the connections they make between the text and their own experiences.

STEP 3: Assess

Check Up

Have students discuss their responses to the question in small groups or with partners. Encourage them to use the photographs on these pages to help them respond.

STEP 1: Monitor Progress

Comprehension Check

Make Connections After reading, discuss with students any connections they made to the reading.

SAY *I think many of you were able to make connections to what you read about.*

- *Have you ever been to the mountains? What did you do there?*
- *Have you stood near a waterfall? How did it feel?*

Applications Explain to students that visitors to national parks often rent equipment for hang gliding or skiing. Give copies of an actual application or copy the one below. Have students practice filling it out.

Rental Application

Date____________

Name__________________________Birthdate __________
Address____
____
____
Phone______________
e-mail____________________

Credit Card___________________ Exp.___________

Type of Equipment_______________________________
Rental Date/Time_________________________________
Return Date/Time_________________________________

_____I certify that I am at least 18 years of age.

I agree to pay to repair or replace damaged, lost, or stolen equipment.

Signature_____________________

Parent or guardian signature (if minor)_______________

Link to Math

Fun Facts About Yosemite The elevation in Yosemite Valley is 4,000 ft. The highest mountain peak in the park is 13,000 ft. At the top of Half Dome, the elevation is 8,842 ft. There is a hiking trail to the top of Half Dome. If you are a strong hiker, you will walk 16 miles round trip for 10–12 hours and climb 4,800 feet in elevation. That means when you reach the top of Half Dome, you can look straight down more than one mile to the valley floor.

Another great place to visit is Yosemite's Glacier Point. It is a high place where visitors can see many of the park's great features. You can see Yosemite Valley. You can see mountains too. Many people go hang gliding there. In winter, you'll need skis or snowshoes to reach it.

Have you ever tried to climb a climbing wall? In Yosemite National Park, people climb real rocks! El Capitan is a 3000-foot high (1000m) vertical rock formation. You can hike to the top of El Capitan on one of the trails in the park. Many people try to climb the face of the cliff itself. Climbing El Capitan is very dangerous. Only experienced rock climbers should try it. It is very difficult for park rangers to rescue climbers who get tired or hurt.

vertical pointing straight up and down

There are easier ways to get to the top of El Capitan!

Hang gliding is popular at Glacier Point.

TESOL Standards

Goal 2, Standard 1—To use English to achieve academically in all content areas: Students will use English to interact in the classroom.
Descriptors—Participating in full-class, group, and pair discussions; Asking and answering questions.

Goal 2, Standard 2—To use English to achieve academically in all content areas: Students will use English to obtain, process, construct, and provide subject matter information in spoken and written form.
Descriptors—Retelling information; Selecting, connecting, and explaining information; Listening to, speaking, reading, and writing about subject matter information; Demonstrating knowledge through application in a variety of contexts.

Yosemite Falls is the seventh highest waterfall in the world.

Yosemite Falls are among the most spectacular waterfalls in the country. The falls are the seventh-highest in the world. The tributaries that form the falls lead to the Merced River. The best time to visit Yosemite Falls is in early spring, when the melting snow really makes the water roar.

The Hetch Hetchy Valley has a funny name, and it's really a fun place! Like Yosemite Valley, it has great views. The Hetch Hetchy Reservoir supplies drinking water to people in San Francisco.

Yosemite National Park is a great vacation place. With all of its great features, there is something for everyone to enjoy.

The natural beauty of Yosemite National Park brings more than three million visitors each year.

spectacular very impressive and exciting

reservoir where water is stored before it is sent to peoples' homes

Practice Book pages 135–136

Reading Strategy

Make Connections

- Have you visited a national park?
- Which activities in the article have you done? Which activities would you like to do?

Think It Over

1. Where is the biggest group of sequoia trees in Yosemite National Park?
2. Which reservoir supplies drinking water to people in San Francisco?
3. How does El Capitan compare to a climbing wall?
4. Why is it difficult to rescue climbers on El Capitan?

275

Differentiated Instruction

Beginning	Have students fill in the blanks: *The El Capitan rock formation is ________ high. The ________ is the best time to visit Yosemite Falls. If you are injured, a ________ will help you.*
Intermediate	Have students select one of the activities shown on pp. 274–275 and research what equipment they would need for the activity.
Greater Challenge	Have students make predictions about what else you might be able to do in Yosemite that was not mentioned in the text or shown in the pictures.
Struggling Reader	Have students locate and read aloud the words in the text that answer these questions: *What activities can you do in parks? What are the large trees that grow there called?*

STEP 2: Teach

Visual Literacy

Photographs Draw students' attention to the photographs on pp. 274–275. Ask volunteers to read aloud the captions.

SAY *Each of the photographs on these pages give the reader information about the importance of setting aside land for national parks.*

- *What can you learn about national parks from the photographs and captions on page 274?*
- *What do the photos and captions on page 275 say about why national parks are important?*

STEP 3: Assess

Reading Strategy

Make Connections Give students an example of how to make connections.

SAY *When readers make connections, they think about what a reading reminds them of. This helps them to better understand what they are reading about or seeing in a photo.*

- *What did you read about in this selection that reminded you of a place you have visited or learned about?*
- *Would you prefer to go rock climbing or hang gliding? Why?*
- *What plants or animals did you learn about from reading this selection?*

Think It Over

Flexible Grouping You may assign this activity as a class discussion, partner activity, or individual writing assignment.

Answer Key

1. The biggest group of sequoias is in Mariposa Grove.
2. The Hetch Hetchy Reservoir supplies San Francisco with drinking water.
3. El Capitan is a vertical rock formation that is far larger and more dangerous than a climbing wall.
4. Rescue is probably hard because the wall is 3,000 feet high and vertical.

STEP 1: Introduce

Phonics and Fluency

Words with *v* and *w* Write the letters *w* and *v* on the board. Explain that while they may look similar, they have very different sounds.

STEP 2: Teach

Read the words in the box aloud as students follow along in their books. Have students repeat each word after you. Then draw students' attention to the Rule Box.

SAY *For words that begin with the letter* v, *narrow your lips, and put your teeth against your lower lip. For words that begin with a* w, *open your lips slightly.*

Reread the list of words from the Student Book. Tell students to raise their right hand if they hear a word with the /v/ sound or their left hand if they hear the sound of a *w*.

was	*waterfall*
vase	*were*
word	*visit*
verb	*valley*

STEP 3: Practice

1. Have students work with partners. Make sure they take turns and that they follow all steps.
2. Encourage students who have finished to write one sentence with as many *w* and *v* words as they can fit.

Reteach

Have students look through another book or magazines to find and list words that begin with the letters *v* or *w*. Have students share their words with the class.

Teaching Resources
- *Practice Book*, p. 137
- *Phonics Workbook*
- *Phonics Flashcards*
- *CD-ROM* • *Audio CD*

Reading 1

Phonics & Fluency

Phonics

Words with *v* and *w*

Read these words aloud. Pay attention to how your lips move.

vase	verb	was	word

Rule Box

- For words that begin with the letter *v*, narrow your lips, and put your teeth against your lower lip.
- For words that begin with a *w*, open your lips slightly.

Practice

Work with a partner. Read the words aloud.

waterfall	were	visit	valley

1. Write three sentences using words with the *v* sound.
2. Write three sentences using words with the *w* sound.
3. Read your sentences aloud to your partner.

Practice Book page 137

276

TESOL Standards

Goal 2, Standard 3—To use English to achieve academically in all content areas: Students will use appropriate learning strategies to construct and apply academic knowledge.
Descriptors—Applying basic reading comprehension skills such as skimming, scanning, previewing, and reviewing text; Using context to construct meaning; Applying self-monitoring and self-corrective strategies to build and expand a knowledge base.

Goal 3, Standard 3—To use English in socially and culturally appropriate ways: Students will use appropriate learning strategies to extend their sociolinguistic and sociocultural competence.
Descriptors—Observing and modeling how others speak and behave in a particular situation or setting; Experimenting with variations of language in social and academic settings; Seeking information about appropriate language use and behavior; Analyzing the social content to determine appropriate language use; Rehearsing variations of language use in different social and academic settings.

Fluency

Look Ahead

Sometimes readers look for hard words before they read. They then try to figure them out.

Practice

Pick one passage. → Find any hard words. → Practice saying those words. → Read the passage aloud.

1 Yosemite National Park was created to help protect the land from damage by builders and tourists. Today there are many beautiful places to visit and many fun things to do in the park.

2 People have lived in the Yosemite region for 8,000 years. In the 1830s, people from other places visited. Some people built hotels and houses there. Environmentalists worried about this. They feared the land would be ruined.

3 Yosemite Valley is a popular destination for visitors. It has cliffs and rock forms. Many guests spend time gazing at its waterfalls. Yosemite Valley is open all year. People often travel to the valley by car.

Yosemite is also famous for its trees. Giant sequoias seem to reach the sky. The biggest group of giant sequoias is found in Mariposa Grove. Between November and March, and sometimes April, the road to Mariposa Grove is closed to cars because of snow.

Linguistic Note

Words with *v, w* In this lesson, students learn how to make the *v* and *w* sounds. Some languages deal very differently with both these sounds. Speakers with backgrounds in Germanic languages will pronounce *w* as *v* and v as *f*. Russian speakers will tend to pronounce an initial consonant *v* as *w*. Most Chinese dialects do not have the *v* sound. Speakers of these dialects will often substitute *w* or *f* for the *v* sound.

STEP 1: Introduce

Fluency

Look Ahead Explain to students that looking for hard words before they read can help them read more smoothly.

Play the Audio CD for this reading to the class, asking students to listen for pacing, intonation, and expression.

STEP 2: Practice

Have students do the following exercise with partners. You may want to assign each student a passage based on difficulty level (1–easy, 2–intermediate, 3–more difficult) or let students select their own passages.

- Have one partner look through his or her paragraph to find any hard words and practice saying those words.
- Then have that student read the passage to his or her partner.
- Have the students change roles.

Have each student write down the words his or her partner had difficulty saying, and repeat the activity if necessary.

Possible Responses–Hard Words

created	damage	tourists
region	hotels	environmentalists
popular	destination	gazing
famous	Mariposa	April

STEP 3: Extend

Study Skills

Internet Have students use the Internet to learn the pronunciation of words they found difficult. Some online dictionaries offer pronunciation keys. Others say the word for you. To complete this activity, have students work with partners to:

- write down three words that were hard to pronounce from these passages;
- look up the words on the Internet;
- say the word at least three times.

Remind students that they can use this study skill at home whenever they need help reading a word.

STEP 1: Monitor Progress

Learning Strategy

Notetaking Taking notes is a good way for students to remember the most important information in a reading. Have students take notes on the selection and share their notes with partners. Then have students discuss their answers to Big Question. Tell them to think of specific reasons why national parks are important.

STEP 2: Teach

Connect Text to Self

Students will learn to use their own experiences to better understand what they read. Prompt students to recognize when they are making a connection between the reading and their own lives.

SAY *Noticing when you have had experiences similar to what is being described in a text can help you to understand and enjoy your reading.*

- *How might having seen a river help you understand what the Merced River is like?*
- *What other experiences helped you imagine features of Yosemite National Park?*
- *When you are in a forest with trees towering over you, what are you thinking about?*

STEP 3: Practice

Flexible Grouping You may assign this activity as a class discussion, partner activity, or individual written assignment.

Before students begin the Practice activity, have them call out suggestions for words that describe feelings. Write the words on the board and tell them to select words from the list when they write their answers.

Teaching Resources

- ***Practice Book***, p. 138
- ***Transparencies***, p. 61
- ***Teachers Resource Book***, p. 159
- ***CD-ROM***

Reading 1

Comprehension

Learning Strategy

Notetaking

Take notes on the features of Yosemite National Park. Share your notes with a partner.

Ask your partner to respond to the Big Question for this reading.

Connect Text to Self

You can use your experience to help you understand what you read. **Experience** is something that you have done, seen, or taken part in.

As you read, ask yourself these questions:

- How are the people, places, and ideas familiar to you?
- In what ways are they different from your experience?
- How are the feelings described in the selection similar to feelings you have had?

Practice

Think about your last visit to a new place.

- Reread the last paragraph on page 274 and look at the small photo. Think about the feelings created in that paragraph.
- Write about a time when you felt those feelings.

Practice Book page 138

278

TESOL Standards

Goal 1, Standard 1—To use English to communicate in social settings: Students will use English to participate in social interactions.
Descriptors—Sharing and requesting information; Expressing needs, feelings, and ideas.

Goal 2, Standard 1—To use English to achieve academically in all content areas: Students will use English to interact in the classroom.
Descriptors—Participating in full-class, group, and pair discussions; Asking and answering questions.

Goal 2, Standard 2—To use English to achieve academically in all content areas: Students will use English to obtain, process, construct, and provide subject matter information in spoken and written form.
Descriptor—Representing information visually and interpreting information presented visually.

Use a 5W Chart

You can use a 5W Chart to help you ask questions about what you read. If you can answer your 5W questions, you will have a good understanding of the selection.

Practice

Write a question about *Yosemite National Park* in each box. Then work with a partner to answer your questions.

Who?	Who likes to visit Yosemite National Park?
What?	
Where?	
When?	
Why?	

Extension

Choose a place you have visited or would like to visit. Create a 5W Chart with questions about that place. Try to find the answers to your questions. Then present your chart to the class.

279

Linguistic Note

Word Analysis Spanish speakers will probably notice that several of the questions in the 5W Chart feature the letter *q* in their native language, rather than *w*. *Who* becomes *quien*, *what* becomes *que*, and *why* becomes *porque*. Recognizing this similarity between languages may help them develop a mnemonic device to help remember the five questions.

Accelerate Language Development

Question Marks Guide students to recognize that in English, a question mark comes at the end of a question. In Spanish, an inverted question mark precedes a question, and a question mark right-side up is the end punctuation mark.

STEP 1: Teach

Use a 5W Chart

Explain to students that when a reporter writes a newspaper article, he or she often uses the 5W questions to make sure the article is complete. Ask students to think of some 5W questions the reporter might have asked in order to write the article. Have students discuss the facts they learned in the article to help them think of the 5W questions.

STEP 2: Practice

You may have students complete the graphic organizer provided as a Blackline Master in the *Teacher's Resource Book*.

Possible Responses

What is the name of the river in the park?

Where can you find the biggest group of giant sequoias?

When did the area become a national park?

Why is the early spring the best time to visit the park?

Link to Social Studies

Have students imagine they are park rangers at Yosemite National Park. Have students research one area of the park where they would like to lead a wilderness hike. Then have students write a script for the tour they would lead. Ask volunteers to present their scripts to the class.

STEP 3: Extend

Oral Presentation Ask students to present the 5W Chart they created to the class. Have them explain how they came up with their own versions of each question. Remind students to listen quietly while their classmates speak. Encourage them to ask questions after each presentation.

STEP 1: Introduce

Tell students that they are going to learn about four different kinds of sentences and the different punctuation they use at the end of each sentence.

STEP 2: Teach

Four Types of Sentences

Write the following sentences on the board. Read aloud each sentence. Then write the word that describes what type of sentence it is and explain the defining characteristic of each type of sentence.

1. These cookies are great! *exclamatory* (expresses strong feelings)
2. Where did Helen and Juan go? *interrogative* (asks a question)
3. Go to your room! *imperative* (gives a command)
4. Alexander does not like to dance. *declarative* (makes a statement)

STEP 3: Practice

Before students begin the Practice activity, have students work in pairs. Ask each pair to write one example of each type of sentence. Have them use their examples and what they learned about each type of sentence to guide them. Remind them that each type of sentence has specific end punctuation. When students have completed the exercise, have them complete the Practice activity on their own.

Answer Key

1. interrogative
2. declarative
3. exclamatory
4. imperative

Teaching Resources

- ***Practice Book,*** pp. 139–140
- ***Transparencies,*** pp. 69–80
- ***Assessments,*** p. 89–92
- ***CD-ROM***

Reading 1

Grammar & Writing

Four Types of Sentences

Writers use different types of sentences to add variety. Notice each sentence has a different type of end punctuation.

> Between November and March the road to Mariposa is closed to cars. Can you think of other ways to reach the grove? You can hike or ski!

There are four types of sentences.

- **Declarative** sentences state something.
- **Interrogative** sentences ask questions.
- **Exclamatory** sentences express strong feelings.
- **Imperative** sentences tell someone to do (or not do) something.

Practice

Tell whether each sentence is *declarative, interrogative, exclamatory,* or *imperative.* Then write your own example sentence for each type.

1. Have you ever tried to climb a climbing wall?
2. Yosemite National Park has cliffs and rock forms.
3. Some people climb that big cliff!
4. Get down from there!

Practice Book page 139

280

TESOL Standards

Goal 2, Standard 3—To use English to achieve academically in all content areas: Students will use appropriate learning strategies to construct and apply academic knowledge.
Descriptors—Using context to construct meaning; Actively connecting new information to information previously learned; Imitating the behaviors of native English speakers to complete tasks successfully.

Goal 3, Standard 1—To use English in socially and culturally appropriate ways: Students will use the appropriate language variety, register, and genre according to audience, purpose, and setting.
Descriptors—Using the appropriate degree of formality with different audiences and settings; Recognizing and using standard English and vernacular dialects appropriately; Using a variety of writing styles appropriate for different audiences, purposes, and settings; Responding to and using slang appropriately; Responding to and using idioms appropriately; Responding to and using humor appropriately; Determining when it is appropriate to use a language other than English; Determining appropriate topics for interaction.

Write a Business Letter

Read the letter Gretchen wrote asking for information about where she wants to go.

Gretchen Koppel
709 Hummingbird Lane
San Francisco, CA 94101

March 7, 2009

Great Smoky Mountains National Park
1420 Little River Road
Gatlinburg, TN 37738

Dear Sir or Madam:

Please send me some information about the Great Smoky Mountains National Park. I would like to know about hiking, camping, and horseback riding. Are there lakes for swimming and boating?

Thank you very much for your help.

Sincerely,
Gretchen Koppel

SPELLING TIP

Learning about prefixes and suffixes will help you be a better speller. For example, the prefix *re* means "again"; *dis* means "not." The suffix *ful* means "full of," and *ness* makes a noun out of an adjective.

Practice Book page 140

Practice

Think of a place you would like to visit. Make a list of questions. Then write a letter asking for information.

Writing Checklist

- ✓ Did you include the reader's address and a formal salutation?
- ✓ Were you specific about the information you want?
- ✓ Did you use a formal closing?
- ✓ Can a partner understand your letter?

281

Differentiated Instruction	
Beginning	Have students add the correct punctuation: *Where do you live; Watch out for the speeding car; My favorite subject is reading*
Early Intermediate	Review the four types of sentences with students. Have students find one example of each type of sentence on pp. 272–275.
Intermediate	Have students reread the chart that shows the four types of sentences. Ask students to write one sentence of each type based on information they learned in the reading.
Standard English Learner CRI	Read aloud various sentences from the reading on pp. 272–275. Have students say out loud the correct type of sentence after you read it.

STEP 1: Introduce

Write a Business Letter

Define a business letter for students. Stimulate class discussion and student questions by talking about the student-written letter on p. 281.

SAY *When you write a business letter, you are often writing to ask for information or for something to be done. Let's look at Gretchen's letter.*

- *What did Gretchen want to know?*
- *What were some specific things she wanted to find out about?*
- *How does Gretchen end her letter?*

Spelling Tip

Read the box to students. Then have students add the prefix *dis*- or *re*-, and/or the suffix *-ful* to the words below to form a new word.

send	*thank*	*respect*
place	*play*	*call*

STEP 2: Practice

Before students write their own business letters asking for information, have them discuss with partners the places they want to visit. Have them ask:

- What would be fun to do there?
- What information would be important to know?
- Is there anything special you'd have to bring?

STEP 3: Monitor Progress

Writing Checklist

- ✓ Check to see that students include a formal salutation and their own address, as well as the addressee's.
- ✓ Have students make sure their questions are specific.
- ✓ Have students circle the closings of their letters.
- ✓ Have students share their letters with their partners and encourage them to ask questions. Remind students to be respectful of others as they share their work.

The Five Step Writing Process in the Writing Handbook reference section of this book provides more student writing instruction.

STEP 1: Introduce

Key Words

Help students learn the skill of defining words by using context.

SAY *All the key words from* How to Prepare for a Trip to Yosemite *are defined in the Words in Context sentences. Let's find the definitions for three words in the passage.*

Point to the key words at random, having students say and spell the word aloud.

STEP 2: Teach

Words in Context

Have students complete this fill-in-the-blanks exercise using the key words.

1. *To protect the* environment*, everyone should conserve our natural resources.*
2. *In a desert* ecosystem*, many small animals live underground.*
3. *During the fall, the leaves in the* alpine *forest are bright yellow.*
4. *After a rainstorm, a* landslide *uprooted trees.*
5. Conservation *is essential for protecting the environment.*
6. *My grandfather built a cabin in a* secluded *grove.*
7. *We went on a* scenic *drive through the mountains.*

Study Skills

Dictionary Students can look up the key words in the dictionary to see if their Words in Context definitions are correct.

Online Dictionary Students can use an online dictionary or the CD that accompanies a learner's dictionary, like the *Longman Basic Dictionary*.
www.LongmanCornerstone.com

Teaching Resources
- ***Practice Book***, pp. 141–142
- ***Transparencies***, p. 53
- ***CD-ROM*** • ***Audio CD***

Reading 2

How to Prepare for a Trip to Yosemite

Vocabulary

How to Prepare for a Trip to Yosemite **describes how two friends get ready for a camping trip.**

Key Words
- **environment**
- **ecosystem**
- **alpine**
- **landslide**
- **conservation**
- **secluded**
- **scenic**

Words in Context

1 An **environment** includes the land, water, and air where people, plants, and animals live.

2 An **ecosystem** is part of the environment. It is a community that includes the plants, animals, and insects in a specific area. This wetland is an ecosystem.

3 Things that are high in the mountains can be called **alpine**. Snowboarding is an alpine sport. An alpine lodge is a lodge high in the mountains.

282

TESOL Standards

Goal 1, Standard 3—To use English to communicate in social settings: Students will use learning strategies to extend their communicative competence.
Descriptors—Testing hypotheses about language; Listening to and imitating how others use English; Exploring alternative ways of saying things; Using context to construct meaning.

Goal 2, Standard 2—To use English to achieve academically in all content areas: Students will use English to obtain, process, construct, and provide subject matter information in spoken and written form.
Descriptor—Understanding and producing technical vocabulary and text features according to content area.

(4) A **landslide** destroyed the house and blocked the road.

(5) There are many ways to practice **conservation**. These students are planting trees.

(6) Marnie hated crowds. She would rather write on this quiet, **secluded** part of the beach.

(7) The park had many **scenic** views that people love to photograph.

Practice

Use each key word in a sentence.

Make Connections

When you go on vacation, do you prefer to sleep in a tent, a cabin, or a hotel? Why? What was your favorite vacation?

Academic Words

specific
precise, exact

features
traits, characteristics

Practice Book pages 141–142

283

Visual Literacy

Photographs Discuss the photographs with students. Tell them that each photograph illustrates or tells more about a key word.

SAY *These photos will help us to understand what the key words mean. They also give us an idea of what we are going to be learning about in the reading.*

Academic Words

Discuss the definitions for *specific* and *features*, then share the following context sentences with students:

The party is this afternoon, but we are not sure of the *specific* time.

Ralph decided to buy that bike because he likes the *features* that it has.

Have students write context sentences for each of the words and share them with the class.

Other Academic Words

Explain to students that some words can be used as more than one part of speech. The word *appropriate* has two pronunciations with different meanings.

appropriate (adjective) suitable or fitting for a person or a situation

The clothes he wore were *appropriate* for the weather.

appropriate (verb) set something aside for a specific purpose

The committee voted to *appropriate* funds for a new recreation center.

STEP 3: Practice

Flexible Grouping You may assign these exercises as a class discussion, partner activity, or individual writing assignment.

Make Connections

Writing Fluency Have students write a short paragraph about their vacation preference and their favorite vacation. Have students draw a picture to go with their writing. Invite volunteers to share their paragraphs and drawings with the class.

Differentiated Instruction

Beginning	Read the list of key words aloud and ask students to repeat each word. Have students find each key word in the context sentences. Encourage students to copy one of the sentences that has a key word.
Intermediate	Ask students to repeat each context word as you read aloud each sentence. Challenge students to make a list of the key words and place them in alphabetical order.
Greater Challenge	Have students write a paragraph using as many key words as possible. Remind students that their paragraphs should have a main idea and supporting details.
Struggling Reader	Have students write down each key word. Have them practice pronouncing and spelling the words with partners.

STEP 1: Introduce

More About The Big Question

The Big Question for this selection is designed to make students think about what they might learn from a visit to a national park.

SAY *We are going to read some e-mails between two friends about a trip one of them is planning.*

- *What supplies do you think you would need for an overnight hike?*
- *What kinds of questions do you have about a trip to Yosemite?*

Have students work in pairs to fill in a 5W Chart with questions they would like to ask about a trip to Yosemite. They can fill in answers to their questions as they read.

Who likes to visit Yosemite?	
What are Yosemite's best features?	
Where is Yosemite located?	
When is the best time to visit?	
Why do people visit Yosemite?	

STEP 2: Teach

Reading Strategy

Draw Conclusions Tell students that to draw a conclusion, readers use clues from the text and what they might already know. Point out that asking questions as they read will help them to better draw conclusions.

Understand Text Structure

Explain that functional writing includes e-mail, letters, journals, posters, and forms. While functional writing is often less formal than the writing students do for school, it is important because it helps people accomplish everyday tasks.

Teaching Resources

- ***Teacher's Resource Book,*** pp. 145–146
- ***Practice Book,*** pp. 143–144
- ***CD-ROM*** • ***Audio CD***

Reading 2

FUNCTIONAL WRITING

E-mail

The Big Question

What can we learn from visiting national parks?

Reading Strategy

Draw Conclusions

You draw conclusions when you put together clues to figure something out.

- What can you conclude about where Jay lives?
- What can you conclude about where Maria lives?

How to Prepare for a Trip to Yosemite

by Jay Rabin and Maria Reyes

From: Jay_Rabin@lincolnschool.net
To: mreyes@californianet.com
Date: May 5
Subject: Yosemite this summer!!!!!

Dear Maria,

Guess what? My family and I are going to Yosemite National Park for **vacation** this summer! I remember you went to Yosemite last year. What are the most scenic spots? What **supplies** do we need to bring?

My dad wants to rent a cabin, but I want to camp in a tent. My mom wonders if we are allowed to fish in the Merced River. My sister wants to hike in secluded spots. My parents want to know if the trails are marked easy or hard. Tell me all about Yosemite!

Your pal,
Jay

vacation trip you take to another place for pleasure

supplies food, clothes, and things needed for a particular activity

284

TESOL Standards

Goal 2, Standard 2—To use English to achieve academically in all content areas: Students will use English to obtain, process, construct, and provide subject matter information in spoken and written form.
Descriptors—Comparing and contrasting information; Persuading, arguing, negotiating, evaluating, and justifying; Listening to, speaking, reading, and writing about subject matter information; Gathering information orally and in writing; Retelling information; Analyzing, synthesizing, and inferring from information.

From: mreyes@californianet.com
To: Jay_Rabin@lincolnschool.net
Subject: Re: Yosemite this summer!!!!!
Date: May 6

Hi Jay,

What great news! You and your family will love Yosemite.

I did go there last year. But I've been to Yosemite many times. I live only a few hours from the park. My family and I go as often as we can.

I will tell you about the spots you really need to see. The first is Yosemite Valley. You will love the waterfalls and cliffs. Don't miss it! If you like giant sequoia trees, you have to go to Mariposa Grove. The best views are at Glacier Point. Long ago, a landslide shaped that part of the park.

Please tell your mom that fishing is allowed in Merced River. Fishing does not disturb the park's ecosystem. There are some rules, but they are clearly posted. They tell where you can fish and the kinds of bait you can use. The trails are marked easy or hard. There are so many trails. Did you decide between renting a cabin or bringing your own tent?

Your friend,
Maria

often regularly or many times
disturb change something in a bad way
bait food used to attract fish

Check Up What do you think Jay will write to Maria about next?

285

Build Vocabulary

Help students recognize how to use the highlighted words that are defined on the bottom of the page.

- Invite a volunteer to read the term and its definition aloud.
- Read the sentence with the highlighted word aloud to the class. Then read the definition aloud. Ask students to work with partners to write two new sentences for each term.

Compound Words Explain to students that *landslide* is a compound word made up of the words *land* and *slide*, and it describes what happens when a hillside gives way and slides downhill. Encourage students to share examples of other compound words they know of or have come across in their reading.

Read Aloud

Have students turn to p. 284. Students should take turns reading the paragraphs on the pages. At the end of each paragraph, work with students to help them draw conclusions about what they have read.

Adapt the Activity

Have students look at the e-mails on pp. 284–285. Have students work with partners to compare and contrast the e-mails with a letter they may have written to a friend. Then have students share with the class their ideas about how e-mails and letters are alike and how they are different.

Differentiated Instruction

Beginning	Write the highlighted words on the board: *vacation*, *supplies*, *often*, *disturb*, *bait*. Have students find the definitions in the reading and write their own sentences for the words.
Early Intermediate	Have students use the highlighted words to fill in the blanks: *Our family ________ takes a ________ so we need ________ to camp and ________ for fishing.*
Intermediate	Have students work with partners to review the e-mails, then retell the events described by Jay and Maria.
Standard English Learner (CRI)	Have students brainstorm a list of gear and supplies they might need for a camping trip.

STEP 3: Assess

Check Up

Tell students to use prior knowledge and what they have read in the selection to make a prediction about what Jay will write about in his next e-mail to Maria.

Choose the Form of Writing

Ask students if they think e-mails are the best way for Jay and Maria to communicate with each other about Jay's trip. Have students brainstorm a list of other ways they could communicate (letters, phone calls, etc.) and discuss the pros and cons of each choice. Students can use a T-Chart to make comparisons, if desired.

STEP 1: Monitor Progress

Comprehension Check

Make Predictions Explain to students that making predictions and drawing conclusions both require the reader to act like a detective. You look for clues in the text, add in what you might already know, and then decide what you think you will learn from the reading.

SAY *Before we finish reading the e-mails, let's discuss what we can predict will be the result.*

- *Why is Jay excited about going to Yosemite National Park?*
- *What can Maria tell Jay to help him get ready for his trip?*
- *Where do you predict Jay will want to stay?*
- *What supplies do you predict he will bring?*

Read a Trail Map Display a map of Yosemite National Park that shows hiking trails. Challenge students to find on the map some of the places in the park they'd like to see. Ask students to select a trail on the map and look for clues about what they will find on that trail. Have students write a descriptive paragraph about what they will see if they hike that trail.

Computer Formatting Draw students' attention to the formatting of Jay's and Maria's e-mails. Explain that when writers use computers, they often put their paragraphs in block form instead of indenting them. If students use this format, remind them to leave a space between each paragraph.

Point out that it is often okay in informal e-mails to omit greetings and closings, and to use lower case *i* for the pronoun *I*. Remind students that such practices are not appropriate for sending e-mails to people with whom they are not friendly.

From: Jay_Rabin@lincolnschool.net
To: mreyes@californianet.com
Subject: Re: Yosemite this summer!!!!!
Date: June 1

Hi Maria,

I'm sorry I haven't written in a while. My family went on a short camping trip this weekend. We went to the Pocono Mountains in Pennsylvania. We wanted to be sure we have everything we need for our big trip.

Here is a picture of my mom and big sister unloading the car after the trip. They were so organized that it was easy for us to unpack the car. Dad put me right to work on cleaning all the equipment and putting it away.

I convinced my parents to rent a tent when we visit Yosemite. I'm so happy! I think we will have such a good time.

Thanks for the information about places to go. I don't know if I like giant sequoias. I've never seen one. I love to be in the wilderness. I really like alpine trees.

We have a map of the park, a compass, and flashlights. Before we leave, can you tell me what other supplies we should bring?

Thanks, my friend!
Jay

---

convinced got someone to agree to do something

286

TESOL Standards

Goal 2, Standard 2—To use English to achieve academically in all content areas: Students will use English to obtain, process, construct, and provide subject matter information in spoken and written form.
Descriptors—Comparing and contrasting information; Persuading, arguing, negotiating, evaluating, and justifying; Listening to, speaking, reading, and writing about subject matter information; Gathering information orally and in writing; Retelling information.

From: mreyes@californianet.com
To: Jay_Rabin@lincolnschool.net
Subject: Re: Yosemite this summer!!!!!
Date: June 8

Dear Jay,

I bet you can't wait for your trip to Yosemite! I think you will love the environment. I hope you and your family can talk to a park ranger about all the conservation projects there.

It's good that you have lots of supplies already. Don't forget a first-aid kit. Bring extra food, water, and clothes. Your parents should bring a knife and matches. They come in handy for emergencies or for cooking outdoors. Avoid sunburn with sunscreen, a hat, and sunglasses. It's good to have a cell phone, two-way radio, or satellite phone in case you get lost.

Have a wonderful time. Send me a postcard if you can!

Your friend,
Maria

Practice Book pages 143–144

Reading Strategy

Draw Conclusions

- Why did Jay's family go on a shorter camping trip first?
- What did you conclude about where Jay and Maria live?
- What hints led you to those conclusions?

Think It Over

1. Why is it important to be prepared when you go camping?
2. What supplies will Jay and his family bring?
3. Why did Jay and his family go camping in the Pocono Mountains?

287

Differentiated Instruction

Beginning	Have children use descriptive words and phrases to describe the items and the activity shown in the photo on p. 286 and describe the things in nature shown in the photo on p. 287.
Intermediate	Have students write a one-sentence caption for each photograph and pp. 286–287. Encourage students to use highlighted words and key words in their writing.
Greater Challenge	Have students create a two-column chart. One column will be a list of supplies, and the second column will be a list of activities. Tell students to carefully review the e-mails to find the information.
Special Needs	Show students the Copy and Paste tools on a computer, and explain that these tools can save students time when students revise their writing.

STEP 2: Teach

Visual Literacy

Photographs Refer students' attention to the photographs on pp. 286–287.

SAY *Let's look at the photographs.*

- *What do they tell you about Yosemite National Park?*
- *How do the photographs help to make the reading more interesting and enjoyable?*
- *What are the two people doing at the back of the car?*

STEP 3: Assess

Reading Strategy

Draw Conclusions Give students an example of how to draw a conclusion.

SAY *Drawing a conclusion helps you better understand what you are reading. When you draw a conclusion, you are thinking about what is happening in the text, and why it is happening.*

- *Where do you think Jay prefers to sleep at Yosemite?*
- *Why does Maria seem to be excited for Jay?*
- *What can you conclude about Jay and his family when you can see from the photograph that they have plenty of camping supplies that they took on their trip to the Poconos?*

Have students write short paragraphs explaining the conclusions they made about Jay's camping trip.

Think It Over

Flexible Grouping You may assign this activity as a class discussion, partner activity, or individual writing assignment.

Answer Key

1. You are far from home and from any store, and there might be emergencies.
2. They have a map, compass, and flashlights, but they will probably also bring what Maria suggested: a first-aid kit, extra food and water, knife, matches, sun protection, and a cell phone or radio.
3. It was a test run to make sure they had everything they needed for the big trip.

STEP 1: Introduce

The photos on these pages are designed to serve as visuals to expand vocabulary related to *How to Prepare for a Trip to Yosemite*.

More About The Big Question

The Closer Look selection also focuses on what people might need to bring on a camping trip. Have students examine the visuals and read the captions on pp. 288–289. Lead a class discussion on preparing for a camping trip.

SAY *Think about different national parks you have learned about in the past. They may be parks you have read about or visited.*

- *What camping or hiking trips have you taken?*
- *What was special about the place you visited?*
- *What special skills or equipment did visiting this place require?*
- *What did you learn that you didn't know before?*

Explain to students that learning from experience is an important habit to have. Point out that when you know you are taking a trip, the better prepared you are, and the more fun you will have.

Build Discussion Before students begin reading through the pages of A Closer Look, have students draw pictures of what they might need on a camping trip. Ask students to label their pictures and write a one-sentence caption that explains why the item is necessary. Display students' illustrations in class. Read aloud the labels and captions to build additional vocabulary relating to camping and experiencing the outdoors.

Link to Social Studies

The First National Park Yellowstone National Park is famous for more than the Old Faithful geyser that shoots steam 50 feet in the air. It is the first area in the country to be declared a national park. Established in 1872 by President Theodore Roosevelt, it is home to bears, elk, buffalo, and wolves, a grand canyon, and many active geysers. Have students write a short report on why President Teddy Roosevelt established national parks.

A Closer Look at...

Things You Might Need On a Camping Trip

It is best to be prepared when you go camping. These are things you should bring on any camping trip. If you go camping in winter, bring warm clothing. If you go to the desert, bring extra water.

▲ **Raingear**
- rain jacket and pants
- poncho
- boots

▲ **Sun Protection**
- sunglasses
- hat
- sunscreen

▲ **Navigation Aids**
- map
- compass

TESOL Standards

Goal 2, Standard 3—To use English to achieve academically in all content areas: Students will use appropriate learning strategies to construct and apply academic knowledge.
Descriptors—Focusing attention selectively; Applying basic reading comprehension skills such as skimming, scanning, previewing, and reviewing text; Using context to construct meaning; Taking notes to record important information and aid one's own learning; Imitating the behaviors of native English speakers to complete tasks successfully.

Goal 3, Standard 1—To use English in socially and culturally appropriate ways: Students will use the appropriate language variety, register, and genre according to audience, purpose, and setting.
Descriptor—Using a variety of writing styles appropriate for different audiences, purposes, and settings.

▲ **Essentials**
- emergency shelter
- first aid kit
- flashlight

▲ **Nourishment**
- GORP (good old raisins and peanuts)
- canteen for water
- dried food

Activity to Do!

- Think of a place you would like to visit.
- Find information about what you need for the trip.
- Create two pages to describe those items.
- Present your work to the class.

289

Differentiated Instruction	
Beginning	Students can act out what they might do on a camping trip, such as chopping wood, putting up a tent, casting a fishing line, or using a flashlight to find their way.
Early Intermediate	Have students study the photos of the camping supplies. Ask them to select three things and write one sentence for each item that describes why the item is useful for campers.
Intermediate	Have students take turns explaining to the class why each item shown on pp. 288–289 is important for a camping trip.
Standard English Learner CRI	Have students prepare a Reader's Theater about camping in the wilderness. Guide them to plan where to go, what to bring, and how to set up camp.

STEP 2: Teach

Visual Literacy

Photographs and Labels Guide students to recognize that these pages use photographs and labels to show the things you would need on a camping trip.

SAY *Look at the photographs and labels on pages 288 and 289 and think about how you would prepare to go on a camping trip.*

- *Why do you think the author used photographs and labels to tell about the things someone might need on a camping trip instead of writing a paragraph about them?*
- *What else might the author have shown on these pages?*

Scaffolding

Have students fill in a Sequence of Events Chart based on the steps in the process of setting up a campsite. Remind students they need a place to sleep, a place to cook, a place to store supplies, and a comfortable place to sit and relax.

STEP 3: Assess

Activity to Do!

Before they begin the activity, have students play a memory game with a camping trip theme. Begin by saying *I'm going on a camping trip, and I'm bringing a flashlight.* Have students take turns repeating each item already said and then adding their own item to the growing list. Play several rounds of the game to give each student the opportunity to play.

Reteach

Two-Column Chart Have students organize the information from these pages into a two-column chart. In the left column, have them write the name of the piece of equipment they see on the pages. In the right column, have them explain how or why it is important for a camping trip. Have students share their completed charts with partners.

STEP 1: Introduce

Phonics & Fluency

Variant Vowel *oo* Write the letters *oo* on the board. Explain that the letters can have two different sounds—*/oo/*, as in *boot*, and */oo/*, as in *book*.

STEP 2: Teach

Ask volunteers to read aloud the words in the box and compare the different sounds. Then draw students' attention to the Rule Box.

SAY *The long /oo/ sound is the sound of /oo/, as in* too. *The short /oo/ sound is the sound of /oo/, as in* took.

- *Can you think of any words with the long /oo/ sound?*
- *Can you think of any words with the short /oo/ sound?*

Possible Responses Long /oo/: moon, spook, spoon, balloon, kook; Short /oo/: look, cook, hook, shook, book, nook

STEP 3: Practice

Answer Key

short /oo/	long /oo/
good	food
cook	cool
looking	soon
redwoods	
Brook	

1. Have students work with partners. Ask each team to come up with as long a list as possible of long and short /oo/ words.
2. Now have them work together to create a silly sentence using as many of the words from their lists as they can. See which team can write the longest sentence.

Teaching Resources
- *Practice Book*, p. 145
- *Phonics Workbook*
- *Phonics Flashcards*
- *CD-ROM* • *Audio CD*

Reading 2

Phonics & Fluency

Phonics

Variant vowel: oo

Words with Letters *oo*	
took	too
hook	food

Each word in the chart has the letters *oo*. Read the words aloud.

What two vowel sounds do the letters *oo* have?

Rule Box

The /ŏo/ sound is the short sound of oo as in **took**.

The /ōo/ sound is the long sound of oo as in **too**.

If you come across a word you do not know, try reading it both ways. Try the long sound first. It is more common.

Practice

Find each word with the letters *oo*. Sort the words into two lists.

Dear Maria,

Here's a picture of the fish I could not catch. It's a good thing we brought our own food to cook.

I have a crick in my neck from looking up at the redwoods! This place is way cool. We'll be back soon.

Your friend,
Jay

Place Stamp Here

Maria Reyes
10 Brook Lane
Sacramento, CA 94211

Practice Book page 145

TESOL Standards

Goal 1, Standard 3—To use English to communicate in social settings: Students will use learning strategies to extend their communicative competence.
Descriptors—Listening to and imitating how others use English; Self-monitoring and self-evaluating language development; Practicing new language; Focusing attention selectively; Exploring alternative ways of saying things; Practicing new language.

Goal 3, Standard 3—To use English in socially and culturally appropriate ways: Students will use appropriate learning strategies to extend their sociolinguistic and sociocultural competence.
Descriptors—Observing and modeling how others speak and behave in a particular situation or setting; Experimenting with variations of language in social and academic settings; Seeking information about appropriate language use and behavior.

Fluency

Read with Expression

When you read aloud, use your voice to show feelings.

Practice

Read silently. → Read aloud. → Get comments. → Read aloud again.

Dear Maria,

Guess what? My family and I are going to Yosemite National Park for vacation this summer. I remember you went to Yosemite last year. What are the most scenic spots? What supplies do we need to bring?

My dad wants to stay in a cabin, but I want to camp in a tent. My mom wonders if we are allowed to fish in the Merced River. My sister said she wants to hike in secluded spots. My parents want to know if the trails are marked easy or hard.

Tell me all about Yosemite!

Your pal,
Jay

291

Sharing Language and Culture

Place Names and History Explain to students that often the history of a given part of the country can be retraced through the names of its geographical features. Yosemite, for instance, is a Paiute Indian word. The Merced (merSED) River that flows through the Yosemite Valley was named by a Spanish explorer in 1806.

Accelerate Language Development

Punctuation and Text Layout Remind students that a question mark at the end of a sentence tells the reader they should raise their voice as they complete a sentence to show that they are trying to find something out. An exclamation point tells the reader that an entire sentence or thought should be read with more emotion. Sometimes words are printed in italics, bold print, or in capital letters. These styles are clues that the word should be read with emphasis because it gives important information.

STEP 1: Introduce

Fluency

Read with Expression Tell students that active readers read with expression, which involves reading important words and phrases with emphasis or heightened emotion.

Play the Audio CD for this reading to the class, asking students to listen to pacing, intonation, and expression.

Model reading with expression using the following sentences from the passage:

Guess what? My family and I are going to Yosemite National Park for vacation this summer. What are the most scenic spots? Tell me all about Yosemite!

STEP 2: Practice

Have students do the following exercise with partners. Ask partners to take turns.

- Have students read the text to each other. Encourage them to think about how they are going to read it with expression.
- The partner listening should mark the sentences where the reader does not use expression, then share them with the reader to practice these sentences together.
- Have students discuss how they read the text. What words, phrases, and sentences did they read with heightened emotion? How did their emphasis of these words or phrases make the reading more enjoyable to listen to? How did it reinforce important information?

STEP 3: Extend

Study Skills

Pronunciation Cards Referring to word families or similar words can help students with the pronunciation of new words. Have students write down a list of three words they found hard to pronounce. Then have them share them with partners who can help them think of similar, easier reference words that may help them remember how to pronounce the words.

STEP 1: Monitor Progress

Learning Strategy

Summarize Summarizing requires students to look closely to identify the most important information in a text. Have students work in pairs, with one student summarizing, and the other responding to the Big Question.

Adapt the Activity

Have students fill in a Main Idea and Details Chart to summarize either Jay or Maria's e-mails. Remind students that the purpose of using the chart is to find the most important information.

STEP 2: Teach

Draw Conclusions

Explain to students that good readers can draw conclusions about what they read from finding clues in the text.

SAY *Asking and answering questions is a good way to better understand a text. Once you have drawn a conclusion, you can test it against information you find out later.*

- *What is the best way to draw a conclusion?*
- *What do the items in the photos suggest to you about what people bring camping? Why do you think they bring what they bring?*

STEP 3: Practice

Flexible Grouping You may assign this activity as a class discussion, partner activity, or individual written assignment.

Possible Response

Maria seemed to like Yosemite Valley the best because that is what she says first and she says Jay should not miss it.

Teaching Resources

- ***Practice Book,*** p. 146
- ***Transparencies,*** p. 59
- ***Teacher's Resource Book,*** p. 157
- ***CD-ROM***

Reading 2

Comprehension

Learning Strategy

Summarize

Summarize Jay or Maria's part of the selection for a partner.

? Ask your partner to respond to the Big Question for this reading.

Draw Conclusions

When you **draw conclusions,** you use the information from the reading to form your own ideas.

- What are some things people worry about when they go camping?
- What do people need to plan for when they go camping?

Practice

Read the paragraph. What site did Maria like best in Yosemite National Park? Tell how you reached your conclusion.

I will tell you about the spots you really need to see. The first is Yosemite Valley. You will love the waterfalls and cliffs. Don't miss it! If you like giant sequoia trees, you have to go to Mariposa Grove. The best views are at Glacier Point. Long ago, a landslide shaped that part of the park.

Practice Book page 146

292

TESOL Standards

Goal 2, Standard 2—To use English to achieve academically in all content areas: Students will use English to obtain, process, construct, and provide subject matter information in spoken and written form.

Descriptors—Listening to, speaking, reading, and writing about subject matter information; Gathering information orally and in writing; Retelling information; Selecting, connecting, and explaining information; Analyzing, synthesizing, and inferring from information; Demonstrating knowledge through application in a variety of contexts; Representing information visually and interpreting information presented visually.

Use a KWL Chart

You can use a KWL Chart to help you relate your knowledge to the ideas in a selection. The letters stand for "What I Know," "What I Want to Know" and "What I Have Learned".

Practice

Complete this KWL Chart about *How to Prepare for a Trip to Yosemite*. Think back to what you knew before you read and what things you would like to know. Then tell what you learned.

K-What I Know	W-What I Want to Know	L-What I Have Learned

Extension

Work with a group. Choose a place to visit. Have each group member place a picture of an item to take on the trip in a box. You may use the actual item if it is available. Write a brief description of each item to explain why you chose it.

293

Linguistic Note

Cognates The word *conclusion* is a cognate in just about every Romance language. In Spanish and French, it is *conclusión/conclusion*. In Italian and Portuguese, it is *conclusione/conclusão*. In still other languages, like Dutch, *conclusion* becomes *conclusive*.

Accelerate Language Development

Tell students that answering the KWL questions is a good strategy for learning. Tell students that a KWL Chart can be especially helpful when reading social studies and science texts.

STEP 1: Teach

Use a KWL Chart

Tell students that thinking about what you know—and what you would like to know—can help them focus more closely on a reading. Read aloud the following imaginary headline from a newspaper:

Snowstorms Hit Yosemite National Park.

Ask students to write *What They Know* from the headline, and *What They Want to Know* from the article. Point out that if they read the article, they would probably be able to answer their questions and write *What They Learned*.

Possible Responses

What I Know: Snowstorms hit Yosemite National Park.

What I Want to Know: Did the park close? How many feet of snow fell? Was there an avalanche? Were any campers stranded in the park?

STEP 2: Practice

You may have students complete the graphic organizer provided as a Blackline Master in the *Teacher's Resource Book*.

STEP 3: Extend

Oral Presentation Ask students to work with the other members of their group to decide what sort of place they would all like to visit. Once they have decided on a place, have them search through magazines or other sources for examples of what they would bring along to put into the box. Then have each member explain to the class why he or she chose that item. Post the images students chose for the class to review.

STEP 1: Introduce

Tell students that writers can write in two different ways—in an active voice, or in a passive voice. Explain that an active voice describes the action as it is happening.

STEP 2: Teach

Active and Passive Voice

Write the following sentence pairs on the board to illustrate the difference between active and passive voice. Guide students to recognize that the first sentence in each pair is in the passive voice; the second sentence is in the active voice.

The land was flooded by the melting ice.
The melting ice flooded the land.

The ball was kicked by the children.
The children kicked the ball.

Guide students to understand that the active voice is preferable because it shows each thing performing the action. Also point out that the second sentences are more fun to read because they make the action more immediate.

STEP 3: Practice

Before students begin the Practice activity, have them works in groups. Give each student a verb from the boxed sentences on p. 294. Have them write a short sentence using the verb in either active or passive voice. Have group members decide which voice the verb is in. Have volunteers share their sentences with the class.

Answer Key

1. active
2. passive
3. active
4. passive

Teaching Resources

- *Practice Book,* pp. 147–148
- *Transparencies,* pp. 69–80
- *Assessments,* pp. 93–96
- *CD-ROM*

Reading 2

Grammar & Writing

Active and Passive Voice

When a verb is in the **active voice**, a person or thing performs an action. These verbs are in active voice.

You **read** my message correctly.
Long ago, a landslide **shaped** Glacier point.

In **passive voice**, the subject receives the action. These verbs are in the passive voice.

The hiking trails **are marked** easy or hard.
The rules about fishing **are posted**.

Practice

Tell whether the verb is in the active voice or the passive voice.

1. Three million people visit the park each year.
2. The park was visited by three million people.
3. Visitors catch fish in the lake.
4. The fish were caught by visitors.

Practice Book page 147

294

TESOL Standards

Goal 1, Standard 3—To use English to communicate in social settings: Students will use learning strategies to extend their communicative competence.
Descriptor—Seeking support and feedback from others.

Goal 2, Standard 1—To use English to achieve academically in all content areas: Students will use English to interact in the classroom.
Descriptors—Following oral and written directions, implicit and explicit; Explaining actions; Expressing likes, dislikes, and needs.

Goal 2, Standard 3—To use English to achieve academically in all content areas: Students will use appropriate learning strategies to construct and apply academic knowledge.
Descriptors—Using context to construct meaning; Actively connecting new information to information previously learned; Imitating the behaviors of native English speakers to complete tasks successfully.

Goal 3, Standard 1—To use English in socially and culturally appropriate ways: Students will use the appropriate language variety, register, and genre according to audience, purpose, and setting.
Descriptor—Using a variety of writing styles appropriate for different audiences, purposes, and settings.

Write a Paragraph in the Active Voice

It is usually better to write sentences in the active voice. Find the active and passive voice sentences in Tami's paragraph.

The Andes Mountains

My parents and I visit our relatives in Peru every year. Our favorite time of year to visit is during Carnival. This holiday period is called Mardi Gras in the United States. The holiday is celebrated by people all over the world. In Peru, we celebrate by having parades and dances. Special food is cooked by families. Some farmers tie ribbons and other decorations to their animals. Everyone has a great time.

Spelling Tip

You can use your computer's spell check to check your spelling, but the computer can't tell whether you meant ***weather*** or ***whether***, or ***your*** or ***you're***. You must still check your spelling carefully.

Practice Book page 148

Practice

Work with a partner. Rewrite the passive voice sentences in Tami's paragraph in the active voice. Then write your own paragraph about a place you visited.

- Think of a place you have visited.
- Write about something that happened to you there.
- Write your sentences in the active voice.

Writing Checklist

✓ Did you indent the first line of your paragraph?

✓ Did you use the active voice?

✓ Was it easier to write in active voice? Why or why not?

✓ Can a partner understand your paragraph?

Differentiated Instruction

Beginning	Read aloud this phrase from Tami's paragraph: *The holiday is celebrated*. Now say the words in active voice, asking students to listen for the difference.
Intermediate	Have students pair up and take turns writing sentences for each other. They can be in either active or passive voice. The partner then rewrites the sentence in the opposite voice.
Greater Challenge	Have pairs of students team up to write a mini-adventure story using entirely the active voice. Suggest they brainstorm characters and a plot, then take turns writing each sentence of the story.
Struggling Reader	Help students out with the words *Mardi Gras*. First, say it out loud, explaining that the *s* is silent. Then, have them sound the word out themselves.

STEP 1: Introduce

Write a Paragraph in the Active Voice

Explain that in the active voice, the subject of the sentence performs the action.

SAY *When you write in the active voice, you carry the reader along with you because the subject of the story is performing the actions. Readers can begin to feel that they are there—hearing or seeing what is actually taking place.*

- *What voice does Tami use more, the active voice or the passive voice?*
- *What might make her paragraph more exciting to read?*

Spelling Tip

Read the box to students. You may want to have students brainstorm together with partners to come up with more words (like *whether* and *weather*) that would pose problems with a computer spell check.

STEP 2: Practice

Before students begin the Practice activity, use an example of passive voice from Tami's paragraph. Put it into active voice and ask a volunteer to explain the difference.

STEP 3: Monitor Progress

Writing Checklist

✓ Remind students to indent the first line.

✓ Have students circle the sentences with active voice.

✓ Some students may need support in describing why it is easier to write in active voice than passive voice.

✓ Encourage students to listen carefully to each other's paragraphs.

The Five Step Writing Process in the Writing Handbook reference section of this book provides more student writing instruction.

STEP 1: Introduce

Key Words

Help students learn the skill of defining words by using context.

SAY *All the key words are in the Words in Context section. Look at the word* forest. *What words helped you to understand the meaning?*

Guide students to recognize that context clues can be words, phrases, or entire sentences.

STEP 2: Teach

Words in Context

Have students complete the fill-in-the-blanks exercise using the key words.

1. We saw the waterfall cascade over the cliff.
2. In the spring, the meadow is filled with wildflowers.
3. Our campsite is at the peak of the mountain.
4. The higher climbers ascend, the harder it is to breathe.
5. On a hike in the forest, you will see birds and animals.
6. Pioneers built their cabins in the valley near the river.

Challenge students to write a descriptive paragraph using all of the key words.

Study Skills

Illustrated Dictionaries Even though some of these dictionaries may be labeled for younger readers, learners of all ages will find them useful.

Online Dictionary Students can use an online dictionary or the CD that accompanies a learner's dictionary, like the *Longman Basic Dictionary*.

www.LongmanCornerstone.com

Teaching Resources

- *Practice Book,* pp. 149–150
- *Transparencies,* p. 54
- *CD-ROM* • *Audio CD*

Reading 3

My Trip To Yosemite

Vocabulary

My Trip to Yosemite **is about Jay's summer trip to Yosemite National Park.**

Key Words

- cascade
- meadow
- peak
- ascend
- forest
- valley

Words in Context

1 I love to watch the water **cascade** down the steps.

2 A **meadow** in summer is one of the prettiest places to be. The grass is tall, and the flowers smell sweet.

3 Sometimes, the **peak** of a high mountain stays covered with snow, even in summer.

296

TESOL Standards

Goal 1, Standard 3—To use English to communicate in social settings: Students will use learning strategies to extend their communicative competence.
Descriptors—Testing hypotheses about language; Listening to and imitating how others use English; Exploring alternative ways of saying things; Using context to construct meaning.

Goal 2, Standard 2—To use English to achieve academically in all content areas: Students will use English to obtain, process, construct, and provide subject matter information in spoken and written form.
Descriptor—Understanding and producing technical vocabulary and text features according to content area.

4 When you **ascend** to the top of a mountain, climbing the last few feet can be the most exciting.

5 It is often cool and dark in the **forest**, even on a warm summer day. The shade from all the tall trees keeps it cool and comfortable.

6 A **valley** often forms between mountains.

Practice

Use each key word in a sentence.

Make Connections

Have you ever watched people climb mountains, go scuba diving, or explore the arctic? Have you seen them on television or in a movie? Talk about whether you would like to do one of those activities.

Academic Words

comment
talk about; say something about

correspond
write messages to other people

Practice Book pages 149–150

297

Differentiated Instruction

Beginning	Have students choose the correct answer: *The (peak/valley) of a mountain has snow. The trees in the (forest/meadow) are tall. We will (cascade/ascend) to the mountain top.*
Early Intermediate	Have students use key words for the following: *What is the highest part of a mountain? Which word can be both a noun and a verb? What is the opposite of* descend*? Where can you stay cool?*
Intermediate	Have students work with partners to write a new context sentence for each of the key words. Encourage them to use a dictionary or thesaurus.
Standard English Learner CRI	Have students use each key word for the activity "Give One, Get One." Select one word at a time and have students call out synonyms until each student has three new words.

Visual Literacy

Photographs Have students study the photos. Point out that they help the reader understand the meanings of the key words. Then have students link each photo to its correct Word in Context. Point to each photo and have students call out words that describe what they see. Encourage students to find as many details as possible.

Academic Words

Have students read the definitions for *comment* and *correspond*. Then share the following context sentences with students:

We were pleased that the judges stopped to *comment* on our science fair project.

Before there was e-mail, writing letters was the only way to *correspond.*

Have students work with partners to use the words *comment* and *correspond* in sentences. If time allows, have volunteers share their comments on things that they have corresponded about.

Other Academic Words

Explain to students that readers may confuse the definitions for two words that sound similar. Write the definitions and context sentences for *maintain* and *obtain* on the board. Then have students suggest context sentences for each word.

maintain keep up or keep in good condition

obtain gain or acquire by planning or effort

STEP 3: Practice

Flexible Grouping You may assign this activity as a class discussion, partner activity, or individual writing assignment.

Make Connections

Writing Fluency Have students write a short answer to each of the questions in the paragraph. Invite volunteers to share their responses with the class. Tie your discussion of students' ideas to the Big Question by pointing out that people often share their vacation experiences with friends through letters, e-mails, and over the telephone.

STEP 1: Introduce

More About The Big Question

The Big Question for this selection is formulated to make students think about how they might share their experience of a national park visit with others.

SAY *In* My Trip to Yosemite, *we are going to learn how Jay shared his experience of his trip to a national park.*

- *When you take a trip or have an adventure, what are you most interested in telling people?*
- *What are some important things we can teach others when we describe our experiences?*

Have students fill in a Main Idea and Details Chart that describes something important they learned on an adventure in nature.

I learned to build a camp fire.

A camp fire requires small, medium, and large dry sticks or pieces of wood.	To start the fire, place the smallest twigs leaning together in a vertical upside down V.	As the fire burns hotter, add the medium sticks, then the larger sticks in a criss-cross over the hot embers from the small sticks.

STEP 2: Teach

Reading Strategy

Review and Retell Tell students that answering the 5W questions as they review a story will help them identify what they would include in a retelling.

Understand Text Structure

Draw students' attention to the genre label. Tell them that a scrapbook is a kind of functional writing—like a letter and an e-mail—because it tells about something that took place.

Teaching Resources

- ***Teacher's Resource Book,*** pp. 147–148
- ***Practice Book,*** pp. 151–152
- ***CD-ROM*** • ***Audio CD***

Reading 3

FUNCTIONAL WRITING

Scrapbook

The Big Question

How could you share what you experienced at a national park with others?

Reading Strategy

Review and Retell

When you review and retell a selection, you pay attention to the major events. As you read:

- Ask yourself the 5W questions to help you remember the most important events.

My Trip To Yosemite

by Jay Rabin

Hey Maria,
Check out my cool Yosemite scrapbook! I am going to show it to my friends at school.
Your friend,
Jay

Half Dome is one of the most famous mountains in Yosemite National Park.

August 7

On our first day, we drove to Glacier Point. Our goal was to ascend to the very top. We had a great view from there. We saw a huge waterfall. We could see Yosemite Valley at the bottom. There were so many trees in the valley! We saw Half Dome mountain. It looks like the top of a circle. We passed rock climbers on the way down. People come from all over the world to climb rocks in Yosemite. It looked fun but also a little scary!

We saw these rock climbers. Yikes!

298

TESOL Standards

Goal 2, Standard 2—To use English to achieve academically in all content areas: Students will use English to obtain, process, construct, and provide subject matter information in spoken and written form.
Descriptors—Listening to, speaking, reading, and writing about subject matter information; Gathering information orally and in writing; Retelling information; Selecting, connecting, and explaining information; Demonstrating knowledge through application in a variety of contexts.

Yosemite Valley is one of the most popular places in Yosemite National Park.

Merced River is where visitors swim. People also go rafting down the river.

August 9

The next day we saw Yosemite Valley again. This time we saw it from the ground. We took a mule ride through the valley. Riding the mule was fun, but bumpy. I was sore afterwards! Many people go on mule tours in Yosemite. There are trees and grass everywhere. We rode to Mirror Lake. When it is filled with water you can see the reflections of mountains in it, like a mirror. We learned that the lake is slowly turning into a meadow. There is not much water there anymore. It is mostly grass and plants. The lake was pretty, but the meadow is, too.

Later we went to a long river called Merced River. The edge of the river is like a beach. Many families sat on the sand. We swam in the water. We also watched some people go rafting.

---

mule a cross between a horse and a donkey

tours short trips through a place to see it

Check Up What did Jay's family do on August 9?

299

Differentiated Instruction

Beginning	Have students find the following terms on pp. 288–289 and copy the sentences where the terms appear: *Glacier Point*, *mule ride*, *meadow*.
Intermediate	Ask students to read the caption beneath the picture of Half Dome. Ask them to look at the picture and discuss how Half Dome probably got its name.
Greater Challenge	Have students work with partners to write an imaginary diary entry about a day in Yosemite. Suggest they use the photographs on these pages for inspiration.
Struggling Reader	Write the following words on the board: *mountain*, *valley*, *river*, *trees*, *beach*. Have students find the words on pp. 298–299. Guide students to point to the picture that the word describes.

Build Vocabulary

Help students recognize how to use the highlighted words that are defined on the bottom of the page.

- Invite a volunteer to read the term and its definition aloud.
- Invite the class to point to the photo on p. 299 that might illustrate the word *tour*.
- Now read the sentence with the word *tour* in it aloud to the class. Then read it again, substituting the words "guided trip" for *tour*.

Words That Are Verbs and Nouns Direct attention to the word *tour* on p. 299. Explain that some words in English—such as *tour*—do double duty as both verbs and nouns. Use *tour* in a sentence as a verb, then as a noun. Ask students to think of other double duty words (*shower*, *paste*, *cast*) and share them with the class.

Read Aloud

Have students turn to p. 298. Students should take turns reading the paragraphs on the pages. At the end of each day in Jay's scrapbook, have students identify important information that they would include in a retelling.

STEP 3: Assess

Check Up

Have students work with partners after they have read up to p. 299. Ask one partner to retell the events of the story so far. Encourage them to use the 5W questions to help find the most important parts to tell. Then have the other partner tell it their way. Have students discuss any differences in how they chose to retell the events in Jay's scrapbook.

Study Skills

Multilingual Online Dictionaries Using students' first languages in class can help them feel represented—as well as appreciated—and can also help them clarify certain vocabulary issues. Use an online dictionary to learn camping words like *tent* and *campfire* in different languages.

STEP 1: Monitor Progress

Comprehension Check

Review and Retell Have students practice the skill of review and retell using the information on these pages.

SAY *Now that we have read these pages, let's look back and identify the most important information. Let's use the 5W questions to find the important information.*

- *Who went on the trip with Jay?*
- *What were two things Jay saw in the park that he had never seen before?*
- *Where did Jay see a rainbow?*
- *When he went to Mariposa Grove, what did he see?*
- *Why is Mirror Lake turning into a meadow?*

Have students fill in a 5W Chart with their answers to the above questions. Then have students exchange their charts with partners and compare and contrast the details in the two charts.

Make Connections

Point out to students that there are different ways to compare natural wonders like trees and waterfalls.

SAY *Think about some amazing things in nature you have seen.*

- *What is the largest living thing you have seen? What is the oldest?*
- *Have you seen a waterfall? What was its biggest dimension? Was it taller or wider?*

Have students write a paragraph about or draw a picture of what they consider to be the most amazing sight they have seen in nature. Have them include an explanation of why they thought it was so amazing.

Study Skills

Internet The Internet is a great resource for information on natural wonders. Students may enjoy visiting many different nature Web sites to learn more about ancient trees.

August 10

We wanted to see the waterfalls in Yosemite National Park. There are eight major waterfalls that people visit. When it rains, many small waterfalls form. Yosemite Falls is the tallest waterfall in the United States. We took a tour and saw two large waterfalls. Vernal Falls and Nevada Falls are not as tall as Yosemite Falls. They are still amazing to see. We watched the water cascade down the sides of the mountains. We could see rainbows in the water. We even felt the mist of water from the falls as we walked by.

We also hiked through the Mariposa Grove. It is a forest filled with only very large trees. These trees are called sequoias. Many people think they are the biggest living things on our planet. They can grow to be over 200 feet tall. These trees are about 3,000 years old.

Wow! Look at how tall these trees are! They are also very old.

My mom took this picture of Vernal Falls. Isn't the rainbow cool?

There are hotels in Yosemite National Park, but we camped in our tent.

300

TESOL Standards

Goal 2, Standard 2—To use English to achieve academically in all content areas: Students will use English to obtain, process, construct, and provide subject matter information in spoken and written form.

Descriptors—Listening to, speaking, reading, and writing about subject matter information; Gathering information orally and in writing; Retelling information; Selecting, connecting, and explaining information; Demonstrating knowledge through application in a variety of contexts.

I heard people love to look at the mountains in the moonlight. Someday, when I am older, I will hike a mountain at night.

Hi Jay,
It looks like you had a really fun time. I can't wait to visit Yosemite again!
Talk to you soon,
Maria

August 11

We slept outside in our tent. The park has a campfire set up for visitors to use. We swam in a lake just as the sun was going down. Then we warmed up by sitting around the fire. We were tired from all the walking. We had seen many things for the first time on this trip. I had never seen rock climbers hanging off the side of a mountain! I had never seen waterfalls so high. I had never seen a forest filled with trees so tall.

When the sun went down we looked for the Moon. It was high in the sky. It was high above the peak of the tallest mountain in Yosemite. When I was in my tent at night, I imagined I could see Half Dome in the distance. This was a great vacation!

campfire a fire made outdoors by people who are camping

Practice Book pages 151–152

Reading Strategy

Review and Retell

Go back and review the selection.

- Retell something Jay did on August 9.
- Retell something Jay did on August 10.

Think It Over

1. What was one place Jay visited?
2. Do you think Jay wants to try rock climbing? Why or why not?
3. How did Jay feel about his family vacation to Yosemite National Park?

Accelerate Language Development

Tell students that answering the 5W questions will help them both as they read, and when they wish to retell a story to someone else. Explain that once you have reviewed the who, what, when, where, and why of a story, telling it to someone else becomes much easier.

STEP 2: Teach

Visual Literacy

Draw students' attention to the photos on pp. 300–301. Point out that these pictures help to tell the story.

SAY *The photos on pages 300 and 301 show the reader what the author has written about. The photos that illustrate a page usually have words that refer to them in the text.*

- *What is at least one sentence in the text that describes what is shown in each photo?*
- *Do you think this scrapbook would be as much fun to read if there were no pictures? Why or why not?*
- *What else could you include in the scrapbook besides words and photographs?*

STEP 3: Assess

Reading Strategy

Review and Retell Give students an example of how to review and retell.

SAY *Reviewing and retelling helps you to make clear in your own head what you know.*

- *As you review what you read, you know that Jay and his family went to Yosemite. You know that they visited Glacier Point, did a mule ride, saw the Merced River, waterfalls, and Mariposa Grove. They also saw Half Dome and had a campfire by moonlight!*
- *Why would it help to retell these things to someone as you read them?*

Think It Over

Flexible Grouping You may assign the activity as a class discussion, partner activity, or individual writing assignment.

Answer Key

1. Mariposa Grove, Merced River, Half Dome, Yosemite Valley
2. He may not want to try rock climbing because he described the climbers as "hanging off the side of a mountain," which sounds pretty scary.
3. He thought it was a great vacation.

STEP 1: Introduce

Word Analysis

Latin Word Roots Help students understand that the English language is made of words with many different origins, including Latin and Greek.

STEP 2: Teach

Review the concept of word roots with students. Explain that a single root can lend itself to many different words.

SAY *The Latin root* circ *appears in many words and as many different parts of speech.*

- *In* circulate, *it refers to how blood moves through the body.*
- *In* circuit, *it refers to an electrical connection.*
- *In* circus, *it refers to a kind of popular entertainment that happens around a round central area.*

STEP 3: Practice

Encourage students to locate the meaning of the Latin root in the sentence, then find that same word among the answers.

Answer Key

1. a. living
2. b. free time
3. c. people
4. c. waterfall

Reteach

Have students look through another book or magazine to make a list of words they think might have Latin roots. Have them work with partners to look through dictionaries or other reference sources to find out if their ideas are correct, and what the exact roots and meanings might be.

Teaching Resources

- ***Practice Book***, pp. 153
- ***Phonics Workbook***
- ***CD-ROM*** • ***Audio CD***

Word Analysis & Fluency

Word Analysis

Greek and Latin Word Roots

Many English words come from Greek or Latin. For example, the word ***circle*** comes from the Latin root, ***circ***. ***Circ*** means "round."

Half Dome is a mountain that looks like the top of a **circle.**

The Latin root in each word is in red.

animal	popular
cascade	vacation

Practice

Complete each statement.

1. The root *anim* means "life, spirit." So, an **animal** is ___.
   a. living b. wild c. tame
2. The root *vac* means "to be empty or free." During a **vacation,** you are likely to have ___.
   a. no time b. free time c. a good time
3. The root *popu* means "people." At a **popular** vacation spot, you're likely to see ___.
   a. plants b. animals c. people
4. The root *cas* means "fall." So, a **cascade** can be a ___.
   a. pool of water b. water fountain c. waterfall

Practice Book page 153

TESOL Standards

Goal 1, Standard 3—To use English to communicate in social settings: Students will use learning strategies to extend their communicative competence.
Descriptors—Listening to and imitating how others use English; Self-monitoring and self-evaluating language development; Practicing new language; Focusing attention selectively; Testing hypotheses about language; Exploring alternative ways of saying things; Using context to construct meaning.

Fluency

Read for Speed and Accuracy

You should read quickly. But never read so quickly that you lose your understanding.

Practice

Read for one minute. ▶ Count the words you read. ▶ Study any hard words. ▶ Read and count again.

We wanted to see the waterfalls in Yosemite National 9
Park. There are eight major waterfalls that people visit. 18
When it rains, many small waterfalls form. Yosemite Falls 27
is the tallest waterfall in the United States. We took a tour 39
and saw two large waterfalls. Vernal Falls and Nevada Falls 49
are not as tall as Yosemite Falls. They are still amazing to 61
see. We watched the water cascade down the sides of the 72
mountains. We could see rainbows in the water. We even 82
felt the mist of water from the falls as we walked by. 94
We also hiked through the Mariposa Grove. It is a forest 105
filled with only very large trees. These trees are called 115
sequoias. Many people think they are the biggest living 124
things on our planet. They can grow to be over 200 feet 136
tall! These trees are about 3,000 years old. 144

Accelerate Language Development

One Root, Many Branches Point out that just as with the Latin root word *circ*, each Latin word can form the basis of very many different English words. The root *vac* in *vacation* means *to be empty or free*, and is also used in the words *evacuate*, *vacant*, and *vacuum*. Ask students to work with partners to find as many words as they can with the Latin roots *popu*, *anim*, and *cas*.

STEP 1: Introduce

Fluency

Read for Speed and Accuracy Explain to students that active readers read for speed and accuracy. Point out that the speed of a reading should sound like regular conversation. All the words should be understandable and the speaker should speak at a normal pace—not too fast and not too slow. Tell students that if a speaker reads too fast, the listener will lose track of what is being said; if the reader speaks too slowly, the listener may lose interest.

Play the Audio CD for this reading to the class, asking students to listen for pacing, intonation, and expression.

STEP 2: Practice

Have students do the following exercise with partners:

- Have one partner look through the paragraph to find any hard words and practice saying those words.
- Then have that student read the passage to his or her partner.
- Have the students change roles.
- Ask students whether dealing with the hard words in advance allowed them to read faster and with more confidence.

Have each student write down the words his or her partner had difficulty saying, and repeat the activity if necessary.

STEP 3: Extend

Study Skills

Internet Have students find the pronunciation of the words they identified as hard on the Internet. To complete this activity, have students work with partners to:

- write down three words that were hard to pronounce from the readings;
- look up the words in on an online dictionary;
- repeat the word at least three times.

STEP 1: Monitor Progress

Learning Strategy

Retell Retelling the story is a way to refresh the students' memory of the story. Have students work in pairs, with one student retelling, and the other responding to the Big Question. Guide students to think about the ways that they share important experiences with friends and family members. You may then have one pair present their retelling and response to the Big Question to the class.

STEP 2: Teach

Review and Retell

Remind students of the difference between review and retell. When they review, they should take notes on the main points of the reading. When they retell, they should explain the information in their own words.

Students will practice reviewing and retelling by writing a two-sentence summary of a paragraph.

SAY *Reviewing the main points of a story can help us to summarize it for others. Retelling can also remind you of things you already know.*

- *What were the basic things that happened?*
- *If you took this trip, what would you choose to tell a friend?*

STEP 3: Practice

Flexible Grouping You may assign this activity as a class discussion, partner activity, or individual written assignment.

Possible Response We drove to the top of Glacier Point and saw a great view of Yosemite Valley and Half Dome mountain. We saw so many trees, a waterfall, and on the way down, we saw rock climbers.

Teaching Resources

- *Practice Book*, p. 154
- *Transparencies*, p. 55
- *Teacher's Resource Book*, p. 153
- *CD-ROM*

Reading 3

Comprehension

Learning Strategy

Retelling

Retell some of the highlights of Jay's trip to a partner.

Ask your partner to respond to the Big Question for this reading.

Review and Retell

What would you do if you wanted to tell a friend about this selection? You can review and retell it!

- When you **review**, you re-read the parts of the selection that tell the main points.
- When you **retell**, you tell the main points of the selection to someone else.

Practice

Write two sentences that retell what happened on August 7.

August 7

On our first day we drove to Glacier Point. Our goal was to ascend to the very top. We had a great view from there. We saw a huge waterfall. We could see Yosemite Valley at the bottom. There were so many trees in the valley! We saw Half Dome mountain. It looks like the top of a circle. We passed rock climbers on the way down. People from all over the world come to climb rocks in Yosemite. It looked fun but also a little scary!

Practice Book page 154

TESOL Standards

Goal 2, Standard 2—To use English to achieve academically in all content areas: Students will use English to obtain, process, construct, and provide subject matter information in spoken and written form.

Descriptor—Representing information visually and interpreting information presented visually.

Use a Main Idea and Details Chart

Reviewing the main idea and details in a selection will help you remember what you have read. Then you can write the main idea and details in a chart. You can use your chart to retell the selection to a partner.

Practice

Copy and complete this Main Idea and Details Chart. Go back and review parts of the text to help you.

Main Idea

Supporting Detail | Supporting Detail | Supporting Detail

Extension

Write a brief description about something you really liked or disliked about a place you have visited. Discuss your description with a partner or group.

Sharing Language and Culture

Global Perspective Students from abroad may have firsthand knowledge about natural wonders in parts of the world other students are unfamiliar with. Have these students talk about their home countries. Encourage them to use what they know about main idea and details and the skill of retelling as they make their presentation. Guide students to recognize that the world has many different climates and landforms—and many different scenic wonders.

STEP 1: Teach

Use a Main Idea and Details Chart

Remind students that a main idea is the main point, or what a reading is about. Details are there to support the main idea. Have students consider how they would describe their day so far. What is the main idea? What are three details? Ask them to write these down.

Possible Response

Main Idea: I got up and came to school.
Detail: The weather was sunny.
Detail: I wore my corduroys.
Detail: I walked instead of riding the bus.

STEP 2: Practice

You may have students complete the graphic organizer provided as a Blackline Master in the *Teacher's Resource Book*.

Possible Responses

We went on a visit to Yosemite National park.

We went to the top of Glacier Point. | We saw a huge waterfall. | We saw rock climbers on Half Dome.

STEP 3: Extend

Oral Presentation Ask students to present the description they wrote to the class. Have them explain what the main idea and details of their description might be. Remind students to listen quietly while their classmates speak. Encourage them to ask questions after each presentation.

Reteach

Have students reread the paragraph on p. 304 from Jay's scrapbook. Ask students to list the main idea of the paragraph and three supporting details.

STEP 1: Introduce

Say the words *the*, *a*, and *an*. Tell students that these words are examples of articles, and that articles are words that refer to nouns.

STEP 2: Teach

Articles

Draw students' attention to the Rule Box.

SAY *Use* a *before nouns that begin with consonants; use* an *before nouns that begin with vowels or vowel sounds. Words that begin with an* h *use* an *if they have a vowel sound:* an hour. *Words that have a long* u *sound use* a, *because long* u *actually sounds like* yoo: a *uniform.*

- The *is called a definite article, because it refers to a specific noun.*
- A *and* an *do not refer to a specific noun; they are indefinite articles.*

Write the following sentences on the board. Have volunteers choose the correct article from the choices and rewrite each sentence using that article.

Lydia owns a *gray horse*. (an/a)

She rides it in the *country*. (an/the)

After a ride, she gives her horse a *bucket of water*. (a/an)

For a reward, he gets an *ear of corn!* (an/the)

STEP 3: Practice

Before students begin the Practice activity, have each student write four sentences that need a different article in each. Tell students to draw a blank line in place of the article. Then have students exchange pages and complete the sentences with the correct article.

Answer Key

1. an/the	4. a/the
2. a/the	5. an/the
3. the	6. a/the

Teaching Resources
- ***Practice Book,*** pp. 155–156
- ***Assessments,*** pp. 97–100
- ***CD-ROM***

Reading 3

Grammar & Writing

Articles

The words ***a***, ***an***, and ***the*** are **articles**. ***The*** is a definite article because you use it before a specific noun, as in ***the*** blue dish. The words ***a*** and ***an*** are indefinite articles because they do not refer to a specific noun, as in ***an*** elephant.

Rule Box

Use ***a*** before nouns that begin with consonants; use ***an*** before nouns that begin with vowels or vowel sounds.

Words that begin with an *h* use ***an*** if they have a vowel sound: ***an hour***.

Words that begin with a long *u* sound, use ***a*** because *u* actually sounds like yoo: ***a uniform***.

Practice

Write the correct article(s) for each noun.

1. honor	4. horse
2. book	5. apple
3. Earth	6. boat

Practice Book page 155

TESOL Standards

Goal 1, Standard 1—To use English to communicate in social settings: Students will use English to participate in social interactions.
Descriptor—Expressing needs, feelings, and ideas.

Goal 1, Standard 3—To use English to communicate in social settings: Students will use learning strategies to extend their communicative competence.
Descriptor—Seeking support and feedback from others.

Goal 2, Standard 1—To use English to achieve academically in all content areas: Students will use English to interact in the classroom.
Descriptors—Following oral and written directions, implicit and explicit; Explaining actions; Expressing likes, dislikes, and needs.

Goal 3, Standard 1—To use English in socially and culturally appropriate ways: Students will use the appropriate language variety, register, and genre according to audience, purpose, and setting.
Descriptors— Recognizing and using Standard English and vernacular dialects appropriately; Using a variety of writing styles appropriate for different audiences, purposes, and settings.

Write a Concluding Paragraph

A concluding paragraph ties the ideas from previous paragraphs together. Aya wrote a concluding paragraph about her vacation to Lake Sebago in her email to Carolina.

From: aya@ansonia.com
To: C_Mendez@workit.com
Subject: Our lake trip
Date: July 21

Hi Carolina,

We spent most of our days swimming, boating, and fishing. One day, we took a cruise around the entire lake and saw interesting birds and animals. We used the outdoor grill for dinner every night. My brother didn't catch any fish, so we ate hamburgers and corn on the cob. All in all, it was a great vacation. I hope we can come back next year.

See you soon,
Aya

SPELLING TIP

Keep a list in your notebook of words that you find hard to spell. Add to your list when you are reading or writing.

Practice Book page 156

Practice

Write an e-mail to a friend that summarizes a trip you took. Discuss your e-mail with a partner or group.

Writing Checklist

- ✓ Did you summarize your trip?
- ✓ Did you make it clear to your reader where you went?
- ✓ Did you give interesting details about your visit?
- ✓ Can a partner understand your e-mail?

307

Differentiated Instruction	
Beginning	Have students find words in the e-mail that correspond to these categories: *foods*, *activities*. Have them write the words and say them aloud.
Early Intermediate	Have each student draw a picture of Aya at the lake on her vacation. Have students write a caption for their pictures.
Intermediate	Have students write an e-mail to Aya telling her about their day at school. Tell students to write in active voice.
Standard English Learner (CRI)	Have students work with partners to write and pronounce the nouns in the e-mail on p. 295.

STEP 1: Introduce

Write a Concluding Paragraph

Define a concluding paragraph for students.

SAY *When you write a concluding paragraph, you tie together the ideas from other paragraphs. In a way, a concluding paragraph is like a summary; it summarizes what you have written for the reader.*

- *Do you think Aya's e-mail gives a good summary of her vacation to Lake Sebago? Why or why not?*
- *What sentence in the e-mail makes a good concluding statement for the way Aya felt about her vacation?*

Spelling Tip

Read the Spelling Tip aloud as students follow along in their books. Have them list words from Aya's e-mail that they would use a computer's spell check feature or a dictionary to check the spelling of—if the e-mail had been read aloud to them and they did not see the words.

STEP 2: Practice

Before students write their own e-mail, have them list the key pieces of information that a summary about a trip should include. Have them discuss their ideas with partners.

STEP 3: Monitor Progress

Writing Checklist

- ✓ Remind students that a summary should only include key points.
- ✓ Have students make sure the name of the place they went to on vacation is mentioned at least once in their writing.
- ✓ Tell students to include at least three details about the vacation spot in their writing.
- ✓ Have students work with partners. Ask them to read one another's e-mail and give feedback if necessary.

The Five Step Writing Process in the Writing Handbook reference section of this book provides more student writing instruction.

STEP 1: Introduce

More About The Big Question

The Big Question for this reading is *Why do we need to know how to write a research paper?* Lead a discussion about writing a research paper.

SAY *You will use the research skills you have learned this year throughout your life. You will have to write research papers throughout middle school, high school, and college.*

Visual Literacy

Photos The photos on pp. 308-309 show Jay and Maria typing on computers. Remind students that the same photos were used in *How to Prepare for a Trip to Yosemite*. Ask students to think of reasons why the photos may have been used again.

STEP 2: Teach

Understand Text Structure

Draw students' attention to the genre label. Tell them that functional writing is usually done in a simple style—as with the newspaper article and Jay and Maria's earlier e-mails.

Read Aloud

Have students stop at the end of each e-mail and discuss whether they think Maria is giving Jay good advice about writing his paper and why.

Computer Literacy

Students should have basic knowledge of how to prepare documents on a computer. Have students who lack computer skills work with more proficient students. If the school provides a technical manual on how to use computers, read the step-by-step instructions on word processing with students. If possible, have a skilled student demonstrate the skills as you read.

Teaching Resources

- *Teacher's Resource Book*, pp. 149–150
- *CD-ROM* • *Audio CD*

Bonus Reading

FUNCTIONAL WRITING

E-mail

Jay Writes a Research Paper

by Jay Rabin and Maria Reyes

From: Jay_Rabin@lincolnschool.net
To: mreyes@californianet.com
Date: June 5
Subject: What's up, Maria?

Hi Maria,

Not much is new in Pennsylvania. I can't wait for summer. We still have to finish the school year, though.

Jay has to write a research paper.

I just found out I have to write a research paper. Our teacher asked us to start thinking of topics. Because I'm going to Yosemite National Park this summer, I want to write about park rangers. Park rangers are important, and they have cool jobs. I think I want to become one!

Have you ever written a research paper? If so, what did you write about? Do you have any tips for me? I know research papers are an important kind of writing. I want to do a great job!

Write back soon if you can. My mom said she would take me to the library on Saturday.

Your friend,
Jay

308

TESOL Standards

Goal 2, Standard 3—To use English to achieve academically in all content areas: Students will use appropriate learning strategies to construct and apply academic knowledge. **Descriptors**—Focusing attention selectively; Applying basic reading comprehension skills such as skimming, scanning, previewing, and reviewing text; Using context to construct meaning; Applying self-monitoring and self-corrective strategies to build and expand a knowledge base; Knowing when to use native language resources (human and material) to promote understanding.

Maria has some great ideas that will help Jay write his paper.

From: mreyes@californianet.com
To: Jay_Rabin@lincolnschool.net
Date: June 6
Subject: Re: What's up, Maria?

Hi, Jay,

Yes, I have written a research paper. It was about community recycling programs. I really learned a lot. Writing about park rangers is a great idea. But, it's a big topic. I think you should make your topic more specific. What interests you the most about park rangers? Write about that. Some good topics might be how to become a park ranger, what park rangers do, or even the history of park rangers.

You should make your topic more specific before you go to the library. Then you'll have an easier time finding information. When I started to research recycling, my topic was too big. I had a stack of books, magazines, and newspaper articles as tall as I am! So, I made my topic more specific: community recycling programs. Then, I needed only the books about my topic. Information about recycling cars or reusing plastic was interesting, but it was too much information for my paper.

Did your teacher say you could use Web sites as sources? If so, ask a librarian to help you find good information. I was amazed at the information we found online.

Your friend,
Maria

309

Differentiated Instruction

Beginning	Have students work in pairs to answer the following question: *How did Jay get help finding a research paper topic?*
Intermediate	Have students work in pairs. Have each pair write a list of things they learned about writing a research paper.
Greater Challenge	Have students discuss other topics about national parks that would be fun to research. Ask each student to select a topic to research then give a brief report to the class.
Struggling Reader	Say aloud the word *research* for students. Have students repeat the term. Write the word on the board then help students say the following words to help them define research: *read*, *learn*, *facts*.

Build Vocabulary

Words with *re-* Explain to students that several words with the prefix *re-* appear in the selection *Jay Writes a Research Paper*. Tell students that the prefix *re-* is Latin for *again*.

SAY *Many of the words on page 309 begin with the prefix* re-.

- *Which* re- *words can you see?* recycling, research, reusing
- *What part of speech can all of these words be?* action word or verb

Have students create a two-column list for words that begin with the prefix *re-*. In one column, have students define the word that begins with *re-*. In the second column, have students define the word without the prefix.

STEP 3: Extend

Students may want to go to the library for their research, as Jay did. Tell students they will need a library card if they want to borrow books. If they don't have one, they will probably need to fill out a form like this one.

Sunny Valley Public Library
Library Card Application

Name ______________________________
Address ______________________________
____
Phone ______________________________
E-mail ______________________________

I agree to pay any fines for overdue, damaged, or lost items.

Signature ______________________________

Parent's signature (if minor)______________________________

Link to Science

Have students research how e-mail began. Ask students to work in small groups and make a presentation to the class on what they learned about the invention and development of e-mail throughout the world.

STEP 1: Monitor Progress

Comprehension Check

Retell Tell students they can refresh their knowledge of what is going on in the selection by retelling the action in their own words. Pair students with partners and have each tell the other what has happened so far in the selection.

SAY *Jay has written Maria with something on his mind.*

- *What does Jay want help with?* He wants help with his research paper.
- *How does Maria help Jay?* She suggests a more specific topic. She suggests he use the Web to do research.

Build Discussion

What's Fun About Parks Lead a class discussion about what some other research topics might be. Students can use the suggestions they developed for writing about parks on p. 309, or they might propose a wider range of topics. Write their ideas on the board. Divide the class in small groups and assign one research topic to each group. Have them decide on a strategy for researching the topic and divide up the work among the group. Invite groups to share their strategies and team structures with the class.

STEP 2: Teach

Understand Text Structure

SAY *Functional writing like e-mails has its own structure with its own rules. Exchanging information by e-mail also takes on a certain kind of pattern.*

- *What has the pattern been with Jay and Maria?* Jay writes Maria, then Maria writes him back.
- *Why do you think the pattern is like this?* Because Jay wrote first; if Maria wrote first, it would be the opposite.

Have students make a list of rules they follow when they are sending an e-mail.

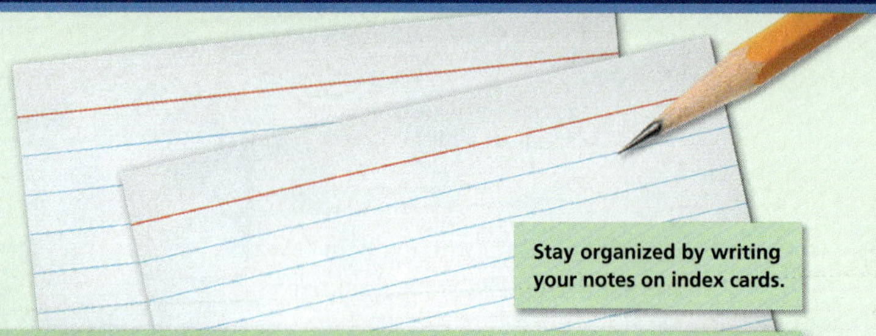

Stay organized by writing your notes on index cards.

From: Jay_Rabin@lincolnschool.net
To: mreyes@californianet.com
Date: June 13
Subject: Research is fun

Hey Maria,

Thanks for the advice. My research is going well. In fact, I'm in the computer lab at the library right now!

The day after I got your message, our teacher talked to us about picking topics that aren't too big or too small. You were right!

I decided to write about what park rangers in Yosemite do. I found lots of books, magazine and newspaper articles, and references at the library. The Internet has lots of stuff too. It can be hard to tell which Web sites have correct information. Sometimes, people make up stuff and post it on the Internet. That's why I'm glad I worked with the librarian. If I look for more sites on the Internet while I'm home, I will ask my mom or dad to help me check them.

When I finish this message, I will start to take notes. It's nice and quiet here in the library. I can really concentrate! I'm going to find the best information, and then put it into my own words. I will write each idea on its own index card. I'm glad I have a big stack of cards!

Your pal,
Jay

310

TESOL Standards

Goal 2, Standard 3—To use English to achieve academically in all content areas: Students will use appropriate learning strategies to construct and apply academic knowledge. **Descriptors**—Focusing attention selectively; Applying basic reading comprehension skills such as skimming, scanning, previewing, and reviewing text; Using context to construct meaning; Applying self-monitoring and self-corrective strategies to build and expand a knowledge base; Knowing when to use native language resources (human and material) to promote understanding.

From: mreyes@californianet.com
To: Jay_Rabin@lincolnschool.net
Date: June 14
Subject: Re: Research is fun

Hey Jay!

It's a great idea to put information in your own words. Also, I wrote the source on the back of each card to help keep track of my sources. List the title, author, publisher, and page or the Web site address. It may take more time, but it's worth it!

It will be helpful to reread your notecards when you are finished with your research. It's fun to put the note cards in order. They will make writing your outline much easier!

Your friend,
Maria

The library is a great place to find information about your topic. Remember to talk quietly.

311

Build Vocabulary

Ask students where on p. 311 they can find another *re-* word.

- Ask a volunteer to come to the board and write the word.
- Invite another volunteer to come up and underline the word's prefix.
- Now have a volunteer circle the word's root.

Subject Lines Explain that in the form of functional writing Jay and Maria are using—e-mail—it is important what you put in the subject line. The subject line tells the person receiving the e-mail what it will be about, and it also lets them know if you are responding to an e-mail you already sent.

STEP 3: Assess

Check Up

Have students work with partners. Ask each partner to tell the other what she or he thinks will learn next about writing a research paper. Ask them to share what clues help them make their predictions.

Differentiated Instruction

Beginning	Have students look at the picture on p. 311 and describe to the class what is happening in the picture and add as many details as possible.
Early Intermediate	Have small groups brainstorm lists of *re-* words. Then have them compose a single silly sentence that uses as many of those words as possible.
Intermediate	Write words with new prefixes on the board. Have students choose a new prefix and find words with that prefix.
Standard English Learner CRI	Lead students in pronouncing each of the words with new prefixes that you have written on the board. Encourage them to add more words to the list.

FYI

The Internet While it seems like the Internet has been around forever, of course it hasn't been. This advanced—and very handy—communications system began in the early 1980s. It was the brainchild of the United States's Advanced Research Projects Agency. At first, the system we now call the Internet—or the Web—was used purely by universities and scientists, but before long, people around the country and the world began to use this system of communication. Today, e-mail has become as important as telephones in helping people stay in touch.

STEP 1: Monitor Progress

Visual Literacy

Photos Draw the students' attention to the photo and caption on p. 312. Ask a volunteer to read the caption aloud.

SAY *When people put together a book like the one you are reading, they use pictures as well as written text to get their message across.*

- *Why do you think this image and caption was used?* The photo shows how you can take written notes; the photo shows someone taking the notes.
- *What does the way the photograph appears on the page suggest about it?* It looks like a snapshot in a scrapbook.

Comprehension Check

Retell Emphasize the idea that the strategy of retelling can be useful at every stage of the writing process. Review with students what the teacher thinks Jay still needs to work on.

SAY *As you write, keep in mind that the retelling strategy can be used at every stage.*

- *What problem does the teacher have with Jay's research paper?* She thinks he needs to work on the conclusion and he needs to indent his paragraphs.
- *How might Jay use the strategy of retelling to work on this problem?* He could try retelling what his paper is about to someone so that he knows what to keep in the conclusion and what to leave out.

Link to Math

If Jay spent 12 hours doing his research and writing note cards, 5 hours writing an outline, and 9 hours writing a rough draft, how many more hours will it take Jay to write his research paper if he takes 75 percent of the time researching, 40 percent of the time writing an outline, plus one-third of the time it took to write the rough draft? 9 + 2 + 3 = 14 hours

Make sure to write down all of your sources and include them in your paper.

From: Jay_Rabin@lincolnschool.net
To: mreyes@californianet.com
Date: June 16
Subject: Rough draft time!

Hi again, Maria,

I got your message at the library. You helped me a lot!

I organized my note cards. But, I didn't have much information about what Yosemite park rangers do in the winter. So I did more research. After that, I wrote my outline. I included all the important ideas. This way, I didn't forget anything.

Then I wrote my rough draft! My teacher looked it over today. It didn't have many spelling or grammar mistakes because I read it a few times before I handed it in. My introduction was clear, and my body paragraphs were organized. My teacher said I need to work on my conclusion. She also reminded me to indent all my paragraphs. I'm going to work on that now. I'll also add my sources.

Do you know why we need sources and a bibliography?

Your friend,
Jay

TESOL Standards

Goal 2, Standard 3—To use English to achieve academically in all content areas: Students will use appropriate learning strategies to construct and apply academic knowledge.
Descriptors—Focusing attention selectively; Applying basic reading comprehension skills such as skimming, scanning, previewing, and reviewing text; Using context to construct meaning; Applying self-monitoring and self-corrective strategies to build and expand a knowledge base; Knowing when to use native language resources (human and material) to promote understanding.

From: mreyes@californianet.com
To: Jay_Rabin@lincolnschool.net
Date: June 20
Subject: Re: Rough draft time!

Hey Jay,

Wow! You sure did a lot of work on your research paper! Don't forget to send me a copy when you are finished.

You know what? I had the same problem with my rough draft. I didn't have a good conclusion. Then I remembered that conclusions sum up the important points from the body paragraphs. That's what I did. It was easy!

You remembered to put all your information in your own words, right? Well, even though you did that, you still have to show where you found the information. The bibliography is a list of the sources you used. It shows each source's title, author, and some other information. If you used a Web site, you include its address.

I'm sure you learned a lot about park rangers at Yosemite. Do you still want to be one someday?

Your friend,
Maria

The librarian can help you find books on your topic.

313

Differentiated Instruction	
Beginning	Challenge students to look through the e-mail on p. 312 for words that name a person, place, or thing. Have students read aloud the words they found.
Intermediate	Have students make a Sequence Chart that shows each step Jay took to write his research paper.
Greater Challenge	Have students discuss with partners what it means to include sources in your paper. Then have students present their ideas to the class and give examples of sources that could be used.
Struggling Reader	Have students look at the picture on p. 312 and say aloud the name of each item in the picture. Write their responses on the board and have them copy the words in their personal thesaurus.

STEP 2: Teach

Words in Context

Help students learn the skill of defining words by using context.

SAY *Whenever you find an unfamiliar word on the page, there is a strategy you can use to figure out what the word means. Take the word* conclusion *on page 313.*

- *What words in Maria's e-mail give you an idea of what she meant when she used the word* conclusion*?* Conclusions sum up the important points from the body paragraphs.
- *What words tell you what* bibliography *means?* The bibliography is a list of the sources that you used.

Study Skills

Dictionary If students need more help with difficult words, they can use a dictionary.

Online Dictionary Students can look up words using the CD that accompanies a learner's dictionary, like the *Longman Basic Dictionary*.

http://www.LongmanCornerstone.com/

STEP 3: Extend

Point of View

Explain to students that the writing style for a research paper is more formal than the writing style for many other types of writing. While research papers are written in both first and third person points of views, students should check with their teachers about which point of view to use in their writing.

E-mail Ask students to think of other ways friends can help each other through e-mail. Then have them write an outline that tells how that e-mail exchange might actually work.

STEP 1: Review

The Big Question

Evidence of Understanding

Read the Big Question with the students to focus attention on this unit's theme in a way that can be answered and assessed in a variety of modalities. The fist tier is the least challenging, and the third tier is the most challenging.

STEP 2: Transfer

Written

Poem Refer to poems you have read in class before and discuss what ideas they are based on.

Brochure Before students start with their own brochures, discuss what a brochure looks like and what content it might contain.

Newspaper Article Make sure students understand that using the 5W questions will help them as they compose their article.

Oral

Conversation Help students prepare for their conversations by reminding them to first respond to what was last said before saying anything new.

Debate Make clear to students that debate has ironclad rules. One team talks, then the other responds, and so forth.

Script Encourage students to conduct research before they write to find a park that really interests them.

Visual/Active

Poster Remind students to choose images for their poster that give a good idea of what the park is like.

Bumper Sticker Before students start with their own bumper stickers, give some examples of effective bumper stickers messages you have seen.

Blueprint Encourage students to think big, and include sights and attractions that *they* would like to see.

UNIT 6 Wrap Up

The Big Question

Why are national parks important?

Written	Oral	Visual/Active
Poem Write a poem about a park you have visited or about Jay's trip to Yosemite. Include details about the park and what people can do there for fun.	**Conversation** With a partner, talk about why national parks are important. Then talk with another pair of students.	**Poster** Design a poster for a national park. Show tourists using the park in a variety of ways.
Brochure Create a brochure for a national park. Include information about its location, activities, and visiting hours. Illustrate your brochure with sketches or photos from the park's Web site.	**Debate** Choose whether you would rather vacation at a national park or in a city. As teams, talk about the reasons for and against choosing each vacation spot.	**Bumper Sticker** Create a bumper sticker that tells about a national park and why people should visit it.
Newspaper Article Research and write a newspaper article about an event or activity that takes place at a national park.	**Script** Write a script a tour guide might use to show tourists around a national park. Be sure to include the park's most popular attractions.	**Blueprint** Use your imagination to design a new national park. Draw a plan for the park that includes its features and activity areas.

314

TESOL Standards

Goal 2, Standard 2—To use English to achieve academically in all content areas: Students will use English to obtain, process, construct, and provide subject matter information in spoken and written form.
Descriptors—Gathering information orally and in writing; Representing information visually and interpreting information presented visually; Understanding and producing technical vocabulary and text features according to content area; Demonstrating knowledge through application in a variety of contexts.

Goal 3, Standard 1—To use English in socially and culturally appropriate ways: Students will use the appropriate language variety, register, and genre according to audience, purpose, and setting.
Descriptors—Using the appropriate degree of formality with different audiences and settings; Recognizing and using Standard English and vernacular dialects appropriately; Using a variety of writing styles appropriate for different audiences, purposes, and settings; Responding to and using slang appropriately; Responding to and using idioms appropriately; Responding to and using humor appropriately; Determining when it is appropriate to use a language other than English; Determining appropriate topics for interaction.

Practice Book pages 157–158

✓ Learning Checklist

Word Analysis and Phonics

- ✓ Distinguish between *v* and *w* sounds.
- ✓ Identify variant vowel /oo/ sounds.
- ✓ Identify Latin word roots.

Comprehension

- ✓ Connect text to self.
- ✓ Use a 5W Chart.
- ✓ Draw conclusions.
- ✓ Use a KWL chart.
- ✓ Review and retell.
- ✓ Use a Main Idea and Details Chart.

Grammar and Writing

- ✓ Identify different types of sentences.
- ✓ Identify active and passive voice.
- ✓ Use articles correctly.
- ✓ Write a business letter.
- ✓ Write a paragraph in active voice.
- ✓ Write a concluding paragraph.

Self-Evaluation Questions

- What do you understand about national parks?
- How easy or difficult was doing research for you?
- What grade or score do you deserve on your research paper? Why?

315

Further Reading

Famous Sports, Cameron Fox
This Penguin Young Reader® is a collection of great stories, facts, and quizzes about American football, basketball, athletics, and more.

John Muir, America's Naturalist, Thomas Locker
Muir's study of nature in Yosemite National Park is highlighted in this biography of the famed naturalist. Full-page landscape paintings augment the text.

Two Bear Cubs: A Miwok Legend from California's Yosemite Valley, Robert D. San Souci
In this story, based on a Miwok Native American legend set in Yosemite National Park, two grizzly bear cubs are stuck on the top of El Capitan rock. Their mother seeks the help of other members of the animal kingdom to rescue her cubs. Surprisingly, the smallest creature succeeds.

STEP 3: Assess

Learning Checklist

Word Analysis and Phonics

- ✓ Words with *v*, *w*: Reading 1, p. 276
- ✓ Variant vowel *oo*: Reading 2, p. 290
- ✓ Latin word roots: Reading 3, p. 302

Comprehension

- ✓ Connect text to self: Reading 1, p. 278
- ✓ Use a 5W Chart: Reading 1, p. 279
- ✓ Draw conclusions: Reading 2, p. 292
- ✓ Use a KWL Chart: Reading 2, p. 293
- ✓ Review and retell: Reading 3, p. 304
- ✓ Use a Main Idea and Details Chart: Reading 3, p. 305

Grammar and Writing

- ✓ Four types of sentences: Reading 1, p. 280
- ✓ Write a business letter: Reading 1, p. 281
- ✓ Active and passive voice: Reading 2, p. 294
- ✓ Write a paragraph in active voice: Reading 2, p. 295
- ✓ Articles: Reading 3, p. 306
- ✓ Write a concluding paragraph: Reading 3, p. 307

Self-Evaluation Questions

The self-evaluation questions provide the teacher with important information about the students' learning process, as well as their self-esteem.

- Encourage students to connect what they have learned about national parks with such science and social studies issues as conservation, ecology, and civic duty.
- Model an answer such as: I used to dislike going to the library to do research. But then I learned to reward myself with a fun book to read every time I finished my research!
- Point out to students that the important thing is to figure out how they can continue to make improvements in their reading and writing.

Teaching Resources

- *Practice Book,* pp. 157–158
- *Transparencies,* p. 86
- *Assessments,* pp. 19–26; 153–161
- *CD-ROM* • *Teacher's CD-ROM*

Writing Workshop

Tell students that this workshop will help them learn how to write research reports. Explain how a research report may differ from other things students have written, such as essays or stories. You may wish to point out that writing research reports is a skill they will use through high school and college.

Research Report

Read aloud the introduction as students follow along. Discuss with students the meaning of the word *research* and the kinds of activities that might be associated with doing research.

Step 1: Choose A Topic

Read aloud the information on how to choose a topic as students follow along. You may wish to discuss the importance of brainstorming to come up with topic ideas.

Scaffolding Demonstrate the process of brainstorming by listing topic ideas on the board. Ask students for additional suggestions. Evaluate each idea as a possible topic for a research report in terms of level of interest, being too simple or too complicated, and how much information may be available.

Step 2: Prewrite and Research

Read aloud this step as students follow along. You may want to arrange a class visit to the school library so the librarian can familiarize students with research sources. (See also *Writing and Research* on pp. 345–350 of this *Handbook*.)

Scaffolding

- **KWL Chart.** Select a simple research topic. Draw a KWL chart on the board and have students copy it. To fill in the K and W columns, ask students, *What do you know about this topic? What do you want to learn?* Have students use classroom materials to find information on the topic. To fill in the L column of the KWL chart, ask students what they learned.
- **Interviews.** If students intend to conduct personal interviews, help them plan and conduct them. Clarify the purpose of the interviews, make appropriate contacts and arrange meetings, prepare questions, and take accurate notes. You may want to demonstrate interviewing and note taking techniques. Stress the importance of writing down accurate information and quotes. Have students practice with each other prior to doing actual interviews. It may be helpful to use audio recorders for interviews. (Students must ask interviewees for permission to tape the interview.)
- **Research notes and sources.** You may wish to demonstrate how to take research notes and write citations on index cards. Some students may need help in determining key ideas, as well as writing notes in their own words instead of copying. Refer to p. 346 for more information on plagiarism and p. 345 for citation formats.

WRITING WORKSHOP

Research Report

Writing a research report is an important skill. In a research report, you explain a topic you have studied in detail.

STEP 1: CHOOSE A TOPIC

The most important step in writing a research report is choosing a topic. Sometimes your teacher will give you the topic to research. Other times you will have to pick it yourself.

If you can choose your own topic, choose a topic you *want* to write about. Be careful that your topic is not too simple or too complicated. If it is, you will have too much, or too little, information to work with.

STEP 2: PREWRITE AND RESEARCH

After you choose your topic, you need to start your research. You can use a KWL chart to help you figure out what you already know about your topic and what you would like to learn.

You can ask the librarian to help you find information. The librarian can show you references, books, magazines, newspapers, and even Web sites! Ask an adult to check the Web sites you use for your research. You may even find people in your community to interview about your topic.

Write down all the information you find on your topic. Get a pack of index cards. Take organized notes on the cards. Make sure the notes are in your own words. Make sure you keep track of your sources. Write what you learn on one side of a card. Then write the source on the back of it. When you list the source, be sure to include the title, author, publisher, and page or Web site address.

316

STEP 3: OUTLINE

If you think you have enough information on your topic, it is time to write an outline. Read all of your index card notes. Set aside any information that you feel is not important.

Put your cards in an order that makes sense. Read your index cards again. Make sure you have all the information you need. Then use the cards to write an outline. The outline should show the ideas you will use in your paper. The ideas should be listed in the order you will write about them. Look at Elena's outline:

I. Why visit San Antonio?
- **A.** We want to visit all 50 states.
- **B.** Many fun things to see and do

II. What is special about the River Walk?
- **A.** walking
- **B.** boat rides

III. What historical places can I visit in San Antonio?
- **A.** The Alamo
- **B.** San Antonio Missions National Historical Park

IV. What other places can I see in San Antonio?
- **A.** Guinness Book of World Records
- **B.** Ripley's Haunted House

V. Conclusion
- **A.** Why I am going in the summer?
- **B.** What if it rains?

Step 3: Outline

Read aloud this step as students follow along in their books. Then call on volunteers to read aloud Elena's outline. Discuss how the outline flows and whether each step in the outline makes sense.

Scaffolding When students read and organize their index cards, it may help to stack them based on main ideas. Students can write main ideas on different index cards and use them to group each stack of cards. This process will also help students write their outline and identify information gaps that will require further research.

Graphic organizers may help some students to organize ideas and create outlines. You may encourage them to use organizers such as T-Charts, Venn Diagrams, Word Webs, Main Idea Charts, Timelines, Flowcharts, or Sequence-of-Events Charts.

Step 4: Write a Draft

Read aloud this step as students follow along. As you read about the report's introduction, body, and conclusion, point out these sections in Elena's first draft. Next, ask student volunteers to read aloud Elena's draft. Discuss each paragraph in terms of the main ideas and supporting details. Ask students, *How do you think Elena used her outline to write her first draft?*

Guide students in using their notes and outlines to write the first draft of their research reports.

Metacognition To help students monitor their comprehension, ask, *What do you think of Elena's first draft? Is there anything she should do to make it better?*

STEP 4: WRITE A DRAFT

Now you are ready to write your first draft. Your paper should start with an introduction. This tells your readers about your topic. Next comes the body of the paper. This has all the information that you researched. The body might be two paragraphs. It might be ten paragraphs. The length of your report will depend on how much research you have done. Finally, you will have a conclusion. This will summarize the topic for your reader. Look at an excerpt from Elena's first draft:

Elena Rodriguez
San Antonio, Texas

My mom and me want to visit all 50 states. We want to visit Texas next. My mom and I picked San Antonio as our spot for Texas. I am really excited to go there cuz it has some cool and fun things like very big water park, a Sea World, the River Walk, and the Alamo. San Antonio also has a zoo and some fun museums.

The River Walk is a place where you can walk or take a boat ride on the San Antonio River. A lot of people call it Paseo de Rio, which means River Walk. The officials city drain the river every January so they can clean the trash from the bottom. You can take a boat ride 35 minutes long. You can even get married there? There are also so many restaurants and stores, I can't wait to do some shopping.

San Antonio also history. The Alamo was a mission where a battle took place. The battle was between a Mexican dictater, Antonio Lopez de Santa Anna with his men and Travis William and his settlers. William Travis outnumbered 189 to 4000. The Alamo be very important to the independence of Texas. I seen pictures of the Alamo but I want to see in person. My mom and me might also visit Spanish missions at San Antonio Missions Park.

STEP 5: REVISE

After you have written your paper, read it carefully. Use the proofreading marks on page 342 to make any corrections. Look up any words you think you spelled incorrectly in the dictionary. Make sure that you have the correct names and dates in your paper. Add any details you may have forgotten. Ask yourself:

- Are the ideas presented in the best order?
- Is there a clear beginning, middle, and end?
- Does each paragraph have a main idea and supporting details?
- Did you cite your sources correctly?

> **Plagiarism**
> Plagiarism is presenting someone else's words, ideas, or work as your own. If the idea or words are not yours, be sure to give credit by citing the source in your work. Plagiarizing can result in your failing the assignment, or worse.

Ask a partner to read your writing and make comments about it. This is called a **peer review**. Decide what changes you want to make. Then rewrite your draft.

STEP 6: EDIT

This is the time to look at word choice, sentence fluency, and writing conventions. Reread your paper. Proofread for mistakes in spelling, grammar, and punctuation. Correct any mistakes you find.

When you edit and proofread your draft, use the editing marks on page 342 of the Writing Handbook to mark the changes.

319

Step 5: Revise

Read aloud the introduction to Step 5 as students follow along. Next, read aloud and discuss each bulleted question. It may be helpful to show a sample of a student's draft report on an overhead transparency and use the bulleted questions to review the report. Refer to the Editing/Proofreading Marks chart on p. 342 and the Modern Language Association's chart on listing sources on p. 347 for citation formats.

Plagiarism Read aloud the definition of *plagiarism* as students follow along. Tell students your school's rules regarding plagiarism and why it is considered a serious offense. For suggestions on how to avoid plagiarizing, see p. 346.

Peer Review For suggestions on showing students how to conduct a constructive peer review, see p. 341. After the peer review, have students work individually to revise their drafts.

Step 6: Edit

In this step, students will check their work and make final corrections. Read aloud step 6 as students follow along in their books.

Guide students as they reread their second drafts, check word choice and sentence fluency, and correct spelling, grammar, and punctuation errors. Refer to p. 342 for an Editing/Proofreading Marks chart and a Proofreading Checklist.

When students are done editing and proofreading their work, they should rewrite or reprint a perfect final draft, ready for publishing.

Elena's Final Research Report. Tell students that the final, edited version of Elena's research report is presented on pp. 320–321. It may be helpful to show a transparency of Elena's report on an overhead projector so you can point to sections and mark it up based on the discussion to follow.

Have student volunteers take turns reading aloud Elena's report. Ask students to use the bulleted questions listed in step 5 to evaluate Elena's report. Discuss what she could have done better. Then ask students to evaluate Elena's report for word choice, sentence fluency, writing conventions, spelling, grammar, and punctuation. Also take a look at her citations on p. 321. Ask students to suggest final edits that Elena may have missed.

You may wish to refer students to the writing rubric on p. 342 or another rubric used in class. Have them score Elena's final draft using the rubric.

After discussing Elena's final draft, students may want to make some additional edits to their own work to prepare for publishing.

Metacognition To monitor student comprehension of the writing process, ask, *When you went through the revision and editing steps, how did you improve your writing? Describe specific examples of how you did this. Why are these steps important in getting your piece ready to publish?*

Look at Elena's final version of her paper.

Elena Rodriguez
San Antonio, Texas

My mom and I want to visit all 50 states. We want to visit Texas next. We chose San Antonio for our Texas visit. I am really excited because it has some cool and fun things like the River Walk and the Alamo. San Antonio also has a zoo and some fun museums.

There is a River Walk in San Antonio. The River Walk is a place where you can walk or take a boat ride on the San Antonio River. A lot of people call it by its Spanish name, Paseo de Rio. The city officials drain the river every January so they can clean the trash from the bottom. You can take a boat ride that is 35 minutes long. There are so many restaurants and stores. I can't wait to do some shopping.

San Antonio also has a lot of history. The Alamo was a mission where a battle took place. The battle was between a Mexican dictator, Antonio Lopez de Santa Anna, with his men and William Travis and his settlers. The Alamo is very important to the independence of Texas. My mom and I might also visit Spanish missions at San Antonio Missions National Historical Park.

I think San Antonio, Texas, is going to be a good place to visit because it has lots of interesting and historic places to see. Mom and I will be going in the summer. Even if it rains I still think it will be fun because there are a few museums you can go to and other places like the Guinness Book of World Records and Ripley's Haunted House. I am looking forward to going. San Antonio is my kind of place.

320

Works cited:

San Antonio Riverwalk May 31, 2007 <www.longmancornerstone.com>

Travel Channel Destination Guides June 1, 2007 <www.longmancornerstone.com>

Convention and Visitors Bureau-San Antonio June 2, 2007 <www.longmancornerstone.com>

Kelly, Kate and Zeman, Anne. *Everything You Need to Know About American History Homework: A Desk Reference for Students and Parents.* New York, NY. Scholastic. 1997. p. 45.

STEP 7: PUBLISH

Once you have revised and proofread your paper, share it with others. Look at these publishing ideas.

- Post your paper on the bulletin board.
- Photocopy your paper. Hand it out to your classmates and family members.
- Attach it to an email and send it to friends.
- Send it to a school newspaper or magazine for possible publication.

Once you have shared your work with others, you may want to put it in your portfolio. A **portfolio** is a folder or envelope in which you keep your writing. If you keep your work in a portfolio, you can look at what you have written over a period of time. This will let you see if your writing is improving. It will help you become a better writer.

Most importantly, don't forget to congratulate yourself on a job well done!

321

Step 7: Publish

In this final step, students share their work with others. Read the bulleted publishing ideas aloud with students. Invite students to think of other ways they can publish their work. You may wish to explore having a class web page where students can post their work.

Have students place their work in their assessment portfolios for comparison with past and future assignments. Sometimes it is helpful for students to keep all their drafts and revisions together with their final published work. This provides evidence of growth, improvement, and learning through use of the writing process.

Handbook

Study Skills and Language Learning

How to Learn Language

Learning a language involves listening, speaking, reading, and writing. You can use these tips to make the most of your language learning.

LISTENING

1. Listen with a purpose.
2. Listen actively.
3. Take notes.
4. Listen to speakers on the radio, television, and Internet.

SPEAKING

1. Think before you speak.
2. Speak appropriately for your audience.
3. Practice reading aloud to a partner.
4. Practice speaking with friends and family members.
5. Remember, it is okay to make mistakes.

READING

1. Read every day.
2. Use the visuals to help you figure out what words mean.
3. Reread parts that you do not understand.
4. Read many kinds of literature.
5. Ask for help.

WRITING

1. Write something every day.
2. Plan your writing before you begin.
3. Read what you write aloud. Ask yourself whether it makes sense.
4. Check for spelling and grammar mistakes.

323

Study Skills and Language Learning Handbook

This Handbook contains valuable information about the study skills and language learning skills students need to succeed in school. It covers the following topics:

- How to learn language
- How to study
- How to build vocabulary
- How to use a book
- How to use a dictionary and thesaurus
- How to take tests

To introduce the Handbook, walk your students through the pages and, together, note the information found under major headings and subheadings. Direct teaching of the Handbook for brief periods will help students become familiar with finding information and understanding content. Point out to students that they may consult the Handbook on their own to find information such as how to use a dictionary.

How to Learn Language

Read the introduction as students follow along in the text. Explain that *Listening*, *Speaking*, *Reading*, and *Writing* are the four key components of learning a language. Then read aloud each tip as students follow along in their books and discuss each item.

Listening

Ask students, *What does it mean to listen with a purpose, and what are some examples? How do you listen actively? When is active listening important? How does taking notes help you listen? How can you use the radio, TV, and Internet to help you learn language?*

Speaking

Ask students, *What are some situations when it's good to think before you speak?* Discuss the importance of speaking your new language at school, at home, in stores, at the doctor's office, and other places. Reassure students that we all make mistakes as part of the learning process, whether it's learning to ride a bike or speak a new language.

Reading

Ask students, *How can you make reading part of your everyday routine? How do visuals (pictures, photos, diagrams) help you figure out what words mean? How does rereading help you understand better?* Explain what literature is. Discuss why reading different kinds of literature improves reading skills.

Writing

Discuss the value of writing every day. Ask, *Why is it important to plan your writing before you start? What do you learn when you read aloud what you write? Why is it important to check spelling and grammar before turning in your work?*

How to Study

Tell students that developing good study habits is important for improving language skills and succeeding in school. Read each tip aloud as students follow along and discuss each item.

- **Schedule a time for studying.** Ask students, *Do you have a special time when you study? Why is this a good habit?*
- **Create a special place for studying.** Ask students, *Do you have a special place where you study? What are some distractions to avoid when you are studying?*
- **Read the directions first.** Ask students, *Why is it important to read directions before you start your work? Do you ask questions when you don't understand something?*
- **Preview the reading.** Ask students, *What do you do before you start reading a book or story? How do these actions help you understand the reading? Do you preview the reading in your math and science classes?*
- **Learn unfamiliar words.** Demonstrate how students can figure out the meanings of unfamiliar words (context, finding smaller words within a word, using a glossary or dictionary, etc.). If students cannot figure out words on their own, they may write them in their reading journals to ask about later.
- **Take notes.** Discuss how taking notes can help them remember what they read. They may want to write notes in their reading journals as they read.
- **Ask questions.** Ask students, *Why is it important to ask questions as you read? How does asking questions help you understand more of what you read?*

How to Study

Here are some tips for developing good study habits.

- **Schedule a time for studying.** It is easier to develop good study habits if you set aside the same time every day to study. Once you have a study routine, it will be easier for you to find time to prepare for larger projects or tests.
- **Create a special place for studying.** Find a study area where you are comfortable and where you have everything you need for studying. If possible, choose an area that is away from telephones or television. You can play music if it helps you to concentrate.
- **Read the directions first.** Make sure you understand what you are supposed to do. Ask a partner or your teacher about anything you do not understand.
- **Preview the reading.** Look at the pictures, illustrations, and captions in the reading. They will help you understand the text.
- **Learn unfamiliar words.** Try to figure out what unfamiliar words mean by finding context clues in the reading. If you still can't figure out the meaning, use a dictionary.
- **Take notes.** Keep notes in a notebook or journal of important things you want to remember from the reading.
- **Ask questions.** Write any questions you have from the reading. Discuss them with a partner or your teacher.

324

Scaffolding Find a short, informational piece in the student book. Read aloud as students follow along. Ask, *What are the most important words in each paragraph?* Demonstrate how to use these key words for taking notes. Tell students to identify the most important ideas, write them in their own words, and avoid copying directly from the text. If students do not understand parts of the reading, they may write questions and follow up later.

How to Build Vocabulary

Use these ideas to help you remember the meanings of new words.

Keep a Vocabulary Notebook Keep a notebook of vocabulary words and their definitions. Test yourself by covering either the word or the definition.

Make Flashcards On the front of an index card, write a word you want to remember. On the back, write the meaning. Use the cards to review the words with a partner or family member.

Say the Words Aloud Use your new words in sentences. Say the sentences to a partner or a family member.

How to Use a Book

The Title Page The title page states the title, the author, and the publisher.

The Table of Contents The table of contents is at the front of a book. The page on which a chapter begins is next to its name.

The Glossary The glossary is a small dictionary at the back of a book. It will tell you the meaning of a word, and sometimes how to pronounce it. Use the glossary the same way you would use a dictionary.

The Index The index is at the back of a book. It lists subjects and names that are in the book, along with page numbers where you can find information.

The Bibliography The bibliography at the back of a book or chapter lets you know the books or sources where an author got information.

325

How to Use a Book

Have students look through the student book. Point out the different sections, such as title page and table of contents. For each section, ask students what information is provided and what clues are given about the reading.

How to Build Vocabulary

Discuss the meaning of the word *vocabulary*. Tell students that building a strong vocabulary is essential for learning a language. Then read aloud each item as students follow along and discuss how they can use each suggestion.

Keep a Vocabulary Notebook. You may want to provide students with blank vocabulary sheets or a format for notebook paper so they can keep a running list of new words and definitions.

Make Flashcards. Show sample flashcards to students. You may wish to give students blank index cards and dictionaries to make their own flashcards. Some students may want to draw pictures to help them remember word meanings.

Cooperative Grouping You may want to have pairs of students use their flashcards to test each other on new vocabulary words.

Say the Words Aloud. Discuss why saying and repeating words aloud helps students learn new words.

Scaffolding Write several key words from a unit in the student book on the board. Say each word aloud and have students repeat. Encourage students to listen closely as you speak the words. It may help students to tape themselves on audio recorders and then listen to how they pronounce words.

Metacognition To help students understand how building vocabularies is already a part of their learning process, ask, *What new word did you learn recently? How did you learn it? Can you use it in a sentence? How can you teach the word to a friend or someone in your family?*

How to Use a Dictionary and Thesaurus

Tell students that knowing how to use a dictionary and a thesaurus will help them improve their reading and writing skills.

The Dictionary

Read the introduction to using a dictionary aloud as students follow along in the text. Discuss the information given in the sample entry—the pronunciation, the part of speech, definitions, and example sentences. Point out that there are two different definitions for the word *letter*.

Students may ask, *How do I look up the spelling of a word that I don't know how to spell?* Write the word *cloud* on the board. Ask, *How would you look up the word cloud if you didn't know how to spell it? What letter or letters have a /k/ sound? (c, k, ch) What letter or letters have an /ow/ sound? (ow, ou)* Explain to students that if a word has more than one potential spelling, they may have to look up various possible spellings before they find the right one.

Metacognition To help students monitor their comprehension, ask, *Who has seen a dictionary page that looks like this? When have you used a dictionary?*

Scaffolding You may want to hand out dictionaries to students to practice looking up words. Point out how guide words at the top of dictionary pages can help them find words. Write a set of key words from the student book on the board. Ask students to look up these words in the dictionary, write down at least one definition for each word, and write a sentence using the word. Depending on students' dictionary skills, you may wish to repeat this exercise on a daily or weekly basis. Also, make sure students use a dictionary every day as they do their reading lessons. Bilingual dictionaries may help some students. If beginning language learners struggle with dictionary usage, check their English alphabet skills.

How to Use a Dictionary and Thesaurus

The Dictionary

You can find the **spelling**, **pronunciation**, **part of speech**, and **definitions** of words in the dictionary.

Pronunciation Part of Speech

Definitions

let•ter /ˈlɛt̬ɚ/ noun ① one of the signs that you use to write words: *A, B, and C are the first three* ***letters*** *in the English alphabet.*
② a written message that you put into an envelope and send to someone: *I wrote a* ***letter*** *to my friend in Texas.*

Example Sentence

The Thesaurus

A thesaurus is a specialized dictionary that lists **synonyms**, or words with similar meanings, and **antonyms**, or words with opposite meanings. Words in a thesaurus are arranged alphabetically. You can look up the word just as you would look it up in a dictionary.

Main entry: sad
Part of speech: adjective[1]
Definition: unhappy
Synonyms: bitter, depressed, despairing, down, downcast, gloomy, glum, heartbroken, low, melancholy, morose, pessimistic, sorry, troubled, weeping
Antonyms: cheerful, happy

326

The Thesaurus

Read the introduction to using a thesaurus aloud as students follow along. Discuss the information given in the sample entry—the pronunciation, the part of speech, definition, and example sentences. Read aloud the synonyms and antonyms for the word *sad*.

Scaffolding Tell students they can replace the word *sad* with the synonyms in the thesaurus sample. Write an example of a sentence on the board using the word *sad*, e.g., *He was sad when his best friend moved away.* Then write the same sentence using a synonym for sad, e.g., *He was depressed when his best friend moved away.* Have students write their own sentences using *sad* and then replace *sad* with synonyms in the same sentences.

How to Take Tests

Taking tests is part of going to school. Use these tips to help you answer the kinds of questions you often see on tests.

True-False Questions

- If a statement seems true, make sure it is *all* true.
- The word *not* can change the meaning of a statement.
- Pay attention to words such as *all*, *always*, *never*, *no*, *none*, and *only*. They often make a statement false.
- Words such as *generally*, *much*, *many*, *sometimes*, and *usually* often make a statement true.

Multiple Choice Questions

- Try to answer the question before reading the choices. If your answer is one of the choices, choose it.
- Eliminate answers you know are wrong.
- Don't change your answer unless you know it is wrong.

Matching Questions

- Count each group to see whether any items will be left over.
- Read all the items before you start matching.
- Match the items you know first.

Fill-In-the-Blank Questions or Completions

- Read the question or incomplete sentence carefully.
- Look for clues in the question or sentence that might help you figure out the answer.
- If you are given possible answers, cross each out as you use it.

Short Answers and Essays

- Take a few minutes to organize your thoughts.
- Give only the information that is asked for.
- Answer as clearly as possible.
- Leave time to proofread your response or essay.

327

How to Take Tests

Read the introduction aloud as students follow along in the text. You may also want to say, *Listen carefully to instructions, and ask questions if you do not understand the instructions. Remember to answer ALL the questions. Do not leave any blanks. Check your work before you turn in the test.*

Then read aloud each tip as students follow along. Discuss how students can use these tips when they are taking tests.

To help students practice using the test-taking tips, you may want to find existing sample practice tests for recent standardized examinations. Make copies of tests, including different types of test items. Review test tips, and guide students through each type of item.

True-False Questions

Write five factual statements on the board. Call on students to read aloud each statement, and then add the word *not* to change the meaning. Ensure that students understand the meanings of words such as *true*, *false*, *all*, *always*, *never*, *no*, *none*, *only*, *generally*, *much*, *any*, *sometimes*, and *usually*.

Multiple Choice Questions

You may want to show students examples of multiple choice questions and make sure they understand the process of logical elimination.

Matching Questions

You may wish to show students examples of matching questions. Tell students they should match the items they know for sure first.

Fill-In-the-Blank Questions or Completions

You may want to provide examples of fill-in-the-blank questions or completions. Give students tips on finding clues to help figure out answers.

Short Answers and Essays

You may want to provide sample short answer questions and essay topics. The process described in the *Writing Handbook* will also help students in writing essays.

Metacognition To help monitor students' comprehension, ask, *What kind of questions have you seen on tests? What types of questions are easy, and what types are hard? Why? How do you get better at taking tests?*

Viewing and Representing Information

This Handbook contains useful information about ways to view and represent different kinds of information. It covers the following topics:

- How to read maps and diagrams
- How to read graphs

How to Read Maps and Diagrams

Read aloud the introduction as students follow along. Discuss how maps, diagrams, graphs, and charts help students understand the readings.

Maps

Read aloud the introduction as students follow along. Ask, *Parts of which two countries are shown on this map?* Have students describe their own experiences using maps.

Explain that the Underground Railroad was used in the United States during the 1800s to help slaves escape from the South to reach freedom in the North. The Underground Railroad was not an actual railroad, but a series of escape routes. (You may also need to explain slavery as a part of United States history.)

Model your observations of some of the map conventions. Ask students to point to words on the map as you mention them. Say, *The names of the states are in capital letters. The name of another country, CANADA, is shown in all capital letters, too.* Point out that names of large bodies of water, such as the Atlantic Ocean, and mountain ranges, such as the Appalachian Mountains, are also shown in capital letters.

Ask students, *If you and your family drive from Florida to New York, which states do you have to go through?* Have students imagine other trips and the states they will travel through.

Point out the compass rose on the map. Ask students, *Why is it called a compass rose?* Have students indicate points on the compass rose when you say a direction.

Ask students if they are more familiar with kilometers or meters. Ask, *Using the scale, how many miles/kilometers is it from Kansas to the Atlantic Ocean?*

Viewing and Representing Information

How to Read Maps and Diagrams

Informational texts often use maps, diagrams, graphs, and charts. These tools help illustrate and explain the topic.

Maps

Maps show the location of places such as countries, states, and cities. They can also show where mountains, rivers, lakes, and streets are located. A compass rose on the map shows which way is north. A scale shows how miles or kilometers are represented on the map.

Routes of the Underground Railroad

Diagrams

Diagrams are drawings that explain things or show how things work. Some diagrams show pictures of how objects look on the outside or on the inside. Others show the different steps in a process.

This diagram shows the steps of the Scientific Method. It helps you understand the order and importance of each step.

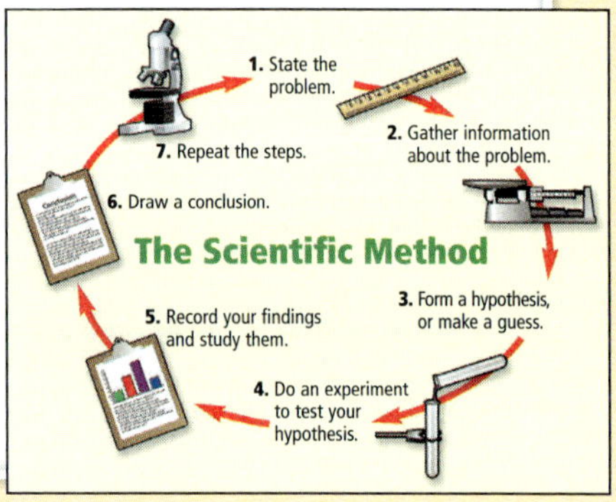

328

Diagrams

Read aloud the introduction as students follow along. Invite students to describe diagrams they have seen in textbooks, newspapers, and magazines.

Explain that the diagram on this page is only one example. Tell students this diagram shows the steps in a process that scientists use to solve science problems. Read aloud each step and explain *scientist*, *hypothesis*, and *conclusion*.

Metacognition To monitor students' comprehension, ask, *What are some examples of diagrams you use in everyday life? Why are they useful? Can you draw a diagram to show someone how to do something or to explain an idea?*

Websites For more information on maps and diagrams, log on to www.LongmanCornerstone.com for links to other interesting websites.

How to Read Graphs

Graphs show how two or more kinds of information are related or alike. Three common kinds of graphs are **line graphs**, **bar graphs**, and **circle graphs**.

Line Graph

A **line graph** shows how information changes over a period of time. This line graph explains how the Native American population of Central Mexico changed over 120 years.

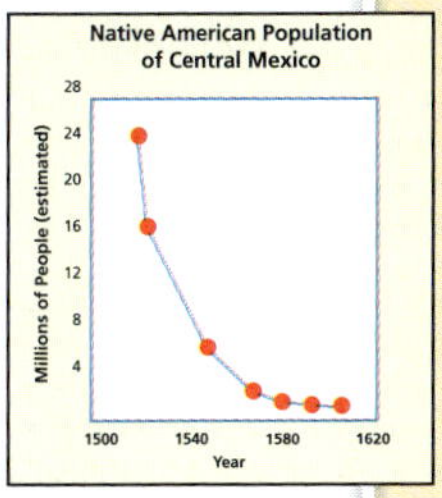

Bar Graphs

We use **bar graphs** to compare information. For example, this bar graph compares the populations of the 13 United States in 1790.

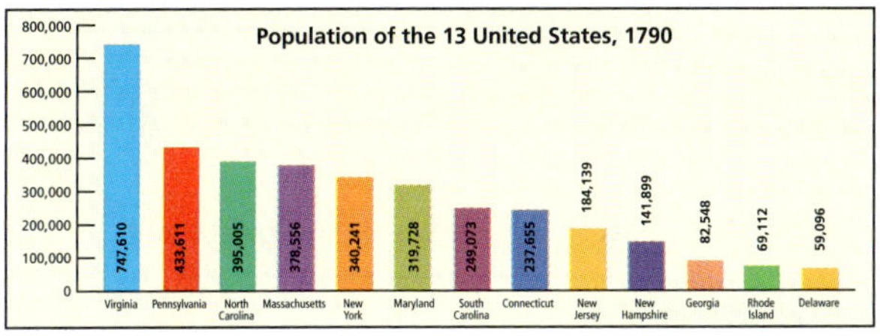

Circle Graphs

A **circle graph** is sometimes called a pie chart because it looks like a pie cut into slices. Circle graphs are used to show how different parts of a whole compare to each other.

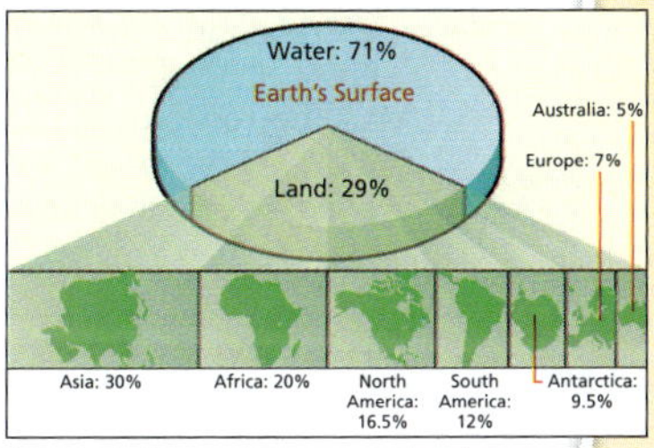

329

How to Read Graphs

Read aloud the introduction as students follow along. Tell them graphs organize and explain different kinds of information. Ask, *Have you ever used or made a graph? How do graphs help you?*

Line Graphs

Look at the line graph. Have a volunteer read aloud the title. Ask, *Have you ever made a graph like this in your math class? What do you remember about that graph?* Point out that the information on this graph might help you understand the history of Native Americans in Central Mexico.

Draw students' attention to the numbers at the bottom of the graph. Say, *These numbers are on the x-axis and represent years. There are forty years in between each of the four numbers shown on the x-axis, even though they are not shown.* Call attention to the numbers on the left-side of the graph. Say, *These numbers are on the y-axis and represent the number of people in millions.* Model how to find points on an x/y-graph.

Have students answer questions based on the graph. Afterwards, ask students to create additional questions that may be answered by looking at the graph.

1. What was the Native American population in Central Mexico in 1520? about 24 million
2. What do you think happened to the number of Native Americans from 1500 to 1620 based on information from the graph? got much smaller

Bar Graphs

Read aloud the introduction to bar graphs and the graph title with students. Ask, *What information is shown in the bar graph? What kind of book might have a graph like this?* United States history Model how to find information on the x-axis and y-axis. Have students answer questions based on the graph. Then ask students to create additional questions that may be answered by looking at the graph.

1. What was the population of Maryland in 1790? 319,728
2. Which state had the biggest population? Virginia

Circle Graphs

Read the definition and chart title aloud. Ask, *Why is pie chart a good name for this chart? What two things does this pie chart show?* land and water Call attention to the information about the continents. Ask, *Which continent takes up 12 percent of the earth's land?* South America *Which takes up 20 percent?* Africa

Websites For more information on reading resources, log on to www.LongmanCornerstone.com for links to other interesting websites.

Grammar Handbook

This Handbook is a valuable guide for your students to use in the classroom or on their own. It contains a concise summary of the grammar and punctuation skills students will use when they speak and write in English. The Handbook covers these topics:

- Parts of Speech
- Punctuation

Parts of Speech

List the nine parts of speech on the board and say them aloud with your students. Explain that students will use these kinds of words to speak and write in English.

Nouns

Read aloud the definition of *nouns* with students. Help students differentiate between the two types of nouns—common and proper nouns. Write the category names *people*, *places*, and *things* on the board. Ask volunteers to say nouns that fit these categories, and write the words on the board. Read aloud the definition of *compound nouns*. Ask volunteers to read aloud the compound words in the box.

Scaffolding Draw two webs on the board. Write *Common Nouns* in the center of the first web and write *Proper Nouns* in the second web. List the following nouns. Then ask students to copy the webs and write each noun in the correct web.

Common Nouns: *desk*, *garden*, *boy*, *month*, *baseball*, *pizza*, *nurse*, *house*

Proper Nouns: *Omar*, *Mexico*, *September*, *Lisa*, *Tuesday*, *Yankees*, *Florida*, *American*

Articles

Read and discuss the definition of *articles* with students. Focus on the indefinite articles *a* and *an* and give examples of usage. Have students use these articles in sentences: *a desk*, *a chair*, *an eraser*, *an e-mail*.

Next, focus on the definite article *the*. Say, *The definite article the is used to talk about one or more specific person, place, or thing.* Give directions, such as *Please bring me the red pen.* Have students take turns giving directions to request specific items.

Grammar Handbook

Parts of Speech

In English there are nine **parts of speech**: nouns, articles, pronouns, verbs, adjectives, adverbs, prepositions, conjunctions, and interjections.

Nouns

Nouns name people, places, or things.

A **common noun** is a general person, place, or thing.

person	thing	place
The **student** brings a **notebook** to **class**.		

A **proper noun** is a specific person, place, or thing.

person	place	thing
Joe went to **Paris** and saw the **Eiffel Tower**.		

Articles

Indefinite articles are *a* or *an*. They refer to a person, place, or thing.

Use *an* before a word that begins with a vowel sound.

> I have **an** idea.

Use *a* before a noun that begins with a consonant sound.

> May I borrow **a** pen?

The is called a **definite article**. Use *the* to talk about specific people, places, or things.

> Please bring me **the** box from your room.

330

Scaffolding Write a list of nouns preceded by definite articles on the board. Then write the same nouns preceded by indefinite articles. Have students take turns underlining each article and using each article and noun in a sentence.

the book	*a book*
the eraser	*an eraser*
the paper	*a paper*

Pronouns

Pronouns are words that take the place of nouns or proper nouns.

proper noun	pronoun
Ana is not home.	She is babysitting.

	Subject Pronouns	Object Pronouns
Singular	I, you, he, she, it	me, you, him, her, it
Plural	we, you, they	us, you, them

A **subject pronoun** replaces the subject of a sentence. A **subject** is who or what a sentence is about.

subject	subject pronoun (singular)
Dan is a student.	He goes to school every day.

Object pronouns replace a noun or proper noun that is the object of a verb. An **object** receives the action of a verb.

object	object pronoun (singular)
Lauren gave Ed the notes.	Lauren gave him the notes.

Possessive pronouns replace nouns or proper nouns. They show who owns something.

	Possessive Pronouns
Singular	mine, yours, hers, his
Plural	ours, yours, theirs

331

Scaffolding Have students place items they own, such as a pen, a book, or a box of markers, on a table. Ask students to say sentences about the items using possessive pronouns. For instance: *This is his pen. These are their markers. This is my book.*

Metacognition To help students understand how they learn, ask, *What worked better for helping you understand pronouns—changing the subjects and pronouns in the sentences or just reading about pronouns?*

Pronouns

Read the definition of *pronouns* aloud with students. Emphasize that pronouns can take the place of the subject of a sentence or the object of the verb in a sentence. Read the chart together and help students distinguish between singular and plural pronouns.

Subject Pronouns Read aloud the definition of *subject pronouns* and the examples in the box with students.

Scaffolding Write the following sentences on the board. Have students take turns completing the second sentence in each pair with a subject pronoun that takes the place of the underlined noun or proper noun in the first sentence.

1. *Mark is playing ball.* ____ *is in the field.*
2. *Ted and I play.* ____ *play after school.*
3. *These books are for Jen.* ____ *are about lions.*
4. *The boys are here.* ____ *are here.*
5. *This school is very clean.* ____ *has a fresh coat of paint on the walls.*

Object Pronouns Read aloud the definition of *object pronouns* with students. Point out the object pronoun *him* that takes the place of the object pronoun *Ed* in the example. Then write these sentences on the board: *Lauren gave Ed the notes. Lauren gave him the notes.* Have students take turns replacing the name *Ed* in the first sentence with other names and then using the correct object pronoun *him* or *her* or *them* to complete the second sentence.

For a discussion of object pronouns used with prepositions, see p. 334.

Possessive Pronouns Read aloud the definition of *possessive pronouns* and the examples in the box. Write on the board: *Alicia put on her coat.* Students may take turns replacing the name *Alicia* with other names and using the correct possessive pronoun in the sentence.

Verbs

Call on a volunteer to act out verbs that you whisper. Ask the other students to identify what the student is doing and record it on the board. For example, *Johnny jumps.* Explain that words that name actions are called *verbs*.

Action Verbs Read aloud the definition and examples with students. Help them distinguish between the action verbs you can see and cannot see. Elicit other verbs to add to each list.

Scaffolding Write the following sentences on the board to review how regular verbs are used. Point out the *-s* endings.

I sit.	*You sit.*	*He sits.*
We sit.	*They sit.*	*She sits.*
		It sits.

Write each verb from the lists on p. 332 on a card. Have students take turns to choose a card, read the verb, and then use the verb in a sentence. Model several sentences that vary the subject. Encourage students to vary sentences in a similar fashion.

Linking Verbs Tell students that *linking verbs* link or connect the subject with another word that describes the subject, but that the linking verbs *themselves* do not show action. Read aloud the examples of linking verbs in the box.

Cooperative Grouping Write the following incomplete sentences on the board. Have students work in pairs to add a word to follow each linking verb and complete each sentence:

I look ____. *The flower smells ____.*

They appear ____. *He seems ____.*

We are ____. *The horse is ____.*

Helping Verbs Read the definition of a *helping verb* aloud with students. Note the examples in the box.

Verbs

Verbs express an action or a state of being.

An **action verb** tells what someone or something does or did.

Verbs That Tell Actions You Can See		Verbs That Tell Actions You Cannot See	
dance	swim	know	sense

A **linking verb** shows no action. It links the subject with another word that describes the subject.

Examples of Linking Verbs		
look	smell	is
are	appear	seem

A helping verb comes before the main verb. They add to a verb's meaning.

	Helping Verbs
Forms of the verb *be*	am, was, is, were, are
Forms of the verb *do*	do, did, does
Forms of the verb *have*	have, had, has
Other helping verbs	can, must, could, have (to), should, may, will, would

332

Cooperative Grouping Write the following incomplete sentences on the board. Have students work in pairs to add an action verb to follow each helping verb and complete each sentence:

I am ____. *We can ____.*

She has ____. *Anna did ____.*

They should ____. *Sam can ____.*

Metacognition To monitor student comprehension, have them compare the differences among action, helping, and linking verbs.

Adjectives

Adjectives describe nouns. An adjective usually comes before the noun it describes.

tall grass	big truck

An adjective can come *after* the noun it describes. This happens in these kinds of sentences.

The bag is **heavy**. The books are **new**.

Adverbs

Adverbs describe the action of verbs. They tell *how* an action happens. Adverbs answer the question *Where?, When?, How?, How much?,* or *How often?*

Many adverbs end in *-ly*.

easily	slowly

Some adverbs do not end in *-ly*.

seldom	fast	very

In this sentence, the adverb *everywhere* modifies the verb *looked*. It answers the question *Where?*

verb adverb
Nicole looked **everywhere** for her book.

333

Scaffolding Write the following words on the board. ***Verbs***: *study, dance, think, play, look*; ***Adverbs***: *beautifully, seldom, fast, everyday, everywhere*. Have students take turns choosing a verb and an adverb to describe it. Students should decide which question the adverb answers *(Where? When? How? How much? How often?)*. Clarify that though many adverbs come after a verb *(He runs quickly)*, some adverbs are used before a verb *(She seldom studies)*.

Metacognition To help students understand how they learn, say, *How do you remember the difference between adverbs and adjectives?*

Websites For more information, log on to www.LongmanCornerstone.com for links to other interesting websites about adjectives and adverbs.

Adjectives

Review with students that nouns name people, places, and things. Then show a crayon. Ask students to suggest words that describe the crayon, such as *red*, *short*, *new*, *broken*, or *pretty*, and list them on the board. Explain that words that describe nouns are called *adjectives*.

Point out that an adjective describes a noun and usually comes before the noun. (This pattern may differ from some students' first languages.) Call on a volunteer to read the examples in the box at the top of the page. Ask students for more examples of adjectives and nouns and write them on the board.

Next, discuss adjectives that come after nouns with students. Read aloud the sentence examples in the box with students. Ask students for additional examples of sentences with adjectives that come after nouns.

Scaffolding Write the words that follow in lists on the board. Have students take turns choosing a noun and an adjective to describe it. ***Nouns***: *weather, sky, person, day, beach, paper, child, dog*; ***Adjectives***: *silly, beautiful, stormy, wonderful, clear, kind, happy, funny*. Then have students select from these nouns and adjectives and use them to write three sentences. Call on volunteers to share sentences.

Adverbs

Read the definition of *adverbs* aloud with students and review the examples. Ask volunteers to use each given adverb in a sentence. Write the sentences on the board. Decide which question the adverb answers: *Where? When? How? How much? How often?*

You may wish to add that some adverbs describe adjectives or other adverbs. Write these examples on the board:

Maria was *terribly lonely* when her best friend moved away.

Justin ran *very fast* down the hill.

Prepositions

Read aloud the definition of prepositions with students. Emphasize that a preposition answers the question *When? Where?* or *In what direction?*

Choose a volunteer to hold a marker and then model giving directions. Use prepositions from the *Place* list to tell the student where to place the marker. *(under the table, below the chair)*

Then ask another volunteer to follow instructions as students use prepositions from the *Direction* list to tell him or her in which direction to walk. *(across the room, to the window)*

Finally, have a third volunteer follow instructions as students use prepositions from the *Time* list to tell the student when to jump three times. *(after counting to two, before you clap)*

Scaffolding Review with students that a preposition shows time, place, or direction, and that it answers the question *When? Where?* or *In what direction?* Write the following prepositions on the board:

after	*above*	*across*
before	*below*	*to*

Model how to use a preposition in a sentence. Then invite volunteers to use each of these prepositions in a sentence, write their responses on the board, and underline the preposition in each sentence. For example, *Jane ran across the field.*

Prepositional Phrases Call attention to the definition of *prepositional phrases*. Help students locate the preposition that begins the prepositional phrase *(near)* and the noun that ends the phrase *(school)*. Tell students that the noun is the *object* of the preposition. Write these prepositional phrases on the board and have students identify the preposition that begins each phrase and the noun that ends it.

before our dinner	*under my desk*
since last year	*into the basket*
near the station	*up the hill*

Explain to students they can also use a *pronoun* as the object of a preposition. Give examples *(near her, above it, after us, below them)*. Ask students for additional examples. (Pronouns were discussed on p. 331.)

Prepositions

Prepositions show time, place, and direction.

Time	Place	Direction
after before	above below	across down

In this sentence, the preposition *above* shows where the bird flew. It shows place.

preposition
A bird flew **above** my head.

In this sentence, the preposition *across* shows direction.

preposition
The children walked **across** the street.

A **prepositional phrase** starts with a preposition and ends with a noun or pronoun. In this sentence, the preposition is *near* and the noun is *school*.

prepositional phrase
The library is **near the new school**.

334

Conjunctions

A **conjunction** joins words, groups of words, and whole sentences. Common conjunctions include *and*, *but*, and *or*.

The conjunction *and* joins two proper nouns: *Allison* and *Teresa*.

> proper noun — proper noun
> Allison **and** Teresa are in school.

The conjunction *or* joins two prepositional phrases: *to the movies* and *to the mall*.

> prepositional phrase — prepositional phrase
> They want to go to the movies **or** to the mall.

The conjunction *but* joins two independent clauses.

> independent clause — independent clause
> Alana baked the cookies, **but** Eric made the lemonade.

Interjections

Interjections are words or phrases that express emotion.

Interjections that express strong emotion are followed by an exclamation point.

> **Wow!** Did you see that catch?

A comma follows interjections that express mild emotion.

> **Gee**, I'm sorry that your team lost.

335

Conjunctions

Explain that *conjunctions* are used to join words, groups of words, and whole sentences. Read aloud the examples of how a conjunction may be used with students. Point out that independent clauses are sentences that can stand alone or be joined to form a new, longer sentence.

Write the following incomplete sentences on the board. Ask students to add a conjunction to complete each sentence:

1. *Leo ____ Joey play baseball on the same team.*
2. *On Saturday, the girls want to go to the movies ____ go shopping.*
3. *My grandmother wants to make tuna sandwiches ____ chicken soup for lunch.*
4. *Beth wants to buy the red dress, ____ her mother wants her to get the blue one.*
5. *Roberto is from Mexico, ____ Kim is from Korea.*

Ask students to write five additional sentences using conjunctions to join nouns, prepositional phrases, and independent clauses. Write selected sentences on the board and read aloud together.

Interjections

Read aloud the definition and examples of interjections with students. Call attention to the exclamation points in the examples.

Hurray!	*Surprise!*	*Hey!*
Wow!	*Amazing!*	*Yikes!*

Discuss situations in which people might use these interjections. Have students take turns making statements that begin with interjections. Then, ask students to pretend that they are at a sports event and make up sentences using that theme. Write the sentences on the board and read them aloud together. Discuss the difference between using an exclamation point and a comma after an interjection.

Sentences

Tell students they will learn about different types of clauses and sentences.

Clauses

Review the meaning of the terms *subject* and *verb*. Explain that clauses are groups of words with a subject and a verb. Then, discuss the meaning of the word *independent* (can stand alone). Read aloud the definition of an *independent clause* with students. Emphasize that an independent clause is a complete sentence. Write several independent clauses on the board and have students name the subject and the verb.

Discuss the meaning of the word *dependent*. Read aloud the definition of a *dependent clause*. Point out that a dependent clause is not a complete sentence.

List the following clauses on the board. Have students determine if the clause is independent or dependent.

After a long time	*The puppy likes to play*
I fed the puppy	*When I was little*

Sentences

Ask students, *What are the things that every sentence has?* Write a list of the attributes of a sentence on the board, discuss, and have students copy the list to keep as a reference.

1. *A sentence has a subject and a verb.*
2. *A sentence tells at least one complete thought.*
3. *A sentence always begins with a capital letter.*
4. *A sentence always ends with a period, question mark, or exclamation point.*

Simple sentence Explain that a simple sentence has one independent clause. Read aloud the example of a simple sentence. Discuss how this sentence has all the attributes of a sentence. Ask students for other examples of simple sentences.

Compound sentence Read aloud the description of a compound sentence with students. Point out that to join two independent clauses into a compound sentence, there must be a comma and a conjunction. Write the following compound sentences on the board. Have a volunteer read each independent clause and then underline the conjunction.

Sentences

Clauses

Clauses are groups of words with a subject and a verb.

- An **independent clause** can stand on its own as a complete sentence.
- A **dependent clause** cannot stand alone as a complete sentence.

Sentences

A simple sentence is an independent clause. It has a subject and a verb.

subject verb The dog barked.

A **compound sentence** is made up of two or more simple sentences, or independent clauses.

independent clause / independent clause The band has a lead singer, **but** it needs a drummer.

Sentence Types

Declarative sentences are statements. They end with a period.

We are going to the beach on Saturday.

Interrogative sentences are questions. They end with a question mark.

Will you come with us?

Imperative sentences are commands. They end with a period or an exclamation point.

Put on your life jacket. Now jump in the water!

Exclamatory sentences express strong feeling. They end with an exclamation point.

I swam all the way from the boat to the shore!

336

1. *We went to the game, but it rained.*
2. *The rain stopped, so we went for a walk.*
3. *We met our friends, and they came home with us.*

Sentence Types

Tell students there are four types of sentences (*declarative*, *interrogative*, *imperative*, and *exclamatory*) and that each type has a different purpose. Read aloud the definitions and examples with students. For each example, ask volunteers to create their own sentences and write them on the board. Then have students identify the sentence attributes.

Punctuation

End Marks

End marks come at the end of sentences. There are three kinds of end marks: periods, question marks, and exclamation points.

Periods

- Use a period to end a statement (declarative sentence).
- Use a period to end a command or request (imperative sentence).
- Use a period after a person's initial or abbreviated title.
- Use a period after abbreviations.

Question Marks and Exclamation Points

- Use an exclamation point to express strong feelings.
- Use a question mark at the end of a question.

Commas

Commas separate parts of a sentence or phrase.

- Use a comma to separate two independent clauses linked by a conjunction.
- Use commas to separate the parts in a series. A series is a group of three or more words, phrases, or clauses.
- Use a comma to set off introductory words or phrases.
- Use commas to set off an interrupting word or phrase.
- Use a comma to set off a speaker's quoted words.
- Use commas to set off the name of the person being addressed in a letter or speech.

337

Punctuation

In this section, students will learn about different kinds of punctuation marks they will see and use when they read and write in English.

End Marks

Read about end marks aloud with students, noting the three kinds of end marks. Call on volunteers to write end marks on the board that are used in their first languages.

Periods

Read aloud with students each bullet point on the different ways periods are used. For each point, write examples on the board. Then write the following on the board. Have students take turns adding a period when necessary and explain their action.

Mrs Green	*JK Rowling*	*Avenue*
Rd	*in*	*kg*
Mr Todd	*ft*	*gal*
cm	*Ave*	*Dr Davis*

Question Marks and Exclamation Points

Read aloud the bullet points with students. For each point, write examples on the board of how question marks and exclamation points are used.

Cooperative Grouping Tell students to work in pairs to copy the following sentences from the board and take turns completing each sentence by adding an end mark. Then have students explain to their partner why that particular mark was used.

1. *Who is the boy running across the street*
2. *They live in the yellow house*
3. *There are so many wonderful things to do on the weekend*
4. *You write so well*
5. *Be careful not to walk on thin ice*

Commas

Read aloud with students the bullet points on commas. Write examples on the board of how commas are used. Next, write the following on the board. Have volunteers take turns adding a comma when necessary and state why they added a comma. Then have all students write their own sentences for each way commas are used.

1. *We waited for the bus but it never came.*
2. *Lucio's bike is red white and blue.*
3. *Yes Jenny likes to go swimming. Olga do you like to swim?*
4. *Tony asked "How do I get the hospital from here?"*
5. *Thank you Ming for putting away the dishes.*

Semicolons and Colons

Semicolons Say the word *semicolon* and write a semicolon on the board. Read aloud the definition of semicolons with students.

Write these independent clauses on the board: *It was a perfect day for a soccer game. The team was ready to play.* Show how two independent clauses can be joined with a comma and the conjunction *and*. Write: *It was a perfect day for a soccer game, and the team was ready to play.* Explain to students that these independent clauses may be joined in another way. Write: *It was a perfect day for a soccer game; the team was ready to play.* Call attention to the semicolon used to join the sentences.

Have students suggest additional pairs of independent clauses. Write them on the board without punctuation. Ask student volunteers to insert semicolons and periods.

Colons Say the word *colon* and write a colon on the board. Tell students that a colon is different from a semicolon in how it looks and how it is used. Read about colons aloud with students. Then write the following on the board:

1. *There are three kinds of end marks: periods, question marks, and exclamation points.*
2. *You must remember this: Always try your best.*
3. *4:30*

Have volunteers locate the colon in each example and state why it is used there.

Quotation Marks

Read aloud bullet points with students. For each point, write examples on the board. Then, ask students to suggest a dialogue between two of their favorite characters from a story, movie, or TV show. Write the lines on the board without punctuation. Invite students to insert quotation marks, commas, periods, question marks, or exclamation points.

Tell students that the rule on quotation marks for titles of short works applies to titles of chapters, short stories, articles, songs, single TV episodes, and short poems. Ask students to suggest items for each category and list them on the board. Explain that titles are <u>underlined</u> for all other written work and artwork, including books, magazines, newspapers, plays, movies, TV series, and paintings.

Semicolons and Colons

Semicolons can connect two independent clauses. Use them when the clauses are closely related in meaning or structure.

Colons introduce a list of items or important information. Also use a colon to separate hours and minutes when writing the time.

Quotation Marks

Quotation marks set off direct quotations, dialogue, and some titles.

- Commas and periods always go inside quotation marks.
- If a question mark or exclamation point is not part of the quotation, it goes outside the quotation marks.
- Use quotation marks to set off what people say in a dialogue.
- Use quotation marks around the titles of short works of writing.

Apostrophes

Apostrophes can be used with singular and plural nouns to show ownership or possession. To form the possessive, follow these rules:

- For singular nouns, add an apostrophe and an *s*.
- For singular nouns that end in *s*, add an apostrophe and an *s*.
- For plural nouns that do not end in *s*, add an apostrophe and an *s*.
- For plural nouns that end in *s*, add an apostrophe.
- Apostrophes are also used in contractions, to show where a letter or letters have been taken away.

Capitalization

There are five main reasons to use capital letters:

- to begin a sentence
- to write the pronoun ***I***
- to write the names of proper nouns
- to write a person's title
- to write the title of a work (artwork, written work)

338

Apostrophes

Read aloud bullet points with students. For each point, write examples on the board. Next, create a web on the board and write *Apostrophes* in the center. Have students give examples in which apostrophes are used and fill in the web.

Capitalization

Read aloud bullet points with students. Discuss each reason and write them on the board. Ask students for examples, including names of people and places, days and months, holidays, languages, religions, and titles. Write these examples under each reason for capitalization. Have students copy the capitalization rules and examples in their notebooks to use for reference.

Writing Handbook

Modes of Writing

Narration is used to tell a story. Here are some types of narration.

- Autobiography is the story of a person's life, told by the writer.
- Biography is the story of a person's life told by another person.
- A short story is a short, fictional narrative.

Exposition gives information or explains something. Here are some types of exposition.

- Compare and Contrast writing analyzes the similarities and differences between two or more things.
- Cause and Effect writing explains why something happened and what happens as a result.
- Problem and Solution writing describes a problem and offers one or more solutions to it.
- How-To writing explains how to do or make something.
- Description paints a picture of a person, place, thing, or event.

Persuasion is writing that tries to convince people to think or act in a certain way.

Functional writing is writing for real-world uses. Here are some types of functional writing.

- You might fill out a form to sign up for lessons, take a field trip, or apply for a library card.
- You might create an invitation to a holiday party.

339

Persuasion Read aloud the definition of persuasive writing. Ask students for examples of situations in which they tried to persuade an adult to let them do something special, such as staying overnight at a friend's house. They should list the reasons to persuade the adult to let them do this activity. Next, they should write a persuasive letter to the adult.

Functional Writing Read aloud the definition and examples. Ask students to provide additional examples of functional writing and write them on the board.

Writing Handbook

This Handbook contains an overview of the writing modes and the writing process. The Handbook is divided into the following sections:

- Modes of Writing
- The Writing Process
- Rubric for Writing
- Writing and Research
- How To Use Technology in Writing

Modes of Writing

Ask students about their previous knowledge of different writing modes from their reading or writing assignments.

Narration Read aloud the definition with students. Ask them to recall autobiographies, biographies, or short stories they have read. Ask, *If someone wanted to learn about your life, what would be some differences between reading an autobiography and a biography?* (The writer, how information is collected, what facts are included or omitted, interviews, opinions, accuracy, etc.)

Exposition Read aloud the definition and descriptions of different types of exposition.

- **Compare and Contrast** To help students understand the difference between *compare* and *contrast*, ask students to compare the similarities between the United States and their home countries. Then ask them to contrast the differences between these countries.
- **Cause and Effect** Draw a two-column chart on the board for *Cause and Effect*. Ask students for ideas to write on the chart. Select one example of cause and effect and discuss how to write an expository piece based on these ideas.
- **Problem and Solution** Draw a two-column chart on the board for *Problem and Solution*. Ask students for ideas to write on the chart. Remind them there could be more than one solution to a problem. Select one example and discuss how to expand on these ideas to write an expository piece.
- **How-to.** Ask students, *What tasks do you know how to do well? Are you an expert at doing something?* Select one example and ask students to provide each step to complete the task. Discuss how to write a how-to piece using these ideas.

The Writing Process

Read aloud the definition of *the writing process* with students. Tell students they will use the writing process to find topic ideas, write a draft, revise their work, and finally publish.

Step 1: Pre-write

Choose a topic Read aloud this section as students follow along. With student input, define the terms *freewrite* and *brainstorm*. Try the different prewriting strategies with students—list, freewrite, and brainstorm. Encourage students to think freely and be creative. Discuss which strategies students prefer and why. Write topic ideas that students generated on the board and have them vote on their top three favorites.

Identify Your Audience Read aloud this section with students. Using the favorite topics written on the board, have students respond to questions about their audience. Discuss why it's important to define who the audience is before starting to write.

Identify Purpose for Writing Read aloud the bullet points as students follow along. Have students select the key word for each bullet (*entertain*, *inform*, *persuade*). Discuss how identifying the purpose helps to guide how a piece is written.

Select the Best Form for Writing The audience and purpose for writing will help determine the best form to use. See *Modes of Writing* for descriptions of some forms.

Gather Information Once students decide on a topic, they need to gather information. The way they collect information depends on what they are writing. For a factual report, for example, they will need to do research at the library or on the Internet. For a fictional story, they will brainstorm ideas for a setting, plot, and characters.

The Writing Process

The writing process is a series of steps that helps you write clearly.

Step 1: Pre-write

When you pre-write, you explore ideas and choose a topic. You identify your audience, and you choose your purpose for writing.

To choose a topic, try one or more of these strategies.

- **List** many ideas that you might want to write about.
- **Freewrite** about some ideas for five minutes.
- **Brainstorm** a list of ideas with a partner.

To identify your audience, think about who will read your writing. What do they already know? What do you need to explain?

To identify your purpose for writing, ask:

- Do I want to entertain my audience?
- Do I want to inform my audience?
- Do I want to persuade my audience?

Now, decide on the best form for your writing. Gather and organize the details that will support your topic.

340

Scaffolding Explain how it may be beneficial to use graphic organizers to generate or organize ideas for a writing assignment. For example, a Venn Diagram or a T-Chart can help students to compare and contrast two things. Here are some common graphic organizers:

- T-Chart
- Word Web
- Venn Diagram
- Main Idea and Details Chart
- Sensory Details Chart
- Timeline
- Flowchart
- Sequence-of-Events Chart

Step 2: Draft

You start writing in this step. Put your ideas into sentences. Put your sentences into paragraphs. Begin to put your paragraphs in order. Don't worry too much about grammar and spelling. You will have a chance to correct any errors later.

Step 3: Revise

This is the time to look at your ideas and the organization of your writing. Read your first draft. Ask yourself:

- Are the ideas presented in the best order?
- Is there a clear beginning, middle, and end?
- Does each paragraph have a main idea and supporting details?

Ask a partner to read your writing and make comments about it. This is called a peer review. Decide what changes you want to make. Then rewrite your draft.

Step 4: Edit/Proofread

This is the time to look at word choice, sentence fluency, and writing conventions. Reread your paper. Proofread for mistakes in spelling, grammar, and punctuation. Correct any mistakes you find.

341

Cooperative Grouping Have students work in pairs to read first drafts to each other. They can conduct a peer review by using the bulleted questions and sharing constructive criticism to improve first drafts. After the peer review, have students work individually to revise their drafts.

Step 4: Edit/Proofread

Read aloud step 4 as students follow along. Guide students as they reread their second drafts and check word choice, sentence fluency, spelling, grammar, and punctuation.

Step 2: Draft

Read aloud step 2 as students follow along. Using one of the topic ideas created in step 1, demonstrate how to write a short first draft. Think aloud as you write on the board, putting ideas into sentences and paragraphs, and using details to support the main idea. Point out that working out ideas and making changes are part of the drafting process. Show how writing a first draft can be a messy process, with cross outs, erasures, and imperfect spelling and punctuation.

Have students write a first draft using a topic idea from step 1. Remind them that the purpose of a draft is to get the ideas down on paper, not to have perfect spelling, grammar, and punctuation. Perfection will come later.

Step 3: Revise

In this step, students will review their first drafts and improve the presentation and organization of ideas.

Review Your Draft Read aloud the bulleted questions with students. Have students use each question to help analyze their first drafts and make appropriate revisions.

Scaffolding Point out that good writers try to put their "personal stamp" on whatever they write. This personal stamp is often referred to as *the author's voice*. Write the following tips on the board. Tell students to use the tips to make sure their personal voice shines through.

–Write about subjects you know well and truly care about.
–Express your enthusiasm for your subject.
–Write directly to your readers.
–Choose words that will help the reader understand exactly what you mean.

Peer Review Prior to the class, make an overhead transparency of a first draft written by a student volunteer. Show the transparency to the class. Model a peer review session with the student author. Demonstrate how to ask questions about the first draft and give positive, constructive criticism on ways to improve the writing.

Step 4: Edit/Proofread (continued)

Go through the editing marks in the chart with students. Students may be unfamiliar with some or all of the marks, so give additional examples for each. You may wish to have students come to the chalkboard, recreate the marks, and write sentences using the marks.

Scaffolding You may want to give students a variety of sentences with mistakes on which they can use editing marks to make corrections. Another way to practice is to give students sentences with editing marks, and then have them rewrite the sentences correctly.

Proofreading Checklist Read aloud the bullet points as students follow along. Have students use the checklist to make a final check of their work before publishing. Ensure that students use dictionaries to check spelling and refer to their Handbooks to correct grammar and punctuation.

When students are done editing and proofreading their work, they should rewrite or reprint a perfect final draft, ready for publishing.

Metacognition To monitor student comprehension ask: *When you went through the revision and editing steps, how did you improve your writing? Give specific examples of how you did this. Why are these steps important in getting your piece ready to publish?*

When you edit and proofread your draft, use these proofreading marks to mark the changes.

Editing/Proofreading Marks		
To:	**Use This Mark:**	**Example:**
add something	∧	We ate rice, bean∧ and corn.
delete something	(delete mark)	We ate rice, beans, and corns.
start a new paragraph	¶	¶ We ate rice, beans, and corn.
add a comma	∧,	We ate rice, beans and corn.
add a period	⊙	We ate rice, beans, and corn ⊙
switch letters or words	∼	We ate rice, baens, and corn.
change to a capital letter	≡	we ate rice, beans, and corn.
change to a lowercase letter	/	WE ate rice, beans, and corn.

Proofreading Checklist

- Check your spelling. Look up words you aren't sure of in the dictionary.
- Check your grammar and usage. Use the Grammar Handbook to help you correct sentences.
- Review capitalization and punctuation. Make sure each sentence begins with a capital letter and uses proper end punctuation.

342

Step 5: Publish

Once you have revised and proofread your paper, share it with others. Look at these publishing ideas.

- Post your paper on the bulletin board.
- Photocopy your paper. Hand it out to your classmates and family members.
- Attach it to an email and send it to friends.
- Send it to a school newspaper or magazine for possible publication.

Once you have shared your work with others, you may want to put it in your portfolio. A portfolio is a folder or envelope in which you keep your writing. If you keep your work in a portfolio, you can look at what you have written over a period of time. This will let you see if your writing is improving. It will help you become a better writer.

Build Your Portfolio

You may want to keep your completed writing in your portfolio. It is a good idea to keep your drafts, too. Keep comments you receive from your teacher or writing partner, as well.

Reflect on Your Writing

Make notes on your writing in a journal. Write how you felt about what you wrote. Use these questions to help you get started.

- What new things did you learn about your topic?
- What helped you organize the details in your writing?
- What helped you revise your writing?
- What did you learn about yourself as you wrote?

343

Step 5: Publish

In this final step, students share their work with others. Read the bulleted ideas aloud as students follow along. Invite students to think of other ways to publish their work. You may wish to explore creating a class web page where students may post their work.

Build Your Portfolio Have students place their work in their assessment portfolios for comparison with past and future assignments. Sometimes it is helpful for students to keep all their drafts and revisions together with their final published work. This provides evidence of growth, improvement, and learning through use of the writing process.

Reflect on Your Writing Read aloud this section as students follow along. Ask students to select a recent, published writing assignment. Have students write answers to bulleted questions in their journal and then share ideas with the class.

Metacognition After students write reflections on their writing, ask them how this activity helps them become better writers. How will they approach their next writing assignment?

Websites For more information, log on to www.LongmanCornerstone.com for links to other interesting websites on the writing process.

Rubric for Writing

Tell students that a *rubric* is a set of rules used to help judge how good something is. Ask students *Have you seen rubrics to grade or score you work before? How do rubrics work?* Read aloud the rubric items for each score level as students follow along in their books.

Pause to explain each item and relate it to the students' work. Make sure students understand why a score of 4 differs from a 2 or 3. Tell them the rubric can give them information about their writing so they know how to improve it and get a better score.

If you have samples of student writing that illustrate the different score levels, review these samples with students. (Organizations that create and publish standardized writing tests often provide scored student writing samples.)

Should you decide to use a rubric to score your students' writing, you may wish to have writing conferences to explain how the rubric was applied and provide specific suggestions to improve student writing. You may want to give students an opportunity to revise or edit their writing so they can meet the criteria set by the rubric.

Rubric for Writing

A rubric is a tool that helps you assess, or evaluate, your work. This rubric shows specific details for you to think about when you write. The scale ranges from 4 to 1, with 4 being the highest score and 1 being the lowest.

4	Writing is clearly focused on the task. Writing is well organized. Ideas follow a logical order. Main idea is fully developed and supported with details. Sentence structure is varied. Writing is free of fragments. There are no errors in writing conventions.
3	Writing is focused, with some unnecessary information. There is clear organization, with some ideas out of order. The main idea is supported, but development is uneven. Sentence structure is mostly varied, with some fragments. Writing conventions are generally followed.
2	Writing is related to the task but lacks focus. Organization is not clear. Ideas do not fit well together. There is little or no support for the main idea. No variation in sentence structure. Fragments occur often. Frequent errors in writing conventions.
1	The writing is generally unfocused. There is little organization or development. There is no clear main idea. Sentence structure is unvaried. There are many fragments. Many errors in writing conventions and spelling.

344

Writing and Research

Sometimes when you write, you need to do research to learn more information about your topic. You can do research in the library, on the Internet, and by viewing or listening to information media.

Library Reference

Encyclopedias contain basic facts, background information, and suggestions for additional research.

Biographical references provide brief life histories of famous people in many different fields.

Almanacs contain facts and statistics about many subjects, including government, world history, geography, entertainment, business, and sports.

Periodicals are past editions of magazines. Use a periodical index to find articles on your topic.

Vertical files contain pamphlets on a wide variety of topics.

Electronic databases provide quick access to information on many topics.

345

Writing and Research

To prepare to teach this section, have examples of different reference materials on hand to share with students. Read aloud the introduction as students follow along in their books.

Library Reference

Read aloud the description of each item. For each item, ask students, *What kind of information would you look up in this reference?* Write these ideas on the board and have students copy the lists for each type of reference.

Scaffolding Tell students to imagine they are doing a research project and looking for specific information. Write the list of required information on the board. Have students identify what reference sources they might use to find this information.

1. *When did dinosaurs live? What are some different kinds of dinosaurs?* encyclopedia
2. *What are the capital cities of every country in Africa?* almanac, electronic database
3. *When was the telephone invented, and who invented it?* encyclopedia
4. *What are some winter holidays that people celebrate in different parts of the world?* almanac, electronic database
5. *Who was Marco Polo, and where did he travel?* biographical reference, encyclopedia, electronic database

Cooperative Grouping Tell students they will help plan a Scavenger Hunt for information at the library. Ask students to come up with ten research questions similar to those listed under Scaffolding. You may want to reserve a specific time at the school library or local public library for the Scavenger Hunt. Guidelines for this activity follow.

- At the library, you or the librarian may want to take the students on a tour of where they can find research resources.
- Working in pairs, students should find research sources and answer each question.
- Give students a specific amount of time in which to complete the activity.
- Back in the classroom, review the research sources and the answers.
- You may wish to award prizes to student pairs with the highest number of correct answers.

Citing Sources

Before you review this section with students, find examples of student research papers that include bibliographies and works cited lists.

Read aloud the material on citing sources as students follow along in their books. Show students the examples of bibliographies and works cited lists in research papers written by other students. Ask students, *Why is it important to cite sources when you write a research paper?* Possible answers are listed below:

- To give credit to people for their ideas and writing.
- People who read my paper will know I used a variety of sources.
- If someone wants to get more information on a topic, they can read a source I cited at the end of the paper.

Plagiarism

Read aloud the definition of *plagiarism* as students follow along. Discuss why plagiarism is considered a serious offense. Tell students the rules in your school regarding plagiarism. Review ways to avoid plagiarizing when working on a research paper:

- Read the research, think about it, and write down the ideas in your own words.
- Do not copy exact sentences or paragraphs from research sources, unless you are going to quote a source.
- When doing Internet research, do not copy and paste information from your source into your notes or your paper (unless you are using a direct quote). Write the information in your own words.
- Avoid depending on one or two people's ideas for your paper. Make sure you use several different sources of information.
- When you are done writing your paper, read it out loud. Do the words sound like your own words, or do they sound like someone else wrote it?

Citing Sources

When you do research, you read what other people wrote. The material you research is called the source or reference. When you tell who wrote the material, this is called citing the source. It is important to cite each source you use when you write.

In your paper, note each place in which you use a source. At the end of the paper, provide a list that gives details about all your sources. A bibliography and a works cited list are two types of source lists.

- A **bibliography** provides a listing of all the material you used during your research.
- A **works cited list** shows the sources you have quoted in your paper.

Plagiarism

Plagiarism is presenting someone else's words, ideas, or work as your own. If the idea or words are not yours, be sure to give credit by citing the source in your work. It is a serious offense to plagiarize.

Look at the chart of the Modern Language Association (MLA). Use this format for citing sources. This is the most common format for papers written by middle and high school students, as well as college students.

346

MLA Style for Listing Sources

Book	Pyles, Thomas. *The Origins and Development of the English Language*. 2nd ed. New York: Harcourt Brace Jovanovich, Inc., 1971.
Signed article in a magazine	Gustaitis, Joseph. "The Sticky History of Chewing Gum." *American History* Oct. 1998: 30–38.
Filmstrips, slide programs, videocassettes, DVDs	*The Diary of Anne Frank*. Dir. George Stevens. Perf. Millie Perkins, Shelly Winters, Joseph Schildkraut, Lou Jacobi, and Richard Beymer. Twentieth Century Fox, 1959.
Internet	*National Association of Chewing Gum Manufacturers*. 19 Dec. 1999. <http://www.longmancornerstone.com> [Indicate the date you found the information.]
Newspaper	Thurow, Roger. "South Africans Who Fought for Sanctions Now Scrap for Investors." *Wall Street Journal* 11 Feb. 2000.
Personal interview	Smith, Jane. Personal interview. 10 Feb. 2000.

347

Scaffolding To help students better understand the kind of information that is included in each type of citation, you may wish to have them look at a magazine and fill in the following information:

Magazine citation
Author (last name, first name):
Title of magazine article (in quotation marks):
Name of magazine (in italics or underlined):
Date of magazine:
Volume number:

Repeat this exercise for other sources, such as newspapers and Internet sources.

Modern Language Association Style for Listing Sources Tell students that the Modern Language Association (MLA) is an organization for language teachers and professors. Explain that the MLA has made a special set of rules for writing and using words. Many students and teachers use the MLA rules when they write papers.

You may want to mention that when students do research, they may see works cited in a style that differs from the MLA. That's because some writers use other style guidelines. Two leading examples include *The Chicago Manual of Style*, published by the University of Chicago and used by many publishers, and *The Associated Press Stylebook*, which is used by many journalists.

In the MLA style chart, read aloud the citation for each type of source as students follow along. Explain the specific information provided in each type of citation. For example, for "Book," you may want to explain as follows:

Pyles, Thomas.	author
The Origins and Development of the English language	title
second	edition
New York	place it was published
Harcourt Brace Jovanovich, Inc.	Publishing company
1971	Year of publishing

Since many students will start their research by using encyclopedias, you may want to show them how to cite this type of source. Write the following entry on the board and have students copy it into their notebooks.

Bergman, P.G. "Relativity." The New Encyclopaedia Brittanica. 15th ed. 1987.

Internet Research

The Internet has become a significant research source for students and professionals. This portion of the Handbook provides useful suggestions for budding researchers.

Read aloud the definitions of *Internet* and *World Wide Web* as students follow along. Ask students, *What are some ways you use the Internet?* (To get information in English and in their first languages, entertainment, games, music, weather, homework help, etc.) Discuss positive and negative things about using the Internet.

Point out that the abbreviation for *World Wide Web* is part of most website addresses, such as *www.weather.com*.

Search Engines Discuss search engines and what they do. You may wish to provide students with lists of age-appropriate search engines that are approved by your school district or school library.

Keywords Read aloud the information and tips on keywords. Stress to students that spelling keywords correctly is essential for productive Internet searches.

Scaffolding Ask students to brainstorm topics for Internet research. Write their ideas on the board. For each idea, ask students to think of important keywords to help them do Internet research. Discuss which keywords are the most important and why.

Internet Research

The Internet is an international network of computers. The World Wide Web is a part of the Internet that lets you find and read information.

To do research on the Internet, you need to open a search engine. Type in a keyword on the search engine page. **Keywords** are words or phrases on the topic you want to learn about. For example, if you are looking for information about your favorite musical group, you might use the band's name as a keyword.

To choose a keyword, write a list of all the words you are considering. Then choose a few of the most important words.

Tips

- Spell the keywords correctly.
- Use the most important keyword first, followed by the less important ones.
- Open the pages at the top of the list first. These will usually be the most useful sources.

348

How to Evaluate Information from the Internet

When you do research on the Internet, you need to be sure the information is correct. Use the checklist to decide if you can trust the information on a Web site.

- ✓ Look at the address bar. A URL that ends in "edu" is connected to a school or university. A URL that ends in "gov" means it is a site posted by a state or federal government. These sites should have correct information.
- ✓ Check that the people who write or are quoted on the site are experts, not just people telling their ideas or opinions.
- ✓ Check that the site is free of grammatical and spelling errors. This is often a hint that the site was carefully designed and researched.
- ✓ Check that the site is not trying to sell a product or persuade people.
- ✓ If you are not sure about using a site as a source, ask an adult.

349

How to Evaluate Information from the Internet
Sometimes it's difficult for students to sift through vast amounts of Internet information to decide what is of value. This section helps students learn how to evaluate Internet sources.

Review of this section would be more effective if you could use a computer that is connected to the Internet and to a projector to show students live examples of specific research tips. Ideally, students should also have Internet access via classroom computers or in a computer lab.

Read aloud the introduction as students follow along. Discuss why information on the Internet is sometimes incorrect or not to be trusted. Ask, *Why is the information you find on the Internet sometimes different from what you read in traditional books, magazines, or newspapers?* (You may want to discuss how people publish information on the Internet compared with how people publish materials in traditional books, magazines, or newspapers.)

Internet Research Checklist Read aloud each point on the checklist. If you have Internet access, provide appropriate examples for each point. (You may wish to find examples before class and add them to your "Favorites" for quick access during the lesson.)

Explain to students that *URL* stands for *Uniform Resource Locator* and refers to the web address for a particular site. In addition to URLs that end in "edu" and "gov," there are URLs that end in "org" (for non-profit organizations) and "com" or "net" (for businesses). Many of these websites provide useful information on topics like art, music, animals, science, health, history, geography, current events, and technology. Check with your school district or school library for a list of approved websites.

Cooperative Learning You may want students to practice their Internet research skills in the computer lab.

- Reserve time for your students in your school's computer lab.
- Create a list of research topics, along with important keywords.
- Give students a list of search engines approved by your school and a copy of the evaluation checklist on this page.
- In the computer lab, have students work in pairs and choose one topic. They can type keywords into the approved search engines to find research sources.
- Have students look at the information on websites and evaluate each source by using the checklist. Students should write down the URL for each source and the reasons why the source seems trustworthy or not.
- At the end of class, discuss what sources the students found and how they evaluated them. Ask, *Which ones seemed valid, and which ones did not. Why?*

Metacognition To monitor students' ability to evaluate and compare source materials, ask *Do you prefer doing research on the Internet or in published books and magazines? Why? How can you judge the accuracy and value of research materials from any source?*

Information Media

Information media is a dominant part of our lives. Students need to understand the different ways they get information from various types of media.

Read aloud the introduction as students follow along in their books. Then read aloud and discuss each type of information media presented in the box.

- **Television News Program** Ask students, *Who watches the news on TV? What are some recent news stories you learned about? What are some times that you really want to watch the news? Do you believe everything you see on the TV news?*
- **Documentary** Ask students, *What documentaries have you watched recently? What are some topics presented by documentaries? What have you learned from documentaries?*

Radio Talk Show Ask students if they or their guardians listen to radio talk shows. *Who talks on these shows? What do you learn from these shows?*

- **Newspaper Article** Ask students what they learn from reading newspaper articles. *Is information in newspapers always accurate? Do newspapers present facts or opinions?*
- **Commercial** Ask students, *What commercials have you seen lately? Do you watch commercials on TV, or do you change channels? What is the main reason that commercials are on TV? How do commercials try to sell you products? Do you think commercials are useful, or are they a waste of time?*

Information Media

Media is all the organizations that provide news and information for the public. Media includes television, radio, and newspapers. This chart describes several forms of information media.

Types of Information Media	
Television News Program	• Covers current news events • Gives information objectively
Documentary	• Focuses on one topic of social interest • Sometimes expresses controversial opinions
Television Newsmagazine	• Covers a variety of topics • Entertains and informs
Radio Talk Show	• Covers some current events • Offers a place for people to express opinions
Newspaper Article	• Covers one current event • Gives details and background about the event
Commercial	• Presents products, people, or ideas • Persuades people to buy or take action

350

How to Evaluate Information from Various Media

Because the media presents large amounts of information, it is important to learn how to analyze this information. Some media sources try to make you think a certain way instead of giving you all the facts. Use these techniques to figure out whether you can trust information from the media.

- ✓ Sort facts from opinions. A fact is a statement that can be proven true. An opinion is how someone feels or thinks about something. Make sure any opinions are supported by facts.
- ✓ Be aware of the kind of media you are watching, reading, or listening to. Is it news or a documentary? Is it a commercial? What is its purpose?
- ✓ Watch out for bias. **Bias** is when the source gives information from only one point of view. Try to gather information from several points of view.
- ✓ Discuss what you learn from different media with your classmates or teachers. This will help you determine if you can trust the information.
- ✓ Read the entire article or watch the whole program before reaching a conclusion. Then, develop your own views on the issues, people, and information presented.

351

How to Evaluate Information from Various Media Students are bombarded with information everyday. It's important for them to be able to analyze this information and discern fact from opinion, truth from fantasy, and objectivity from bias. The checklist in the box provides tips to help students evaluate information from media.

Read aloud the introduction as students follow along in their books. Then read aloud and discuss each checklist item. When possible, provide examples, or ask students for examples to illustrate each item.

Scaffolding You may want to help students practice how to evaluate media. Find a documentary approved by your school district about a controversial topic, such as civil rights or global warming. Preview it and note examples of fact vs. opinion, bias, exaggeration, or inaccuracies. Determine the purpose of this documentary. At the end, think of different conclusions that viewers might reach based on watching this documentary.

Introduce the documentary to your students. Ask them to follow along on the media checklist as they watch and to take notes if they spot examples of facts/opinions, bias, or other issues. You may wish to stop the documentary from time to time to point out examples from the checklist or other things that students should question or evaluate.

At the end of the documentary, discuss what students learned from the documentary and how they evaluated it in terms of facts, opinions, bias, purpose, and accuracy of information. Ask students, *What did the documentary makers want you to learn? What conclusions did you reach? What did you see in the documentary to support those conclusions?* Discuss why some students may have reached different conclusions.

How To Use Technology in Writing

This section provides useful tips to students on how to use computers for writing. You may find a wide range of computer skills among your students, depending on prior training and access to computers at home and at school.

Review of this section would be more effective if you could use a computer that is connected to a projector so students could see live examples. Ideally, students should also have access to computers in the classroom or in a computer lab.

Writing on a Computer

Read aloud the introduction and tips as students follow along in their books. If you are using a computer and a projector, demonstrate how to save documents and how to revise by using cut, copy, and paste commands.

You may also want to show students how to use the grammar and spell check functions. Point out that students must use their own grammar and spelling skills when they write and should not depend on these software functions to correct their work. Also, the grammar and spell check functions are not always correct.

Keeping a Portfolio

You may want to create a simple, logical folder system for students to use for saving documents. Give them naming protocols and specify which documents should go into the folders.

Computer Tips

Read aloud the tips as students follow along. In addition to saving drafts using the SAVE AS function, it may be helpful to show students how computer file manager functions show the date and time of their most recent work.

Emphasize the importance of saving and backing up as part of the computer writing process. Discuss the consequences of failing to do this. At the end of each computer writing session, have students save and back up before they are allowed to leave the class.

How To Use Technology in Writing

Writing on a Computer

You can write using a word processing program. This will help you when you follow the steps in the Writing Process.

- When you write your first draft, save it as a document.
- As you type or revise, you can move words and sentences using the cut, copy, and paste commands.
- When you proofread, you can use the grammar and spell check functions to help you check your work.

Keeping a Portfolio

Create folders to save your writing in. For example, a folder labeled "Writing Projects—September" can contain all of the writing you do during that month.

Save all the drafts of each paper you write.

Computer Tips

- Rename each of your revised drafts using the SAVE AS function. For example, if your first draft is "Cats," name the second draft "Cats2."
- If you share your computer, create a folder for only your work.
- Always back up your portfolio on a server or a CD.

352

Glossary

A

accompany go with (p. 233)

adapt change to fit a new situation (p. 167)

adversary person you are fighting or competing against (p. 112)

alpine in or related to the Alps or other high mountains (p. 282)

area part of a place (p. 271)

arena large building used for sports and entertainment (p. 76)

ascend move higher (p. 296)

assess decide how good or significant something is (p. 63)

assist help someone (p. 233)

assistance help or support (p. 194)

attitude point of view; state of mind (p. 37)

authorities people who are in charge of an area (p. 195)

B

biome community of plants, animals, and insects–like a rain forest or a desert (p. 166)

blister swelling on a surface (p. 86)

bore carried something (p. 62)

broad wide (p. 86)

C

carry take something somewhere (p. 36)

cascade small waterfall (p. 296)

charge run toward something quickly (p. 36)

chased ran after someone or something (p. 76)

classify put into groups (p. 167)

cliffs areas of high steep rock (p. 270)

clumsy moving awkwardly (p. 8)

cobblestone small round stone set in the ground to make a street (p. 126)

code words, letters, or numbers used to send secret messages (p. 232)

colonies countries that are controlled by other countries (p. 112)

comment talk about; say something about (p. 297)

compensate make payment (p. 113)

complete whole; with nothing left out (p. 8)

complexity complicated or detailed (p. 245)

conduct lead or direct (p. 9)

confidential not intended to be shown or told to other people (p. 126)

conservation saving or protecting of animals or plants (p. 282)

consume eat or use something (p. 183)

contained held something inside (p. 86)

context situation, events, or information related to something (p. 221)

contract legal agreement (p. 113)

convention formal meeting for a specific purpose (p. 139)

cooperate work together with someone else to get something done (p. 62)

correspond write messages to someone (p. 296)

cottage small house in the country (p. 36)

courageous brave (p. 22)

criminal someone who has done something wrong and is punished by the law (p. 76)

crown special hat made of gold and jewels worn by a king or queen (p. 112)

curious wanting to know or learn about something (p. 126)

D

damage harm something (p. 194)

debate public talk at which people give opinions about a subject (p. 139)

delegates people who are chosen to speak, vote, and make decisions for a group (p. 126)

demonstrate show how to do something (p. 221)

desert large area of land where it is hot and dry (p. 166)

distinct separate; different from others (p. 87)

E

ecosystem all the animals and plants in a particular area (p. 282)

emergency unexpected and dangerous situation (p. 22)

environment world of land, sea, and air that you live in (p. 282)

equator imaginary line around the middle of Earth (p. 166)

error mistake (p. 63)

escape get out of a place (p. 232)

establish start a company, system, situation, etc. (p. 195)

evaluate look at a situation carefully (p. 23)

exclaimed said something loud and suddenly because you were surprised (p. 8)

F

features traits or characteristics (p. 283)

federal relating to the central government of a country that controls a group of states (p. 138)

flea market market, usually in the street, where old or used goods are sold (p. 244)

forest area where there are a lot of trees (p. 296)

G

goal something you want to achieve (p. 183)

grasslands large areas of land covered with wild grass (p. 166)

grateful thankful (p. 62)

grove piece of land with trees growing on it (p. 270)

H

handle hold or touch something (p. 194)

harmonies combinations of musical notes that sound good together (p. 244)

hearing ability to hear (p. 220)

I

important very useful or valuable (p. 8)

improve become better, or make something better (p. 8)

improvisation something done without any preparation (p. 244)

individual separate from others in the same group (p. 127)

instruments objects used for making music (p. 220)

interact act upon or with another (p.87)

intervene try to stop an argument, problem, or war (p. 22)

item single piece or thing (p. 37)

K

kazoo simple musical instrument that you play by holding it to your lips and making sounds into it (p. 244)

L

landmarks things that help you recognize where you are, such as a famous building (p. 232)

landslide sudden falling of a lot of soil and rocks down the side of a hill, cliff, or mountain (p. 282)

legal allowed by law (p. 127)

legislature institution that has the power to make or change laws (p. 138)

liberty freedom (p. 112)

M

marvelous very good (p. 62)

meadow field with wild grass and flowers (p. 296)

merchants people who buy and sell large quantities of goods (p. 126)

merry happy and having fun (p.86)

midst in the middle of something (p. 86)

migrated moved from one place to another (p. 182)

millet plant like grass with small seeds that are used for food (p. 62)

motive underlying reason for doing something (p. 77)

musicians people who play musical instruments very well (p. 220)

N

national parks large areas of land throughout the United States that the government has set aside for nature (p. 270)

O

ocean very large area of water (p. 166)

orphan child or animal without parents (p. 182)

P

peak pointed top of a hill or mountain (p. 296)

peeked quickly looked at something (p. 36)

percussion drums and other musical instruments which you play by hitting or shaking them (p. 220)

pods family group of marine animals (p. 182)

predator animal that kills and eats other animals (p. 182)

principle rule or idea that you believe is right and that makes you behave in a particular way (p. 77)

privy bathroom or outhouse (p. 126)

project plan or activity (p. 9)

R

refugees people who have to leave their own countries, especially because of war (p. 22)

region area or location (p. 271)

relief assistance in time of difficulty (p. 194)

representation having someone speak, vote, or make decisions for you (p. 112)

republic a government with an elected head of state (p. 138)

reunite come together again (p. 182)

rhythms strong patterns of sound (p. 244)

riverbank land on the sides of a river (p. 232)

S

scarce not enough of something (p. 36)

scenic beautiful views of nature (p. 282)

secluded private and quiet (p. 282)

secrecy keeping information secret (p. 126)

secret idea or plan that you do not tell other people about (p. 232)

separate not connected to each other; apart (p. 138)

sequoias very tall trees that grow near the coast in Oregon and California (p. 270)

share have or use something together with other people (p. 36)

sounds things that you hear (p. 220)

specific precise; exact (p. 283)

startle make someone suddenly surprised or shocked (p. 86)

starvation suffering or death from lack of food (p. 182)

stranded needing help because you cannot move from a particular place (p. 194)

surrender stop fighting because you know you cannot win (p. 138)

suspicious not willing to trust someone or something (p. 8)

swollen became larger because of injury or sickness (p. 76)

T

tailors people whose job is to make suits, coats, etc. (p. 126)

task job or piece of work that must be done (p. 23)

taxes money you must pay to the government (p. 112)

teamwork ability of a group to work well together, or the effort the group makes (p. 22)

tracks marks made on the ground by an animal, person, or vehicle (p. 232)

training process of being taught how to do a particular job (p. 22)

tributaries rivers or streams that flow into a larger river (p. 270)

tropical coming from the hottest and wettest part of the world (p. 166)

tundra large flat lands in northern areas where it is very cold and there are no trees (p. 166)

V

valley area of lower land between two lines of hills or mountains (p. 296)

variety differences within something (p. 245)

veteran someone who has been a soldier in a war (p. 138)

vibrations continuous shaky movements (p. 220)

virtue good quality of someone's character (p. 62)

W

wander move or travel with no particular purpose (p. 76)

Index

Credits

ILLUSTRATORS: Meredith Johnson 10–16, **Julie Downing** 38–43 **Soud** 64–69 **TK** 92 **Gary Torrisi** 100–103 **Doris Ettlinger** 153–157 **middle Richard Ward** 166 **Jennifer Emery** 258–261.

COVER: Terry Kovalcik

ICONS: Bill Melvin

LETTER LOGOS: Jan Bryan-Hunt

UNIT 1: 2–3 TK; 5 top ©Dana White/PhotoEdit Inc.; 5 upper middle ©Steve Gorton/ Dorling Kindersley; 5 lower middle PhotoEdit Inc.; 5 bottom ©David Young-Wolff/ PhotoEdit Inc.; 6 left top © Mark Richards/PhotoEdit Inc.; 6 left bottom ©Tony Freeman/ PhotoEdit Inc.; 6 right top © Danilo Balducci/Peter Arnold; Inc.; 6 right bottom ©David Young-Wolff/PhotoEdit Inc.; 7 left top © Cindy Miller Hopkins/Danita Delimont Photography; 7 left bottom © Michele Molinari/ Danita Delimont Photography; 7 right bottom © Demetrio Carrasco/Stone Allstock/Getty Images; 7 right top © Michael Dunning/ Photo Researchers Inc; 8 top © Jonathan Nourok/PhotoEdit Inc.; 8 middle; Managed Photographs; 8 bottom © Jeff Greenberg/PhotoEdit Inc.; 9 top © Donna Day/ Stone Allstock/Getty Images; 9 middle © Vicky Kasala Productions/Image Bank/Getty Images; 9 bottom Masterfile; 17 © Cleo Photography/ PhotoEdit Inc.; 18 Alami Images; 19 © Frank Siteman/Omni-Photo Communications Inc.; 20 Will Hart; 21 Bettman/CORBIS; 22 top © Dwayne Newton/PhotoEdit Inc.; 22 bottom © Vince Streano/NY/CORBIS; 23 top © Blair M. Seitz Creative Eye/MIRA.com; 23 right © Bill Aron/PhotoEdit Inc.; 23 bottom AP World Wide Photos; page 24 MSF Sygma/CORBIS; 25 Kieran Doherty/Reuters/CORBIS;26 Philippe Desmazes/ Getty Images; 27 Robert Harding World Imagery; 28 top © Ton Koene/Peter Arnold Inc.; 28 bottom left © Keren Su National Geographic Image Collection; 28 bottom right ©Hoang Dinh Nam/ Getty Images; 29 top Liason/Getty Images; 29 bottom Ian Berry/Magnum Photos; 30 National Geographic Image Collection; 31 Liason/Getty Images; 32 © Antonia Reeve/Photo Researchers Inc.; 33 © Patrick Robert Sygma/CORBIS; 34 © Jimin Lai/Getty Images; 35 © Jorgen Schytte/ Peter Arnold Inc.; 36 top © Don Mason/CORBIS; 36 middle Taxi/Getty Images; 36 bottom © G. Baden Gerhard Steiner/CORBIS; 37 top National Geographic Image Collection; 37 right © Nelly Boyd/Robert Harding World Imagery; 37 bottom © Martin Harvey/Peter Arnold Inc.; 44 © David Young-Wolff/PhotoEdit Inc.; 45 © Clive Streeter/ Dorling Kindersley; 46 © Ralph Talmont/Aurora and Quanta Productions; 47 © Jerry Mason/Photo Researchers Inc.; 48 © Robert E. Daemmrich/Stone Allstock/Getty Images; 50 © Al Grillo/AP World Wide Photos; 52–53 © Clark J. Mishler/Creative Eye/Mira.com

UNIT 2: 56–57 Anton Vengo/Superstock; 59 top © Dave King/Dorling Kindersley; 59 upper middle © Annabella Bluesky/Photo Researchers Inc.; 59 middle © Mark Richards/ PhotoEdit Inc.; 59 bottom PhotoEdit Inc.; 60 top left © A. Ramey/Stock Boston; 60 bottom left ©Ellen Sensei 60 top right Ryan's Well Foundation; 60 bottom right;© Mark Richards/PhotoEdit Inc.; 61 top left Victor Englebert; 61 bottom left © Claire Liembach/ Robert Harding World Imagery; 61 top right Picture Desk/Kobal Collection; 61 bottom right © David Young-Wolff/PhotoEdit Inc.; 62 top © David Young-Wolff/PhotoEdit Inc.; 62 middle © Peter Anderson/Dorling Kindersley; 62 bottom © Richard Morrell/CORBIS; 63 top © Charlotte Thege/Peter Arnold Inc.; 63 middle © Gary Ombler/Dorling Kindersley; 63 bottom Lawrence Migdale; 70 Dorling Kindersley; 71 © Betty Press/Woodfin Camp and Associates; 72 © Christopher and Sally Gable/Dorling Kindersley; 73 © Chad Ehlers/ Stock Connection; 74 © Kristin Mosher/Danita Delimont Photography; 75 © Roger de la Harpe/Dorling Kindersley; 76 top © Peter Blackwell Nature Picture Library; 76 bottom © Susan Van Etten/PhotoEdit Inc.; 77 top © David Shale Nature Picture Library; 77 middle © Chad Ehlers Stock Connection; 77 bottom © John Boykin/PhotoEdit Inc.; 78–79 Hulton Archive/ Getty Images; 80 CORBIS; 81 Hulton Deutsch/ CORBIS; 82 Hulton Archive/Getty Images; 83 Hulton Archive/Getty Images; 84 Hulton Archive/ Getty Images; 85 Canali Photobank; 86 top National Geographic Image Collection; 86 middle © Peter Reali CORBIS; 86 bottom Stockbyte/ Getty Images; 87 top © David Lok Superstock Inc.; 87 right © Stewart Cohen/Photo Library.

com; 87 bottom right © Jane Burton/Dorling Kindersley; 89 (background) Bettman/CORBIS; 89 (inset) © Cinema Photo/CORBIS; 90 © Arni Katz/PhotoLibrary.com; 91 Library of Congress; 92 © Donna Day Stone/Allstock/Getty Images; 93 Picture Desk Inc./Kobal Collection; 94 CORBIS; 95 Bettman/CORBIS; 96 Picture Desk Inc./ Kobal Collection; 97 Photofest; 98 content.answers.com; 99 Everett Collection

UNIT 3: 106–107 The Granger Collection; 109 top © Jeff Greenberg/PhotoEdit Inc. 109 top middle © Tony Perottet/Ambient Images; 109 middle © Steve Gorton/Dorling Kindersley; 109 bottom © Ahmad Masood/Reuters America/CORBIS; 110 top left © Martin Beebe/CORBIS; 110 bottom left EMG Education Management Group; 110 top right © Greg Johnston/Danita Delimont Photography; 110 bottom right © Patricia Jordan/ Peter Arnold Inc.; 111 top left © Joseph Nettis/ Photo Researchers Inc.; 111 bottom left Pearson Learning Photo Studio; 111 top right © Mark Antman/The Image Works; 111 bottom right © Steve Gorton/Dorling Kindersley; 112 top right © Atsuko Tanaka/ CORBIS; 112 middle right © Ron Bell/AP World Wide Photos; 112 bottom CORBIS; 113 top © Mark C. Burnett/Photo Researchers Inc. 113 top right © Michael John O'Neill/ Image Bank/Getty Images; 113 bottom © Mike Theiler Bettman/CORBIS; 114 Bettman/CORBIS; 115 Pearson Education Modern Curriculum; 116 Bettman/CORBIS; 117 The Granger Collection; 118 top AP World Wide Photos; 118 bottom left Bettman/CORBIS; 118 right © Najlah Feanny Bettman/CORBIS; Bettman/CORBIS; 119 top left Hulton Archive/Getty Images; 119 top right AP World Wide Photos; 119 center AP World Wide Photos; 119 bottom AP World Wide Photos; 120 The Granger Collection; 121 Viesti Associates; 122 Library of Congress; 123 The Granger Collection; 124 The Anne S.K. Military Collection; 125 © Lisa Poole/AP World Wide Photos; 126 top right Architect of the Capitol; 126 right; Stockbyte/ Getty Images; 126 bottom left © David Mager/ Pearson Learning Photo Studio; 126 bottom National Geographic Image Collection; 127 top © Robert Fried Photography; 127 top right © Michelle D. Bridwell/ PhotoEdit Inc. Inc.; 127 middle right © Tony Souter Dorling Kindersley; 127 bottom © Mark Johnson/Creative Eye/MIRA. com; 128 The Granger Collection NY © Eduardo Garcia/Getty Images; 129 The Granger Collection NY © Eduardo Garcia/Getty Images; 130 The Granger Collection NY © Eduardo Garcia/Getty Images;131 Independence National Historical Park; 132 © Cary Wolinsky/Aurora & Quanta Productions Inc.; 133 Hulton Archive/Getty Images; 134 William H. Sadler; 135 Metropolitan Museum of Art; 136 © David Merewether/Dorling Kindersley; 137 Hulton Archive/Getty Images; 138 top right Photodisc/Getty Images; 138 right © Paul Conklin/PhotoEdit Inc.; 138 bottom left Art Resource NY; 139 middle right © Jeff Greenberg/ PhotoEdit Inc.; 140 Library of Congress; 141Bridgeman Art Library International; 142 New York Historical Society; 143 Hulton Archive/Getty Images; 144 Photo Researchers Inc.; 145 Hulton Archive/Getty Images; 146 © Les Riess/Omni-Photo Communications; 147 © Mary Steinbacher/ PhotoEdit Inc.; 148 © Joe Sohm/The Stock Connection; 149 © Paul Conklin/ PhotoEdit Inc. ; 150 Hulton Archive/Getty Images; 151 PhotoEdit Inc.

UNIT 4: 160–161 Felicia Martinez/Photoedit Inc. 163 top © Bill Bachman/Creative Eye/MIRA.com; 163 top middle Omni-Photo Communications Inc. 163 middle © David Noton/Nature Picture Library; 163 bottom left © Jose B. Ruiz/Nature Picture Library; 163 bottom right © Charlotte Thege/Peter Arnold Inc.; 164 top left The Image Works; 164 bottom left © Esben/Anderson/Omni-Photo Communications Inc. 164 top right © Mark Edwards/Peter Arnold Inc. 164 bottom right © Adam Buchanan/Danita Delimont Photography; 165 top left © Yva Momatiuk/Stock Boston; 165 bottom left © Eascott-Momatiuk/The Image Works; 165 top right © Pete Oxford/Nature Picture Library; 165 bottom right Ellen Sinisi; 166 top © David Parker Photo Researchers Inc.; 166 middle right © Ben Osborne/Nature Picture Library; 166 bottom © Chad Ehlers/The Stock Connection; 167 top © David Noton/Nature Picture Library; 167 middle right © Glen Allison Photodisc/Getty Images; 167 bottom © Dave Fleetham Pacific Stock; 168–169 © Barbara Nelson Creative Eye/MIRA.com; 169 (inset)© Pete Oxford/Nature Picture Library; 170 top National Geographic Image Collection; 170 bottom © Marc Bernardi/The Stock Connection; 171

(background) DeAgostini Editore Picture Library; 171 (inset) © Simon Fraser/Photo Researchers Inc.; 172–173 (background)© Peter Scoones/Photo Researchers Inc.; 172 (inset) © Annie Griffiths Belt National Geographic Image Collection; 174 top left © Damien Moore Dorling Kindersley; 174 top right © Wyman Meinzer/Peter Arnold Inc.; 174 bottom left Viesti Associates; 174 bottom right © Pete Oxford /Nature Picture Library; 175 top left © Mark Payne-Gill/Nature Picture Library; 175 top right © Jeffrey Rotman/ Photo Researchers Inc.; 175 middle © Chad Ehlers/The Stock Connection; 175 bottom © Kenneth M. Highfill/Photo Researchers Inc.; 176 Viesti Associates; 177 © Peter Oxford Nature Picture Library; 178–179 National Geographic Image Collection; 180 © John Hyde/Creative Eye/MIRA.com; 181 © Rob Blakers/Photo Library.com; 182 top right © John Hyde/Creative Eye/ MIRA.com; 182 middle left © David Hosking/ Photo Researchers Inc.; 182 bottom © Terry Andrewartha/Nature Picture Library; 183 top © Dietmar Nill Nature Picture Library; 183 middle right © Tom Nebbia/ CORBIS; 183 bottom center © Skjold Image Works; 184–185 (background) © John Hyde/ Pacific Stock; 184 (inset) © Tom Walmsley/Nature Picture Library; 186 Seattle Post Intelligencer; 188 © Tom Brakefield/The Stock Connection; 189 CORBIS; 190 © John Hyde/Pacific Stock; 191 © Joel Rogers/Stone Allstock/Getty Images; 192 Animals Animals/Earth Scenes; 194 top right © David Purdy/Biloxi Sun Herald Newscom; 194 middle © Bruce Ayres Stone Allstock/Getty Images; 194 bottom National Oceanic and Atmospheric Administration; 195 top © Najlah Feanny Bettman/CORBIS; 195 middle right © Pavel Rahman/AP World Wide Photos; 195 bottom © Jeff Greenberg/PhotoEdit Inc.; 197 top ©Reza Webistan/CORBIS; 197 bottom/Reuters/CORBIS; 198 ©Frank Siteman/ Getty Images; 199 ©Chris Graythen/Getty Images; 200 Bettman/CORBIS; 201 Viviane Moos/CORBIS; 202 PhotoEdit Inc.; 203 NASA Headquarters; 204–205 Getty Images; 206 Bettman/CORBIS; 209 top © Bill Curtsinger/National Geographic Image Collection; 209 top middle© Andrew Syred/Photo Researchers Inc.; 209 middle © Matthew Oldfield/ Photo Researchers Inc.; 209 bottom © Ralph Lee Hopkins/National Geographic Image Collection; 210 top © Denis Scott Bettman/CORBIS; 210 bottom left © Marc Moritsch/National Geographic Image Collection; 210 bottom right © Peter Scoones/Photo Researchers Inc.; 211 top left © Howie Gather Creative Eye/MIRA.com; 211 top right © John Hyde Pacific Stock; 211 bottom © Ken Findlay Dorling Kindersley

UNIT 5: 214–215 Image Source/Punchstock; 217 top © Michelle D. Bridwell/PhotoEdit Inc.; 217 top middle © Chris Stock/Lebrecht Music & Arts Library; 217 © Ulrich Perrey/ NY/CORBIS; 217 © Michael Newman/PhotoEdit Inc.; 218 top left Getty Images; 218 bottom left © Dallas and John Heaton/The Stock Connection; 218 top right © Sam Yeh/ Getty Images; 218 bottom right © Richard Haynes/Silver Burdett Ginn Needham; 219 top left © Jacques Jangoux /The Stock Connection; 219 bottom left Photolibrary.com; 219 top right © Pete Saloutos Bettman/CORBIS; 219 bottom right Lawrence Migdale Pictures; 220 Geri Engberg Photography; 221 top © Jan Persson/Lebrecht Music & Arts Library; 221 bottom Dorling Kindersley; 222 J. Wilson ©/EG Images; 223 © Richard H. Smith/ Lebrecht Music & Arts Library; 224 © Chris Christodoulou/Lebrecht Music & Arts Library; 225 J. Wilson ©/EG Images; 226 © Mike Albans/AP World Wide Photos; 227 CORBIS; 228 © Jan Persson/Lebrecht Music & Arts Library; 230 CORBIS; 232 top right Image Bank/Getty Images; 232 middle right CORBIS; 232 bottom © Mark E. Gibson/ Creative Eye/MIRA.com; 233 top Geri Engberg Photography; 233 middle right © Thomas Kitchin/Tom Stack and Associates Inc.; 233 bottom left © Ralph Lee Hopkins/National Geographic Image Collection; 233 bottom middle © Don King/Pacific Stock; 233 bottom right © Dave King/Dorling Kindersley; 234–235 Nativestock/Getty Images; 236 Peter Arnold/Getty Images; 237 Getty Images; 238 © Eckhard Slawik/Photo Researchers Inc.; 239 Art Resource/Metropolitan Museum of Art; 241 © Kayte M. Deioma/PhotoEdit Inc.; 243 The Granger Collection; 244 top right © Michael Newman PhotoEdit Inc.; 244 middle © Stephen Oliver Dorling Kindersley; 244 middle right © Phillippe Giraud Sygma/CORBIS; 244 bottom Robert Fried Photography; 245 top © Peter Peevers Dorling Kindersley; 245 bottom Dorling Kindersley; 246 © Ken Gillham/Robert Harding World Imagery; 247 top Photodisc/Getty Images; 248 top ©

Akhil Bakshi/Dorling Kindersley; 248 bottom Dorling Kindersley; 249 Jonathan Knowles/Getty Images; 250 top © Peter Chadwick Dorling Kindersley; 250 bottom left © Dave King/Dorling Kindersley; 250 bottom right © Mike Dunning Dorling Kindersley; 251 top © Dave King Dorling Kindersley; 251 bottom © Mike Dunning/Dorling Kindersley; 252 © Dave King/Dorling Kindersley; 253 Photodisc/Getty Images; 254 © Chris Stock/ Lebrecht Music & Arts Library; 255 © David Young-Wolff/PhotoEdit Inc.

UNIT 6: 264–265 Corbis/Punchstock; 267 top © Peter Frischmuth/Peter Arnold Inc; 267 top middle © W. Lynn Seldon Jr./Omni-Photo Communications Inc.; 267 middle © Greg Huglin/ The Stock Connection; 267 bottom left Photodisc/ Getty Images; 267 bottom right © Andrew J. Martinez/Photo Researchers Inc.; 268 top left © Pekka Parviainen/Photo Researchers Inc.; 268 bottom left © Arthur Tilley/Getty Images; 268 top right © Marc Bernardi/The Stock Connection; 268 bottom right © Tim Bewer/The Stock Connection; 269 top left © Art Wolfe/Danita Delimont Photography; 269 bottom left © Charlotte Thege/ Peter Arnold Inc.; 269 top right © E.A. Kuttapan Nature Picture Library; 269 bottom right © John and Lisa Merrill/Stone Allstock/Getty Images; 270 top © Jim Wark Airphoto; 270 middle © Andy Holligan/Dorling Kindersley; 270 bottom © Paul Harris/ Stone Allstock/Getty Images; 271 top right EMG Education Management Group; 271 bottom © Lewis Kemper Phototake NYC; 272 © Gerald French Bettman/CORBIS; 273 right Frans Lanting/ Minden Pictures; 273 bottom © John Heseltine/ Dorling Kindersley; 274 top right © Jimmy Chin/National Geographic Image Collection; 274 bottom © Bill Lies/Ambient Images; 275 top © Jian Chen/The Stock Connection; 275 bottom © Cosmo Condina/The Stock Connection; 276 © Peter Oxford/Nature Picture Library; 277 DeAgostini Editore Picture Library/Getty Images; 278–279 © Jacques Jangoux/The Stock Connection; 280 Tom Till Photography Inc.; 282 top right © Chad Ehlers/The Stock Connection; 282 middle right © Lynn Betts/U.S. Department of Agriculture; 282 bottom © Richard Price/Taxi/ Getty Images; 283 top Ken Hamblin; 283 middle © Tony Freeman/ PhotoEdit Inc.; 283 middle right ©Michele Westmoreland/Danita Delimont Photography; 283 bottom © Brad Mitchell Creative Eye/MIRA.com; 284–287 (background) © Christopher T. Frank /Ambient Images; 284 (inset)© Spencer Grant/PhotoEdit Inc.; 285 (inset) © David Young-Wolff/PhotoEdit Inc.; 286 © David Young-Wolff PhotoEdit Inc.; 287 © David Noton/Nature Picture Library; 288 left © Inga Spence/D. Donne Bryant Stock Photography; 288 right top Dorling Kindersley; 288 right middle © Gary Ombler/ Dorling Kindersley; 288 bottom DK Images; 289 all but canteen DK Images; 289 canteen © John Lei Omni-Photo Communications Inc.; 290 © Skip Brown/National Geographic Image Collection; 291 © Jimmy Chin/National Geographic Image Collection; 293 © Bill Stevenson/The Stock Connection; 294 © Kennan Ward Bettman/CORBIS; 295 © Mark Moritsch/ National Geographic Image Collection; 296 top © Jack Hollingsworth Photodisc/Getty Images; 296 middle © Geoff Dann/Dorling Kindersley; 296 bottom © Kim Sayer/Dorling Kindersley; 297 top © Mike Powell/Allsport Photography/Getty Images; 297 middle Alistair Duncan/Dorling Kindersley; 297 bottom © Christopher and Sally Gable/Dorling Kindersley; 298 top © Robert W. Ginn/PhotoEdit Inc.; 298 bottom © Gordon Wiltsie/National Geographic Image Collection; 299 both images © Larry Brownstein/Ambient Images; 300 top right © Gavin Hellier/Robert Harding World Imagery; 299 bottom left © Cosmo Condina/The Stock Connection; 299 bottom right © Skip Brown/ National Geographic Image Collection; 301 © Larry Brownstein/Ambient Images; 302 © Bill Lies/Ambient Images; 303 © Marc Moritsch/ National Geographic Image Collection; 304 © Robert W. Ginn/PhotoEdit Inc.; 305 © Bill Hatcher/National Geographic Image Collection; 306 © Marc Moritsch/National Geographic Image Collection; 307 © Marc Moritsch/ National Geographic Image Collection; 308 © Spencer Grant/PhotoEdit Inc.; 309 © David Young-Wolff/PhotoEdit Inc.; 310 © Jeffrey Coolidge/ CORBIS; 311© Andrew M. Levine/ Photo Researchers Inc.; 312 © David Young-Wolff/ PhotoEdit Inc.; 313 © Ellen Senisi/The Image Works